VENICE &
THE VENETIAN ARC

3RD EDITION

Where to Stay and Eat
for All Budgets

Must-See Sights
and Local Secrets

Ratings You Can Trust

Fodor's Travel Publications   New York, Toronto, London, Sydney, Auckland
www.fodors.com

FODOR'S VENICE & THE VENETIAN ARC

Editors: Matthew Lombardi, Jane Onstott

Editorial Production: Tom Holton
Editorial Contributors: Linda Cabasin, Elaine Eliah, David Graham, Christina Knight, Patricia Rucidlo
Maps: David Lindroth, *cartographer;* Bob Blake and Rebecca Baer, *map editors*
Design: Fabrizio La Rocca, *creative director;* Guido Caroti, *art director;* Melanie Marin, *senior picture editor*
Production/Manufacturing: Angela L. McLean
Cover Photo (Rialto Bridge, Venice): Bob Krist

Third Edition

ISBN 1–4000–1288–0

ISSN 1547–9269

SPECIAL SALES

This book is available for special discounts for bulk purchases for sales promotions or premiums. Special editions, including personalized covers, excerpts of existing books, and corporate imprints can be created in large quantities for special needs. For more information, write to Special Markets/Premium Sales, 1745 Broadway, MD 6-2, New York, New York 10019 or e-mail specialmarkets@randomhouse.com.

AN IMPORTANT TIP & AN INVITATION

Although all prices, opening times, and other details in this book are based on information supplied to us at press time, changes occur all the time in the travel world, and Fodor's cannot accept responsibility for facts that become outdated or for inadvertent errors or omissions. So **always confirm information when it matters,** especially if you're making a detour to visit a specific place. Your experiences—positive and negative—matter to us. If we have missed or misstated something, **please write to us.** We follow up on all suggestions. Contact the Venice editor at editors@fodors.com or c/o Fodor's at 1745 Broadway, New York, New York 10019.

PRINTED IN THE UNITED STATES OF AMERICA

10 9 8 7 6 5 4 3 2 1

DESTINATION VENICE & THE VENETIAN ARC

Rising up from its lagoon, shimmering in the sun, or wrapped in mist, Venice could be mistaken for a mirage. But rub your eyes and look again. The city is no illusion—it's simply unlike anyplace you've ever seen, without an automobile or a bit of modern architecture in sight. Canals are its streets and gondolas its taxicabs. Climb in, and you glide past cathedrals and palaces that mix Renaissance refinement and Oriental exoticism. Standing in the Piazza San Marco, the heart of this once-great maritime power, you feel as though you're straddling the axis of the Eastern and Western worlds. When you depart the lagoon and travel inland through the Venetian Arc—the surrounding region once ruled by the Republic of Venice—a sense of the extraordinary still prevails. To the west are coolly symmetrical Palladian villas, to the north the jagged Dolomites, and to the east the refined cafés of Trieste. Wonders await at every turn. *Buon viaggio!*

Karen Cure, Editorial Director

CONTENTS

Understanding Venice & the Venetian Arc 254

Index 273

Maps

CloseUps

ABOUT THIS BOOK

There's no doubt that the best source for travel advice is a like-minded friend who's just been where you're headed. But with or without that friend, you'll have a better trip with a Fodor's guide in hand. Once you've learned to find your way around its pages, you'll be in great shape to find your way around Venice and the Venetian Arc.

SELECTION

Our goal is to cover the best properties, sights, and activities in their category, as well as the most interesting communities to visit. We make a point of including local food-lovers' hot spots as well as neighborhood options, and we avoid all that's touristy unless it's really worth your time. You can go on the assumption that everything you read about in this book is recommended wholeheartedly by our writers and editors. Flip to On the Road with Fodor's to learn more about who they are. It goes without saying that no property mentioned in the book has paid to be included.

RATINGS

Orange stars ☆ denote sights and properties that our editors and writers consider the very best in Venice and the Venetian Arc. These, the best of the best, are listed in the Fodor's Choice section in the front of the book. Black stars ★ highlight the sights and properties we deem Highly Recommended, don't-miss sights and properties. Fodor's Choice and Highly Recommended options in each chapter are listed on the title page of that chapter. Use the index to find complete descriptions. Sights pinpointed with numbered map bullets ❶ in the margins tend to be more important than those without bullets.

SPECIAL SPOTS

Pleasures & Pastimes in the front of the book focuses on types of experiences that reveal the spirit of Venice and the Venetian Arc. Watch for Off the Beaten Path sights. Some are out of the way, some are quirky, and all are worth your while. If the munchies hit while you're exploring, look for Need a Break? suggestions.

TIME IT RIGHT

Wondering when's the best time to take your trip? Check When to Go up front for weather and crowd overviews and a list of seasonal events.

SEE IT ALL

Use Fodor's exclusive Great Itineraries as a model for your trip. Good Walks guide you to important sights in each neighborhood; ▶ indicates the starting points of walks in the text and on the map.

BUDGET WELL

Hotel and restaurant price categories from ¢ to $$$$ are defined in the opening pages of the Where to Stay and Where to Eat chapters—expect to find a balanced selection for every budget. For attractions, we always give standard adult admission fees; reductions are sometimes available for children, students, and senior citizens.

BASIC INFO

Smart Travel Tips lists travel essentials. To find the best way to get around, look under individual modes of travel ("Boat & Ferry," "Car," "Train") for details. At the end of listings we give phone numbers, addresses, and Web sites so you can check on particulars.

ON THE MAPS

Maps throughout the book show you what's where and help you find your way around. Black and orange numbered bullets ❶ ❶ in the text correlate to bullets on maps.

BACKGROUND	In general, we give background information in the course of explaining sights as well as in CloseUp boxes.
FIND IT FAST	Within the Exploring Venice chapter, sights are grouped by neighborhood, starting with the Piazza San Marco in the heart of the city. Where to Eat and Where to Stay are also organized by neighborhood. The Nightlife & the Arts and Sports & the Outdoors chapters are arranged alphabetically by entertainment type. Within Shopping, a description of the city's main shopping districts is followed by a list of specialty shops grouped according to their focus. The Southern Veneto, Northern Veneto, and Friuli-Venezia Giulia chapters explore the regions that surround Venice, subdivided by town, with the towns covered in logical geographical order. Heads at the top of each page help you find what you need within a chapter.
DON'T FORGET	Restaurants are open for lunch and dinner daily unless we state otherwise; we mention dress only when there's a specific requirement and reservations only when they're essential or not accepted—it's always best to book ahead. Hotels have private baths, phones, TVs, and air-conditioning unless otherwise indicated. We always list facilities but not whether you'll be charged extra to use them, so when pricing accommodations, find out what's included.

SYMBOLS

Many Listings

★ Fodor's Choice
★ Highly recommended
⊠ Physical address
✦ Directions
🕮 Mailing address
☎ Telephone
🖷 Fax
⊕ On the Web
✉ E-mail
💳 Admission fee
🕗 Open/closed times
⚑ Start of walk/itinerary
Ⓥ Vaporetto stops
⊟ Credit cards

Hotels & Restaurants

🏨 Hotel
🛏 Number of rooms
⚒ Facilities
🍽 Meal plans
✕ Restaurant
⚓ Reservations
🏛 Dress code
✕🏨 Hotel with restaurant that warrants a visit

Other

☾ Family-friendly
🔢 Contact information
⇨ See also
⊠ Branch address
☞ Take note

ON THE ROAD WITH FODOR'S

A trip takes you out of yourself. Concerns of life at home disappear, driven away by more immediate thoughts—about, say, what marvels will beguile the next day, or where you'll have dinner. That's where Fodor's comes in. We make sure that you know all your options, so that you don't miss something that's just around the next bend. Because the best memories of your trip might well have nothing to do with what you came to Venice and the Venetian Arc to see, we guide you to sights large and small all. You might set out with visits to the Basilica di San Marco and the Palazzo Ducale at the top of your list, but back at home you find yourself unable to forget a wonderful meal at a tiny *bacaro* just off the Rialto fish market. With Fodor's at your side, serendipitous discoveries are never far away.

Our success in showing you every corner of Venice and the Venetian Arc is a credit to our extraordinary writers. Although there's no substitute for travel advice from a good friend who knows your style, our contributors are the next best thing—the kind of people you would poll for travel advice if you knew them.

From African war zones to Asian mountaintops, writer and journalist Elaine Eliah has captured pieces of the world in words. Since settling in Venice in 1999, she's rowed nearly every canal and sailed many of the Venetian Republic's Adriatic trade routes. She currently writes, teaches English, and helps travelers discover the magic of her adopted home.

David Graham was a tour guide in Europe, Southeast Asia, and the Middle East before moving to Vicenza in the 1980s. During his years in the Venetian Arc region he's been particularly inspired by the hand-tended vineyards, the spectacular mountains, and Trieste's sparkling coastline. David now lives in Venice, where he is a translator specializing in art and architecture.

Food maven and Florence resident Patricia Rucidlo holds master's degrees in Italian Renaissance history and art history. When she's not extolling the virtues of a Pontormo masterpiece or angrily defending the Medici, she's leading wine tours, catering private dinner parties, or working on a cookbook.

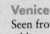

Venice

Seen from the window of a plane, Venice looks like a fish arranged on a blue tray, with Piazza San Marco located exactly at its belly. The tail consists of the picturesque neighborhood of Castello, where the workers of the Republic's legendary Arsenal once lived. The fins would correspond to the long Giudecca island to the south and the *sestieri* (neighborhoods) of San Polo and Santa Croce in the middle. The train station stands in place of the imaginary fish's eye, while the commercial harbor is where its mouth would be. On a clear day you can just catch a glimpse of the glittering ribbon of water drawing an inverted "S" across the city—the celebrated Grand Canal. The four dots of land swimming off the back of the fish are the islands of the northern lagoon: San Michele, Murano, Burano, and Torcello.

Although Venice is smaller in size than most major Italian towns—you can walk from head to tail in about an hour—a warren of some 2,300 alleys multiplies your walking options, and the choice of itineraries is wide. An efficient water-transportation system led French architect Le Corbusier to conclude that Venice is the perfect city of the future, with two distinct networks of "streets," which allow for relaxed pedestrian circulation as well as speedy delivery of goods.

The Grand Canal Venice's incomparable main street testifies to the genius and expertise of its builders and architects and to the desires of its nobility, who had their showcase palaces built one after another. Among the landmarks you float by are the imposing facade of Palazzo Vendramin-Calergi, now the winter site of the town's casino; the finely wrought Ca' d'Oro, once covered in gold; and the baroque Santa Maria della Salute, built by Venetians to thank the Virgin Mary for having brought an end to a terrible plague. You'll pass under the Rialto Bridge and then the Ponte dell'Accademia, and as you catch sight of Palazzo Ducale you'll want to turn the boat around and do it all over again. But why not wait until nightfall, and sail across magic Venice under the moonlight?

Piazza San Marco No matter how you arrive in Venice, keep in mind that Piazza San Marco was the grand gateway of the Republic. It's easy to see why Napoléon called the square "Europe's stupendous drawing-room." Almost nothing has changed since then—even the four Byzantine horses that the emperor stole from the Basilica's loggia were kindly returned to the city—and a bit of the courteous atmosphere of the past comes back during Carnevale. An estimated 35,000 visitors a day come to this corner of the Mediterranean to admire the sights that made Venice world famous well before the days of mass tourism: the Basilica di San Marco, with its 4,000 sq m (42,985 sq ft) of glittering mosaics, built to treasure the relics of the Evangelist that were stolen from Alexandria in 828; and the exquisite Palazzo Ducale, the Gothic residence of the democratically elected doge and headquarters of the government.

San Marco The sestiere of San Marco is the most central of Venice's six districts, and one of the most expensive neighborhoods in Italy. It's no wonder high-fashion designers opened boutiques and shops here that rival the best in Rome and Milan. Art galleries, jewelry shops, and glass showrooms thrive as well. Some of the city's grandest hotels, all with a view of the Bacino di San Marco, are along the quarter mile between Campo Santa Maria del Giglio and San Zaccaria. Windows and the famous Piazza are not the only attractions of this busy sestiere. To start with, it claims one of the most-photographed bridges in the world, the Ponte di Rialto, heavy with history and souvenir stalls. Tucked away in an alley off Campo Manin is the Scala del Bovolo, perhaps the most graceful spiral staircase ever built. Nearby is the large Campo Santo Stefano, with cafés and usually a soccer match or two played up against the side of the church. The Teatro La Fenice, with a rich season of operas, concerts, and lectures, served as Venice's center of musical culture until it was devastated by fire in 1996. Restoration work has been bogged down in delays, but it is hoped that the *fenice* (phoenix) will rise again from its ashes.

Dorsoduro The sestiere of Dorsoduro was a favorite of American and English expatriates from the days of the Grand Tour. The one who made the most lasting impression was American heiress and art collector Peggy Guggenheim, who settled in a palace on the Grand Canal and got around in her private gondola. Her small but choice collection of modern art is now one of the most pleasant museums to visit in town. The engaging Gallerie dell'Accademia nearby contain many masterpieces of Western painting of the 14th through 19th centuries; and the Museo del Settecento Veneziano, housed in baroque Ca' Rezzonico, opens a dramatic window on the lifestyle of 18th-century Venice. As with the Grand Canal, it's hard to get enough of the Zattere promenade, which skirts the wide Canale della Giudecca and at night offers some of Venice's most romantic views. Make a point of coming here for a cup of gelato or a glass of prosecco at one of the outdoor cafés. The city's prettiest budget hotels cluster along the silent *fondamente* (streets) of Dorsoduro. An array of artisans' shops, including mask workshops, book binderies, and wood carving shops, has sprouted in recent years to cater to the increasing numbers of independent tourists that explore the city at a relaxed pace.

San Polo & Santa Croce Although attractions like the Frari, with two paintings by Titian, and the Scuola di San Rocco, lavishly decorated by Tintoretto, draw big crowds, the surrounding areas don't have the touristy feel or souvenir shops reserved for the main drag leading to the Rialto Bridge. A visit to the Rialto market, with its produce stalls and large *pescheria* (fish market), is an essential part of any visit to Venice. A few steps away are worthwhile sites: have a look at Palazzo Mocenigo, a Venetian noble apartment dating from the 18th century, the Renaissance Scuola Grande di San Giovanni Evangelista, and the San Giacomo dell'Orio. In the summer, the large Campo San Polo hosts the Cinema all'Aperto, with open-air shows of first-run movies (often international productions with Italian subtitles).

Cannaregio A short distance from the bustle of the train station, Cannaregio offers some of the quietest and prettiest canal-side walks in town. You won't see any great-looking palaces, but the colorful boats and picturesque canals make up for the lack of architectural splendor. Too few visitors see the parish church of Renaissance painter Tintoretto, Chiesa della Madonna dell'Orto. And it seems only younger folks in search of wine and live music tread the Fondamenta della Misericordia after dark. The Jewish Ghetto has a fascinating history and tradition all its own. Here you can take a tour of some of the world's oldest synagogues and eat and drink kosher.

Castello For those who have been to Rome and visited the once working-class quarter of Trastevere, perhaps it makes sense to hear that the east side of Castello has been called "the Trastevere of Venice" for its lack of palaces and concentration of humble houses around which neighborhood life turns. Adventurous tourists who get out to Sant'Elena, San Pietro di Castello, and the Arsenale face an almost total absence of bars and shops, with the exception of Via Garibaldi and its tiny morning produce market, low-key shops, and watering holes. The Giardini della Biennale comes to life in the summer of odd years, when the Biennale dell'Arte draws crowds of intellectuals and art dealers from all over the world.

Churches that could make a Renaissance pope jealous await as you head back west from the mighty gate of the Arsenale, and the streets partially resume a more familiar appearance. San Francesco della Vigna, Santi Giovanni e Paolo, Santa Maria dei Miracoli, and, near Piazza San Marco, San Zaccaria, all deserve a visit, as does the Scuola di San Giorgio degli Schiavoni for its remarkable paintings by Carpaccio.

San Giorgio & the Giudecca Technically islands off the city's southern edge, San Giorgio and the Giudecca are within such an easy reach from San Zaccaria and the Zattere that they seem like extensions of central Venice. The view from the top of San Giorgio's Campanile on a clear day is the real reason to make the trip. The only other thing to see on San Giorgio is Palladio's church, San Giorgio Maggiore, which is rather bland on the inside, although worth a look for two important works by Tintoretto: *The Gathering of Manna* and *The Last Supper.*

The Giudecca, a forlorn neighborhood that became Venice's industrial center in the 19th century, now holds the Art Deco remains of a gigantic flour mill, the Molino Stucky, and of the Dreher beer factory. The accommodation options are few: you can sleep in a $1,300 suite at the Cipriani Hotel, or spend 20 bucks for a bed in Venice's largest hostel. Bars are almost as scarce as in the east side of Castello, but some make the trip just to visit Harry's Dolci, the closest you can get in Venice to a Viennese café. On the third weekend in July, the island celebrates the Festa del Redentore with a sumptuous display of fireworks and the building of a pontoon across the Canale della Giudecca to facilitate the pilgrimage to Palladio's Chiesa del Redentore.

Islands of the Lagoon A trip to Murano, home to Venice's glass-blowing industry, will introduce you to this centuries-old art by means of a well-arranged glass museum and the many free demonstrations that the smaller furnaces use to draw tourists inside their showrooms.

Burano looks a bit like a toy town—the low fishermen's houses are traditionally painted with the brightest colors possible to make them visible even in the thickest of the lagoon's fogs. The Museo del Merletto contains paragons of antique lace made with threads as fine as cobwebs. They look nothing like the machine-made, often imported lace sold as "made in Burano" throughout Venice. The farther-flung Torcello was a lagoon power in the days before Venice was born; now its dreamlike atmosphere fosters legends like that of the Ponte del Diavolo, where the Devil, in the shape of a black cat, is believed to appear at the center of the unfenced arch every Christmas Eve at midnight.

The Lido is part of the narrow strip of land to the south that separates the Adriatic Sea from the lagoon, and since the beginning of the 20th century has served as Venice's fashionable beach resort. A sprinkle of stardust inebriates the island for the 10 days of the Biennale del Cinema in late August, the international film festival that rivals Cannes.

Southern Veneto

In the green plains to the west of the Venetian lagoon lie the art cities of Padua, Vicenza, and Verona, each with their own unique attractions, yet all bearing the Venetian patina of chic. Padua draws art-lovers for the cycle of Giotto frescoes in the Scrovegni chapel, and Donatello's imposing bronze statue of *Il Gattamelata,* splendidly sited outside the Basilica di Sant'Antonio. Elegant Vicenza bears the hallmark of the 16th-century architect Andrea Palladio, as do the nearby Villa La Rotonda, Villa Pisani, and Villa Barbaro, where Venetian aristocrats vied with one another in the opulence of their holiday haunts. The most westerly city, Verona, is known the world over for its legendary lovers, Romeo and Juliet, though it's the breathtaking Roman arena that really steals the show—and still packs operagoers in for thrilling performances. Some of Italy's best shopping is concentrated here, with all the fashion names you could wish for. Verona is also the gateway to Lake Garda, with azure water and mountain vistas that provide some of the most stunning settings in Italy.

Northern Veneto

The north of the region is presided over by the Dolomites, a magnet for connoisseurs of scenery attracted by the lush meadows of the valleys, the crystal waters of the lakes, and, most of all, the giant jagged teeth of the magnificent peaks. For others, this is the place to vaunt the latest Italian fashion accessories, for to be seen in Cortina d'Ampezzo is just as important as to ski here. But more enduring pleasures await a little further south—the Palladian bridge over the river at Bassano del Grappa, the enchanting vistas from Asolo, the perfectly preserved walls of Cittadella, and the checkerboard square of Marostica. All these are matched by the artistic delights of the region's capital, Treviso, whose medieval streets and churches are enlivened by striking frescoes from as early as the 13th century.

Friuli-Venezia Giulia

In the northeastern spur of Italy, sipping coffee in an Art Nouveau coffee house, swimming in the Adriatic, and visiting one of the oldest centers of Christianity is all possible in one day. The grand buildings of Trieste bear the imprint of Maria Theresa, empress of the Austrian Habsburg dynasty for which the city was the principal maritime outpost. Farther west, past the coastal haunts of Rilke and Dante and the saltwhite castle of Miramare, stands Aquileia, whose basilica took shape in the early 4th century and contains the most extensive early Christian mosaics in the West. Due north, the Tempietto Longobardo in Cividale del Friuli is unique for its Lombard art. Udine boasts works by the Venetian master Tiepolo. After feasting the eye, feasts for the stomach await in Western Carnia, a mountainous zone of forests and tiny hamlets where wild game, herbs, and the freshest greenery are cooked over a heartening *fogolar* (central fireplace).

You could easily spend 10 days visiting Venice's monuments, wandering in the less-central neighborhoods, taking trips to the islands of the lagoon, shopping, and eating good fish. But Venice is also a popular weekend destination, and it fills two days to the brim with sights, walks, and wonder.

If You Have Two Days

The best introduction to the city is an early morning cruise along the **Grand Canal** from Piazzale Roma to San Zaccaria. You'll treasure seeing **Piazza San Marco** for the first time from the water as travelers before you have for hundreds of years. Spend the morning visiting the **Basilica** and **Palazzo Ducale**, allowing time to climb the **Campanile**. After lunch, take Salizzada San Moisè and Calle Larga XXII Marzo—lined with fashionable shops—to reach the *traghetto* (gondola ferry) in Campo Santa Maria del Giglio. Once across the Grand Canal, bear left and walk to the baroque **Chiesa della Madonna della Salute**, with several paintings by Titian. The Punta della Dogana, to the right as you come out of the church, opens to one of the best panoramas in town. Head for the **Peggy Guggenheim Collection**, home of first-rate 20th-century art, and then stretch your legs on the Zattere promenade while having a gelato. After dinner, splurge on a romantic gondola ride.

On day two, start early to beat the crowds at the **Rialto Bridge** and market. Don't miss the lively pescheria, where fish have been sold for more than 1,000 years. Follow the main drag to Campo San Polo and the **Chiesa dei Frari**, with two important works by Titian. Visit the **Scuola Grande di San Rocco**, famous for a series of more than 50 paintings by Tintoretto—Venice's answer to the Sistine Chapel. After lunch, jump into 18th-century Venice at **Ca' Rezzonico**, home of the Museo del Settecento Veneziano. Finish your day with a visit to the **Gallerie dell'Accademia**, with masterpieces of Western painting dating from the 14th to 19th century, or stroll to the center along the Ponte dell'Accademia for late-afternoon shopping.

If You Have Four Days

Start day three at the **Museo Correr**, dedicated to the art and history of Venice, before exploring the sestiere of Castello. On a clear morning, an alternative to the museum is the **Isola di San Giorgio**, with breathtaking views of the lagoon and the city. From Piazza San Marco, go to the church of **San Zaccaria**, with a famous altarpiece by Giovanni Bellini. Then visit the Greek church of **San Giorgio dei Greci**, lined with Byzantine icons. Time your walk to hit the **Scuola di San Giorgio degli Schiavoni** before it closes at midday. Head to the graceful **Santa Maria Formosa**, and then take Calle del Paradiso via Campo Santa Marina toward a miracle born of marble, **Santa Maria dei Miracoli**. After a late lunch, visit **Campo Santi Giovanni e Paolo** and its Gothic abbey; then take Barbaria delle Tole to the **Campo dell'Arsenale**, only a short walk from the picturesque island of **San Pietro di Castello**. Take vaporetto Line 82 from the Giardini della Biennale to the **Giudecca**, where you can have dinner, or return to Piazza San Marco along the Riva degli Schiavoni, particularly beautiful at sunset.

On your final morning, take a guided tour of the **Jewish Ghetto**. Board vaporetto Line 42 (Ponte delle Guglie landing) by 11 AM, cruising to the islands of the lagoon: **Murano** and its glass museum, where you should stop for lunch; **Burano** and its lace museum, where you should have a *merenda* (afternoon tea) with the local cookies called *buranelli*; and romantic **Torcello**, wrapped in the mists of the lagoon. Unless you are dining at Locanda Cipriani, plan for dinner in central Venice.

Venice is most crowded from April to October, during Christmas, and of course during Carnevale, so serious sightseers might want to consider a winter visit. This so-called low season is cooler and inevitably rainier, but though you may encounter a high tide, you're unlikely to encounter a high tourist density. You'll have less waiting in line, unhurried viewing of sights, substantial hotel discounts, and you'll find local people far less tourist-fatigued.

Climate

Weather-wise, the best sightseeing months are March, April, May, June, September, and October—generally pleasant and not too hot. In July and August, when southeasterly *scirocco* winds sweep Venice, days can get hot and sticky. Brief afternoon thunderstorms are common (and welcome) throughout the Veneto region. Venetian winters are relatively mild but always include foggy days, some rainy spells, and the risk of *acqua alta* (high water, when portions of the city flood). Inland towns are generally colder in winter and hotter in summer than Venice but less humid.

🛈 Forecasts **Weather Channel Connection** ☎ 900/932–8437, 95¢ per minute from a Touch-Tone phone ⊕ www.weather.com.

VENICE

Jan.	42F	6C	May	70F	21C	Sept.	75F	24C
	33	1		56	13		61	16
Feb.	46F	8C	June	76F	25C	Oct.	65F	19C
	35	2		63	17		53	12
Mar.	53F	12C	July	81F	27C	Nov.	53F	12C
	41	5		66	19		44	7
Apr.	62F	17C	Aug.	80F	27C	Dec.	46F	8C
	49	10		65	19		37	3

ON THE CALENDAR

Contact the Italian Government Tourist Board (⇨ Visitor Information, *in Smart Travel Tips*) for exact dates and further information on all the festivals held in Venice and the Venetian Arc.

WINTER	
Jan.	Art movies from central and eastern Europe are shown at the Alpe-Adria Film Festival (⊕ www.alpeadriacinema.it/edizioneX/den.htm) in Trieste.
Jan. 6	For the Regata delle Befane, senior members of historical Bucintoro rowing club get dressed as the witch of the Befana to race along the Grand Canal.
10–12 days preceding Lent	Carnevale, dating from the Middle Ages, is celebrated in Venice with plays, masked balls, concerts, and fireworks.
SPRING	
Sun. in Mar. or Apr.	Su Zo per i Ponti. In this family fun run, you can choose the distance you'd like to cover while you join thousands of others climbing "up and down the bridges" as the race's name translates.
First weekend of Spring	FAI Day of Springtime. Throughout Italy, monuments normally closed to the public are open for free visits. ⊕ www.fondoambiente.it
Apr. 25	For the Festa di San Marco a solemn Mass is held in the Basilica di San Marco to honor the city's patron saint, and red roses are sold.
Sun. in May (depends on tide)	Crews bring their own boats for La Vogalonga, an amateur rowing race.
May (coincides with Vogalonga)	Mediterranean wooden boats are celebrated at Navalis, held in Arsenale.
Last Sun. in May or 1st in June	The Sagra delle Ciliege (Cherry Festival) is held in the castle yard at Marostica.
6th Sun. after Easter	On Festa della Sensa (Ascension Day) a procession of boats leaves San Marco for the Lido, and the mayor, doge for a day, throws a golden ring in the water to celebrate the wedding of Venice and the Adriatic.
May & June	Vicenza's Teatro Olimpico hosts a concert season (⊕ www.olimpico.vicenza.it/it/festival.html) A Jazz Festival featuring internationally renowned performers is staged at various venues in Vicenza.
SUMMER	
June	The International Jazz Festival (☎ 0458077201 ⊕ www.estateteatraleveronese.it) takes place in Verona. Classical, traditional, and contemporary musicians perform for Venezia Suono in dozens of campi around the city one Sunday in June.
2nd wk of June	Arquà Petrarca's Festa della Sacra Trinità features local food and wine tastings, theater performances, and music.

3rd wk of June	La Maciliana is celebrated in Chioggia with medieval fun and games.
Mid-June to early Nov.	In even-numbered years, La Biennale brings together contemporary artists from around the world for an exhibition in Venice.
End of June.	The Dama Castellana (⊕ www.dama.tv.it) in Conegliano has a human chess match with processions, flag waving, and fireworks.
End of June to early Sept.	Verona's Festival dell'Opera brings several spectacular productions to the city's historic arena.
3rd weekend of July	On the eve of the Festa del Redentore, commemorating the end of a 16th-century plague, *foghi* (fireworks) explode above the Giudecca and the following morning crowds of pilgrims cross the Canale della Guidecca over a pontoon bridge built for the event.
Third week of July	The Sagra del Pesce (Fish Festival) in Chioggia has fish tasting, music, poetry, and theater.
July & Aug.	A Shakespeare Festival is staged at the Teatro Romano in Verona. The Festival Internazionale dell'Operetta is held at various venues in Trieste. Bassano del Grappa's Opera Estate Festival includes classical and jazz music, dance, opera, cinema, and theater.
1st weekend in Aug.	The Palio di Feltre combines a series of medieval games with fine wine and good food.
Mid-Aug.	Le Nozze Carsiche is a one-week reenactment of 19th-century weddings at Monrupino, near Trieste (held in odd-numbered years).
End of Aug.– early Sept.	Biennale del Cinema, Venice's international film festival, takes place on the Lido, where first runs of movies are shown in the Palazzo del Cinema.
FALL	
First Sun. of Sept.	A procession of historic boats with crews in Renaissance costumes opens the Regata Storica rowing competition.
Second weekend in Sept.	The *partita a scacchi* is a giant chess game played out by humans in Marostica in even-numbered years.
Sun. in Sept.	A palio with ten competing districts is run in Montagnana one Sunday in September.
Second & Third weekends. in Sept.	The Giostra della Rocca in Monselice relives medieval feasting games, climaxing with the *quintana* (medieval competition).
Third weekend in Sept.	A *palio* (horse race) run by Roman chariots takes place in the streets of Asolo.
Sept. & Oct.	The Teatro Olimpico in Vicenza hosts a classical drama season.
Oct.	Watch from hills as nearly 2000 boats compete in Trieste's annual Barcolana sailing regatta, the second weekend of October. On the last Sunday of October, the Venice Marathon begins in Stra and follows the Brenta River into Venice.
Nov. 21	Festa della Madonna della Salute traditional thanksgiving pilgrimage to light candles at the Chiesa della Madonna della Salute.

PLEASURES & PASTIMES

The Art of Enjoying Art

Travel veterans will tell you that the endless series of masterpieces in Venice's churches, palaces, and museums can cause first-time visitors—eyes glazed over from a heavy downpour of images, dates, and names—to lean, Pisa-like, on their companions for support. After a surfeit of Tiepolo and Tintoretto and the 14th Titian, even the greatest of the Venetian masters may begin to pall. The secret, of course, is to act like a turtle—not a hare—and take your sweet time. Instead of trotting after briskly efficient tour guides, allow the splendors of the age to unfold—slowly.

Museums are only the most obvious places to view art; there are always the trompe l'oeil renderings of Assumptions that float across church ceilings and campo scenes that might be Carpaccio paintings brought to life. Of course, there may be many art treasures that will not quicken your pulse, but one morning you may see a Veronese so perfect, so beautiful, that your knees will buckle.

Carnevale

" . . . All the world repaire to Venice to see the folly and madnesse of the Carnevall . . .'tis impossible to recount the universal madnesses of this place during this time of licence," commented traveler John Evelyn in 1646. Indeed, Carnevale was once an excuse for all manner of carnal indulgence. In its 18th-century heyday, festivities began on December 26 and lasted two months; the festival has since traded some of its more outlandish flavor for commercialization and lasts only for the 12 days preceding Ash Wednesday.

If you plan to join the revelers, give some thoughts to your fancy dress, as even visitors there just to observe can feel quite naked without a costume. Do pack Grandma's Charleston dancing gown, spruce up your best Halloween suit, or cut and sew a brand-new garment—the more color and sparkles and out-of-this-worldness the better—but if you are short of time and can't pilfer from an attic, Venice has, of course, a bevy of costume rental shops (⇨ Specialty Shops *in* Chapter 6).

Concerts & Opera

Chances are you'll have to choose between concerts in Venice—most nights there are different performances in various theaters and churches. The love of Italian culture need not stop at Venice. Verona, Trieste, and Vicenza offer some of the most spectacular opportunities for indulging in a passion for open-air opera and concerts. An opera in the Roman arena at Verona is a spectacle overflowing with exuberance and flair. Stars of the opera world are regular fixtures—José Carreras and Placido Domingo have graced the stage in past years. Verona and Vicenza also have free concerts in the villas and churches, much lower-key affairs but still extravagantly performed. The festival season runs from July to August, when you can also attend the international operetta festival held in Trieste and jazz festivals in Verona and Vicenza.

Delicious Fish

The old Italian saying "Fish needs to swim three times: in water, in oil, and in wine" applies here, and although there is some meat to be found on local menus, consider your trip to Venice in part an opportunity to eat local fish, much of it strange to foreign eyes—fried, baked, grilled, simmered, stewed, marinated, and even whipped. The average standard of Venetian restaurants has suffered from the effects of tourism, but fine restaurants are still to be found, and the kind of family-run trattoria called *bacaro con cucina* makes it possible to eat well at a fair price.

Getting Lost

There's no escaping the fact that Venice is a difficult place to navigate. Narrow, winding streets, a shortage of easily visible landmarks to orient yourself by, and near-meaningless address numbers all add to the confusion. Fortunately, getting lost in Venice can be a pleasure. You may not find the Titian masterpiece you'd set out to see, but instead you might come across an ageless bacaro or a charming shop that makes your afternoon; opportunities for such serendipity abound. And the city is nothing if not self-contained—sooner or later, perhaps with the help of a patient native, you can rest assured that you'll regain your bearings.

Shopping

You'll find all the style and quality you want in the streets of Venice and the main cities of the Veneto, lined with the heavyweight fashion names. Leather goods, shoes, clothing, jewelry, and ceramics of a superior quality are also specialties. In Venice look out for glassware, lace, and paper goods; in Bassano, colorful ceramics; in the Dolomites, hand-crafted wooden items. But take time to veer off the well-frequented tourist trails; for the best finds, let fate be your guide. Poking about in the narrow streets will often unearth original gift shops, where you might find that little item for the kitchen, or that lovely embroidered curtain or tablecloth that you admired in a restaurant the night before. Before buying any bulky or heavy items, check on how much it will cost to have them shipped home. Most pleasurable of all are the local markets, works of art in themselves, bulging with a vivid variety of greenery, mounds of rich red cherries, and sculptures of glittering fish. Every town also has a general market, which can be bargain-hunting grounds. On specific days of the week there's usually also an antiques-and-curios market.

Villas & Palazzos

Countless villas and palaces are sprinkled throughout the Venetian hinterland—none more notable than those designed by of Andrea Palladio, the Renaissance architect responsible for such masterpieces as Villa la Rotonda (near Vicenza) and Villa Barbaro (near Maser). The region's gracious country homes, Palladian or otherwise, give insight into how wealthy Venetians used to (and still do) get away from it all. Many of the villas are privately owned but are open to the public at certain times or by special request.

FODOR'S CHOICE

The sights, restaurants, hotels, and other travel experiences on these pages are our editors' top picks—our Fodor's Choices. They're the best of their type in the area covered by the book—not to be missed and always worth your time. In the destination chapters that follow, you will find all the details.

LODGING

$$$$ **Colombina,** Castello, Venice. A 16th-century palazzo has been converted into a quiet, romantic inn minutes from San Marco.

$$$$ **Duchi d'Aosta,** Trieste, Friuli-Venezia Giulia. Venetian Renaissance elegance pervades this gracious waterfront hotel in the heart of Trieste.

$$$$ **Gabbia d'Oro,** Verona, Southern Veneto. Romanticism reigns at this historic hotel filled with antique furnishings and sumptuous fabrics.

$$$$ **Il Palazzo at the Bauer,** San Marco, Venice. The last word in Venetian luxury includes a terrace and hot tub with views over the entire city.

$$$$ **Metropole,** Castello, Venice. The most intimate of Venice's luxury hotels is filled with antiques and character.

$$–$$$ **Pensione Accademia Villa Maravege,** Dorsoduro, Venice. A garden with a view of the Grand Canal is just one of the pleasures at this exemplary Venetian villa.

$$ **Due Mori,** Marostica, Northern Veneto. The elegant, modern rooms here are an ideal base for visiting the hills of the northern Veneto.

$$ **Villa Igea,** Castello, Venice. An intimate feel still lingers at this former private home in a central, yet quiet location.

$$ **Villa Pisani,** near Este, Southern Veneto. Staying in a grand 16th-century villa surrounded a 15-acre park makes for something more than a typical B&B experience.

BUDGET LODGING

$–$$ **La Calcina,** Dorsoduro, Venice. Impeccable, no-nonsense rooms with original Art Deco furnishings, a lovely reading room, and a floating deck all contribute to the experience here.

$ **Bernardi Semenzato,** Cannaregio, Venice. In a city markedly short on good budget options, this is a welcome exception.

¢   **Istituto San Giuseppe,** Castello, Venice. Rooms are spartan at this convent, but the nuns maintain them with pride.

RESTAURANTS

$$$$ **Antico Pignolo,** San Marco, Venice. Dine on pitch-perfect renditions of classic Venetian cuisine served in a 13th-century spice shop; when the weather's warm, nab a table in the garden.

$$$$ **Arquade,** near Verona, Southern Veneto. Chef Bruno Barbieri creates *nouveau* Italian cuisine that's a pure pleasure.

$$$$	**Osteria da Fiore**, San Polo, Venice. A gastronomic temple that bloomed in the city's back streets, Da Fiore tops the list of Venice's fine fish restaurants.
$$$–$$$$	**Alle Testiere**, Castello, Venice. The food is as sophisticated as the atmosphere is informal at this tiny, five-table trattoria.
$–$$	**Osteria Terraglio**, Bassano del Grappa, Northern Veneto. Come here for creative, modern cuisine that puts a premium on freshness.
$–$$	**Toni del Spin**, Treviso, Northern Veneto. At this local favorite with a homey wood Art Noveau interior, you order your meal from a list of specials scrawled on a chalkboard.

BUDGET RESTAURANTS

$	**Antipastoteca di Mare**, Trieste, Friuli-Venezia Giulia. Order up a smorgasbord of sublime seafood in this cozy osteria.
$	**Bancogiro**, Santa Croce, Venice. This osteria with contemporary flair takes full advantage of its location next to the Rialto market.
$	**Da Bastian**, Maser, Northern Veneto. The changing menu here gives you the best of whatever is in season; you can take your meal in a pleasant garden when weather permits.
$	**Trattoria Ca' d'Oro**, Cannaregio, Venice. Settle at one of the long tables for a meal of Venetian specialties and hearty pastas.
¢	**Cantina Do Mori**, San Polo, Venice. Workers from the Rialto market have been refueling at this bacaro for more than 500 years.
¢	**Cantinone**, Dorsoduro, Venice. You won't find cicheti here; the specialty is *panini*—sandwiches made with top-quality meat and cheese.
¢	**Enoteca la Mascareta**, Castello, Venice. This bacaro is a favorite evening haunt for locals.

CHURCHES

Cappella degli Scrovegni, Padua, Southern Veneto. Brilliant frescoes by Giotto, impeccably restored and preserved, decorate Italy's second-most famous chapel.
Basilica di San Marco, Venice. This one building above all others best defines the character of Venice.
San Zeno Maggiore, Verona, Southern Veneto. The rose window and bronze doors are of special note at what is quite possibly the finest Romanesque church in Italy.
Santa Maria dei Miracoli, Cannaregio, Venice. Renaissance master builder Pietro Lombardo created here a tiny marble gem.
Santa Maria Gloriosa dei Frari, San Polo, Venice. The blazing colors of two of Titian's most spectacular altarpieces illuminate this monumental Gothic church.

MUSEUMS

Gallerie dell'Accademia, Dorsoduro, Venice. During the French occupation of the city, Napoléon managed to found this incomparable collection of Venetian art.

Ca' Rezzonico, Dorsoduro, Venice. The Museum of 18th-Century Venice, housed in this palace, provides a fascinating glimpse into a world of elegant decadence.

ONLY IN THE VENETIAN ARC

Arena di Verona, Southern Veneto. Sit under the stars in this "second Colosseum" and enjoy world-class opera on a stage big enough for teams of horses.

Castello di Miramare, Friuli-Venezia Giulia. The Austrian influence over Trieste and the surrounding area is lavishly displayed at this castle for built for the Archduke Maximilian of Habsburg.

Cortina d'Ampezzo, Northern Veneto. You'll feel far from Venice as you soar in a different sort of gondola at this old-school ski resort.

PALACES

Ca' d'Oro, Cannaregio, Venice. The most regal of the palaces lining the Grand Canal doubles as a fine art museum.

Palazzo Ducale, San Marco, Venice. The home of the doges stands as an awesome testiment to a time when Venice was a great maritime power.

Villa La Rotonda, Vicenza, Southern Veneto. A kind of Renaissance update of the Pantheon in Rome, Palladio's most famous villa was the inspiration for Thomas Jefferson's Monticello, as well as numerous capitol buildings.

QUINTESSENTIAL VENICE

Biennale del Cinema. Part of the grand Biennale series of art exhibits, this film festival may rank second to Cannes in prestige, but it's unequaled for fun.

Festa del Redentore. The third Sunday in July marks Venice's most jubilant annual celebration, capped by fireworks over the Bacino di San Marco.

Gondola Ride. From daybreak to the depths of a moonlight night, it's magical to ply Venice's surreal waterways, where fairytale palazzi waltz by, veiled in silvery mist.

Ponte di Rialto. Climb Venice's most famous bridge for a classic view of the Grand Canal—then descend into the bustling markets that neighbor it.

SHOPPING

Barbieri, Castello, Venice. This has been *the* place for scarves and shawls in Venice since 1945.

Fruttaverdure, Cannaregio, Venice. Women's accessories here come in a rainbow of colors.

Gilberto Penzo, San Polo, Venice. Signor Penzo makes gondola souvenirs that are definitely not kitsch, including model kits and authentic *forcole* (oarlocks).

Scheggi di Arlecchino, Castello, Venice. The return of Carnevale has meant the revival of Venetian mask-making; here they sell the traditional styles and creative variations.

Venetia Studium, San Marco, Venice. The tradition of fine Venetian fabrics lives on at this shop, which, among other things, uses its wears to create Fortuny lamps.

SPORTS

Biking on the Lido, Venice. For a breath of fresh air, spend a day pedaling along the scenic (and flat) Lido.

Regata Storica, Venice. With its parade and four races, this annual September event is the Olympics of Venetian rowing.

Voga alla Veneta, Venice. If you're feeling adventurous, take a lesson in Gondolier-style rowing, the lagoon's quintessential sport.

SMART TRAVEL TIPS

Finding out about your destination before you leave home means you won't squander time organizing everyday minutiae once you've arrived. You'll be more streetwise when you hit the ground as well, better prepared to explore the aspects of Venice and the Venetian Arc that drew you here in the first place. The organizations in this section can provide information to supplement this guide; contact them for up-to-the-minute details, and consult the A to Z sections that end the Southern Veneto, Northern Veneto, and Friuli-Venezia Giulia chapters for facts on the various topics as they relate to the areas around Venice. Happy landings!

ADDRESSES

Venice addresses give the name of one of the city's six *sestieri* or neighborhoods (San Marco, Cannaregio, Castello, Dorsoduro, Santa Croce, and San Polo) followed by a number. The hitch is that the numbers don't necessarily run in sequential order, so San Marco 3672 and 3673 might well be several winding streets away from one another. Accordingly, Venetian addresses in this book include the nearest campo, bridge, calle, or vaporetto stop when helpful. A street that runs along a canal is called either a *riva* or a *fondamenta*.

Yellow signs, posted on many corners, point toward the major landmarks—San Marco, Rialto, Accademia, etc.—but don't count on finding these once you're deep into residential neighborhoods. Even buying a good map at a newsstand—the kind showing all street names and vaporetto routes—won't insure you don't get lost. However, getting lost in Venice may mean you've also lost most of the other tourists; patience with yourself and the Venetians you ask for help can go a long way in making the experience part of the adventure.

Italian addresses outside of Venice are fairly straightforward: the street is followed by the street number. However, you might see an address with a number plus "bis" or "A" (e.g., Via Verdi 3/bis or Via Mazzini 8/A). This indicates that 3/bis or 8/A is the next entrance or door down from Via Verdi 3 and Via Mazzini 8, respectively.

In rural areas, some addresses give only the route name or the distance in kilometers along a major road (e.g. Via Fabbri, km 4.3), or sometimes only the name of the small village in which the site is located.

AIR TRAVEL

BOOKING

When you book, look for nonstop flights and remember that "direct" flights stop at least once. Try to avoid connecting flights, which require a change of plane. Two airlines may operate a connecting flight jointly, so ask whether your airline operates every segment of the trip; you may find that the carrier you prefer flies you only part of the way. To find more booking tips and to check prices and make on-line flight reservations, log on to www.fodors.com.

CARRIERS

When flying internationally, you must usually choose between a domestic carrier, the national flag carrier of the country you are visiting, and a foreign carrier from a third country. You may, for example, choose to fly Alitalia to Italy. National flag carriers have the greatest number of nonstops. Domestic carriers may have better connections to your home town and serve a greater number of gateway cities. Third-party carriers may have a price advantage.

Alitalia—in addition to other major European airlines and smaller, privately run companies such as Meridiana and Air One—has an extensive network of internal flights in Italy. Ask your domestic or Italian travel agent about discounts, which include a 50% family reduction and up to 30% off certain night flights.

There are not many direct flights to Venice because most visitors include the city on an Italian tour that covers more commonly served airports (Rome and Milan, for instance). After landing elsewhere, many travel by train to Venice. Delta Airlines has a direct flight to Venice from the United States. Direct service from Heathrow to Venice is provided daily by Alitalia and British Airways. From Manchester there are three direct BA flights daily to Milan, and daily flights to Rome.
To & from Italy Alitalia ☎ 800/223-5730 in the U.S., 020/7602-7111 in the U.K., 06/65641 in Rome, 848/865641 elsewhere in Italy ⊕ www.alitalia.it to Rome, Milan, and Venice. **American Airlines** ☎ 800/433-7300 in the U.S., 02/679141 in Milan ⊕ www.aa.com to Milan and Rome. **British Airways** ☎ 800/247-9297 in the U.S., 0345/222-111 in the U.K., 06/65011575 in Rome, 848/812266 elsewhere in Italy ⊕ www.britishairways.com to Rome, Milan, and Venice. **Continental Airlines** ☎ 800/

231-0856 in the U.S., 06/47675205 in Rome, 800/296230 elsewhere in Italy ⊕ www.flycontinental.com to Rome and Milan. **Delta Air Lines** ☎ 800/241-4141 in the U.S., 800/864114 in Italy ⊕ www.deltaairlines.com to Rome, Milan, and Venice. **Easyjet** ⊕ www.go-fly.com **Meridiana** ☎ 020/7839-2222 in the U.K., 06/478041 in Italy ⊕ www.meridiana.it from London to Florence, Bologna, Turin, and Catania. **Northwest Airlines** ☎ 800/225-2525 in the U.S., 02/218981 in Italy ⊕ www.nwa.com to Rome and Milan. **Ryanair** ⊕ www.ryanair.com **United Airlines** ☎ 800/538-2929 in the U.S., 02/667481 in Italy ⊕ www.ual.com to Milan. **US Airways** ☎ 800/428-4322 in the U.S., 848/813177 in Italy ⊕ www.usairways.com to Rome.
Around Italy Air One ☎ 06/488800 in Rome, 848/848880 elsewhere in Italy ⊕ www.air-one.it. **Alitalia** ☎ 800/223-5730 in the U.S., 020/7602-7111 in the U.K., 06/65641 in Rome, 848/865641 elsewhere in Italy ⊕ www.alitalia.it. **Alpieagles** ☎ 041/599777 ⊕ www.alpieagles.com. **Meridiana** ☎ 020/7839-2222 in the U.K., 06/478041 in Italy ⊕ www.meridiana.it.

CHECK-IN & BOARDING

Always **find out your carrier's check-in policy.** Plan to arrive at the airport about two hours before your scheduled departure time for domestic flights and 2½ to 3 hours before international flights. You may need to arrive earlier if you're flying from one of the busier airports or during peak air-traffic times. In Venice, only Delta insists that passengers arrive two hours before their international flight. Other airlines are more flexible and in fact, negotiating security is faster and simpler in Venice than in other cities. To avoid delays at airport-security checkpoints, try not to wear any metal. Jewelry, belt and other buckles, steel-toe shoes, barrettes, and underwire bras are among the items that can set off detectors.

Assuming that not everyone with a ticket will show up, airlines routinely overbook planes. When everyone does, airlines ask for volunteers to give up their seats. In return, these volunteers usually get a several-hundred-dollar flight voucher, which can be used toward the purchase of another ticket, and are rebooked on the next flight out. If there are not enough volunteers, the airline must choose who will be denied boarding. The first to get bumped are passengers who checked in late and those flying on discounted tickets, so get to the gate and check in as early as possible, especially during peak periods.

Always **bring a government-issued photo I.D.** to the airport; even when it's not required, a passport is best.

CUTTING COSTS

The least expensive airfares to Venice and other Italian destinations are priced for round-trip travel and must usually be purchased in advance. Airlines generally allow you to change your return date for a fee; most low-fare tickets, however, are nonrefundable. It's smart to call a number of airlines and check the Internet; when you are quoted a good price, book it on the spot—the same fare may not be available the next day, or even the next hour. Always check different routings and look into using alternate airports. Also, price off-peak flights, which may be significantly less expensive than others. Travel agents, especially low-fare specialists (⇨ Discounts and Deals), are helpful.

Consolidators are another good source. They buy tickets for scheduled flights at reduced rates from the airlines, then sell them at prices that beat the best fare available directly from the airlines. Sometimes you can even get your money back if you need to return the ticket. Carefully read the fine print detailing penalties for changes and cancellations, purchase the ticket with a credit card, and confirm your consolidator reservation with the airline.
⛏ Consolidators AirlineConsolidator.com ☎ 888/468-5385 ⊕ www.airlineconsolidator.com; for international tickets. **Best Fares** ☎ 800/576-8255 or 800/576-1600 ⊕ www.bestfares.com; $59.90 annual membership. **Cheap Tickets** ☎ 800/377-1000 or 888/922-8849 ⊕ www.cheaptickets.com. **Expedia** ☎ 800/397-3342 or 404/728-8787 ⊕ www.expedia.com. **Hotwire** ☎ 866/468-9473 or 920/330-9418 ⊕ www.hotwire.com. **Now Voyager Travel** ✉ 45 W. 21st St., 5th floor, New York, NY 10010 ☎ 212/459-1616 🖷 212/243-2711 ⊕ www.nowvoyagertravel.com. **Onetravel.com** ⊕ www.onetravel.com. **Orbitz** ☎ 888/656-4546 ⊕ www.orbitz.com. **Priceline.com** ⊕ www.priceline.com. **Travelocity** ☎ 888/709-5983, 877/282-2925 in Canada, 0870/111-7060 in the U.K. ⊕ www.travelocity.com.

ENJOYING THE FLIGHT

State your seat preference when purchasing your ticket, and then repeat it when you confirm and when you check in. For more legroom, you can request one of the few emergency-aisle seats at check-in, if you are capable of lifting at least 50 pounds—a Federal Aviation Administration require-

ment of passengers in these seats. Seats behind a bulkhead also offer more legroom, but they don't have under-seat storage. Don't sit in the row in front of the emergency aisle or in front of a bulkhead, where seats may not recline.

Ask the airline whether a snack or meal is served on the flight. If you have dietary concerns, request special meals when booking. These can be vegetarian, low-cholesterol, or kosher, for example. It's a good idea to pack some healthful snacks and a small (plastic) bottle of water in your carry-on bag. On long flights, try to maintain a normal routine, to help fight jet lag. At night, get some sleep. By day, eat light meals, drink water (not alcohol), and **move around the cabin** to stretch your legs. For additional jet-lag tips consult *Fodor's FYI: Travel Fit & Healthy* (available at bookstores everywhere).

Smoking policies vary from carrier to carrier. Many airlines prohibit smoking on all of their flights; others allow smoking only on certain routes or certain departures. Ask your carrier about its policy.

FLYING TIMES

Most flights to Venice will be routed through another European hub. Flying time from New York to Venice is 9 hours, and to Milan is 8½ hours. Flying time to Milan is 10–11 hours from Chicago, and 11½ hours from Los Angeles. It's 2½ hours to fly from London to Venice. It takes travelers from Sydney 23½ hours to reach Rome.

HOW TO COMPLAIN

If your baggage goes astray or your flight goes awry, complain right away. Most carriers require that you **file a claim immediately.** The Aviation Consumer Protection Division of the Department of Transportation publishes *Fly-Rights,* which discusses airlines and consumer issues and is available on-line. You can also find articles and information on mytravelrights.com, the Web site of the nonprofit Consumer Travel Rights Center.
⛏ Airline Complaints Aviation Consumer Protection Division ✉ U.S. Department of Transportation, C-75, Room 4107, 400 7th St. SW, Washington, DC 20590 ☎ 202/366-2220 ⊕ airconsumer.ost.dot.gov. **Federal Aviation Administration Consumer Hotline** ✉ for inquiries: FAA, 800 Independence Ave. SW, Washington, DC 20591 ☎ 800/322-7873 ⊕ www.faa.gov.

RECONFIRMING

Check the status of your flight before you leave for the airport. You can do this on your carrier's Web site, by linking to a flight-status checker (many Web booking services offer these), or by calling your carrier or travel agent. Always confirm international flights at least 72 hours ahead of the scheduled departure time. Reconfirmation by phone is necessary in Venice.

AIRPORTS & TRANSFERS

Venice's Aeroporto Marco Polo (VCE) is served by domestic and international flights, including connections from 21 European cities, plus direct flights from Moscow and New York's JFK. Treviso Airport, some 20 miles north of Venice, receives Ryan Air's daily arrivals from London's Stansted Airport. The ATVO operates a connecting bus to and from Venice's Piazzale Roma for every Ryan arrival and departure.

The major gateways to Italy are Rome's Aeroporto Leonardo da Vinci, better known as Fiumicino (FCO), and Milan's Aeroporto Malpensa (MXP), which handle domestic, intercontinental, and European traffic. If you land in Rome or Milan and plan to take a train to Venice, you must first get to the main train stations in either town. In Rome you will need to take a train or a taxi to Stazione Termini; in Milan, take the convenient buses to Stazione Centrale. Trains for Venice are frequent during the day. The trip takes four to five hours from Rome, three hours or less from Milan, on the Eurostar, the fastest train. Smaller, minor gateways are served by domestic and some international flights.

🛈 Airport Information **Aeroporto Malpensa 2000** ✉ 50 km [31 mi] north of Milan ☎ 02/74852200 ⊕ www.sea-aeroportimilano.it. **Aeroporto Marco Polo** ✉ 10 km [6 mi] north of Venice, Tessera ☎ 041/2609260, 041/2609222 lost baggage ⊕ www.veniceairport.it. **Aeroporto Leonardo da Vinci/Fiumicino** ✉ 32 km [20 mi] southeast of Rome) ☎ 06/65951 ⊕ www.adr.it. **Aeroporto Treviso** ✉ 32 km [20 mi] north of Venice) ☎ 0422/315131

AIRPORT TRANSFERS

By Boat: This is the most convenient (and scenic) way to get to Venice from Aeroporto Marco Polo. A shuttlebus or 10-minute walk takes you from the terminal to a dock where public and private boats leave directly for Venice historic center. For €10 per person, including bags, Alilaguna operates service from predawn until nearly midnight. It takes about an hour to reach the landing near Piazza San Marco, stopping at the Lido on the way. A sleek *motoscafo* (water taxi), a modern powerboat, carries up to four people and four bags to city center for about €78. Each additional person, bag, or stop costs extra, so it's essential to **agree on a water-taxi fare before boarding.** The trip takes from 25 to 40 minutes, depending on your specific destination and traffic.

By Bus: Blue ATVO shuttle buses make the 20-minute nonstop trip from the airport to Piazzale Roma; from here you can get a vaporetto to the landing nearest your hotel. The ATVO fare is €2.70 and tickets are available on the bus when the airport ticket booth is closed. The yellow ACTV local bus (Line 5) leaves the airport at 10 and 40 minutes past every hour (hourly service after 11:10 PM) and takes about 30 minutes to reach Piazzale Roma; before boarding, you must buy a €1 ticket at the airport tobacconist-newsstand, open daily 6:30 AM–9 PM, or from designated ATVO/ACTV booths. During rush hour, luggage can be a hassle on the local bus.

By Taxi: A land taxi from the airport to Piazzale Roma costs about €30 and takes 15–20 minutes.

🛈 ACTV/Vela bus/vaporetto information ☎ 899/909090 ⊕ www.velaspa.com. **Alilaguna** ☎ 041/5235775. **ATVO** ☎ 041/929500 ⊕ www.atvo.it. **Radio (land) Taxi** ☎ 041/936222. **Motoscafo** ☎ 041/5415084 airport transfers.

DUTY-FREE SHOPPING

The duty-free shopping area for travelers leaving Venice for the U.S. and other non-EU countries is very small and not particularly exciting.

BEACHES

In the Veneto and Friuli regions, the tame landscape features sandy beaches with well-maintained facilities, catering mostly to crowds of locals and sunbathers from Austria and Germany. The lack of rocks and cliffs, and the shallowness of the sea, makes them ideal for families with small children. As you go from south to north, the most popular sea resorts in the area are Venice beaches on the Lido; Jesolo (40 km [25 mi] from Venice), famous for its vibrant nightlife in summer; Lignano

Sabbiadoro, named after the "golden sand" that attracts more than 100,000 visitors a day (located a few miles from the mouth of the Tagliamento River in Friuli); and the historic town of Grado, which makes a great day trip from Trieste. Inland, the shores of Lago di Garda bring together natural beauty with a low-key worldliness that includes discos, spas, and stylish restaurants; Torbole, to the north of Monte Baldo on the eastern shore, is a sailing and wind-surfing center. .

For most Italians who live along the coast, going to the beach is more a part of the regular summer routine than a vacation activity: locals head to the nearest beach during the long Italian lunch break and for the evening *passeggiata* (stroll). In Italy a healthy suntan is still much sought after, although awareness of the dangers of long-term overexposure is spreading. Creams and sunblocks are available, but read the labels carefully to make sure you are getting the protection you desire, and don't underestimate the scorching power of the Italian sun. The "tanning" season begins in early May, when bathing suits by the major designers begin to appear in the windows of Italian shops, and the beach season starts in earnest in early June, with the opening of beaches run by concessionaires.

It is essential to distinguish between the private and public beaches. The former are free and open to the public but offer no services. Although on the most popular public beaches it's sometimes possible to buy sandwiches and soft drinks from kiosks or roaming vendors, as a general rule you shouldn't expect such comforts, let alone pay telephones, toilets, or showers. Private beaches charge admission and range from spartan (cold showers and portable toilets) to luxurious (with gardens, stylish bars, fish restaurants, and private guest huts). Admission policies and prices vary accordingly: although most establishments offer day passes that cost €5–€26 per person and include a chaise lounge and an umbrella, some of the more exclusive places cater only to patrons who pay by the week or month. Inquire at local tourist offices for details.

The summer season ends on September 15. During weekends, holidays, and throughout August, sea resorts and beaches are very crowded, some posting no-vacancy signs by 10 AM. Nowhere in Italy, except in the rare nudist beach, is it common practice to walk around topless, and wearing beach attire (bare chests and thighs) in town can get you fined. Men or women pay a €40 fine for going topless in Venice, even aboard boats in the Grand Canal.

BIKE TRAVEL

Italians are great bicycling enthusiasts—in the flatlands and historical centers of the Veneto region, locals often commute by bike, and they are proud of it. Those who enjoy touring have fine bicycling itineraries at their disposal throughout Italy. One such itinerary is The Federazione Italiana Amici della Bicicletta's (FIAB) *Bicycle route of the Sun,* which runs from south to north Italy. The Web site www.cycling.it contains an interesting selection of articles (in Italian) from the publication *La Bicicletta,* with detailed descriptions of itineraries across national parks and areas of natural beauty.

Local Resources **FIAB** ✉ Viale Col Moschin 1, 30170 Mestre ☎ 041/921515 ⊕ www.fiab-onlus.it.

BIKES IN FLIGHT

Most airlines accommodate bikes as luggage, provided they are dismantled and boxed; check with individual airlines about packing requirements. Some airlines sell bike boxes, which are often free at bike shops, for about $15 (bike bags can be considerably more expensive). International travelers often can substitute a bike for a piece of checked luggage at no charge; otherwise, the cost is about $100. U.S. and Canadian airlines charge $40–$80 each way.

BOAT & FERRY TRAVEL

The only way to get around Venice is by boat or by foot, so try to learn the various canal transportation options.

GONDOLA RIDES

If you can lose the feeling you're on a Disney ride, forget the price you're paying per minute, and block out any scents or sights that hardly seem hygienic, then you're ready for Venice by gondola. Late afternoons and evenings are lovely, but can get chilly. Scenic though the Grand Canal may be, you see it from a vaporetto, whereas tiny canals are accessible only by private boat. You'll have no trouble finding boats near San Marco—it's loaded with gondola stations—but if you'd like to get off the circuit, maybe even have a canal all to yourself, try the San Tomà or Santa Sofia (near Ca' d'Oro) gondola stations. The price of fifty-minute rides is supposed to be fixed at €62 for up to six passengers, rising to €77.50 between 8 PM and 8 AM, but these are minimums and you may have difficulty finding a gondolier who'll work for that unless the city is empty. Bargaining can help, but in any case, come to terms on cost and duration before you start and make it clear that you want to see smaller canals, which aren't as crowded as the Grand Canal.

TRAGHETTI

Few tourists know about the two-man gondola ferries that cross the Grand Canal at various fixed points. At €.40, they're the cheapest and shortest gondola ride in Venice, but they can save a lot of walking. TRAGHETTO signs point the way and you hand your fare to the gondolier when you board. Note that although there are several traghetti along the Grand Canal, only San Tomà and Santa Sofia operate every day (except on major holidays) from about 7 AM to 7 PM. Don't depend on the others, which might run only mornings or weekdays, or shut down due to rain, fog, strong currents, or even for lack of passengers. Starting from the train station end of the Grand Canal, traghetto links include Ferrovia–S. Simeon Piccolo; Campo San Marcuola–Fondaco dei Turchia; Rialto Pescheria–Campo Santa Sofia (near Ca' d'Oro); Fondamenta del Vin–Riva del Carbon (near Rialto); Campo San Tomà–Calle del Traghetto (near Campiello dei Morti); San Samuele (Palazzo Grassi)–Ca' Rezzonico; Santa Maria del Giglio (Gritti Palace)–Calle Lanza (near Madonna della Salute); Dogana Point (Salute)–Calle Vallaresso.

VAPORETTI

ACTV water buses run the length of the Grand Canal and circle the city. There are several lines, some of which connect Venice with the major and minor islands in the lagoon. Vaporetti costs vary depending on the line. A one-way trip along the Grand Canal costs €5, but a one-way passage on any other line costs only €3.50 with children under 4 riding free. A traghetto ticket allows you to cross the Grand Canal, one stop only, for €1.80. Save money with *Travel Cards*, good for all ACTV vaporetti

and buses (including the Line 5 bus to the airport), which allow 24 hours of unlimited travel for €10.50 and 72 hours for €22. Line information is posted at each landing, but complete timetables for all lines are available for €.60 at ACTV/Vela ticket booths, located at most major stops. Buy tickets before getting on the boat and remember to **validate them in the yellow time-stamp machines.** Single fare tickets are sold onboard but you must ask to buy one immediately upon boarding. When inspectors come aboard, ticket-less riders are fined, as are those who didn't validate tickets. Ignorance will not spare you the €23 fine. The law says you must also buy tickets for dogs, bags over 28", and baby strollers left unfolded, and though enforcement has been minimal, ACTV has been operating in the red for some time and is expected to intensify collection efforts.

Line 1 is the Grand Canal local, making all stops except San Samuele and continuing via San Marco to the Lido. (It takes about 45 minutes from the train station to San Marco.)

Line 3 is the *morning* express connection between Tronchetto–San Marco Giardinetti from April through September. It follows the Grand Canal, stopping only at Ferrovia (train station), San Samuele, and Accademia; note that it does not stop at Piazzale Roma or Rialto (see Line 82 below). Line 3 continues in a loop, returning nonstop to Tronchetto via the Canale della Giudecca.

Line 4 is the *afternoon* express, also April through September, running nonstop Tronchetto–San Marco Giardinetti via the Canale della Giudecca and returning through the Grand Canal with stops at Accademia, San Samuele, Rialto, Ferrovia, and Piazzale Roma.

Line 12 connects the Fondamente Nuove with Murano (Faro stop only), Burano, and Torcello, but does not stop at San Michele cemetery. (See Lines 41 and 42, *below*.)

Line 41 (counterclockwise) and **Line 42** (clockwise) circle the entire city: for example, take Line 42 clockwise from San Zaccaria (near San Marco) to Redentore, but Line 41 counterclockwise to return to San Zaccaria. Taking Line 42 clockwise from the Ferrovia (train station), stops to the north include Guglie (near Jewish Ghetto), Sant'Alvise (near Sant'Alvise church),

Fondamente Nuove (connect to Burano and Torcello), Cimitero (Isola di San Michele), and several stops in Murano. Continuing clockwise from Fondamente Nuove, Line 42 rounds Sant'Elena, stops at Giardini (home of the Biennale d'Arte), Arsenale, and San Zaccaria, before making four stops on the Giudecca (Zitelle, Redentore, Palanca, and Sacca Fisola) and returning via Piazzale Roma to the Ferrovia. Before getting on board, you're wise to confirm with the boat operator that you are going in the right direction.

Line 51 makes a counterclockwise loop from the railway station to San Zaccaria via Piazzale Roma and Zattere then continues to the Lido. The reverse route leaving Lido becomes **Line 52**, which stops at Sant'Elena, Giardini, San Zaccaria, Zattere, Santa Marta, Piazzale Roma, the train station, Guglie, Tre Archi (near San Giobbe church), Sant'Alvise, Orto (near Madonna dell'Orto church), Fondamente Nuove, Ospedale, Celestia (near San Francesco della Vigna church), San Pietro di Castello, and back to the Lido.

Line DM (Direct Murano), as its name implies, connects Piazzale Roma and Ferrovia to Murano (and reverse) in about 20 minutes. In summer the boat also connects with Tronchetto.

Line 61 starts at Piazzale Roma and runs express to the Lido via Zattere; note that it does not stop at San Zaccaria. **Line 62** follows the reverse, clockwise route.

Line 5 is a nonstop boat connecting San Zaccaria–Murano from April through September. On Murano, it stops at Navagero, Faro, and Colonna before returning to San Zaccaria.

Line 82 leaves the most easterly San Zaccaria landing (Pensione Wildner), to call at San Giorgio, Giudecca, Zattere, Tronchetto, Piazzale Roma, and Ferrovia. From there, it becomes a Grand Canal express to Rialto, with some boats, between 9 AM and 9 PM, continuing to Vallaresso (San Marco) and some even servicing the Lido beaches in summer. As Line 82 runs both clockwise and counterclockwise, check with the boat operator that you're going in the right direction, especially when boarding at Ferrovia or Piazzale Roma.

Line LN loops from San Marco to Fondamente Nova (and reverse), connecting the islands of the North Lagoon. The large, triple-decker *motonave* leaves very 20 minutes from San Zaccaria (Palazzo Ducale), runs nonstop to the Lido then continues to the northern mainland at Punta Sabbione. There you can connect immediately with a smaller boat, which stops at Torcello, Burano, and Murano before landing at Fondamente Nuove and reversing direction.

Line N is the night or "notte" line with boats leaving every 20 minutes from the Lido to San Zaccaria and back, and from Rialto to Piazzale Roma and back. Every second boat leaving Lido, after making its stop at San Zaccaria (near Hotel Danieli), continues up the Grand Canal. Calling at major landings, it rounds Tronchetto, and stops at Zattere and the Giudecca before returning to San Zaccaria near Hotel Jolanda). Reversing direction, it runs via Giudecca-Tronchetto-Grand Canal-San Zaccaria en route to the Lido.

The **Servizio Notturno Laguna Nord** runs very limited night service from Fondamente Nuove to Murano and Burano, and back. 🅰 **ACTV** ☎ 041/5287886, 🌐 www.actv.it. **Vela** information and tickets ☎ 041/2424 €.40/min 🌐 www.hellovenezia.it.

WATER TAXIS

The stylish powerboat *motoscafi* aren't cheap; you'll spend €75 per hour to visit the islands. The fare system is convoluted, with luggage handling, waiting time, early or late hours, and even ordering a taxi from your hotel adding expense. Always agree on price first. Twenty-four-hour service is available through a number of companies and cooperatives. 🅵 **Motoscafi** ☎ 041/5222303, 041/5224281. **Water taxis for airport transfers** ☎ 041/5415084.

BUSINESS HOURS

Religious and civic holidays are frequent in Italy. Depending on their local importance, businesses may close for the day (businesses do not close on a Friday or Monday if the holiday falls on the weekend).

BANKS & OFFICES

Banks are open weekdays 8:30 to 1:30 and 2:45 to 3:45. Venice's main post office, known as Fondaco dei Tedeschi, is open Monday through Saturday 8:15 to 7 for stamps and registered mail, until 6 for other operations.

GAS STATIONS

Gas stations are generally open Monday through Saturday from 7 to 7 with a break at lunch. Many stations have automatic self-service pumps that accept bills (some also take credit cards). Gas stations on autostrade are open 24 hours.

MUSEUMS & SIGHTS

In Venice, the 15 churches belonging to the Chorus Association are open Monday through Saturday 10 to 5 and Sunday 1 to 5 (with a few minor variations). Other churches usually open early in the morning, close at noon or 12:30, then reopen late in the afternoon until about 7 PM. The Basilica di San Marco closes at 4:30 from November through April; 5:30 the rest of the year. It opens Monday through Saturday at 9:45 and Sunday at 1 PM. Sightseeing in churches is discouraged during services, usually held at 7 AM, noon, and 6:30 PM.

Museum hours vary and change with the seasons. Venice's major museums (Museo Correr, Palazzo Ducale, and the Gallerie dell'Accademia) are open daily, but weekend visits can be crowded. Other museums are closed one day a week: always check ahead.

PHARMACIES

Most pharmacies are open weekdays 9 to 12:30 and 4 to 7:30 and Saturday 9 to 12:30. Pharmacists take turns being on call overnights and holidays; you'll find their names and addresses posted at pharmacies, or listed in local newspapers and tourist publications.

SHOPS

Shops generally open weekdays 9:30 to 1 and 3:30 to 7 and on Saturday morning. In Venice, tourist-oriented shops often stay open seven days a week and do not close at midday. Food shops open 8 to 1 and 5 to 7:30 and close Sunday and Wednesday afternoon, but butchers generally work only mornings. Bars and pastry shops usually close one day a week. Barbers and hairdressers, with some exceptions, are closed Sunday and Monday. Throughout the month of August, many businesses of all kinds close for holiday.

BUS TRAVEL TO & FROM VENICE

ACTV buses to Padua (€3.30) leave at 25 and 55 minutes past each hour, and stop along the Brenta River. ATVO has daily buses to Cortina (€10.20) June–September and throughout the Christmas–New Year holidays. Buses leave Venice at 7:50 AM, and depart Cortina 3:15 PM. September–May service is only available on weekends. Bus networks throughout the Veneto and Friuli-Venezia Giulia are extensive. Though Italian trains are generally low-priced and convenient, in some areas buses can be faster and more direct, so it's worth comparing prices and timetables. *Eurolines* is especially worth looking into for intercity travel in Europe. Their network of buses runs from Portugal to Turkey, Ireland to Morocco, and many are overnight connections. Passes good from two weeks to two months can be cheaper than rail passes, especially for those over 25.

Frequent ACTV buses leave Piazzale Roma for Mestre and other destinations in the province. Line 5 runs to Aeroporto Marco Polo and Line 2 to Mestre train station. To Mestre city center, Lines 4 and 4/ follow Corso del Popolo but Line 12, using a back route, arrives quicker. Night buses run every 30 minutes between midnight and 5 AM, with Line N1 serving Mestre train station and the city's periphery; Line N2 follows Corso del Popolo through town center. Tickets, good for 60 minutes after validation, cost €1 or €9 for a book of 10. They're sold at ACTV's Piazzale Roma office from 7:30 AM to 8 PM, at tobacco shops, and at night you can buy them from coin-operated machines.

FARES & SCHEDULES

Time tables and fare schedules are available by phoning or stopping by the offices of the specific bus lines, where you'll usually find someone who speaks English. Though bus companies have Web sites, information is not always kept up to date.

RESERVATIONS

Reservations are recommended for Eurolines buses, especially during summer. ATVO buses rarely fill up but riders can guarantee a place, especially for ski weekends to Cortina, by booking ahead.

🚌 Bus Information **Bus Terminal** ✉ Piazzale Roma, across the Grand Canal from the train station, Santa Croce. **ACTV** ☎ 041/5287886 🌐 www.actv.it

✉ Lost property; ACTV office, Piazzale Roma ☎ 041/2722179. **ATVO** ☎ 041/5205530, ⊕ www. atvo.it. **Eurolines** ✉ Viale Stazione 1, Mestre Train Station ☎ 041/5382118 ⊕ www.eurolines.it.

BUS TRAVEL ON THE LIDO

Buses on the Lido leave from the vaporetto landing at Santa Maria Elisabetta. Orange Line *A* goes to San Nicolò and back. Dark blue Line *B* goes to the Alberoni/Faro Rocchetta (Malamocco) and, in the opposite direction, to the Ospedale al Mare. Blue Line C serves long Via Sandro Gallo. Green Line *V* goes to Malamocco (Via Parri). Line 11 goes to Pellestrina.

The lost-property office is open daily 7:30 AM–8 PM.

FARES & SCHEDULES

Lido bus routes and schedules are included in the same guide that lists vaporetto information. You'll find these on sale at ACTV/ Vela ticket sellers for €.60 and the staff there generally speaks English, French, and Spanish.

🚌 Bus Information **ACTV** ☎ 041/5287886 ⊕ www.actv.it ✉ Lost property; ACTV office, Piazzale Roma ☎ 041/2722179.

PAYING

The driver does not sell tickets. Buy them at ticket offices or at tobacco shops before boarding. These tickets must then be validated when entering the bus.

CAMERAS & PHOTOGRAPHY

The *Kodak Guide to Shooting Great Travel Pictures* (available at bookstores everywhere) is loaded with tips. Taking photos is discouraged in many churches and being the subject of a snapshot is a sore point with some of the Venetians. If you want to single someone out for a photo, be it an eldery woman or vendor, ask permission first.

🚌 Photo Help **Kodak Information Center** ☎ 800/ 242–2424 ⊕ www.kodak.com.

EQUIPMENT PRECAUTIONS

Silica gel packs may help keep gear free of moisture buildup during Venice's humid summers and winters. Cameras moved from air-conditioned rooms into humid weather may experience condensation problems and the lens may need drying.

Fog and mist can also be dense enough to cause some electronic cameras to fail.

Don't pack film or equipment in checked luggage, where it is much more susceptible to damage. X-ray machines used to view checked luggage are extremely powerful and therefore are likely to ruin your film. Try to ask for hand inspection of film, which becomes clouded after repeated exposure to airport X-ray machines, and keep videotapes and computer disks away from metal detectors. Always keep film, tape, and computer disks out of the sun. Carry an extra supply of batteries, and be prepared to turn on your camera, camcorder, or laptop to prove to airport security personnel that the device is real.

FILM & DEVELOPING

In Venice and most major cities you'll see scores of photo developing shops, many with service in one hour (or less). One-hour shops will develop and print a 36-exposure roll for between €10–€13. Photography stores sell film starting at €4 (24-exposure Kodak ASA 100), but you'll pay much more at kiosks and souvenir shops.

VIDEOS

While VHS videotapes and players are common, be forewarned that Italy, like other countries in Europe, uses a different video system (PAL) than that used in the United States (NTSC). Newer VCRs can often play either system.

CAR RENTAL

Rates in Venice begin at €50 a day and €200 a week for an economy car with air-conditioning, a manual transmission, and mileage limited to 150 km (93 mi) a day. This includes the 20% IVA tax on car rentals. Most major American car-rental companies have offices or affiliates in Italy, but the rates are generally better if you make a reservation from abroad rather than from within Italy. In Italy, you can save up to 30% by renting your car on-line pretending you are still abroad. Weekend rates with limited mileage are usually good deals. Note that in Italy car-rental companies usually make it mandatory to purchase the collision-damage waiver, regardless of what coverage may be provided by your credit card.

🚌 Major Agencies **Alamo** ☎ 800/522-9696 ⊕ www.alamo.com. **Avis** ☎ 800/331-1084, 800/ 879-2847 in Canada, 0870/606-0100 in the U.K.,

02/9353-9000 in Australia, 09/526-2847 in New Zealand ⊕ www.avis.com. **Budget** ☎ 800/527-0700, 0870/156-5656 in the U.K. ⊕ www.budget.com. **Dollar** ☎ 800/800-6000, 0124/622-0111 in the U.K., where it's affiliated with Sixt, 02/9223-1444 in Australia ⊕ www.dollar.com. **Hertz** ☎ 800/654-3001, 800/263-0600 in Canada, 0870/844-8844 in the U.K., 02/9669-2444 in Australia, 09/256-8690 in New Zealand ⊕ www.hertz.com. **National Car Rental** ☎ 800/227-7368, 0870/600-6666 in the U.K. ⊕ www.nationalcar.com.

CUTTING COSTS

For a good deal, book through a travel agent who will shop around. Do look into wholesalers, companies that do not own fleets but rent in bulk from those that do and often offer better rates than traditional car-rental operations. Prices are best during off-peak periods. Rentals booked through wholesalers often must be paid for before you leave home.

🚗 **Local Agencies Avis** ✉ Piazzale Roma ☎ 041/5225825 ✉ Aeroporto Marco Polo ☎ 041/5415030, 199/100133 countrywide ⊕ www.avis.com. **Hertz** ✉ Piazzale Roma ☎ 041/5284091 ✉ Aeroporto Marco Polo ☎ 041/5416075, 199/112211 countrywide ⊕ www.hertz.com. **Sixt Rent-a-Car** ✉ Aeroporto Marco Polo ☎ 041/5415654 ⊕ www.sixt.it. **Thrifty** ✉ Aeroporto Marco Polo ☎ 041/5415032 ⊕ www.italybycar.it.

🚗 **Wholesalers Auto Europe** ☎ 207/842-2000 or 800/223-5555 ☎ 207/842-2222 ⊕ www.autoeurope.com. **Europe by Car** ☎ 212/581-3040 or 800/223-1516 ☎ 212/246-1458 ⊕ www.europebycar.com. **Destination Europe Resources** (DER) ✉ 9501 W. Devon Ave., Rosemont, IL 60018 ☎ 800/782-2424 ⊕ www.der.com. **Kemwel** ☎ 800/678-0678 ☎ 207/842-2124 ⊕ www.kemwel.com.

INSURANCE

When driving a rented car you are generally responsible for any damage to or loss of the vehicle. Collision policies that car-rental companies sell for European rentals typically don't cover stolen vehicles. Indeed, all car-rental agencies operating in Italy require that you buy a theft-protection policy. Before you rent—and purchase collision coverage—see what coverage you already have under the terms of your personal auto-insurance policy and credit cards.

REQUIREMENTS & RESTRICTIONS

In Italy your own driver's license is acceptable. An International Driver's Permit is a good idea; it's available from the American or Canadian Automobile Association and, in the United Kingdom, from the Automobile Association or Royal Automobile Club. These international permits are universally recognized, and having one in your wallet may save you a problem with the local authorities. In Italy you must be 21 years of age to rent an economy or sub-compact car and at least 25 years of age to rent a bigger car. Upon rental, all companies require credit-card numbers as a warranty.

SURCHARGES

Before you pick up a car in one city and leave it in another, ask about drop-off charges or one-way service fees, which can be substantial. Note, too, that some rental agencies charge extra if you return the car before the time specified in your contract. To avoid a hefty refueling fee, fill the tank just before you turn in the car, but be aware that gas stations near the rental outlet may overcharge. It's almost never a deal to buy the tank of gas that's in the car when you rent it; the understanding is that you'll return it empty, but some fuel usually remains.

CAR TRAVEL

There is an extensive network of *autostrade* (toll highways), complemented by equally well-maintained but free *superstrade* (expressways). All are clearly signposted and numbered. The ticket you are issued upon entering an autostrada must be returned when you exit and pay the toll; on some shorter autostrade, mainly connecting highways, the toll is paid upon entering. Viacard cards, on sale at many autostrada locations, make paying tolls easier and faster. A *raccordo* is a connecting expressway. *Strade statali* (state highways, denoted by *S* or *SS* numbers) may be single-lane roads, as are all secondary roads; directions and turnoffs are not always clearly marked. Venice is on the east–west A4 autostrada, which connects with Padua, Verona, Brescia, Milan, and Turin.

Roads just outside of Venice are notoriously crowded and lines of 30–50 km are not uncommon during holiday weekends. Count on parking your car and leaving it during your stay in the city.

Automobil Club Italiano (ACI) gives travel tips and information in English about rules of the road, road conditions, and car insurance.

🚗 **ACI** ☎ 06/49982389 ⏱ 8 AM–8 PM.

EMERGENCY SERVICES

It's advisable to call your rental company first—look for a free "numero verde" green number in the paperwork. If that fails, Automobil Club Italiano (ACI) has 24-hour emergency service.

F **ACI emergency service** ☎ 803116.

GASOLINE

Gas stations are generally open Monday–Saturday 7–7 with a break at lunchtime. Many stations have automatic self-service pumps that accept only bills of 5, 10, 20, and 50 euros; some, but not all, also take credit cards. Gas stations on autostrade are open 24 hours. Gas costs about €1.05 per liter.

PARKING

If you bring a car to Venice, you will have to pay for a garage or parking space. Warning: do not be waylaid by illegal touts, often wearing fake uniforms, who may try to flag you down as you approach Venice and offer to arrange parking and hotels; their activities have become a scandal in a city generally free of con men and criminals. Ignore them and continue on until you reach the automatic ticket machines.

Do not leave valuables in the car. There is a luggage storage office, open 6 AM–9 PM, next to the Pullman Bar on the ground floor of the municipal garage at Piazzale Roma. You can take your car to the Lido—the car ferry (Line 17) makes the half-hour trip about every 50 minutes from a landing at Tronchetto, but in summer there can be long lines. It costs €8.78 to €18.08, depending on the size of the car.

Parking at Autorimessa Comunale costs €18.59 for 24 hours. The private Garage San Marco costs €19 for up to 12 hours, and €26 for 12–24 hours plus a €1 supplement Sundays, holidays, and nights. To reach Tronchetto parking (€18 for 1–24 hours), watch for signs coming over the bridge from the mainland; you'll have to turn right before you get to Piazzale Roma. Many hotels have negotiated guest discounts with San Marco or Tronchetto garages; get a voucher when you check in your hotel and present it when you pay the garage. Line 82 connects Tronchetto with Piazzale Roma, Piazza San Marco, and also goes to the Lido in summer. When there's thick fog or extreme tides, a bus runs to Piazzale Roma instead. Avoid private boats—they're a rip-off. Garage San Marco and Autorimessa Comunale accept reservations.

Parking space in most cities is at a premium, but in historic town centers where streets are closed to most traffic, peripheral parking areas are usually full. Parking in an area signposted ZONA DISCO is allowed for limited periods (from 30 minutes to two hours or more—the limit is posted); if you don't have the cardboard disk, you can use a piece of paper to indicate what time you parked. The *parcometro*, the Italian version of metered parking, has been introduced in some major cities (not in Venice).

F **Autorimessa Comunale** ✉ Piazzale Roma, Santa Croce end of S11 road, ☎ 041/2727301, ⊕ www.asmvenezia.it. **Garage San Marco** ✉ Piazzale Roma 467/f, Santa Croce turn right into bus park, ☎ 041/5232213 ⊕ www.garagesanmarco.it. **Tronchetto** ☎ 041/5207555.

ROAD CONDITIONS

Autostrade are well maintained, as are most interregional highways. The condition of provincial (county) roads varies, but road maintenance at this level is generally good in Italy.

ROAD MAPS

Street and road signs are often challenging—a good map and patience are essential. Local road maps can be obtained at the point of rental pickup. Alternatively, most bookstores such as Feltrinelli sell them as do most highway gas stations. In major cities, look for the Touring Club Italiano's shop. They sell maps (road, bicycle, hiking, among others). Probably the best road maps are those produced by Michelin.

RULES OF THE ROAD

Driving is on the right, as in the United States. Regulations are largely as in Britain and the United States, except that the police have the power to levy on-the-spot fines. In most Italian towns the use of the horn is forbidden in certain, if not all, areas; a large sign, ZONA DI SILENZIO, indicates where. Italians drive fast and are impatient with those who don't. Speed limits are 130 kph (80 mph) on autostrade and 110 kph (70 mph) on state and provincial roads, unless otherwise marked.

Handheld mobile phones are illegal while driving; fines can exceed €100. The blood-alcohol content limit for driving is

0.5 gr/ with fines up to €5,000 for sur-passing the limit and the possibility of six months' imprisonment. Though enforce-ment of laws varies depending on region, fines for speeding are uniformly stiff: 10 kph over the speed limit can warrant a fine of up to €500; over 10 kph, and your li-cense could be taken away from you.

CHILDREN IN VENICE & THE VENETIAN ARC

Italians love children and are generally very tolerant and patient with them, but there are few amenities provided specifi-cally for them. Some discounts exist, such as children under 4 riding free on va-poretti, municipal buses and trains, and children 4–12 paying 50% on Italian trains. It never hurts to **ask about a *sconto bambino o studente*** (child or student dis-count) before purchasing tickets. Certain museums and galleries may offer discounts only to students who are EU citizens, but in other places, any student might be eligi-ble. Venice caters more to art and history lovers than people on family vacations.

If you are renting a car, don't forget to ar-range for a car seat when you reserve. For general advice about traveling with chil-dren, consult *Fodor's FYI: Travel with Your Baby* (available in bookstores everywhere).

BABY-SITTING

Most hotel concierges can help you locate a baby-sitter, often as not a young English-speaking woman with whom they may be personally acquainted. Prices range from €7–€25 per hour depending on the hotel. During holiday periods when the student population is vacationing, finding a sitter could prove difficult.

FLYING

If your children are two or older, ask about children's airfares. As a general rule, infants under two not occupying a seat fly at greatly reduced fares or even for free. But if you want to guarantee a seat for an infant, you have to pay full fare. Consider flying during off-peak days and times; most airlines will grant an infant a seat without a ticket if there are available seats. When booking, confirm carry-on al-lowances if you're traveling with infants. In general, for babies charged 10% to 50% of the adult fare you are allowed one carry-on bag and a collapsible stroller; if the flight is full, the stroller may have to be checked or you may be limited to less.

Experts agree that it's a good idea to use safety seats aloft for children weighing less than 40 pounds. Airlines set their own policies: if you use a safety seat, U.S. carriers usually require that the child be ticketed, even if he or she is young enough to ride free, because the seats must be strapped into regular seats. And even if you pay the full adult fare for the seat, it may be worth it, especially on longer trips. Do **check your airline's policy about using safety seats during takeoff and landing.** Safety seats are not allowed everywhere in the plane, so get your seat assignments as early as possible.

When reserving, request children's meals or a freestanding bassinet (not available at all airlines) if you need them. But note that bulkhead seats, where you must sit to use the bassinet, may lack an overhead bin or storage space on the floor.

SIGHTS & ATTRACTIONS

Places that are especially appealing to chil-dren are indicated by a rubber-duckie icon (🦆) in the margin. Feeding pigeons in San Marco seems to be a favorite with kids as is the view from atop the Campanile. Young ones might also enjoy the Scala Contarini del Bovolo—and you'll enjoy it, too, unless you happen to be carrying them up this long spiral climb. Watching glass come to life in Murano fascinates old and young alike. If the Museum of Naval History's collection of model ships doesn't interest your child, perhaps their collection of seashells will. Or you can take the child to the beach at Lido to start his or her own shell collection.

SUPPLIES & EQUIPMENT

The cost of diapers in Italy is similar to that in other places, though American brands such as Pampers and Huggies are slightly higher than in the United States. COOP is a reliable brand; you'll pay about €10 for 50 diapers.

Italian formula (both in premixed and powder forms) generally contains more vitamins than its American counterparts; Plasmon is a good brand. Italian bottles are identical to American ones, but it is difficult to find no-spill glasses for tod-dlers; it's best to bring a couple along with you.

COMPUTERS ON THE ROAD

Getting on-line in Venice isn't difficult; Internet points and Internet cafés, sometimes open 24 hours a day, are becoming more and more common. Prices and deals vary—franchise-operators may charge more initially, but you'll be able to carry unused time to Florence or Rome. Some hotels have Internet access in the lobby; others have in-room modem lines, but as with phones, using the hotel's line is relatively expensive. **Always check modem rates before plugging in.** You may need an adapter for your computer for the European-style plugs. As always, if you are traveling with a laptop, carry a spare battery and an adapter. Never plug your computer into any socket before asking about surge protection. IBM sells a pea-size modem tester that plugs into a telephone jack to check if the line is safe to use.

⚏ Internet Cafés Internet Cafe net house ⊠ Campo Santo Stefano, San Marco 2967/2958 ☎ 041/2771190 ⏱ 24 hours. **Planet Internet** ⊠ 5 minutes from train station Strada Nova, Cannaregio 1519 ☎ 041/5244188 ⏱ 9 AM–midnight.

CONCIERGES

Concierges, found in many hotels, can help you with theater tickets and dinner reservations: a good one with connections may be able to get you seats for a hot show or prime-time dinner reservations at the restaurant of the moment. You can also turn to your hotel's concierge for help with travel arrangements, sightseeing plans, services ranging from aromatherapy to zipper repair, and emergencies. **Always tip** a concierge who has been of assistance (⇨ Tipping).

CONSULATES

⚏ Australia Australian Consulate, Milan ⊠ Via Borgogna 2 ☎ 02/777041.
⚏ Canada Canadian Embassy, Rome ⊠ Via G.B de Rossi 27 ☎ 06/445981.
⚏ New Zealand New Zealand Embassy, Rome ⊠ Via Zara 28 ☎ 06/4417171.
⚏ United Kingdom U.K. Consulate, Venice ⊠ Campo della Carità, 1051 Dorsoduro ☎ 041/5227207. **U.K. Consulate, Rome** ⊠ Via Venti Settembre 80A ☎ 06/42200001.
⚏ United States U.S. Consulate, Rome ⊠ Via Veneto 121 ☎ Rome 06/46741, Milan 02/290351, Florence 055/266951.

CONSUMER PROTECTION

Whether you're shopping for gifts or purchasing travel services, **pay with a major credit card** whenever possible, so you can cancel payment or get reimbursed if there's a problem (and you can provide documentation). If you're doing business with a particular company for the first time, contact your local Better Business Bureau and the attorney general's offices in your state and (for U.S. businesses) the company's home state as well. Have any complaints been filed? Finally, if you're buying a package or tour, always consider travel insurance that includes default coverage (⇨ Insurance).

⚏ BBBs Council of Better Business Bureaus ⊠ 4200 Wilson Blvd., Suite 800, Arlington, VA 22203 ☎ 703/276-0100 🖷 703/525-8277 🌐 www.bbb.org.

CUSTOMS & DUTIES

When shopping abroad, keep receipts for all purchases. Upon reentering the country, **be ready to show customs officials what you've bought.** Pack purchases together in an easily accessible place. If you think a duty is incorrect, appeal the assessment. If you object to the way your clearance was handled, note the inspector's badge number. In either case, first ask to see a supervisor. If the problem isn't resolved, write to the appropriate authorities, beginning with the port director at your point of entry.

IN AUSTRALIA

Australian residents who are 18 or older may bring home A$400 worth of souvenirs and gifts (including jewelry), 250 cigarettes or 250 grams of cigars or other tobacco products, and 1,125 ml of alcohol (including wine, beer, and spirits). Residents under 18 may bring back A$200 worth of goods. Members of the same family traveling together may pool their allowances. Prohibited items include meat products. Seeds, plants, and fruits need to be declared upon arrival.

⚏ Australian Customs Service 🕾 Regional Director, Box 8, Sydney, NSW 2001 ☎ 02/9213-2000 or 1300/363263, 02/9364-7222 or 1800/803-006 quarantine-inquiry line 🖷 02/9213-4043 🌐 www.customs.gov.au.

IN CANADA

Canadian residents who have been out of Canada for at least seven days may bring in C$750 worth of goods duty-free. If you've been away fewer than seven days but more than 48 hours, the duty-free allowance drops to C$200. If your trip lasts 24 to 48 hours, the allowance is C$50. You may not pool allowances with family members. Goods claimed under the C$750 exemption may follow you by mail; those claimed under the lesser exemptions must accompany you. Alcohol and tobacco products may be included in the seven-day and 48-hour exemptions but not in the 24-hour exemption. If you meet the age requirements of the province or territory through which you reenter Canada, you may bring in, duty-free, 1.5 liters of wine *or* 1.14 liters (40 imperial ounces) of liquor *or* 24 12-ounce cans or bottles of beer or ale. Also, if you meet the local age requirement for tobacco products, you may bring in, duty-free, 200 cigarettes and 50 cigars. Check ahead of time with the Canada Customs and Revenue Agency or the Department of Agriculture for policies regarding meat products, seeds, plants, and fruits.

You may send an unlimited number of gifts (only one gift per recipient, however) worth up to C$60 each duty-free to Canada. Label the package UNSOLICITED GIFT—VALUE UNDER $60. Alcohol and tobacco are excluded.

F Canada Customs and Revenue Agency ⊠ 2265 St. Laurent Blvd., Ottawa, Ontario K1G 4K3 ☎ 800/461-9999, 204/983-3500, 506/636-5064 ⊕ www.ccra.gc.ca.

IN ITALY

Of goods obtained anywhere outside the EU the allowances are as follows: (1) 200 cigarettes or 100 cigarillos or 50 cigars or 250 grams of tobacco; (2) 2 liters of still table wine or 1 liter of spirits over 22% volume or 2 liters of spirits under 22% volume or 2 liters of fortified and sparkling wines; and (3) 50 ml of perfume and 250 ml of toilet water.

Of goods obtained (duty and tax paid) within another EU country, the allowances are as follows: (1) 800 cigarettes or 400 cigarillos or 400 cigars or 1 kilogram of tobacco; (2) 90 liters of still table wine plus (3) 10 liters of spirits over 22% volume plus 20 liters of spirits under 22% volume plus 60 liters of sparkling wines plus 110 liters of beer.

F Dogana Sezione Viaggiatori ⊠ Aeroporto Leonardo da Vinci, Fiumicino, 00054 Rome ☎ 06/65954343. Ministero delle Finanze, Direzione Cen-

trale dei Servizi Doganali, Divisione I ⊠ Via Carucci 71, 00143 Rome ☎ 06/50242117.

IN NEW ZEALAND

All homeward-bound residents may bring back NZ$700 worth of souvenirs and gifts; passengers may not pool their allowances, and children can claim only the concession on goods intended for their own use. For those 17 or older, the duty-free allowance also includes 4.5 liters of wine or beer; one 1,125-ml bottle of spirits; and either 200 cigarettes, 250 grams of tobacco, 50 cigars, *or* a combination of the three up to 250 grams. Meat products, seeds, plants, and fruits must be declared upon arrival to the Agricultural Services Department.

F New Zealand Customs ⊠ Head office: The Customhouse, 17–21 Whitmore St., Box 2218, Wellington ☎ 09/300–5399 or 0800/428–786 ⊕ www.customs.govt.nz.

IN THE U.K.

If you are a U.K. resident and your journey was wholly within the European Union, you probably won't have to pass through customs when you return to the United Kingdom. If you plan to bring back large quantities of alcohol or tobacco, check EU limits beforehand. In most cases, if you bring back more than 200 cigars, 3,200 cigarettes, 10 liters of spirits, 110 liters of beer, and/or 90 liters of wine, you have to declare the goods upon return.

F HM Customs and Excise ⊠ Portcullis House, 21 Cowbridge Rd. E, Cardiff CF11 9SS ☎ 0845/010–9000 or 0208/929–0152, 0208/929–6731 or 0208/910–3602 complaints ⊕ www.hmce.gov.uk.

IN THE U.S.

U.S. residents who have been out of the country for at least 48 hours may bring home, for personal use, $800 worth of foreign goods duty-free, as long as they haven't used the $800 allowance or any part of it in the past 30 days. This exemption may include 1 liter of alcohol (for travelers 21 and older), 200 cigarettes, and 100 non-Cuban cigars. Family members from the same household who are traveling together may pool their $800 personal exemptions. For fewer than 48 hours, the duty-free allowance drops to $200, which may include 50 cigarettes, 10 non-Cuban cigars, and 150 ml of alcohol (or 150 ml of perfume containing alcohol). The $200 allowance cannot be combined with other individuals' exemptions, and if you exceed it, the full value of all the goods will be taxed. Antiques, which the U.S. Bureau of Customs and Border Protection defines as objects more than 100 years old, enter duty-free, as do original works of art done entirely by hand, including paintings, drawings, and sculptures. This doesn't apply to folk art or handicrafts, which are in general dutiable.

You may also send packages home duty-free, with a limit of one parcel per addressee per day (except alcohol or tobacco products or perfume worth more than $5). You can mail up to $200 worth of goods for personal use; label the package PERSONAL USE and attach a list of its contents and their retail value. If the package contains your used personal belongings, mark it AMERICAN GOODS RETURNED to avoid paying duties. You may send up to $100 worth of goods as a gift; mark the package UNSOLICITED GIFT. Mailed items do not affect your duty-free allowance on your return.

To avoid paying duty on foreign-made high-ticket items you already own and will take on your trip, register them with Customs before you leave the country. Consider filing a Certificate of Registration for laptops, cameras, watches, and other digital devices identified with serial numbers or other permanent markings; you can keep the certificate for other trips. Otherwise, bring a sales receipt or insurance form to show that you owned the item before you left the United States.

🛂 **U.S. Bureau of Customs and Border Protection** ⊠ for inquiries and equipment registration, 1300 Pennsylvania Ave. NW, Washington, DC 20229 ⊕ www.customs.gov ☎ 877/287-8667, 202/354-1000 ⊠ for complaints, Customer Satisfaction Unit, 1300 Pennsylvania Ave. NW, Room 5.5D, Washington, DC 20229.

DISABILITIES & ACCESSIBILITY

Italy has only recently begun to provide facilities such as ramps, telephones, and rest rooms for people with disabilities; such things are still the exception, not the rule. In Venice, bridges, historic buildings that cannot be modernized, and traveling by boat complicate matters for people with mobility problems. Don't rely on tourist maps that indicate lifts on certain bridges around town; these rarely if ever work. Kiosks in the airport, train station, and parking areas that book hotels, can only dispense information member hotels provide; there is no set criteria for designating one's own "hotel accessible." *Informahandicap* has a website with helpful information for wheelchair users, and questions you e-mail to them in English will be answered.

Contact the nearest Italian consulate about bringing a Seeing Eye dog into Italy; this requires an import license, a current certificate detailing the dog's inoculations, and a letter from your veterinarian certifying the dog's health.

🛈 Local Resources **Informahandicap** ⊠ Viale Giuseppe Garibaldi 155 30174, Mestre ☎ 041/5341700 🖷 041/5342257 ⊕ www.comune.venezia.it/handicap

WHERE TO STAY

Despite the Americans with Disabilities Act, the definition of accessibility seems to differ from hotel to hotel. Some properties may be accessible by ADA standards for people with mobility problems but not for people with hearing or vision impairments, for example.

If you have mobility problems, ask for the lowest floor on which accessible services are offered. If you have a hearing impairment, check whether the hotel has devices to alert you visually to the ring of the telephone, a knock at the door, and a fire/emergency alarm. Some hotels provide these devices without charge. Discuss your needs with hotel personnel if this equipment isn't available, so that a staff member can personally alert you in the event of an emergency.

If you're bringing a guide dog, get authorization ahead of time and write down the name of the person with whom you spoke.

Choose a hotel that has access to a Line 1 or Line 82 vaporetto landing without having to cross a bridge. Newer and newly restored buildings are more likely to meet the latest legal specifications. Some of the better choices in Venice include San Zulian and Ca' Pisani.

RESERVATIONS

When discussing accessibility with an operator or reservations agent, **ask hard questions.** Are there any stairs, inside *or* out? Are there grab bars next to the toilet *and* in the shower/tub? How large is the elevator? How wide is the door to the room? To the bathroom? To the shower? If you reserve through a toll-free number, consider also calling the hotel's local number to confirm the information from the central reservations office. Get confirmation in writing when you can.

SIGHTS & ATTRACTIONS

Most major historic buildings and museums are accessible without having to cross a bridge if you plan ahead and **you use the correct vaporetto stop.** Palazzo Ducale, Museo Correr, the Campanile di San Marco, Ca' Rezzonico, Palazzo Grassi, Ca' d'Oro, and Scuola di San Rocco have either elevators or stair-climbing machines that accommodate wheelchairs. Gallerie dell'Accademia has one such machine, but visitors must still overcome a few steps connecting exhibit rooms. Most churches, including the Basilica di San Marco, have at least a few steps at their entrances.

TRANSPORTATION

From the airport, the yellow ACTV bus 5 is ramped for chair loading or you can use a land taxi. Once in Venice, vaporetto Lines 1, 82, and LN (for Laguna Nord) have plenty of deck space and easy cabin entry, however, unless you can navigate a few steps aboard Lines 41, 51, and 61, you'll be forced to ride outdoors, or if the boat is very crowded, you won't even be allowed to board. Boarding water taxis is not easy. Floating docks are rare, and even when the boat can mechanically raise its deck level with the dock, waves can make the transfer exciting, to say the least. Private boats with a driver plus an assistant are available; they arrive equipped to lift and carry disabled passengers safely, and comfortably. This service is best arranged by contacting a local tour operator experienced in such transfers who can also help you find rental wheelchairs, crutches, and other mobility aides.

Venice Santa Lucia station is an end-of-the-line train terminal, which means that you won't have to climb down stairs to walk underneath platforms. Though there are plenty of steps at the front door, these are easily bypassed by a ramped exit to your left as you leave the platform. Trenitalia, the Italian rail system, tries hard to accommodate travelers with mobility problems and, at least in Venice and 15 other major cities, they do quite well. If notified ahead of time, porters will meet arriving or departing passengers with a cart that lifts wheelchairs to the level of the train car. Visit its website to find out what services might make your trip easier. ⁊ **Trenitalia** ☎ 041/785570, 041/785913, 8488-88088 (local call anywhere in Italy) ⎁ Fax 041-785167 ⊕ www.trenitalia.it **Kele Teo** ⊠ Ponte dei Bareteri, San Marco 4930 between San Marco and Rialto ☎ 041/5208722 ⎁ 041/5208913 ⊕ www.keleteo.com. ⁊ Complaints **Aviation Consumer Protection Division** (⇨ Air Travel) for airline-related problems. **Departmental Office of Civil Rights** ⊠ for general inquiries, U.S. Department of Transportation, S-30, 400 7th St. SW, Room 10215, Washington, DC 20590 ☎ 202/366-4648 ⎁ 202/366-9371 ⊕ www.dot.gov/ost/docr/index.htm. **Disability Rights Section** ⊠ NYAV, U.S. Department of Justice, Civil Rights Division, 950 Pennsylvania Ave. NW, Washington, DC 20530 ☎ ADA information line 202/514-0301, 800/514-0301, 202/514-0383 TTY, 800/514-0383 TTY ⊕ www.ada.gov. **U.S. Department of Transportation Hotline** ☎ for disability-related air-travel problems, 800/778-4838 or 800/455-9880 TTY.

TRAVEL AGENCIES

In the United States, the Americans with Disabilities Act requires that travel firms serve the needs of all travelers. Some agencies specialize in working with people with disabilities.

⁊ Travelers with Mobility Problems **Access Adventures/B. Roberts Travel** ⊠ 206 Chestnut Ridge Rd., Scottsville, NY 14624 ☎ 585/889-9096 ⊕ www.brobertstravel.com ✎ dltravel@prodigy.net, run by a former physical-rehabilitation counselor. **CareVacations** ⊠ No. 5, 5110-50 Ave., Leduc, Alberta, Canada, T9E 6V4 ☎ 780/986-6404 or 877/478-7827 ⎁ 780/986-8332 ⊕ www.carevacations.com, for group tours and cruise vacations. **Flying Wheels Travel** ⊠ 143 W. Bridge St., Box 382, Owatonna, MN 55060 ☎ 507/451-5005 ⎁ 507/451-1685 ⊕ www.flyingwheeltravel.com.

DISCOUNTS & DEALS

Be a smart shopper and compare all your options before making decisions. A plane ticket bought with a promotional coupon from travel clubs, coupon books, and direct-mail offers or purchased on the Internet may not be cheaper than the least expensive fare from a discount ticket agency. And always keep in mind that what you get is just as important as what you save.

DISCOUNT RESERVATIONS

To save money, look into discount reservations services with Web sites and toll-free numbers, which use their buying power to get a better price on hotels, airline tickets (⇨ Air Travel), even car rentals. When booking a room, always **call the hotel's local toll-free number** (if one is available) rather than the central reservations number—you'll often get a better price. Always ask about special packages or corporate rates.

When shopping for the best deal on hotels and car rentals, look for guaranteed exchange rates, which protect you against a falling dollar. With your rate locked in, you won't pay more, even if the price goes up in the local currency.

Ⓐ Airline Tickets **Air 4 Less** ☎ 800/AIR4LESS; low-fare specialist.

Ⓐ Hotel Rooms **Accommodations Express** ☎ 800/444-7666 or 800/277-1064 ⊕ www.accommodationsexpress.com. **Hotels.com** ☎ 800/246-8357 ⊕ www.hotels.com. **Steigenberger Reservation Service** ☎ 800/223-5652 ⊕ www.srs-worldhotels.com. **Turbotrip.com** ☎ 800/473-7829 ⊕ www.turbotrip.com.

PACKAGE DEALS

Don't confuse packages and guided tours. When you buy a package, you travel on your own, just as though you had planned the trip yourself. Fly/drive packages, which combine airfare and car rental, are often a good deal. In cities, ask the local visitor's bureau about hotel packages that include tickets to major museum exhibits or other special events. If you **buy a rail/drive pass,** you may save on train tickets and car rentals. All Eurailpass holders get a discount on Eurostar fares through the Channel Tunnel and often receive reduced rates for buses, hotels, ferries, and car rentals.

EATING & DRINKING

The restaurants we list are the cream of the crop in each price category. Properties indicated by a ✕⌂ are lodging establishments whose restaurant warrants a special trip. For further information about dining in Venice, see *Know-How* in Chapter 2.

CATEGORY	COST
$$$$	over €22
$$$	€17–€22
$$	€12–€17
$	€7–€12
¢	under €7

Prices are for a second course (secondo piatto) and are given in euros.

A few pointers on Italian dining etiquette: Italians diners tend to know exactly how they want their food, so **don't be afraid to ask the waiter for what you want** (salt, extra Parmesan cheese, or olive oil on the side) or to have a dish prepared without ingredients you do not care for (for example, sens'aglio, per favore—without garlic, please). Although mineral water makes its way to almost every table, you can always order a carafe of tap water (acqua di rubinetto or acqua semplice) instead. Italians order their food first, then wine and beverages. Wiping your bowl clean with a small piece of bread is considered a sign of appreciation, not bad manners. Spaghetti should be eaten with a fork only, although a little help from a spoon will not horrify the locals the way cutting spaghetti into little pieces might. When you finish eating and are ready to have your plate cleared, rest your utensils together on your plate at about five o'clock. Order your espresso (Italians do not drink a cappuccino after midday) after dessert, not with it. You must ask for a check when you are ready to leave; unless it's well past closing time, no waiter will put a bill on your table without your having asked first. Doggy bags are not the norm in Italy.

MEALS & SPECIALTIES

What's the difference between a *ristorante* and a *trattoria*? Can you order food at an *enoteca*? Can you go to a restaurant just for a snack, or order just a salad at a *pizzeria*? The following definitions should help.

Not too long ago, restaurants tended to be more elegant and expensive than trattorie and *osterie,* which served more traditional, home-style fare in an atmosphere to match. But the distinction has blurred considerably, and an osteria in the center of town might be far fancier (and pricier) than a ristorante across the street. An enoteca menu is often limited to a selection of cheese, cured meats, pickles, salads, and desserts, but if there is a kitchen, you'll also find vegetable soups, pasta, meat, and fish preparations. Venetian *bacari* are something between an old-style osteria and a wine bar: here it's possible to grab a fast snack (*cicheto*) at the counter to be swallowed down with a glass of wine (*ombra*), or sit down for a fast meal. Most pizzerie don't offer just pizza, and although the other dishes on the menu are supposed to be starters, there's no harm in skipping the pizza. The typical pizzeria fare includes *affettati misti* (selection of cured meat), simple salads, and various kinds of *bruschetta* and *crostino* (similar to bruschetta, but baked). Pizzerie generally have fresh fruit, ice cream, and simple desserts.

Throughout the region, the handiest and least expensive way to grab a quick snack between sights is to hit a *bar, caffè,* or *pizza al taglio*. Most bars have a selection of *panini* (sandwiches), *toast,* (grilled sandwiches), and *tramezzini* (untoasted sandwich triangles). In cities, you may also find prepared salad, cold pasta dishes, and yogurt around lunchtime. Most bars have beer and a variety of alcohol, but few, except in Venice, sell wine by the glass. A caffè is like a bar but usually with more tables to sit down. Many caffès have limited restaurant licenses that allow them to serve hot pasta dishes, but choose carefully as some simply dispense microwaved portions. Pizza as well, is often reheated. If you place your order at the counter, ask if you can sit down: some places, especially in Venice, charge extra for table service. In a self-service bar and caffè, it's good manners to clean up your table before you leave. Note that in some places you must pay before you place the order and be ready to show your *scontrino* (receipt) when you move to the counter. Few shops that sell *pizza al taglio* (by the slice) have places to sit down. Some pizzerie sell 1/8 of a large pizza as a slice, whereas in others, you'll pay by weight—just point out which kind you want and indicate how big a piece.

ELECTRICITY

To use electric-powered equipment purchased in the U.S. or Canada, **bring a converter and adapter.** The electrical current in Italy is 220 volts, 50 cycles alternating current (AC); wall outlets take Continental-type plugs, with two round prongs.

Most laptops operate equally well on 110 and 220 volts and so require only an adapter.

EMERGENCIES

No matter where you are in Italy, **dial 113 for all emergencies,** or find someone, such as a concierge, to call for you, as not all 113 operators speak English. The Italian word to use to draw people's attention in an emergency is *aiuto* (meaning "help,"

pronounced ah-*you*-toh). *Pronto soccorso* means "first aid" and will get you an ambulance (*ambulanza*). If you just need a doctor, ask for *un medico*. (Most hotels will be able to refer you to an English-speaking doctor.) Don't forget to ask the doctor for *una ricevuta* (receipt) to show to your insurance company for reimbursement. Other useful emergency words in Italian words are *al fuoco* ("fire," pronounced ahl fuh-*woe*-co), and *Al ladro* ("Follow the thief," pronounced ahl *lah*-droh).

Italy has a national police force (*carabinieri*) as well as local police (*polizia,* also known as *questura*). Both are armed and have the power to investigate crimes and make arrests. Always report the loss of your passport to either the carabinieri or the police (in addition to your consulate or embassy). *Polizia Municipale,* usually referred to as *vigili,* are the local police to call if you're involved in a minor traffic accident. They also hand out parking tickets and clamp cars, so before you even consider parking the Italian way, at least be able to spot the uniforms of these men and women who wear white in summer and black in winter.

Historic Venice has one hospital, SS. Giovanni e Paolo, in the Campo of the same name (vaporetto 41/42/51/52 stop Fondamente Nuove), which is used for emergencies and equipped with a decent emergency room. One can never count on finding an English speaker in the middle of the night. Serious problems are generally sent to Mestre where the hospital is better equipped and staffed.

🚩 Emergency Services **Carabinieri (militarized police)** ☎ 112. **Fire** ☎ 115. **Italian Automobile Club** ☎ 116. **Medical emergency and ambulance** ☎ 118. **Police** ☎ 113. **Vigili (Polizia Municipale)** ☎ 041/2748111 Venice, 049/8205111 Padua, 045/8077111 Verona, 0444/221111 Vicenza, 040/366111 Trieste, 0422/6581 Treviso, 0432/271111 Udine.
🚩 Hospitals **SS. Giovanni e Paolo** ✉ Campo SS. Giovanni e Paolo, Castello ☎ 041/5294111.

ENGLISH-LANGUAGE MEDIA

Cafoscarina, close to Università Ca' Foscari, has a large selection of English literature, mainly classics. Emiliana and Studium stock books about Venice and Italian food with a few fiction paperbacks. The Venice Pavilion, off Piazza San Marco near the Giardini Reali, has a good selection of books and novels featuring the city.

For books about Venice's maritime culture, lagoon, and environment, try Maredicarta. A number of hotels around the city offer their guests the *Herald Tribune* or *USA Today*. Newsstands are likely to carry the Tribune but your best bet for UK's *Guardian, Times,* or *Financial Times* is the stall beside the San Marco post office (behind Museo Correr) or the one in Campo SS. Apostoli, between Rialto and Ca' d'Oro.

⚠ Bookstores **Cafoscarina** ⊠ Campiello Squellini, 3259 Dorsoduro ☎ 041/5229602. **Emiliana** ⊠ Calle Goldoni, 4487 San Marco, between Piazza San Marco and Campo San Luca ☎ 041/5220793. **Maredicarta** ⊠ Fondamenta dei Tolentini, Santa Croce 222, across from train station ☎ 041/716304 **Studium** ⊠ Calle de la Canonica, 337/c San Marco, off Piazzetta dei Leoncini ☎ 041/5222382. **Venice Pavilion** ⊠ 2 San Marco ☎ 041/5225150.

ETIQUETTE & BEHAVIOR

Most churches require knees and shoulders be covered and many forbid cameras of any kind. A dress code is actively enforced at Basilica di San Marco and the Chorus group of churches, so it's wise to carry a sweater, or scarf, to wrap around your shoulders before entering a church. **Do not enter a church with food,** and do not drink from your water bottle while inside. **Do not go in if a service is in progress.** And if you have a cellular phone, **turn it off before entering.**

Italians who are friends greet each other with a kiss, first on the left cheek, and then on the right. When you meet a new person, shake hands.

Residents and shopkeepers are plagued by visitors who don't respect right-of-way courtesy in the narrow streets and on bridges (keep to the right). When strolling two or three abreast in a tiny calle, be aware of the local who may need to get by.

Posted around Piazza San Marco are signs detailing what the city considers polite comportment. Regardless of how hot the weather might be, shirtless men or women in the historic city, including on the Grand Canal, can be fined €40. Lying down in streets or squares is prohibited as is sitting around your picnic lunch, unless you happen to be in one of the city's parks. Swimming or even dipping feet into canals is not permitted.

BUSINESS ETIQUETTE

Showing up on time for business appointments is expected in Italy, but have some reading material handy is not a bad idea. Business is done more over lunch than dinner. Business cards are used throughout Italy, and business suits are the norm for both men and women. Certainly a person is scrutinized down to their shoes by men and women alike.

Loud communication doesn't necessarily mean heated argument. That said, a calm voice may be a nice thing to have but a hike in volume can sometimes be necessary. A procrastination ("I'll call you tomorrow") in giving a negative response is considered more polite than saying an outright "No."

VAPORETTO ETIQUETTE

The vaporetto rules forbid men with tank tops (muscle shirts) and riders must remove backpacks. When boarding the vaporetto, wait in the entry area instead of blocking the boarding ramp. Once aboard, move away from the entrance and don't block aisles with luggage. A significant number of Venice's residents are elderly—be considerate about yielding seats.

GAY & LESBIAN TRAVEL

Same-sex couples won't raise any eyebrows in Venice but public displays of affection are rare. Clubs and bars in Venice and the Veneto are usually mixed rather than exclusively gay or lesbian.

⚠ Local Contacts **Archigay Help Line** ☎ 041/5384151, Mon. 7 PM–9 PM and Thurs. 9 PM–11 PM. **Casa de Uscoli** ☎ 349/7941393 ⊕ www.casadeuscoli.com. **Venice à la Carte** ⊕ www.tourvenice.org.

⚠ Gay- & Lesbian-Friendly Travel Agencies **Different Roads Travel** ⊠ 8383 Wilshire Blvd., Suite 520, Beverly Hills, CA 90211 ☎ 323/651-5557 or 800/429-8747 (Ext. 14 for both) 🖷 323/651-3678 ✉ lgernert@tzell.com. **Kennedy Travel** ⊠ 130 W. 42nd St., Suite 401, New York, NY 10036 ☎ 212/840-8659, 800/237-7433 🖷 212/730-2269 ⊕ www.kennedytravel.com. **Now, Voyager** ⊠ 4406 18th St., San Francisco, CA 94114 ☎ 415/626-1169 or 800/255-6951 🖷 415/626-8626 ⊕ www.nowvoyager.com. **Skylink Travel and Tour** ⊠ 1455 N. Dutton Ave., Suite A, Santa Rosa, CA 95401 ☎ 707/546-9888 or 800/225-5759 🖷 707/636-0951; serving lesbian travelers.

GUIDEBOOKS

Plan well and you won't be sorry. Guide-books are excellent tools—and you can take them with you. You may want to check out color-photo-illustrated *Fodor's Exploring Venice*, thorough on culture and history, and pocket-size *Citypack Venice,* which includes a foldout map. Both are available at on-line retailers and book-stores everywhere.

HEALTH

Though Italians are mineral water addicts, the "rubinetto" or tap water in and around Venice is not bad. It may be a bit overchlorinated for some and certainly contains its share of calcium, but it won't hurt anyone unless they happen to be stay-ing in a home that still has old lead pipes.

FOOD & DRINK

Although few Italian cows have been found infected with *mucca pazza,* (mad cow disease), concern has prompted many Italians to limit their consumption of beef. European Union guidelines consider *vitello* (veal), *vitellone* (young beef), and *manzo* (beef) safe to eat as long as the cuts don't come in contact with spinal marrow. Ini-tially banned, Tuscany's thick T-bone *bis-tecca alla fiorentina,* has reappeared, but only animals under 12 months old are used. Traditional *osso buco* (braised shank), has not been affected as it uses only leg bones. *Cavallo* (horse meat, which is sweet and lean), and *coniglio* (rabbit) have always been part of the Italian diet and are well worth trying. Some restau-rants experimented with "alternative meats" such as *struzzo* (ostrich) and *can-guro* (kangaroo), but Italians don't change dietary habits readily.

OVER-THE-COUNTER REMEDIES

It's always best to **travel with your own tried and true medicines.** The regulations regarding what medicines require a pre-scription are not likely to be the exact same in Italy as in your home country—all the more reason to bring what you need with you. Aspirin (*l'aspirina*) can be pur-chased at any pharmacy, but Tylenol and Advil are unavailable.

PESTS & OTHER HAZARDS

Mosquitoes can be a problem in Venice. In many hotel rooms you'll find a *fornelletto antizanzare,* an electrical device that uses mosquito-repellent tablets. Insert a fresh tablet in the metal slot and plug the fornel-letto in the wall (ideally in the vicinity of an open window): it should warm up after one minute. Leave at least one window open while the fornelletto is on and wash your hands carefully after touching the tablets. One tablet is good for one night.

HIKING & WALKING

The Dolomites have an extensive network of trails with many huts and hostels along the way. **CAI,** Club Alpino Italiano's Web site, is in Italian only and though your calls won't be answered in English, they promise to respond to faxes. Local tourist-information offices can also be helpful.
🄷 Hiking Organization **CAI** ✉ via Petrella 19, 201124 Milan ☎ 02/2057231 🖷 02/205723201 ⊕ www.cai.it.

HOLIDAYS

National holidays include New Year's Day (January 1); Epiphany (January 6); Easter Sunday and Monday; Liberation Day (April 25); St. Mark's Day in Venice (April 25); Labor Day or May Day (May 1); Festa della Repubblica (June 2), Assump-tion of Mary, also known as Ferragosto (August 15); All Saints' Day (November 1); Immaculate Conception (December 8); Christmas Day and Boxing Day (Decem-ber 25 and 26).

The feast days of patron saints are ob-served locally. Many businesses and shops may be closed in Venice on November 21 (Madonna della Salute).

INSURANCE

The most useful travel-insurance plan is a comprehensive policy that includes cover-age for trip cancellation and interruption, default, trip delay, and medical expenses (with a waiver for preexisting conditions).

Without insurance you'll lose all or most of your money if you cancel your trip, re-gardless of the reason. Default insurance covers you if your tour operator, airline, or cruise line goes out of business. Trip-delay covers expenses that arise because of bad weather or mechanical delays. Study the fine print when comparing policies.

If you're traveling internationally, a key component of travel insurance is coverage for medical bills incurred if you get sick on the road. Such expenses aren't generally covered by Medicare or private policies. U.K. residents can buy a travel-insurance policy valid for most vacations taken during the year in which it's purchased (but check preexisting-condition coverage). British and Australian citizens need extra medical coverage when traveling overseas.

Always **buy travel policies directly from the insurance company**; if you buy them from a cruise line, airline, or tour operator that goes out of business you probably won't be covered for the agency or operator's default, a major risk. Before making any purchase, review your existing health and home-owner's policies to find what they cover away from home.

🔳 Travel Insurers In the U.S.: **Access America** ✉ 6600 W. Broad St., Richmond, VA 23230 ☎ 800/284-8300 🖶 804/673-1491 or 800/346-9265 🌐 www.accessamerica.com. **Travel Guard International** ✉ 1145 Clark St., Stevens Point, WI 54481 ☎ 715/345-0505 or 800/826-1300 🖶 800/955-8785 🌐 www.travelguard.com.

🔳 In the U.K.: **Association of British Insurers** ✉ 51 Gresham St., London EC2V 7HQ ☎ 020/7600-3333 🖶 020/7696-8999 🌐 www.abi.org.uk. In Canada: **RBC Insurance** ✉ 6880 Financial Dr., Mississauga, Ontario L5N 7Y5 ☎ 800/565-3129 🖶 905/813-4704 🌐 www.rbcinsurance.com. In Australia: **Insurance Council of Australia** ✉ Insurance Enquiries and Complaints, Level 3, 56 Pitt St., Sydney, NSW 2000 ☎ 1300/363683 or 02/9251-4456 🖶 02/9251-4453 🌐 www.iecltd.com.au. In New Zealand: **Insurance Council of New Zealand** ✉ Level 7, 111-115 Customhouse Quay, Box 474, Wellington ☎ 04/472-5230 🖶 04/473-3011 🌐 www.icnz.org.nz.

LANGUAGE

In Venice, language is not a big problem. You can always find someone who speaks at least a little English. Remember that the Italian language is pronounced exactly as it is written. (Many Italians try to speak English the same way, enunciating every syllable, with disconcerting results.) You may run into a language barrier in the countryside, but a phrase book and close attention to the Italians' astonishing use of pantomime and expressive gestures will go a long way. Try to **master a few phrases for daily use**, and familiarize yourself with the terms you'll need to decipher signs and museum labels.

More than a dialect, locally spoken *veneziano* is a real language with a rich history. All the Republic's official documents, all commercial transactions, and even many diplomatic missions to foreign states were written or conducted in the Venetian language. Unless you know some Italian, you may not realize how much of what you hear on the street is actually local language. If you listen closely, especially to the boatmen, or people in Castello or Cannaregio, you might notice a difference in tone, less enunciation, or the sound of a hard "g" or "z," normally not heard in Italian. Venetians also tend to drop consonants, so perhaps that's how an old Venetian greeting *sciavo* (literally "slave"), pronounced without the "v," became the Italian word *ciao*, used for both "hi" and "see you."

LANGUAGES FOR TRAVELERS

A phrase book and language-tape set can help get you started. *Fodor's Italian for Travelers* (available at bookstores everywhere) is excellent.

LODGING

The lodgings we list in this guide are the cream of the crop in each price category. We always list the facilities that are available—but we don't specify whether they cost extra: when pricing accommodations, always ask what's included and what costs extra.

At the end of each review we indicate the meal plan the hotel uses: European Plan (EP, with no meals), Continental Plan (CP, with a Continental breakfast daily), Modified American Plan (MAP, with breakfast and dinner daily), or the Full American Plan (FAP, with all meals). All hotels listed have private bath unless otherwise noted.

CATEGORY	VENICE	ELSEWHERE
$$$$	over €300	over €210
$$$	€225-€300	€160-€210
$$	€150-€225	€110-€160
$	€75-€150	€60-€110
¢	under €75	under €60

Prices are for two people in a standard double room in high season, including tax and service. and are given in euros.

APARTMENT RENTALS

If you want a home base that's roomy enough for a family and comes with cooking facilities, consider a furnished rental. These can save you money, especially if you're traveling with a group. Home-exchange directories sometimes list rentals as well as exchanges.

International Agents At Home Abroad ✉ 405 E. 56th St., Suite 6H, New York, NY 10022 ☎ 212/421-9165 ⊟ 212/752-1591 ⊕ www.athomeabroadinc.com. **Drawbridge to Europe** ✉ 98 Granite St., Ashland, OR 97520 ☎ 541/482-7778 or 888/268-1148 ⊟ 541/482-7779 ⊕ www.drawbridgetoeurope.com. **Hideaways International** ✉ 767 Islington St., Portsmouth, NH 03801 ☎ 603/430-4433 or 800/843-4433 ⊟ 603/430-4444 ⊕ www.hideaways.com, membership $145. **Hometours International** ✉ 1108 Scottie La., Knoxville, TN 37919 ☎ 865/690-8484 or 866/367-4668 ⊕ http://thor.he.net/~hometour/. **Interhome** ✉ 1990 N.E. 163rd St., Suite 110, North Miami Beach, FL 33162 ☎ 305/940-2299 or 800/882-6864 ⊟ 305/940-2911 ⊕ www.interhome.us. **Solemar** ✉ 1990 N.E. 163rd St., Suite 110, North Miami Beach, FL 33162 ☎ 305/940-2299 or 800/882-6864 ⊟ 305/940-2911 ⊕ www.visit-toscana.com. **Villanet** ✉ 1251 N.W. 116th St., Seattle, WA 98177 ☎ 206/417-3444 or 800/964-1891 ⊟ 206/417-1832 ⊕ www.rentavilla.com. **Villas and Apartments Abroad** ✉ 370 Lexington Ave., Suite 1401, New York, NY 10017 ☎ 212/897-5045 or 800/433-3020 ⊟ 212/897-5039 ⊕ www.ideal-villas.com. **Villas International** ✉ 4340 Redwood Hwy., Suite D309, San Rafael, CA 94903 ☎ 415/499-9490 or 800/221-2260 ⊟ 415/499-9491 ⊕ www.villasintl.com.

Italy-Only Agencies Cuendet USA ✉ 165 Chestnut St., Allendale, NJ 07041 ☎ 201/327-2333 ✉ Suzanne T. Pidduck, c/o Rentals in Italy, 1742 Calle Corva, Camarillo, CA 93010 ☎ 800/726-6702. **Vacanze in Italia** ✉ 22 Railroad St., Great Barrington, MA 01230 ☎ 413/528-6610 or 800/533-5405. **In the U.K. CV Travel** ✉ 43 Cadogan St., London SW3 2PR, England ☎ 020/7581-0851. **Magic of Italy** ✉ 227 Shepherds Bush Rd., London W6 7AS, England ☎ 020/8748-7575.

HOME EXCHANGES

If you would like to exchange your home for someone else's, join a home-exchange organization, which will send you its updated listings of available exchanges for a year and will include your own listing in at least one of them. It's up to you to make specific arrangements.

Exchange Club HomeLink International ⌂ Box 47747, Tampa, FL 33647 ☎ 813/975-9825 or 800/638-3841 ⊟ 813/910-8144 ⊕ www.homelink.org; $110 yearly for a listing, on-line access, and catalog; $70 without catalog.

HOSTELS

No matter what your age, you can save on lodging costs by staying at hostels. In some 4,500 locations in more than 70 countries

around the world, Hostelling International (HI), the umbrella group for a number of national youth-hostel associations, offers single-sex, dorm-style beds and, at many hostels, rooms for couples and family accommodations. There is one large HI hostel in town that has only dorm rooms. It takes advance bookings, but doesn't allow kitchen use. The other hostels are smaller church-operated places and Valdese is probably the best choice for families. All these hostels have curfews. As there are so few cheap places to stay in Venice, these are often booked ahead by large youth groups.

Membership in any HI national hostel association, open to travelers of all ages, allows you to stay in HI-affiliated hostels at member rates; one-year membership is about $28 for adults (C$35 for a two-year minimum membership in Canada, £13.50 in the U.K., A$52 in Australia, and NZ$40 in New Zealand); hostels charge about $10–$30 per night. Members have priority if the hostel is full; they're also eligible for discounts around the world, even on rail and bus travel in some countries.

Local Hostels Foresteria Valdese ✉ 5170 Castello, off Campo Santa Maria Formosa, 30122 ☎ 041/5286797 ⊟ 041/2416238 ⊕ chiesavaldese.org/venezia. **Istituto Canossiano** ⊕ Ponte Piccolo 428, Giudecca, 30133 Venice ☎ 041/5222157, women only; no bookings, show up in the morning. **Ostello di Venezia** ✉ Fondamenta delle Zitelle 86, Giudecca, 30133 Venice ☎ 041/5238211 ⊟ 041/5235689 ⊕ www.hostelbooking.com.

Organizations Hostelling International–USA ✉ 8401 Colesville Rd., Suite 600, Silver Spring, MD 20910 ☎ 301/495-1240 ⊟ 301/495-6697 ⊕ www.hiayh.org. **Hostelling International–Canada** ✉ 205 Catherine St., Suite 400, Ottawa, Ontario K2P 1C3 ☎ 613/237-7884 or 800/663-5777 ⊟ 613/237-7868 ⊕ www.hihostels.ca. **YHA England and Wales** ✉ Trevelyan House, Dimple Rd., Matlock, Derbyshire DE4 3YH, U.K. ☎ 0870/870-8808, 0870/ 770-8868, 0162/959-2700 ⊟ 0870/770-6127 ⊕ www.yha.org.uk. **YHA Australia** ✉ 422 Kent St., Sydney, NSW 2001 ☎ 02/9261-1111 ⊟ 02/9261-1969 ⊕ www.yha.com.au. **YHA New Zealand** ✉ Level 4, Torrens House, 195 Hereford St., Box 436, Christchurch ☎ 03/379-9970 or 0800/278-299 ⊟ 03/365-4476 ⊕ www.yha.org.nz.

HOTELS

Italian hotels are classified from five-star (deluxe) to one-star (very basic hotels and small inns). Stars are assigned according to standards set by regional boards (there are 20 in Italy), but rates are set by each hotel. During slack periods, or when a hotel is not full, you can often negotiate a discounted rate. In the major cities, room rates are on a par with other European capitals: deluxe and four-star rates can be quite extravagant. In these categories, **ask for one of the better rooms,** since less desirable rooms—and there usually are some—don't give you what you're paying for. Except in deluxe and some four-star hotels, rooms may be very small by U.S standards.

A lovely canal view may come at a price—noise. For a city without cars, diesel boats and vaporetto landings can become unnervingly noisy. Also beware of booking a room directly opening onto a campo or busy calle, especially during Carnevale season.

In all hotels there is a rate card inside the door of your room, or inside the closet door; it tells you exactly what you will pay for that particular room (rates in the same hotel may vary according to the location and type of room). On this card, breakfast and any other optionals must be listed separately. Any discrepancy between the basic room rate and that charged on your bill is cause for complaint to the manager and to the local tourist office.

Although, by law, breakfast is supposed to be optional, most hotels quote room rates including breakfast. When you book a room, specifically **ask whether the rate includes breakfast** (*colazione*). You are under no obligation to take breakfast at your hotel, but in practice most hotels expect you to do so. The trick is to "offer" guests "complimentary" breakfast and have its cost built into the rate. However, it is encouraging to note that many of the hotels we recommend are offering generous buffet breakfasts instead of simple, even skimpy "Continental breakfasts." Remember, if the latter is the case, you can **eat for less at the nearest coffee bar.**

Hotels that we list as ($$) and ($)—moderate to inexpensively priced accommodations—may charge extra for optional air-conditioning. In older hotels the quality of the rooms may be very uneven; if you don't like the room you're given, request another. This applies to noise, too. Front rooms may be larger and have a view, but they also may have a lot of street noise. If you're a light sleeper, **request a quiet room when making reservations.** Rooms in lodgings listed in this guide have a shower and/or bath, unless noted otherwise. Remember **to specify whether you care to**

have a bath or shower, since not all rooms, especially in lodgings outside major cities, have both.

You can save considerably on hotel rooms in Venice during low season, especially November through March (except during Carnevale and from December 22 to January 6, both periods considered high-season). In July and August, prices are slightly lower than in the spring and autumn months.

Associazione Veneziana Albergatori, an association of hotel keepers, operates a booking service by phone, fax, and at booths serving entry points around Venice. There's a kiosk inside Santa Lucia train station (open 8 AM–9 PM), one at Marco Polo airport (open 8 AM–10 PM), and one kiosk in each of the two Piazzale Roma parking garages (open 9 AM–10 PM). This service is free, but you'll have to pay a deposit (€11–€47 per person; Visa and Master Card accepted), which will be deducted from your hotel bill. Alternatively, Venezia Sì offers free reservations over the phone Monday–Saturday 9–7.

⊡ Reserving a Room **AVA hotel-reservation service booths** ✉ Piazzale Roma ☎ 041/5231397 and 041/5228640 ✉ Santa Lucia train station ☎ 041/715288 and 041/715016 ✉ Marco Polo airport ☎ 041/5415133. **Venezia Sì** ☎ 800/843006 in Italy [toll-free, Mon.–Sat. 9 AM–7 PM], 0039/0415222264 from abroad 🖷 0039/0415221242.

⊡ Toll-Free Numbers **Best Western** ☎ 800/528–1234 ⊕ www.bestwestern.com. **Choice** ☎ 800/424–6423 ⊕ www.choicehotels.com. **Comfort Inn** ☎ 800/424–6423 ⊕ www.choicehotels.com. **Hilton** ☎ 800/445–8667 ⊕ www.hilton.com. **Holiday Inn** ☎ 800/465–4329 ⊕ www.sixcontinentshotels.com. **Jolly** ☎ 800/247–1277 in New York state, 800/221–2626 elsewhere in U.S., 800/237–0319 in Canada, 800/017703 in Italy. **Quality Inn** ☎ 800/424–6423 ⊕ www.choicehotels.com. **Radisson** ☎ 800/333–3333 ⊕ www.radisson.com. **Ramada** ☎ 800/228–2828, 800/854–7854 international reservations ⊕ www.ramada.com or www.ramadahotels.com. **Sheraton** ☎ 800/325–3535 ⊕ www.starwood.com/sheraton. **Westin Hotels & Resorts** ☎ 800/228–3000 ⊕ www.starwood.com/westin.

MAIL & SHIPPING

The Italian mail system isn't the world's fastest and it can take up to 15 days for mail to or from the United States and Canada, and a week to or from the United Kingdom (or even within Italy). Though Posta Prioritaria and Postacelere are faster, they rarely meet their "guarantee" of delivery within 24 hours in Italy and 3–5 days abroad.

Venice's main post office is open Monday–Saturday 8:30–6:30.
🚩 Post Offices **Venice main post office** ✉ Fondaco dei Tedeschi, near Rialto Bridge ☎ 041/5289257, 160 countrywide postal information.

OVERNIGHT SERVICES

Private courier companies make international shipping from major cities in Italy fast and fairly easy. Most couriers have a morning deadline for next-day or two-day delivery. DHL and FedEx both have convenient offices near San Marco. For information on rates, drop-off points, or to schedule a pick-up, call the services' toll-free numbers.
🚩 Major Services **DHL** ☎ 199/199345, 24 hours a day. **Federal Express** ☎ 800/123800, weekdays 8 AM–7 PM. **SDA** ☎ 800/016027, weekdays 8:30 AM–7:30 PM and Saturday 8:30 AM–1:30 PM.

POSTAL RATES

Airmail postcards and lightweight letters to the United States and Canada cost €.52 for the first 20 grams; €1.03 for up to 100 grams. If in doubt about weight, you should go to the post office. Always stick the blue airmail tag on your mail, or write "Airmail" in big, clear characters to the side of the address. Postcards and letters (for the first 20 grams) to the United Kingdom, as well as to any other EU country, including Italy, cost €.41. In addition to post offices, you can generally find *francobolli* (stamps) at tobacconists.

Posta Prioritaria (envelopes and small packages up to 2 kilograms) and the more expensive *Postacelere* (up to 20 kilograms) are Poste Italia's special services that promise delivery within 24 hours in Italy and three to five days abroad. Letters sent Posta Prioritaria to the United States and Canada cost €.77 for the first 20 grams and €1.55 for parcels up to 100 grams; to the United Kingdom, Italy, and all other EU countries it costs €.62. As regular stamps are not valid for this service, make sure you buy the special golden Posta Prioritaria stamps. Postacelere rates to the United States and Canada range between €27.89 for parcels up to 500 grams (a little over a pound) and €102.27 for 10 kilograms (about 22 pounds). Prices for

the United Kingdom and Europe cost about half.
🚩 **Informazioni Poste Italiane** ☎ 803/160 for information in Italian or English about rates and local post offices' opening hours, as well as about Postacelere ⊕ www.poste.it.

RECEIVING MAIL

Correspondence can be addressed to you care of the Italian post office. Letters should be addressed to your name, "c/o Ufficio Postale Centrale," followed by "Fermo Posta" on the next line, and "30124 Venice" on the next. You can **collect it at the central post office** by showing your passport or photo-bearing I.D. and paying a small fee. American Express also has a general-delivery service. There's no charge for cardholders, holders of American Express traveler's checks, or anyone who booked a vacation with American Express.

SHIPPING PARCELS

You can ship parcels via air or surface. Air takes about two weeks, and surface anywhere up to three months. If you have purchased antiques, ceramics, or other objects, **inquire to see if the vendor will do the shipping** for you; in most cases, this is a possibility.

MONEY MATTERS

Italy's prices are in line with those in the rest of Europe, with costs in the main cities comparable to those in other major capitals, such as Paris and London. Venice is the most expensive city in Italy, and is therefore one of Europe's priciest tourist destinations. Efforts are being made to hold the line on hotel and restaurant prices that have become inordinately high by U.S. standards. Depending on season and occupancy, you may be able to obtain unadvertised lower rates in hotels; always inquire.

In Venice, admission to Palazzo Ducale is €9.50, but that ticket includes entrance to Museo Correr, Museo Archeologico, and Biblioteca Marciana. Admission to the Gallerie dell'Accademia is €6.50 (free for children under 12). A vaporetto ride costs €3.10, a 50-minute gondola ride starts at €62 (but goes much higher). An English-language newspaper is €1.50. An inexpensive hotel room for two, including breakfast, is about €90 in low season, nearly twice as much during spring and fall, and can go even higher during

Carnevale. An inexpensive restaurant dinner for two is €30, with a simple pasta dish on the menu running about €8 and ½-liter carafe of house wine €3. A *bacaro* (wine bar) lunch is €15, including a glass of good wine. A Coca-Cola (standing) at a caffè is €1.90, a cup of coffee €.80, and a pint of beer from a pub or pizzeria (at the table) €4.80.

Prices throughout this guide are given for adults. Substantially reduced fees are almost always available for children, students, and senior citizens. For information on taxes, *see* Taxes.

ATMS

There are bancomat (ATM) machines all over Venice and the Veneto, but you won't find one in Venice's train station. ATMs are the easiest way to get euros in Italy. The term for PIN is *codice segreto*. Most machines accept four-digit codes; some will accept a larger number of digits. Keypads have only numbers, no letters.

CREDIT CARDS

All over Italy, Visa and MasterCard are preferred to American Express, but in tourist areas American Express is usually accepted. While increasingly common, not all establishments and stores take credit cards, and some require a minimum expenditure. If you want to pay with a card in a small hotel, store, or restaurant, it's a good idea to make your intentions known early on.

Throughout this guide, the following abbreviations are used: **AE**, American Express; **DC**, Diners Club; **MC**, MasterCard; and **V**, Visa.

🖪 Reporting Lost Cards **American Express** ☎ 336/668-5110 international collect. **Diners Club** ☎ 702/797-5532 collect, 800/864034 toll-free in Italy. **MasterCard** ☎ 800/870866 toll-free in Italy. **Visa** ☎ 800/819014 toll-free in Italy.

CURRENCY

The European Union (EU) currency, the euro, is used in Italy. There are seven notes—5, 10, 20, 50, 100, 200, and 500 euros (practically impossible to change outside of banks)—and eight coins: 1 and 2 euros, plus 1, 2, 5, 10, 20, and 50 centimes, or cents, which are 100 to the euro.

CURRENCY EXCHANGE

For the most favorable rates, **change money through banks**. Although ATM

transaction fees may be higher abroad than at home, ATM rates are excellent because they're based on wholesale rates offered only by major banks. You won't do as well at exchange booths in airports or rail and bus stations, in hotels, in restaurants, or in stores. To avoid lines at airport exchange booths, get a bit of local currency before you leave home.

At press time, the exchange rate was about 0.83 euros to the U.S. dollar; 0.64 euros to the Canadian dollar; 1.44 euros to the pound sterling; 0.61 euros to the Australian dollar; and 0.54 euros to the New Zealand dollar.

🖪 Exchange Services **International Currency Express** ✉ 427 N. Camden Dr., Suite F, Beverly Hills, CA 90210 ☎ 888/278-6628 orders 🖷 310/278-6410 🌐 www.foreignmoney.com. **Thomas Cook International Money Services** ☎ 800/287-7362 orders and retail locations 🌐 www.us.thomascook.com.

TRAVELER'S CHECKS

Do you need traveler's checks? It depends on where you're headed. If you're going to rural areas and small towns, go with cash; traveler's checks are best used in cities. Lost or stolen checks can usually be replaced within 24 hours. To ensure a speedy refund, buy your own traveler's checks—don't let someone else pay for them: irregularities like this can cause delays. The person who bought the checks should make the call to request a refund.

PACKING

The weather is considerably milder in the Veneto region than in the north and central United States or Great Britain. In summer, stick with clothing that is as light as possible, though its wise to carry a lightweight "modesty" shirt when touring religious sites. At dusk, even in mid-summer, that shirt, or a sweater can come in handy, especially in the mountains. An umbrella can spare you a sudden drenching from the all too common summer afternoon thundershowers (and it's handy in winter as well). Do not underestimate the humid cold of Venetian winters; a waterproof coat is a must, and it should be well-lined. A hat, scarf, gloves and comfortable, watertight shoes or boots will make walking tours more enjoyable. Some museums and most churches lack central heating, but elsewhere you should be able to escape the cold indoors.

Venetians may be less fashion-conscious than Romans, Florentines, and Milanese, but Italians in general dress exceptionally well. Though even the best restaurant in Venice wouldn't throw out a diner wearing rubber boots (during *acqua alta*, of course), you likewise won't see Venetians wearing shorts and tennis shoes around town. Men aren't required to wear ties or jackets anywhere, except in some of the grander hotel dining rooms and top-level restaurants, but they are expected to look reasonably sharp—and they do. Italian women usually wear skirts even in winter, but if trousers are worn, they're generally the dressy sort. Formal wear has become the exception rather than the rule at the opera, though people in expensive seats usually do dress up.

For sightseeing, **pack a pair of binoculars**; they will help you get a good look at painted ceilings and domes. If you stay in budget hotels, **take your own soap**; many such hotels do not provide it, or give guests only one tiny bar per room.

If you're tempted to take advantage of the generous luggage allowance American carriers permit, do think again. Getting around Venice is difficult even when unencumbered, and can become a nightmare when toting large bags. The wheeled variety help, except when crossing bridges and when flooded streets force you to lift them onto raised walkways. **Porters are notoriously hard to find** even at the train station and crosstown porterage is expensive. When riding the vaporetto, if you're bag exceeds 50 cm (28 in), you can be forced to buy an extra €3.10 ticket for the bag.

In your carry-on luggage, pack an extra pair of eyeglasses or contact lenses and enough of any medication you take to last a few days longer than the entire trip. You may also ask your doctor to write a spare prescription using the drug's generic name, as brand names may vary from country to country. In luggage to be checked, **never pack prescription drugs, valuables, or undeveloped film.** And don't forget to carry with you the addresses of offices that handle refunds of lost traveler's checks. Check *Fodor's How to Pack* (available at on-line retailers and bookstores everywhere) for more tips.

To avoid customs and security delays, carry medications in their original packaging. Don't pack any sharp objects in your carry-on luggage, including knives of any size or material, scissors, and corkscrews, or anything else that might arouse suspicion.

To avoid having your checked luggage chosen for hand inspection, don't cram bags full. The U.S. Transportation Security Administration suggests packing shoes on top and placing personal items you don't want touched in clear plastic bags.

CHECKING LUGGAGE

You're allowed to carry aboard one bag and one personal article, such as a purse or a laptop computer. Make sure what you carry on fits under your seat or in the overhead bin. Get to the gate early, so you can board as soon as possible, before the overhead bins fill up.

Baggage allowances vary by carrier, destination, and ticket class. On international flights, you're usually allowed to check two bags weighing up to 70 pounds (32 kilograms) each, although a few airlines allow checked bags of up to 88 pounds (40 kilograms) in first class. Some international carriers don't allow more than 66 pounds (30 kilograms) per bag in business class and 44 pounds (20 kilograms) in economy. On domestic flights, the limit is usually 50 to 70 pounds (23 to 32 kilograms) per bag. In general, carry-on bags shouldn't exceed 40 pounds (18 kilograms). Most airlines won't accept bags that weigh more than 100 pounds (45 kilograms) on domestic or international flights. Check baggage restrictions with your carrier before you pack.

Airline liability for baggage is limited to $2,500 per person on flights within the United States. On international flights it amounts to $9.07 per pound or $20 per kilogram for checked baggage (roughly $640 per 70-pound bag), with a maximum of $634.90 per piece, and $400 per passenger for unchecked baggage. You can buy additional coverage at check-in for about $10 per $1,000 of coverage, but it often excludes a rather extensive list of items, shown on your airline ticket.

Before departure, itemize your bags' contents and their worth, and label the bags with your name, address, and phone number. (If you use your home address, cover it so potential thieves can't see it readily.) Include a label inside each bag and **pack a copy of your itinerary.** At check-in, make sure each bag is correctly tagged with the destination airport's three-letter code. Because some checked bags will be opened for hand inspection, the U.S. Transportation Security Administration recommends that you leave luggage unlocked or use the plastic locks offered at check-in. TSA screeners place an inspection notice inside searched bags, which are re-sealed with a special lock.

If your bag has been searched and contents are missing or damaged, file a claim with the TSA Consumer Response Center as soon as possible. If your bags arrive damaged or fail to arrive at all, file a written report with the airline before leaving the airport.

🖪 Complaints **U.S. Transportation Security Administration Consumer Response Center** ☎ 866/289-9673 ⊕ www.tsa.gov.

PASSPORTS & VISAS

When traveling internationally, carry your passport even if you don't need one (it's always the best form of I.D.) and **make two photocopies of the data page** (one for someone at home and another for you, carried separately from your passport). If you lose your passport, promptly call the nearest embassy or consulate and the local police.

U.S. passport applications for children under age 14 require consent from both parents or legal guardians; both parents must appear together to sign the application. If only one parent appears, he or she must submit a written statement from the other parent authorizing passport issuance for the child. A parent with sole authority must present evidence of it when applying; acceptable documentation includes the child's certified birth certificate listing only the applying parent, a court order specifically permitting this parent's travel with the child, or a death certificate for the non-applying parent. Application forms and instructions are available on the Web site of the U.S. State Department's Bureau of Consular Affairs (⊕ www.travel.state.gov).

ENTERING ITALY

AUSTRALIAN CITIZENS

Citizens of Australia need only a valid passport to enter Italy for stays of up to 90 days.

CANADIAN CITIZENS

You need only a valid passport to enter Italy for stays of up to 90 days.

NEW ZEALAND CITIZENS

Citizens of New Zealand need only a valid passport to enter Italy for stays of up to 90 days.

U.K. CITIZENS

Citizens of the United Kingdom need only a valid passport to enter Italy for an unlimited stay.

U.S. CITIZENS

All U.S. citizens, even infants, need only a valid passport to enter Italy for stays of up to 90 days.

PASSPORT OFFICES

The best time to apply for a passport or to renew is in fall and winter. Before any trip, check your passport's expiration date, and, if necessary, renew it as soon as possible.

🖪 Australian Citizens **Passports Australia** ☎ 131-232 ⊕ www.passports.gov.au.

🖪 Canadian Citizens **Passport Office** ✉ to mail in applications: 200 Promenade du Portage, Hull, Québec J8X 4B7 ☎ 819/994-3500 or 800/567-6868 ⊕ www.ppt.gc.ca.

🖪 New Zealand Citizens **New Zealand Passports Office** ☎ 0800/22-5050 or 04/474-8100 ⊕ www.passports.govt.nz.

🖪 U.K. Citizens **U.K. Passport Service** ☎ 0870/521-0410 ⊕ www.passport.gov.uk.

🖪 U.S. Citizens **National Passport Information Center** ☎ 900/225-5674 or 900/225-7778 TTY (calls are 55¢ per minute for automated service or $1.50 per minute for operator service), 888/362-8668 or 888/498-3648 TTY (calls are $5.50 each) ⊕ www.travel.state.gov.

REST ROOMS

Public rest rooms aren't common around Italy, but Venice does have pay toilets scattered throughout the city, including on the Lido and the other islands. They're well posted and strategically located along the main tourist routes: at Piazzale Roma; near Rialto Bridge (both sides); on Strada Nova, near Ponte delle Guglie; near Accademia Bridge vaporetto landing; and next to the tourist information office at the Giardinetti Reali, close to Piazza San Marco. The charge is €.50 and nearly all are accessible to wheelchairs. While private businesses rarely permit passersby to use their toilets, most bars will allow you if you ask politely, or alternatively, buy a little something—a mineral water or espresso—in exchange for their kindness. Standards of cleanliness and comfort vary greatly. While hotels, department stores like La Rinascente and Coin, and restaurants, including McDonald's, tend to have the cleanest rest rooms, those in pubs and bars rank among the worst. It is always best to carry your own tissue. You'll find well-kept pay toilets (for €.25–€.50) in airports, major train stations, and in most museums. There are also bathrooms at highway rest stops and gas stations where a small tip to the cleaning person is always appreciated. Churches, post offices, public beaches, or subway stations rarely have public facilities.

SAFETY

Day or night, violent crime is extremely rare in Venice, however this is a city ripe for crimes of opportunity. Expert thieves couldn't find a better place to work than where vacationing spenders are too busy ogling to be aware of stealthy pickpockets. Concentrating in busy streets and squares, jam-packed vaporetti, and chaotic train stations, these pros, generally working in teams, can stall traffic, jostle a person and pass colleagues the wallet too fast for anyone's reflexes to respond. **Protect yourself before going out:** A money belt or a pouch hung around the neck works as long as strings or bulges are not visible, otherwise these too have disappeared. Slinging bags or cameras across your body bandolier-style, and even covering them with your coat are not bad ideas, but are not guarantees. Nothing protects better than **awareness**.

WOMEN IN ITALY

The difficulties encountered by women traveling alone in Italy are often overstated. Younger women have to put up with much male attention, but it is rarely dangerous. Ignoring whistling and questions is the best way to get rid of unwanted attention.

SENIOR-CITIZEN TRAVEL

EU citizens over 60 are entitled to free admission to state museums, as well as to many other museums—always ask at the ticket office. Older travelers may be eligible for special fares on Alitalia.

To qualify for age-related discounts, mention your senior-citizen status up front when booking hotel reservations (not when checking out) and before you're seated in restaurants (not when paying the bill). Be sure to have identification on hand. When renting a car, ask about promotional car-rental discounts, which can be cheaper than senior-citizen rates.

🎓 Educational Programs **Elderhostel** ✉ 11 Ave. de Lafayette, Boston, MA 02111-1746 ☎ 877/426-8056, 978/323-4141 international callers, 877/426-2167 TTY 🖶 877/426-2166 🌐 www.elderhostel.org.

SHOPPING

The notice PREZZI FISSI (fixed prices) means just that; in shops displaying this sign it's a waste of time to bargain unless you're buying a sizable quantity of goods or a particularly costly object. Always try to bargain, however, at outdoor markets (except food markets) and when buying from street vendors. For information on VAT refunds, *see* Taxes.

SIGHTSEEING TOURS

BOAT TOURS

Boat tours to the islands of Murano, Burano, and Torcello leave various docks around Piazza San Marco daily. These 3–3½-hour trips cost €15–€17 and can be annoyingly commercial, often emphasizing glass-factory showrooms, and pressuring you to buy at prices even higher than normal. April–October trips depart at 9:30 and 2:30 and November–March at 2.

Over a dozen major travel agents in Venice have grouped together to provide frequent, quality tours of the city. One of these is a serenaded gondola trip, with dinner (€68) or without (€31), which can be purchased at any of their offices or at American Express. Nightly tours leave at 7:30 and 8:30 May–September; at 7:30 in April and October; and at 3:30 November–March.

The Venetian lagoon itself is expansive, but though rich in islands, culture, and wildlife, it's only one part of the system of rivers, canals, and secondary lagoons that stretch for over 100 miles. For those interested in getting off the main waterways and away from the masses, several Venetian operators offer lagoon tours aboard privately owned wooden boats. You'll dine impeccably aboard Mauro Stoppa's **Eolo,** a traditional sailing *bragozzo,* which after decades of working the lagoon, has been restored and retired to the cruising life. **Sior Bepi** is a smaller sailing bragozzo making less expensive day trips. For motor tours, try **Bragozzo Moretto.**

EXCURSION TOURS

American Express and other agencies offer several excursions in the Veneto region. A boat trip to Padua along the Brenta River makes stops at three Palladian villas, and you return to Venice by bus. The tours run three times a week (Tuesday, Thursday, and Saturday) from March through October and cost €62 per person (€86 with lunch); bookings should be made a few days in advance.

The Palladio Villa Tour (by minibus, maximum eight people), includes villas plus a walking tour of Vicenza (Wednesdays; €108 per person, optional lunch €13).

The Hills of the Veneto tour (by minibus, maximum eight people) visits the picturesque hill towns of Marostica, Bassano del Grappa, and Asolo, with stops at Villa Barbaro at Maser and at a vineyard along Strada del Prosecco for Prosecco wine tasting (Tuesday, Thursday, and weekends; €104 per person, optional lunch €13).

For a break from the heat, consider the Dolomite Tour (by minibus, maximum eight people) through the stupendous scenery in the Dolomite mountains; stops include Titian's birthplace Pieve di Cadore, Lakes Santa Caterina and Misurina, the famous Cime di Lavaredo peaks, and Cortina d'Ampezzo (Monday and Friday, €113 per person, including a packed lunch). For these last three tours it is essential to make reservations at least a week in advance in high season.

WALKING TOURS

The same group of travel agents (mentioned above) offers a two-hour walking tour of the San Marco area (€24), which ends with a glassblowing demonstration (daily; no Sunday tour in winter). From April through October, there's also an afternoon walking tour that ends with a gondola ride (€29). Book at most local travel agents or through American Express.

Venicescapes, an Italo-American cultural association offers several themed itineraries focusing on history and culture as well as tourist sights. Their three- to seven-hour tours, are private and groups are small (generally six to eight people). Reservations are recommended during busy seasons and prices start at US$200 for two people. For those who want to travel their own way, yet take advantage of local expertise, the goal of Venice à la Carte is to individualize the Venice experience to fit your particular taste.

📧 **American Express** ✉ Salizzada San Moisè 1471, San Marco 1417, ☎ 041/5200844, 📠 041/5229937. **Cooperativa Guide Turistiche Autorizzate** ✉ San Marco 750, near San Zulian ☎ 041/5209038 📠 041/5210762 ✉ guideve@tin.it. **Kele Teo** ✉ Ponte dei Bareteri, San Marco 4930 between San Marco and Rialto ☎ 041/5208722 📠 041/5208913. **Venice à la Carte** ☎ 349/1447818 📠 240/208-7273 (US) ⊕ www.tourvenice.org. **Venicescapes** ✉ Campo San Provolo, Castello 4954 ☎📠 041/5206361 ⊕ www.venicescapes.org.

📧 Contacts: Boat Tours **Bragozzo Moretto** ☎ 347/4205004 ✉ dellatoffolac@interfree.it. **Consorzio San Marco** ☎ 041/2406712. **Eolo** ☎ 049/8078032 ⊕ www.cruisingvenice.com. **Serenissima Motoscafi** ☎ 041/5224281. **Sior Bepi** ☎ 041/2410636 or 347/2682027 ✉ siorbepi@tin.it.

SMOKING

In 2002, laws were enacted banning smoking in many public places, including bars and restaurants, but Italians are unrepentant smokers and compliance is arbitrary. If you ask someone to smoke elsewhere or not to smoke in no-smoking areas, don't expect them to respond or respect your request. Smokers should check to see if there's a "Vietato Fumare" (No Smoking) sign before lighting up. For as smoke-free an environment as possible, stick to large establishments and, weather permitting, eat outside. All FS trains have no-smoking cars: always specify when you make reservations.

SPORTS & OUTDOORS

Italians are sports lovers, and several daily newspapers are devoted solely to sports. *Calcio* (soccer) is fiercely popular in Italy, and if you make the effort to get tickets to a match, you won't be denied fancy footwork and raving fans. This climate makes it tough to resist the temptation to serve a cannonball on a red-clay tennis court, putt a birdie on a scenic green, or just climb a hill to savor the fresh air and view. Come winter, skiers hit the slopes of the Apennines and the Alps, including the Veneto's Dolomite Alps, for world-class conditions.

STUDENTS IN VENICE & THE VENETIAN ARC

The "Rolling Venice" Pass, costing €2.58 and valid throughout a calendar year, buys youths 14–29 discounts on vaporetto passes, lots of museums, and assorted ho-

tels, restaurants, and shops. You can buy this pass upon presentation of your passport or ID at Vela ticket offices (major vaporetto stops), at the Assessorato alla Gioventù (open weekdays 9:30–1, plus Tuesday and Thursday afternoons 3–5), or at the Associazione Italiana Alberghi per la Gioventù (open Monday through Saturday 8–2), or at the Centro Turistico Studentesco e Giovanile (CTS; open weekdays 9:30–1:30 and 3–7). During summer months, they're even sold at a special booth in the train station (daily 8–8). You must show your passport to qualify.
🖪 **Rolling Venice** ☎ 041/2714747 ⊕ www.comune. venezia.it. **Assessorato alla Gioventù** ⊠ Corte Contarina, San Marco 1529, behind Piazza San Marco post office ☎ 041/2747651. **Associazione Italiana Alberghi per la Gioventù** ⊠ Calle Castelforte, San Polo 3101, near San Rocco ☎ 041/5204414. **Centro Turistico Studentesco (CTS)** ⊠ opposite Ca' Foscari University, Dorsoduro 3252 Venezia ☎ 041/5205660 ⊕ www.cts.it.

TRAVEL AGENCIES

To save money, **look into deals available through student-oriented travel agencies.** To qualify you'll need a bona fide student I.D. card. Members of international student groups are also eligible.

The Centro Turistico Studentesco (CTS) is a student and youth travel agency with offices in major Italian cities; CTS helps its clients find low-cost accommodations and bargain fares for travel in Italy and elsewhere. CTS is also the Rome representative for EuroTrain International.
🖪 IDs & Services **Centro Turistico Studentesco (CTS)** ⊠ opposite Ca' Foscari University, Dorsoduro 3252 Venezia ☎ 041/5205660 ⊕ www.cts.it. **STA Travel** ⊠ 10 Downing St., New York, NY 10014 ☎ 212/627-3111, 800/777-0112 24-hr service center 🖨 212/627-3387 ⊕ www.sta.com. **Travel Cuts** ⊠ 187 College St., Toronto, Ontario M5T 1P7, Canada ☎ 800/592-2887 in the U.S., 416/979-2406 or 866/246-9762 in Canada 🖨 416/979-8167 ⊕ www. travelcuts.com.

TAXES

VALUE-ADDED TAX

Value-added tax (VAT, or IVA in Italian) is 20% on clothing, wine, luxury goods, and most services. On all consumer goods it is already included in the amount shown on the price tag, whereas on services it may not be. IVA is always included in restaurant bills, and only a few five-star deluxe

hotels treat IVA as a separate 10% item added to the bill at departure.

To **get a VAT refund,** when you are leaving Italy take the goods and the invoice to the customs office at the airport or other point of departure and have the invoice stamped. (If you return to the United States or Canada directly from Italy, go through the procedure at Italian customs; if your return is via any of the EU countries, for instance, via Britain, take the Italian goods and invoice to British customs.) Under Italy's VAT-refund system, a non-EU resident can obtain a refund of tax paid on consumer goods. Shop with your passport and ask the store for an invoice itemizing the article(s), price(s), and the amount of tax. Once back home—and within 90 days of the date of purchase—mail the stamped invoice to the store, which will send the VAT rebate to you. The VAT on services is not refundable.

When making a purchase, **ask for a V.A.T. refund form** and find out whether the merchant gives refunds—not all stores do, nor are they required to. Have the form stamped like any customs form by customs officials when you leave the country or, if you're visiting several European Union countries, when you leave the EU. Be ready to show customs officials what you've bought (pack purchases together in your carry-on luggage); budget extra time for this. After you're through passport control, take the form to a refund-service counter for an on-the-spot refund, or mail it back to the store or a refund service after you arrive home.

A refund service can save you some hassle, for a fee. Global Refund is a Europe-wide service with 190,000 affiliated stores and more than 700 refund counters—located at every major airport and border crossing. Its refund form is called a Tax Free Check. The service issues refunds in the form of cash, check, or credit-card adjustment, minus a processing fee. If you don't have time to wait at the refund counter, you can mail in the form instead.
🖪 VAT Refunds **Global Refund** ⊠ 99 Main St., Suite 307, Nyack, NY 10960 ☎ 800/566-9828 🖨 845/348-1549 ⊕ www.globalrefund.com.

TAXIS

The only land taxi service is to and from the airport. Taxi stands are located in Pi-

azzale Roma, and they also line up at the vaporetto landing as people arrive in Lido.
F Taxi Companies **Radio (land) Taxi** ☎ 041/936222.

TELEPHONES

CALLS WITHIN ITALY

For all calls within Italy—local and long distance—you must dial the area code (*prefisso*), including the "0," such as 041 for Venice or 06 for Rome. If you are calling from a public phone you must deposit a coin or use a calling card to get a dial tone.

AREA & COUNTRY CODES

The country code for Italy is 39. A personal phone number in Italy can range from 5 digits to 8 digits depending on area. Area codes (*prefissi*) for major cities in the Veneto region are as follows: Venice, 041; Verona, 045; Treviso, 0422; Padua, 049; Belluno, 0437; Vicenza, 0444; Rovigo, 0425. Note that in Italy, all calls, including local ones, must be preceded by the appropriate regional area code, zero included. Calls from abroad must be preceded by 39 and the regional area code, zero included. For example, a call from New York to Venice would be dialed as 011 + 39 + 041 + local phone number; from Venice to another number in Venice, dial 041 + local phone number; from Rome to Venice, 041 + local phone number. Country codes are 1 for the United States and Canada, 61 for Australia, 64 for New Zealand, and 44 for the United Kingdom.

CELL PHONES

In Italy, you're rarely beyond earshot of ringing *telefonini* ("little phones" or "cell phones"), which have become a national compulsion and are left on in restaurants, theaters, museums, trains, and buses. The three major service companies are Tim, Omnitel, and Wind. Each company has a series of prefixes (328, 338, 345), which never begin with a "0." For example, from New York, you dial an Italian cell phone with: 011 + 39+ 338 + personal phone number; in Italy, dial 338 + personal number. Receiving calls on Italian cell phones is free, unless the phone is outside of Italy and using another phone carrier for "roaming."

DIRECTORY & OPERATOR ASSISTANCE

For general information in English, dial 4176. To place international telephone calls via operator-assisted service, dial 170 or long-distance access numbers (⇨ Long-Distance Services, *below*).

INTERNATIONAL CALLS

Since hotels tend to overcharge, sometimes exorbitantly, for long-distance and international calls, it is best to make such calls from public phones, using telephone cards (⇨ Public Phones, *below*). You can **make collect calls from any phone by dialing 800/172444**, which will get you an English-speaking operator. Rates to the United States are lowest around the clock on Sunday and 10 PM to 8 AM (Italian time) on weekdays.

From major Italian cities, you can place a direct call to the United States by reversing the charges or using your phone credit-card number. When calling from pay telephones, insert a coin, which will be returned upon completion of your call. You automatically reach an operator in the country of destination and thereby avoid all language difficulties.

LONG-DISTANCE SERVICES

AT&T, MCI, and Sprint access codes make calling long distance relatively convenient, but you may find the local access number blocked in many hotel rooms. First ask the hotel operator to connect you. If the hotel operator balks, ask for an international operator, or dial the international operator yourself. One way to improve your odds of getting connected to your long-distance carrier is to travel with more than one company's calling card (a hotel may block Sprint, for example, but not MCI). If all else fails, call from a pay phone.
F Access Codes **AT&T Direct** ☎ 800/172444. **MCI WorldPhone** ☎ 800/905825. **Sprint International Access** ☎ 800/172405.

PHONE CARDS

More convenient than coins, prepaid Telcom *carte telefoniche* (calling cards), used throughout Italy, can be found at post offices, tobacconists, most bars and news stalls, and in vending machines at airports or train stations. Tear off a corner of the card and insert it in the slot. When you dial, its value appears in the window and after you hang up, the card is returned so you can use it until its value runs out. Also popular are long-distance phone cards, which offer up to an hour of calling for €5. To use these, scratch off a coating and dial in your hidden code. Shops sell many different types, some more reliable than others, but the market changes too fast to recommend any one card.

PUBLIC PHONES

Some pay phones accept only coins, others only *carte telefoniche*, so be smart and always have both ready in your pockets (⇨ Phone Cards, *above*).

TIME

Venice is 6 hours ahead of New York. Venice is 1 hour ahead of London, 10 hours behind Sydney, and 12 hours behind Auckland. Italy keeps time using the 24-hour (or "military") method, which means that after 12 noon you continue counting the hours forward: 1 PM is 13:00, 2 PM is 14:00, and so on.

TIPPING

Among Italian travelers, tipping until recently was considered the exception rather than the rule; however, the influx of foreigners in Venice has seriously raised expectations among service industry workers. The following guidelines, which apply to Venice, could be reduced in smaller cities and towns. In an osteria or trattoria, unless the menu states that service is included, a service charge of about 12% may appear as a separate item on your bill. Either way, it's customary to leave an additional 5% to 10% tip, depending on the quality of service and the number of servers involved. Higher-priced restaurants rarely charge for service, relying on diners' generosity to compensate their staff. Tip checkroom attendants €.50 per person, rest room attendants €.20–€.30 (more in expensive hotels and restaurants). When seated at a bar, tip about 10% of the bar bill.

Italians tip taxi drivers only under exceptional circumstances but in Venice, where boat drivers are often expected to hoist very heavy bags on and off the boat, €5–€10 is reasonable per couple. Railway and airport porters charge a fixed rate per bag but if porters are very helpful, tip an additional €1 per person. On sightseeing tours, tip guides about €1–€2 per person for a half-day group tour, more if they are very good. In museums and other places of interest where admission is free, helpful assistants should be tipped €1.

In Venice, though the hotel *portiere* (concierge) usually receives compensation from restaurants and taxis booked on your behalf, he still expects to be tipped, based on service you received, €10–€20. For two people in a double room in a moderately priced hotel, leave the chambermaid about €1–€2 per day and tip a minimum of €1 for valet or room service. Double those amounts in an expensive hotel. In expensive hotels, tip doormen €1 for calling a cab and a minimum of €2 for carrying bags to the check-in desk, bellhops €3–€4 for carrying your bags to the room.

TOURS & PACKAGES

Because everything is prearranged on a prepackaged tour or independent vacation, you spend less time planning—and often get it all at a good price.

BOOKING WITH AN AGENT

Travel agents are excellent resources. But it's a good idea to collect brochures from several agencies, as some agents' suggestions may be influenced by relationships with tour and package firms that reward them for volume sales. If you have a special interest, find an agent with expertise in that area; the American Society of Travel Agents (ASTA; ⇨ Travel Agencies) has a database of specialists worldwide. You can log on to the group's Web site to find an ASTA travel agent in your neighborhood.

Find a travel agent who has been to Venice or at least knows the accommodations and other services they recommend. Ask about the hotel's location, room size, beds, and whether it has a pool, room service, or programs for children, if you care about these. Has your agent sent others whom you can contact?

Do some homework on your own, too: local tourism boards can provide information about lesser-known and small-niche operators, some of which may sell only direct. Shopping on the Internet can indeed save you money, but bear in mind, the person on the other end of your e-mail or 800 phone call is working as a sales agent, and may never have traveled internationally.

BUYER BEWARE

Each year consumers are stranded or lose their money when tour operators—even large ones with excellent reputations—go out of business. So check out the operator.

Ask several travel agents about its reputation, and try to **book with a company that has a consumer-protection program.** (Look for information in the company's brochure.) In the United States, members of the National Tour Association and the United States Tour Operators Association are required to set aside funds to cover payments and travel arrangements in the event that the company defaults. It's also a good idea to choose a company that participates in the American Society of Travel Agents' Tour Operator Program; ASTA will act as mediator in any disputes between you and your tour operator.

Remember that the more your package or tour includes, the better you can predict the ultimate cost of your vacation. Make sure you know exactly what is covered, and beware of hidden costs. Are taxes, tips, and transfers included? Entertainment and excursions? These can add up.

Tour-Operator Recommendations **American Society of Travel Agents** (⇨ Travel Agencies). **National Tour Association** (NTA) ✉ 546 E. Main St., Lexington, KY 40508 ☎ 859/226-4444 or 800/682-8886 🖷 859/226-4404 🌐 www.ntaonline.com. **United States Tour Operators Association** (USTOA) ✉ 275 Madison Ave., Suite 2014, New York, NY 10016 ☎ 212/599-6599 🖷 212/599-6744 🌐 www.ustoa.com.

TRAIN TRAVEL

The fastest, most expensive trains on *Trenitalia,* also referred to as Ferrovia dello Stato (FS), the Italian national rail system, are Eurostar trains, operating on several main lines, including Rome–Milan; Rome–Venice (via Florence and Bologna); and Milan–Venice (via Verona, Vicenza, and Padua). Seat reservation is mandatory and included in ticket price. Nonsmokers should request seats far from smoking areas, as poorly designed partitions are not smoke-proof. On most Eurostar trains, only small bags fit above or below seats. There is space for large bags near each car entrance and to avoid having to squeeze through narrow aisles, board only at your car—your reservation ticket shows train number, car number, and seat number.

The next-fastest trains are the intermediate-priced Intercity (IC) trains. *Interregionale* trains usually make more stops and are a little slower. Often serving local commuters, *Regionale* and *locale* trains are the slowest and are the only trains in which you cannot reserve seats.

There is refreshment service on most long-distance trains, with mobile carts and a cafeteria or dining car. Tap water on trains is not drinkable.

Venice has rail connections with every major city in Italy and Europe, however, some Continental trains do not enter historic Venice but stop only at the mainland Mestre station. As all trains traveling to and from Venice Santa Lucia stop at Mestre, it's just a 10-minute hop on the next passing train. Remember if you swap a regional train for an Intercity or Eurostar, you'll need to upgrade with a *supplemento* (extra charge) or be liable for a hefty fine. You'll also be fined if before boarding you forget to purchase and validate train tickets in the yellow machines found on or near platforms.

Saving a night's lodging by traveling at night is cost effective but you should be vigilant about security. Never leave your belongings unattended (even for a minute) and remember that even locking your compartment door won't protect against a thief in the next bunk. More comfortable trains serve the longer routes (Sicily–Rome, Sicily–Milan, Sicily–Venice, Rome–Turin, Lecce–Milan); ask for the good-value T3, the Intercity Notte, and the Carrozza Comfort lines. The Vagone Letto Excelsior (available only to/from Paris) has private bathrooms, coffee machines, microwave ovens, refrigerators, and suites with double bed and VCR.

CLASSES

Almost all Italian trains have first and second classes. On local trains the higher first-class fare gets you little more than a clean doily on the headrest of your seat, but on long-distance trains you get wider seats, more legroom, and better ventilation and lighting. At peak travel times, first-class train travel is worth the difference. Reservations, even when not obligatory, are advisable during busy periods for either class.

CUTTING COSTS

You can save money with **rail passes,** but be aware that unless you're planning to cover a lot of miles, especially in Italy where train fares are lower than in other parts of Europe, you may spend less buying individual tickets.

If Italy is your only destination in Europe, **consider purchasing a Trenitalia Pass,** which allows unlimited travel on the entire Italian Rail network. The Trenitalia Pass allows a designated number of travel days (four to ten) within two months: a four-day adult second-class ticket costs $191; a ten-day one costs $305.

Once in Italy, **inquire about the Cartaverde (Green Card) if you're under 26** (€25.82 for one year), which entitles the holder to a 15% discount on train tickets. Also in Italy, **those over 60 can purchase a Carta d'Argento (Silver Card)** (€25.82 for one year), which lets you buy tickets discounted 15%. On all Italian trains, **children under 4 ride free and children 4–12 pay 50%.** With the **Family Group plan, one child 4–12 rides free** when accompanied by two adults (don't have to be parents). More information is available on Trenitalia's Web site (⊕ www.trenitalia.it).

You can travel in Italy with a standard **Eurailpass,** which permits unlimited travel within their 17-country network for the number of consecutive days you opt to purchase. Eurailpass also allows free travel or discounted fares on some ferry lines.

If your plans call for only limited train travel, **you'll save money with Eurail Select Pass,** which allows you to select three, four, or five countries you wish to visit, and then select the number of **nonconsecutive days** (six to ten) you wish to travel. Prices for travel within three countries range from $336 for six days to $460 for ten days. With both Eurailpass and Eurail Select Pass, discounts abound so **ask about special rail-pass plans.** There are bargains for youth under 26, for two or more people traveling together, and also a EurailDrive Pass, which combines travel by train and rental car. There's even a special pass for those who plan to confine their train travel to Italy and France. Note that fares are subject to change. Whichever pass you choose, remember that you must **purchase any Eurailpass before you leave** for Europe.

Many travelers assume that rail passes guarantee them seats on any train they wish to ride. Not so. To guarantee a seat or sleeping space, you must **book ahead even if you are using a rail pass.** Seat reservations are mandatory on some European trains, including most overnight and high-speed trains. Though other trains may not require reservations, booking

ahead is advisable, particularly on popular routes during summer and holiday travel. With all railpasses, you'll have to upgrade and book to use a Eurostar (€11 for 1st class and €8 for 2nd class).

TICKETING

To avoid long lines at station windows, **buy tickets and make seat reservations up to two months in advance** at any train station, or at travel agencies displaying the FS emblem. Agents stop making reservations about five hours before the train departs from its city of origin. For trains that require a reservation (Eurostar, Cisalpino, and International overnight), seats may be available from the conductor just before boarding, but do not count on this.

You must **date-stamp your ticket in the small yellow machines on the platform before you board.** Once stamped, your ticket is valid for 6 hours if your destination is within 200 km (124 mi) and for 24 hours for destinations beyond that. You can get on and off at will at stops in between for the duration of the ticket's validity. If you forget to stamp your ticket in the machine, or you didn't make it in time to buy the ticket, you must actively seek out a conductor and pay a €6 penalty. Don't wait for the conductor to find out that you are without a valid ticket (unless the train is overcrowded and walking becomes impossible), as he might charge you a much heavier fine. You can buy train tickets for nearby destinations (within a 200-km [125-mi] range) at tobacconists and at ticket machines in stations.

🚆 Train Information/Italian Rail Passes **Trenitalia** (Ferrovia dello Stato) ☎ 892021 local call in Italy ⊕ www.trenitalia.it.
🚆 Eurailpasses **CIT Rail** ✉ 9501 W. Devon Ave., Suite 502, Rosemont, IL 60018 ☎ 800/248-7245. **DER Travel Services** ✉ Box 1606, Des Plaines, IL 60017 ☎ 800/782-2424 🖷 800/282-7474. **Rail Europe** ✉ 226-230 Westchester Ave., White Plains, NY 10604 ☎ 914/682-5172 or 800/438-7245 ⊕ www. raileurope.com ✉ 2087 Dundas E., Suite 105, Mississauga, Ontario L4X 1M2 ☎ 416/602-4195.

TRAVEL AGENCIES

A good travel agent puts your needs first. Look for an agency that has been in business at least five years, emphasizes customer service, and has someone on staff who specializes in your destination. In addition, **make sure the agency belongs to a**

professional trade organization. The American Society of Travel Agents (ASTA)—the largest and most influential in the field with more than 20,000 members in some 140 countries—maintains and enforces a strict code of ethics and will step in to help mediate any agent-client disputes involving ASTA members if necessary. ASTA (whose motto is "Without a travel agent, you're on your own") also maintains a Web site that includes a directory of agents. (If a travel agency is also acting as your tour operator, *see* Buyer Beware *in* Tours and Packages.)

⬚ Agents in Venice Albatravel ✉ Calle dei Fabbri San Marco 4538 ☎ 041/5210123 🖶 041/5200781. **American Express** ✉ Salizzada San Moisè, San Marco 1471 ☎ 041/5200844 🖶 041/5229937. **Gran Canal** ✉ Ponte del Ovo, near the Rialto Bridge, San Marco 4759 ☎ 041/2712111 🖶 041/5223380. **Kele Teo** ✉ Ponte dei Bareteri, San Marco 4930 between San Marco and Rialto ☎ 041/5208722 🖶 041/5208913.

⬚ Local Agent Referrals American Society of Travel Agents (ASTA) ✉ 1101 King St., Suite 200, Alexandria, VA 22314 ☎ 703/739-2782 or 800/965-2782 24-hr hot line 🖶 703/739-3268 ⊕ www.astanet.com. **Association of British Travel Agents** ✉ 68–71 Newman St., London W1T 3AH ☎ 020/7637-2444 🖶 020/7637-0713 ⊕ www.abta.com. **Association of Canadian Travel Agencies** ✉ 130 Albert St., Suite 1705, Ottawa, Ontario K1P 5G4 ☎ 613/237-3657 🖶 613/237-7052 ⊕ www.acta.ca. **Australian Federation of Travel Agents** ✉ Level 3, 309 Pitt St., Sydney, NSW 2000 ☎ 02/9264-3299 🖶 02/9264-1085 ⊕ www.afta.com.au. **Travel Agents' Association of New Zealand** ✉ Level 5, Tourism and Travel House, 79 Boulcott St., Box 1888, Wellington 6001 ☎ 04/499-0104 🖶 04/499-0786 ⊕ www.taanz.org.nz.

VISITOR INFORMATION

Learn more about foreign destinations by checking government-issued travel advisories and country information. For a broader picture, consider information from more than one country.

⬚ At Home Italian Government Tourist Board (ENIT) ⊕ www.italiantourism.com ✉ 630 5th Ave., New York, NY 10111 ☎ 212/245-4822 🖶 212/586-9249 ✉ 401 N. Michigan Ave., Chicago, IL 60611 ☎ 312/644-0990 🖶 312/644-3019 ✉ 12400 Wilshire Blvd., Suite 550, Los Angeles, CA 90025 ☎ 310/820-0098 🖶 310/820-6357 ✉ 1 Pl. Ville Marie, Ste 1914, Montréal, Québec H3B 3M9 ☎ 514/866-7667 🖶 514/392-1429 ✉ 1 Princes St., London W1R 8AY ☎ 020/7408-1254 🖶 020/7493-6695. **⬚ Local Tourist Offices Venice Tourist Offices** ⊕ www.turismovenezia.it ✉ Train Station

Cannaregio, ☎ 041/5298727 ✉ Procuratie Nuove San Marco 71/f, near Museo Correr ☎ 041/5298740 ✉ Venice Pavilion San Marco near Giardini Reali ☎ 041/5225150 ✉ Garage Comunale, Piazzale Roma ☎ 041/2411499 ✉ S. Maria Elisabetta 6/a, Lido ☉ Summer only ☎ 041/5265721.

Marostica ✉ Piazza Castello 1, 36063 ☎ 0424/72127 ⊕ www.marosticascacchi.it. **Padua** ✉ Stazione Ferroviaria, 35100 ☎ 049/8752077 ⊕ www.turismopadova.it. **Treviso** ✉ Piazzetta Monte di Pietà 8, 31100 ☎ 0422/547632 ⊕ www.provincia.treviso.it. **Trieste** ✉ Piazza Unita, ☎ 040/3478312 ✉ Via San Nicola 20 between train station and Piazza Unita ☎ 040/67961 ⊕ www.triestetourism.it. **Udine** ✉ Piazza Primo Maggio 7, 33100 ☎ 0432/295972 ⊕ www.turismo.fvg.it. **Verona** ✉ Piazza Bra, 37100 ☎ 045/8068680 ✉ Stazione FS ☎ 045/8000861 ⊕ www.tourism.verona.it. **Vicenza** ✉ Piazza Matteotti 12, 36100 ☎ 0444/320854 ⊕ www.vicenzae.org.

⬚ Government Advisories U.S. Department of State ✉ Overseas Citizens Services Office, Room 4811, 2201 C St. NW, Washington, DC 20520 ☎ 202/647-5225 interactive hot line or 888/407-4747 ⊕ www.travel.state.gov; enclose a cover letter with your request and a business-size SASE. **Consular Affairs Bureau of Canada** ☎ 800/267-6788 or 613/944-6788 ⊕ www.voyage.gc.ca. **U.K. Foreign and Commonwealth Office** ✉ Travel Advice Unit, Consular Division, Old Admiralty Building, London SW1A 2PA ☎ 020/7008-0232 or 020/7008-0233 ⊕ www.fco.gov.uk/travel. **Australian Department of Foreign Affairs and Trade** ☎ 02/6261-1299 Consular Travel Advice Faxback Service ⊕ www.dfat.gov.au. **New Zealand Ministry of Foreign Affairs and Trade** ☎ 04/439-8000 ⊕ www.mft.govt.nz.

WEB SITES

Do check out the World Wide Web when planning your trip. You'll find everything from weather forecasts to virtual tours of famous cities. Be sure to visit Fodors.com (⊕ www.fodors.com), a complete travel-planning site. You can research prices and book plane tickets, hotel rooms, rental cars, vacation packages, and more. In addition, you can post your pressing questions in the Travel Talk section. Other planning tools include a currency converter and weather reports, and there are loads of links to travel resources.

⬚ Suggested Web Sites For Venice: ⊕ www.elmoro.com, ⊕ www.meetingvenice.it, ⊕ www.aguestinvenice.com; for Italy: ⊕ www.initaly.com, ⊕ www.wel.it

EXPLORING VENICE

FODOR'S CHOICE

Basilica di San Marco, *Piazza San Marco*

Ca' d'Oro, *Cannaregio*

Ca' Rezzonico, *Dorsoduro*

Gallerie dell'Accademia, *Dorsoduro*

Palazzo Ducale, *Piazza San Marco*

Ponte di Rialto

Santa Maria dei Miracoli, *Cannaregio*

Santa Maria Gloriosa dei Frari, *San Polo*

HIGHLY RECOMMENDED

Arsenale, *Castello*

Burano

Campanile, *Piazza San Marco*

Jewish Ghetto, *Cannaregio*

Madonna dell'Orto, *Cannaregio*

Museo Correr, *Piazza San Marco*

Peggy Guggenheim Collection, *Dorsoduro*

Piazza San Marco

Querini-Stampalia, *Castello*

San Francesco della Vigna, *Castello*

San Giorgio Maggiore, *Isola di San Giorgio*

San Nicolò dei Mendicoli, *Dorsoduro*

San Sebastiano, *Dorsoduro*

San Zaccaria, *Castello*

Santi Giovanni e Paolo, *Castello*

Scuola di San Giorgio degli Schiavoni, *Castello*

Scuola Grande dei Carmini, *Dorsoduro*

Scuola Grande di San Rocco, *San Polo*

Torcello

Updated by
Elaine Eliah

IT WAS CALLED LA SERENISSIMA REPUBBLICA, "the most serene republic," a name suggesting the power and majesty of the city that was for
centuries the unrivaled mistress of trade between Europe and the Orient and the staunch bulwark of Christendom against the tides of Turkish expansion.

No matter how many times you've seen it in movies or TV commer-
cials, the real Venice is more surreal and dreamlike than you could ever
have imagined. Its landmarks—the Basilica di San Marco, the Palazzo
Ducale—hardly seem Italian. Delightfully idiosyncratic, they are exotic
mélanges of Byzantine and Gothic styles. Sunlight shimmers and silvery
mist softens every perspective. It is full of secrets, ineffably romantic,
and at times, given over entirely to pleasure.

Venice was founded in the 5th century when the Veneti, inhabitants of
the mainland region roughly corresponding to today's Veneto, fled their
homes to escape invading barbarians. The city rose from the marshes
to dominate the Adriatic and hold the gorgeous East in fee. Early in its
history the city called in Byzantine artists to decorate its churches with
brilliant mosaics, still glittering today. From the 13th through 15th centuries, the influence of Gothic architecture produced the characteristic
type of palace in the Florid Gothic style, with ogival windows and finely
wrought facades for which the town is famous the world over. The Renaissance arrived in Venice relatively late, at a time when the city had
peaked in power and prosperity. In its early phase the style is referred
to as Lombardesque, after the Lombardo family of masons and sculptors, who created distinctive intertwined discs, roundels, and crosses made
of red, green, and dark yellow marble. The city's greatest Early Renaissance
artists—Carpaccio, Giorgione, and the Bellini brothers, Giovanni and
Gentile—were all active between the late 15th and early 16th centuries.
Along with the stars of the next generation—Veronese, Titian, and Tintoretto—they played a decisive role in the development of Western art,
and their work still covers walls and ceilings all over the city.

Venice's participatory democracy, established in the 7th century, featured
a ruler, the doge, who was elected to a lifetime term. However, starting
in the 12th century the doge's power was increasingly limited by a
growing number of councils, commissions, and magistrates, and in
1268 a complicated procedure for his election was established to prevent nepotism. By this point, power really rested with the Great Council, which once had over 2000 members, and though originally an
elected body, from 1297 onward was an aristocratic stronghold, members inheriting seats from their noble ancestors. Laws were passed by
the Senate, a group of 200 elected from the Great Council, and executive powers belonged to the College, a committee of 25 leaders. In
1310, the Council of Ten was formed to protect state security. When
circumstances abroad or at home endangered the Republic's democracy,
the doge could expedite decision making and guarantee greater secrecy
by consulting only the Council of Ten. In order to avoid too great a concentration of power, these ten served only one year and had to be chosen from different families.

Another Venice institution that you'll hear mentioned frequently is the
scuola (plural *scuole*). The scuole were not schools, as the word today
translates, but an important network of institutions that were established
by different social groups—enclaves of foreigners, tradesmen, followers of a particular saint, and parishioners. For the most part secular despite their devotional activities, the scuole were charitable institutions
that concentrated on helping their own membership or helping society's
neediest citizens. The tradesmen's or servants' scuole formed social se-

curity nets for their elder or disabled members. Wealthier scuole assisted orphans or provided dowries so poor girls could marry. By 1500, there were more than 200 major and minor scuole in Venice, some of which contributed substantially to arts and crafts guilds. The Republic was in favor of their existence, because the scuole kept strict records on the names and professions of contributors to the brotherhood, which helped when it came time to collect taxes.

The decline of Venice came slowly. For 400 years the powerful maritime city-republic held sway, but after the 16th century the tide changed. The Ottoman Empire blocked Venice's Mediterranean trade routes, and newly emerging sea powers such as Britain and the Netherlands ended Venice's monopoly by opening oceanic trading routes.

You must walk almost everywhere in Venice, and where you cannot walk you go by water. Occasionally, you have to walk *in* water. When normally higher winter tides are exacerbated by falling barometers and south-easterly *scirocco* winds, the result is *acqua alta,* or flooding in lower lying parts of the city—especially Piazza San Marco; falling tide brings relief a few hours later. Work has begun on the Moses Project, which would dam off the lagoon when high tides threaten, but it is a much-debated response to a complex problem. In general, protecting Venice and its lagoon from high tides, high use, and the damaging wave action caused by powerboats, is among the the city's most highly contested issues. Progress is being made, however. Police are using radar to enforce speed limits, and while dredging continues periodically throughout the city, the canalside walkways are systematically being reinforced and raised one stretch at a time.

It's practically a given that at some point you'll find yourself lost in Venice. The narrow streets make it difficult to navigate by way of a fixed point of reference such as a church dome or bell tower, and the winding paths tend to leave you without any sense of which way north is, much less where your restaurant might be. Streets and canals look deceptively familiar until they suddenly dead end. Consider that on a detailed map you can count more than 100 separate islands, divided by a network of roughly 150 canals and crossed by over 400 bridges. Even Venetians can find themselves challenged in an unfamiliar neighborhood.

To minimize confusion, yellow signs, posted prominently all over town, point you toward Ferrovia (train station), Piazzale Roma, Rialto Bridge, Accademia Bridge, and Piazza San Marco. Place-names are neatly hand-painted at nearly every square and bridge, but they don't always agree with maps, and they may look nothing like names you've seen in other Italian towns. Here, a street is a *calle* but becomes *riva* or *fondamenta* if it runs alongside a canal. A street with shops can be a *ruga,* and the word *salizzada* means it was among the first to be cobbled, or paved. A small canal is a *rio* (*rii* plural), and a *rio terà* is a street created when a canal has been filled in. San Marco is the only square called a piazza in Venice—all the rest are called *campo, campiello,* or *corte* (field, little field, or yard), harking back to a time when they were used to grow vegetables and raise poultry.

Don't depend on addresses to clarify things. In 1170 the government divided central Venice into six *sestieri* (neighborhoods): San Marco, Castello, Dorsoduro, Cannaregio, San Polo, and Santa Croce. What began as a rather artificial dissection of the city now seems almost as natural a feature of Venice as its hundreds of man-made islands and canals; over the course of time, each neighborhood developed its own distinctive atmosphere and layout. Because street names repeat from one sestiere to an-

Rialto to Cannaregio

Canale delle Sacche

Canale di S. Girolamo

Rio d. Madonna dell'O.

Rio di S. Sensa

Sacca della Misericordia

San Polo & Santa Croce to San Marco

CANNAREGIO

Campo del Ghetto Nuovo

Canale Cannaregio

C. Riello

Ponte Guglie

R. T. S. Leonardo

R. di S. Nobile

(Canalazzo)

C. Muazza

Strada Nuova

Stazione Ferroviaria Santa Lucia

Lista di Spagna

Ponte degli Scalzi

Grand Canal

Lista d. Bari

Campo S. Giac

C. Larga

C. d. Pintor

San Marc

Ponte di Rialto

NUOVA ISOLA DEL TRONCHETTO

Bridge to Mainland

C. d. S. Simeon Piccolo

C. della Lana

Corte Canal

Rio di S. Zan Degola

SANTA CROCE

Rio di S. Cassiano

C. dei Botteri

Riva del Vin

V. d. Aprile

Mercerie

Bacino Stazione Marittima

Canale di S. Chiara

C. d. S. Andrea

Piazzale Roma

C. d. Lacca

C. d. Fondero d. Chiovere

SAN POLO

Campo dei Frari Rio della Frescada

Terra

Campo S. Polo

P. Sar

Canale Scomenzera

Canale di S. Marta Maggiore

Rio di S. Marta

Rio Nuova

F. Minotto

Rio Foscari

Grand Canal (Canalazzo)

S. Luca

Fond. del Cereri

Fond. Rossa S. Margherita

Campo di S. Margherita

C. d. Carrozze

Campo S. Angelo

Campo S. Stefano

SAN MARCO

Cap. d. S. Luca

Fond. d. Farine

Rio di S. Nicolò

Calle Avogaria

Rio d. S. Barnaba

Campo S. Barnaba

Calle della Teletta

Ponte dell'Accademia

San Marco to Dorsoduro

Saliz. San Baségio

Rio d. Ognissanti

Fondamenta delle Zattere

Rio Terà A. Foscarini

Rio d. Fornaci

Fond. della Fornace

DORSODURO

C. della Scuola

Sacca Fisola

Canale della Giudecca

Fond. S. Biagio

Fond. S. Eufemia

R. d. Convertite

Chiesa del Redentore

Rio d. S. Biagio

GIUDECCA

San Giorgio Maggiore & the Giudecca

Laguna Veneta

Exploring Venice

Murano

Canale delle Navi

San
Michele

Cimitero
San
Michele

*Sacca
della
ericordia*

& co

C.po dei
Gesuiti

R. d. Gesuiti

Fondamente Nuove

C. d. Squero

Canale delle Fondamente Nuove

Castello Alto

Marco

Rio d. S. Marina

R. Mendicanti

Barbaria delle Tole

Campo
S. Marina

Campo
S. Maria

Salizz. di S. Lio

Campo
S. Maria

Sal. di S. Lio

Ruga Giuffa

R. d. S.
Francesco

C. Lion

R. d. Greci

R. d. Giorgio

Canale d. Galeazze

R. d. Vergini

C. d. Cannaria

San
Zaccaria

CASTELLO

Darsena
Grande

Rio d. S.
Daniele

San Pietro

**Piazza
San Marco**

Molo Riva degli Schiavoni

Rio della Tana

Rio d. S.
Anna

S.in Pietro (Can.)

San
Pietro

di d.

Marine

Bacino di San Marco

R. d. Arsenale

V. Garibaldi

Riva dei Sette Martiri

R. d. S. Giuseppe

Darsena
di
Sant' Elena

**S. Giorgio
Maggiore**

Rio dei Giardini

Viale
vientiquattro
Maggio

Sant'Elena

Fondamenta
Piave

Viale
Sant' Elena

Fond.
delle Zitelle

Riva dei Partigiani

Viale
quattro
Novembre

Viale
Sant' Elena

Calle
Michelangelo

Viale Vittorio Veneto

Castello Basso

0   440 yards

0   400 meters

other, the address system was "simplified" in 1841, when houses were numbered by sestiere rather than street. Except for churches, which go only by their saint's name, all Venetian addresses consist of the name of the sestiere and a number. The hitch is that the numbers don't run sequentially, so San Marco 3672 and 3673 might be several narrow winding streets away from one another. When getting directions, be sure to ask at the nearest campo, bridge, or calle.

Unlike other towns in Italy, Venice rarely has streets and squares dedicated to places or great figures in Italian history. Many streets retain names from establishments that once stood nearby, such as Calle del Cafetier (named for a coffee shop) or Ponte Tette (Bridge of Breasts, named for a nearby brothel). Others were named for saints or noble families, such as Corner, Morosini, and Tron. No one is certain what prompted such names as Ponte delle Maravegie (Bridge of the Wonders) or Ponte della Donna Onesta (Bridge of the Honest Woman); Ponte dei Pugni (Bridge of Fists), crossing Canale San Barnaba, earned its name for the ritual fistfights it once hosted, and you can still see on it the footprints that marked the fighters' starting corners.

Although the smaller canals are often spanned by several bridges, the Grand Canal can only be crossed on foot at three points: Ponte degli Scalzi, near the train station (Ferrovia); Ponte di Rialto, at the Rialto; and at Ponte dell'Accademia, between Campo Santo Stefano and the Gallerie dell'Accademia. If you find yourself on the wrong bank with no bridge in sight, look for signs that say *traghetto* (gondola ferry) and hop across in style, saving your legs and your mood. The two-minute Grand Canal crossing may be the shortest gondola ride in town, but at €.40 each way, it's also the least expensive, even cheaper than using the *vaporetto* (water bus).

The vaporetti that circulate through the city on set routes are easy to use. If you plan to jump on and off boats frequently, you can save money by purchasing a 24-hour, three-day, or weekly pass. You can pick up a vaporetto route map and schedule for €.50 at the ticket booths located in front of many stops.

In 1997, a group of parish priests founded a nonprofit organization to raise money for maintenance and protection of Venetian churches. The fifteen **Chorus Churches** (☎ 041/2750462. ⊕ www.chorus-ve.org), including Santa Maria del Giglio, Santo Stefano, Santa Maria Formosa, Santa Maria dei Miracoli, Santa Maria Gloriosa dei Frari, San Polo, San Giacomo dell'Orio, San Stae, Sant'Alvise, Madonna dell'Orto, San Pietro di Castello, SS. Redentore, San Sebastiano, Gesuati, and San Giovanni Elemosinario, are open to visitors all day except Sunday mornings. There's usually someone to provide information and a free leaflet (available in English), and postcards and booklets are on sale. Single church entry costs €2, or you can buy an €8 Chorus pass that allows you one admission to each church and is good for a year. The pass includes use of audio guides except in Basilica dei Frari, where guides cost €.50. The artwork in Chorus churches is labeled, and the staff can show you where to switch on special lighting for certain paintings.

Eleven museums currently make up Venice's **Musei Civici** (☎ 041/2715911 ⊕ www.museiciviciveneziani.it), and a Museum Pass for €15.50 (valid three months) lets you make one visit to each museum. For access to only the Piazza San Marco group—Palazzo Ducale, Museo Correr, Museo Archeologico, and Biblioteca Marciana—you can purchase a Museum Card for €11. An €8 ticket buys entry to all three "museums of 18th-century culture"—Ca' Rezzonico, Palazzo Mocenigo, and Casa

Goldoni. A €6 ticket will allow you to visit both the Burano Lace Museum and the Murano Glass Museum.

Some Venice museums, including Gallerie dell'Accademia, have no cafés inside and don't permit you to bring in food or drink. The staff might allow you to run to the nearest bar and return without paying a second admission, but this is left to their discretion. There are refreshments available in Palazzo Ducale, Museo Correr, Ca' Rezzonico, Querini-Stampalia, and the Guggenheim.

THE GRAND CANAL

There's no better introduction to Venice than a cruise on the Grand Canal, or as Venetians refer to it, Canalazzo. Without a doubt one of the world's great "avenues," Venice's main thoroughfare competes with Piazza San Marco for the honor of being the city's most famous landmark. For 4 km (2½ mi.) it winds its way in a backward "S," past 12th- to 18th-century palaces built by the city's richest families. A handful still belong to the descendants of those who built them, but many have been converted to other uses. A dozen museums, several five-star hotels, a few modest inns, government and city offices, courts, university departments, a post office, a casino, and even a TV station, are housed in Renaissance studios and baroque ballrooms, hiding behind those Byzantine and Gothic facades.

There is a definite theatrical quality to the Grand Canal, something particularly noticeable as you pass in a vaporetto or a gondola; it's as if each facade had been designed to steal your attention from its rival across the way. The most romantic way to see the canal is from a gondola. Take a ride from Rialto to San Marco an hour or so before sunset, or at daybreak when dreamlike scenery will be there just for you. The next best thing—at a fraction of the cost—is to take in the view from vaporetto Line 1, especially if you manage to sit in one of the coveted seats at the prow, which offers a clear view of both banks. Although you can board at any of the 16 stops along the canal, it makes sense to begin your voyage from Piazzale Roma or the train station (Ferrovia) and take the full 45-minute ride to San Marco or San Zaccaria. Lean back in your seat, take in the view, and marvel at the history steeped in the grand past of this Grand Canal. Below is a description of what you'll see. For more detailed information about the major sights, see the neighborhood tours that follow.

Don't leave Venice until you have seen it by night from the water—but bring a warm scarf in winter and mosquito repellent in summer. Once off the vaporetto, keep in mind that traghetti at many points along the Grand Canal will ferry you from one bank to the other for just €.40.

Numbers in the text correspond to numbers on the Grand Canal map.

Timing

From Piazzale Roma to San Zaccaria, vaporetto Line 1 takes about 45 minutes; service runs between 5 AM and midnight, with departures every 10 minutes during the day, and every 20 minutes early in the morning and after 9:30 PM. There is *servizio notturno* (night service) from midnight to 5 AM, with "N" boats running between Piazzale Roma and San Zaccaria every 40 minutes (to and from Rialto every 20 minutes). A trip down the Grand Canal by gondola takes about an hour and a half. Never let a gondolier help you climb down into his gondola without having discussed the duration and cost of the ride.

From Piazzale Roma to Rialto

If you arrive in Venice by train or car, you'll immediately encounter this first tract of the Grand Canal, which flows between the sestieri of Cannaregio and Santa Croce. Highlights include the baroque San Stae church, Venice's fabulous casino, and the sensational Ca' d'Oro.

Vaporetto Line 1 starts at Piazzale Roma, the beginning of the Grand Canal, and its first stop is the train station or **Ferrovia** ❶ (officially called "Stazione Ferroviaria Santa Lucia"). Piazzale Roma and Ferrovia are among the city's more modern areas, but more classically Venetian architecture isn't far off. Near the Ferrovia stop is the baroque **Chiesa degli Scalzi** ❷, named after the order of barefoot friars who founded it. The church was partially rebuilt after being struck by an Austrian bomb in World War I that destroyed two Tiepolo ceiling frescoes. Venice's last, rather inept doge, Ludovico Manin, was aptly buried here on the edge of town. The first of the Grand Canal's three bridges, **Ponte degli Scalzi** ❸, is also its newest, built in the 1930s.

Opposite the landing of Riva di Biasio, a plaque on the wall near the church of **San Geremia** ❹ is a memorial to the Church of Santa Lucia, which was demolished to make room for the train station. The reliquary of the patron saint of eyesight (according to Catholics, Lucia tore her eyes out after being complemented on their beauty by one of her pagan jailers) was moved to San Geremia. The imposing palace half-hidden behind the bell tower is the famous **Palazzo Labia** ❺ (⇨ Rialto to Cannaregio, *below*), with magnificent frescoes by Tiepolo. A left turn into the Canale di Cannaregio would bring you to the north side of the lagoon facing the town of Mestre and the industrial complex of Marghera.

The uncompleted facade of the church of **San Marcuola** ❻, lets you see what's behind the marble decorations of similar 18th-century churches. On the other riva, flanked by two *torricelle* (side wings in the shape of small towers) and a triangular *merlatura* (crenellation), is the **Fondaco dei Turchi** ❼. It was once the largest palazzo on the Grand Canal and has a checkered history of occupants and restorations (⇨ San Polo and Santa Croce to San Marco, *below*). Next comes the plain brick **Depositi del Megio** ❽, a 15th-century millet granary; a lion marks it as Serenissima property. Next door is obelisqued **Ca' Belloni-Battagia** ❾ designed by Baldassare Longhena after the Belloni family bought itself into aristocracy. It's somewhat overshadowed by **Palazzo Vendramin-Calergi** ❿ on the other bank. Charismatic Doge Leonardo Loredan led Venice to victory against the League of Cambrai, which was formed in 1508 by the pope, the Holy Roman Emperor, and the kings of France and Spain with the intention of destroying the Republic. He commissioned this Renaissance gem from Mauro Codussi (1440–1504) in the 1480s, at a time when the late-Gothic style was still fashionable. German composer Wagner died here in 1883 soon after the success of his *Parsifal*. A banner with gilded lettering heralds this as the home of Venice's casino.

White and whimsically baroque, the church of **San Stae** ⓫ welcomes visitors with a host of marble saints. Another example of the baroque awaits farther down the bank at **Ca' Pesaro** ⓬. Today it's home to a gallery of contemporary paintings and a collection of Oriental art, but it was once home to the man who declared war against Napoléon (⇨ San Polo and Santa Croce to San Marco, *below*). One block and two *rii* (small canals) ahead stands a tall, balconied palace named for a queen, **Ca' Corner della Regina** ⓭. In 1468, 13-year-old Caterina Cornaro, the "daughter of the Republic," was married to the king of Cyprus in a foreign policy maneuver by the Serenissima. Although her descendents demolished the

THE WORLD'S MOST ELEGANT TAXI

MORE THAN WINGED LIONS or Carnevale masks, gondolas have become the symbol of Venice, re-created en masse as plastic toys, snow globes, and virtually every other tchotchke known to man. But if you can look beyond all the kitsch, you'll discover an austerely beautiful and elegantly designed boat that has evolved over centuries to meet Venice's unique demands.

The gondola is among the most enduring of numerous flat-bottomed craft that were developed to navigate the lagoon's shallow waters. The first written reference to a gondola dates to the 11th century, and images of the boats appear in Venetian art as early as the 1300s. At the height of their popularity in the 17th century, more than 5,000 gondolas were active on Venice's waterways. (Their number has now dwindled to around 500.) They were made slim to maneuver the narrowest canals and topped with felzi, small cabins that allowed a city full of Casanovas to travel incognito. Originally the color of gondolas wasn't regulated, though they were predominantly black from the pitch used to keep them water tight. When in the 16th century private boats started to become exceptionally lavish, sumptuary laws were enacted mandating that they be the uniform black you still see today.

The Republic's fall in 1797 and the subsequent economic decline triggered experiments in gondola construction that would allow the boats to be handled by one gondolier rather than two. Boat-builder Domenico Tramontin perfected the design in the late 1800s, creating an ingenious asymmetrical hull that keeps the gondola traveling in a straight line even though it's being rowed by a single oar. This would be the last genetic modification to one of the world's loveliest dinosaurs— for within fifty years, the gondola would be driven to the brink of extinction by engine-driven boats, most notably the vaporetto, the water bus that's now Venice's primary means of transportation.

Gondolas are made and repaired in a workshop called a squero. Starting with well-seasoned wood, boat-builders can construct a gondola body in about a month, but embellishments, carved and gilded, can take much longer. The finishing touch is the ferro, the ornament that adorns the bow. According to common wisdom, the ferro's graceful "S" curve is meant to mimic the bends of the Grand Canal, its six prongs represent Venice's six sestieri, and its rounded top echoes the shape of the doge's hat. This elaborate explanation was most likely invented by gondoliers in the early 20th century to impress their passengers, but it's ingenious enough to have endured for 100 years and become a part of gondola lore.

The most conspicuous squero of the few that remain is at San Trovaso, just down the small canal near the Zattere boat landing. Not far from there is the squero **Domenico Tramontin and Sons** (✉ Fondamente Ognissanti, near Giustinian Hospital ☎☎ 041/5237762 ⊕ www.tramontingondole.it), where Domenico's great grandson Roberto and grandson Nedis continue to practice the family trade. Tours with a translator can be arranged by contacting Roberto via fax or through the web site. While there, you can inquire about ordering your own gondola. Prices start at €26,000. North Carolinian Thom Price came to Venice with a fellowship to study gondola making and never went back. At his **Squero Canaletto** (☎☎ 041/2413963 ⊕ www.squero.com) he not only builds boats but also conducts weeklong workshops on gondola construction and Venetian rowing. If you want to take up gondola building as a vocation, consider applying for a nine-month apprenticeship.

The shapely forcola (oarlock) used in Venetian-style rowing is itself a work of refined engineering. To see forcole being made, visit the shop of **Saverio Pastor** (✉ Fondamenta Soranzo, Dorsoduro 341 ☎ 041/5225699 ⊕ www.forcole.com), which is open weekdays 8–6. While there you can buy a forcola for yourself; architects I. M. Pei and Frank Gehry are counted among the visitors who have taken one home.

The
Grand Canal

queen's birthplace in the 1720s to build this Ca' Corner, the old name stuck. In the 1970s, it became a library and *cineteca* (film archive) for the Biennale.

The **Ca' d'Oro** ⑭, or "Golden House," takes its name from the gilding that once accentuated the marble carvings of its facade. One of the most striking palazzi on the Canal, it holds a good collection of antiquities and paintings (⇨ Rialto to Cannaregio, *below*). Opposite is one of the oldest outdoor food markets in Europe. The loggia-like, neo-Gothic **Pescheria** ⑮ marks the spot where fish from the lagoon and the Dalmatian coast have been sold for the last 1,000 years. Fruit and vegetable stalls fill the spacious fondamenta, and cheese shops and butchers pack the buildings in the background. Next is the porticoed edifice built by Sansovino in 1555 to house the Republic's equivalent of a stock exchange and chamber of commerce. Today it contains Venice's Tribunal and Court of Justice. Opposite, the 13th-century Byzantine **Ca' da Mosto** ⑯, with its water porch, looks like it could use a face-lift, but in the 18th century it was the fashionable Leon Bianco hotel. The canal narrows and boat traffic increases as you approach Rialto, a commercial hub with a concentration of souvenir booths and inexpensive retail stores. On the left, just before your boat passes under the bridge, is the central post office, once frescoed with alluring female figures by Giorgione and Titian. It was apt decoration for what was then the busiest trading center of the Republic—the **Fondaco dei Tedeschi** ⑰—where merchants from Germany, Austria, Bohemia, and Hungary kept warehouses, shops, and sleeping quarters. The curiously angled **Ca' dei Camerlenghi** ⑱ stands opposite. Built in 1525 to accommodate the powerful State Treasury, it had a jail for tax evaders on the ground floor. The **Rialto Bridge** ⑲, arched high to allow galleys to pass beneath, dates from the late 16th century (⇨ Rialto to Cannaregio, *below*). As the vaporetto pulls over to stop on the left, it passes Sansovino's **Ca' Dolfin-Manin** ⑳, designed in the 1560s. The home of Venice's last doge is today occupied by the Banca d'Italia.

From Rialto to the Ponte dell'Accademia

Heading toward more noble quarters, the Grand Canal continues its loop through the southern part of town, encircling sestiere San Marco. Mansions of the many families that gave the Republic its doges line the San Polo and Dorsoduro side, vying with homes on the San Marco side for the passersby's glance. Wavering reflections on the canal's jade green water seem to echo the question of the wicked witch in *Snow White*: Who's the fairest one of all? . . .

Rialto is the only point along the Grand Canal where buildings do not have principle entrances on the water, a consequence of the two long and spacious *rive* (streets), which were once used for unloading two vital staples: coal and wine. On your left along Riva del Carbon stand **Ca' Loredan** ㉑ and **Ca' Farsetti** ㉒, 13th-century Byzantine works that today make up Venice's city hall. On Riva del Vin, just past the San Silvestro landing, is the 12th–13th-century facade of **Palazzo Barzizza** ㉓, an elegant example of Veneto-Byzantine architecture that managed to survive a complete renovation of the building in the 17th century. Across the water is the sternly Renaissance **Ca' Grimani** ㉔, an intimidating presence that seems the appropriate location for today's Court of Appeals. Just past a canal, the white-and-red-striped Casetta Tron (small house) is sandwiched between the 15th-century **Ca' Corner-Contarini dei Cavalli** ㉕, named for the horses on its coat of arms, and massive **Ca' Martinengo** ㉖. This was the residence of Conte Volpi, who modernized the city during the first half of the 20th century. Venice has him to thank for innovations such as electricity, the nearby industrial zone in Porto Marghera, the foundation of Mestre, the chain of five-star CIGA hotels, and the now-famous Biennale film festival.

Cruising into the landing at Sant'Angelo, the vaporetto passes close to **Ca' Corner-Spinelli** 27 built by Mauro Codussi. It became a prototype for other Grand Canal buildings; Codussi himself copied its windows when building Palazzo Vendramin-Calergi. The building opposite, **Palazzo Barbarigo della Terrazza** 28, home of the German Institute, has an expansive terrace with an unsurpassed view of the canal. Standing grandly next door, dressed in a salmon color that seems to change with the time of day, is elegant **Palazzo Pisani Moretta** 29, with twin water entrances where modern-day revelers arrive for candlelit dinner parties. On the other bank, four-storied **Ca' Garzoni** 30, part of the Università di Venezia Ca' Foscari, is beside the San Tomà *traghetto* (gondola ferry), which has operated since 1354. As the vaporetto stops on the right at San Tomà, you can look across at **Ca' Mocenigo** 31, where a plaque notes that Lord Byron lived there (1818–1819), but neglects to mention that he shared the apartment with two monkeys, a bear, two parrots, and a fox, and had 14 servants, a butler, and a gondolier at his service. The boat makes a sharp turn, and on the right passes one of the city's tallest Gothic palaces, **Ca' Foscari** 32. Built for 15th-century Doge Francesco Foscari—under whose reign the Republic reached its greatest size—it's been a part of Venice's university since the 1870s. Positioned at one of the busiest junctures along the Grand Canal, this palace has suffered severe foundation damage from relentless waves. It was evacuated in 1996 and may wear its painted shroud quite a while before it is repaired. Richard Wagner lived next door in **Ca' Giustinian** 33 while he was working on *Tristan and Isolde*.

The vaporetto passes **Ca' Rezzonico** 34 so closely that you get to look inside one of the most fabulous entrances along the canal. The architect Longhena began work on the palace in 1649, but it wasn't completed until almost a century later. Today it houses the Museo del Settecento Veneziano (⇨ San Marco to Dorsoduro, *below*). Opposite stands the Grand Canal's youngest mansion, **Palazzo Grassi** 35, commissioned in 1749 by a Bolognese tycoon from architect Giorgio Massari—who also completed Ca' Rezzonico after Longhena's death. Just beyond Grassi and Campo San Samuele, the first house past the garden was once Titian's studio. It's followed by **Palazzo Falier** 36, instantly recognizable by its twin loggias (windowed porches). It's said to have been the home of Doge Martin Falier, who was beheaded for treason in 1355.

Ahead, **Accademia Bridge** 37, like the Eiffel Tower, with which it shares a certain structural grace, was never intended to be permanent. Built in 1933 as a quick alternative to a rusting iron bridge built by the Austrians, it was so well liked by Venetians that a perfect replica with steel bracing was created in 1986. Among the scores of religious institutions suppressed by Napoléon were the church, convent, and scuola of Santa Maria della Carità. As the vaporetto stops at the bridge, on your right you'll see the **Gallerie dell'Accademia** 38 (⇨ San Marco to Dorsoduro, *below*), which grew out of the Accademia di Belle Arti (founded in 1750 with Tiepolo as director), installed in the former church buildings in 1807. Its original collection of paintings quickly grew with works collected from other suppressed churches and confraternities.

From the Ponte dell'Accademia to San Zaccaria

You're only three stops from the end of the the Grand Canal, but this last tract is like a rich dessert after a delicious meal: a baroque creation resembling a wedding cake topped with meringue and whipped cream marks the end of what Charles VIII's ambassador to Venice called the *"plus belle rue en tout le monde"* (the most beautiful street in all the world).

Lovely **Ca' Franchetti** ㊴, with a central balcony made in the style of Palazzo Ducale's loggia, dates from the late Gothic period, but its gardens are no older than the cedar tree that stands at their center—until the late 19th century, this was a *squero* (workshop) where gondolas were made and repaired. **Ca' Barbaro** ㊵ next door was the residence of the illustrious family who rebuilt the church of Santa Maria del Giglio (⇨ San Marco to Dorsoduro, *below*). In more recent times it hosted guests such as Monet, Henry James, and Cole Porter (who later lived aboard a boat in Giudecca Canal). Farther along on the left bank, a garden, vibrant with flowers in summer, surrounds **Casetta Rossa** ㊶ (small red house) as if it were the centerpiece of its bouquet. Across the canal, bright 19th-century mosaics on **Ca' Barbarigo** ㊷ gives you some idea how the frescoed facades of many Venetian palaces must have looked in their heyday. A few doors down are the lush gardens growing within the walls of the unfinished **Palazzo Venier dei Leoni** ㊸. A scale model of the palace in the Museo Correr gives some credit to the theory that Venier's construction was somehow sabotaged by the family living in Sansovino's **Ca' Grande** ㊹ across the canal, who didn't want the new house obstructing their view of the lagoon. In 1951 Venier was bought by American heiress and art collector Peggy Guggenheim, who kept her private gondola parked at the door and left her ever-present dogs standing guard in place of roaring lions (⇨ Peggy Guggenheim Collection *in* San Marco to Dorsoduro, *below*).

Lovely, leaning **Ca' Dario** ㊺ is more notable for its colorful marble facade than for its structural engineering. However tilted Dario might be, it has outlasted its many owners, who seem plagued by misfortune, including Italian industrialist Raul Gardini, whose 1992 suicide followed charges of corruption and his unsuccessful bid for the America's Cup. Ca' Dario has been on the real estate market for some time. Past the landing of Santa Maria del Giglio stands the 15th-century **Ca' Pisani-Gritti** ㊻, best known as the Gritti Palace Hotel. On the other bank, narrow **Palazzo Salviati** ㊼, with its 20th-century mosaic facade, was among the last glass factories to operate within the Venice city center. As you approach the cupola of **Santa Maria della Salute** ㊽ (⇨ San Marco to Dorsoduro, *below*), save a glance or two for the picturesque Rio di San Gregorio, and what's left of the namesake Gothic abbey, now privately owned.

Leaving **Punta della Dogana** ㊾ and its Palla della Fortuna (golden ball, topped by a windvane depicting Fortune) shining against the sky, the vaporetto stops on the left at the famous Harry's Bar, near **Giardinetti Reali** ㊿, planted by Napoléon after he tore down the Republic's grain warehouse. The Grand Canal has officially ended, but stay on board one more stop (to San Zaccaria) for the greatest view of all: **Piazzetta San Marco** �51, **Basilica di San Marco** �52, and **Palazzo Ducale** �53 (⇨ Piazza San Marco, *below*). This sight moved Thomas Mann to claim that arriving in Venice over the bridge from the mainland (he had taken the train) was like entering the house of a beautiful woman through the service entrance.

PIAZZA SAN MARCO

One of the world's most evocative squares, Piazza San Marco is the heart of Venice, a vast open space bordered by an orderly procession of arcades marching toward the fairy-tale cupolas and marble lacework of the Basilica di San Marco. Perpetually animated during the day, when it's crowded with people and fluttering pigeons, it can be magical at night, especially in the winter, when melancholy mists swirl around the lampposts and bell tower.

Numbers in the text correspond to numbers in the margin and on the San Marco map.

a good walk

The area around **Piazza San Marco ❶** ▶ offers enough interesting sights to fill up the better part of a day. Begin with a morning visit to the **Basilica di San Marco ❷**, home of the Pala d'Oro and the Museo Marciano. Next, get a bird's-eye view of the piazza and city from the **Campanile ❸**. Move on to the smaller **Piazzetta San Marco ❹** for a visit to the glorious **Palazzo Ducale ❺** and a look at the Ponte dei Sospiri. Return to Piazza San Marco, and cross to the side opposite the Basilica, the Ala Napoleonica—so named because it was Napoléon who closed off the piazza. Inside is the **Museo Correr ❻**.

Allow some time between sights to browse in the shops under the arcades of the Procuratie and the adjoining streets, particularly in the Mercerie district, reachable through the passage under the **Torre dell'Orologio ❼**. The Frezzeria and Salizzada San Moisè, which both begin near the Correr Museum (the former is to the right; the latter is straight ahead), also make for good shopping strolls.

TIMING   It takes a full day to really see everything, so if time is limited, you'll have to prioritize. Plan on 1½ hours to see the Basilica di San Marco and its Pala d'Oro, Galleria, and Museo Marciano. You'll want at least two hours to do justice to Palazzo Ducale. Be sure to take time to appreciate the piazza itself from a café table, or on a clear day, from atop the Campanile. The view is enchanting (unless the bells are ringing the hour); allow at least 40 minutes.

What to See

❷ **Basilica di San Marco.** An opulent synthesis of Byzantine and Romanesque styles, this church, Venice's gem, is laid out in a Greek-cross (four arms of equal length) floor plan and topped with five plump domes. The basilica did not actually become the cathedral of Venice until 1807, but its role as the Chiesa Ducale (doge's private chapel) gave it immense power and wealth. The original church was built in 828 to house the body of St. Mark the Evangelist. His remains were stolen from Alexandria by two agents of the doge and, so the story goes, hidden in a barrel beneath layers of pickled pork to sneak them past Muslim guards. The escapade is depicted in the 13th-century mosaic above the front entrance door to the farthest left. This semicircular arch is the earliest mosaic on the heavily decorated facade; look closely and you'll see an image of the basilica as it appeared at that time.

Fodor'sChoice
★

A 976 fire destroyed most of the original church; rebuilding began in 1063 and it reopened in 1094. Over the centuries it stood as a symbol of Venetian wealth and power, endowed with all the riches the Republic's admirals and merchants could carry off from the Orient, becoming so opulent it earned the nickname Chiesa d'Oro (Golden Church). The four bronze horses that prance and snort over the entrance are copies of sculptures that victorious Venetians took from Constantinople in 1204 (the originals are in the Museo Marciano). Look for a medallion of red porphyry set in the porch floor, just inside the central doorway. It marks the spot where in 1177 a great political coup by Doge Sebastiano Ziani brought reconciliation between Barbarossa, the Holy Roman Emperor, and Pope Alexander III. The basilica's dim light, the *matroneum* (women's galleries) high above the naves, the *iconostasis* (altar screen), and the single massive Byzantine chandelier all seem to wed Christianity with the Orient, giving San Marco its exotic blend of majesty and mystery.

The basilica is famous for its 43,055 square ft of stunning mosaics, made possible by an innovative roof made of brick vaulting rather than wood. Many of the original windows were filled in to make room for even more artwork. Only between 11:30 AM and 12:30 PM, when the interior is fully illuminated, do these mosaics come alive—their tiny gold tiles are nothing short of magical. The earliest mosaics are from the 11th and 12th centuries and the last were added in the early 1700s. One of the most recent is the *Last Judgment* on the arch between the porch and the nave, said to be based on drawings by Tintoretto (1518–94). Inside the main entrance, turn right on the porch to see the Book of Genesis depicted on the ceiling. Ahead, **Cappella Zen** (Zen Chapel)—named for a local cardinal, not a form of Buddhism—shows St. Mark's life in 13th-century mosaics. Cappella Zen, like the basilica's **Battistero** (Baptistery), and underground **Crypt** is open only to scholars.

Two chapels in the left transept are worth a special look: the **Cappella della Madonna di Nicopeia** (Chapel of the Madonna of Nicopeia) takes its name from a precious icon that many consider Venice's most powerful protector. In the nearby **Cappella della Madonna dei Mascoli** (Chapel of Madonna of the Males), the life of the Virgin Mary is depicted in fine 15th-century mosaics, possibly based on drawings by Jacopo Bellini (circa 1400–70), and his son-in-law, Andrea Mantegna.

In the **Santuario** (Sanctuary), the main altar is built over the tomb of St. Mark, its green marble canopy lifted high on carved alabaster columns. Even more impressive is the extraordinary **Pala d'Oro**, a dazzling gilded silver screen encrusted with 1,927 precious gems and 255 enameled panels. Originally commissioned in Constantinople by Doge Pietro Orseolo I in the 10th century, it was continually enlarged and embellished over the next four hundred years by master craftsmen and wealthy merchants. The bronze door leading from the sanctuary back into the sacristy is another Sansovino work. In the top left corner the artist included a self-portrait and, above that, a picture of his friend and fellow artist Titian (circa 1485–1576). The **Tesoro** (Treasury), entered from the right transept, contains many treasures carried home from Constantinople and other conquests.

From the atrium, climb the steep stairway to the **Galleria** and the **Museo Marciano.** From here you get the best possible overview of the basilica's interior, and you can step outdoors for a sweeping panorama of Piazza San Marco and the Piazzetta dei Leoncini. The highlight of the museum is a close-up look at the original four gilded bronze horses that once pranced upon the outer gallery. They were probably cast in Rome and taken to Constantinople. When Napoléon (1769–1821) conquered Venice in 1797, he took them back to Paris with him. They were returned after the fall of the French Empire, but came home "blind": their big ruby eyes had been sold.

Be warned: guards at the entrance to the basilica turn away anyone wearing shorts, short skirts, tank tops, and other attire considered inappropriate (no bare shoulders or knees). If you want to take a free guided tour in English during summer months (with less certainty in winter, as the guides are volunteers), look for groups forming on the porch inside the main door. You might also arrange a free tour by appointment. ⊠ *Piazza San Marco* ☎ *041/5225205 Basilica, 041/5225697 tours* 🖻 *Basilica free, Tesoro €2; Santuario and Pala d'Oro €1.50, Galleria and Museo Marciano €2* ☉ *May–Oct., Mon.–Sat. 9:45–5, Sun. 2–5; Nov.–Apr., Mon.–Sat. 9:45–4, Sun. 2–4; last entry ½ hr before closing* Ⓥ *Vallaresso/San Zaccaria.*

Biblioteca Marciana (Marciana Library). There's a wondrous collection of centuries-old books and illuminated manuscripts at this library, located across the Piazzetta from Palazzo Ducale in two buildings designed by Renaissance architect Sansovino, **Libreria Sansoviniana** and the adjacent **Zecca**. Unfortunately, the books can only be viewed by written request and are primarily the domain of scholars. But the **Gilded Hall** in the Sansoviniana is worth visiting for the works of Veronese, Tintoretto, and Titian that decorate its walls. You reach the Gilded Hall, which often hosts special exhibits relating to Venetian history, through Museo Correr. ✉ *Piazza San Marco, enter through Museo Correr* ☎ *041/5224951* 🖅 *€11 Piazza San Marco museums, €15.50 Musei Civici pass* 🕓 *Apr.–Oct., daily 9–7; Nov.–Mar., daily 9–5; last tickets sold 1½ hrs. before closing* Ⓥ *Vallaresso/San Zaccaria.*

★ ☾ ❸ **Campanile.** Venice's famous brick bell tower (325 ft tall, plus the angel) had been standing nearly 1,000 years when in 1902, practically without warning, it collapsed, taking with it Jacopo Sansovino's 16th-century marble loggia at the base. The crushed loggia was promptly restored and the new tower, rebuilt to the old plan, reopened in 1912. In the 15th century, clerics found guilty of immoral behavior were suspended in wooden cages from the tower. Some were forced to subsist on bread and water for as long as a year, while others were left to starve. The stunning view from the tower on a clear day includes the Lido, the lagoon, and the mainland as far as the Alps but, strangely enough, none of the myriad canals that snake through the city. ✉ *Piazza San Marco* ☎ *041/5224064* 🖅 *€6* 🕓 *June–Sept., 9 AM–sunset but not later than 9 PM; Oct.–May, 9–4; last entry 30 mins. before closing* Ⓥ *Vallaresso/San Zaccaria.*

Chiostro di Sant'Apollonia. Behind the Basilica and over a bridge, a short fondamenta leads right toward the unassuming entrance of the **Museo Diocesano** (upstairs), housed in a former Benedictine monastery. Its peacefully shady 12th-century cloister has been modified over the centuries, but it remains the only surviving example of a Romanesque cloister in Venice. The brick pavement is original, and the many inscriptions and fragments on display (some from the 9th century) are all that remain of the first Basilica di San Marco. The museum contains an array of sacred vestments, reliquaries, crucifixes, ex-votos, and paintings from various Venetian churches. ✉ *Ponte della Canonica, Castello 4312* ☎ *041/5229166* 🖅 *Free (donations welcomed)* 🕓 *Mon.–Sat. 10:30–12:30; ring bell* Ⓥ *Vallaresso/San Zaccaria.*

Museo Archeologico. This museum was first conceived in 1523, when Cardinal Domenico Grimani, a noted humanist, left his collection of original Greek (5th–1st centuries BC) and Roman (mostly from the imperial era) marbles to the Republic. Highlights include the statue of Kore (420 BC), an Attic original known as Abbondanza Grimani; the 1st-century BC Ara Grimani, an elaborate Hellenistic altar stone with a bacchanalian scene; a tiny but refined 1st-century BC crystal woman's head, which some say depicts Cleopatra; and a remarkable gallery of Roman busts. Don't miss the small collection of Egyptian and Assiro-Babylonian relics, including two mummies and a brick bearing the name of King Nebuchadnezzar. ✉ *Piazza San Marco, enter through Museo Correr* ☎ *041/5225978* 🖅 *€11 Piazza San Marco museums; €15.50 Musei Civici pass. Contact the museum for information about free guided tours in English* 🕓 *Apr.–Oct., daily 9–7; Nov.–Mar., daily 9–5; last tickets sold 1½ hrs before closing* Ⓥ *Vallaresso/San Zaccaria.*

★ ❻ **Museo Correr.** Exhibits in this museum of Venetian art and history range from the absurdly high-soled shoes worn by 16th-century Venetian ladies (who walked with the aid of servants) to old master paintings. Visit Correr after you've seen a bit of the town as it looks today—so much the better to appreciate La Serenissima's glorious past. From the first 1830 donation by Teodoro Correr, the museum has become so richly endowed that many of its treasures are warehoused and rotated into exhibits as time and space permit. Don't miss the huge, intricate *Grande Pianta Prospettica* in which Jacopo de' Barbari (circa 1440–1515) details in carved wood every inch of 16th-century Venice, including the old version of the Rialto Bridge and the neighborhood that once stood in the Giardini della Biennale before Napoléon demolished it. Whole rooms are devoted to Admiral Francesco Morosini (doge from 1688 to 1694), to intriguing objects and garments used by the doges through the ages, and even to antique games. In the second floor **Quadreria** (Picture Gallery) Room 36 is entirely given over to the talented Bellini family of Renaissance painters, Jacopo and his sons, Giovanni (1430–1516) and the lesser known Gentile (1429–1507). Room 30 houses a small but evocative Pietà by Cosmè Tura (1430–95). In Room 38 is Carpaccio's (circa 1465–1525) *Two Venetian Ladies,* formerly referred to as *The Courtesans.* Experts are still debating whether this painting is an extension of a larger Carpaccio work. If the *Hunt in the Valley* (J. P. Getty Museum, Malibu) depicts another part of the same scene, these two ladies may in fact be waiting for the return of their gentlemen hunters. ✉ *Piazza San Marco, Ala Napoleonica* ☎ *041/5225625* ☑ *€11 Piazza San Marco museums; €15.50 Musei Civici pass* ⊙ *Apr.–Oct., daily 9–7; Nov.–Mar., daily 9–5; last tickets sold 1½ hrs before closing* Ⓥ *Vallaresso/San Zaccaria.*

❺ Palazzo Ducale (Doge's Palace). Rising above the Piazzetta San Marco, this Gothic-Renaissance fantasia of pink-and-white marble is a majestic expression of the prosperity and power attained during Venice's most glorious period. Some architectural purists contend that the building is top-heavy, with dense upper floors resting awkwardly upon the

FodorsChoice
★

TO LIVE LIKE A DOGE

T WASN'T EASY BEING THE DOGE.
Called the Serenissimo ("Most Serene"), he led a life that was anything but.

In the 1,100 years of the Republic (697–1797), 121 men were elected to lifetime terms as doge through a convoluted election process: first, 41 electors, all belonging to noble Venetian families, were chosen through a series of random drawings and secret votes. Sequestered in a wing of the Palazzo Ducale, they deliberated in absolute secrecy until at least 25 votes concurred on the selection, a process that took anywhere from a few hours to several months. This complicated procedure, designed to prevent tyranny and nepotism, was nonetheless not perfect; during the late period of the Republic, many of the less-wealthy electors sold their votes.

When a new doge was finally chosen, the cannons of the galleys anchored in the Bacino di San Marco would sound and the city's bells would ring. On Coronation Day, 80 arsenal workers would carry the doge through the crowds that had gathered in Piazza San Marco. The throngs cheered him as they pocketed the silver coins he tossed to them out of a silver bucket.

Severe measures were taken to ensure that such a cautiously elected prince did not abuse his office. He wasn't allowed to send notes (not even to his wife), a measure taken to prevent the creation of secret alliances. To discourage bribery and collusion, he could not accept any gifts other than flowers and rosewater. He didn't have a royal stall in theaters—in fact, he wasn't even allowed to go to theaters and cafés, where he might have a chance to plot against democracy. He had to pay all his office bills out of his own pocket, but couldn't engage in any money-making activities. And for all their splendor, dogal garments such as those on display at the Museo Correr were nothing more than a set of grand uniforms to be worn according to rigid etiquette for state occasions only. The doge was expected to lead the Venetian fleet into battle, literally; bad health and old age did not excuse him from the duty. The 90-year-old, blind Enrico Dandolo proudly laid siege to Constantinople in 1203 and 1204, making off with the four horses that now adorn the Basilica and the famous icon of the Madonna Nicopeia.

Even the resting place of the doge was determined according to a rigid protocol: for much of the history of the Republic, the doges were mummified and put on display in the Chiesa dei Santi Giovanni e Paolo. But Venetian taxonomists were not as expert as their ancient Egyptian counterparts, and after several centuries of unpleasant odors, "symbolic" mummies replaced the real ones, which were interred in family chapels. Though eulogized as the most serene, the Serenissimo of Venice had, in reality, a dog's life.

— Carla Lionello

---

graceful ground-floor colonnade, but it's hard to imagine the Piazza with any other design. Always much more than a residence, this Palazzo was White House, Senate, torture chamber, and prison rolled into one.

Though a fortress for the doge existed on this spot in the early 9th century, the building you see today began in the 12th century, and like the basilica next door, was continually remodeled over the centuries. You can exit through the ornately Gothic **Porta della Carta** (Gate of the Paper), where official decrees were traditionally posted, but the main visitor entrance is under the portico facing the water. It opens onto an immense courtyard with the city's only two bronze *pozzi* (wellheads). Ahead is the **Scala dei Giganti** (Stairway of the Giants), guarded by huge statues of Mars and Neptune by Sansovino. Being an ordinary mortal, you won't get to climb these stairs, but if you walk along the arcade to reach the central interior staircase, you'll be dazzled by the sumptuously gilded

Scala d'Oro (Golden Staircase), also designed by Sansovino. Although it may seem odd that the government's main council rooms and reception halls would be so far upstairs, imagine how this extraordinary climb must have impressed and even intimidated foreign emissaries.

The rooms are no less impressive than the climb. Even though goldsmiths at that time could hammer one gram of gold into one square yard of gold leaf, there's still been an amazing amount of gold lavished on the palace ceilings—those that aren't covered with works by Venice's greatest artists. In the **Anticollegio**, a waiting room outside the Collegio's chamber, you can see Tintoretto's *Bacchus and Ariadne Crowned by Venus* and Veronese's (1528–88) *Rape of Europa*. Veronese also painted the ceiling of the adjacent **Sala del Collegio** (College Chamber). The ceiling of the **Sala del Senato** (Senate Chamber) features *Triumph of Venice* by Tintoretto, magnificent in its own right but dwarfed by his masterpiece *Paradise* in the **Sala del Maggiore Consiglio** (Great Council Hall). A vast work commissioned for a vast hall, this dark, dynamic mural is the world's largest oil painting (23 by 75 ft). The room's carved and gilded ceiling is breathtaking, even dizzying, as you wheel around searching for the best vantage point from which to admire Veronese's majestic *Apotheosis of Venice* filling one of the center panels. Around the upper part of the walls, study the frieze of portraits of the first 76 doges and you'll notice one picture is missing near the left corner of the wall opposite *Paradise*. A black painted curtain marks the place where Doge Marin Falier's portrait should be. A Latin inscription bluntly explains that Falier was beheaded for treason in 1355, when, at age 71 and less than a year into his reign, he was accused of plotting to establish an autocracy.

A narrow canal separates the Palace's east side from the cramped, gloomy cell blocks of the so-called **Prigioni Nuove** (New Prisons). High above the water arches the enclosed marble **Ponte dei Sospiri** (Bridge of Sighs), which earned its name from the sighs of those being led to prison or execution. Look out its windows and you'll see the last earthly view many of these prisoners had. During the Romantic era of the 19th century, the bridge's melancholy history made it a tourist must-see, and the sight still backs up pedestrian traffic as visitors crowd to take pictures.

The palazzo's "secret itinerary" guided tour takes you to the doge's private apartments, through hidden passageways to the torture chambers, where prisoners were "interrogated," and into the rooftop *piombi* prison, named for the building's leaded roofing. Giacomo Casanova (1725–98), Venetian-born writer and libertine, was imprisoned here in 1755, having offended someone in power. (He was officially charged with being a Freemason). He and an accomplice made a daring escape 15 months later and Casanova fled to France, where he continued his career of intrigue and scandal. They were the only prisoners ever to escape, and their guard was imprisoned for 10 years. ⊠ *Piazzetta San Marco* ☎ *041/5224951* ✆ *€11 Piazza San Marco museums, €15.50 Musei Civici pass* ☉ *Apr.–Oct., daily 9–7; Nov.–Mar., daily 9–5; last tickets sold 1½ hrs before closing* ⊠ *English guided tours* ✆ *€6* ☉ *Tues.–Thurs., Sat. 11:30 "Secret Itinerary" tour* ✆ *€12.50* ☉ *English tours daily 10 and 11:30; reservations advisable* Ⓥ *Vallaresso/San Zaccaria.*

★ ☺ ⌐ ❶ **Piazza San Marco.** (St. Mark's Square). If you face the basilica from in front of the Correr Museum, you'll notice that rather than being a strict rectangle, this square opens wider at the basilica end, distorting the perspective and creating the illusion that it's even larger than it is. On your left, the long, arcaded building is the **Procuratie Vecchie,** built in the early 16th century as offices and residences for the powerful Procurators of San Marco—the Republic's only magistrates, elected for life. They were responsible for administering the basilica's funds and supervising the doge's chaplains. On your right is the **Procuratie Nuove,** built a half century later in more grandiose classical style. Venice's great Renaissance architect Sansovino planned the building but died before construction had begun. His design was executed by Vincenzo Scamozzi (circa 1552–1616), a pupil of Andrea Palladio (1508–80) and a devout neoclassicist. Later sections were completed by Baldassare Longhena (1598–1682), Venice's other great architect, who belonged firmly to the baroque tradition.

When Napoléon entered Venice with his troops in 1797, he called Piazza San Marco "the world's most beautiful drawing room"—and promptly gave orders to redecorate it. His architects demolished a church with a facade designed by Sansovino to build the **Ala Napoleonica** (Napoleonic Wing), or Fabbrica Nuova (New Building), which linked the two 16th-century procuratie and effectively enclosed the piazza.

need a break?

Coffee, which for centuries had been a popular drink throughout countries to the East, may have first arrived in Europe aboard Venetian cargo ships. Merchants were regularly importing beans in the early 1600s, and coffee shops opened in Venice, Paris, and Vienna shortly thereafter. Since **Caffè Florian** (☎ 041/5205641), located in the Procuratie Nuove, brewed its first cup, it has served the likes of Casanova, Dickens, and Proust. It's Venice's oldest café, continuously open since 1720 (though you'll find it closed on Wednesday in winter). Counter seating is less expensive than taking a table, especially when there's live music. In the Procuratie Vecchie, **Caffè Quadri** (☎ 041/5289299), exudes almost as much history as Florian across the way and is similarly pricey. It was shunned by 19th-century Venetians when the occupying Austrians made it their gathering place. During slow season, it closes Monday.

❹ Piazzetta San Marco. This "little square" leads from Piazza San Marco to the waters of *Bacino San Marco* (St. Mark's Basin) and has great views of the islands of the Giudecca and San Giorgio. The *molo* (landing), now lined with gondolas, once served as the grand entrance to the Republic. Two columns on the waterfront seem to form a doorway to the larger piazza behind. On one column is San Todaro—St. Theodore, the first patron saint of Venice—and his dragon. Atop the other is the winged lion, a traditional emblem of St. Mark, which became the symbol of Venice itself. These two pieces are also emblematic of the architectural and artistic growth of the city, which was in large part driven by art imported from the Near East. In this case, the lion was likely to have once been a 4th-century BC chimera (a mythological creature with a lion's head and body, goat's head attached to its back, and serpent's tail) to which the Venetians attached the wings, which may be of Etruscan, Persian, or even Chinese origin. Theodore is no less a patchwork, having been assembled from a beautiful statue of King Mithridates mounted on a later Roman trunk, with "new" 15th-century legs. Despite the fact that a third column was lost when it fell in the lagoon while being unloaded, the architect in charge of the operations was paid with the only gambling license in Venice, to be used "between the Lion and St. Theodore." A stage was also set up here for public executions.

❼ Torre dell'Orologio. Erected between 1496 and 1499, the Clock Tower has an enameled timepiece and animated Moorish figures that strike the hour. On Epiphany (January 6) and during Ascension Week (40 days after Easter), an angel and three wise men go in and out of the doors and bow to the Virgin Mary. The complicated clock mechanism also indicates the phase of the moon and the path of the sun across the signs of the zodiac. If the tower's inscription is true—HORAS NON NUMERO NISI SERENAS ("I only count happy hours")—then perhaps happy times may again come to Venice if they ever manage to fix the clock; it's been under restoration since 1999 and there's no completion date in sight. You can however visit the famous three wise men on the ground floor of Palazzo Ducale where parts of the clock are on display. ⊠ *Northern side of Piazza San Marco.*

SAN MARCO TO DORSODURO

The long, narrow sestiere Dorsoduro, literally "hardback," may owe its name to the hard clay that gives support to the southern side of town. Its eastern end, Punta della Dogana, was for centuries the Serenissima's customs office. Its western area of Santa Marta, formerly a poor fishermen's neighborhood, is now part of the Port of Venice's busy passenger terminal. Dorsoduro also includes the Giudecca (⇨ San Giorgio Maggiore and the Giudecca, *below*), which is actually a string of small islands that lie just far enough apart to feel like a world of their own. Spread between the southern stretch of the Grand Canal and the broader, deeper Giudecca Canal, this part of the city is prone to great changes in color and weather; extremely blue and warm under the sun, it becomes creamy white and icy when the fog rolls in, hazy gray under a summer storm, and tinged with fiery orange at sunrise or sunset.

Except perhaps for Lido beach, there's no sunnier spot in Venice than Fondamenta delle Zattere. It's the city's gigantic public terrace, with bustling bars and gelaterie. It's the place to stroll, read in the open air, go for a run, or play hooky from sightseeing. The call of the seagulls or the whistle of the boats on their way to port recalls days gone by. This vaguely intellectual and cosmopolitan part of town is home to the Università degli Studi di Venezia and the Accademia di Belle Arti. At the border of the small sestiere of Santa Croce is a prestigious institute of architecture, frequented by students from all over Europe. Campo Santa Margherita, the largest square in Dorsoduro, is lively from early morning fishmarket to late-night cafés.

Numbers in the text correspond to numbers in the margin and on the San Marco to Dorsoduro map.

a good walk

Leave Piazza San Marco from the Museo Correr side, taking upscale Salizzada San Moisè and Calle Larga XXII Marzo—home to some of the most fashionable shops in town—to reach **Santa Maria del Giglio** ❽ ▶, with a *Madonna* by Rubens and a spruced-up collection of silver reliquaries. Often, the simplest way to reach Dorsoduro from here is by hopping on the traghetto across the Grand Canal. However, as operation of these boats depends heavily on weather, time of day, and the whims of the boatmen on duty, you may have to use a vaporetto instead. Either way you'll arrive at **Santa Maria della Salute** ❾, where several paintings by Titian await you in the sacristy. The easternmost, and often the windiest, point in Dorsoduro is Punta della Dogana. It has one of the best views in Venice, especially of the waterways in and out of town. It's no surprise that this was the site of the Republic's maritime customs office—they didn't want to miss the chance to tax imported goods aboard merchants' galleys—and no surprise that Fortune stands atop the windvane on the *Palla della Fortuna*, symbolizing a republic that sailed not for conquest but for commerce. Backtracking past Salute and the *Abbazia* (abbey), a narrow calle and a couple of bridges will take you to the **Peggy Guggenheim Collection** ❿, a small but first-rate museum of 20th-century paintings and sculpture. From there, take Fondamenta Venier right to Campo San Vio, where benches not only let your feet rest, but let your eyes slow down as you watch traffic drift by on the Grand Canal. Leaving the Grand Canal behind you, walk south along Canal San Vio until you reach the Zattere. Overlooking Giudecca Canal, this promenade is one of the sunniest spots in town and on clear days, summer or winter, you'll swear that half the city is out for a *passeggiata,* or stroll. Visit the church of **Gesuati** ⑪ to your right, if only to peek at the Tiepolo ceiling, and don't miss the *bocca di leone* (lion's mouth), between the church and its older sibling, Santa Maria della Visitazione. During the time of Venice's infamous Council of Ten, a bocca was used to make anonymous accusations against fellow citizens; this particular bocca, one of the few that remain, was fed complaints about sanitation. Up ahead at the next rio, tucked away in one of Venice's most picturesque corners, is the Squero di San Trovaso, where wooden boats have been built and repaired for centuries. Campo San Trovaso, just beyond the squero, is still grassy, as all Venetian campi at one time were. The church here is worth a brief stop for the *Adoration of the Magi* by Tintoretto's son, Domenico (1565–1637).

Returning to Zattere, continue to the San Basilio vaporetto stop. Ahead lies Stazione Marittima, where in summer cruise ships line the dock. Turn right on Calle del Vento alongside the canal. Across the rio at the second bridge is **San Sebastiano** ⑫, with a number of astounding paintings by Veronese, as well as the artist's grave. This church's campo connects with the Campo l'Angelo Raffaele. Cross the bridge beside this campo's church to reach Fondamenta Barbarigo. A left here will take you to the church of **San Nicolò dei Mendicoli** ⑬, isolated on a little square surrounded by water. Return to Fondamenta Barbarigo and follow it to Ponte del Soccorso. Across this bridge you'll pass an inconspicuous building numbered 2590, today used as university housing, but originally established by the famous 16th-century courtesan and poetess Veronica Franco as a home for fallen women. You'll also pass Palazzo Zenobio, formerly an Armenian school, as you work your way to **Carmini** ⑭ church (also known as Santa Maria del Carmelo) and the **Scuola Grande dei Carmini** ⑮, not to be missed for its Tiepolo paintings. To the left as you leave the scuola is Campo Santa Margherita, Venice's only large square that doesn't have a church. That hasn't always been the case; look for the stubby remains of an old bell tower, and the former patron saint Margherita carved in triumph over her emaciated dragon. The monolithic cube of a building, seemingly dropped in the middle of the square, once headquartered a company of furriers. Carved on the building is a weathered sign that stipulates minimum sizes for selling fish. You may notice the *masegni* (gray paving stones) are laid in different directions; that's because several canals, now filled in, once crossed this campo.

Zigzag toward **Ca' Rezzonico** ⑯ through a maze of alleys that leads to Campiello Squellini. If you climb up the bridge near there you can peek in at the Venice Fire Department boats. Also in this area are two of Venice's leading mask workshops, Ca' Macana on Calle Pedrocchi and Mondonovo on Rio Terà Canal. After visiting the Museo del Settecento Veneziano, you can hop on vaporetto Line 1 at the museum's own landing, or you can walk through Campo San Barnaba and sample some good wine at the *enoteca* (wineshop) or buy some fruit from the boat moored in the rio—one of the last such boat vendors in Venice. The bridge here, Ponte dei Pugni (Bridge of Fists), is a former battleground of the Nicolotti (westsiders) and Castellani (east-enders), Venice's Hatfields and McCoys. The **Gallerie dell'Accademia** ⑰, is the city's most important art museum and merits an extended visit—maybe on a rainy morning or when the Quadreria is open.

TIMING This walk takes about two hours without stops and a full day to cover all the sites, excluding the Gallerie dell'Accademia. A few hours will allow you to see a good sampling at the Gallerie, but if time is short, an audio

San Marco to Dorsoduro

Piazza San Marco

KEY
▲ Start of walk
▲ Vaporetto Stop

VENICE

0   1/8 km
0   1/8 mile

guide can help you zip through the highlights in about an hour. Give yourself at least 1½ hours for the Peggy Guggenheim Collection—although the gardens, gift shop, café, and air-conditioning might tempt you to linger even longer. The churches and Scuola dei Carmini are not large, and unless something grabs your attention, a half hour should be enough for each one. Ca' Rezzonico deserves a couple of hours.

What to See

16

FodorśChoice

★

Ca' Rezzonico. English critic John Ruskin (1819–1900) may have called this "the silliest palace" on the Grand Canal, but today a visit to its **Museo del Settecento Veneziano** (Museum of 18th-Century Venice) provides a fascinating peek into the lives of Venetian nobles and commoners of a bygone era. The palace was given a 17th-century baroque design by Longhena, but wasn't completed until nearly 100 years later by Giorgio Massari (1686–1766). It was acquired by the city in 1935. Its frescoes, gilded salons, and marble fixtures show how elegance held on in Venice despite the city's declining fortunes. Bought and sold frequently over the centuries, Ca Rezzonico once belonged to English poet Robert Browning's son. During a visit Browning caught a cold and died here. His epitaph-like quip, "Open my heart and you will see graven inside of it Italy," is still visible on the facade. The mansion is loaded with sumptuous brocade, fine furniture, and chandeliers of Murano glass. Concerts, often held in the elegant ballroom, call to mind parties from a bygone era, and a lovely alcoved bedroom might have welcomed Casanova and his intrigues. The carefully reconstructed **Farmacia ai Do San Marchi** (Pharmacy at the Two St. Marks), with its jars full of powders and potions, gives a sense of how 18th-century people dealt with health and medicine. A worthwhile art gallery includes genre pictures by Pietro Longhi (1702–85) showing life in the parlors and kitchens behind the Grand Canal's facades. Donations have added nearly 300 works to the collection, most from various schools of Venetian painting. Alongside more sombre pieces by Tintoretto and Bonifacio, Sebastiano Ricci's (1659–1734) *Venus with Sartyr and Cupid,* and Gaspare Diziani's (1689–1767) *Pan and the Sleeping Nymph* seem lighthearted, even magical. Several portraits by Rosalba Carriera (1675–1757), one of Venice's few female painters, deserve attention, as do cityscapes by Francesco Guardi (1712–93), a great painter whose misfortune was being a contemporary of the more popular Canaletto. ⊠ *Fondamenta Rezzonico, Dorsoduro 3136* ☎ *041/2410100* 🎟 *€6.50; €8 Museums of 18th-Century Culture pass; €15.50 Musei Civici pass* ⊙ *Apr.–Oct., Wed.–Mon. 10–6; Nov.–Mar., Wed.–Mon. 10–5; last entry 1 hr before closing* Ⓥ *Ca' Rezzonico.*

14

Carmini. This rather simple Gothic red-brick basilica has two remarkable altarpieces: a *Nativity* by Cima da Conegliano (circa 1459–1517), and *Sts. Nicholas, John the Baptist, and Lucy,* by Lorenzo Lotto (circa 1480–1556). The church is named after Santa Maria del Carmelo, who was left for several centuries without even a painting in her honor, until her followers finally managed to build the scuola nearby. ⊠ *Campo dei Carmini, Dorsoduro* ☎ *041/5226553* 🎟 *Free* ⊙ *Mon.–Sat. 8–noon and 2:30–6:30, Sun. 4:30–6* Ⓥ *Ca' Rezzonico.,*

17

FodorśChoice

★

Gallerie dell'Accademia (Accademia Galleries). Napoléon founded these galleries in 1807 on the site of a religious complex he'd suppressed, and what he initiated amounts to the world's most extraordinary collection of Venetian art. Many works come from churches, convents, and scuole that either were suppressed by the French leader or were judged unsuitable places to house such treasures.

Byzantium was an early influence on the art of Venice, as evidenced by the gold, enamel colors, and unreal narrative structure that became part of Venetian Gothic style, which is on display in Room 1 of the galleries. The 14th-century polyptychs by Paolo Veneziano (circa 1290–1360) and Lorenzo Veneziano (active 1356–72)—no relation—you see the distinct influence of the Byzantine Church. Further into Room 1 are works by masters of the 15th-century Gothic style, Jacobello del Fiore (circa 1370–1439) and Antonio Vivarini (circa 1415–1476/84).

Room 2 demonstrates a second characteristic central to Venetian painting, rich color. The emphasis on color can be attributed to the city itself: light reflected off the lagoon often seems to blur contours and melt colors together. While Italian Renaissance painters elsewhere concentrated on perfect drawing, balanced arrangement, and perspective, their colleagues in Venice became masters of color, using it to bring figures together and give unity to their works.

Jacopo Bellini (circa 1400–1470), father of artist sons Giovanni and Gentile, is also considered the father of Venetian Renaissance. Apprenticing in Perugia under Gentile da Fabriano, Jacopo practiced perspective drawing and sketching from life, and he would carry these techniques home to Venice. Study his harmonious *Madonna and Child with Saints*; comparing this to Room 2's other large altarpieces—Cima da Conegliano's touching *Madonna of the Orange Tree,* or Carpaccio's narrative *Ten Thousand Martyrs of Mt. Ararat*—shows how Venice's early Renaissance masters built on Jacopo's foundation.

Works by Bellini's son Giovanni (circa 1430–1516) draw your eye not with their subject matter but with their mellowness and richness of color. Rooms 4 and 5 are full of his Madonnas, many painted for shrines in private homes. Though the subject is the same, they're far from repetitive; note the contrast between the young Madonna with baby hanging beside the grieving, elderly Madonna whose son has just died—you'll see the colors of dawn and dusk in Venice.

Color was often more important than content for Giorgione (circa 1478–1510); his enigmatic *Tempest* (Room 5), which has intrigued centuries of viewers and critics, depicts a storm approaching as a nude woman nurses her child and a soldier looks on. According to 20th-century art historian E. H. Gombrich, "Though the figures are not particularly carefully drawn, and the composition is somewhat artless, the picture is clearly blended into a whole simply by the light and air that permeates it all . . . ; for the first time, it seems, the landscape is not just a background. . . ." Giorgione broke away from the tradition of painting only beautiful figures; in his *Old Woman,* the subject holds in her right hand a piece of paper reading *col tempo* (with time), reminding viewers that everyone must age. Next door in Room 7, Lorenzo Lotto's *Young Man in his Study,* with his intense expression of melancholy, is one of the most compelling portraits in the Galleries.

In the 16th century, only Michelangelo was more famous than Titian (circa 1487–1576). Giorgione's heir and the official painter of the Venetian Republic, he was the guest of royal courts throughout Europe; though he traveled south to paint a portrait for Pope Paul III, he refused to remain in Rome. His *Presentation of the Virgin* (Room 24) is the only work in the collection that was originally created for the building in which it hangs. He was finishing *Pietà* (Room 10) for his tomb in Chiesa dei Frari when he died of the plague in 1576. Over this masterpiece's shadowy background you can see how Titian applied glowing colors with his hands, often his tools of choice. You can also see a self-portrait of the artist as an old man—he's pictured to the viewer's right of Jesus.

Tintoretto and Veronese, two more Venetian Renaissance giants, are featured in Room 10. The first of Jacopo Tintoretto's (1518–1594) four scenes from the *Life of San Marco* shows the saint dreaming of Venice. Tintoretto was often at odds with critics, who described his work as crude and carelessly executed; he strove to show emotion and felt the incomparable beauty of Titian's works rendered them more pleasing than moving. Perhaps the artist believed a careful "finish" impeded the drama of his painting. Paolo Veronese (1528–1588), on the other hand, wanted his work to be attractive and pleasing. *Feast in the House of Levi* shows the Venetian high Renaissance in all its richness and glamour. Commissioned as a *Last Supper* by Dominican friars, this painting was rejected and the artist was reported to the Inquisition, which took issue with the painting's jesters, dogs, and German (therefore Protestant) soldiers. Veronese cleverly avoided the charges of profanity by changing the painting's title to the *Feast in the House of Levi,* representing a bawdy but nonetheless biblical event.

Rooms 20 and 21 feature series of canvases by Gentile Bellini (1429–1507) and Vittore Carpaccio, masters of Renaissance narrative painting. These renderings of Venetian life are exceptional sources of historical information, detailing everything from shoe and hair styles to boat design. Bellini's *Procession of the Relic of the Cross* (circa 1496), painted for the Scuola Grande di San Giovanni Evangelista, serves as a snapshot of Piazza San Marco, circa 1496—it's fascinating to see how things have changed, and how they've stayed the same. Carpaccio's *Miracle of the True Cross at Rialto* (also known as *Healing of a Lunatic*), shows the old wooden bridge at Rialto, which opened to let large boats pass. If the people depicted in the paintings are particularly realistic, it's because they were often painted from life. Monks and nobles of the 15th century frequently sat for the artist; note Caterina Cornaro, Queen of Cyprus, at the lower left of the *Recovery of the Relic from the Canal of San Lorenzo,* and the red-haired Patriarca di Grado witnessing the *Miracle at Rialto.*

In the 1700s, fresco and stucco became popular art forms, exemplified by Giambattista Tiepolo (1696–1770). Sections of a Tiepolo fresco, salvaged from Chiesa dei Scalzi after a World War I bombing, hang in Room 11. Another trend of the 1700s was landscape painting; travelers wanted souvenirs of their trips to Venice, and a new school of painters rose to the occasion. Two of the greatest had their destinies written in their names: Antonio Canal (1697–1768), called Canaletto, which literally translates as "Small Canal," and Francesco Guardi (1712–1793) whose surname means "You Look." Their styles couldn't have been more different. Canaletto, whose work is on display in Room 17, became official landscape painter of the Republic and was courted throughout Europe for his remarkable verisimilitude and precise Flemish details. Guardi (Room 15) left your eye to imagine that which he didn't reveal in paint; in *Island of San Giorgio,* his gondoliers consist of a few deftly placed patches of color. So popular was Canaletto that little of his work remained in Venice; so precise was his work that modern researchers are tracing rising tides by studying buildings in his paintings. In the adjacent room hang portraits by Rosalba Carriera (1675–1758), one of Venice's best known female artists. She imported colors from Paris, where soft shades, like powdered skin, had become fashionable. The aging artist went mad, which you may be able to sense in her self-portrait.

Though not essential, prebooking your tickets to the Gallerie allows you to bypass the line during busy seasons and costs only an additional €1. Booking is necessary to see the **Quadreria,** a narrow exhibition room where additional works by Venetian masters cover every inch of the walls. It's open for limited, irregular hours (another reason to call ahead); a free map identifies the art and artists, and the bookshop sells an English-language booklet with additional information. In the main Gallerie, a €4 audio guide saves reading but adds little to each room's excellent English annotation; audio/video guides (€6) are more exhaustive and ease navigating. ☒ *Campo della Carità, near Accademia Bridge, Dorsoduro 1050* ☎ *041/5222247, 041/5200345 reservations* ⊕ *www.gallerieaccademia.org* ☒ *€6.50; €11 also includes Ca' d'Oro and Oriental* ☉ *Tues.–Sun. 8:15–7:15, Mon. 8:15–2* Ⓥ *Accademia.*

⑪ Gesuati. As soon as the Dominicans took over the church of Santa Maria della Visitazione from the suppressed order of Gesuati laymen, Giorgio Massari was commissioned to build this church in its place. Venice's favorite architect of the day, Massari had a populist attitude, saying, "An architect who doesn't want to starve must by necessity adapt himself to see and think according to classical norms and models." Inside, Gesuati is a triumph of 18th-century baroque. Images of saints in Dominican attire are rendered by Giambiattista Piazzetta (1683–1754), Sebastiano Ricci (1659–1734), and Giambattista Tiepolo, whose works here include the splendid ceiling. Sadly, only during holidays dedicated to the Virgin does the church display Stefano di Sant'Agnese's beautiful 15th-century *Madonna delle Grazie.* ☒ *Zattere, Dorsoduro* ☎ *041/2750462 Chorus* ☒ *€2; €8 Chorus pass* ☉ *Mon.–Sat. 10–5, Sun. 1–5.* Ⓥ *Zattere.*

need a break? If ice cream is the food of gods, then heaven's as close as the Zattere, where generations of Venetians have chosen **Gelateria Nico** (☒ Dorsoduro 922 ☎ 041/5225293). Grab a chocolaty *gianduiotto,* their famous nutty slab of chocolate ice cream floating on a cloud of whipped cream, and relax on the biggest, most welcoming deck in town.

★ ⑩ Peggy Guggenheim Collection. Extremely rich, provocative, and extravagant, Peggy Guggenheim (1898–1979)—wife of Max Ernst and niece of Solomon Guggenheim, founder of the New York museum bearing their name—was among the 20th-century's greatest collectors of modern art. On display in Palazzo Venier dei Leoni, her residence for 30 years, are works representing the most important artistic movements from the early 20th century through the postwar period: Cubism (Picasso and Braque); Futurism (Balla, Severini, and Boccioni); metaphysical painting (*The Red Tower* by De Chirico); abstract painting (Kandinsky); and a large group of Surrealist masterpieces, including Magritte's *Empire of Light,* Max Ernst's outstanding large Dada canvases *The Kiss, The Attirement of the Bride,* and *The Anti-Pope* (he gave the last two to Guggenheim as a wedding present), and Miró's *Dutch Interior II* and *Seated Woman II.* The modernist generation of painters is represented by Rothko, Motherwell, Pollock, and Bacon. A room is dedicated to the lively little pictures made by the heiress's daughter Pegeen, who disappeared under mysterious circumstances. Scattered around the two beautiful gardens of the villa are sculptures ranging from Giacometti's ethereal bronze figures to a giant phallus pointing out to the Grand Canal. (Beverages, snacks, and light meals are served in the gardens.) In a tiny family cemetery, several tombstones indicate the resting place of Guggenheim herself and her beloved dogs. Don't miss the gift shop, with large black-and-white pictures (not for sale) of the young heiress living her dazzling life, and an array of thematic gifts such as mugs and neckties designed by architect Frank Lloyd Wright, Mondrianesque umbrellas, and Modigliani pins. ☒*Calle San Cristoforo, Dorsoduro 701* ☎ *041/2405411* ⊕ *www.guggenheim-venice.it*

✉ €8 ⏱ *Wed.–Mon. 10–6; Apr.–Oct., Sat. open until 10 PM; last entry 15 mins before closing* Ⓥ *Accademia.*

★ ⑬ **San Nicolò dei Mendicoli.** Padovans fleeing the Lombard invasion in the 7th century chose this scrap of an island called *Mendigola* to found their church. A humble fishing village grew up around it and became the west end haunt of the Nicolotti, one of the town's two historic "gangs." A community unto itself, it had its its own lion atop a column (wingless but still there), its own flag, and even a leader dubbed the Doge of the Nicolotti. The current 12th-century church of San Nicolò has had enough renovations as to document changing fashions of church architecture. The bell tower has survived since the 12th century but only just—it took a stray shell during the German withdrawal in World War II. The facade and its 13th-century windows were rediscovered only when 18th-century restoration shucked the bad remodeling that had covered them over interim centuries. The Gothic-style porch was a popular 15th-century feature among Venetian churches, built to shelter the *pinzocchere* (female beggars). The interior, brilliantly restored after Venice's 1966 flood by the Venice in Peril Fund, is covered with paintings by Veronese's pupils, including Alvise Dal Friso (1554–1608). Also worth seeing is Palma il Giovane's (1544–1628) *Resurrection.* ✉ *Campo San Nicolò dei Mendicoli, Dorsoduro* ☎ *041/2750382* ✉ *Free* ⏱ *10–noon and 4–6* Ⓥ *San Basilio.*

★ ⑫ **San Sebastiano.** The treasure this dull facade conceals is an example of what you could miss hidden behind Venice's many masks. This jewel is an extraordinary collection by Paolo Caliari, better known as Veronese (1528–1588), who in his early twenties came to Venice from his hometown of Verona (hence the nickname). The first frescoes he painted in San Sebastiano launched an intense and celebrated career for this grand-scale decorator, famous for glowing colors. A contemporary of Tintoretto, Veronese lived in the salizzada nearby and took great pride in embellishing this, his parish church. He began in the period 1555–56 with Old Testament scenes in the Sacristy and episodes from the Book of Esther in the coffered ceiling. He progressed to the upper part of the nave, choir, organ doors, and frontispiece. Between 1562–70, he created *Madonna in Glory with St. Sebastian, Saints Mark and Marcellino Led to their Martyrdom,* and the *Martyrdom of St. Sebastian.* The artist, not surprisingly, was buried here; beneath his bust near the organ. ✉ *Campo San Sebastiano, Dorsoduro* ☎ *041/2750462 Chorus.* ✉ *€2; €8 Chorus pass* ⏱ *Mon.–Sat. 10–5; Sun. 1–5.* Ⓥ *San Basilio.*

▶ ⑧ **Santa Maria del Giglio.** This white, airy church is one of the most remarkable examples of Venetian Baroque. If you step back and look up at the facade's upper-left corner, the angel seems about to take flight. Santa Maria del Giglio is often referred to as Santa Maria Zobenigo, after the family that built the original 9th-century church, but this present building is dedicated to the the painting *Virgin with the Lily,* which hangs inside In the iconography of the Annunciation, the angel offers Mary a white lily, a symbol of purity and inside you will see a painting showing this scene. Virgin and lilies aside, this church seems more like one large monument to the five Barbaro brothers, who financed its reconstruction. Along with their statues decorating the facade, are the maps of Zara, Candia, Padua, Rome, Corfu, and Spalato, the cities where Antonio Barbaro spent his life in service to the Republic. The interior has more the feeling of an art gallery than a place of worship, as the walls and ceiling are packed with paintings of all sizes and shapes, including a good stations-of-the-cross series by various artists. Ask the doorkeeper to light the area behind the main altar to better appreciate Tintoretto's *Four Evangelists,* and the moving *Annunciation,* by Salviati (died 1575). The cozy Cappella Molin is full of exquisite gold and silver reliquaries containing everything from fragments of bones to fingernails. Newly encased in its protective frame is the only work by Rubens in Venice, *Madonna and Child with Young St. John*. The **Sacristy**, open only 10–11:30, contains several lesser known works. ⊠ *Campo Santa Maria del Giglio, San Marco* ☎ *041/2750462 Chorus.* 🎫 *€2; €8 Chorus pass* ⊙ *Mon.–Sat. 10–5, Sun. 1–5.* Ⓥ *S. Maria del Giglio.*

❾ Santa Maria della Salute. The view of "La Salute," as Venetians affectionately call it, from the Riva degli Schiavoni at sunset or from the Accademia Bridge under the moonlight is simply unforgettable. Early birds should also go for a walk to the Piazzetta at the break of dawn to see the lines of the temple's dome slowly emerge from the morning mist. The architect Baldassare Longhena was only 32 years old when, together with 10 colleagues, he participated in the design competition to build a great shrine in Venice dedicated to the Virgin Mary in gratitude for liberation from a terrible plague that from 1630 to 1631 killed 47,000 people in Venice alone. Presenting his project, Longhena spoke of it as an "unprecedented work which had never been even imagined in total or in part by other churches in this city." His plan for a classically inspired white octagonal temple covered by a colossal cupola, with a Palladian-style facade and bizarre Baroque decorations, effortlessly conquered the avant-garde judges of the competition.

The grandiose temple is made of *marmorino* (brick covered with marble dust) and Istrian stone, an inexpensive material used in Venice for framing windows and lining steps on bridges. Building it was no easy task: about 100,000 trunks of oak were used to reinforce the muddy terrain. The luminous interior features six chapels with one altar each and a beautiful polychrome marble floor. Look for Titian's *Pentecost* across the aisle to the left. Since it was brought from Crete by Francesco Morosini in 1672, the Byzantine icon above the main altar has been venerated as the Madonna della Salute (of Health). (A small-scale silver replica still hangs in many Venetian bedrooms.) To its side is a remarkable sculpture group showing Venice on bended knee, asking the Virgin for protection from the plague, represented as a fleeing old woman. The **Sacrestia Maggiore** contains a wealth of art, including five works by Titian, the best of which are the *Five Saints* altarpiece; a large *Nozze di Canaan* by Tintoretto; and a precious 15th-century *paliotto* (tapestry), made from a drawing in the style of Mantegna (1431–1506) and Bellini on wool, silk, and silver thread that represents the Pentecost against a naturalistic background. A traditional thanksgiving pilgrimage during November's Festa della Madonna della Salute is one of the most evocative Venetian festivals. ⊠ *Punta della Dogana, Dorsoduro* ☎ *041/5225558* 🎫 *Church free, sacristy €1.50* ⊙ *June–Sept., daily 9–noon and 3–6; Oct.–May, daily 9–noon and 3–5:30* Ⓥ *Salute.*

★ ⓯ Scuola Grande dei Carmini. By the time Longhena completed this scuola in the 1670s, the brotherhood of Santa Maria del Carmelo had grown to 75,000 members, making it the largest fraternal order of the period. It was also one of the wealthiest, so little expense was spared in the decorating, which includes stuccoed ceilings, carved ebony paneling, and choice paintings. The real show, however, began in 1739 when the **Sala Capitolare** was entrusted to Tiepolo. Many consider the nine canvases that adorn the vault to be his best work. Using vivid techniques, Tiepolo was able to transform some rather unpromising religious themes into flamboyant displays of color and movement. Mirrors in the rooms may make it easier for ceiling-viewers' necks. ⊠ *Campo dei Carmini, Dorsoduro 2617* ☎ *041/5289420.* 🎫 *€5* ⊙ *Nov.–Mar., 9–4; Apr.–Oct., Mon.–Sat. 9–6, Sun. 9–4* Ⓥ *Ca' Rezzonico.*

SAN POLO & SANTA CROCE
TO SAN MARCO

The smallest of Venice's six sestieri, San Polo and Santa Croce are named after their main churches, though the Chiesa di Santa Croce was demolished in 1810. San Polo, with the Rialto market and the busy shopping streets nearby, is livelier than Santa Croce, where, especially near Piazzale Roma, you might feel removed from the swing of things. Rialto Bridge connects San Polo with the sestiere of San Marco, which stretches from Rialto to the rio beneath Ponte dei Sospiri, and is the part of town considered most fashionable and most expensive to sleep, eat, and shop. San Marco's fairly straight main drag runs between Campo San Bartolomeo, at the foot of the Rialto Bridge, and Campo Santo Stefano, at the foot of Accademia Bridge. Both squares are popular meeting places, with monuments and bars where Venetians break for an espresso and the inevitable *telefonino* (cell phone) chat while waiting for their friends. Between this last campo and Calle Larga XXII Marzo are the Teatro La Fenice and the gloomy network of alleys where Visconti's *Death in Venice* was shot.

After a day spent looking at the sights of San Polo and Santa Croce, which include major attractions such as the Frari and the Scuola Grande di San Rocco, and worthwhile but lesser-known churches and museums such as San Pantalon and Palazzo Mocenigo, it's nice to stroll back to the busy center, stopping along the way for an aperitivo. In Venice ask for a "spritz" (white wine, Aperol or Campari, and soda), Campari (served with soda and a green olive), or *prosecchino,* a short glass of prosecco, either *dolce* (sweet), or *secco* (dry). By request a prosecchino can be prepared with fresh fruit juice.

Numbers in the text correspond to numbers in the margin and on the San Polo and Santa Croce to San Marco map.

a good walk

If you are planning to visit Ca' Pesaro or Palazzo Mocenigo, your best bet is to take vaporetto Line 1 to San Stae. The boat lands at the church of **San Stae** ⑱ ▶, small, white and richly adorned with baroque statues. Signs will direct you over a bridge and down an alley to **Ca' Pesaro** ⑲, where you'll find both the Museum of Modern Art and the Oriental Museum. Walking straight ahead from San Stae landing, you'll arrive at **Palazzo Mocenigo** ⑳, its entrance on Salizzada San Stae. From this palazzo turn right on Calle del Tintor, cross the bridge at Zucca restaurant, and ahead on Calle dello Spezier, you'll zigzag to the small church of **San Zandegolà** ㉑, open to visitors Monday through Saturday 10 to noon. Nearby is **Fondaco dei Turchi** ㉒, home to the Museo di Storia Naturale, which has been under restoration for years with no end in sight. Backtracking along Calle dello Spezier, a right at the bridge leads you to **Campo San Giacomo dall'Orio** ㉓ and its church, **San Giacomo dall'Orio** ㉔. This large and quiet square is a good place to rest. Take Calle del Tintor to Ponte del Parrucchetta, which offers a picturesque view of Campo San Boldo, its ruined bell tower discreetly converted into a block of apartments. Continue down the bridge and make a right onto Calle della Chiesa, which leads to Campo San Stin. A calle angling diagonally to the right from where you enter this campo leads to the superb Renaissance entrance of the **Scuola Grande di San Giovanni Evangelista** ㉕. Pass through this small campo and follow Calle della Laca to a large bridge; turn left instead of crossing. The next bridge will lead you past the school of architecture to the seemingly out-of-place pillared church of **San Nicola da Tolentino** ㉖. A left leaving the church and a second left as the canal branches leads along Salizzada San Pantalon. Before you reach the bridge, turn right and angle your way across tiny, aptly named Campiella Mosca. Just over the small bridge stands **San Pantalon** ㉗; if you happen to come across it when it's open, don't miss a chance to see its incredible ceiling. A left out of the church leads to Calle della Crosera where if you haven't yet walked up a hunger, one glimpse in Pasticceria Tonolo could change your mind. Right around the corner from Tonolo, Calle della Scuola will lead you to the **Scuola Grande di San Rocco** ㉘, lavishly decorated by Tintoretto, and from here you'll be able to see the walls of the imposing Franciscan church of **Santa Maria Gloriosa dei Frari** ㉙, which holds two of Titian's finest paintings. Calle Larga leads out of Campo dei Frari near the left nave and belltower. Ahead is Campo San Tomà, with its closed church on one end and Scuola dei Calegheri (of the shoemakers) on the other. Left of the neoclassical church, over the Ponte di San Tomà, is the birthplace of 18th-century playwright Carlo Goldoni, whose works, written in the Venetian dialect, have been likened to Shakespeare's crowd-pleasing comedies. The house is open to the public. Just beyond, you'll reach one of Venice's largest campi, **Campo San Polo** ㉚, where the church of **San Polo** ㉛ has a remarkable ship's keel roof and its fair share of artwork. Backtrack past Casa Goldoni and follow signs to the traghetto landing at San Tomà, where you can hop a ride across the Grand Canal. Take narrow Calle del Traghetto and turn right to reach Salizzada San Samuele. It leads back toward the Grand Canal to **Palazzo Grassi** ㉜. Italian car maker Fiat acquired this 18th-century mansion in 1984, and now the rococo rooms are the site of some of Europe's most prestigious traveling art exhibitions. Calle Malpiero leads out of Campo San Samuele, and a short maze of backstreets and *sottoportici* (underpasses) will take you to the church of **Santo Stefano** ㉝ in **Campo Santo Stefano** ㉞. This is a good place for a sweet fix: the campo is home to Caffè Paolin, a gelato institution, and Le Café, which serves pastries and other snacks. Take the calle near the church to Campo Sant'Angelo, from where you'll really be able to appreciate just how much San Stefano's bell tower is leaning. Finish your day by visiting, and perhaps climbing, the **Palazzo Contarini del Bovolo** ㉟.

TIMING   The walk by itself would only take about an hour—two hours if you factor in window shopping, meandering, and the obligatory getting lost. Depending on how many of the sights you see, you could while away a pleasant half day to a day. Late starters will miss San Zandegolà and San Giovanni Evangelista, both open only mornings, and those who wish to shorten their tour might choose to omit San Stae, San Polo, and San Nicola da Tolentino. To appreciate both museums in Ca' Pesaro takes a couple hours, as might Palazzo Grassi if there's an exhibit there that catches your interest. Allow at least 40 minutes for the Scuola Grande di San Rocco, more if you are a real Tintoretto fan. The Frari will take another 30 to 40 minutes, and the rest of the churches will need an average of 20 minutes each, with San Pantalon being the most engaging.

What to See

㉓ **Campo San Giacomo dell'Orio.** Perhaps it is fitting that the name of this campo and its church is derived not from some torturous saintly martyrdom, but from the *orio* (laurel tree) that once provided the area shade. Trees today give the pleasantly odd-shaped campo character, and when you add a few benches and a fountain (with drinking bowl for dogs), it becomes a welcoming place for meeting friends, having picnics, and watching neighborhood kids at play. Several streets lead into it at odd angles, and the church sits nicely among the houses rather than towering above them. On the south side of the campo you can cross over the Ponte dell'Anatomia, into secluded Corte dell'Anatomia. Early scientists and students were reputed to hide here when authorities raided

San Polo
& Santa Croce
to San Marco

KEY

► *Start of walk*
▲ *Vaporetto Stop*

their anatomy classes. Although an anatomy theater was officially established here in 1507—some 87 years before the more famous Università di Padua theater opened—itinerant anatomical experiments were taking place in Venice as early as 1368.

30 **Campo San Polo.** Not long ago this campo, second in size only to San Marco, was a throbbing center of activity, hosting shows, bull races, fairs, military parades, and packed markets. Today the activity has dissipated, and children zooming around on bikes and scooters, their voices echoing off surrounding palaces, make San Polo feel even more cavernous. The campo only really comes alive on summer nights, when it hosts the city's outdoor cinema. A stone's throw from the Grand Canal, this neighborhood was settled by some of the richest families of the city. The early 15th-century Palazzo Soranzo (at No. 2170–1) was entirely decorated with frescoes by Giorgione; the baroque building at No. 1957 took the place of the Gothic mansion of the Bernardo family, covered with frescoes by Salviati. The facade of the Renaissance **Palazzo Corner Mocenigo**, facing the canal, is best seen by looking right from Ponte San Polo on the way to the Frari. If you leave the campo through the Sottoportico dei Cavalli (No. 1957), cross the bridge, take a left, and then cross another bridge and take another left, you'll reach the 17th-century **Palazzo Albrizzi**, occasionally open to the public for temporary exhibits. **Ⓥ** *San Tomà.*

34 **Campo Santo Stefano.** Although Venetians steadfastly refer to this campo by its old saint designation, on maps and walls it bears the name of Francesco Morosini (1618–92). Morosini came from a family that had already given the Republic four doges; he became captain of a galley at age 23 and supreme commander of the Venetian navy at 39. Fondly remembered by Venetians as their last great sea hero, he made his mark on the world when in 1687 a cannon under his command fired a direct hit that practically obliterated the Parthenon in Athens, which the Turks had been using as a powder magazine. Elected doge while he was taking the Peloponnese, Morosini returned home to a 125-ft-tall triumphant arch that spanned Piazzetta San Marco. Wine flowed through two enormous fountains, and the Republic placed his bronze bust inside Palazzo Ducale, an honor previously granted only posthumously.

Santo Stefano's doesn't have a statue of Morosini, but there is one of Nicolò Tommaseo (1802–74), an important figure in the rebellion against Austria in 1848. **Ca' Morosini** (at No. 2802–3) was sold after the last heir died in 1884, and the city acquired the family's records and personal effects, which are now in Museo Correr. To the right, **Palazzo Pisani,** once the largest private home in Venice, has been a conservatory of music since 1897 and is closed to the public. A very busy crossroad, this campo is a favorite meeting point for Venetians and visitors. During Carnevale and Christmas it hosts popular outdoor fairs. Ⓥ *Accademia.*

⑲ **Ca' Pesaro.** Designed by Baldassare Longhena in grand baroque style, this impressive mansion was completed in 1710, nearly thirty years after both its commissioner and architect had died. After trading hands several times, the palace was turned over to the city on the condition that it be used to exhibit the works of young Venetian artists. Initially, the **Galleria Internazionale d'Arte Moderna** (Gallery of Modern Art) fulfilled this condition by exhibiting paintings and sculpture from the Biennale, an international art event that, with few interruptions, has taken place in Venice every two years since 1895. Years of acquisitions and donations have turned it into one of Italy's most varied collections of modern art, with works by such artists as Klimt, Kandinsky, Matisse, and Miró. Reopened in 2002 after several years of restoration, the building is well lit and the works are well presented. Ca' Pesaro's upper floors house the **Museo d'Arte Orientale,** (Oriental Art Museum), an assortment of art, garments, armor, and musical instruments from China and Japan. Poor lighting and labeling detract from otherwise interesting exhibits, but the view across neighborhood rooftops is lovely. ✉ *San Stae, Santa Croce 2076* ☎ *041/5240695 Galleria, 041/5241173 Museo Orientale* ◷ *Apr.–Oct., Tues.–Sun. 10–6; Nov.–Mar., Tues.–Sun. 10–5* 🎟 *€5.50 includes both museums; €15.50 Musei Civici pass; €11 includes only Museo Orientale, Ca' d'Oro, Accademia* Ⓥ *San Stae.*

㉒ **Fondaco dei Turchi.** Built in 1225 by an immigrant from Pesaro, this palace was so beautiful that in 1381 it was bought by the Republic. They loaned it to the Duke of Ferrara, from whom it was periodically confiscated in conflicts, and at the same time used it as a hotel for visiting emissaries. Ownership passed through a number of families, until in 1621 it was leased to Turkish merchants, who used it as a warehouse and residence, even installing a mosque and bathhouse.

From the Grand Canal, Fondaco dei Turchi is striking, with its pink and white marble facade and crenellated top. It was the original 19th-century home of Museo Correr but now contains the city's **Museo di Storia Naturale** (Museum of Natural History). Its collections of flora and fauna native to the lagoon and the skeletons of two prehistoric reptiles haven't been seen in some time: it's been closed for years for renovation, and there's no projected date for reopening. In the meantime, you must content yourself with looking upon this lovely building from the vaporetto. ✉ *Salizzada del Fontego dei Turchi, Santa Croce 1730.*

㉟ **Palazzo Contarini del Bovolo.** Easy to miss despite its vicinity to Piazza San Marco, this Renaissance-Gothic palace is accessible only through a narrow backstreet that connects Campo Manin with Calle dei Fuseri.

Built around 1500 by the renowned Contarini family, it was closed for decades in the late 20th century, until structural reinforcement made its striking six-floor spiral staircase (*bovolo* means "snail" in Venetian dialect) climbable again. From the rooftop you can try to identify all of the bell towers you've seen around town. ⊠ *Corte del Bovolo, San Marco 4299* ☎ *041/2702464* 🎫 *€2.50* ⊙ *Apr.–Oct., daily 10–6; Nov.–Mar. weekends 10–4* Ⓥ *Rialto.*

㉜ Palazzo Grassi. Having bought their way into Venetian aristocracy in 1718, the Bolognese Grassi family became the new kids on the Grand Canal block thirty years later, when architect Giorgio Massari began work on their neoclassical palazzo; it was to be the canal's last grand addition. Fiat, Italy's leading auto maker, acquired the palazzo in 1985 and restored it as a venue for temporary art exhibits. Shows in the past have featured artists Picasso, Modigliani, and Balthus, and historical subjects such as the Phoenicians and Etruscans. ⊠ *Campo San Samuele, San Marco 3231* ☎ *041/5231680* ⊕ *www.palazzograssi.it* Ⓥ *San Samuele.*

⑳ Palazzo Mocenigo. So well preserved it looks like a movie set, this palazzo gives a sense of how wealthy families lived in the last years of the Republic. Bequeathed to the city in 1945 by the last surviving Mocenigo heir, the home is richly decorated with polished floors, fabric-covered walls, and glass chandeliers from Murano. The *portego* (entry hall), typical of Venetian palazzi, occupies about one-third of the total floor space; once used for receptions and balls, it now occasionally hosts classical concerts. Sparsely furnished, it's lined with portraits of the seven Mocenigo family doges and other notables. Doors on both sides of the portego open onto bedrooms and salons, where visitors were received with a cup of hot chocolate in the early morning hours after nights typically spent at parties or seated at gambling tables. Furniture and paintings are all original and constitute a permanent exhibit. The mannequins' clothing, lace, fabrics, and accessories on display come from the **Center for the History of Textiles and Costumes** (housed in a wing of the palace) which organizes 15th- to 18th-century thematic exhibits. ⊠ *Salizzada San Stae, Santa Croce 1992* ☎ *041/721798* 🎫 *€6.50; €8 Museums of 18th-Century Culture pass; €15.50 Musei Civici pass* ⊙ *Apr.–Oct., Tues.–Sun. 10–5; Nov.–Mar., Tues.–Sun. 10–4* Ⓥ *San Stae.*

㉔ San Giacomo dell'Orio. Founded according to legend in the 9th century on an island still populated by wolves, the church as it presently stands was built in 1225. Its short, unmatched Byzantine columns survived renovation during the Renaissance, and the church never lost the feel of an ancient pagan temple sheltering beneath its 15th-century ship's keel roof. A religious sense is restored in the sanctuary with large marble crosses surrounded by a bevy of small medieval Madonnas. Above the main alter is one of the few works by Lorenzo Lotto that remained in Venice, *Madonna with Child and Saints* (1546). The sacristies contain several works by Palma il Giovane (circa 1544–1628). ⊠ *Campo San Giacomo dell'Orio, Santa Croce* ☎ *041/2750462 Chorus.* 🎫 *€2; €8 Chorus pass* ⊙ *Mon.–Sat. 10–5, Sun. 1–5.* Ⓥ *San Stae.*

㉖ San Nicola da Tolentino. When San Gaetano da Thiene arrived in Venice in 1528 with a handful of monks and even less cash, he was given a small oratory. Years of contributions allowed the monks to hire Vincenzo Scamozzi (1552–1616), whose projects included Piazza San Marco's Procuratie Nuove, to work on their church from 1591 to 1602. The Corinthian portico with very tall columns was added in the early 18th century and gives character to an otherwise plain building. Also giving it character is the cannonball lodged in the facade, an Austrian souvenir of the siege of 1849. There's so much scrollwork inside that it's hard to tell where stucco ends and similar painted work begins. Most of the artwork is by lesser-known painters. Worth noting are *Charity of St. Lawrence* by Bernardo Strozzi (1581–1644) near the third chapel in the left transept, and *St. Jerome Visited by an Angel* by Giovanni Lys (circa 1597–1630) in the right transept. The interior is too dark to be seen after sundown. ✉ *Fondamenta Tolentino, Santa Croce* ☎ 041/5222160 ⊙ *Mon.–Sat. 8–noon and 5–6:30, Sun. 5–6:30* Ⓥ *Piazzale Roma.*

㉗ San Pantalon. Say the name Pantalon in Venice and most people think of a theater character popular in traditional commedia dell'arte—a greedy old merchant with a hooked nose, a cantankerous personality, and a weakness for *le belle putte* (pretty girls), who love to tease him. This church is named for a very different sort of character, a poor doctor martyred by Roman Emperor Diocletian. Do not come here without a supply of €.50 pieces for the coin-operated lights; this is one of the least illuminated churches in town, and it's open only in the late afternoon.

Put some coins in the slot in the right nave marked *illuminazione soffitto* (ceiling illumination), and out of the darkness emerges the *Martyrdom of St. Pantaleo,* Gian Antonio Fumiani's (circa 1643–1710) colossal (443-sq-m) masterpiece. It's actually made up of 40 separate canvases joined together to look like a large fresco. This technique was not unheard of, but the enormity of the work demanded tremendous mastery of perspective, and consumed the last 24 years of the little-known artist's life. Legend says he fell to his death while applying finishing touches. The **Cappellina del Sacro Chiodo** (Little Chapel of the Holy Nail) holds a splendid *Coronation of the Virgin* by Antonio Vivarini; the custodian sells a book that can help sort out who's who in the picture's dense world of Gothic symbolism. There are also four small works by Paolo Veneziano: *Madonna with Child, Annunciation, Sleeping Virgin,* and *Presentation to the Temple.* Often overlooked in this chapel is a beautiful gilded alabaster carving of the Virgin and Child, dating from the late 1300s by an unknown artist. One of the last works by Veronese, *St. Pantalon Healing a Child,* is in the second chapel to the right. ✉ *Campo San Pantalon, Santa Croce* ☎ 041/5235893 ▧ *Free* ⊙ *Mon.–Sat. 4–6* Ⓥ *San Tomà.*

㉛ San Polo. Founded in the 9th century, the church of San Polo underwent a major reconstruction in the late Gothic period and a neoclassical makeover in the early 1800s. Extensive restoration in the 1930s brought back the wonderful wooden ship's keel roof, as well as the earlier Byzantine window on the facade. The artwork inside is not particularly engaging, as the 19th-century alterations were so costly that the friars had to sell the best paintings in order to pay the bills. Though Giambattista Tiepolo is represented here, his work is outdone by 16 works by his son Giandomenico (1727–1804), including the *Stations of the Cross* in the oratory to the left of the entrance. The younger Tiepolo also created a series of remarkably expressive and theatrical paintings of the saints. Look for the altarpieces by Tintoretto and Veronese, which managed to escape auction. San Polo's sturdy bell tower has remained unchanged through the centuries—don't miss the two lions guarding it, playing with a detached human head. ✉ *Campo San Polo* ☎ 041/2750462 *Chorus* ▧ *€2; €8 Chorus pass* ⊙ *Mon.–Sat. 10–5, Sun. 1–5.* Ⓥ *San Tomà.*

▶ ⑱ San Stae. The most renowned sculptors of the time decorated the facade here, paid with a legacy left by Doge Alvise Mocenigo II, who's buried in the center aisle. San Stae's painting collection is small, but it has one of the best assortments of works by Venice's early 18th-century masters, from Giambattista Tiepolo, Gregorio Lazzarini, and Sebastiano Ricci to the lesser known Giovanni Pellegrini, Giambattista Piazzetta, and Giambattista Pittoni. ⊠ *Campo San Stae, Santa Croce* ☎ *041/2750462 Chorus* 💻 *€2; €8 Chorus pass* 🕙 *Mon.–Sat. 9–5, Sun. 1–5.* Ⓥ *San Stae.*

②⑨ **Santa Maria Gloriosa dei Frari.** St. Francis was still alive when a group

Fodor'sChoice of friars from his order arrived in Venice in 1222. They remained with-
★ out a fixed residence for about 30 years, until the Doge Tiepolo gave
them an abandoned abbey on a vast tract of land in the San Polo sestiere. The Friars replaced the abbey's old church with a newer building
which served them until the huge Gothic temple you see today was completed in the 1400s, culminating a century of work. Known locally as
I Frari, it's believed to have been designed by architect and Franciscan
friar Scipione Bon, also known as Beato Pacifico, whose portrait is in
the right transept beneath his funeral monument.

Abstinence and poverty were fundamental tenets of the Franciscan
order, an austerity that echoes from plain russet-color walls. (Look
closely and you'll find them painted in a faux-brick pattern.) Save for
its richly carved choir stalls, the church was always known for its relative absence of artwork, but paradoxically, I Frari does contain a few
of the most sumptuously brilliant paintings in any Venetian church, including the magnificent Titian altarpieces, which are among the most
dazzling works this prolific artist produced. Visit the sacristy first, to
see Giovanni Bellini's 1488 triptych *Madonna and Child with Saints* in
all its mellow luminosity, painted for precisely that spot. Contrast this
with the heroic energy of Titian's large *Assumption* over the main
altar—painted little more than 30 years later—to appreciate the rapid
development of Venetian Renaissance painting. This work caused a
sensation when unveiled in 1518 and was immediately acclaimed for
its winning combination of Venetian color—especially the glowing
reds—and classical Roman figure style. It was said that this piece raised
Venetian painting to the level of art being produced for the pope. Many
believe Titian made an even greater artistic stride in his subsequent painting, the *Madonna di Ca' Pesaro* (in left nave). It took almost 10 years
to complete and was created for nobleman Jacopo Pesaro in gratitude
for victory over the Turks. Looking at the Madonna, modeled after the
artist's wife who died soon afterward in childbirth, it's hard to appreciate the radical break from convention she represented, but it was unheard of in Titian's time to move the Virgin out of picture center and
portray the surrounding saints as active participants in the scene.

The church lost some of its asceticism when a number of grandiose 19th-
century mausoleums were added. Especially conspicuous is the pyramid-
shaped tomb of sculptor Antonio Canova (1757–1822), with its sleepy
lion (perhaps hinting at Venice's captivity under the Austrians). Opposite this is an equally ponderous monument to Titian, a man so revered
that Venetians exhumed his body from a communal grave used for
plague victims. Conclude your visit with a look at the arrestingly realistic wooden sculpture *St. John the Baptist,* which Donatello made for
the Florentine community in 1438. ⊠ *Campo dei Frari, San Polo*
☎ *041/2728618, 041/2750462 Chorus.* 💻 *€2; €8 Chorus pass*
🕙 *Mon.–Sat. 9–6, Sun. 1–6.* Ⓥ *San Tomà.*

need a break? On a narrow passage between Frari and San Rocco, **Gelateria Millevoglie** (a Thousand Desires; ☎ 041/5244667) has pizza slices, calzones, and gelato so popular it backs up traffic. It's closed in December and January, but the rest of the year it's open 10 AM to midnight, seven days a week.

③③ **Santo Stefano.** The third-largest convent building in Venice after the Frari
and San Zanipolo, the church of Santo Stefano was founded by Au-

gustinian hermits in the 13th century. Perhaps there was something wrong from the very beginning—the church had to be entirely rebuilt in the 14th century, and the story goes that it was reconsecrated six times because of bloodstains that appeared on the ceiling. The church's entrance portal by Bartolomeo Bon is striking, and tall interior pillars make this an excellent example of florid Gothic style. Here you appreciate the Venetian ingenuity in lightening structures that otherwise would have sunk into their muddy foundations: in place of the typically heavy roofs that bore down on static walls, the master shipbuilders of the lagoon envisioned and created a wooden roof shaped like a ship's keel. Three paintings by Tintoretto are on display in the sacristy, and Doge Francesco Morosini (died 1694), the city's most celebrated admiral, is buried beneath a huge marble slab in the main aisle. ⊠ *Campo Santo Stefano, San Marco* ☎ *041/2750462 Chorus* ▨ *€2; €8 Chorus pass* ☾ *Mon.–Sat. 10–5, Sun. 1–5* Ⓥ *Accademia.*

㉑ San Zandegolà. Founded in 1007, this frequently overlooked little church is among the lagoon's oldest. It was dedicated to San Giovanni Decollato (St. John the Beheaded), and many still refer to it by that name. In keeping with the Romanesque style, the church exterior is very simple, but there's great detail inside, with Greek marble columns and remnants of the frescoes that once covered walls and ceiling. For about a century, starting in 1818, the church was closed for worship and used as a warehouse. Restoration initiated in the 1940s revealed many Byzantine frescoes, and as recently as 1993 workmen moving a marble altarpiece for restoration stumbled upon a Gothic fresco of St. Michael the Archangel believed to date back to about 1380. ⊠ *Campo di San Zandegolà, Santa Croce* ▨ *Free* ☾ *Mon.–Sat. 10–noon* Ⓥ *Riva de Biasio.*

㉕ Scuola Grande di San Giovanni Evangelista. Starting from Campo San Stin, two turns bring you to a rather magical Lombardesque marble wall; the great intimidating eagle perched on top signals the sacred territory of the apostle St. John. Founded in 1349 by the powerful brotherhood of St. John the Evangelist, the Scuola Grande was closed by Napoléon and then bought from the Austrian government in 1857 by the Guild of Arti Edificatorie (Guild of Building Arts), which still runs the place. Its lovely facade and front yard are captivating examples of Lombardesque-Renaissance style, and since 1998 the Guild—for the first time in its long history—has opened its doors to the public (for very limited hours, by appointment only). The layout inside suits the standard requirements of any Venetian scuola, whose primary function was to host crowds of petitioners as well as the wealthier members of the fraternal order. The plain, spacious entry hall was meant to welcome the needy. It now contains architectural fragments and sculptures from around town, which were dumped here "for storage" after the suppression of the brotherhood in the 1800s. Note a rare 14th-century sculpture of the beloved *Madonna della Misericordia,* with the faithful gathered beneath her ample mantel; and the Gothic capitals with the pastoral symbol of St. John in Ephesus inserted between the portraits of different praying brothers to signify the intercession of the Apostle. The double flight of stairs, skillfully designed by Codussi, takes care of the narrow space with a simple perspective trick, in which the steps incrementally increase in height, creating the illusion of depth. The engravings on the marble threshold representing the tools of the guild were added in the 20th century. The richer scuole would typically commission the decoration of their main meeting hall, called the **Sala del Capitolo,** from the best available artists. But here, Tintoretto painted only some of the episodes from the *Life of St. John* that cover the walls. Although Tiepolo had discussed redoing the ceiling with the famous architect Massari, the painter left for Spain (where he ultimately died) and the job was eventually given to a group of minor artists. The addition of several extra rooms, the Albergo (sort of a deluxe hostel for pilgrims), and a small chapel, dedicated to the relics of the Holy Cross. The carved pole to the left of the altar was used to carry these relics across town, as you can see in Carpaccio and Gentile Bellini's *Miracles of the Holy Cross* series now hanging in Gallerie dell'Accademia. The scuola's scale-model shows where these paintings originally hung. In the 14th-century painting *Madonna with Child and Saints Peter, John the Baptist, and John,* the most significant work the scuola retained, you'll immediately recognize the headless St. John. Stepping outside, note the stone marker set about waist high into the corner of the courtyard showing the level water reached in the city's 1966 flood. ⊠ *Campiello della Scuola, San Polo 2454* ☎ *041/718234 call ahead* 💰 *Free (donation welcomed)* ☉ *most weekday mornings* Ⓥ *Ferrovia.*

★ ㉘ **Scuola Grande di San Rocco.** The Brotherhood of San Rocco grew up around a French-born medical student who renounced career and wealth to make a pilgrimage to Italy. He dedicated himself to helping plague sufferers and in the process became infected. Legend says that he hid in a forest, and each day a dog brought him bread until he healed miraculously. Upon return to France, he was not recognized by his family and died in prison at age 32, but he'd already planted a seed in Italy and a sect dedicated to San Rocco was recognized by the Republic in 1478. The cult of St. Rocco, invoked against the plagues that decimated Europe, was particularly strong in Venice, and after the grave epidemic of 1576, the saint was made co-patron of the city. Generous donations to the brotherhood led to the construction of a church and one of the most sumptuous scuole in the city.

Apart from being a great example of Venetian Renaissance architecture, the Scuola Grande di San Rocco is famous for a series of more than 60 paintings by Tintoretto that some have referred to as Venice's Sistine Chapel. More mystical and devout than his contemporaries, Tintoretto sought pathos and emotional tension rather than refined brushstrokes. He carried Titian's love of motion and unusual composition to highly dramatic ends: his wall-size *Crucifixion* left even tough-skinned critic Ruskin speechless. The story goes that in 1564 Tintoretto won the competition to decorate the Albergo of the scuola by submitting a finished work—*St. Rocco in Glory* at the center of the ceiling—instead of a sketch. He offered the painting for free "not to win, but to honor St. Rocco" and spent the next 23 years on the cycle of paintings. Start from the Albergo on the first floor, which also houses two intense works on easels attributed to Giorgione and Titian. Then return to the large adjoining hall, where Tintoretto worked from 1576 to 1588, after the scuola agreed to pay him an annual pension for life. On the ceiling are episodes from the Old Testament; the three larger, central subjects are *Moses Striking Water from the Rock to Quench the People's Thirst; The Brazen Serpent* (serpent wrapped around a staff); and *The Fall of Manna.* These represent humanity's three bodily sufferings—thirst, disease, and hunger—which San Rocco and later his brotherhood worked to eliminate. The walls feature New Testament scenes and some conspicuous wood carvings by 17th-century sculptor Francesco Pianta. The mildly satirical, bizarre figures are allegories of the sentiments, such as Fury (the winged youth with the blindfold, flask of wine, and cannon); of activities like Espionage (the man wrapped in a large scarf); and of the arts—symbolized by a bad-tempered Tintoretto, with a bunch of brushes. The eight canvases on the ground floor, conceived when Tintoretto was in his sixties, show his innovative use of light and shadow, which play a key role in the economy of his masterpiece *Flight into Egypt.* The Old and New Testament works were restored in the 1970s, making all the more evident Tintoretto's inventive use of light. ⊠ *Campo di San Rocco, San Polo 3052* ☎ *041/ 5234864.* ⌦ *€5.50* ⊙ *Nov. 3–Mar. 27, daily 10–4; Mar. 28–Nov. 2, daily 9–5:30; last entrance ½ hr. before closing.* Ⓥ *San Tomà.*

need a break? The music may get loud at **Café Noir** (⊠ Calle Crosera, Dorsoduro 3805 ☎ 041/710925), but the sandwiches are good, and buying food gives you discounts on Web surfing. It's open until 2 AM but is closed Sunday. **Pasticceria Tonolo** (⊠ Dorsoduro 3764 ☎ 041/5237209), has been fattening Venetians since 1886. During Carnevale, it's still the best place in town for *fritelle*, fried doughnuts (traditional raisin or cream-filled); during acqua alta, the staff dons rubber boots and keeps working. The place is closed on Monday, and there's no seating anytime.

RIALTO TO CANNAREGIO

Cannaregio's main drag, which is also the longest street in Venice, winds its way parallel to the Grand Canal. Lined with fruit and vegetable stalls near Ponte delle Guglie, quiet shops, gelaterias, and bakeries, the Strada Nova (literally, "New Street," as it was opened in 1871) serves as a pedestrian expressway from the train station to Ca' d'Oro. A number of nightspots, including Venice's only disco, have cropped up along this paved ribbon, which, although bereft of sights itself, is a convenient point of reference while exploring Cannaregio. Seen from above, this part of town seems like a wide field plowed by several long, straight canals that are linked by intersecting straight streets—not typical of Venice, where the shape of the islands usually defines the shape of the canals. But these canals were cut through a vast bed of reeds (hence the name Cannaregio, which means "Reed Place"), and not even the Venetians could overlook such an opportunity to make long, straight thoroughfares. What also sets Cannaregio apart from the rest of the town are its relatively clean canals and a distinct absence of odors you sometimes encounter in other parts of Venice. The daylight reflected off the bright-green canals, wooden boats painted vivid red or blue, and the big sky visible from the fondamente make this a particularly luminous area of town. It's no surprise, perhaps, that Titian and Tintoretto had houses nearby.

Though Cannaregio has noble palaces built along the Grand Canal, the northern part of the sestiere was, and still is, a typical working-class neighborhood, where many *bacari* (wine bars) fill up with old card players every afternoon. The Jewish Ghetto, with its rooftop synagogues, and several striking churches are architectural highlights, while Ca' d'Oro's Galleria Franchetti and the Tiepolo Ballroom in Palazzo Labia add color to your walk.

Numbers in the text correspond to numbers in the margin and on the Rialto to Cannaregio map.

a good walk Start your day at Campo San Bartolomio, guarded by a statue of the good-natured, witty Venetian playwright Carlo Goldoni, responsible for resurrecting the commedia dell'arte, and browse through the lively stalls on the **Ponte di Rialto** ㊱ ▶ as visitors to Venice have done for centuries. Ahead, half-hidden behind heaps of fruit and vegetables in the market area, stands **San Giacometto** ㊲ church. Don't miss the arcade that runs parallel to it, with faded 16th-century ceiling frescoes. Before you dive into the market, head left down Ruga Vecchia S. Giovanni that leads south away from Rialto. Look for a gate on your left marking the entrance to the church of **San Giovanni Elemosinario** ㊳, which is completely devoid of facade because it always leased its outdoor space to vendors. Leaving the church, return to the main street heading right into Campo delle Beccarie, once the butchers' quarter, with the adjoining— and still thriving—*pescheria* (fish market) on Campo della Pescheria. Have a look at the nearby produce stalls facing the Grand Canal. Not long ago, the area between the Rialto Bridge and the pescheria was entirely devoted to food, but as the local population shrunk from 300,000 at the end of World War II to 200,000 in the late '50s, and finally to 60,000 today, souvenir and mask shops moved in. Still, while shops on the San Marco side sell everything that's hip, this side sells everything that's edible. Come early to beat the crowds and bear in mind that "metà kilo" is about a pound and an "etto" is a few ounces. Take the traghetto from the pescheria to Campo Santa Sofia and follow Strada Nova left to **Ca' d'Oro** ㊴, with its collection of antiques and paintings in Galleria Franchetti.

Continuing on Strada Nova toward the train station, you'll pass through Campo della Maddalena (after Ponte Sant'Antonio), where you'll see Venice's only round church, Chiesa della Maddalena, a finely carved Renaissance wellhead, and an impressive block of medieval houses with towering chimney pots. Looking left from Ponte delle Guglie, you can see the Grand Canal and one side of **Palazzo Labia** ㊵, with Tiepolo's celebrated frescoed ballroom (entrance in Campo San Geremia). Turning right after the bridge, stroll along the canal until you come to the church of **San Giobbe** ㊶. This off-the-beaten-track neighborhood offers some relaxing meandering, with one of the city's largest hidden parks and a view of the western lagoon and Ponte della Libertà connecting Venice to the mainland. You can reach the **Jewish Ghetto** ㊷ via Ponte dei Tre Archi, built tall because the canal below was once Venice's most trafficked entryway. Turn right over the bridge and look for Calle del Ghetto Vecchio, with Gam-Gam, Venice's only kosher restaurant, on the corner. This calle leads to Campiello delle Scuole (also called Campiello del Ghetto Vecchio) and to Campo del Ghetto Nuovo, home to some of Europe's oldest synagogues. Here, to the right, is the entrance to the Museo Ebraico. Go over Ponte del Ghetto Nuovo and walk right along the canal. At the first bridge, turn left onto Calle Malvasia. Follow straight ahead over two bridges to the church of **Sant'Alvise** ㊸.

When you leave the church, cross back over the bridge and walk ahead until you reach the first canal. A left on Fondamenta della Sensa leads straight into Campo dei Mori, which gets its name from an Arab warehouse that once stood here. The building's cornerstone carvings are said to be three Arab brothers who came to Venice in 1112. Tintoretto lived down the fondamenta at No. 3399, and his old studio is still used by printing artists today. You can see some of the painter's best works in his parish church, **Madonna dell'Orto** ㊹, which stands across the rio from Campo dei Mori. Walking left as you leave the church, you can look across the canal and see a camel carved in the Arab warehouse. As the fondamenta ends, cross the bridge and continue until the next canal, where you again turn left. Stroll beneath the portico of Gothic Scuola Vecchia della Misericordia and into the Campo dell'Abbazia. Walk around Chiesa di Santa Maria di Valverde to your left, and the fondamenta will lead to a small boat harbor. The building you'll see at the far left-most point is Casino degli Spiriti; rather than a gambling casino, this was a gathering place for men of great minds. (It was also, according to popular lore, a house of ill repute and the sight of more than one suspicious death, and seen at night, its mystery and intrigue are almost palpable.) Cross the bridge at Campo dell'Abbazia and walk alongside the

ODES TO VENICE

SINCE THE EARLY 19TH CENTURY, Venice has been a stop on every sensitive scribe's Grand Tour, and the result has been a centuries-long serenade sung by some of English literature's greats. Lord Byron, for one, was so enchanted that he moved to Venice in 1817, trailed by his literary companion Percy Bysshe Shelley. Charles Dickens, on a break from documenting the social ills of industrial England, visited Venice in 1844, and it seems that he, too, fell head over heels for the city. In a letter to a friend he wrote, "The gorgeous and wonderful reality of Venice is beyond the fancy of the wildest dreamer; it is a thing you would shed tears to see."

Among the other literary giants enticed by Venice were Edith Wharton, George Eliot, Henry James, and Marcel Proust—who came to Venice on a visit with his mother and refused to leave. Mark Twain visited in 1867, and, unlike Proust, failed to be seduced; in Innocents Abroad he dismissed the fabled gondola and gondolier as "the one an inky, rusty old canoe with a sable hearse-body clapped on to the middle of it, and the other a mangy, barefooted gutter-snipe. . . ." In the 20th century, such varied talents as Ernest Hemingway, Erica Jong, and Ezra Pound (who is buried in the cemetery on San Michele) all adored the place. Thomas Mann's 1913 novel Death in Venice is the city's most bittersweet love song.

Exploring Venice's literary past—unlike that of, say, Paris—doesn't require falling in with a circle of bereted bohemians or passing late nights in a smoky coffeehouse. Venice's literati have for the most part been tourists like the rest of us, and the Venice that spurred them to poetic heights is the traveler's Venice, the one that you can see every day. Henry James, who described Venice in Portraits of Place (1883) and Italian Hours (1892), waxed poetic not only about Venice's great monuments, but also its simple street scenes: "it is charming to disembark at the polished steps of a little campo—a sunny, shabby square with an old well in the middle, an old church at one side and tall Venetian windows looking down." Ezra Pound was moved by nothing greater than the play of light on an evening gondola ride: "The prows rose silver on silver, taking light in the darkness."

If Venice inspires you to take pen to paper, you certainly won't be the first, and if it eludes you, you're also not alone. In a letter to a friend, Dickens wrote "with your foot upon its stones, its pictures before you, and its history in your mind, it is something past all writing or speaking of—almost past all thinking of." On the other hand, William Shakespeare set two plays in Venice (the beginning of Othello, and The Merchant of Venice) without ever having set foot here—proof that for some, at least, the Venice of the imagination is inspiration enough.

— Valerie Hamilton

Scuola Nuova della Misericordia, a work of Sansovino that was never quite finished. Take the bridge to your left; straight ahead you'll see one of Venice's only surviving bridges without parapets. It's hard to imagine now, but until the 11th century, Venetians preferred riding horses to walking or rowing, so they built their first bridges flat. Only later were they rebuilt so that boats could pass underneath, and it was centuries before railings were built. This particular bridge leads to a private home, but take the next bridge and turn left at Calle Racchetta to reach Fondamenta Nuova, where you look across at the lighthouse of Murano and the cypress trees of San Michele. On a clear day you can see Burano and Torcello floating in the distance and sometimes even the snow-topped Dolomites towering above the entire lagoon.

You won't be able to miss the elaborately baroque facade of **Gesuiti** ㊺, a church that is truly unique among Venice's rich collection of religious shrines. The bridge on the south end of this campo will connect you to a series of calle that leads to Campo Santi Apostoli, where Strada Nova officially ends. It's not really an end of the road by any means, for if you cross over the tiny bridge you'll notice the main drag continues to San Giovanni Crisostomo church, which houses two remarkable paintings by Sebastiano dal Piombo and Giovanni Bellini. Past the church, take the Sottoportico to the left leading to Corte del Milion—some believe Marco Polo was born here in 1254, but no one can say in which of the three houses. The courtyard takes its name from his nickname, "Milion," because many ridiculed the million different stories he told about his travels to China. While imprisoned by the rival city of Genoa, he dictated some of these stories to his literate cell mate, and the resulting book—which is actually a serious historical document—became famous as *Il Milione*. Cross Ponte Storto to Calle Scaletta, where a right will lead you to Campo San Lio, and you can reach Rialto or the Piazza San Marco in time for sunset.

TIMING Make an early start to beat the crowds that clog the Rialto Bridge and market for most of the day, and try to make it to the Ca' d'Oro around mid-morning. Allow about one hour to see the Galleria Franchetti, then visit San Giobbe before getting an early lunch. If you want to take the guided tour of the Jewish Ghetto's synagogues, make sure you'll be done by 4 o'clock—the churches of Sant'Alvise and the Madonna dell'Orto close at 5. If you are late, the latter is a more engaging site and should be given priority. The rest of the walk, including a visit to the Chiesa dei Gesuiti, will take about an hour. If you are counting on seeing the Tiepolo Ballroom in Palazzo Labia, call ahead to make a reservation.

What to See

39 **Ca' d'Oro.** This exquisite Venetian Gothic palace was once literally a
Fodor'sChoice "Golden House," when its marble traceries and ornaments were em-
★ bellished with pure gold. Created in 1434 by the enamored patrician Marino Contarini for his wife, Ca' d'Oro became a love offering a second time when a 19th-century Russian prince gave it to Maria Taglioni, a celebrated classical dancer who collected palaces along the Grand Canal. The last proprietor, perhaps more taken with Venice than with any of his lovers, left Ca' d'Oro to the city, after having had it carefully restored and filled with antiquities, sculptures, and paintings that today make up the **Galleria Franchetti.** Besides Mantegna's celebrated *St. Sebastian* and other first-rate Venetian works, the Galleria Franchetti contains the type of fresco that once adorned the exteriors of Venetian buildings (commissioned by those who could not afford a marble facade). One such detached fresco displayed here was made by a young Titian for the (now grayish-white) facade of the Fondaco dei Tedeschi, now the main post office. ⊠ *Calle Ca' d'Oro, Cannaregio 3933* ☎ *041/5222349.* ⊠ *€5; €11 includes Accademia and Museo Orientale* ☉ *Tues.–Sun. 8:15–7:15, Mon. 8:15–2; last entry 30 mins. before closing* Ⓥ *Ca' d'Oro.*

45 **Gesuiti.** Extravagantly baroque, this 18th-century church completely abandoned classical Renaissance straight lines in favor of flowing, twisting forms. Its interior walls resemble brocade drapery, and only touching will convince skeptics that rather than paint, the green-and-white walls are actually inlaid marble. Over the first altar on the left, the *Martyrdom of St. Lawrence* is a dramatic example of Titian's feeling for light and movement. ⊠ *Campo dei Gesuiti, Cannaregio* ☎ *041/5286579* ☉ *Daily 10–noon and 3–5* Ⓥ *Fondamente Nuove.*

★ **42** **Jewish Ghetto.** The neighborhood that gave the world the word "ghetto" is today a quiet warren of backstreets that is still home to Jewish institutions, a kosher restaurant, a rabbinical school, and several syna-

Rialto to Cannaregio

KEY
▶ Start of walk
▲ Vaporetto Stop

gogues. Jews may have come to Venice as early as the 11th century, but the first synagogues weren't built, nor was a cemetery founded, until the Askenazim, or Eastern European Jews, arrived in the late 1300s. Over the centuries, Jews would be alternately welcomed and expelled. In return for the right to live and work in Venice, protection in case of war, and religious freedom, the Jews paid increasingly heavier taxes and were forced to lend money at low interest. Throughout the Middle Ages, Rialto's commercial district, as vividly recounted in Shakespeare's *The Merchant of Venice,* depended on Jewish merchants and moneylenders for trade and to help cover ever-increasing war expenses.

Relentless local opposition forced the Senate in 1516 to confine Jews to the periphery of town. An island in Cannaregio was selected, then named for its foundry (*geto* in Venetian), which produced cannon. Gates at the entrance to the neighborhood were locked at night, and boats patrolled the surrounding canals. The first settlers were Central Europeans, whose German accents changed "geto" into "ghetto." They were allowed only to lend money, operate government-controlled pawnshops, trade in textiles, and practice medicine. Jewish doctors were highly respected for their skills and could leave the ghetto at any hour when on duty. Men were required to wear yellow circles stitched on their coats, and women had to wear yellow scarves. Jews were nevertheless safe, and in the 16th century the community grew considerably with refugees from the Near East, southern and central Italy, Spain, and Portugal. The Ashkenazim built their two synagogues, **Schola Grande Todesca** (1528) and **Schola Canton** (1531), on the top floors of adjacent houses. The Levantine Jews were wealthy enough to purchase land on the island across the rio and in 1541 built sumptuous **Schola Levantina,** currently used for worship in winter. A third atticlike synagogue was built by the poor Italian Jews in 1575, its tentative dome barely visible from the campo below. Finally, in 1589, the ghetto became refuge for Sephardic Jews fleeing from Spain. Their **Schola Spagnola** stands just across from Schola Levantina in the Campiello delle Scuole and is used for summer services.

In the early 17th century about 5,000 Jews lived in the ghetto. It had been allowed to expand twice, but still had the city's densest population and consequently ended up with the city's highest buildings (nine stories); notice the slanting apartment blocks on Campo del Ghetto Nuovo. Although the gates were pulled down after Napoleon's 1797 arrival, Jews realized freedom only in the late 19th century with the founding of the Italian state. On the eve of World War II there were about 1,500 Jews left in the ghetto: 247 were deported by the Nazis. Eight returned.

The area has Europe's highest density of ancient synagogues, and visiting them is a unique cross-cultural experience. Though each is marked by the tastes of its individual builders, Venetian influence is clearly evident. Women's galleries resemble theater galleries typical of the times, and some were decorated by artisans who were simultaneously working in local churches. Tours in Italian and English leave hourly from the **Museo Ebraico.** The small but well-arranged museum highlights centuries of Jewish culture with splendid silver Hanukkah lamps and torahs and handwritten, beautifully decorated wedding contracts in Hebrew. You might complete your tour of Jewish Venice with a visit to the **Antico Cimitero Ebraico** (⊠ Ancient Jewish Cemetery, Via Cipro ☎ 041/715359 ☒ €8 ◷ tour Sun. 2:30, call for arrangements Ⓥ Lido–S.M.E.) on the Lido, full of fascinating old tombstones half-hidden by ivy and grass. The cemetery was in use until the end of the 18th century, and the earliest grave dates to 1389. *Museo Ebraico ⊠ Campo del Ghetto Nuovo, Cannaregio 2902/b* ☎ *041/715359.* ⊕ *www.museoebraico.it* ☒ *€3 museum only; €8 museum, synagogues* ◷ *Sun.–Fri., Oct.–May, 10–5:45; June–Sept., 10–6:45. Last hourly tour 5:30 in summer (winter; 4:30 or on Fri. sunset).* Ⓥ *San Marcuola or Guglie.*

---

need a break?

You'll find authentic Venetian refreshment where Calle del Cristo (San Marcuola) crosses Strada Nova. **Enoteca Do Colonne** (☎ 041/ 5240453) stocks dozens of Veneto wines and an array of *cicheti* (snacks) that will dazzle eyes and taste buds. They're closed Saturday, but open all winter, when you shouldn't miss the chance to try *musetto*, a Venetian specialty sausage.

★ ④ **Madonna dell'Orto.** From a campo elegantly parqueted in red brick and white Istrian stone rises an Oriental-style campanile complete with its own cupola. There, captured between earth and sky are the 12 Apostles, hovering upon the facade of this 14th-century church. Though squatly Romanesque and sporting a later pre-Renaissance doorway, Madonna dell'Orto remains one of the most typical Gothic churches in Venice. Built near a busy shipping area that served merchants and pilgrims sailing the often treacherous northern lagoon, it was suitably dedicated to St. Christopher, patron saint of travelers and boatmen. But after a statue that had been in a nearby *orto* (garden) became renowned as a miracle worker, St. Christopher was displaced by the Madonna dell'Orto as the church's namesake. The statue is believed to be the work of Giovanni di Santi, and though years outdoors took their toll on its soft white stone, the faces of mother and child, now displayed inside the **Cappella di San Mauro,** are still captivating.

Tintoretto lived nearby, and this, his parish church, contains some of his most powerful work. Lining the chancel are two huge (45 ft by 20 ft) canvases, *Adoration of the Golden Calf* and *Last Judgment.* In the latter, a dramatic scene of heavenly justice, there hardly seems enough space to contain the flurry of activity. As the holy ascend, converging with the celestial court, the damned are violently swept downward by a wildly gushing river, which uproots trees and piles sinners along the shore to await Charon's boat, sailing in from the flames in the lower right. In glowing contrast to this awesome spectacle is Tintoretto's *Presentation at the Temple* and the simple chapel where Tintoretto and his children, Marietta and Domenico, are buried. Several paintings by Domenico also hang in the church, though the son's work pales alongside that of his famous father. Of a totally different texture and scope than Tintoretto's paintings is the fresh and luminous masterpiece by Cima da Conegliano, *St. John the Baptist and Saints,* which seems to be a concentrated effort to represent peace, both within the soul and in the surrounding world. Finally, the first chapel to the left displays a photographic reproduction of a precious *Madonna with Child* by Giovanni Bellini. The original was stolen one night in March 1993. ✉ *Campo della Madonna dell'Orto, Cannaregio* ☎ *041/2750462 Chorus* 🎫 *€2; €8 Chorus pass* 🕙 *Mon.–Sat. 10–5, Sun. 1–5* Ⓥ *Orto.*

⓿ Palazzo Labia. Once among Venice's showiest 18th-century families, the Labias bought their way into the city's aristocracy. At their palace, boasting facades on two canals and a campo, they were famous for serving meals on golden plates and then throwing them out of the window to the cry of: *"L'abia o no l'abia, sarò sempre Labia"* ("With or without it, I'll always be a Labia")—although it seems that a net strung across the bottom of the canal recovered the plates in time for the next dinner party. Today the palace is the Venetian headquarters of RAI, the Italian national radio and television network. It's hard to imagine a modern broadcasting company set among such baroque splendor, but in Italy it somehow makes sense. The gorgeous **Tiepolo Ballroom,** which after the decline of the Labias was turned into a school and then a laundry room, exhibits the final flowering of Venetian painting: Giambattista Tiepolo's frescoes of *Anthony and Cleopatra,* dressed like noble Venetians of the time, teeming with dwarfs, Barbary pirates, and toy dogs. Note that the palazzo is only open by appointment for limited hours. ✉ *Campo San Geremia, Cannaregio 275* ☎ *041/781277* 🎫 *Free, reservation required* 🕙 *Wed.–Fri. 3–4* Ⓥ *Ferrovia.*

▶ ㊱ Ponte di Rialto (Rialto Bridge). It is rather startling to consider that Venice,
which by the end of the 12th century had already produced its first version of Palazzo Ducale and most of Basilica di San Marco, didn't build a permanent stone bridge across the Grand Canal until the late 1500s. It was not as if there hadn't been a need: earlier there had been an inconvenient toll bridge, replaced in the 13th century by a rickety wooden bridge (which collapsed twice). In the 15th century a larger bridge was built, this time with shops and an open central corridor, but a century later it had deteriorated so badly that the Republic finally gave up on wood. The competition to design the Grand Canal's first stone bridge attracted the best architects, including Michelangelo, Palladio, and Sansovino, but the job went to the appropriately named Antonio da Ponte. His pragmatic design featured shop space and was high enough for galleys to pass beneath; it kept decoration and cost to a minimum at a time when the Republic's coffers were low due to continual wars against the Turks and the opening of oceanic trade routes. A single arcade, more than 91 ft in length, supports two rows of shops selling jewelry, leather, lace tablecloths, and souvenirs, with windows that open onto the central passage. Along the railing you'll find one of the city's most famous views: the Grand Canal vibrant with gondola and motorboat traffic. Ⓥ *Rialto.*

㊲ San Giacometto. Legend says a church was founded here in the 5th century by some of the lagoon's earliest refugees, but this building was probably constructed in the 11th and 12th centuries, the same time as the neighboring market. Doges traditionally paid visits here every Good Friday. Across from the church's front door is a squat marble pedestal where public announcements were read. Beneath the steps to the pedestal stands what people have long referred to as the Rialto *gobbo* (hunchback); the figure is now thought to represent a working man, symbolically bent from the weight of the steps. The conspicuous 24-hour clock has had a horrible reputation for timekeeping since it was installed—it hasn't worked for years. Behind the church is a cross-shaped inscription that entreats merchants to be honest in law, exact in weights and measures, and faithful in contracts. The church is rarely open except for evening concerts. ⊠ *Rialto Market* Ⓥ *Rialto.*

㊶ San Giobbe. Like San Pietro di Castello, Sant'Elena, and San Francesco della Vigna, San Giobbe once marked the city limits, yet even in this peripheral church you'll find the remains of a doge. Cristoforo Moro had San Giobbe built for the poor residents of a nearby hospice, testimony to just how far the Venetian Republic went to protect even its humblest citizens. Begun in Gothic style (note the brick bell tower, the well, and what survives of the cloister) and finished by Pietro Lombardo in the early 1470s, this church is Venice's first example of Renaissance church architecture. A triptych by Antonio Vivarini in the **Sanctuary** is especially worth seeing as is the **Cappella Martini,** with its blue and yellow *majolica* (glazed earthenware) decorations. Jacopo Bellini's *Madonna with Saints* (better known as the *Pala di San Giobbe*) and Carpaccio's *Presentation to the Temple* once hung here, and though efforts were begun in the late 1990s to reclaim them from Gallerie dell'Accademia, they've so far proved futile. They have however revived a long-standing controversy in Italy about the display of artistic masterpieces out of the context for which they were created. In their absence, the best Renaissance picture here is a nativity scene by Gian Girolamo Savoldo (circa 1485–1548). ⊠ *Campo di San Giobbe (near Tre Archi bridge), Cannaregio* ☎ *041/5241889* 🎟 *Free* ☉ *Weekdays 10–noon and 3:30–6; Sat. 3:30–6; Sun. 8–noon.*

㊳ San Giovanni Elemosinario. Intimately bound to Rialto Market, this church has storefronts for a facade and the altars built by market guilds—poultry sellers, messengers, and fodder merchants. During San Giovanni Elemosinario's restoration, workers found frescoes by Pordenone (1484–1539) that had been painted over centuries earlier (as well as the bones of 80 unidentified people). Look for Titian's *St. John the Almsgiver* and Pordenone's *Saints Catherine, Sebastian and Roch,* which were returned after 30 years by Gallerie dell'Accademia, a rarity for Italian museums. ⊠ *Ruga Vecchia S. Giovanni, Rialto* ☎ *041/2750462 Chorus.* 🎟 *€2, €8 Chorus pass* ☉ *Mon.–Sat. 10–5, Sun. 1–5* Ⓥ *San Silvestro or Rialto.*

㊸ Sant'Alvise. Founded by young patrician Antonia Venier in the late 14th century after St. Louis, the bishop of Toulouse, had appeared to her in a dream, the church of Sant'Alvise takes its name from the Venetian dialect version of the saint's name. Three canvases depicting Christ's passion, which Giambattista Tiepolo originally created as a triptych, now hang here separated. The *Ascent to Calvary* in the chancel looks all the more painfully tragic because of its veritable parade of spectators. To the right, the pathos continues with *Crowning with Thorns* and the *Flagellation.* The ceiling's trompe l'oeil, a late-1600s work attributed to Pietro Antonio Torri and Pietro Ricchi, is striking for its use of color and perspective—it seems to break right through the roof. In the back, supported by pillars, is the nuns' *barco* (choir stall), which connected directly to the convent. Below the barco are eight tempera paintings with biblical scenes that Ruskin enthusiastically identified as "baby Carpaccios." However, it turns out Carpaccio truly was little more than an infant at the time they were created; they've now been attributed to Lazzaro Bastiani (active 1449–1512), and the so-called Carpaccio signature identified as a 19th-century forgery. ⊠ *Campo Sant'Alvise, Cannaregio* ☎ 041/ 2750462 *Chorus.* ▨ €2; €8 *Chorus pass* ☉ *Mon.–Sat. 10–5, Sun. 1–5.* Ⅴ *Sant'Alvise.*

CASTELLO ALTO

Castello, Venice's largest sestiere, includes all of the land from east of Piazza San Marco to the city's easternmost tip. Its name probably comes from a fortress that once stood on one of the eastern islands. Venetians divide the sestiere into Castello Basso (low), the southernmost area following Riva dei Sette Martiri to Sant'Elena, and Alto (high), which runs along the northern shore of Fondamente Nuove, with its eastern edge at Arsenale and its western along Piazza San Marco. Roughly speaking, the low-numbered addresses are in Castello Basso and higher numbers in Castello Alto. Not every well-off Venetian family could afford to build a palazzo on the Grand Canal. Many that couldn't instead settled in Castello Alto, taking advantage of its proximity to the Rialto and San Marco, and built the noble palazzi that today distinguish this neighborhood from the fishermen's enclave in the adjacent streets of Castello Basso.

Castello Alto isn't lacking in colorful history. In the early 15th century, large Greek and Dalmatian communities moved into the area along the Riva degli Schiavoni, where many of them sold dried fish and meat; the Confraternity of San Marco, based in what is now the hospital on Campo Santi Giovanni e Paolo, was patronized by Venetian high society in the 16th to 18th centuries; and nearby Campo Santa Maria Formosa served as a popular open-air theater for shows of various kinds, some involving bulls, until Napoléon conquered the Republic. When 12th-century Doge Michiel's diplomatic trip to Byzantium resulted in nothing but a plague (which had already decimated his crew and proceeded to infect the city), the general assembly turned against him and the public called for blood. Michiel fled for the safe haven of Castello Alto's San Zaccaria Church but was killed before he could get there. His assassin, though acting out the will of the people, was executed nonetheless, and orders were given to raze not only the killer's home, where he hid after the crime, but the entire neighborhood along Calle delle Rasse. This 1172 edict prevented any permanent construction in the area until 1948; you can't help but notice one part of the Danieli Hotel is too modern to blend in with the surroundings.

Numbers in the text correspond to numbers in the margin and on the Castello Alto map.

A Good Walk

Start your day in front of Chiesa della Pietà, along the water east of Piazza San Marco. The calle to its right leads you into the areas originally settled by immigrants from Greece and Dalmatia. The church of **San Giorgio dei Greci** 46 ⌐ and the **Museo dei Dipinti Sacri Bizantini** 47 pay homage not only to the Greek Orthodox tradition, but also to the Serenissima's tradition of tolerating, even welcoming, newcomers. Leaving the museum, turn right onto Salizzada dei Greci, cross the Rio della Pietà, and follow the canal left to the **Scuola di San Giorgio degli Schiavoni** 48, where you'll find nine remarkable works by Carpaccio, whose shades of red gave the owner of Harry's Bar the name for his famous *carpaccio* (marinated, thinly sliced raw beef). A left leaving the scuola leads into Campo delle Gate, and a left leaving the campo's opposite end will put you on Salizzada delle Gate. When its name changes to San Francesco you've almost reached the church of **San Francesco della Vigna** 🟤. Behind its somewhat stern Palladian facade are quiet, peaceful cloisters. Follow Calle San Francesco west to a small canal; while crossing the bridge of Santa Giustina, look right to see the island of San Michele. Walk through a campo, then follow Calle del Cafetier as it becomes Barbaria delle Tole. Here you'll pass the ornate facade of Ospedaletto before arriving at one of Venice's truly grand campi, **Campo Santi Giovanni e Paolo** 🟤 with its magnificent basilica of **Santi Giovanni e Paolo** 🟤, referred to by locals as San Zanipolo. You'll be right in front of the equally impressive **Scuola Grande di San Marco** 🟤, which couldn't be a better disguise for the city hospital, or its little-known Medical Museum. Leaving the campo with your back to the main church door, you'll cross three bridges to arrive at the fairy-tale church of **Santa Maria dei Miracoli** 🟤, a marble jewel worth returning to under moonlight.

After lunch, you can catch San Zanipolo when it reopens if you've missed it, or visit **Ospedaletto** 🟤 and its Sala della Musica (open only three afternoons a week). Calle dell'Ospedaletto, nearly opposite the building, crosses a bridge and becomes one of the narrowest alleys in town. You'll cross one more bridge before bearing right as Calle Lunga Santa Maria Formosa, which leads to the white marble church of **Santa Maria Formosa** 🟤. Just behind the church is the bridge leading to **Querini-Stampalia** 🟤, a palazzo and gallery that stays open late to host concerts on weekends. Walk along Rio del Mondo Nuovo, which runs along the right side of the church, and cross it at Calle del Paradiso. The name of this street, lined with some of the oldest houses in Venice, refers to the splendid *luminarie* (decorative lights) once displayed here on Good Friday. Note the tilting Gothic arch over the bridge, and the well-preserved wooden *barbacani* (buttresses) running along the walls of the buildings, an architectural scheme to enlarge rooms. Turn left onto Salizzada San Lio, then right at the dead end, and cross the canal over Ponte della Guerra. There should be time left to end your walk with a visit to **San Zaccaria** 🟤, a church that's half-Gothic, half-Renaissance. It features a 10th-century, water-logged crypt with the bones of eight early doges as well as one of Giovanni Bellini's most impressive works.

TIMING   You will need to budget a full day and get an early start, for although the walking time is no more than 1½ hours, there is a lot to see. San Giorgio dei Greci and Carpaccio's paintings at the Scuola di San Giorgio degli Schiavoni are worth a long look. San Francesco della Vigna, with its comforting cloister, is a 30-minute stop. Santi Giovanni e Paolo and San Zaccaria are both closed during lunch hours, but Santa Maria dei Miracoli and Santa Maria Formosa are open, as is Querini-Stampalia, which has a café on the premises. You can spend about an hour visiting the museum after lunch, then make a short backtrack to Santi Giovanni e Paolo, and be right on time for Ospedaletto.

What to See

🟤 **Campo Santi Giovanni e Paolo.** This large, attractive square is the site of three city landmarks: the imposing namesake Gothic church; the Scuola Grande di San Marco, with one of the loveliest Renaissance facades in Italy; and the only equestrian monument ever erected by La Serenissima. The rider, Bartolomeo Colleoni, served Venice well as a *condottiere*, or mercenary commander—the Venetians preferred to pay others to fight for them on land. When he died in 1475, he left his fortune to the city

Castello Alto

KEY

▶ Start of walk
▲ Vaporetto Stop

0 _____ 1/8 mile
0 _____ 1/8 km

on the condition that a statue be erected in his honor "in the piazza before San Marco." The Republic's shrewd administrators coveted Colleoni's
ducats but had no intention of honoring anyone, no matter how valor-
ous, with a statue in Piazza San Marco. So they collected the loot, commissioned a statue by Florentine sculptor Andrea del Verrocchio
(1435–88), and put it up before the Scuola Grande di San Marco,
which, before becoming part of the city hospital, was headquarters of
a powerful fraternal order.

need a break? Baking and catering since 1879, the **Rosa Salva** family today has
several outposts bearing their name scattered around Venice. Visit
their bar in Campo Santi Giovanni e Paolo (☎ 041/5227949) for
pastries and coffee or homemade gelato.

47 **Museo dei Dipinti Sacri Bizantini** (Museum of Sacred Byzantine Painting).
Housed in the former hospital of Baldassare Longhena's Scuola di San
Nicola dei Greci, this rich post-Byzantine collection is one of a kind in
Europe. Though at first glance the icons may seem identical in color and
style, careful inspection reveals a variety of subjects. Elegantly gilded
Madonnas date back to the 14th century. Several Last Judgment scenes
elaborately detail the poor sinners' fates. Other Biblical scenes include
Theodore Poulakis's whimsical 17th-century depiction of Noah's ship-
mates arriving for their cruise. ⊠ _Scuola di San Nicola dei Greci (near
Ponte dei Greci), Castello 3412_ ☎ _041/5226581_ ⊠ _€4_ ⊙ _Mon.–Sat.
9–12:30 and 1:30–4:30, Sun. 9–5_ Ⓥ _San Zaccaria._

54 **Ospedaletto.** This 16th-century "little hospital" (as the name translates)
was one of four church foundling homes, each of which had an orchestra
and choir of orphans. Entering through the church of **Santa Maria dei**

Derelitti (St. Mary of the Destitute), you'll see a large gallery built for the young musicians. The orphanage is now a home for the elderly, but its beautiful 18th-century **Sala della Musica** (Music Room), the only one of its kind to survive, has been carefully restored. On the far wall, Jacopo Guarana's (1720–1808) fresco depicts Apollo, god of music, surrounded by the orphan musicians and their conductor, Pasquale Anfossi. ✉ *Calle Barbaria delle Tole, Castello* ☎ *041/2702464* 💶 *€2* ⊙ *Thurs.–Sat. 3:30–6:30* Ⓥ *Fondamente Nuove.*

★ **56** **Querini-Stampalia.** Home to the venerable Querini family for centuries, this Renaissance palace now contains a library and a fine collection of Venetian art. Highlights include Giovanni Bellini's *Presentation in the Temple,* and Sebastiano Ricci's triptych *Dawn, Afternoon, and Evening.* Portraits of newlywed Francesco Querini and Paola Priuli were left unfinished by the death of Palma Il Vecchio in 1528 (note the groom's hand and the bride's dress). The home's original 18th-century furniture and stucco work are a fitting background for Pietro Longhi's period portraits. Not mentioned among artist stars, Gabriele Bella (1730–99) captured Venetian streetlife in a style more resembling that of a photojournalist than painter; his nearly 70 works displayed here tell stories beyond the Republic's pomp and parades. Museum admission on Friday and Saturday includes evening concerts performed on antique instruments at 5 and 8:30. The library is open only for research. ✉ *Campo Santa Maria Formosa, Castello 5252* ☎ *041/2711411.* ⊕ *www.querinistampalia.it* 💶 *€6* ⊙ *Tues.–Thurs. and Sun. 10–6; Fri. and Sat. 10 AM–10 PM* Ⓥ *San Zaccaria.*

> **need a break?** Florian Art e Caffè (✉ Campo Santa Maria Formosa ☎ 041/ 5206675), inside Querini-Stampalia, is an offshoot of the famed San Marco café and offers a way to enjoy Florian hospitality without paying uptown prices. Drinks, specialty pastries, and full lunches are available every day except Monday.

★ **49** **San Francesco della Vigna** (St. Francis of the Vineyard). Legend says this is where an angel awakened St. Mark the Evangelist with the famous words, "Pax tibi Marce Evangelista meus" (Peace to you Mark, my Evangelist), which became the motto of the Venetian Republic. The land was given in 1253 to the Franciscans, who kept the vineyard but replaced the ancient church with a new one dedicated to St. Francis. Nearly three centuries later the Franciscan church was enlarged and rebuilt by Sansovino in 1534. Be sure to come here with a pocket full of coins—you'll need them to illuminate the surprising artwork inside. Antonio Vivarini's (circa 1415–84) triptych of Saints Girolamo, Bernardino da Siena, and Ludovico hangs to your right as you enter the main door. Giovanni Bellini's *Madonna with Saints* is down some steps to the left, inside the Cappella Santa. The glittering gold *Madonna Adoring the Child* by Antonio da Negroponte, near the church's side door, is an inspiring work that invites contemplation. Painted in the second half of the 15th century, this masterpiece marks the transition from Gothic style, of which it preserves a certain formal rigidity, to the Renaissance style revealed in its elaborately detailed decoration and naturalistic subjects. Two pretty cloisters open out from the left nave, their pavement constructed entirely of tombstones of patricians, admirals, and cardinals, testimony to San Francesco della Vigna's former popularity among noble Venetians. ✉ *Campo di San Francesco della Vigna, Castello* ☎ *041/5206102* 💶 *Free* ⊙ *8–12:30 and 3–7* Ⓥ *Celestia.*

▶ **46** **San Giorgio dei Greci.** With the fall of the Byzantine Empire in 1453, Venice's Greek Orthodox community grew considerably with refugees fleeing the Turks. La Serenissima allowed them to found a fraternal order and a scuola, and a papal bull entitled them to build a church in the 16th century to celebrate their own rites. Over the centuries, the scuola became the richest and most important center of Greek Orthodoxy in the Western world, before losing its property when Napoléon conquered Venice. The interior of the church of San Giorgio is luminously gold, its walls covered by intense icons and mosaics. These are mostly the work of little-known 17th-century artists from Crete, whose figurative style has been passed down to the workshops of the monks of Mt. Athos. Among the images of saints, madonnas, and prophets, it is the extremely rich yet subtle iconostasis with a large *Annunciation* mosaic that draws your attention. The second focal point of this jewel box of a church is the stunning ceiling fresco by 16th-century artist Giovanni di Cipro, representing a tidy *Last Judgment* with Christ the Pantocrator at the center surrounded by scenes of *Preparation of the Throne* (first ring), *Apostles and Angels* (second ring), and *Prophets* (third and largest ring). ⊠ *Ponte dei Greci, Castello 3412* ☎ *041/5226581* ⬚ *Free* ⊙ *Wed.–Mon. 9–1, 2:30–4:30* Ⓥ *San Zaccaria.*

★ ❺⓻ **San Zaccaria.** When 12th-century doge Giustiniano Partecipazio payed a visit to Constantinople as a gesture of submission, Emperor Leo V was so pleased by the visit that he presented Venice with the remains of St. Zachary, father of St. John the Baptist. Leo went even further when he sent along a group of masons, decorators, *scalpellini* (stonecutters), and mosaic artists to build a church dedicated to the saint. The adjacent Benedictine convent quickly became the richest—and least chaste—in the city. This was the convent where girls whose families couldn't afford marriage dowries ended up, by misfortune rather than choice or devotion. San Zaccaria always enjoyed the protection of the doge, who attended Easter Mass here every year. The tilted square bell tower dates from the 13th century.

The striking Renaissance facade, with central and upper portions representing some of Codussi's best work, is only the last chapter in the long story of the building, which features a coronet of four chapels instead of the apse—a Gothic layout typical of the great northern European cathedrals but unusual for Italy. Where the apse of the original church once was there's now a crypt, with tombs of eight of the earliest doges. Be sure to bring with you a pocket full of €.50 coins, which you'll need to turn on the lighting for the major artwork. Giovanni Bellini's celebrated altarpiece is easily recognizable in the left nave. It portrays one of the artist's best Madonnas, this time in the company of an angel playing an ancient viola and four very silent saints. Ask the custodian to show you to the **Cappella di Sant'Atanasio,** also called Cappella del Coro, to see a copy of the magnificent choir stalls that once belonged to the church of Sant'Elena in Castello Basso. The five gilded chairs on the right were used by the doge and his entourage during his annual visit. The **Cappella di San Tarasio** displays frescoes by Tuscan Renaissance artists Andrea del Castagno (1423–57) and Francesco da Faenza (circa 1400–1451). The three outstanding Gothic polyptychs attributed to Antonio Vivarini earned it the nickname "Golden Chapel." From here, you might want to descend to the spooky crypt, as long as the tide is low and it's not flooded. ⊠ *Campo San Zaccaria, 4693 Castello* ☎ *041/5221257* ⬚ *Church free, chapels and crypt €1* ⊙ *Mon.–Sat. 10–noon and 4–6, Sun. 4–6* Ⓥ *San Zaccaria.*

❺❸ **Santa Maria dei Miracoli.** Tiny, yet perfectly proportioned, this early Renaissance gem has a marble-sheathed exterior and inside is decorated with exquisite marble reliefs. Architect Pietro Lombardo (circa 1435–1515) seems to have compressed Miracoli into its confined space and then made it look bigger through various optical illusions: the varied color of the marble exterior creates the effect of greater distance; extra pilasters make the building's canal side looks longer than it is; offsetting the arcade windows makes the arches appear deeper. From Ponte dei Miracoli you can appreciate how the church actually hangs out over a rio.

The church was built in the 1480s to house Nicolò di Pietro's 1408 painting of the Virgin Mary, *I Miracoli* (look for it on the high altar), which is said to perform miracles. At one time it was Venice's most important shrine to the Virgin Mary, celebrating more than 40 masses daily. The church's only other paintings are on the coffered ceiling, but if you're here when afternoon sun filters through the large round window, the marble decoration seems to come alive with soft pink shades. The immaculate flight of stairs leading to the altar's holy icon is a favored Venetian wedding stage. On the parapet are four small, detailed sculptures by Tullio Lombardo (1455–1532), among them *Saint Francis* and *Santa Chiara*, both known for their devotion to the Madonna. ⊠ *Campo Santa Maria Nova, Cannaregio* ☎ *041/2750462 Chorus.* ⊡ *€2; €8 Chorus pass* ☉ *Mon.–Sat. 10–5, Sun. 1–5* Ⓥ *Rialto.*

need a break? Grab an outdoor table at **Bar ai Miracoli** (⊠ Campo Santa Maria Nova ☎ 041/5231515) and gaze across the canal at Maria dei Miracoli, Lombardo's miracle in marble.

⑤⑤ Santa Maria Formosa. Directed by his vision of a beautiful Madonna, 7th-century St. Magno followed a small white cloud and built a church where it settled. Gracefully white, the marble building you see on the same spot today dates from 1492, when Mauro Codussi grafted it onto the 11th-century foundations of the church that had replaced Magno's original. The interior is an architectural blend of Renaissance decoration and Codussi's Byzantine cupola, barrel vaults, and narrow-columned screens. Of interest are two fine paintings: Bartolomeo 's *Madonna of the Mercy,* sheltering a group of petitioners under her cloak, and Palma Il Vecchio's *Santa Barbara,* the patron saint of gunpowder. Outside, the surrounding square bustles with sidewalk cafés and a produce market on weekday mornings. ⊠ *Campo Santa Maria Formosa, Castello* ☎ *041/ 5234645, 041/2750462 Chorus* ⊡ *€2; €8 Chorus pass* ☉ *Mon.–Sat. 10–5, Sun. 1–5* Ⓥ *Rialto.*

★ ㊑ Santi Giovanni e Paolo. While Franciscan friars were laboring away on Santa Maria Gloriosa dei Frari in San Polo, the Dominicans were similarly busy in Castello. Some say San Zanipolo, as the church here is commonly called, is better proportioned and more luminous than the Frari, and it is the only church in Venice to have benefited from the work of the glass masters of Murano. The 15th-century stained glass window near the side entrance is breathtaking for its brilliant colors and beautiful figures, made from drawings by Bartolomeo Vivarini and Gerolamo Mocetto (their signatures appear near St. Theodore). The second official church of the Republic after San Marco, this is the Venetian equivalent of London's Westminster Abbey, with a great number of important people, including 25 doges, buried here. Artistic highlights include an outstanding polyptych by Giovanni Bellini (right nave, second altar), Alvise Vivarini's *Christ Carrying the Cross* (sacrestia), and Lorenzo Lotto's *Charity of St. Antonino* (right transept). Don't miss the *Cappella del Rosario* (Rosary Chapel), off the left transept. It was built in the 16th century to commemorate the 1571 victory of Lepanto in western Greece, when Venice led a combined European fleet to defeat the Turkish navy. The chapel was devastated by a fire in 1867 and restored in the early years of the 20th century with works from other churches, among them the sumptuous Veronese ceiling paintings.

However quick your visit, be sure to see the tomb Pietro Mocenigo, to the right of the main entrance, a monument built by the ubiquitous Pietro Lombardo and his sons. Also worth seeking out is the sepulchre of Doge Michele Morosini, in the choir, which was described by Ruskin as "the richest monument of the Gothic period in Venice." Oddities include a foot of St. Catherine of Siena and an urn containing the skin of commander Marcantonio Bragadin, tortured and flayed alive by the Turks during the siege of Cyprus in 1571. ⊠ *Campo Santi Giovanni e Paolo, Castello* ☎ *041/5235913* ⊠ *Free* ⊙ *Mon.–Sat. 7:30–12:30 and 3:30–6, Sun. 3:30–6.* Ⓥ *Fondamente Nuove or Rialto.*

★ ㊽ **Scuola di San Giorgio degli Schiavoni.** Founded in 1451 by the Dalmatian community, which still owns it today, this scuola served as a social and cultural headquarters for migrants who crossed the Adriatic Sea from what is now Croatia. The small scuola is lavishly decorated, yet somehow unpretentious and harmoniously balanced. Not well known outside Venice, where he spent all his life, Vittore Carpaccio painted devotional *teleri* (large narrative canvases of legendary and religious scenes) against a background of Venetian architecture. He combined observation with fantasy, a sense of warm color with a sense of humor (don't miss the body parts in the dragon's lair). In Scuola di San Giorgio, Carpaccio concentrated on three saints especially venerated in Dalmatia: St. George, St. Tryphone, and St. Jerome. The two paintings to the left and the one opposite the entrance tell the story of St. George, who was passing through Selene (in Libya) when he found a beautiful virgin princess had been offered as a sacrifice to a dragon. The exuberant *St. George Charging the Dragon* is a contrast to the more somber baptism of the king and queen—St. George wouldn't slay the dragon until the royals became Christians. In the central painting, the saint stands triumphantly over his adversary, while the king and queen, with their newly freed princess, look on. The fourth painting shows the child St. Tryphone freeing the emperor's daughter from the devil. Paintings five and six are called, respectively, the *Agony in the Garden* and the *Calling of St. Matthew.* The remaining three teleri are dedicated to St. Jerome, who in the seventh painting is about to take a thorn out of the lion's paw while monks flee in terror. The *Funeral of St. Jerome* and the *Vision of St. Augustine* follow. This last work—especially vivid in detail—is the faithful representation of the "office" of a 15th-century humanist. Augustine is writing a letter to his dear friend Jerome, when the latter appears and delivers the news that he'd died and gone to heaven.

The adjoining small room displays old garments and other objects used by the brotherhood. The first floor features many portraits of brothers and sisters. Try to visit in the morning, as the fraternal order sometimes closes the church in the afternoon for its own use. ⊠ *Calle dei Furlani, Castello 3259/a* ☎ *041/5228828* ⊠ *€3* ⊙ *Apr.–Oct., Tues.–Sat. 9:30–12:30 and 3:30–6:30, Sun. 9:30–12:30; Nov.–Mar., Tues.–Sat. 10–12:30 and 3–6, Sun. 10–12:30* Ⓥ *San Zaccaria.*

㊾ **Scuola Grande di San Marco.** Where else but in Venice will you find a city's main public hospital with a Lombardo marble facade? The building started out as a scuola in 1260 and became one of the city's six *scuole grandi* (a term applied to Venice's most wealthy confraternities, which took on the responsibility of caring for some of the city's poorest residents). Fire destroyed a substantial part of it in 1485, and though much of the remainder is closed to the public, it's worth a look behind the striking facade at the ballroomlike main entry. Also in the scuola is the **Medical Museum**—not for the young or squeamish, but adults, especially those in the medical professions, are likely to find the displays entertaining and enlightening. Itinerant anatomical experimenting was going on in Venice as early as 1368, some 100 years before Venice founded a reputable anatomical theater and more than 200 years before the famous Università di Padua theater opened. The elaborately illustrated books on display perfectly depict not only complex anatomy, but also some of the clandestine, backwoods operating theaters. There's a collection of tools of the trade that, lacking specific labeling, often seem less therapeutic than torturous. To find the museum, walk through the main hospital entrance, past the front desk, through the lobby, and go up the stairway on the right-hand side. (You can also ask the doorman for directions.) ⊠ *Campo San Giovanni e Paolo, Castello* ☎ *041/5294323* ▣ *Free* ☉ *Weekdays 8:30–2.*

CASTELLO BASSO

Until about 100 years ago, the neighborhood of Castello Basso was occupied by fishermen, lace artisans, pearl stringers, and shipbuilders who worked at the Arsenale. Nobles never chose this area for their palaces, nor have today's designer boutiques and souvenir shops chosen to infiltrate. Castello Basso is a chance to see Venice unmasked, with its laundry hanging across narrow streets and its butchers and bakers going about their business. Early in the evening, the neighborhood around Via Garibaldi, the city's widest street, is a vision of Venetians conducting their daily lives: kids too young to ride scooters or play tag are pushed in carriages, men prop up one bar or another, and elderly ladies hold forth on park benches.

The large eastern quarter, known as Sant'Elena, was once an island hermitage. As its church grew, so too did the island by repeatedly building then backfilling new, more distant bulwarks. It was further enlarged by the Austrians in the 19th century to create a parade ground for staging military exercises. Continuing military tradition, this is now home to the Italian Navy's Morosini Naval Military School. It's also the home of Venice's soccer team, which has bounced into and out of the Italian League's first division so often that even fans have trouble keeping track. The football stands look more like temporary scaffolding than anything that should be trusted to support 10,000 fans. Plans for a new facility near Mestre on the mainland have blossomed and subsequently wilted.

The presence of trees and the relative scarcity of bridges and canals makes a visit to Sant'Elena seem almost like a walk on the mainland. During Austrian occupation, its open spaces became a favorite Sunday retreat for Venetians who didn't happen to have country villas. The 1920s Fascist government enlarged the islands by building upon refuse dumps and turned it into working-class, residential housing. You'll notice how relatively modern some of the buildings look and how the streets, instead of being calle, are called *viali*, as in other Italian towns. A small monument amid a breezy pine grove recalls a disaster that struck the area on a warm September afternoon in 1970, when the sky blackened suddenly and a tornado uprooted trees, tore off roofs, and capsized a vaporetto, killing 89 passengers.

Numbers in the text correspond to numbers in the margin and on the Castello Basso map.

a good walk

Starting from Piazzetta San Marco, cross Ponte della Paglia near Palazzo Ducale and continue along Riva degli Schiavoni—Venetian dialect for the people who came from Schiavonia, the Dalmatian coast of today's Croatia. Its wide promenade, crowded with vendors, is popular with Venetians and tourists alike for the evening *passeggiata* (stroll). At **Chiesa della Pietà** 58 ▶, stop in to see the collection of baroque musical instruments, which includes a violin that once belonged to Antonio Vivaldi. Crenellated facades mark the 15th-century naval bakery and bread storehouse between Calle dei Forni and Ponte dell'Arsenale. Until 1936, this bridge opened so ships could enter Arsenale. Beyond it is the **Museo Storico Navale** ㊾, and though it may not do justice to the Venetian Republic's rich, maritime history, its collection of modern and ancient ship models is certainly worth a visit. Continuing along the waterside promenade, circle around Gardini before crossing a bridge into the pine grove of Sant'Elena, officially called the Parco delle Rimembranze. Take the main boulevard through the park; directly ahead, across a small canal, is Morosini Scuola Militare Navale, which though not open to the public, has an interesting lion perched on its gate. Walk left along the canal and take the next bridge, which leads to the church of **Sant'Elena** ㉖. Leaving the church, a right turn brings you alongside the rather rickety-looking soccer stadium and then to the small boat harbor of Diporto Velico, where you can look across to the area where vaporetti are hauled out for repairs. A winding course through backstreets and over bridges (Via Calle del Pasubio, Paludo Sant'Antonio, San Giuseppe, and Fondamenta Sant'Anna) leads to the island of **San Pietro di Castello** ㉑, Venice's first Cathedral. After visiting the church, stroll back across the bridge and straight ahead to Via Garibaldi, where you can mingle with the locals and have a snack and a drink at one of several unpretentious bars with outdoor tables. Fondamenta della Tana runs parallel to Via Garibaldi on the side opposite the gardens. A small bridge will lead you directly to **Arsenale** ㉒, with a veritable pride of lions guarding its mighty gateway. From here, head to Campo Bandiera e Moro, walking past the church of San Martino, and visit the late-Gothic **San Giovanni in Bragora** ㉓, with a wonderful painting by Cima da Conegliano.

TIMING On a fine day this walk makes a very scenic wander that's not too heavy on sights. Allow a full morning if you want to include the Museo Storico Navale (which adds an hour). After lunch at a nearby restaurant or a quick snack from one of the several bars in Via Garibaldi, you can have a sit-down coffee or gelato along the Riva, and then spend the rest of the afternoon visiting the Giudecca and the Isola di San Giorgio, where from atop the bell tower you have a panoramic view of the buildings and domes you walked past in the morning.

What to See

★ ☺ ㉒ **Arsenale.** The immense Arsenal dockyard was founded, according to tradition, by Doge Falier in 1104 and was built up considerably throughout the 16th century. For a republic founded on sea power, having a huge, state-of-the-art shipyard was of paramount importance, and this one was legendary for its size and efficiency. Galleys 200 ft long were built here, capable of carrying 300 tons of ginger, pepper, silk, and silver. Until the middle of the 16th century, when slaves began to be used in the galleys, the crew was made up of men who volunteered in exchange for an opportunity to amass pounds of precious merchandise from ports all around the Eastern Mediterranean, to be resold if they survived the perils of the trip. With 16,000 "Arsenalotti" on the payroll, a perfectly armed warship could be built in just 12 hours; 100 ships were built in 60 days in 1597 for the battle against the Turks at Cyprus. After that war, the old Venetian word *arzanà* (from the Arabic *darsina'a*, meaning workshop) was adopted by another 14 languages. Dante visited the shipyards several times, and the half-naked bodies of the workers, armed with pitches and boiling tar, inspired his vision of the seventh plane of Hell for his *Inferno*.

The impressive Renaissance **gateway** (1460) is guarded by four lions, war booty of Francesco Morosini, who took the Peloponnese from the

Turks in 1687. The 10-ft-tall lion to the left has had a 2,000-year career standing sentinel, beginning in a harbor near Athens. Experts say
its mysterious inscription is Scandinavian runic "graffiti" left by one of
the Viking mercenaries hired by the Byzantine emperor to suppress
11th-century revolts in Piraeus. If you look at the winged lion above
the doorway, you'll notice that the Gospel at his paws is open but lacks
the customary *Pax* inscription; praying for peace perhaps seemed inappropriate above a factory that manufactured weapons.

Modernization under the Austrians and the Kingdom of Italy enabled
the Arsenale to make several World War I battleships, and though these
marked the end of its shipbuilding career, the shipyard still has active
dry-docks that haul out and service sizable ships. Some buildings inside
have been restored and are used by the Italian Navy, but there are many
more in urgent need of care. The debate over what to do with this massive, historically important sight is ongoing. The Arsenale isn't regularly
open to the public, but it's open for the Biennale and for Venice's festival of traditional boats, held every May. If you're here during those times,
don't miss the chance for a look inside. ✉ *Campo dell'Arsenale, Castello*
Ⓥ *Arsenale.*

> **need a
> break?**
>
> Castello's **Via Garibaldi** is the bazaar of bars, cafés, and osterie. The
> farther from the water you get the less touristy these become, and
> with choices on both sides of this, Venice's widest street, you can pick
> between sunny and shady to fit your whim.

▶ ❺❽ **Chiesa della Pietà.** Unwanted babies were left on the steps of this religious
institute, founded by a Franciscan friar in 1346. The girls were immediately taken in at the adjoining orphanage, which provided the children

with a musical education. The church flourished during the years of the Venetian Republic, when it was traditionally visited by the doge on Palm Sunday, protected by the pope, and supported by generous benefactors. The quality of the performances here reached continental fame—the in-house conductor was none other than Antonio Vivaldi (1675–1745), who wrote some of his best compositions here for the hospice. The original church was rebuilt in the 15th century, and again after the death of the great musician. Today, with its ceiling frescoes by Tiepolo, it is an elegant example of a Venetian sacred site, and more like a small theater than a church. In an adjoining room to the left of the entrance is a tiny collection of Baroque instruments, including the violin played by Vivaldi. Often closed during the day, the Pietà hosts Baroque concerts, usually with Venetian composers such as Vivaldi, Galuppi, and Marcello on the program. Some are performed in 17th-century costume. ⊠ *Riva degli Schiavoni, Castello* ☎ *041/5222171* ⊠ *Free* ◷ *June–Oct., weekdays 10–noon and 4–6, weekends 10–noon and 4–5:30* Ⓥ *San Zaccaria.*

☾ ❺❾ **Museo Storico Navale** (Museum of Naval History). A 12-ft replica of the doge's ceremonial boat, the *Bucintoro,* and Peggy Guggenheim's private gondola, complete with *felze,* the romantic cabin popular in Casanova's time, are among the highlights of this museum. Models, parts from galleys, old and modern naval weapons, fishermen's ex-votos, and even a few real boats round out the collection. Maps and scale models of the Arsenale will help you appreciate this "town within the town." The museum also houses a large seashell collection, donated to the city by Venetian-born fashion designer Roberta da Camerino. ⊠ *Campo San Biagio, Castello* ☎ *041/5200276.* ⊠ *€1.55* ◷ *Weekdays 8:45–1:30; Sat. 8:45–1* Ⓥ *Arsenale.*

❻❸ **San Giovanni in Bragora.** This humble redbrick church is said to have been one of the lagoon's first churches—it's so old that no one is sure what the word *bragora* means. At the beginning of the 8th century, St. Magno, the same bishop whose vision of a beautiful Madonna led to the building of Santa Maria Formosa, wanted to dedicate a church to St. John the Baptist, but the relics in the second chapel to the right are those of St. John the Almsgiver. After undergoing two restorations, the church was completely redone in a light Gothic style in 1475. You'll find works by two sons of Antonio Vivarini. *Madonna with Child* in the left nave is by Alvise (circa 1445–1503), but it's his *Christ Risen,* right of main altar, that shows the freedom and movement that would lead him to become a leader in the late 15th-century Veneto school of painting. His brother Bartolomeo's (1432-99) *Madonna with Child and Saints* is clearly Gothic by comparison. Contrast these works with Cima da Conegliano's (circa 1459–1517) altarpiece *Baptism of Christ.* This luminous scene is realistic not only in its gaunt St. John administering sacrament, but in the beautifully rendered Veneto countryside. Be sure to bring €.50 coins for lighting the paintings. ⊠ *Campo Bandiera e Moro, Castello* ☎ *041/5205906* ⊠ *Free* ◷ *Weekdays 8:30–11 and 3:30–6, Sat. 8:30–11, Sun. 9:30–11* Ⓥ *Arsenale.*

❻❶ **San Pietro di Castello.** A 7th-century church dedicated to Byzantine saints Sergio and Bacchus was replaced two centuries later with a new church honoring St. Peter the Apostle. Palladio redesigned the facade at the end of the 16th century and added its stark campanile, the first in Venice built from marblelike Istrian stone rather than brick. It stands out against the picturesque, workaday slips along the Canale di San Pietro and the peaceful Renaissance cloister, which for years was a sort of squatters colony. Veneti lived on this island long before Venice was officially founded as a city, but now it's a sleepy, almost forgotten place, with little to suggest that for more than 1,000 years this church was Venice's cathedral—until the Basilica di San Marco replaced it in 1807. The interior has some minor 17th-century art and San Pietro's ancient *cattedra* (thrown) in the right nave. According to legend, this marble seat, inscribed with verses from the Koran, was used by Peter at Antioch. ⊠ *Campo San Pietro, Castello* ☎ *041/2750462 Chorus.* ⊡ *€2; €8 Chorus pass* ☉ *Mon.–Sat. 10–5, Sun. 1–5.* Ⓥ *San Pietro di Castello or Giardini.*

60 **Sant'Elena.** Hermit monks in the ninth century built the first chapel on what was then a scrap of land flanked by mud flats. The church here today was a 13th-century creation built to receive pilgrims bound for the Holy Land and was aptly dedicated to Emperor Constantine's mother, Sant'Elena, who legend says, chose this island herself as a final resting place—it seems the Venetian galley transporting Sant'Elena's reliquary from Constantinople mysteriously ran aground near the island. Monks from Mt. Olive in Tuscany rebuilt the church and added its Renaissance doorway with Commander Vittore Cappello kneeling before St. Helen in Antonio Rizzo's sculptural group. The interior, touching in its simplicity, has faded frescoes with floral and angelic motifs awaiting restoration. There are ceiling nets strung to protect worshippers from loose debris; they make it hard to appreciate three medallions on the cross vault representing San Marco, San Benedetto, and San Nicola da Bari, patron saint of navigators. Sant'Elena wasn't nearly as stark before Napoléon closed the church and spirited away 60 carved wooden choir stalls, for which the church was renowned, and much of the other artwork as well. He might have taken the saint herself if someone hadn't stashed her in nearby San Pietro di Castello. You can see her now in the chapel to the right of the front door.

Work on Sant'Elena's foundation revealed a history few had even guessed when a number of *forni* (ovens) were uncovered. It seems the monks were in business baking bread for sea voyages and cooking for crews anchored nearby. Historians believe Sant'Elena was used to offload precious cargo, often as not pilfered, during Serenissima naval excursions. The land around the church grew considerably in the last century due to the deposit of the city's refuse as landfill, which makes the foundation for the nearby naval school and soccer stadium. The church's 1950s cement bell tower, though not a great match for the rest of the structure, has become a fixture in the skyline for so long it's unlikely to disappear anytime soon—at least not like a former one did. Though old drawings show a bell tower, it vanished without a trace, never to be seen nor written about after the 1700s. ⊠ *Sant'Elena, Castello* ☎ *041/5205144* ⊡ *Free* ☉ *Mon.–Sat. 5–7, Sun. 9–noon* Ⓥ *Sant'Elena.*

| need a break? | A short calle inland from Sant'Elena's park is **Osteria Sant'Elena** (⊠ Campo Stringare ☎ 041/5208419), where with the peace and quiet of this grassy square, you'll swear you've found an oasis in Venice. |

SAN GIORGIO MAGGIORE & THE GIUDECCA

Beckoning travelers across St. Mark's Basin, sparkling white through the mist, is the island of San Giorgio Maggiore, separated by a small channel from the Giudecca. A tall brick campanile on that distant bank perfectly complements the Campanile of San Marco. Beneath it looms the stately dome of one of Venice's greatest churches, San Giorgio Maggiore. the island of Giudecca, a crescent cupped around the southern shore of Venice, has a history shrouded in mystery, but today it's about as down to earth as you can get and one of the city's few remaining neighborhoods that feel truly Venetian.

Numbers in the text correspond to numbers in the margin and on the San Giorgio Maggiore and the Giudecca map.

a good boat trip

Take Line 82 from San Zaccaria across St. Mark's Basin to the island of San Giorgio to visit Palladio's **San Giorgio Maggiore** ➅ ⏵. In the adjacent monastery, Fondazione Cini operates a music institute and a school of art restoration. It's only open to the public for exhibitions, conferences, and performances at its lovely outdoor amphitheater, Teatro Verde. The next three vaporetto stops are on the **Giudecca** ➅. Visit **Santissimo Redentore** ➅, another church by Palladio and another built to commemorate a plague. Thanks to several bridges, you can walk the entire length of Giudecca's promenade, relaxing at one of several eateries or just taking in the lively atmosphere.

TIMING A half day should give you plenty of time to enjoy the sights. Allow at least an hour to visit each of the churches and another hour or two to visit the Giudecca neighborhood.

What to See

➅ **Giudecca.** Seeing Venice from the Giudecca is a bit like seeing the earth from the moon. On a clear day you can take in the city's full panorama, from the Giardini della Biennale to your right (east) to the fuming factories of Marghera industrial complex on the mainland to your left. The island is delightfully mysterious in light fog, but rain or northerly *bora* winds can turn an otherwise perfect walk into cold misery. Few tourists venture beyond the main fondamenta, and few Venetians bother coming to Giudecca at all, unless it's to visit Sacca Fisola's Friday market or the public swimming pool. The original name for the island was *Spinalunga* (long spine), and how it came to be called Giudecca is something of a mystery. It may derive from a possible 14th-century Jewish settlement, or it may be the result of 9th-century nobles being condemned to *giudicato* (exile) here.

Giudecca became a pleasure garden for wealthy Venetians during the Republic's long and luxurious decline. Through much of the 20th century it was largely working-class, but of late it has become increasingly gentrified. The island is the site of the exclusive Cipriani hotel, but also the International Youth Hostel and a women's prison. Here and there the ruins of an industrial past—watchmaking, beer brewing, textiles, and a granary—all dating from the 19th century, are being resurrected into housing. Mulino Stucky, an 1895 neo-Gothic flour mill, abandoned for years, is being slowly transformed into a hotel and condominiums overlooking the city's port. Other renovated properties are offering special terms to help make it affordable for Venetians to remain in their city of birth.

off the beaten path

LIDO – Separating the lagoon from the sea, this long sandbar of an island was once a garden plot providing vegetables to Venice. Only its southern end, Malamocco, which was the Republic's 8th-century administrative center, was inhabited, the rest being cultivated. But from the 1850s through World War II, the Lido became a fashionable sea resort, and its name was subsequently borrowed by many seaside resorts throughout the world. This was where Austrian Archduke Maximilian built his summer residence, where Thomas Mann wrote *Death in Venice*, and where Iran's former Shah Reza Pahlavi came to water-ski. The Lido's popularity peaked in the late 1930s, following the launch of the Biennale film festival, the building of one of Italy's first airports (now used only for private traffic), and the opening of

San Giorgio Maggiore & the Giudecca

Bacino di S. Marco

San Giórgio Maggiore

64

San Giorgio Maggiore

SAN GIORGIO ▲

Canale della Grázia

VENICE

Fond. S. Giovanni

ZITELLE ▲

Fond. d. Zitelle

Calle Michelangelo

Calle Esterna

C.d. Ld.

Cooperativa

Squero

C.d. Gran

C. dello

F. della Croce

Fond. Dogana

SALUTE ▲

DORSODURO

Fondamenta Zattere ai Saloni

REDENTORE

Fond. Zattere allo Spirito Santo

Campo del Redentore

65

Rio della Croce

C.d. Fratti

C.S. Giacomo

C.d. Pesce

Fond. San Giacomo

A

Fond. Zattere ai Gesuati

Rio di S. Vio

R. Terrà a Foscarini

Campo della Carità

Rio d. Ponte Lungo

Fond. de Ponte Piccolo

C

C

Campo S. Trováso

R. d. S.

R. d. S. Trovaso

ZATTERE ▲

PALANCA ▲

Fond. Santa Eufémia

Ponte Lungo

Fond. de Ponte Piccolo

T. d. Scuole

Corte Grande

dell'Accademia dei Nobili

Calle Lunga

65

C

Rio d. Sa. Eufémia

D

U

Fond. San Biágio

Rio d. Convertite

Rio d. S. Biágio

S. BASILIO ▲

Canale della Giudecca

SACCA FISOLA ▲

Canale d. Lavranéri

Calle della Sacca

Calle Larga d. Lavranéri

SACCA FISOLA

Fontam. Baéta Giuliana

Calle Rimini

Fontam. S. Gerardo Sagredo

SACCA SAN BIÁGIO

G

0 — 1/8 km
0 — 1/8 mile

KEY

▲ Start of walk

▲ Vaporetto Stop

the casino (now closed). Some of the glamour and architecture of those days remains in the Moorish-looking Grand Hotel Excelsior and on the quiet streets branching from Gran Viale Santa Maria Elisabetta, adorned with many Art Deco villas. Today, the Lido is where locals keep holiday houses and crowds of commuters from Venice and the mainland spend a good portion of their summer. The water looks murky because of the fine sand, celebrated by Byron and Shelley, but it's actually quite clean. Small waves make for relatively safe swimming, even for children. The best way to explore the Lido is by renting a bicycle, alternating sight-seeing with sunbathing. (⩔ S. M. Elisabetta Lido, Lines 1, 6/14, 51, 61, and in summer 82)

★ ⌐ ⑥④ **San Giorgio Maggiore.** There's been a church on this island since the late 8th century, with a Benedictine monastery added in the 10th century. The present neoclassical church of red brick and white marble was begun in 1566 by Palladio, and it displays his architectural hallmarks of mathematical harmony and affinity for classical antiquity. Inside, it's refreshingly airy and simply decorated. *The Last Supper* and *The Gathering of Manna,* two of Tintoretto's later works, line the chancel. Right of the entrance hangs *Adoration of the Shepherds* by Jacopo Bassano (1517–92); his foothills home, Bassano del Grappa, is evident in his portrayal of nature and country life and earth-tone colors he chooses. Ask the monks to see Carpaccio's *George and Dragon*; it hangs in a private room, but they're happy to escort you if they have time. The campanile is so high that it was struck by lightning in 1993. Take the elevator to the top for some of the finest views in town. ⊠ *Isola di San Giorgio* ☎ *041/5227827* ✆ *Church free; €3 campanile* ☼ *June–Sept., daily 9:30–12:30 and 2–7; Oct.–May, daily 9:30–12:30 and 2–5* ⩔ *San Giorgio.*

> off the
> beaten
> path

SAN LAZZARO DEGLI ARMENI – When a leprosy epidemic hit Venice in 1185, those infected were confined to a hospital on this island in the lagoon, which was subsequently dedicated to San Lazzaro (St. Lazarus), the leper of biblical fame. San Lazzaro later served as a shelter for beggars. In 1717 Doge Giovanni Corner II gave the island to Peter of Manug, better known as Father Mekhitar ("the Consoler"), an Armenian priest who had founded an order of monks in Morea, today's Peloponnese. (Armenia had been the first country in the world to adopt Christianity as its state religion, though it did not recognize the pope's authority.) Following the Turkish invasion of Greece, Mekhitar fled to Venice, where a small but wealthy Armenian community had thrived since the 13th century. On San Lazzaro he built the monastery that still stands today, more than tripled the size of the island with landfill, and established what was then the world's largest center of Armenian culture outside of Armenia.

Only 15 minutes from the San Zaccaria vaporetto stop, San Lazzaro feels a world apart from the touristy hubbub of San Marco. Its 322,920 sq ft are covered with trees, orchards, and gardens impeccably kept by a community of some 20 Mekhitarist priests and seminarians. Apart from the monastery, San Lazzaro houses a flock of sheep, a church, a picture gallery, a museum, two libraries, and a collection of precious manuscripts.

The daily afternoon tour—led by guides fluent in several languages, including English—begins with a brief lesson on Armenian history beneath the turquoise ceiling of the 14th-century **church.** It was partially rebuilt by Mekhitar, and today features rococo decorations and Austrian stained glass. In the refectory is an 18th-century *Last Supper* inspired by Leonardo da Vinci's masterpiece. Mekhitar's staircase leads to the **picture gallery,** with about 100 paintings by Armenian artists from the 18th through 19th centuries, and to Mekhitar's room, which still contains his personal possessions. With nearly 200,000 volumes, the main library holds the world's richest collection of Armenian writing, some of which belonged to the founder himself. Unlike other Venetian monasteries, which Napoléon destroyed, this one was spared because the French conqueror believed it to be more of a learning center than a religious institution. Tiepolo's *Peace and Justice* painting is on the ceiling as you enter the eclectic **museum collection,** where you can appreciate the encyclopedic Mekhitarist passion for culture. Here Armenian pottery, swords, and silver artwork share space with an Egyptian mummy, an Indian wooden and ivory throne, a Sanskrit Buddhist manuscript, Chinese ivory carvings, and fragments of Roman urns. A few steps lead down to **Byron's room,** displaying his portrait. The poet spent months here in 1816 and 1817 recovering from his separation from England and Anne Isabelle Milbanke. To appease the soul and pass the time, Byron studied the Armenian language—he even helped write an Armenian-English grammar book (still printed by the island's press), which you'll find in the gift shop, right next to the monk's famous homemade *marmellata di rose* (rose jam). Finally, the **round library** contains nearly 4,000 mostly Armenian 8th- to 18th-century manuscripts, some brilliantly illuminated with gold. ☎ *041/5260104* ✆ *€6* ☉ *One tour daily, 3:25–5* Ⓥ *Line 20 from San Zaccaria (near Pensione Wildner) at 3:10 only.*

66 **Santissimo Redentore.** After a 16th-century plague claimed 50,000 people, one-third of the city's population, Andrea Palladio was asked to design a commemorative church. Giudecca's Capucin friars offered land and their services, provided the building was in keeping with the simplicity of their hermitage. Consecrated in 1592, Palladio's creation is dominated by a dome and a pair of slim, almost minaretlike bell towers. Its simple, stately facade leads to a bright, airy interior, perfectly proportioned like San Giorgio Maggiore and in distinct contrast to the dusky Byzantine mystery of the Basilica di San Marco.

For hundreds of years, on the third weekend in July the doge would make a pilgrimage here to give thanks to the Redeemer for ending a 16th-century plague. The event has become the Festa del Redentore, a favorite Venetian festival featuring boats, fireworks, and outdoor feasting. It's the one time of year you can walk to Giudecca—across a temporary pontoon bridge connecting Redentore with the Zattere. ⊠ *Fondamenta San Giacomo, Giudecca* ☎ *041/5231415, 041/2750462 Chorus* ✆ *€2; €8 Chorus pass* ☉ *Mon.–Sat. 10–5, Sun. 1–5* Ⓥ *Redentore.*

ISLANDS OF THE LAGOON

The perfect vacation from your Venetian vacation is an escape to Murano, Burano, and Torcello, the islands of the northern lagoon. Torcello offers greenery, breathing space, and picnicking opportunities, as long as you remember to pack a lunch. Burano is a toy town of houses painted in a riot of color—blue, yellow, pink, ocher, and dark red. Visitors still love to shop here for "Venetian" lace, despite the fact that these days it's almost all machine made in Taiwan. Just as Murano is renowned for its glass, Murano tours, even those organized by top hotels, are notorious for high-pressure sales. Vaporetto connections aren't difficult, and for the price of a boat ticket you'll buy your freedom and more time to explore. The Murano "guides" herding new arrivals follow a rotation so that factories take turns giving tours, but you can avoid the hustle by just walking away.

Numbers in the text correspond to numbers in the margin and on the Islands of the Lagoon map.

a good boat trip

Vaporetto Line 41 leaves San Zaccaria (in front of Jolanda hotel) every 20 minutes, circling the east end of Venice and stopping at Fondamente Nuove before making the five-minute hop to **San Michele** ⑥⑦ ▶, the island cemetery with its church of San Michele in Isola. Another five minutes and you're in **Murano** ⑥⑧. To see glass blowing, get off at Colonna; the Museo stop will put you near the Museo Vetrario, with its fascinating display of glass dating from AD 1st–3rd century to the 19th century. A bit farther down Fondamenta Giustinian you'll see Basilica di Santi Maria e Donato, which has a mosaic floor complete with Murano glass. Make your way to the island's *faro*, a lighthouse that still guides boats into the lagoon. From the Faro stop, Line 12 runs to **Burano** ⑥⑨, about 30 minutes farther, where you can see traditional lace making at the Scuola di Merletti di Burano. Line 12 then continues to the sleepy green island of **Torcello** ⑦⓪, only five minutes away. A paved lane from the landing follows a canal across the island. You'll pass elegantly reclusive Locanda Cipriani before reaching a grassy square and the beautifully eerie Cathedral of Santa Maria Assunta, the island's most significant surviving monument.

TIMING From April through October, San Zaccaria is connected to Murano by Line 5, an express boat stopping at Navagero, Faro, and Colonna before returning to San Zaccaria; the trip takes about 30 minutes. Local Line 41 takes about 45 minutes to get from San Zaccaria to Murano; it doesn't go to Burano or Torcello, but does stop at San Michele. From Fondamente Nuove boats leave every 10 minutes. Line LN (for Lagoon North) goes from Fondamente Nuove direct to Murano, Burano, and Torcello; the full trip takes 45 minutes each way. Hitting all the sights on all the islands takes a full day. If you limit yourself to Murano and San Michele, a half day will suffice. If you enjoy riding boats, try an alternate route back; continue on Line 12 another 30 minutes to Punta Sabbione on the mainland, where Line 6/14 connects directly to San Marco.

What to See

★ ⑥⑨ **Burano.** Colorfully painted houses line the canals of this quiet fishing village where centuries ago lace-making rescued a faltering economy. As you walk the 100 yards from the dock to Piazza Galuppi, the main square, you pass stall after stall of lace vendors. These good-natured ladies won't press you with a hard sell, but don't expect precise product information or great bargains. Remember that real handmade Burano lace is very rare and costs €1,000 to €2,000 for a 10-inch doily. What you see in the stalls is almost certainly made elsewhere.

Museo del Merletto (Lace Museum) lets you marvel at the intricacies of Burano's lace-making. Try to imagine the hours it took to produce the articles on display and you'll understand why genuine handmade lace commands the price it does. The museum is also a skills center—more a sewing circle than a school—so on weekdays you'll often find women continuing the centuries-old tradition that made the island famous throughout Europe. They sometimes have authentic pieces for sale privately. ✉ *Piazza Galuppi 187* ☎ *041/730034* 🖃 *€4, €6 with Museo Vetrario, €15.50 Musei Civici pass* ⏱ *Apr.–Oct., Wed.–Mon. 10–5; Nov.–Mar., Wed.–Mon. 10–4* Ⓥ *Burano.*

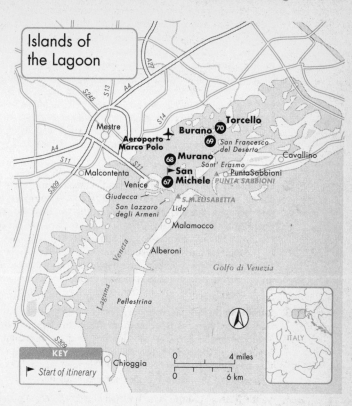

**Islands of
the Lagoon**

KEY
▶ Start of itinerary

🖐 ⑥⑧ **Murano.** As in Venice, bridges here link a number of small islands, dotted with houses that once were workmen's cottages. The republic, concerned about fire hazard in the 13th century, moved its glassworks to Murano, and today you can visit the factories and watch glass being made. Many of them line the Fondamenta dei Vetrai, the canal-side walkway leading from the Colonna vaporetto landing. Before you reach Murano's Grand Canal (250 yds from the landing) you'll pass the **Chiesa di San Pietro Martire.** Reconstructed in the 16th century, it houses Giovanni Bellini's *Madonna and Child* and Veronese's *St. Jerome.* ⊠ *Fondamenta dei Vetrai* ☎ *041/739704* 🕐 *Mon.–Sat. 9–12:30 and 2–5* Ⓥ *Colonna.*

The collection at **Museo Vetrario** (Glass Museum) ranges from priceless antiques to only slightly less expensive modern pieces. You'll see authentic Venetian styles and patterns, including the famous Barovier wedding cup (1470–80). ⊠ *Fondamenta Giustinian 8* ☎ *041/739586* 💳 *€4, €6 with Museo del Merletto, €15.50 entry to all Musei Civici, including Palazzo Ducale.* 🕐 *Apr.–Oct., Thurs.–Tues. 10–5; Nov.–Mar., Thurs.–Tues. 10–4; last tickets sold ½ hr before closing.* Ⓥ *Museo.*

Basilica dei Santi Maria e Donato, just past the glass museum, is among the first churches founded by the lagoon's original inhabitants. The elaborate mosaic pavement includes the date 1140; its ship's keel roof and Veneto-Byzantine columns add to the air of an ancient temple. ⊠ *Fondamenta Giustinian* ☎ *041/739056* 💳 *Free* 🕐 *Daily 8–noon and 4–7* Ⓥ *Museo.*

off the beaten path

SAN FRANCESCO DEL DESERTO – Legend says St. Francis of Assisi visited the lagoon in 1220 with his follower Illuminato on their way back from a preaching tour of Palestine. They'd thought about settling on Torcello, but found it too rich for their tastes. Instead, they rowed to this tiny deserted island, then known as Due Vigne ("Two Vineyards"). When Francis planted his pilgrim's stick into the ground, it miraculously grew into a pine tree and birds came to sing for him. Reaching Assisi, he sent some friars to the island, who in 1228 built the first church. Today the island is a floating grove of cypress trees, with a peaceful monastery and cloisters—it's about as far from Venice's bustle as you can get. You'll learn more about Franciscan lore while being shepherded around by one of the 10 resident friars. ☎ 041/5286863 ⌧ *Donation welcomed; water taxi from Burano landing to San Francesco del Deserto, €25–30 round-trip* ✆ *Tues.–Sun. 9–11 and 3–5* Ⓥ *Burano.*

☛ ⑥⑦ **San Michele.** This cypress-lined island is home to the pretty Renaissance church of **San Michele in Isola**—and to some of Venice's most illustrious deceased. The church was designed by Codussi; the graves include poet Ezra Pound (1885–1972), impresario and art critic Sergey Diaghilev (1872–1929), and composer Igor Stravinsky (1882–1971). Surrounded by the living sounds of Venice lagoon, this would seem the perfect final resting place. However, these days newcomers are exhumed after 10 years and transferred to a less grandiose location. ☎ 041/2730111 ⌧ *Free* ✆ *Apr.–Sept., daily 7:30–6; Oct.–Mar., daily 7:30–4* Ⓥ *San Michele.*

★ ⑦⓪ **Torcello.** In their flight from barbarians 1,500 years ago, the first Venetians landed here, prospering even after many left to found the city of Venice. As malaria took its toll and the island's wool-manufacturing was priced out of the market, Torcello became a ghost town. In the 16th century there were 10 churches and 20,000 inhabitants; today you'll be lucky to see one of the island's 16 permanent residents.

Santa Maria Assunta was built in the 11th century, and Torcello's wealth at the time is evident in the church's high-quality Byzantine mosaics. The massive *Last Judgment* shows sinners writhing in pain, while opposite, above the altar, the Madonna looks calmly down from her field of gold. Ask to see the inscription dated 639 and a sample of mosaic pavement from the original church. The adjacent **Santa Fosca** church, added when the body of the saint arrived in 1011, is still used for religious services. It's worth making the climb up the adjacent **Campanile** for an incomparable view of the lagoon wetlands. ⌧ *Torcello* ☎ *041/730119* ⌧ *Santa Maria Assunta €3; Campanile €2* ✆ *Apr.–Oct., daily 10:30–6; Nov.–Mar., daily 10–5* Ⓥ *Torcello.*

WHERE TO EAT

2

FODOR'S CHOICE

Alle Testiere, *Castello*

Antico Pignolo, *San Marco*

Bancogiro, *Santa Croce*

Cantina Do Mori, *San Polo*

Cantinone, *Dorsoduro*

Enoteca la Mascareta, *Castello*

Osteria da Fiore, *San Polo*

Trattoria Ca' d'Oro, *Cannaregio*

HIGHLY RECOMMENDED

Ai 4 Feri, *Dorsoduro*

Ai Gondolieri, *Dorsoduro*

Al Prosecco, *Santa Croce*

Altanella, *Giudecca*

Bentigodi da Andrea, *Cannaregio*

Cipriani, *Giudecca*

Corte Sconta, *Castello*

Il Sole sulla Vecia Cavana, *Cannaregio*

L'Incontro, *Dorsoduro*

Tiziano, *Cannaregio*

Vini da Gigio, *Cannaregio*

Updated by
Patricia Rucidlo

THE CATCHWORD IN VENICE, at both fancy restaurants and holes in the wall, is fish, often at its tastiest when it looks like nothing you've seen before. How do you learn first-hand about the catch of the day? An early morning visit to the Rialto's *pescheria* (fish market) is more instructive than any book.

There's no getting around the fact that Venice has more than its share of overpriced, mediocre eateries that prey on tourists. Avoid places with cajoling waiters standing outside, and beware of restaurants that don't display their prices. At the other end of the spectrum, showy *menu turistico* (tourist menu) boards make offerings clear in a dozen languages, but for the same 15–20 euros you'd spend at such places you could do better at a *bacaro* (the local version of a wine bar) making a meal of *cicheti* (savory snacks).

Dining options in Venice range from the ultra-high end, where jackets and ties are required, to the super-casual, where the clientele (almost all of them tourists) won't notice if you're wearing shorts. Some of Venice's swankiest restaurants—the ones that usually have only male waiters wearing white jackets and bow ties—trade on longstanding reputations and might seem a little stuffy and faded. The food at such places tends toward interpretations of international cuisine and, though often expertly prepared, can seem as old-fashioned as the waiters who serve it. On the other hand, midrange restaurants are often more willing to break from tradition, incorporating ingredients such as ginger and wasabi in their creations.

Budget-conscious travelers, and those simply looking for a good meal in unpretentious surroundings, might want to stick to trattorie and bacari. Trattorie often serve less highfalutin versions of classic Venetian dishes at substantially reduced prices; bacari offer lighter fare, usually eaten at the bar (though sometimes tables are available), and wine lists that offer lots of choices by the glass.

Although pizzerias are not hard to find, Venice is not much of a pizza town—standards aren't what they are elsewhere in Italy, and local laws impede the use of wood-burning ovens. Beware of the gooey, soggy pizza at bar-pizzerias, which is commonly precooked and reheated. *Tramezzini*, the triangular white-bread sandwiches served in bars all over Italy, however, are particularly good in Venice. Many bars here still make their own mayonnaise, and few skimp on the fillings.

Tiramisu lovers will have ample opportunity to sample this creamy concoction made from ladyfingers soaked in espresso and covered with sweetened mascarpone cheese. It was invented here in the Veneto. In addition to sorbets and *semifreddi* (frozen ice cream and cake desserts), other sweets that frequently appear on Venetian menus are almond cakes and strudels, as well as dry cookies served with sweet white wine. Ice cream is sold at every corner but, with a few notable exceptions, rarely rises above mediocrity.

Burano

$$–$$$ ✕ **Al Gatto Nero da Ruggero.** Even cats know that this restaurant dedicated to one of their own offers the best fish on the island. The "Black Cat," with its vivid blue facade, stands out among the low, brightly colored buildings animating the picturesque Fondamenta della Giudecca. All pastas and desserts are made in-house; the flavors come alive in chef/owner Ruggero's spaghetti *alla scogliera,* which teems with treats from the sea. The *fritto misto* (fish fry) is outstanding for its lightness and variety of fish. ✉ *Fondamenta della Giudecca 88, Burano* ☎ *041/730120* 🖃 *AE, DC, MC, V* ☻ *Closed Mon. and 3 wks in Nov.* Ⓥ *Burano.*

When you sit down for a meal in a *ristorante, trattoria,* or *osteria,* you're generally expected to order at least a two-course meal, such as: a *primo* (first course) and a *secondo* (second course) or a *contorno* (vegetable side); an antipasto (starter) followed by a primo or secondo; or a secondo and a *dolce* (dessert). In a *bacaro* or pizzeria, it's common to order just one dish.

The handiest places for a snack between sights are bars, cafés, and the quintessentially Venetian bacari. Bars are places for a quick coffee and a *panino* (sandwich, often warmed on a griddle) or *tramezzino* (sandwich on untoasted white bread), rather than drinking establishments. A café (*caffè* in Italian) is like a bar but usually with more seating. If you place your order at the counter, ask if you can sit down: some places charge considerably more for table service. Often you'll pay a cashier first, then give your *scontrino* (receipt) to the person at the counter who fills your order.

Mealtimes & Closures

Breakfast (*la colazione*) is usually served from 7 to 10:30, lunch (*il pranzo*) from 12:30 to 2, dinner (*la cena*) from 7:30 to 10. Many bacari open as early as 8 AM, but they do not serve typical breakfast items or coffee; some Venetians partake of cicheti and tramezzini for their morning meal.

Reservations & Dress

Reservations are always a good idea in restaurants and trattorias, especially on weekends. We mention them in reviews only when they are essential or not accepted. We mention dress only when men are required to wear a jacket or a jacket and tie. Keep in mind that Italian men never wear shorts or running shoes in a restaurant or bacaro, no matter how humble. The same "rules" apply to ladies' casual shorts, running shoes, and plastic sandals. Shorts are acceptable in pizzerias and cafés.

Prices & Tipping

All prices include tax. Restaurant menu prices include service (*servizio*) unless indicated otherwise on the menu. It's customary to leave a small tip (from a euro to 10% of the bill) in appreciation of good service. Tips are always given in cash. Most restaurants have a "cover" charge, usually listed on the menu as *"pane e coperto."* It should be modest (€1–€2.50 per person) except at the most expensive restaurants. Some restaurants instead charge for bread, which should be brought to you (and paid for) only if you order it. When in doubt, ask about the servizio, pane, and coperto policy upon ordering. The price of fish dishes is often given by weight (before cooking); the price on the menu will be for 100 grams, not for the whole fish. An average fish portion is about 350 grams. Be sure to keep some cash on hand, because osterie, bacari, and pizzerias usually do not take credit cards.

WHAT IT COSTS In euros				
$$$$	**$$$**	**$$**	**$**	**¢**
AT DINNER over €22	€17–€22	€12–€17	€7–€12	under €7

Prices are for a second course (secondo piatto).

Where to Eat in Venice

KEY

ℹ️ Tourist Information

▲ Vaporetto Stop

Cannaregio

$$$$ ✕ **Al Bacco.** Located not far from the Ghetto, this ancient osteria caters to young locals and those tourists who make the effort to seek it out. Among the classic Venetian dishes, sample the *sarde sotto sale* (salted sardines) or the old favorite *bigoli in salsa* (rough-shaped spaghetti in an anchovy sauce). For alfresco dining, the charming garden has a few tables. ✉ *Fondamenta Capuzine, Cannaregio 3054* ☎ *041/717493* ▤ *AE, DC, MC, V* ⊘ *No lunch; closed Mon.* Ⓥ *San Marcuola.*

$$–$$$$ ✕ **Fiaschetteria Toscana.** Contrary to what the name suggests, there's nothing Tuscan about this restaurant's menu. It was formerly a Tuscan wine and oil storehouse, and it's worth a visit for its cheerful and courteous service, fine *cucina* (cooking), and noteworthy cellar. The owners, Albino and Mariuccia Busatto, make their presence felt as they walk among the well-appointed tables, opening special bottles of wine and discussing the menu. Gastronomic highlights include a light *tagliolini neri al ragù di astice* (thin spaghetti served with squid ink and mixed with a delicate lobster sauce), and zabaglione. ✉ *Campo San Giovanni Crisostomo, Cannaregio 5719* ☎ *041/5285281* ▤ *AE, DC, MC, V* ⊘ *Closed Tues. and 4 wks July–Aug. No lunch Mon.* Ⓥ *Rialto.*

★ **$$$** ✕ **Il Sole sulla Vecia Cavana.** Owner Stefano Monti opened this spot in 2001, and it immediately became a star of the Venice dining scene. The young talented kitchen staff create winning Italian and Venetian dishes such as *filetti di pesce a cottura differenziata* (fish fillet, cooked on one side and seared on the other), tender baby cuttlefish, and, among desserts, *gelato al basilico* (basil ice cream). The 18th-century *cavana* (boathouse) maintains its original low columns, arches, and brick walls, but has been decorated with contemporary flair. ✉ *Rio Terà SS. Apostoli, Cannaregio 4624* ☎ *041/5287106* ▤ *AE, DC, MC, V* ⊘ *Closed Mon., 2 wks in Jan., and in Aug.* Ⓥ *Ca' d'Oro.*

$$ ✕ **Antica Mola.** You'll find a warm welcome at this family-run trattoria. Whether you choose the terrace overlooking the canal or the shaded garden in back, owners Antonietta and Franco will entertain you with their lively presence. The cooking is reliably good, homey fare with the accent on seafood—spaghetti *coi caparozzoli* (with carpet-shell clams) is a favorite. ✉ *Fondamenta dei Ormesini, Cannaregio 2800* ☎ *041/717492* ▤ *AE, DC, MC, V* ⊘ *Closed Wed. and Aug.* Ⓥ *San Marcuola.*

$$ ✕ **Osteria del Bomba.** It's a bacaro and a trattoria; take a table if you can, as it's more pleasurable to enjoy the food while sitting down. Locals (mostly middle-age men) flock here to have a glass of wine and a plate of pasta while bantering with genial proprietors Marco and Giacomo. Here they do saor three ways, and the *gamberetti* (small shrimp) in saor might even be better than the classic version with sardines. The grilled vegetables provide a fine counterpoint to delicacies from the sea. ✉ *Calle dell'Oca, off Campo Santa Sofia Cannaregio* ☎ *041/241146* ▤ *MC, V* ⊘ *Closed Sat. lunch and Mon.* Ⓥ *Ca' d'Oro.*

★ **$$** ✕ **Vini da Gigio.** A quaint, friendly, family-run trattoria on the quay side of a canal just off the Strada Nuova, da Gigio is very popular with Venetians and other visiting Italians, who appreciate the affable service; the well-prepared homemade pasta, fish, and meat dishes; the imaginative and varied cellar; and the high-quality draft wine. It's good for a simple lunch at tables in the barroom. ✉ *Fondamenta de la Chiesa, Cannaregio 3628/a* ☎ *041/5285140* ▤ *AE, DC, MC, V* ⊘ *Closed Mon., 3 wks Jan.–Feb., 1 wk in June, and 3 wks Aug.–Sept.* Ⓥ *Ca' d'Oro.*

$–$$ ✕ **Anice Stellato.** Hidden away on one of the most romantic fondamente of Cannaregio, this family-run bacaro-trattoria is the place to stop for fairly priced, great-tasting food in a part of town that doesn't teem with restaurants. The space has plenty of character: narrow columns rise from the

NAVIGATING THE VENETIAN MENU

THE SEAFOOD PILED HIGH at the Rialto pescheria (fish market) comes from local waters and carries names peculiar to Venice. Inevitably, much of it finds its way to Venetian tables: moeche (soft-shell crabs) are caught at molting time (spring and fall) and fried in an egg-and-Parmesan batter. Seppie in tecia (tender baby cuttlefish) turn deep black after being stewed in their ink and a dash of tomato sauce and are customarily served with golden yellow polenta.

A vast array of tasty shellfish, including caparozzoli (carpet-shell clams), garusoli (snail-like mollusks), and peoci (mussels), are tossed with pasta, stirred into risotto or soups, or simply boiled and dressed with olive oil, lemon juice, and parsley. Capesante (sea scallops) are usually baked, either plain or with bread crumbs, Parmesan, and parsley. Crustaceans include gamberetti (shrimp), scampi (king prawns), schie (tiny gray shrimp), granseola (spider crab), and canocie (mantis shrimp). One very traditional preparation for fish, found on just about every bacaro, osteria, and restaurant menu, is sarde in saor, or just saor (boned sardines fried in olive oil, then marinated in a sauce of sautéed onion, vinegar, raisins, and pine nuts).

Less strictly Venetian but nevertheless often found on menus throughout the city are dishes featuring fish from the Mediterranean such as branzino (sea bass, also called spigola), orata (gilthead), sogliola (sole), rombo (turbot), and dentice (sea bream). Common preparations include ai ferri (grilled), al forno (baked, usually with potatoes), al sale (baked under a sea-salt crust), and a filetti (as fillets).

A Venetian specialty savored all over Italy is fegato alla veneziana (thin slices of calf's liver quickly sautéed and dressed with onion, then briefly stewed in olive oil and butter and sprinkled with parsley). Adventurous diners should try bisatto all'ara, a local variety of fleshy eel with a thin skin cooked on a bed of bay leaves. Bisatto can also be deep-fried or stewed.

Although pasta with seafood sauce is generally well prepared, other pasta dishes are better elsewhere in Italy. Venice is justifiably proud of its rice dishes, including risottos and a springtime specialty called risi e bisi made with arborio rice and baby peas. The fertile, salty soil of the larger islands of the lagoon is legendary for the quality of the vegetables that grow from it. Now just a few stalls at the Rialto market sell locally grown crops, but produce from the inland regions surrounding Venice is itself of high quality.

Spring treats are the fat white asparagus from Bassano and artichokes, either called castraure (baby artichokes sautéed with olive oil, parsley, and garlic) or fondi (hearts of globe artichokes, simmered in olive oil, parsley, and garlic). From mid-December to early March, red radicchio di Treviso (from Treviso) comes to market and is best grilled or used as a base for risotto. Fall brings small, brown wild mushrooms called chiodini and zucca barucca, a bumpy squash often baked, used in soups, or stuffed into ravioli. In the cooler months, keep an eye out for pasta e fasioi, a thick bean soup enriched with fresh pasta, known elsewhere in the region as pasta e fagioli.

Tiramisu is the most popular dessert in town, but no matter how many times you try it it's always a bit different, as each restaurant follows its own tiramisu creed. Just to mention a few of the possible variations, sweet liqueur can be added to the coffee, whipped cream or crème anglaise stirred in the basic mascarpone and egg-yolk filling, or bits of bitter chocolate scattered on top instead of cocoa.

Sparkling prosecco, a wine from the Veneto, is a popular aperitif that's sometimes mixed with fresh fruit juice. Prosecco di Valdobbiadene is one of the region's favorites. Finer restaurants offer wide selections of Italian and French wines. Osterie usually have a more limited choice of wines from the region. Popular reds include merlot, Valpolicella, Raboso, Bardolino, and the more-refined Cabernet Pramaggiore and Amarone. Good table whites are Recioto, Tocai Lison, Soave, and the sauternes-like Torcolato.

Buon appetito!

colorful mosaiclike floor, dividing the room into cozy booths. Traditional Venetian fare is enriched with such offerings as *carpacci di pesce* (thin slices of raw tuna, swordfish, or salmon dressed with olive oil and fragrant herbs), tagliatelle with king prawns and zucchini flowers, and several tasty fish stews. ⊠ *Fondamenta de la Sensa, Cannaregio 3272* ☏ *041/720744* ▭ *AE, DC, MC, V* ⊙ *Closed Mon., Tues., and in Aug.* Ⓥ *Sant'Alvise.*

$–$$ ✕ **Da Bepi.** This neighborhood hangout teems with regulars who clearly appreciate the home-style cooking. At peak times you might have to wait a few minutes before receiving any attention, but you'll be consoled by the inviting aromas wafting through the busy dining room. All dishes are fresh and well prepared: try the *tortelli con spinaci, patate, e ricotta* (ravioli filled with spinach, potato, and ricotta cheese) or, for a break from the usual Venetian fare, the *spiedini di pollo* (chicken on skewers). ⊠ *Salizzada del Pistor, off Campo Santi Apostoli, Cannaregio 4550* ☏ *041/5285031* ▭ *MC, V* ⊙ *Closed Thurs. and 2 wks in July* Ⓥ *Ca' d'Oro.*

$–$$ ✕ **Gam-Gam.** At the edge of the Jewish Ghetto near Ponte delle Guglie is one of the very few kosher restaurants in Italy, with a name that in Hebrew means "more-more" and recalls the Italian word *gnam-gnam* ("yum-yum"). The informal dining room is narrow and pink. The Orthodox staff is helpful in explaining the blend of Israeli and other Middle Eastern dishes highlighting the menu, which include falafel with tahini sauce and cous cous prepared several different ways. Vegetarians might create their own salad from the salad bar or try the *piatto di melanzane* (eggplant plate). ⊠ *Sottoportico del Ghetto Vecchio, Cannaregio 1122* ☏ *041/715284* ▭ *No credit cards* ⊙ *Closed Sat. No dinner Fri., and closed 1st week in Feb.* Ⓥ *San Marcuola.*

★ $ ✕ **Bentigodi da Andrea.** *Bentigodi* is Venetian for "you'll enjoy yourself," and such a jaunty name is well suited to this trendy osteria, decorated with fishing-boat lamps and old-fashioned prints on whitewashed walls. The menu includes tartare of tuna and swordfish, steamed orata with green apple and lemon, *masorini con alici e capperi* (duck with anchovies and capers), and game in winter. Good homemade desserts include cakes made with pumpkin and almond or chocolate and walnut, a rich bread pudding, and simple *panna cotta* served with fresh fruit. ⊠ *Calesele, Cannaregio 1423* ☏ *041/716269* ▭ *No credit cards* ⊙ *Closed Sun., Mon., and 3 wks in Jan.* Ⓥ *San Marcuola.*

$ ✕ **Da Alberto.** An amicable trattoria that doubles as a bacaro, Alberto is always packed with locals. The faux-antique decor makes the place look old, but missing is the characteristic bacaro odor that comes from years of serving wine. However, what you cannot smell, you see: heaping barrels and demijohns full of vino da ombra. Vegetarians will appreciate the range of nonmeat dishes on the menu. Pasta is made to order, and fish can be better here than in most of the city center's pricier restaurants. ⊠ *Calle Giacinto Gallina, Cannaregio 5401* ☏ *041/5238153* ▭ *MC, V* ⊙ *Closed Sun., 1st wk in Feb., and 3 wks July–Aug.* Ⓥ *Ca' d'Oro.*

$ ✕ **Trattoria Ca' d'Oro.** Known commonly as La Vedova (the Widow), this warm trattoria not far from the Ca' d'Oro was opened as a low-key bacaro by the owner's great-grandparents. A rough Venetian floor, old marble counter, and long tables invite conviviality. Cicheti include tender *seppie roste* (grilled cuttlefish), *polpette* (meatballs), and baccalà mantecato. The house winter pasta is the *pastisso de radicio rosso* (lasagna with sausage, radicchio, and béchamel sauce). In spring, the chef switches to pastisso *de asparagi* (with asparagus). ⊠ *Calle del Pistor, Cannaregio 3912* ☏ *041/5285324* ▭ *No credit cards* ⊙ *Closed Thurs., no lunch Sun.* Ⓥ *Ca' d'Oro.*

Fodor'sChoice ★

★ ¢ ✕ **Tiziano.** They serve inexpensive salad plates and daily pasta specials at this tavola calda, but concentrate instead on the staggering array of *tramezzini* (sandwiches) that line the display cases. It's a handy place for a quick detour and snack at very modest prices. Vegetarians will delight in Tiziano's version of the classic Italian toast which, in this case, is a grilled cheese sandwich with eggplant slices and roasted zucchini. ⊠ *Salizzada San Giovanni Crisostomo, Cannaregio 5747* ☎ *041/ 5235544* ▬ *No credit cards* Ⓥ *Rialto.*

Castello

$$$$ ✕ **Al Covo.** This small charming osteria changes its menu according to the day's bounty—mostly local seafood caught just hours before and specialties from other European waters. Cesare Benelli and his American wife, Diane, insist on only the freshest ingredients. Try the *zuppa di pesce* (fish soup) followed by the fish of the day (grilled, baked, or steamed). Desserts are homemade, and the wine list is extensive. At lunch, only a fixed-price menu (€33, with several options) is served; dinner is à la carte. Given the steep prices here, it's more than a pity that it's cash only. ⊠ *Campiello della Pescaria, Castello 3968* ☎ *041/5223812* ▬ *No credit cards* ☾ *Closed Wed.–Thurs., 1 wk in Aug., and 4 wks Dec.–Jan.* Ⓥ *Arsenale.*

$$$$ ✕ **Do Leoni.** The Two Lions, located in the Hotel Londra Palace, is a sumptuous candlelight setting in which to sample Venetian and other Italian cuisine. Young Sicilian chef Stefano Mazzone is a veteran of stints in luxury hotels throughout Italy; his seasonal menu is inventive and indulges in savory flights of fantasy. He elevates such earthy soups as zuppa di fagioli to new levels; his seven-course tasting menu utilizes such non-Italian ingredients as vanilla and ginger. The summer terrace occupies a good portion of the Riva. ⊠ *Riva degli Schiavoni, Castello 4171* ☎ *041/ 5200533* 🪑 *Reservations essential* ▬ *AE, DC, MC, V* Ⓥ *San Zaccaria.*

$$$–$$$$ ✕ **Alle Testiere.** A strong local following can make it tough to get one of
Fodor'sChoice the five tables at this tiny trattoria near Campo Santa Maria Formosa.
★ With its decidedly unglamorous ceiling fans, the place feels as informal as a bistro (or a saloon); the food, however, is much more sophisticated. Chef Bruno Gavagnin's dishes stand out for lightness and balance: try the *gnocchetti con moscardini* (little gnocchi with tender baby octopus) or the linguine with *coda di rospo* (monkfish), or inquire about the carpaccio of the day. The well-assembled wine list is particularly strong on local whites. ⊠ *Calle del Mondo Novo, Castello 5801* ☎ *041/5227220* 🪑 *Reservations essential* ▬ *MC, V* ☾ *Closed Sun. and Mon.* Ⓥ *Rialto or San Marco.*

★ **$$–$$$** ✕ **Corte Sconta.** What happens when a hotel porter and a trade union leader open up a bacaro near the Arsenal? They choose an old tavern, where the poor once brought food from their unheated homes in order to drink a glass of wine and share the warmth of a roaring stove, and leave the decor as is. Cicheti, served as starters, come by the dozen, but save room for primi such as spaghetti *neri alle capesante e zucchine* (cuttlefish-ink pasta with scallops and zucchini) and secondi such as squid stuffed with radicchio di Treviso. The house dessert is a warm zabaglione with cookies. ⊠ *Calle del Pestrin, Castello 3886* ☎ *041/5227024* 🪑 *Reservations essential* ▬ *AE, DC, MC, V* ☾ *Closed Sun.–Mon., 4 wks Jan.–Feb., 4 wks July–Aug.* Ⓥ *Arsenale.*

$–$$$ ✕ **Da Bruno.** A country *taverna* (tavern) in the center of Venice, this popular restaurant grills its meat over an open fire. First, though, don't overlook the cicheti at the counter, such as the paper-thin prosciutto wrapped around *grissini* (thin bread sticks). For main courses, take your pick from such Italian specialties as fillet of beef with pepper sauce or veal with wild mushrooms. Fish fans may gravitate toward the scampi, calamari, or squid with polenta. ⊠ *Calle del Paradiso, Castello 5731* ☎ *041/ 5221480* ▬ *AE, DC, MC, V* Ⓥ *San Marco or Rialto.*

$$ ✕ **Al Mascaron.** The convivial, crowded Al Mascaron, with its paper table-cloths and informal atmosphere, is always filled with Venetians who drop in to gossip, drink, play cards, and eat cicheti at the bar. You can bet on delicious fish, pastas, risottos, and seafood salads. Locals complain that the prices have become somewhat inflated, but grudgingly admit that the food is good. ⊠ *Calle Lunga Santa Maria Formosa, Castello 5225* 🕾 *No credit cards* ⊘ *Closed Sun. and mid-Dec.–mid-Jan.* Ⓥ *Rialto or San Marco.*

$–$$ ✕ **Dai Tosi.** Finding a restaurant in Castello Basso can be difficult; this neighborhood trattoria is the only fairly priced place near San Pietro di Castello. The red, hand-painted sign above the window reflects the homey interior and also the cheerfulness of service: *tosi* refers to the "young lads" on the waitstaff, as opposed to the grumpy, aging career waiters you might encounter elsewhere. The menu offers the usual array of Vene-tian primi at lower-than-usual prices. In the evening and on Thursday at lunch you can opt for pizza; on Monday, Tuesday, and Thursday evenings there's only pizza. ⊠ *Seco Marina, Castello 738* 🕾 *041/ 5237102* 🖃 *No credit cards* ⊘ *Closed Wed. and 2–3 wks in Aug.* Ⓥ *Riva dei Partigiani.*

$ ✕ **Da Remigio.** They may seat the foreigners in the first room and the later-arriving Venetians in the second, but that's a minor complaint, and it's clear why Venetians come here: the food is good, the service prompt, and the atmosphere lively. The *canocchio bollite* (boiled, then chilled, shredded mantis shrimp) is a perfect starter, particularly when paired with an effervescent local white wine. Though seconds are strong on fish, Da Remigio also turns out respectable nonfish dishes such as the spaghetti *con porcini* (with mushrooms) and grilled meats. ⊠ *Salizzada dei Greci, Castello 3416* 🕾 *041/5230089* 🕭 *Reservations essential* 🖃 *AE, DC, MC, V* ⊘ *Closed Mon. dinner, closed Tues., 2 wks July–Aug., and 4 wks Dec.–Jan. No dinner Mon.* Ⓥ *Riva Schiavoni.*

$ ✕ **Osteria al Portego.** At this bacaro, located on a calle where bacari have thrived for centuries, the emphasis is more on food than on wine. Reg-ulars swear by the gelatinous *nervetti* (veal cartilage) served with beans; it's an acquired taste, but once you've developed a taste for it, it's hard to resist. Equally good, but less daring, are the deep-fried crab claws, *folpetti* (baby octopus), and hard-boiled eggs with pickles and anchovies. A big pot of risotto is made once or twice a day and served on the spot. ⊠ *Calle della Malvasia, Castello 6015* 🕾 *041/5229038* 🖃 *No credit cards* ⊘ *June–Sept., closed weekends; Oct.–May, closed Sun., no dinner Sat.; closed over Christmas, 2 wks in June, and 2 wks in Aug.* Ⓥ *Rialto.*

$ ✕ **Rivetta.** A reasonably priced trattoria among sandwich shops and tourist traps, Rivetta is a safe bet for a bite to eat near Piazza San Marco. Crowded and not particularly charming, it is redeemed by fast service and a solid selection at the counter: try *insalata di mare* (seafood salad) and *un bianco* (a glass of house white wine). If you take a seat, con-sider the *pasticcio* (fish lasagna) pasta special. If you have recently taken a gondola ride, there's a fair chance you will run into your gondolier: those who park at the nearby Ponte della Canonica, San Zaccaria, and Bacino di San Marco are regulars here. ⊠ *Ponte San Provolo, Castello 4625* 🕾 *041/5287302* 🖃 *MC, V* ⊘ *Closed Mon. and three wks in July–Aug.* Ⓥ *San Zaccaria.*

Dorsoduro

★ $$$–$$$$ ✕ **Ai Gondolieri.** If you're somewhat sick of fish, this is the place to come, as meat and food of the mainland are menu mainstays. Despite the tourist-trap name, it's a favorite with Venetians. Feast on *filetto di maiale con castraure* (pork fillet with baby artichokes), duck breast with apple and sweet onion, or more traditional dishes from [...] horse meat and game, gnocchim, and polent[...] average in quality and variety. ⊠ *Fondament[...] soduro 366* ☎ *041/5286396* ⊟ *AE, DC, M[...] lunch July–Aug.* Ⓥ *Accademia.*

$$–$$$$ ✕ **Locanda Montin.** Peggy Guggenheim used t[...] including Jackson Pollock and Mark Rothko—to this [...] tian inn not far from her Palazzo Venier dei Leoni. The walls are still covered with modern art, but it's far from the haute bohemian hangout it used to be, except for when the Biennale crowd takes over. Outside, you can dine under an elongated arbor and enjoy such specialties as rigatoni *ai quattro formaggi* (with four cheeses), spaghetti Adriatica (with fish sauce), and antipasto Montin (seafood antipasto). ⊠ *Fondamenta di Borgo, Dorsoduro 1147* ☎ *041/5227151* ⊟ *AE, DC, MC, V* ◷ *Closed Wed., Jan. to Carnival, and Tues.–Wed. in July and Aug.* Ⓥ *Accademia.*

$$–$$$ ✕ **Cantinone Storico.** On a quiet, romantic canal near the Accademia, this comfortable trattoria with alfresco tables serves well-prepared specialties such as risotto *terra mare* (with seafood, vegetables, and porcini mushrooms) and tagliolini *alla granseola* (with spider-crab sauce, available only with advance notice). The place draws mostly tourists, but it's hard to beat for location and reasonable prices. The house stocks a good selection of wines. ⊠ *Fondamenta di Ca' Bragadin, Dorsoduro 660/1* ☎ *041/5239577* ⊟ *AE, MC, V* ◷ *Closed Sun., Nov., and Jan.* Ⓥ *Accademia.*

$$–$$$ ✕ **Enoteca Onega.** With its outside tables in summer and a good, informal restaurant open for dinner, this enoteca is an ideal spot for some satisfying food and a glass of wine. The decor is modern but warm and comfortable, and behind the counter you can see the cooks at work in the kitchen. They might be preparing old Venetian favorites such as baked sardines or saor, but also lasagna, gnocchi *ai cinque formaggi* (in a rich cheese sauce), lamb on skewers, and home-smoked fish. ⊠ *Campo San Barnaba, Dorsoduro 2852 (near the Accademia Gallery)* ☎ *041/5224410* ⊟ *AE, DC, MC, V* ◷ *Closed Sun. and Tues. No lunch Mon.* Ⓥ *Accademia.*

$$–$$$ ✕ **La Furatola.** The name means simply "The Restaurant" in Old Venetian dialect, reflecting the plain style of the decor, but it hardly does justice to the fine fish available within. There's a selection of seafood cicheti on display as you enter, and for the main course, the fish are presented for your approval before being cooked. When it's available, the John Dory is truly remarkable. It's a small place—just one room—and they will only seat you if you have reserved in advance. ⊠ *Calle Lunga San Barnaba, Dorsoduro 2870* ☎ *041/5208594* ⌂ *Reservations essential* ⊟ *AE, DC, MC, V* ◷ *Closed Thurs., last 3 wks in Jan., and Aug. No lunch Mon.* Ⓥ *Ca' Rezzonico.*

★ $$ ✕ **L'Incontro.** This trattoria between San Barnaba and Campo Santa Margherita has a faithful clientele of Venetians and visitors, attracted by flavorful Sardinian food, sociable service, and reasonable prices. Starters include Sardinian sausages, but you might sample the delicious traditional primi like *culingiones* (large ravioli filled with pecorino, saffron, and orange peel). The selection of secondi is heavy on herb-crusted meat dishes such as *coniglio al mirto* (rabbit baked on a bed of myrtle sprigs) and the *costine d'agnello con rosmarino e mentuccia* (baby lamb ribs with rosemary and wild mint). ⊠ *Rio Terrà Canal, Dorsoduro 3062/a* ☎ *041/5222404* ⊟ *AE, DC, MC, V* ◷ *Closed Mon., Jan., and 2 wks in Aug. No lunch Tues.* Ⓥ *Ca' Rezzonico.*

$–$$ ✕ **Anzolo Rafael.** A long way from the madding crowd, this trattoria has a clientele evenly divided between locals and visitors, all eager to eat something simple and authentic at a fraction of the price of comparable Venetian restaurants. Take a seat at a wooden table in the no-nonsense back room and listen to the kind signora (her husband is a few steps away in the kitchen) recite the short menu. Choose from two pastas or a fish soup, two vegetable side dishes, and a main course of fish, either grilled or fried. Plan on dessert elsewhere—the signore doesn't make sweets. ⊠ *Campo Anzolo Rafael, Dorsoduro 1722* ☎ *041/ 5237456* ⊟ *No credit cards* ☉ *Closed Mon.–Tues.* Ⓥ *Zattere.*

$–$$ ✕ **Taverna San Trovaso.** A wide choice of Venetian dishes served in robust portions, economical fixed-price menus, pizzas, and house wine by the glass or pitcher keep this two-floor, no-nonsense tavern abuzz with young Venetians and budget-conscious visitors in the know. It's always packed, and table turnover is fast. Not far from the Gallerie dell'Accademia, this is a good place to slip into while sightseeing in Dorsoduro. ⊠ *Fondamenta Priuli, Dorsoduro 1016* ☎ *041/5203703* ⊟ *AE, MC, V* ☉ *Closed Mon. and 1 wk Dec.–Jan.* Ⓥ *Zattere.*

★ $ ✕ **Ai 4 Feri.** The paper tablecloths and cozy, laid-back ambience are all part of this small restaurant's charm. The menu varies according to what's fresh that day; imaginative combinations of ingredients in the primi— herring and sweet peppers, salmon and radicchio, giant shrimp and broccoli (with pumpkin gnocchi)—are the norm. A meal here followed by after-dinner drinks at Campo Santa Margherita, a five-minute walk away, makes for a lovely evening. The kitchen closes early on weekdays. ⊠ *Calle lunga San Barnaba, Dorsoduro 2754/a* ☎ *041/5206978* ⊟ *No credit cards* ☉ *Closed Sun. and June* Ⓥ *San Basilio or Ca' Rezzonico.*

¢–$ ✕ **Alla Dona Onesta.** The virtue of the "Honest Woman" is still maintained by the owners of this small, neat trattoria perched along the rio. Through the glass door you'll see a well-kept old structure with no frills— the style is dark-brown wooden chairs and white tablecloths. The menu posted outside offers a reasonable choice of staple Italian pasta dishes, fish, and meat. Few tourists stop here, and the little English you'll hear is likely to be a conversation among professors of the nearby Università Ca' Foscari, who are lunchtime regulars. ⊠ *Ponte de la Dona Onesta, Dorsoduro 3922* ☎ *041/710586* ⊟ *AE, DC, MC, V* Ⓥ *Accademia.*

Giudecca

★ $$$$ ✕ **Cipriani.** A cut above most Italian restaurants in ambience, service, and view, the Cipriani is an expensive, world-class experience worth having once. In white-peach season (July to early September), start with the famous blossom-scented Bellini. The cuisine is rooted in Venetian tradition, prepared with a star chef's hand, and matched with a superb wine list. Sole fillets instead of whole sardines are used for the saor; deep-fried prawns, coated in semolina flour, stay wonderfully crisp. Desserts are spectacular: a decadent tiramisu is served in a bitter-chocolate shell topped by a gondola. ⊠ *Fondamenta San Giovanni 10, Giudecca* ☎ *041/5207744* ♨ *Reservations essential* ⊟ *AE, DC, MC, V* ☉ *Closed mid-Nov.–mid-Mar.* Ⓥ *Zitelle.*

★ $–$$ ✕ **Altanella.** This Giudecca institution facing a large canal is the right place to taste some of the strange-looking fish sold at the stalls in the Rialto's *pescheria* (fish market). The Altanella is a favorite among locals, although a trilingual menu makes it clear that visitors find their way here as well. Start with a salad of folpetti, followed by a creamy risotto or gnocchi with a seppie (cuttlefish) sauce. Secondi include grilled or deep-fried fish, or seppie *in umido* (in a stew with its black ink and a dash of tomato sauce), served with polenta. Wine is not this rustic place's strong suit. ⊠ *Calle delle Erbe 268, Giudecca* ☎ *041/5227780* ⊟ *No credit cards* ☉ *Closed Mon.–Tues., most of Aug., and last 3 wks in Jan.* Ⓥ *Redentore or Palanca.*

Lido

$$–$$$ ✕ **Trattoria Favorita.** This neighborhood eatery has been in the same family's hands since the 1920s and offers you the choice between a wood-beamed dining room and a vine-covered garden. Seafood is the specialty, always fresh and lovingly prepared; you won't go wrong ordering the tagliolini with shrimp and zucchini or the divine gnocchi con granseola. ⊠ *Via Francesco Duodo 33, Lido* ☎ *041/5261626* ⌖ *Reservations essential* ▤ *AE, DC, MC, V* ⊘ *Closed Mon. and Jan.–mid-Feb. No lunch Tues.* Ⓥ *Lido.*

$$ ✕ **Al Vecio Cantier.** The wild scenery, with intersecting canals and reeds, contributes to the appeal of one of the liveliest places on the Lido, always filled to the gills during the film festival. There's efficient cicheti service, but the restaurant deserves a longer visit for a relaxing meal in the best Venetian tradition: try whipped baccalà with polenta, or tagliolini *con gamberetti e carciofi* (with shrimp and artichokes) in spring. Homemade desserts include lemon and almond tarts, or you can dip cookies in a glass of *vino passito,* a dessert wine. Outside dining is in a pretty garden. ⊠ *Via della Droma 76, Lido* ☎ *041/5268130* ▤ *AE, DC, MC, V* ⊘ *Closed Mon. No lunch Tues., Nov., or Jan.* Ⓥ *Lido.*

$–$$ ✕ **Le Garzette.** A small, family-run trattoria inside the agriturismo of the same name, Le Garzette serves very fresh fish, homegrown vegetables, and home-raised poultry, including duck. Meals are available to those not rooming here only at Friday dinner and lunch and dinner on weekends. You won't find anything new on the menu, but everything tastes genuine, and the staff won't look down on you if you are wearing shorts. ⊠ *Lungomare Alberoni 32, Lido* Ⓥ *vaporetto Lines 1, 6, 14, 51/52, or 82, Lido stop* ☎ *041/731078* ⌖ *Reservations essential* ▤ *No credit cards* ⊘ *Closed Dec.–Feb. No lunch weekdays* Ⓥ *Venice Lido.*

$ ✕ **Bar Trento.** This neat, old-style osteria 10 minutes from Piazzale Santa Maria Elisabetta has a soft spot for meat and innards (one of the owners was a *bechèr,* or butcher). Lunch is the only meal served, but it stays open from 8 to 8 for ombre and cicheti. Descriptions of tasty snacks from century-old recipes are omitted, as they might put off nonnatives. More recognizable options include baccalà *alla vicentina* (stewed with onion, milk, and Parmesan); pasta with seafood; and several seasonal risottos. As a secondo, fish can be cooked any way you want. ⊠ *Via Sandro Gallo 82, Lido* ▤ *No credit cards* ⊘ *Closed Sun. No dinner except during Biennale* Ⓥ *Lido.*

Murano

$$–$$$$ ✕ **Valmarana.** The most upscale restaurant on Murano is housed in a palace on the *fondamenta* (street) across from the Museo Vetrario. Stuccoed walls and glass chandeliers complement well-appointed tables, and although the menu contains no surprises, the cuisine is more refined than at other places here. Try the baked sea scallops, the crab with fresh herbs, or the rich risotto *alla pescatora,* containing all kinds of fish. In warm weather, reserve a table in the back garden or on the terrace overlooking the canal; inside, there's a no-smoking room. ⊠ *Fondamenta Navagero 31, Murano* ☎ *041/739313* ▤ *AE, DC, MC, V* ⊘ *Closed 3 wks in Jan. No dinner* Ⓥ *Navagero.*

$–$$ ✕ **Ai Frati.** A walk along the Fondamenta dei Vetrai brings you to the large iron bridge spanning Murano's Grand Canal; down to the left, hanging over the Canale degli Angeli, is the attractive terrace of Ai Frati. As elsewhere in Venice, the key word here is fish, prepared any way you want. The risottos are nicely done. If you want to taste a famous dish from Murano and you're lucky enough to be here in November, ask when

WITH CHILDREN?

DINING IN VENICE can present some obstacles if you're traveling with children. Most notable is the fish factor: the notorious non-favorite with kids dominates Venetian menus. Most—though not all—restaurants will have other offerings; if fish is going to be a problem, it's a good idea to check what alternatives are available before booking or taking your seat.

Generally, children will feel welcome at casual establishments such as trattorias, but only very well-behaved children should go to higher-end restaurants; indeed, it's rare to see Italian children in them. Some restaurants and trattorias will have high chairs or cushions for children to sit on, but you won't find a children's menu. Instead, ask the waiter for a mezza porzione (half portion) or porzione da bambino (child's portion) of any dish. Though spaghetti and meatballs isn't found on menus, other pasta dishes such as spaghetti al pomodoro (with tomato sauce) may prove to be suitable substitutions. Italian children are fond of pasta in bianca (with butter) and con olio e parmigiano (with olive oil and Parmesan); even if they're not on the menu, most chefs will be happy to prepare them. Many restaurants serve prosciutto e melone (cured ham and melon, available in season) and insalata caprese (mozzarella, tomatoes, and basil), both of which can be attractive alternatives for a child confronted with calf's liver and cuttlefish.

Venetian pizza is a last resort, or nearly so; though most of it is forgettable at best, the familiar wedge of dough and cheese may be the closest thing to comfort food a young diner will find. That is, unless you count McDonald's, which has found its way to La Serenissima, to the chagrin of many natives and visitors alike. The most central location is near the Rialto bridge.

you book for the *bisatto sull'ara*, a local variety of fleshy eel traditionally cooked on a bed of bay leaves. ⊠ *Fondamenta Sebastiano Venier 4, Murano* ☎ *041/736694* ⊟ *V* ⊘ *Closed Thurs. and Feb. No dinner* Ⓥ *Venier.*

$–$$ ✕ **Antica Trattoria.** This lunch-only trattoria can be easily spotted by the bright red walls close to the Grand Canal on the island of Murano. For company you'll probably find local glass workers with a *caffè corretto con grappa* (espresso with grappa) in front of them. If it's more solid nourishment you're after, go for the freshly grilled fish or the seppie in tecia, served in the rear garden. ⊠ *Riva Longa 20, Murano* ☎ *041/739610* ⊟ *AE, DC, MC, V* ⊘ *Closed Sat. and Feb. No dinner* Ⓥ *Murano.*

$–$$ ✕ **Busa alla Torre da Lele.** A pretty square with olive trees and a well sets the stage for Da Lele, a favorite of the Muranese. On the ground floor of a dark-red building with a loggia, the restaurant stretches out on the campo, where you eat in the shade of large umbrellas. Check the blackboard for such daily specials as antipasto Busa, with granseola and garusoli; *bavette alla busara* (flat spaghetti with a hot spicy shrimp and tomato sauce); and baked rombo or branzino with potato. Homemade cookies are served with *fragolino*, a sweet, sparkling wine redolent of strawberries. ⊠ *Campo Santo Stefano 3, Murano* ☎ *041/739662* ⊟ *AE, MC, V* ⊘ *No dinner* Ⓥ *Faro.*

San Marco

$$$$ ✕ **Al Graspo de Ua.** Opened in the 19th century as a small osteria, the "Bunch of Grapes" became the meeting place of artists and movie stars back in the 1960s. Today, it serves a faithful clientele of wealthy Italians. The decor is a miscellanea of plants, sculpture, candlelight, and paintings set against brick and white-stucco walls. The owner, Lucio

Zanon, speaks fluent English and will introduce you to a wide-ranging menu of fresh pasta, seasonal risotto, and meat and seafood. A treat in late spring is the thick white asparagus from Bassano, which, with a couple of fried eggs, is eaten as a main course. ⊠ *Calle dei Bombaseri, San Marco 5094* ☎ *041/5223647* ▤ *AE, DC, MC, V* ◷ *Closed Mon. and 1 wk in Jan.* Ⓥ *Rialto.*

$$$$ ✕ **Antico Martini.** It was born as a caffè in 1792 for those artists, intellectuals, singers, and conductors loitering around the opera house La Fenice. It's changed management only twice, and since 1921 the Baldi family have been the proprietors. If you're after Old World Venetian elegance, then look no further. Intimate candle-lit tables, antique oil paintings, and a patrician air complement traditional yet inventive dishes. Salmon rolls filled with caviar and sour cream might be followed by homemade tagliatelle with prawn and arugula or angelfish with black peppercorns. ⊠ *Calle del Cafetier, off Campo San Fantin, San Marco 1983* ☎ *041/5224121* ⚄ *Reservations essential* ⛨ *Jacket required* ▤ *AE, DC, MC, V* ◷ *Closed Tues. No lunch Wed.* Ⓥ *San Marco or Santa Maria del Giglio.*

$$$$ ✕ **Antico Pignolo.** The "Old Pine Nut" occupies a former spice shop dating from the 1200s; adventurous types might want to arrive by boat, as the place has its own private landing. If you're lucky enough to be in town when it's warm, book a table in the exquisite garden, where white flowers match the table settings. Top-notch staff, also clad in white, serve creative interpretations of Venetian classics. The *crostino di polenta con baccalà mantecato* (creamy salt cod served on polenta) may be the definitive version. The carefully culled wine list alone is worth the trip. ⊠ *Calle degli Specchieri, San Marco 451* ☎ *041/5228123* ▤ *AE, DC, MC, V* Ⓥ *San Marco.*

FodorśChoice
★

$$$$ ✕ **Da Arturo.** This tiny eatery on the Calle degli Assassini has the distinction in Venice of *not* serving seafood. Instead you can choose from salads and fresh vegetable dishes; tasty, tender, meat courses in generous portions, including the subtly pungent *braciola alla veneziana* (pork chop schnitzel with vinegar); and an authentic creamy homemade tiramisu to finish. Noncarnivores make their way here as well, as the *antipasti* and *primi* offerings are more than hospitable. ⊠ *Calle degli Assassini, San Marco 3656* ☎ *041/5286974* ⚄ *Reservations essential* ▤ *No credit cards* ◷ *Closed Sun., 10 days after Carnevale, and 4 wks in Aug.* Ⓥ *San Marco or Rialto.*

$$$$ ✕ **Da Ivo.** An enclave of Tuscan cuisine two minutes from Piazza San Marco, this is a cozy, relaxing—and very expensive—spot, with paintings and copper pots hanging on white walls and candlelight at dinner. Start with the less-Tuscan tagliolini *alla bottarga* (with roe). The reputation of the restaurant has been built on its famous *bistecche fiorentine* (2-pound Chianina beef steaks grilled over olive-wood charcoal), but game and fish are also reliable standards. ⊠ *Ramo dei Fuseri, San Marco 1809* ☎ *041/5285004* ▤ *AE, DC, MC, V* ◷ *Closed Sun. and Jan.* Ⓥ *San Marco.*

$$$$ ✕ **Grand Canal.** The restaurant of the Hotel Monaco & Grand Canal is a favorite with Venetians, who enjoy eating on the lovely canal-side terrace in summer and in the cozy dining room in winter. All the pasta is made fresh daily on the premises, and the smoked and marinated salmon are also prepared here. The chef's traditional Venetian cuisine is top-flight; you'll marvel over savory dishes such as *scampi alla Buséra* (shrimp in a cognac sauce). Jackets are required for men at dinner. ⊠ *Hotel Monaco & Grand Canal, Calle Vallaresso, San Marco 1325* ☎ *041/5200211* ▤ *AE, DC, MC, V* Ⓥ *San Marco.*

$$$$ ✕ **Harry's Bar.** The humble door of this famed watering hole leads to the legendary Venetian hangout of such notables as Hemingway, Maugham, and Onassis. Such company doesn't come cheap, but Harry's

Where to Eat in San Marco

is still known for the driest martinis and the most h[...] v
town, as well as decent, though overpriced, *cucina v[...]*
boring beige-on-beige, but the view upstairs—lookin[...]
ular Chiesa di Santa Maria della Salute—competes w[...]
Canaletto *vedute* (scenic paintings). Remember, you come to Harry [...]
the phenomenal atmosphere, not for the less-than-phenomenal food.
⊠ *Calle Vallaresso, San Marco 1323* ☏ *041/5285777* ⌕ *Reservations essential* ▭ *AE, DC, MC, V* Ⓥ *San Marco.*

$$$$ ✕ **La Caravella.** It's been a Venetian classic for the past forty years, and even though the decor, made to suggest the interior of a seagoing vessel, might evoke a theme restaurant, there's nothing gimmicky about the cuisine. The seasonal menu offers such treats as *ravioli con scampi, zafferano, e noce* (ravioli with shrimp, saffron, and walnuts), and variations on Ventian standards such as *bigola con anatra* (a thick pasta with a fragrant duck sauce). The pretty garden courtyard is open from May through September. ⊠ *Saturnia Internazionale, Calle Larga XXII Marzo, San Marco 2397* ☏ *041/5208901* ⌕ *Reservations essential* ▭ *AE, DC, MC, V* Ⓥ *Santa Maria del Giglio.*

$$$$ ✕ **Quadri.** In the 19th century, princes, dukes, and countesses dined here, and you'll feel like one when you walk into the gilded salons of Venice's most beautiful restaurant. The decor is stunning—Quadri's second-floor aerie gives you a pigeon's-eye view of Piazza San Marco—and the cuisine is classic Venetian, with lots of fish. (Truffles are a major draw in the fall.) Come September, when the Biennale is in session, the sequins-and-sunglasses set takes over. ⊠ *Piazza San Marco, San Marco 120–124* ☏ *041/5289299* ⌕ *Reservations essential* ▭ *AE, DC, MC, V* ☉ *Closed Mon. Nov.–Apr. except during Christmas and Carnevale* Ⓥ *San Marco.*

$$$$ ✕ **Taverna la Fenice.** The lovely (and bilingual) Odette Zora presides over this Old Venetian restaurant steps away from La Fenice. Though the velvet-laden interior may feel somewhat dated, the menu is up-to-the-minute. The *carpaccio di branzino di mare* (thinly sliced raw sea bass) benefits from the judicious addition of ginger and, yes, wasabi. Avocado and asparagus adorn the *insalata di granchio* (crab salad). The wine list, particularly strong on wines from the Veneto, is well thought out. When it's warm, you can dine alfresco. ⊠ *Campo San Fantin, San Marco 1939* ☏ *041/5223856* ▭ *AE, DC, MC, V* Ⓥ *San Marco.*

$$$–$$$$ ✕ **Canova.** The restaurant of the Hotel Luna Baglioni is on the pricey side, but the excellent service, tasteful surroundings, and inventive dishes all make for one of the most reliably good dining experiences close to Piazza San Marco. Fresh, nicely presented dishes might include a warm salad of scallops and cannellini beans in a lemon rosemary sauce, or veal medallions with champagne vinegar, capers, and herbs. ⊠ *Luna Baglioni, San Marco 1243* ☏ *041/5289840* ▭ *AE, DC, MC, V* Ⓥ *San Marco.*

¢–$ ✕ **Vino Vino.** The annex of the extremely expensive Antico Martini restaurant is an informal wine bar where you can sample wines by the glass from an impressive list. You can also partake of a light lunch or dinner buffet style. Typical offerings include pastas of the day, vegetables, and a couple of meat dishes. Service is incredibly friendly and patient: given its location, it attracts crowds who come for a quick bite to eat before heading off to another museum. If you're traveling with children, consider stopping here. ⊠ *Calle delle Veste, near Campo San Fantin, San Marco 2007/a* ☏ *041/2417680* ⌕ *Reservations not accepted* ▭ *No credit cards* ☉ *Closed Tues.* Ⓥ *San Marco or Santa Maria del Giglio.*

¢   ✕ **Enoteca al Volto.** Just steps away from the Rialto Bridge, this bar has been around since 1936; the fine cicheti and primi have a lot to do with its staying power. Two small, dark rooms with wooden tables and chairs provide the backdrop to enjoy simple fare. The place prides itself on its considerable wine list of both Italian and foreign wines; if you stick to the panini and a cicheto or two, you'll eat very well for very little. If you opt for one of the primi of the day, the price category goes up a notch. ⊠ *Calle Cavalli, San Marco 4081* ☎ *041/5228945* ▤ *No credit cards* ☯ *Closed Sun.* Ⓥ *Rialto.*

San Polo

$$$$ ✕ **Osteria da Fiore.** Tucked away on a little calle off the top of Campo
Fodor'sChoice San Polo, Da Fiore is a favorite among high-end diners for its superbly
★ prepared Venetian cuisine and refined yet relaxed atmosphere. A superlative seafood lunch or dinner here might include delicate hors d'oeuvres of moeche, scallops, and tiny octopus, followed by a succulent risotto or tagliolini *con scampi e radicchio* (with shrimp and radicchio), and a perfectly cooked main course of *rombo* (turbot) or *tagliata di tonno* (tuna steak). ⊠ *Calle del Scaleter, San Polo 2202/a* ☎ *041/721308* ⬡ *Reservations essential* ▤ *AE, DC, MC, V* ☯ *Closed Sun.–Mon., Aug., and Dec. 25–Jan. 20* Ⓥ *San Tomà.*

$$–$$$$ ✕ **Poste Vecie.** A tiny wooden bridge connects this historic osteria with the Rialto pescheria. In the 16th century, Poste Vecie (Old Post Office) served as a base for Venetian couriers, who stopped here to sort the mail between a glass of wine and a bowl of risotto. The place went upscale, but the large fireplaces are still here, along with the wooden ceiling, hand-painted plates, and some bizarre frescoes depicting allegories of vices (gluttony has been left out). Besides the usual Venetian specialties, you'll find the more rare bisatto *in umido* (stewed with polenta) and moeche in spring-time. An inner garden opens up in warm weather. ⊠ *Pescheria, San Polo 1608* ☎ *041/721822* ▤ *AE, DC, MC, V* ☯ *Closed Tues.* Ⓥ *Rialto.*

$$–$$$ ✕ **Da Ignazio.** Conveniently located on the route from Campo San Polo to the Frari, this pleasant family restaurant serves good, honest Venetian cuisine. The house specialty is a generous portion of creamy white polenta topped by shelled scampi, in the fall served with porcini. Poorly prepared elsewhere in town, the *capesante gratinate* (scallop gratin) here is made with just enough bread crumbs to make it nice and crusty on top. Desserts—standards such as crème caramel—are homemade and light. The garden is a charming spot to dine in fair weather. ⊠ *Calle dei Saoneri, San Polo 2749* ☎ *041/5234852* ▤ *AE, DC, MC, V* ☯ *Closed Sat., 2 wks over Christmas, and 1st 2 wks in Aug.* Ⓥ *San Tomà.*

$ ✕ **Alla Madonna.** It's true that many hotels in town send their guests here, and that sometimes there are more foreigners present than locals, but for quality and price, this osteria is hard to beat. In short, it's a rare Venetian bargain. Ubiquitous copper pots line the ceilings, walls are covered with paintings and prints, and bow-tied waiters in white jackets rush among tables delivering plates filled with hefty portions. The *granseola* (crab) is particularly winning here; make sure to ask for some extra-virgin olive oil. If possible, try to save room for the tiramisu. ⊠ *Calle della Madonna, San Polo 594* ☎ *041/5223824* ▤ *AE, MC, V* ☯ *Closed Wed. and part of Aug.* Ⓥ *Rialto.*

Santa Croce

$$–$$$ ✕ **Ribò.** Signor Martini loves thoroughbreds, so when he took over this spot he renamed it after the champion European horse Ribot. His kitchen puts out purebred Venetian cuisine—food that's fanciful but not fancy. Several homemade pasta dishes are always on the menu, and the fish rolls with eggplant, when available, are worth a medal. The pleasant interior garden is a rarity for Venetian restaurants. ⊠ *Fondamenta Minotto, Santa Croce 158* ☎ *041/5242486* ▤ *AE, DC, MC, V* ☯ *Closed Mon., 10 days in Jan., and 2 wks in Aug. No dinner Sun.* Ⓥ *Stazione.*

$$–$$$ ✕ **Vecio Fritolin.** Until not so long ago, fish was fried and sold "to go" throughout Venice just as in London, except that it was paired with polenta rather than chips. An old sign advertising fish to go still hangs outside the "Old Fry Shop," but nowadays you can only dine in. A second sign, announcing cicheti available to go, still holds true. At this neat bacaro con cucina you can have a traditional meal featuring such dishes as bigoli in salsa, baked fish with herbs, and non-Venetian lamb chops. ⊠ *Calle della Regina, Santa Croce 2262* ☎ *041/5222881* ▭ *AE, DC, MC, V* ⊗ *Closed Mon., 2 wks in Jan., and 2 wks in Aug. No lunch Tues.* Ⓥ *San Stae.*

$$ ✕ **Antica Besseta.** Tucked away in a quiet corner of Santa Croce, with a few tables under an ivy shelter, the Antica Besseta dates from the 18th century, and it retains some of its old feel. The menu focuses on vegetables and fish, according to what's at the market: spaghetti with caparozzoli or cuttlefish ink, *schie* (tiny gray shrimp with polenta), and plenty of grilled fish. ⊠ *Salizzada de Ca' Zusto, Santa Croce 1395* ☎ *041/5240428* ▭ *AE, MC, V* ⊗ *Closed Mon.–Tues. No lunch Wed.* Ⓥ *Rive di Biasio.*

$$ ✕ **La Zucca.** The place feels like as much like a typical vegetarian restaurant as you could expect to find in Venice, what with its simple place settings, exposed wood walls, and mélange of languages being spoken. Though the menu does have superb meat dishes such as the *sfilacci di cavallo con radicchio trevigiano* (smoked horse meat with radicchio), more attention is paid to dishes from the garden: try the *sedano rapa gratina al pecorino* (celery root gratin with pecorino cheese) or the *finocchi piccanti con olive* (fennel in a spicy tomato-olive sauce). Friendly service in a number of languages is the norm. ⊠ *Calle del Tintor, Santa Croce 1762* ☎ *041/5241570* ▭ *AE, DC, MC, V* ⊗ *Closed Sun., 1 wk in Aug., and over Christmas.* Ⓥ *S. Stae.*

$ ✕ **Bancogiro.** Come to this casual spot for a change from standard Venetian food. Yes, fish is on the menu, but offerings such as *mousse di gamberoni con salsa di avocado* (shrimp mousse with an avocado sauce) and Sicilian-style *sarde incinte* (stuffed, or "pregnant," sardines) are far from typical fare. The wine list and the cheese plate are both divine. The location is in the heart of the Rialto market in a 15th-century loggia, with tables upstairs in a carefully restored no-smoking room with a partial view of the Grand Canal; when it's warm, you can sit outdoors and get the full canal view. ⊠ *Campo San Giacometto 122 (under the porch), Santa Croce* ☎ *041/5232061* ▭ *No credit cards* ⊗ *Closed Mon. No dinner Sun.* Ⓥ *Rialto.*

FodorśChoice
★

$ ✕ **Do Spade.** A rough Venetian floor and the motto *Vinum bonum fortificat cor hominis* (good wine fortifies the man's heart) are tip-offs to the character of this classic bacaro that was once the haunt of Casanova. The plump host, Giorgio Lanza, is the town's unofficial authority on little sandwiches. He coined the term *paperini* for his own creations— cicheti served *on* bruschetta—and after tasting one you'll happily add the word to your Venetian vocabulary. At mealtimes, the bacaro doubles as a trattoria; stick to more authentic dishes such as *salsicce* (sausage) di secole, bean soup, baccalà, and cuttlefish. ⊠ *Calle Do Spade, San Polo 860* ☎ *041/5210574* ▭ *No credit cards* ⊗ *Closed Sun., 2 wks in Aug., and 10 days in Jan.* Ⓥ *Rialto.*

¢–$ ✕ **Ae Oche.** There's nothing Venetian about this saloonlike pizzeria with shelves of imported stouts and a no-smoking room. Seventy-nine pizza combinations include the Campagnola, lavishly topped with a mix of tomato, mozzarella, mushroom, Brie, and *speck* (smoked prosciutto). Purists can stick to the *margherita,* with tomato, mozzarella, and basil. A selection of 16 salads plus a few pasta dishes make the Oche an ideal stop for a light meal between sights. ✉ *Calle delle Oche, Santa Croce 1552/a–b* ☎ *041/5241161* ▭ *MC, V* Ⓥ *San Stae.*

★ ¢–$ ✕ **Al Prosecco.** Locals stream into this place, order the "spritzer bitter" (a combination of white wine, Campari, and seltzer water), and continue on their way; contemplate trying the drink while chewing on one of the fine panini, such as the *porchetta romane verdure* (roasted pig, Roman style, with greens). Proprietors Davide and Stefano preside over a young and friendly staff who reel off the day's specials with ease. When the weather's warm, you can eat outside on a beautiful campo. ✉ *Campo S. Giacomo da l'Orlo, Santa Croce 1503* ☎ *041/5240222* ▭ *No credit cards* ⊘ *Closed Sun.* Ⓥ *San Stae.*

Torcello

$$$$ ✕ **Locanda Cipriani.** Owned by a nephew of Arrigo Cipriani–the founder of Harry's Bar—this inn profits from its idyllic location on the island of Torcello. Hemingway, who loved the silence of the lagoon, came here often to eat, drink, and brood under the green veranda. The food is not exceptional, especially considering the price, but dining here is more about getting lost in Venetian magic. The menu features pastas, *vitello tonnato* (chilled poached veal in a tuna and caper sauce), baked orata with potatoes, and lots of seafood. A vaporetto service runs until 11:30 PM, and then upon request; service is sporadic. ✉ *Piazza Santa Fosca 29, Torcello* ☎ *041/730150* ▭ *AE, DC, MC, V* ⊘ *Closed Tues. and early Jan.–early Feb.* Ⓥ *Torcello.*

Bacari

While the list below covers some of the best of Venice's bacari, it's by no means exhaustive. Venetians themselves don't know how many bacari thrive in their hometown, and often the perfect one is the one you happen upon when hunger strikes.

¢ ✕ **Aciugheta.** Though the "tiny anchovy" (as the name translates) doubles as a pizzeria, stick to the tasty cicheti offered at the bar. The selection of wines by the glass changes daily, but there are always the ubiquitous local whites on hand, as well as some Tuscan and Piedmontese choices thrown in for good measure. Don't miss the *tonno con polenta* (tuna with polenta) if it's offered. ✉ *Campo SS. Filippo e Giacomo, Castello 4357* ☎ *041/5224292* ▭ *MC, V* Ⓥ *San Zaccaria.*

¢ ✕ **Cantina Do Mori.** This bacaro par excellence—cramped but warm and FodorśChoice cozy under hanging antique copper pots—has been catering to the ★ workers of the Rialto market since the 15th century. In addition to young, local whites and reds, the well-stocked cellar offers about 600 more-refined labels, many available by the glass. Between sips you can munch on crunchy grissini draped with prosciutto or a few well-stuffed, tiny tramezzini, appropriately called *francobolli* (stamps). Don't leave without tasting the delicious baccalà mantecato. ✉ *Calle dei Do Mori, San Polo 429* ☎ *041/5225401* ▭ *No credit cards* ⊘ *Closed Sun., 3 wks in Aug., and 1 wk in Jan.* Ⓥ *Rialto.*

¢ ✕ **Cantinone.** A beautiful 19th-century osteria opposite the *squero* (gon-FodorśChoice dola repair shop) of San Trovaso, this bacaro has original furnishings ★ and one of the best wine cellars in town. No cicheti are offered here, but you won't regret trying one of the huge *panini* (sandwiches) filled with first-rate cheeses and cured pork. Particularly tasty is the mortadella slathered with ricotta and Parmesan, topped with lettuce and a walnut or two, which is then rolled and eaten with the fingers. ✉ *Fondamenta Nani, Dorsoduro 992* ☎ *041/5230034* ▭ *No credit cards* ⊘ *Closed Sun. after 2 PM and 2 wks in Aug.* Ⓥ *Zattere.*

BACARI: ANDAR PER OMBRE

BACARI (the name harkens back to Bacchus, the Greek god of wine) provide the most quintessentially Venetian dining experience, and they aren't to be missed. They're the pillars of the city's social life: here fishermen and bankers alike line up for a glass of the house vino da ombra—"wine of the shadow," so named because in the past wine merchants kept their demijohns cool in the shadow of the Campanile. In a bacaro, ombre are enjoyed with cicheti, served at the counter, usually made of fish, inexpensive cuts of meat, grilled vegetables, boiled eggs, and onions. In recent years, a good number of Venice's bacari have become rather refined, adding some of northern Italy's best wines to their more typical local offerings.

An upsurge of bacari con cucina, family-run trattorias with limited menus catering mostly to Venetians, has made it possible to eat a full, well-prepared meal without spending a fortune. Tablecloths are often considered a luxury in these places, but the atmosphere is friendly, allowing you to catch a glimpse of the local way of life. Service is fast without being brusque, and there's no need to dress up.

Not all bacari double as bacari con cucina. Some do not even have tables for eating your cicheti. But even when they are little more than holes in the wall with blackened beams and rustic trappings, they qualify as the redeeming counterpart to all those tourist-oriented fast-food joints and bars lining the city's main streets. More often than not, bacari are hard to find. Tucked away in narrow calli, few have signs on the doors or storefront windows. Although in some cases plastic chairs and veneered tables have replaced generations-old furnishings, the spirit of bacari is still rooted in diehard traditions. A real bacaro would never dream of selling soft drinks, beer, or mineral water, and hosts would find it inconceivable to offer green salads and "lite" preparations.

All bacari serve wine by the glass and have at least a dozen cicheti available, from baccalà mantecato (a delicious whipped cod spread, served on bread or polenta squares) and folpetti (baby octopus, boiled and tossed with olive oil, lemon, and parsley) to polpette (meat loaf), melanzane alla griglia (grilled eggplant), and cipolline (sweet-and-sour pearl onions). Table service is the exception rather than the rule; normally you go to the counter and pick what you want. Keep track of what you eat and drink, and pay for everything (in cash only) at the end. Plan on spending €10–€15 for a hearty helping of cicheti. Hours of operation vary. Some bacari are open nonstop from 8 in the morning to 8 or 9 in the evening; others take a lunch break, closing around 1 or 1:30 and reopening at 5. Still others observe the same opening and closing times of osterie and restaurants. Most are closed on Sunday.

¢ ✕**Da Dante Alle Alpi.** A little oasis thriving in the deserted lands of Castello, this bacaro has the usual fish cicheti, including folpetti *consi* (with olive oil, parsley, and boiled potatoes). Locals flock here to play the gambling machines and to savor Dante's divine *calamari fritti* (fried squid). Plan to arrive around lunchtime, when succulent fish dishes start emerging from the kitchen. ⊠ *Corte Nova, near the Scuola di San Giorgio degli Schiavoni, Castello 2877* ☎ *041/5285163* ▭ *No credit cards* ☉ *Closed Sun.* Ⓥ *San Zaccaria.*

¢ ✕**Da Pinto.** At the heart of the Rialto market and with tables outside, Da Pinto has its cicheti all ready by 8 in the morning. A necessary stop for curious visitors and a second home of stall vendors and clerks of the nearby Tribunale (Court of Justice), this ever-packed bacaro is worth elbowing your way into. ⊠ *Campo delle Becarie, San Polo 367* ☎ *041/5224599* ▭ *No credit cards* ☉ *Closed Mon. and 2 wks in Nov.* Ⓥ *San Marco.*

¢ ✕ **Enoteca la Mascareta.** An offspring of the popular casual restaurant
FodorsChoice   Al Mascaron, the Mascareta offers refined cicheti and a selection of cured
  ★   pork and cheeses, washed down with quality ombre such as Chardonnay Friuliano. The place doesn't open till 6 PM, but doesn't close till past
midnight. ⊠ *Calle Lunga Santa Maria Formosa, Castello 5183* ☎ *041/
5230744* ⊟ *No credit cards* ⊘ *No lunch; closed Sun. and over Christmas* Ⓥ *Rialto or San Marco.*

¢ ✕ **Minibar da Lele.** A three-minute stroll from Piazzale Roma, Lele's 6-
by-10-ft place is a blessing for hungry commuters on their way to work.
Not strictly a bacaro, it offers equally good food and wine. Try the freshly
made, enormous tramezzini and tiny panini filled with vegetables and
cured pork. ⊠ *Campo dei Tolentini, Santa Croce 183* ☎ *no phone*
⊟ *No credit cards* ⊘ *Closed weekends* Ⓥ *Stazione.*

¢ ✕ **Osteria da Toni.** This unpretentious bar-bacaro sits on the western edge
of the Zattere promenade, near a pretty and breezy side canal. It caters
mainly to workers from the harbor over the bridge, and you might luck
into a dish of homemade lasagna if you show up during lunch hours.
⊠ *Fondamenta San Basilio, Dorsoduro 1642* ☎ *041/5286899* ⊟ *No
credit cards* ⊘ *Closed Mon. and 3 wks Aug.–Sept.* Ⓥ *Zattere.*

Pasticcerie

Venetians have always loved pastry, not so much in the way of desserts
at the end of a meal but rather as something that could go well with a
glass of sweet wine or a cup of hot milk. Traditional cookies are sold
in *pasticcerie* (pastry shops) throughout town, both by weight and by
the piece, and often come in attractive gift packages. Search for *zaeleti*
(cookies made with yellow corn flour and raisins), *buranelli* (S-shape
cookies from Burano, which also come in heavy, fat rings), or *baicoli*
(crunchy cookies made with yeast). Many bakeries also sell pastry by
the portion: from apple strudel to *crostate* (jam tarts) and *torta di man-
dorle* (almond cake)—just point out what you want. After Christmas
and through Carnevale, a great deal of frying takes place behind the
counter to prepare the tons of pastries annually devoured by Venetians
and tourists alike in the weeks preceding Lent: *frittole* (doughnuts with
pine nuts, raisins, and candied orange peel, rolled in sugar), best eaten
warm; the ribbonlike *galani* (crunchy, fried pastries sprinkled with con-
fectioners' sugar); and walnut-shape *castagnole* (fried pastry dumplings
rolled in sugar).

Dal Col. This is a good spot near Piazza San Marco for coffee and pas-
try on the run, with bar (coffee and beverage) service at the counter.
⊠ *Calle dei Fabbri, San Marco 1035* ☎ *041/5205529* ⊟ *AE, V* ⊘ *Closed
Aug. 5–20.* Ⓥ *San Marco.*

Dal Mas. Crisp croissants, pastries such as *kranz* (a braided pastry filled
with almond paste and raisins) and strudel from the Friuli region, and
bar service make this a great place for breakfast. ⊠ *Lista di Spagna,
Cannaregio 150/a* ☎ *041/715101* ⊟ *MC, V* ⊘ *Closed Tues.* Ⓥ *Stazione.*

Didovich. Here you'll find all the usual amenities of a pasticceria, and
also some sublime vegetable tortes. ⊠ *Campo di Santa Marina, Castello
5909* ☎ *041/5230017* ⊟ *No credit cards* ⊘ *Closed Sun. June–Sept.;
closed Sun. afternoon Oct.–May* Ⓥ *Rialto.*

Giovanni Volpe. This is the only place in town that all year round still
bakes traditional Venetian-Jewish pastry and delicious *pane azimo*
(matzo bread), although the days of operation give it away that the shop
is not kosher. ⊠ *Calle del Ghetto Vecchio, Cannaregio 1143* ☎ *041/
715178* ⊟ *No credit cards* ⊘ *Closed Sun.* Ⓥ *San Marcuola.*

Harry's Dolci. With tables outside in warm weather and an elegant room inside, Harry's makes for a perfect break while exploring the Giudecca, or you can fill your bag to go. ☒ *Fondamenta San Biagio 773, Giudecca* ☎ *041/5208337* ▭ *AE, V* ⊘ *Closed Tues. and Nov.–Mar.* Ⓥ *Santa Eufemia.*

Maggion. It's worth the trip to the Lido even in bad weather for celebrated, custom-made fruit tarts (to be ordered one day ahead; no bar service). ☒ *Via Dardanelli 48, Lido* ☎ *041/5260836* ▭ *AE, DC, MC, V* ⊘ *Closed Mon.–Tues.* Ⓥ *Lido.*

Marchini. The best-known and most expensive pasticceria in town has a fantastic display of tarts and gifts (no bar service). ☒ *Spadaria, San Marco 676* ☎ *041/5229109* ▭ *AE, MC, V* ⊘ *Closed Tues.* Ⓥ *San Marco.*

Rizzardini. This is the tiniest and prettiest pastry shop in Venice, with a counter dating from the late 18th century. Frittole and *pastine di riso* (pastry with a creamy rice filling) are especially good. ☒ *Calle Fibuera, San Marco 951* ☎ *041/5223835* ▭ *No credit cards* ⊘ *Closed Tues.* Ⓥ *San Marco.*

Rosa Salva. There are several branches to this venerable pasticcerie in town; the headquarters is a small shop on Calle Fiubera in San Marco with a wide selection of pastry and savory snacks as well as bar service at the counter. ☒ *Calle Fiubera, San Marco 951* ☎ *041/5210544* ☒ *Campo San Luca, San Marco 4589* ▭ *AE, DC, MC, V* ☎ *041/5225385* ⊘ *Closed Sun.*

Tonolo. Students from the nearby Università di Ca' Foscari crowd the counter at Tonolo, which makes for a nice break while visiting the Frari district. ☒ *Calle San Pantalon, Dorsoduro 3764* ☎ *041/5237209* ▭ *No credit cards* ⊘ *Closed Mon., Aug.* Ⓥ *San Tomà.*

Vio. Besides the usual selection of small pastry and drinks, here you can get a piece of *crostata di marroni* (chestnut tart) or a bag of spicy cookies made with chili. ☒ *Fondamenta Rio Marin, Santa Croce 784* ☎ *041/718523* ▭ *No credit cards* ⊘ *Closed Wed.*

Gelaterie

According to Venetians, Marco Polo imported from China a dessert called *panna in ghiaccio* (literally, "cream in ice"), a brick of frozen cream between wafers. There's no documentation to support the claim, but the myth lives on. Several local *gelaterie* (gelato shops) sell panna in ghiaccio, the supposed "ancestor" of gelato, but you'll have to ask around for it, because it's almost never kept on display. On a hot summer day, nothing is better than a cup of fruit-flavored gelato to restore your energy: light and refreshing, it will help you go that extra mile before you call it a day. Most gelaterie are open nonstop from mid-morning to late evening; some keep longer business hours in the summer.

Boutique del Gelato. Good value and a long list of flavors have won this gelateria a dedicated following. ☒ *Salizzada San Lio, Castello 5727* ☎ *041/5223283* ⊘ *Closed Jan.* Ⓥ *Rialto.*

Caffè Paolin. The morning sun draws crowds of all ages and nationalities to take a seat on busy Campo Santo Stefano and enjoy a little cup at this favorite bar-gelateria. Ask for an extra topping of whipped cream and *amarene* (sour cherries). ☒ *Campo Santo Stefano, San Marco 3464* ☎ *041/5220710* ⊘ *Closed Sat.* Ⓥ *San Samuele or Sant'Angelo.*

Da Titta. On the Lido, strategically located on the main drag between the vaporetto stop and the most central beaches, Titta is one of the oldest gelaterie in Venice. Get your receipt at the *cassa* (register) for a cone to go, or enjoy one of the special combinations while lolling in a swinging chair under the trees that line the Gran Viale. There's also bar service. ☒ *Gran Viale Santa Maria Elisabetta 61, Lido* ☎ *041/5260359* ⊘ *Closed Nov.–early Mar.* Ⓥ *Venice Lido.*

Gelateria Ca' d'Oro. Here you'll find the usual array of flavors, plus panna in ghiaccio and some chocolate-covered specialties in the freezer to the side of the counter. ☒ *Strada Nova, near Campo Santi Apostoli, Cannaregio 4273/b* ☎ *041/5228982* Ⓥ *Ca' d'Oro.*

Gelateria Il Doge. This popular take-out gelateria, just off Campo Santa Margherita, offers a good selection of flavors, from a few low-calorie options to the extra-rich *strabon* (Venetian for "more than good," which in this case means made with cocoa, espresso, and chocolate-covered almonds), as well as granitas in summer. It's open late most of the year. ☒ *Campo Santa Margherita, Dorsoduro 3058/a* ☎ *041/5234607* ⊘ *Closed Nov.–Feb.*

Le Café. On Campo Santo Stefano across from Paolin, with see-and-be-seen tables outside year-round, Le Café is something of a nightspot. It also has bar service and afternoon tea and offers a variety of hot chocolate drinks and desserts. ☒ *Campo Santo Stefano, San Marco 2797* ☎ *041/5237201* Ⓥ *San Samuele or Sant'Angelo.*

Nico. With an enviable terrace on the Zattere, Nico is the city's gelateria with a view. The house specialty is the *gianduiotto,* a brick of dark chocolate ice cream flung into a tall glass filled with freshly whipped cream. There's also bar service. ☒ *Zattere, Dorsoduro 922* ☎ *041/5225293* ⊘ *Closed Thurs., Dec. 21–Jan.8* Ⓥ *Zattere.*

WHERE TO STAY

FODOR'S CHOICE

Bernardi Semenzato, *Cannaregio*

Colombina, *Castello*

Il Palazzo at the Bauer, *San Marco*

Istituto San Giuseppe, *Castello*

La Calcina, *Dorsoduro*

Metropole, *Castello*

Pensione Accademia Villa Maravege, *Dorsoduro*

Villa Igea, *Castello*

HIGHLY RECOMMENDED

Dalla Mora, *Santa Croce*

Galleria, *Dorsoduro*

Hotel Antico Doge, *Cannaregio*

La Residenza, *Castello*

Messner, *Dorsoduro*

Monaco & Grand Canal, *San Marco*

Quattro Fontane, *Lido*

San Cassiano-Ca' Favretto, *Santa Croce*

San Zulian, *San Marco*

Updated by
Patricia Rucidlo

VENETIAN MAGIC CAN STILL LINGER when you retire for the night, whether you're staying in a grand hotel or budget find. Many Venetian hotel rooms are swathed in brocades and glitter with Murano chandeliers, and even in the less grand *pensioni* you stand a chance of finding antiques, Oriental carpets, and a canal view. No satellite TV to keep you company? Just open the window and listen to the gondoliers' serenades or watch the ebb and flow of city life in the campo below.

There are hotels in Venice catering to all tastes and price ranges. Deluxe and upscale hotels are often filled with antiques and art collections and retain much of the feel of the past, with coffered ceilings, frescoes, stucco, and fireplaces in the best rooms. Renovations are usually made as discreetly as possible, paying respect to Gothic and Renaissance structures. With a few exceptions, there's a widespread dislike for modern design among Venetian hoteliers, and even the moderately priced establishments usually opt for 18th-century Venetian style. This means curvaceous, carved furnishings and wallpaper in soft colors—pale yellow and green are big favorites—with gilded or flowery decorations.

Before choosing a hotel, decide in advance what's important to you and don't be afraid to ask detailed questions. The staff members at most Venetian hotels will be able to converse with you in English. Space is at a premium, and even exclusive hotels have some small, dowdy, Cinderella-type rooms. Rooms tend to be different even on the same floor: windows with canal views and windows looking onto bleak alleyways are both common. If you're not happy with the room you've been given, ask to be moved.

Although the city has no cars, it does have boats plying the canals and pedestrians chattering in the streets, even late at night, so request a quiet room if noise bothers you—but be aware that you could be sacrificing a view for the quiet. During the summer months, don't leave your room lights on *and* your window wide open at night: mosquitoes can descend en masse.

Cannaregio

$$$$ 🏨 **Grand Hotel dei Dogi.** Dei Dogi, housed in an old Venetian palace that once served as the French embassy, offers easy access to the northern lagoon, a private garden, lounges with tall Renaissance-style windows, and majestic Murano chandeliers. Well-appointed rooms featuring red Venetian floors, Oriental carpets, and antique-looking furnishings are all here at two-thirds the price of comparable hotels in Venice. The quiet and romantic beauty of the surroundings makes the (relative) splurge worth the stay. ⊠ *Fondamenta Madonna dell'Orto, Cannaregio 3500, 30121* ☎ *041/2208111* 🖷 *041/722278* ⊕ *www.boscolohotels.com* ⤴ *58 rooms, 11 suites* ⚒ *Restaurant, bar, cable TV, concierge, dry cleaning, laundry service, meeting room, some pets allowed, no-smoking rooms* 🖃 *AE, DC, MC, V* ⬛ *CP* ⬛ *Madonna dell'Orto.*

$$$–$$$$ 🏨 **Giorgione.** Tucked away in a little-visited part of town not far from Rialto Bridge, the Giorgione is a dignified cross between old and new. A 15th-century palace and a modern building with many common areas are set around a private garden with a lily pond. Guest rooms feature golden brocades on the walls, carpeted floors, and unusual furnishings in a Venetian-Chinese style: red lacquered headboards decorated with Oriental motifs, rounded chests of drawers, and nightstands. Some split-level rooms come with the lovely bonus of a small, private balcony. ⊠ *Calle dei Proverbi, near Campo Santi Apostoli, 4587 Cannaregio, 30121* ☎ *041/5225810* 🖷 *041/5239092* ⊕ *www.hotelgiorgione.com*

3

It is *essential* to know how to get to your hotel when you arrive. Unless you take a (very expensive) water taxi that deposits you at your hotel's door, you may find yourself wandering down side streets—luggage in hand—with relapses of déjà vu. Although in Venice you can't go terribly wrong in terms of "good" areas to stay, each neighborhood offers different advantages. The area in and around San Marco is always the most crowded and often more expensive: even two- and three-star hotels cost more here than in other parts of town. If you want to stay in less-trafficked surroundings, consider the usually quieter hotels in Dorosudoro and Cannaregio (though hotels near the train station in Cannaregio have their own noise issues.) A stay in the Lido in shoulder season offers peace and serenity, but it also includes about a half-hour traghetto ride to San Marco. The Lido in the summer is crowded with beach-goers.

Facilities

Most hotels occupy old buildings, and preservation laws prohibit elevators in some, so ask ahead if an elevator is essential. In the ¢–$$ price categories, hotels may not have lounge areas, and some rooms may be cramped. Bathrooms are on the small side (tubs are considered a luxury) but are usually well equipped. Carpeted floors are rare, so pack slippers if you dislike wood and marble under your bare feet. Air-conditioning can be essential in summer; note that some hotels charge a supplement for it. If you're pestered by mosquitoes, ask at your hotel's desk for a Vape, an antimosquito device.

Reservations

You're well served to book your room far in advance. Planning your trip four to five months ahead will give you much greater freedom of room choice. Double-booking is not uncommon, so ask for a written confirmation of your reservation with a description of any special requirements (tub or shower, first or top floor, and so on). Many hotels accept reservations on-line; the Web site ⊕ www.veniceinfo.it offers information (with photographs) about most hotels in town. If you don't have reservations when you arrive, try **Venezia Sì** (☎ 800/843006 toll-free in Italy, Mon.–Sat. 9–7), which offers a free reservation service by phone. It's the public relations arm of **AVA** (Venetian Hoteliers Association) and has booths where you can make same-day reservations at Piazzale Roma (☎ 041/5231397 ⊙ Daily 9 AM–10 PM), Santa Lucia train station (☎ 041/715288 or 041/715016 ⊙ Daily 8 AM–9 PM), and Marco Polo Airport (☎ 041/5415133 ⊙ Daily 9 AM–10 PM).

Prices

You can find hotels in all price ranges in Venice, but in general prices run higher here than elsewhere in Italy for the same quality of facilities. You can save off-season—November through March, excluding Christmas and Carnevale.

WHAT IT COSTS In euros				
	$$$$	**$$$**	**$$**	**$**	**¢**
FOR 2 PEOPLE	over € 300	€225–€300	€150–€225	€75–€150	under €75

Prices are for two people in a standard double room in high season.

➦ *56 rooms* ⚇ *Bar, in-room safes, minibars, cable TV, billiards, Internet, no-smoking floor* 🖃 *AE, DC, MC, V* ⦿*CP* Ⓥ *Ca' d'Oro.*

$$ 🖼 **Abbazia.** The only Venetian abbey turned into a hotel, the Abbazia is not recognizable as such from the outside. The guest rooms are in the former convent—a low, white stucco structure with no exposed brick or Gothic windows. Numerous details survive from the building's religious past: tiny wooden pulpits hang on the walls, and holy-water bowls await around many corners. Brass chandeliers befit the austerity of the place, as does the cream-white and beige decor of the rooms (considerably larger than monks' cells), although some touches of gaudy colors are found in the tapestries and couches. ⊠ *Calle Priuli dei Cavaletti, 68 Cannaregio, 30121* ☎ *041/717333* 🖶 *041/717949* ⊕ *www. abbaziahotel.com* ➦ *40 rooms* ⚇ *In-room safes, minibars, cable TV, no-smoking rooms* 🖃 *AE, DC, MC, V* ⦿*CP* Ⓥ *Stazione.*

★ $$ 🖼 **Hotel Antico Doge.** If you're looking for a small, intimate hotel in a quiet yet central location, look no further. This delightful palazzo was once home to Doge Marino Falier; since then, it's been modernized with lovely results. Some rooms have *baldacchini* (canopied beds); all have fabric walls and hardwood floors. Located on a small canal, and only minutes away from San Marco and the Rialto Bridge, this is an oasis of tranquillity. An ample buffet breakfast is served in a room with a frescoed ceiling and Murano chandelier. ⊠ *Campo SS. Apostoli, Cannaregio 5643, 30131* ☎ *041/2411570* 🖶 *041/2443660* ⊕ *www.anticodoge. com* ➦ *13 rooms, 2 suites* ⚇ *Bar, in-room safes, minibar, cable TV, Internet* 🖃 *AE, DC, MC, V* ⦿*CP* Ⓥ *San Marco.*

$–$$ 🖼 **Hesperia.** A quiet, friendly hotel housed in a two-floor building (no elevator) just across from the Jewish Ghetto, the Hesperia is within walking distance to the train station but also safely removed from the noise and commercial clutter. Half the rooms offer a beautiful view of the wide (and clean) Cannaregio Canal. The decor doesn't lend much atmosphere, with basic furniture, spare tapestry in pastel shades, and humble, black-and-white versions of Venetian floors, but the space is less cramped than in comparable hotels. Its not-so-central location makes it a possibility when the rest of town is booked solid. ⊠ *Calle Riello, Cannaregio 459, 30121* ☎ *041/715251* 🖶 *041/715112* ➦ *15 rooms, 13 with bath* ⚇ *Restaurant, cable TV, Internet, some pets allowed* 🖃 *AE, DC, MC, V* ⦿*CP* Ⓥ *Stazione.*

$ 🖼 **Bernardi Semenzato.** This is a particularly inviting little place just off

Strada Nova and near the gondola ferry to the Rialto market. Rooms are well maintained, with exposed ceiling beams, matching headboard-bedspread sets, and tiled bathrooms. The nearby *dipendenza* (annex) has more the feeling of a private apartment, with large rooms featuring inlaid wooden floors, Murano chandeliers, and several 19th-century antiques. ⊠ *Calle dell'Oca, Cannaregio 4366, 30121* ☎ *041/5211052* 🖶 *041/5222424* ⊕ *www.hotelbernardi.com* ➦ *24 rooms, 14 with bath* ⚇ *Cable TV, some pets allowed, no-smoking rooms* 🖃 *AE, MC, V* ⊗ *Closed Dec. 8–Dec. 20* ⦿*CP* Ⓥ *Ca' d'Oro.*

$ 🖼 **Minerva e Nettuno.** This friendly, family-run place located near the train station is popular with backpackers and Italian families. It offers spotless rooms with solid wood furniture. The "vippina" treatment (Italian for "V.I.P.") for €20 extra entitles you to a soft bathrobe, and your own copy of a booklet with literary extracts about Venice, and lunch or dinner at I Quattro Rusteghi, located in the heart of the Jewish Ghetto. ⊠ *Lista di Spagna, Cannaregio 230, 30121* ☎ *041/715968* 🖶 *041/5242139* ⊕ *www.minervaenettuno.it* ➦ *27 rooms, 11 with bath* ⚇ *In-room data ports, some pets allowed; no a/c, no room TVs* 🖃 *AE, DC, MC, V* ⦿*CP* Ⓥ *Stazione.*

$ ▣ **Rossi.** Most guests stay here for the reasonable price and the convenient, if not central, location not far from the train station. Rooms are comfortable and clean, with tile floors and dark, solid wood furniture. Some face an adjacent private garden that houses a colony of songbirds, others the dead-end street below. Skip the house breakfast and instead take advantage of the hotel's vicinity to Cannaregio's best pastry shop, Dal Mas. ⊠ *Off Lista di Spagna, Cannaregio 262, 30121* ☎ *041/ 715164* 🖷 *041/717784* 🛏 *14 rooms* ♨ *Cable TV, Internet* ▤ *MC, V* ⦿ *CP* Ⓥ *Stazione.*

$ ▣ **Santa Lucia.** Set in a narrow alleyway just off the Lista di Spagna— steps from the train station and a stone's throw from a vaporetto stop— this small and plain hotel makes a quiet oasis in the midst of the hustle and bustle. The best feature is the surprisingly spacious garden, where you can picnic (there's a fountain for washing fruit) or take breakfast. Rooms (some without private bathroom) are simply furnished but benefit from facing the garden. ⊠ *Calle della Misericordia, Cannaregio 358, 30121* ☎ *041/715180* 🖷 *041/710610* ⊕ *www.hotelslucia.com* 🛏 *15 rooms, 9 with bath* ♨ *Fans, some pets allowed; no a/c, no room TVs* ▤ *AE, DC, MC, V* ☽ *Closed Jan. 10–Feb. 10* ⦿ *CP* Ⓥ *Stazione.*

Castello

$$$$ ▣ **Bisanzio.** Managed by the Busetti family since 1969, this fine hotel is in a restored 16th-century building, right by the church of La Pietà, where Vivaldi was choirmaster and violin master. The peaceful rooms are decorated in Venetian antique style. Generous buffet breakfasts are served in a bright and airy salon, and a lounge opens onto an old courtyard, close to a private mooring for gondolas and other boats. Better rooms have private balconies. ⊠ *Calle della Pietà, Castello 3651, 30122* ☎ *041/5203100* 🖷 *041/5204114* ⊕ *www.bisanzio.com* 🛏 *40 rooms* ♨ *Bar, in-room data ports, some in-room safes, minibars, cable TV, babysitting, dry cleaning, laundry service, concierge, some pets allowed, nosmoking rooms* ▤ *AE, DC, MC, V* ⦿ *CP* Ⓥ *San Zaccaria.*

$$$$ ▣ **Colombina.** In the 16th century it was a private palazzo, and now it's

★ an intimate and romantic inn. Minutes away from the bustle of San Marco, Colombina is on a quiet side canal. Many of the rooms, all with deep bathtubs and most with dramatic Murano chandeliers, face this canal; at night, all you can hear is the lapping of the water. There's an ample breakfast buffet, which you can supplement with extras (such as scrambled eggs) à la carte for an additional charge. The stellar staff provides the perfect complement to this enchanting spot. ⊠ *Calle del Remedio, Castello 4416, 30122* ☎ *041/2770525* 🖷 *041/2776044* ⊕ *www. hotelcolombina.com* 🛏 *33 rooms* ♨ *Bar, in-room data ports, in-room safes, minibar, cable TV with movies, dock, baby-sitting, concierge, meeting room, dry cleaning, laundry service, some pets allowed* ▤ *AE, DC, MC, V* ⦿ *CP* Ⓥ *San Marco.*

$$$$ ▣ **Danieli.** You'll feel like a doge in Venice's largest luxury hotel, a complex of newer buildings and a 14th-century palazzo. Sumptuous Venetian decor prevails from the moment you set foot in the soaring atrium, with its sweeping staircase. Long favored by world leaders and movie stars, it's predictably chic and expensive. The rooftop terrace restaurant has a heavenly view but unexceptional food. May through October, guests have access to the pool, tennis courts, and beach of the Hotel Excelsior on the Lido via a private (free) launch running on the hour. ⊠ *Riva degli Schiavoni, Castello 4196, 30122* ☎ *041/5226480, 041/2961222 reservations in English* 🖷 *041/5200208* ⊕ *www.luxurycollection.com/danieli* 🛏 *221 rooms, 12 suites* ♨ *Restaurant, bar, room service, in-room safes, in-room data ports, minibars, cable TV, baby-sitting, dry clean-*

Where to Stay in Venice

SAN MICHELE

Cimitero San Michele

Sacca della Misericordia

F. NUOVE

Canale delle Navi

0   1/8 mile
0   1/8 km

KEY

ℹ️ Tourist Information

▲ Vaporetto Stop

Canale delle Navi

OSPEDALE CIVILE

Campo Santi Giovanni e Paolo

CELESTIA

BACINI

Bacini di Carenàggio

Barbaria delle Tole

R. d. S. Francesco

RIALTO

Darsena Grande

Campo S. Lorenzo C. Lion

C.d. Furlani

CASTELLO

San Pietro

Piazza San Marco

SAN ZACCARIA

See Inset

Molo Riva d. Schiavoni

S. ZACCARIA

CAMPO DELLA TANA

ARSENALE

R. della Tana della Tana

San Pietro

SAN MARCO

P. de Sospiri

Riva Ca' di Dio

V. Garibaldi

R. d. S. Anna F. Sant'Anna

SALUTE

S. MARCO VALLARESSO

Bacino di S. Marco

Viale Garibaldi

GIARDINI

Marina

Secco

R. d. S. Giuseppe

Paludo S. Antònia

C.po S. Giuseppe

F. Dogana

SAN GIÓRGIO

Canale d. Grazia

San Giórgio Maggiore

Bacino d. S. Giórgio

Bacino di S. Marco

Riva dei Sette Martiri

ZITELLE

Fond S. Giovanni

F. d. Zitelle

F. della Croce

C. d. Vin

Rio del Vin

Riva degli Schiavoni

R. d. Grazia

Detail

42

36 - 41

ing, laundry service, concierge, Internet, business services, meeting rooms, some pets allowed, no-smoking rooms ▭ *AE, DC, MC, V* ❍❘ *CP* Ⓥ *San Zaccaria.*

$$$$ ⊡ **Hotel Londra Palace.** A hundred windows overlooking the lagoon and the island of San Giorgio impart a hearty dash of sunlight to many of the finely decorated rooms of this luxury hotel. The view must have been pleasing to Tchaikovsky, who wrote his 4th Symphony here in 1877. Neoclassical public rooms, with splashes of blue and green glass suggesting the sea, play nicely off guest rooms, which have fine fabric, damask drapes, Biedermeier furniture, and Venetian glass. A change in management in 2003 has brought a breath of fresh air to the place; the staff is top-notch, as are the restaurant and bar. ⊠ *Riva degli Schiavoni, Castello 4171, 30122* ☎ *041/5200533* 🖷 *041/5225032* ⊕ *www.hotelondra.it* ↘ *36 rooms, 17 suites* ⚘ *Restaurant, room service, in-room data ports, in-room fax, in-room safes, minibars, cable TV, wine bar, piano bar, babysitting, dry cleaning, laundry service, concierge, Internet, business services, meeting room* ▭ *AE, DC, MC, V* ❍❘ *CP* Ⓥ *San Zaccaria.*

$$$$ ⊡ **Metropole.** Eccentrics, eclectics, and fans of Antonio Vivaldi (who taught

Fodor'sChoice
★ music here) love the Metropole, the most intimate and affordable of the high-end hotels stretching along the Riva degli Schiavoni. The owner, a lifelong collector of odd objects, displays his collection of oil paintings and enough antiques to fill a dealer's shop—some of which make their way into the beautifully appointed rooms. Honeymooners should consider a stay in the just-this-side-of-kitsch Room of the Angels. ⊠ *Riva degli Schiavoni, Castello 4149, 30122* ☎ *041/5205044* 🖷 *041/5223679* ⊕ *www.hotelmetropole.com* ↘ *43 rooms, 26 suites* ⚘ *Restaurant, bar, room service, in-room data ports, in-room safes, minibars, cable TV, baby-sitting, dry cleaning, laundry service, meeting room, concierge, some pets allowed* ▭ *AE, DC, MC, V* ❍❘ *CP* Ⓥ *San Zaccaria.*

$$$$ ⊡ **Santa Marina.** In the small neighborhood campo that's home to this hotel, five minutes from the Rialto Bridge, you will probably see more Venetians than tourists passing by. Immaculate rooms are outfitted with pastel colors and lacquered Venetian-style furniture. There are no sitting areas, but in summer a cheerful veranda is set up on the square and breakfast is served behind rows of pink geraniums by the kind and helpful staff. ⊠ *Campo Santa Marina, Castello 6068, 30122* ☎ *041/5239202* 🖷 *041/5200907* ⊕ *www.hotelsantamarina.it* ↘ *41 rooms, 2 suites* ⚘ *In-room safes, minibars, room TVs, concierge, dry cleaning, laundry service, some pets allowed, no-smoking rooms* ▭ *AE, DC, MC, V* ❍❘ *CP* Ⓥ *Rialto.*

$$$–$$$$ ⊡ **Savoia e Jolanda.** The location and views are the best features of this hotel, facing San Giorgio Maggiore on one side, the church of San Zaccaria on the other. All guest rooms are decorated with sumptuous tapestries and Murano glass chandeliers; all have high ceilings—some are coffered—and many get a great deal of light. There's a copious buffet breakfast. ⊠ *Riva degli Schiavoni, Castello 4187, 30122* ☎ *041/ 5206644* 🖷 *041/5207494* ⊕ *www.hotelsavoiajolanda.com* ↘ *36 rooms, 15 suites* ⚘ *Restaurant, bar, room service, in-room data ports, in-room safes, in-room hot tubs, minibars, cable TV, baby-sitting, dry cleaning, laundry service, concierge, Internet, some pets allowed, no-smoking rooms* ▭ *AE, DC, MC, V* ❍❘ *CP* Ⓥ *San Zaccaria.*

$$$ ⊡ **Da Bruno.** A fairly priced hotel in a very central location, Da Bruno is just a five-minute walk from Piazza San Marco and the Rialto. Rooms are simple and well maintained, done up in Venetian style with chairs and bed stands in carved wood, mirrors set in glass frames, and glass chandeliers. You can sip hot and cold drinks on the *terrazzino* (terrace) upstairs in perfect quiet—it's so tiny it holds just one table (first come, first served). If you find it picturesque to watch the flow of pedestrians from your window, ask for a room with a view of the Salizzada. There are two floors but no elevator. ⊠ *Salizzada San Lio, Castello 5726/a, 30122* ☎ *041/5230452* 🖷 *041/5221157* ⊕ *www.hoteldabruno.it* ⇔ *32 rooms* ⚇ *Bar, in-room safes, cable TV, concierge, dry cleaning, laundry service, some pets allowed, no-smoking rooms* ⊟ *AE, DC, MC, V* ⍾◦l *CP* Ⓥ *Rialto or San Marco.*

$$ 🏨 **Al Piave.** This is a stylish little hotel with modest rates, set on a busy street but not too noisy inside. Rooms are a bit cramped but tastefully furnished, though with no views to speak of. It's a good choice if you're traveling with children, as they have family suites–two connecting rooms–that can sleep up to five people. ⊠ *Ruga Giuffa, Campo Santa Maria Formosa, Castello 4838–40, 30132* ☎ *041/5285174* 🖷 *041/5238512* ⊕*www.hotelalpiave.com* ⇔*8 rooms* ⊟*AE, DC, MC, V* ⍾◦l*CP* Ⓥ *San Zaccaria or Rialto.*

$$ 🏨 **Bucintoro.** The Bucintoro is halfway down the promenade from Piazza San Marco to the Isola di Sant'Elena and a few steps away from the Museo Storico Navale (where the original Bucintoro, the doge's ceremonial boat, is on display). Many Venetian hotel brochures show striking panoramas that are visible from only a few choice rooms, but here nearly every room has an expansive view of the lagoon, the Isola di San Giorgio, and the Bacino di San Marco. The decor, however, does not enhance the view: modern wood furniture, plain white walls and bedcovers, faux lace curtains, and linoleum floors. ⊠ *Riva San Biagio, Castello 2135, 30122* ☎ *041/5223240* 🖷 *041/5235224* ⇔ *28 rooms* ⚇ *Fans; no room TVs* ⊟ *No credit cards* ⍾◦l *CP* Ⓥ *Ca' di Dio San Biagio.*

$$ 🏨 **Campiello.** The good location, old-fashioned appointments, and modest prices are the best reasons to come to this hotel. Marble floors and gracious furnishings add a certain luster to the public rooms, and guest rooms are functional if unexceptional. There is a bar but no restaurant, though plenty of dining choices exist in the neighborhood. ⊠ *Campiello del Vin, Castello 4647, 30122* ☎ *041/5205764* 🖷 *041/5205798* ⊕ *www.hcampiello.it* ⇔ *15 rooms* ⚇ *Bar, in-room safes, cable TV, Internet, no-smoking rooms* ⊟ *AE, MC, V* ⊙ *Closed 2 weeks in Jan.* ⍾◦l *CP* Ⓥ *San Zaccaria.*

$$ 🏨 **Casa Verardo.** Close to the Campo Santa Maria Formosa and just a few minutes from San Marco, this hotel is one of the best bargains in the district. Rooms, three of which have canal views (two others look onto a small courtyard), are spotless and have a predominantly antique tone. ⊠ *Calle della Chiesa, Castello 4765, 30122* ☎ *041/5286127* 🖷 *041/5232765* ⊕ *www.casaverardo.it* ⇔ *8 rooms, 15 suites* ⚇ *In-room safes, minibars, cable TV, baby-sitting, dry cleaning, laundry service, some pets allowed, no-smoking rooms* ⊟ *AE, MC, V* ⍾◦l *CP* Ⓥ *San Zaccaria.*

★ $$ 🏨 **La Residenza.** The word *residenza* in Italian suggests a good deal of aristocratic elegance, and this hotel, with more the feeling of a private noble house than a hotel, does not disappoint. The hall occupies the whole *portego* (entryway) of the patrician apartment of Palazzo dei Badoari-Partecipazi già Gritti and looks almost disproportionately opulent for this quiet hotel. Well-preserved 18th-century stuccowork adorns the ceilings and walls, along with precious oil paintings. Oriental carpets partially hide the beautiful Venetian floor. ⊠ *Campo Bandiera Re Moro, Castello 3608, 30122* ☎ *041/5285315* 🖷 *041/5238859* ⇔ *14 rooms* ⚇ *In-room safes, minibar, room TVs* ⊟ *MC, V* ⍾◦l *CP* Ⓥ *Arsenale.*

$$ 🏨 **Paganelli.** The lagoon views here so impressed Henry James that he wrote the Paganelli up in the preface to his *Portrait of a Lady.* This enchanting small hotel on the waterfront near Piazza San Marco is tastefully decorated in the Venetian style. The quieter annex in Campo San Zaccaria is a former convent, and some rooms preserve the original cof-

fered ceilings. ✉ *Riva degli Schiavoni, Castello 4687, 30122* ☎ *041/ 5224324* 🖷 *041/5239267* ⚘ *Bar, cable TV, baby-sitting* ▤ *AE, MC, V* ⏐⃝⏐ *CP* Ⓥ *San Zaccaria.*

$$ ▥ **Scandinavia.** Central but off the main tourist arteries, the Scandinavia is housed in a building dating from the 11th century. Despite the name, the rooms are done in Venetian style, with brocade tapestry and Murano chandeliers. The top suite has a beautiful, private, covered veranda with a view of the nearby church. ✉ *Campo Santa Maria Formosa, Castello 5240, 30122* ☎ *041/5223507* 🖷 *041/5235232* ⊕ *www. scandinaviahotel.com* ↬ *33 rooms, 1 suite* ⚘ *Cable TV, baby-sitting, dry cleaning, laundry service, some pets allowed, no-smoking rooms; no a/c in some rooms* ▤ *AE, MC, V* ⏐⃝⏐ *CP* Ⓥ *San Zaccaria or Rialto.*

$$ ▥ **Villa Igea.** The villa offers all the intimacy of a private home (albeit a somewhat large one), which is what it was in the 19th century. It looks on to the church and square of San Zaccaria and, despite its rather central location, is an oasis of tranquility. Rooms are decorated in light pastels; some of them have tiny private balconies, and one has its own terrace. Six rooms have extra beds, making them particularly well-suited for families. The hotel is the annex of the more expensive Savoia e Jolanda just around the corner, which is where breakfast is served. ✉ *Riva degli Schiavoni, Castello 4187, 30122* ☎ *041/5206644* 🖷 *041/5207494* ↬ *27 rooms* ⚘ *Restaurant, room service, In-room safes, minibar, cable TV, dry cleaning, laundry service, concierge, Internet, parking (fee), some pets allowed* ▤ *AE, DC, MC, V* ⏐⃝⏐ *CP* Ⓥ *San Zaccaria.*

FodorsChoice ★

$$ ▥ **Wildner.** Right between the superdeluxe Danieli and Londra Palace hotels, this pleasant, unpretentious, family-run pensione enjoys the same views. The rooms are spread over four floors (no elevator), half with a view of San Giorgio and half looking out onto the quiet Campo San Zaccaria. The simple, no-nonsense decor features parquet floors and solid, dark furniture matched by brown leather headboards. Light, white curtains and creamy bedspreads further enhance the Wildner's understated ambience. ✉ *Riva degli Schiavoni, Castello 4161, 30122* ☎ *041/5227463* 🖷 *041/2414640* ⊕ *www.veneziahotels.com* ↬ *16 rooms* ⚘ *In-room safes, cable TV, some pets allowed; no room phones* ▤ *AE, DC, MC, V* ⏐⃝⏐ *CP* Ⓥ *San Zaccaria.*

$ ▥ **Doni.** This former palace occupies a prime position on a canal a couple of stone's throws from Piazza San Marco. The rooms at the front look out onto gondolas through ogee windows. It's a family-run place with wooden floors, solid if uninspiring furniture, and old-fashioned wallpaper to match, although some rooms have frescoed ceilings and chandeliers. ✉ *Calle del Vin, Castello 4656, 30122* ☎☎ *041/5224267; 041/ 5206682 in Jan.* ⊕ *www.albergodoni.it* ↬ *13 rooms, 4 with bath* ⚘ *Fans, baby-sitting, some pets allowed, no-smoking rooms; no room phones, no a/c, no room TVs* ▤ *MC, V* ⊙ *Some years closed Jan.* ⏐⃝⏐ *CP* Ⓥ *San Zaccaria.*

$ ▥ **Riva.** This small hotel, close to San Marco, is at the junction of three canals much used by all manner of Venetian watercraft. Although they are endlessly fascinating to watch, here you take the good with the bad—the passing gondolier at sunset travels the same waters as the buzzing water taxi at dawn. Rooms differ in size, and climbing up to the fourth floor (no elevator) wins you a better view. The decor is typical of Venetian hotels—a mix of Murano chandeliers, 18th-century-style furniture, exposed ceiling beams, and beds lacquered in pastel shades. ✉ *Ponte dell'Angelo, Castello 5310, 30122* ☎ *041/5227034* 🖷 *041/ 5285551* ↬ *12 rooms, 10 with bath* ⚘ *No a/c in some rooms* ▤ *No credit cards* ⊙ *Closed mid-Nov.–Carnevale (except 2 wks at Christmas)* ⏐⃝⏐ *CP* Ⓥ *San Marco.*

¢   🏠 **Istituto San Giuseppe.** This religious institution, in an excellent loca-
Fodor'sChoice   tion north of Piazza San Marco, is one of several lodgings in Venice run
★   by nuns. Rooms are spartan in decor but spotless and very quiet, overlooking the inner cloister. Book well ahead, as the unbeatable prices draw
crowds, mostly Italians in the know. Curfew is at 11 (10:30 in the winter), and no breakfast is served. Couples must be prepared to prove that
they are married, and patience should be observed if making reservations over the phone; language barriers aside, this convent is a remarkable deal. ⊠ *Ponte della Guerra, Castello 5402, 30122* ☎ *041/5225352*
🖷 *041/5224891* ⇋ *12 rooms* ♨ *No room phones, no a/c, no room TVs*
⊟ *No credit cards* ⫧ *CP* Ⓥ *San Marco.*

Dorsoduro

$$$$ 🏠 **Ca' Pisani.** Here's a breath of fresh air: a Venetian hotel with no brocades and chandeliers to be found. Instead there's a tasteful mix of modern design and well-chosen antique pieces. The entrance hall has marble
floors and an interesting play of colors and lights; the rooms contain
original art deco pieces from the '30s and '40s (every bed is different).
The no-smoking wine bar La Rivista serves light meals all day, and upstairs are a Turkish bath and a wooden rooftop terrace where you can
take the sun. ⊠ *Rio Terà Antonio Foscarini, Dorsoduro 979/a, 30123*
☎ *041/2401411* 🖷 *041/2771061* ⊕ *www.capisanihotel.it* ⇋ *25 rooms,
4 suites* ♨ *Restaurant, room service, in-room data ports, in-room safes,
minibars, cable TV with movies, Turkish bath, wine bar, concierge, dry
cleaning, laundry service, Internet, some pets allowed, no-smoking floor*
⊟ *AE, DC, MC, V* ⫧ *CP* Ⓥ *Accademia.*

$$$ 🏠 **American.** At first sight, it's hard to pick out this quiet, family-run
hotel from the houses along the fondamenta: there are no lights, flags,
or big signs on the hotel's yellow stucco facade. A hall decorated with
reproduction antiques, Oriental rugs, and contemporary images of
Venice on the walls leads to a breakfast room reminiscent of a theater
foyer, with red velvet chairs and gilded wall lamps. A 2002 overhaul
has given the place some zip, with new carpets and updated bathrooms.
Rooms vary in size and shape, but sage green and delicate pink fabrics
and lacquered Venetian-style furniture are found throughout. ⊠ *San Vio,
Dorsoduro 628, 30123* ☎ *041/5204733* 🖷 *041/5204048* ⊕ *www.
hotelamerican.com* ⇋ *28 rooms, 2 suites* ♨ *In-room safes, in-room data
ports, minibars, cable TV, baby-sitting, Internet, no-smoking rooms*
⊟ *AE, DC, MC, V* ⫧ *CP* Ⓥ *Accademia.*

$$$ 🏠 **Hotel Pausania.** From the moment you ascend the grand staircase ris-
ing above the fountain of this 14th-century palazzo, you sense the com-
bination of good taste and modern comforts that characterizes Hotel
Pausania. Light-colored rooms are spacious, with comfortable furniture
and carpets with rugs thrown over them. Some rooms face the small canal
(which can become a bit noisy early in the morning) in front of the hotel,
while others look out over the large garden courtyard. The hotel has a
convenient car service (€40) to and from the airport. ⊠ *Fondamenta
Gherardini, Dorsoduro 2824, 30123* ☎ *041/5222083* 🖷 *041/5222989*
⊕ *www.hotelpausania.it* ⇋ *26 rooms* ♨ *Bar, minibars, cable TV, baby-
sitting, dry cleaning, laundry service, concierge, airport shuttle, some
pets allowed* ⊟ *AE, MC, V* ⫧ *CP* Ⓥ *Ca' Rezzonico.*

$$$ 🏠 **Pensione Seguso.** This venerable establishment, run by the third gen-
eration of the Seguso family and housed in a modern building with good
views of the Giudecca Canal, is the last true pensione in Venice. The re-
quired half-board adds character to your stay, with meals served in a
dining room adorned with heirloom silver plate and old wall lamps.
Rooms are spare—no TV, minibars, or phones, and some don't have

CloseUp

WITH CHILDREN?

An extra bed or a crib for children can usually be added in Venetian hotel rooms, but it rarely comes free of charge—expect to pay between 20% and 40% extra. Some hotels in Venice allow children under a certain age to stay in their parents' room at no extra cost, but others charge for them as extra adults; be sure to find out the cutoff age for children's discounts. Good family choices include Al Piave, Sturion, Villa Igea, and Sofitel.

While a pool is a blessing—for adults as well as kids—in the heat of summer, it comes at a cost: Venice's only hotel with a pool is the high-end Cipriani. Hotels on the Lido provide beach access, but they put you a fair distance (about a half-hour boat ride) from the heart of the city. The Hotel Des Bains is right on the water and has a parklike area for children.

their own bathrooms—but they're decorated with attractive wooden furniture that will charm the flea-market-lover in you. Persian rugs, leather couches, and dark-wood paneling set the tone for the intimate reading salon. ⊠ *Zattere, Dorsoduro 779, 30123* ☎ *041/5286858, 041/5222472 when closed* 🖷 *041/5222340* 🗗 *36 rooms, 16 with bath* ⌕ *Restaurant, bar, some pets allowed* ⊟ *AE, DC, MC, V* ⑩ *MAP* ⊘ *Closed Dec.–Carnevale* Ⓥ *Zattere or Accademia.*

$$–$$$
FodorsChoice
★

Pensione Accademia Villa Maravege. A secret garden awaits just beyond an iron gate, complete with a mini Palladian-style villa, flower beds, stone cupids, and verdant trees—all rarities in Venice. Aptly nicknamed "Villa of the Wonders," this patrician retreat once served as the Russian embassy and was the residence of Katharine Hepburn in the movie *Summertime.* Conservative rooms are outfitted with Victorian-era antiques and fine tapestry. The location is on a promontory where two side canals converge with the Grand Canal, which can be seen from the garden. Book well in advance. ⊠ *Fondamenta Bollani, Dorsoduro 1058, 30123* ☎ *041/5210188* 🖷 *041/5239152* ⊕ *www.pensioneaccademia. it* 🗗 *27 rooms* ⌕ *Bar, in-room safes, minibar, cable TV, baby-sitting, dry cleaning, laundry service* ⊟ *AE, DC, MC, V* ⑩ *CP* Ⓥ *Accademia.*

$–$$

Agli Alboretti. The Alboretti is one of the many hotels clustered at the foot of the Ponte dell'Accademia. Its unpretentious, rather small rooms are blessed with plenty of light. Their nautical decor, with original pieces taken from old ships' cabins, goes well with the cries of seagulls living along the nearby Giudecca Canal. Some steep climbing might be part of your stay, as there are four floors and no elevator. In warm weather, breakfast is served in an inner courtyard under a rose bower; a small terrace with potted plants is open during the warmer months. ⊠ *Rio Terrà Foscarini, Dorsoduro 884, 30123* ☎ *041/5230058* 🖷 *041/5210158* ⊕ *www. aglialboretti.com* 🗗 *20 rooms* ⌕ *Restaurant, bar, in-room data ports, cable TV, dry cleaning, laundry service, concierge, some pets allowed, no-smoking rooms* ⊟ *AE, DC, MC, V* ⑩ *MAP* Ⓥ *Accademia.*

$–$$
FodorsChoice
★

La Calcina. La Calcina sits in an enviable position along the sunny Zattere, with views across the wide Giudecca Canal. You can sunbathe on the *altana* (wooden terrace) or enjoy an afternoon tea in one of the reading corners of the shadowy, intimate hall with flickering candlelight and barely perceptible classical music. A stone staircase (no elevator) leads to the rooms upstairs, with shiny wooden floors, original Art Deco furniture and lamps, and firm beds. Some rooms suffer from a lack of storage space. A few of the single rooms have a shared bath. ⊠ *Zat-*

tere, Dorsoduro 780, 30123 ☎ 041/5206466 🖷 041/5227045 ⊕ *www.lacalcina.com* 🛏 *29 rooms, 26 with bath, 5 suites* ⚓ *Restaurant, bar, room service, in-room safes, cable TV, baby-sitting, dry cleaning, laundry service* ▱ *AE, DC, MC, V* ⦿ *CP* Ⓥ *Zattere.*

$ 🏨 **Antica Locanda Montin.** Only a street lamp hanging above the entrance marks this waterway inn, which, in spite of its low-key looks, won the hearts of John Ruskin, Peggy Guggenheim, and Italian poet Gabriele d'Annunzio. Rooms have somewhat worn decor, inexpensive furniture, and good contemporary paintings left by the many artists who have stayed here in years past. Though a romantic view of the canal or the pretty internal garden and a durable reputation as a den for artists and literati keep the Locanda full all year long, the bargain rates are its primary appeal. ⊠ *Fondamenta delle Eremite, Dorsoduro 1147, 30123* ☎ *041/5227151* 🖷 *041/5200255* ⊕ *www.locandamontin.com* 🛏 *12 rooms, 6 with bath* ⚓ *Restaurant, fans, bar, concierge, Internet, some pets allowed; no a/c, no room TVs* ▱ *AE, DC, MC, V* ⦿ *CP* Ⓥ *Accademia or Zattere.*

★ $ 🏨 **Galleria.** For atmosphere and location, this hotel is the gem of its price range, but the secret is out, and you will probably need to book months ahead for the sensational view of the Grand Canal and the Accademia Bridge. Rooms differ in size and shape but are all classically Venetian, with a few whimsical touches, such as huge cane armchairs, faux liberty-style lamps, and sumptuous brocades on the walls. Although there is no breakfast room, a small Italian-style *colazione* (breakfast) of croissants and hot drinks is served in the rooms. The Galleria is a few steps away from the convenient Accademia vaporetto landing. ⊠ *Accademia Bridge, Dorsoduro 878/a, 30123* ☎ *041/5232489* 🖷 *041/5204172* ⊕ *www.hotelgalleria.it* 🛏 *9 rooms, 7 with bath* ⚓ *Fans, cable TV, concierge, no-smoking rooms; no a/c* ▱ *AE, MC, V* ⦿ *CP* Ⓥ *Accademia.*

$ 🏨 **Locanda Ca' Foscari.** Although an unprepossessing choice, this is a homey and relaxed pensione between Dorsoduro and San Polo where the English-speaking owner will proudly show you to your modest-size but surprisingly well-decorated and comfortable room. Booking ahead may ensure you get one of the few rooms with a pleasant view. ⊠ *Calle della Frescada, Dorsoduro 3887/b, 30123* ☎ *041/710401, 041/5211365 when closed* 🖷 *041/710817* ⊕ *www.locandacafoscari.com* 🛏 *11 rooms, 5 with bath* ⚓ *Concierge, baby-sitting; no a/c, no room phones, no room TVs* ▱ *MC, V* ⊗ *Closed Dec.–mid. Jan.* ⦿ *CP* Ⓥ *San Tomà.*

★ $ 🏨 **Messner.** Located in a modest, two-story palace on a luminous fondamenta, this is a budget hotel that fulfills all your best expectations. Several rooms, the best featuring Gothic-style balconies, face the clean and sunny *rio* (canal) below. All rooms have sturdy wooden furniture, white curtains, and blue carpeting. You can opt for the half-board plan by paying just €13 more per day. An annex has 23 less-expensive rooms without a view. ⊠ *Fondamenta Ca' Balà, Dorsoduro 216, 30123* ☎ *041/5227443* 🖷 *041/5227266* ⊕ *www.hotelmessner.it* 🛏 *34 rooms, 6 suites* ⚓ *Dining room, bar, a/c in some rooms, in-room safes, some pets allowed, no-smoking rooms* ▱ *AE, DC, MC, V* ⊗ *Closed Dec.–Jan. (except 1 wk at Christmas)* ⦿ *CP* Ⓥ *Salute.*

Giudecca

$$$$ 🏨 **Cipriani.** It's impossible to feel stressed in this oasis of stunning rooms and suites, some with garden patios. The hotel launch whisks you to Giudecca from San Marco and back at any hour; those dining at the exceptional Ristorante Harry Cipriani can use it as well. The restored 17th-century-style Palazzo Vendramin is preferable to the main hotel and the Palazzetto, a modern annex facing the Canale della Giudecca.

Prices are high even by Venetian standards, but this is the only place in town with such extensive facilities and services, from an Olympic-size pool and tennis courts to cooking courses and fitness programs. ⊠ *Giudecca 10, 30133* ☎ *041/5207744* 🖷 *041/5207745* 🌐 *www. hotelcipriani.it* 🛏 *54 rooms, 50 suites* ♨ *2 restaurants, bar, room service, in-room safes, minibars, cable TV, tennis court, saltwater pool, health club, massage, sauna, spa, baby-sitting, concierge, dry cleaning, laundry service, Internet, meeting room, no-smoking rooms* 🚍 *AE, DC, MC, V* ☺ *Closed Dec.–Apr.; Palazzo Vendramin closed 2nd wk Nov.–early Mar.* ⵏⵟ *CP* Ⓥ *San Marco or Zitelle.*

Lido

$$$$ 🏨 **Hotel des Bains.** This is a classic spot to soak up some of the atmosphere in Venice's Lido district. Thomas Mann wrote his haunting novella *Death in Venice* here, and it appeared in the book's film adaptation. The art deco tone has survived pretty much intact, making this a favorite stopover for the beautiful people during the Biennale. Rooms are sumptuously furnished, overlooking either the garden or the sea, and the facilities, including the beach, are superb. A minibus links the hotel with the nearby Excelsior, from which shuttle boats cross to San Marco every 30 minutes. ⊠ *Lungomare Marconi 17, Lido, 30126* ☎ *041/ 5265921 041/2961222 reservations in English* 🖷 *041/5260113* 🌐 *www. sheraton.com/desbains* 🛏 *172 rooms, 19 suites* ♨ *2 restaurants, 2 snack bars, pool, wading pool, 2 tennis courts, gym, sauna, beach, bar* 🚍 *AE, DC, MC, V* ☺ *Closed mid-Nov.–mid-Mar.* ⵏⵟ *CP* Ⓥ *Venice Lido.*

$$$$ 🏨 **The Westin Excelsior.** The Excelsior's imposing, Moorish-style building with its green cupolas and inner courtyard comes complete with potted lemon trees and fountains; the feel is decidedly southern Mediterranean. No longer a haunt of the noble and famous of the dolce vita days (except during the Biennale), the hotel nonetheless offers the same panache, luxury, and space as ever. Rooms are tastefully modern, done in bright colors, and face either the inner garden or the beach below. A shuttle boat between the hotel and San Zaccaria is at guests' disposal. ⊠ *Lungomare Marconi 41, Lido, 30126* ☎ *041/5260201* 🖷 *041/ 5267276* 🌐 *www.westin.com/excelsiorvenicelido* 🛏 *197 rooms, 19 suites* ♨ *3 restaurants, in-room data ports, in-room safes, minibar, in-room movies, 6 tennis courts, pool, wading pool, hair salon, beach, windsurfing, waterskiing, 3 bars, baby-sitting, dry cleaning, laundry service, concierge, meeting rooms, parking (fee), some pets allowed, no-smoking rooms* 🚍 *AE, DC, MC, V* ☺ *Closed mid-Nov.–mid-Mar.* ⵏⵟ *CP* Ⓥ *Venice Lido.*

★ $$–$$$$ 🏨 **Quattro Fontane.** This fine hotel in a well-maintained mansion run by Danish sisters Bente and Pia Bevilacqua offers the serenity of the Lido in a location that's a 15-minute walk and a 20-minute boat ride from Piazza San Marco. Well-decorated rooms, with period furniture and tasteful tapestries, overlook the surrounding garden. Common areas contain an odd collection of mason's aprons, pipes, ex-votos, masks from Jakarta, Roman seals, and seashells. A huge fireplace adds warmth and character in the colder months. After a full day you can relax in the library, stocked with books in many languages. ⊠ *Via delle Quattro Fontane 16, Lido, 30126* ☎ *041/5260227* 🖷 *041/5260726* 🌐 *www. quattrofontane.com* 🛏 *54 rooms, 4 suites* ♨ *Restaurant, bar, air-conditioning in some rooms, in-room safes, minibar, cable TV, library, baby-sitting, dry cleaning, laundry service, meeting room* 🚍 *AE, DC, MC, V* ☺ *Closed Nov.–Mar.* ⵏⵟ *CP* Ⓥ *Venice Lido.*

$$$ 🏨 **Hotel Hungaria Palace.** Art Nouveau lovers, and those simply in search of a non-Venetian hotel in Venice, should consider a stay at this

one-of-a-kind place. It was built in 1905, and its fanciful facade and colorful majolica tiles are a glamorous throwback to a bygone age. Simply furnished public rooms have some of the hotel's original furniture; the curvaceous bar is also original. Most rooms, some with furniture dating to the turn of the 20th century, have deep, tiled bathtubs, and prints and photographs of Venice adorning the walls. Note that the fourth floor is done in a rustic style—not unattractive, but radically different from the rest of the hotel. ⊠ *Gran Viale S.M. Elisabetta 28, Lido, 30126* ☎ *041/2420060* 🖷 *041/5264111* ⊕ *www.hungaria.it* ⟷ *78 rooms, 3 suites* ⌂ *Restaurant, bar, room service, in-room data ports, minibar, cable TV, bicycles, baby-sitting, playground, dry cleaning, laundry service, concierge, meeting room, free parking, some pets allowed, no-smoking rooms* ⊟ *AE, DC, MC, V.*

$$$ 🏨 **Villa Mabapa.** Built as a private house in the 1930s and subsequently converted into a hotel, this lodging is still run by the original owners and conserves its air of a family home. A charming rustic atmosphere prevails, and the shady garden is an excellent spot for an alfresco dinner of classic Venetian dishes. The name, in case you're wondering, is a combination of *mamma, bambini,* and *papa.* ⊠ *Riviera San Nicolò 16, Lido, 30126* ☎ *041/5260590* 🖷 *041/5269441* ⊕ *www.villamabapa. it* ⟷ *69 rooms* ⌂ *Restaurant, bar, in-room safes, minibar, cable TV, baby-sitting, concierge, dry cleaning, laundry service, meeting room, some pets allowed* ⊟ *AE, DC, MC, V* 🍴 *CP* Ⓥ *Venice Lido.*

$ 🏨 **Le Garzette.** As the only *agriturismo* (working farm with guest accommodations) available in Venice, this place is a bit of an oddity, situated at the greener end of the island about a half hour from San Marco. The quiet guest rooms, some of which have balconies facing the sea, are furnished with 19th-century antiques. The restaurant—which is open to nonguests on weekends—takes its ingredients directly from the surrounding orchards and gardens. Bicycles are available free, and the beach is literally steps away. With so few rooms available, you'd do well to book early. A one-week stay is mandatory in July and August. ⊠ *Lungomare Alberoni 32, Lido, 30010* ☎ *041/731078* 🖷 *041/2428798* ⊕ *www.welcome.to/legarzette* ⟷ *5 rooms* ⌂ *Restaurant, fans, bicycles, some pets allowed; no a/c* ⊟ *No credit cards* ⊗ *Closed 2 wks at Christmas* 🍴 *CP* Ⓥ *Venice Lido.*

San Marco

$$$$ 🏨 **Bonvecchiati.** The owner here is a passionate collector of contemporary paintings, and the works adorning the walls contribute to the hotel's character. Guest rooms are in cool shades of blue, green, or salmon, with wooden floors, Oriental rugs, and either smart modern furniture or antique-looking pieces with elaborate carvings. A few small but choice rooms on the fifth floor overlook the domes of the Basilica di San Marco. From sunset to midnight there is intense gondola traffic outside, with noisy singers entertaining tourists. Avoid rooms on lower floors facing the mezzanine terrace restaurant. ⊠ *Calle Goldoni, San Marco 4488, 30124* ☎ *041/5285017* 🖷 *041/5285230* ⊕ *www.hotelbonvecchiati.it* ⟷ *104 rooms* ⌂ *Restaurant, bar, room service, in-room data ports, minibars, cable TV, concierge, dry cleaning, laundry service, some pets allowed* ⊟ *AE, DC, MC, V* 🍴 *CP* Ⓥ *San Marco.*

$$$$ 🏨 **Cavalletto & Doge Orseolo.** The curved, yellow stucco facade was clearly remade in recent times, but this choice spot next to Piazza San Marco has been familiar to travelers and visitors since 1308, when the earliest version of the Cavalletto was founded here under the Latin name Taberna ad Cavaletum. The French windows of the bright hall and breakfast room open onto the largest gondola parking lot in town.

The same view is enjoyed from all the "superior" rooms (well worth the supplement), which feature king-size beds and spacious marble bathrooms, some with bathtubs. The decor varies from room to room: expect soft colors, warm parquet floors, and lacquered furniture. ⊠ *Calle del Cavalletto, San Marco 1107, 30124* ☎ *041/5200955* 🖷 *041/5238184* ⊕ *www.sanmarcohotels.com* 📞 *107 rooms, 7 junior suites* ⌂ *Restaurant, bar, room service, in-room data ports, in-room safes, minibars, cable TV, baby-sitting, dry cleaning, laundry service, some pets allowed, no-smoking rooms* ⊟ *AE, DC, MC, V* 🍴 *CP* Ⓥ *San Marco.*

$$$$ 🏨 **Concordia.** Half of the rooms in this attractive, well-run hotel catch a side view of the Basilica di San Marco, as does the spacious breakfast room–bar, where light meals and snacks are served all day. Rooms are decorated with brocade tapestry and have cream, aqua, or peach color schemes. The romantic *mansarda* (rooftop room) has a panoramic view over the Piazza San Marco. The management offers good deals at off-peak times, so check when booking. ⊠ *Calle Larga San Marco, San Marco 367, 30124* ☎ *041/5206866* 🖷 *041/5206775* ⊕ *www.hotelconcordia. com* 📞 *54 rooms, 3 suites* ⌂ *Room service, in-room safes, minibars, cable TV, laundry service, dry cleaning, baby-sitting, concierge, meeting room, some pets allowed* ⊟ *AE, DC, MC, V* 🍴 *CP* Ⓥ *San Marco.*

$$$$ 🏨 **Gritti Palace.** Queen Elizabeth, Greta Garbo, and Winston Churchill made this their Venetian address. The feeling of being in an aristocratic private home pervades this legendary hotel, replete with fresh flowers, fine antiques, sumptuous appointments, and old-fashioned service. The dining terrace on the Grand Canal is best enjoyed in the evening when the boat traffic dies down. Guests have access to pool and tennis courts. ⊠ *Campo Santa Maria del Giglio, San Marco 2467, 30124* ☎ *041/794611* 🖷 *041/5200942* ⊕ *www.luxurycollection.com* 📞 *87 rooms, 6 suites* ⌂ *Restaurant, bar, room service, cable TV with movies, in-room data ports, in-room safes, in-room fax on request, in-room VCRs on request, minibars, baby-sitting, dry cleaning, laundry service, concierge, Internet, business services, meeting rooms, some pets allowed, no-smoking rooms* ⊟ *AE, DC, MC, V* 🍴 *CP* Ⓥ *Santa Maria del Giglio.*

$$$$ 🏨 **Il Palazzo at the Bauer.** A $38 million restoration has turned il Palazzo, under the same management as the larger Bauer Hotel, into the ultimate word in luxury. Bevilacqua and Rubelli fabrics cover the walls, and no two rooms are decorated the same. What they have in common, however, are high ceilings, many with sweeping views, Murano glass, marbled bathrooms, and damask drapes. Breakfast is served on Venice's highest terrace, appropriately named il Settimo Cielo (Seventh Heaven). The outdoor hot tub, also on the seventh floor, offers views that won't quit of La Serennissima. ⊠ *Campo San Moisè, San Marco 1459, 30124* ☎ *041/5207022* 🖷 *041/5207557* ⊕ *www.bauervenezia.it* 📞 *35 rooms, 40 suites* ⌂ *Restaurant, bar, room service, in-room data ports, in-room fax, in-room safes, some in-room hot tubs, minibars, cable TV with movies, golf privileges, health club, outdoor hot tub, massage, sauna, Turkish bath, dock, baby-sitting, dry cleaning, laundry service, concierge, Internet, some pets allowed, no-smoking rooms* ⊟ *AE, DC, MC, V* 🍴 *CP* Ⓥ *San Marco.*

FodorsChoice
★

$$$$ 🏨 **Luna Baglioni.** Two minutes from San Marco, this handsome hotel has elegant rooms, several with a view of the Grand Canal. Breakfast is served in a salon fit for a king, adorned with frescoes by the school of Tiepolo, 18th-century furniture, and Venetian floors. Most suites are lavish affairs, with fireplaces, jetted tubs, and terraces. Restaurant Canova offers modern Venetian cuisine. ⊠ *Calle Vallerosso, San Marco 1243, 30124* ☎ *041/5289840* 🖷 *041/5287160* ⊕ *www.baglionihotels.com* 📞 *107 rooms, 11 suites* ⌂ *Restaurant, bar, room service, in-room data ports, in-room safes, in-room hot tubs, minibars, cable TV, dock, piano bar,*

Where to Stay in San Marco

baby-sitting, dry cleaning, laundry, concierge, Internet, some pets allowed, no-smoking rooms ⊟ *AE, DC, MC, V* ⍥ *CP* Ⓥ *San Marco.*

★ $$$$ ⊞ **Monaco & Grand Canal.** Between the view onto the Bacino di San Marco and the touches of elegance and comfort found at this luxurious hotel, you may find little motivation to leave. The common rooms on the ground floor are flooded with the shimmering light coming off the lagoon, and the piano bar, with velvety light-sage couches, comes alive every night. Rooms are spacious but warm and intimate, with carpeted floors, satin-lined walls, handsome antique-style furniture, and ample terra-cotta bathrooms. The half-board option, with meals à la carte in the worthwhile Grand Canal restaurant, is a good choice. ⊠ *Calle Vallaresso, San Marco 1325, 30124* ☎ *041/5200211* ⌨ *041/5200501* ⬩ *64 rooms, 7 suites* ⌂ *Restaurant, bar, room service, in-room data ports, in-room safes, some in-room hot tubs, minibars, cable TV, dock, piano bar, baby-sitting, concierge, dry cleaning, laundry service, some pets allowed* ⊟ *AE, DC, MC, V* ⍥ *CP* Ⓥ *San Marco.*

$$$$ ⊞ **San Moisè.** The closest you can get to staying in an 18th-century Venetian house, the San Moisè deserves special mention for its warm decor and choice location. Rooms share the same motifs as the cozy portego: Oriental rugs, glass chandeliers, rich tapestries, handsome furniture, and in some cases pleasantly irregular dimensions. Some rooms have a view of the rio, and others face a small inner courtyard, home to a lush wisteria tree. There is no elevator, but you won't have to climb any higher than the second floor. ⊠ *Piscina San Moisè, San Marco 2058, 30124* ☎ *041/5203755* ⌨ *041/5210670* ⊕ *www.sanmoise.it* ⬩ *16 rooms* ⌂ *Minibar, bar, baby-sitting, dry cleaning, laundry service, concierge, some pets allowed* ⊟ *AE, DC, MC, V* ⍥ *CP* Ⓥ *Calle Vallerosso.*

$$$$ ⊞ **Saturnia Internazionale.** You'll find lots of old-fashioned charm and tranquillity in this historic palace near Piazza San Marco. Beamed ceilings, damask-hung walls, and authentic Venetian decor impart character to the comfortable rooms and salons. Many rooms have glamorous, large bathrooms. La Caravella restaurant, which serves traditional Venetian dishes, is of special note, as is the fine staff at the front desk. ⊠ *Calle Larga XXII Marzo, San Marco 2398, 30124* ☎ *041/5208377* ⌨ *041/5207131* ⊕ *www.hotelsaturnia.it* ⬩ *91 rooms* ⌂ *Restaurant, bar, in-room data ports, in-room safes, minibar, cable TV, baby-sitting, dry cleaning, laundry service, Internet (fee), meeting room, some pets allowed, no-smoking rooms* ⊟ *AE, DC, MC, V* ⍥ *CP* Ⓥ *San Marco.*

$$$–$$$$ ⊞ **Ala.** The Ala is in the "aristocratic" part of town, between Piazza San Marco and Campo Santo Stefano a few steps from the Santa Maria del Giglio vaporetto and traghetto stop. The owner's collection of armor is displayed in the hall and sitting rooms, where daily English-language newspapers are at your disposal. Some rooms are large, with coffered ceilings and old-style furnishings; others are smaller with more modern decor. Most come with a view of either the campo below or of the side canal. ⊠ *Campo Santa Maria del Giglio, San Marco 2494, 30124* ☎ *041/5208333* ⌨ *041/5206390* ⊕ *www.hotelala.it* ⬩ *85 rooms* ⌂ *In-room safes, minibar, cable TV with movies, concierge, Internet, no-smoking rooms* ⊟ *AE, DC, MC, V* ⍥ *CP* Ⓥ *Santa Maria del Giglio.*

$$$ ⊞ **Flora.** The Flora is distinguished by its many sitting rooms and pretty courtyard. It's in a quiet but central spot near San Moisè and Piazza San Marco. Rooms have Venetian period decor and are a bit dark; a handful are small, with tiny bathrooms. Ask for a room with a view of the courtyard or the garden. ⊠ *Calle Bergamaschi, off Calle Larga XXII Marzo, San Marco 2283/a, 30124* ☎ *041/5205844* ⌨ *041/5228217* ⊕ *www.hotelflora.it* ⬩ *44 rooms* ⌂ *Bar, in-room safes, cable TV, baby-sitting, concierge, dry cleaning, laundry service* ⊟ *AE, DC, MC, V* ⍥ *CP* Ⓥ *Calle Vallerosso.*

$$$ ▣ **Montecarlo.** There's plenty of atmosphere in this hotel housed in a 17th-century palazzo behind Piazza San Marco and only a short stroll from the Rialto Bridge. Typical Venetian-style rooms are well equipped; chandeliers and paintings by old Venetian masters add to the refined ambience. The well-regarded Antico Pignolo restaurant serves traditional Venetian fare. ⊠ *Calle degli Specchieri, San Marco 463, 30124* ☎ *041/5207144* 🖷 *041/5207789* 🖘 *48 rooms* ⊕ *www.venicehotelmontecarlo.com* ⌕ *Restaurant, bar, room service, in-room data ports, in-room safes, cable TV, baby-sitting, concierge, dry cleaning, laundry service, some pets allowed, no-smoking rooms* ⊟ *AE, DC, MC, V* ⍾ *CP* ⓥ *San Marco.*

$$–$$$ ▣ **La Fenice et des Artistes.** The timeworn facade of this hotel on Campo San Fantin hides a rather unusual interior layout. The building was once divided into a fashionable atelier, a warehouse, and private apartments. Rambling corridors and common areas lead to the rooms, some of which overlook the two inner gardens, where breakfast is served in fair weather. Try to reserve an antique-style room (several have balconies), as a few bedrooms have modern, rather disappointing furniture. Ask in advance if you require air-conditioning, which isn't available in all rooms. ⊠ *Campo San Fantin, San Marco 1936, 30124* ☎ *041/5232333* 🖷 *041/5203721* ⊕ *www.fenicehotels.com* 🖘 *65 rooms* ⌕ *Restaurant, bar, in-room data ports, in-room safes, cable TV, concierge, meeting room, no-smoking rooms; no a/c in some rooms* ⊟ *AE, DC, MC, V* ⍾ *CP* ⓥ *Sant'Angelo.*

$$ ▣ **Palazzo del Giglio.** A whole block of orange stucco houses overlooks Campo Santa Maria del Giglio at this hotel and short-term residence with modern, if not too charming, decor. Guest rooms lack views and are rather overpriced in high season. The real appeal lies in the apartments, which have hotel service, house two to six people, and offer views of the campo below. The larger units are outfitted with two bedrooms, two bathrooms, a spacious common area, and a fully equipped kitchen. It's essential to reserve months ahead. Fortunately, there's no minimum stay. ⊠ *Campo Santa Maria del Giglio, San Marco 2462, 30124* ☎ *041/2719111* 🖷 *041/5205158* ⊕ *www.hotelgiglio.com* 🖘 *24 rooms, 19 apartments* ⌕ *Room service, cable TV, in-room safes, minibars, baby-sitting, concierge, dry cleaning, laundry service* ⊟ *AE, DC, MC, V* ⍾ *CP* ⓥ *Santa Maria del Giglio.*

★ $$ ▣ **San Zulian.** A minimalist entrance hall leads to rooms that are a refined variation on the Venetian theme, with lacquered 18th-century-style furniture and parquet floors. Room 304 is on two levels and has its own delightful covered veranda. Two ground-floor rooms have bathrooms equipped for people with disabilities. The handy location near San Marco and the Rialto and the top-notch staff make a stay here eminently worthwhile. ⊠ *Campo della Guerra, San Marco 534/535, 30124* ☎ *041/5225872 or 041/5226598* 🖷 *041/5232265* ⊕ *www.hotelsanzulian.com* 🖘 *25 rooms* ⌕ *In-room safes, minibars, cable TV, some pets allowed* ⊟ *AE, DC, MC, V* ⍾ *CP* ⓥ *San Marco.*

$$ ▣ **Serenissima.** Run with pride by the amiable Dal Borgo family since 1960, the Serenissima offers quiet rooms in the heart of town at very fair prices. An effort to create some warmth has been made in the common areas, but the waxed wooden floors, Oriental rugs, and dark-burgundy leather couches don't lend too much to the atmosphere. A similar style characterizes the guest rooms, which, within their category, stand out for good maintenance and comfort. As busy Calle Goldoni below does not really count as a view, your best bets are the quieter rooms at the back, all facing an inner courtyard. ⊠ *Calle Goldoni, San Marco 4486, 30124* ☎ *041/5200011* 🖷 *041/5223292* ⊕ *www.hotelserenissima.it* 🖘 *38 rooms* ⌕ *In-room data ports, cable TV, concierge, Internet,*

some pets allowed ⊟ *AE, MC, V* ⊘ *Closed mid-Nov.–Carnevale* ❙⊘❙ *CP*
Ⓥ *Rialto or San Zaccaria.*

$ ▣ **Albergo San Samuele.** Near the Grand Canal and Palazzo Grassi, this
friendly hotel has clean, sunny rooms in surprisingly good shape for the
price. Five of the bathrooms, with white and gray-blue tiles, are relatively new, and the walls are painted in crisp, pleasant shades of pale
pink or blue. Curtains and bedspreads are made from antique-looking
fabrics, and although the furniture is of the boxy modern kind, the owners are gradually adding more interesting-looking pieces. ⊠ *Salizzada
San Samuele, San Marco 3358, 30124* ▦▦▦ *041/5228045* ⏎ *10 rooms,
7 with bath* ⚭ *Fans, some pets allowed, no-smoking rooms; no a/c* ⊟ *No
credit cards* ❙⊘❙ *CP* Ⓥ *San Samuele.*

$ ▣ **Locanda Fiorita.** This welcoming, small hotel is tucked away in a
sunny little square near the Ponte dell'Accademia. The entrance is
through a vine-covered porch, a section of which belongs to the best
guest room. Beamed ceilings give some character to otherwise bland but
practical furnishings. Eight of the rooms are in an annex on Campo Santo
Stefano. Air-conditioning is available in some rooms. ⊠ *Campiello
Novo o dei Morti, San Marco 3457/a, 30124* ☎ *041/5234754* 🖷 *041/
5228043* ⊕ *www.locandafiorita.com* ⏎ *18 rooms, 14 with bath*
⚭ *Cable TV, baby-sitting, Internet; no a/c in some rooms* ⊟ *AE, MC,
V* ❙⊘❙ *CP* Ⓥ *Accademia.*

San Polo

$$$$ ▣ **Marconi.** With its location next to the Rialto Bridge in the Riva del
Vin area—once renowned for its taverns—it is no surprise to learn that
the Marconi was itself an *osteria* until its conversion in the 1930s into
one of the most elegant hotels in town. Rooms are furnished in antique
style but equipped with up-to-date facilities. Two of the guest rooms enjoy
outstanding views overlooking the Grand Canal, though they are on the
small side. The bustling produce market is steps away. ⊠ *Rialto, Riva
del Vin, San Polo 729, 30125* ☎ *041/5222068* 🖷 *041/5229700* ⊕ *www.
hotelmarconi.it* ⏎ *26 rooms* ⚭ *Restaurant, bar, room service, in-room
safes, minibars, baby-sitting, concierge, dry cleaning, laundry service,
Internet, some pets allowed* ⊟ *AE, DC, MC, V* ❙⊘❙ *CP* Ⓥ *Rialto.*

$$–$$$ ▣ **Sturion.** At the end of the 13th century this building housed foreign
merchants selling their wares at the Rialto, and Carpaccio depicted it
in his 1494 *Mircale of the Cross* (on view at the Accademia). Now it's
decorated in 18th-century Venetian style and run with great care by a
Venetian family. Rooms are done in red and gold brocade (two with views
of the Grand Canal); there's also a small but inviting breakfast room.
Two of the rooms comfortably sleep four and are perfect for families.
Be warned that the stairs are steep here, and there's no elevator. ⊠ *Calle
del Sturion, San Polo 679, 30125* ☎ *041/5236243* 🖷 *041/5228378*
⊕ *www.locandasturion.com* ⏎ *11 rooms* ⚭ *Restaurant, in-room safes,
minibar, library, Internet, some pets allowed, no-smoking rooms* ⊟ *AE,
MC, V* ❙⊘❙ *CP* Ⓥ *Rialto.*

Santa Croce

$$$$ ▣ **Sofitel.** Housed inside a new, well-maintained pink palazzo just 300
yards from Piazzale Roma and with access to all main vaporetto lines,
the Sofitel is the luxury hotel of choice for travelers with children, as
kids under 12 stay free in their parents' bedroom. You'll find an efficient staff and modern comforts, including soft carpets, noise insulation,
and spacious bathrooms with tubs and windows. The tasteful decor mixes
wooden furniture, large mirrors, glass chandeliers, and pastel-shade
walls. ⊠ *Giardini Papadopoli, Santa Croce 245, 30135* ☎ *041/710400*

⌨ 041/710394 ⊕ *www.sofitel.com* ↩ *92 rooms, 5 suites* ⚓ *Restaurant, bar, room service, in-room data ports, in-room safes, minibars, cable TV with movies, dock, baby-sitting, concierge, Internet, meeting room, some pets allowed, no-smoking floor* ▭ *AE, DC, MC, V* ⍾ *CP* Ⓥ *Stazione.*

★ **$$$$** 🏨 **San Cassiano-Ca' Favretto.** This Renaissance-era red-stucco and stone building was home to the families of several doges before being purchased by the Venetian painter Giacomo Favretto (1849–87). The spacious portego preserves the original 20-ft beamed ceiling, from which hang two huge Murano chandeliers fit for a royal ballroom; old tapestries arranged high on the walls add glamour and a medieval feel. All rooms are furnished with either real antiques or well-made replicas. Nearly every window frames a great view; those facing the Grand Canal open on the lacy facade of the Ca' d'Oro, which at sunset picks up magic shades of pink. ⊠ *Calle della Rosa, Santa Croce 2232, 30135* ☎ *041/5241768* ⌨ *041/721033* ⊕ *www.sancassiano.it* ↩ *35 rooms* ⚓ *Bar, in-room safes, minibar, cable TV, baby-sitting, dry cleaning, Internet* ▭ *AE, DC, MC, V* ⍾ *CP* Ⓥ *S. Stae.*

$$ 🏨 **Santa Chiara.** You can drive your car to the entrance of the Santa Chiara and yet still find yourself staying in a room overlooking the Grand Canal. The hotel was built where the convent and church of Santa Croce once stood; a surviving wall is incorporated into the present-day structure. Wood-beam ceilings and red-and-white-checked floors give character to the common areas. Rooms are bright and well appointed and generally larger than average within this price category. The most coveted room is the attic, with a private terrace and panoramic view. Twelve rooms in the nearby annex are wheelchair-friendly. ⊠ *Piazzale Roma, Santa Croce 548, 30135* ☎ *041/5206955* ⌨ *041/5228799* ⊕ *www.hotelsantachiara.it* ↩ *40 rooms* ⚓ *Bar, in-room safes, minibars, concierge, dry cleaning, laundry service, Internet, free parking* ▭ *AE, DC, MC, V* ⍾ *CP* Ⓥ *Stazione.*

$$ 🏨 **Falier.** The name Falier (recalling a former doge) is a bit misleading for this simple, decidedly undogelike hotel. In fact, if it weren't for the red-and-white checked floor of the portego, the decor wouldn't be at all Venetian. Terra-cotta floors and basic wood furniture recall a budget mountain chalet; in most rooms the feeling is enhanced by rustic wooden ceilings and short curtains. Bathrooms are on the small side and have showers only. Views are not great, and the first floor is rather dark. The exception is room 41, with a lovely little terrace set amid the neighboring roofs. ⊠ *Salizzada San Pantalon, Santa Croce 130, 30135* ☎ *041/710882* ⌨ *041/5206554* ⊕ *www.hotelfalier.com* ↩ *19 rooms* ⚓ *Bar, cable TV, baby-sitting, Internet, some pets allowed* ▭ *AE, DC, MC, V* ⍾ *CP* Ⓥ *Stazione.*

★ **$** 🏨 **Dalla Mora.** On a quiet calle beyond the main flow of traffic, this hotel occupies two simple, well-maintained houses, both with views. The cheerful, tiny entry hall leads upstairs to a terrace lined with potted geraniums, the perfect place to catch the breeze on summer evenings. Rooms are all quite spacious, with basic wooden furniture and tile floors. The annex across the calle has rooms without private bathrooms and others with only showers and sinks. The excellent price and good views make this an attractive place to stay if you're on a budget. ⊠ *Off Salizzada San Pantalon, Santa Croce 42, 30135* ☎ *041/710703* ⌨ *041/723006* ↩ *14 rooms, 6 with bath* ⚓ *Baby-sitting; no a/c in some rooms* ▭ *MC, V* ⍾ *CP* Ⓥ *San Tomà.*

NIGHTLIFE & THE ARTS

FODOR'S CHOICE

Festa del Redentore

Biennale del Cinema

HIGHLY RECOMMENDED

Caffè Florian, *Piazza San Marco*

Gelateria il Doge, *Dorsoduro*

Il Caffè, *Dorsoduro*

Palazzo Grassi, *San Marco*

Piccolo Mondo, *Dorsoduro*

Updated by
Elaine Eliah

YOUR FIRST IMPRESSION may well be that Venice doesn't have a nightlife. As the last rays of daylight slip away, so too do most signs of a bustling town. Boat traffic drops to the occasional vaporetto, shutters roll down, and signs go dark. Even though *bacari* (wine bars) would seem to be natural after-hours gathering spots, most close around 9 PM. Yet sprinkled judiciously around the city's residential-looking calli and campi, you'll stumble upon *locali* (nightspots) that stay open until 1 or 2 AM. Some even offer live music, though rarely past midnight—a city ordinance prohibits too much wildness except during Carnevale. Though there are no suitable venues for rock shows, Piazza San Marco has hosted some less rambunctious concerts on summer evenings. Except for a couple of lounge bars with dancing, nightlife tends to be student oriented.

Venice is a stop for major traveling art exhibits, from Mayan to contemporary. From mid-June to early November in odd-numbered years, the Biennale dell'Arte attracts several hundred contemporary artists from around the world. Classical music buffs can rely on a rich season of concerts, opera, chamber music, and some ballet. Minor venues and churches offer lower-priced, occasionally free performances, often highlighting Venetian composers. Though the city has no English-language theater, during Carnevale foreign companies act in their mother tongue. All films screened at the Venice Film Festival are shown in the original language, with subtitles in English, Italian, or both. During winter months, the movie theater Giorgione Movie d'essai screens English-language films on Tuesday nights.

A Guest in Venice, a monthly bilingual booklet, free at hotels, is probably your most accessible, up-to-date guide to Venice happenings. It also includes information about pharmacies, vaporetto and bus lines, and the main trains and flights. You can visit their website, ⊕ www.aguestinvenice.com, for a preview of musical, artistic, and sporting events. *Venezia News,* available at newsstands, has similar information but also includes in-depth articles about noteworthy events; listings are bilingual but most articles are in Italian. The tourist office publishes *Leo* and *Bussola,* bimonthly brochures in Italian and English listing events and updated museum hours. *Venezia da Vivere* is a bilingual guide that comes out seasonally listing night spots and live music. Venice information websites give you a chance to scan the cultural horizon before you arrive; try ⊕ www.veniceonline.it and ⊕ www.venicebanana.com. Italian speakers can find useful information at ⊕ www.comune.venezia.it and ⊕ www.veneziacultura.it. Last but not least, don't ignore the posters you see everywhere in the streets; they're often as current as you can get.

THE ARTS

Art has been a way of life in Venice for so many centuries that it seems you need only inhale to enjoy it. While the Biennale is a whirlwind of contemporary arts, Carnevale masks and costumes let revelers dance with history. But though costumed musicians entice you to performances in the finest churches and palaces, don't ignore the opera wafting from the gondolas or the conservatory students practicing with open windows.

Art Exhibitions

★ Venice's major site for temporary exhibits is **Palazzo Grassi** (⊠ Campo San Samuele 3231 ☎ 041/5231680 ⊕ www.palazzograssi.it Ⓥ San Samuele), a stately 18th-century palace on the Grand Canal that hosts art and cultural shows of international importance, ranging from contemporary painting to Etruscan finds. Banners flying on the Island of San Giorgio Maggiore herald an exhibit by the **Cini Foundation** (☎ 041/5289900 ⊕ www.cini.it), which occasionally hosts artistic and cultural shows. If you're near Campo Santa Margherita, visit **Fondazione Bevilacqua La Masa** (✉ Rio San Barnaba, Dorsoduro 2826 ☎041/5207797 Ⓥ Ca' Rezzonico), which often exhibits contemporary artists.

From time to time, museums such as Palazzo Ducale, Ca' Rezzonico, Museo Correr, Querini-Stampalia, Galleria di Palazzo Cini, and the Peggy Guggenheim Collection host temporary exhibits. There's usually no extra charge to visit such shows. Exhibits are advertised with banners, on city walls, and at museum entrances. Publications such as *A Guest in Venice* (free in hotels), *Leo* (free at tourist office), and *Venezia News* (sold at news kiosks) also list these events.

Carnevale

The first historical evidence of Carnevale (Carnival) in Venice dates from 1097, and for centuries the city marked the days preceding *quaresima* (Lent, the 40 days of abstinence leading up to Palm Sunday) with abundant feasting and wild celebrations. The word *carnival* is derived from the words for meat (*carne*) and to remove (*levare*), as eating meat was prohibited during Lent. Venice earned its international reputation as the "city of Carnevale" in the 18th century, when partying would begin right after Epiphany (January 6) and the city seemed to be one continuous decadent masquerade. With the Republic's fall in 1797, the city lost a great deal of its vitality, and the tradition of Carnevale celebrations was abandoned.

Carnevale was revived in the 1970s when residents took to the calli and campi in their own impromptu celebrations. Informality was the key, with friends and neighbors coming together to break the winter doldrums. It didn't take long for moneymakers to capitalize on the holiday to stimulate business and tourism during low season. The revival has been successful, though not without its problems. While the well-off are well catered by hotels and elegant balls, revelers here only for the day often complain there are few low-cost activities for them. Each year over the 10–12-day Carnevale period, more than a half million people attend concerts, theater and street performances, masquerade balls, historical processions, fashion shows, and contests. **A Guest in Venice** (⊕ www.aguestinvenice.com) gives free advertising to public and private event festivities and is therefore one of the most complete Carnevale guides. For general Carnevale information, contact **Consorzio Comitato per il Carnevale di Venezia** (✉ Santa Croce 1714, 30135 ☎ 041/717065, or 041/2510811 during Carnevale 🖷 041/5200410 ⊕ www.meetingeurope.com).

The **Tourist Office** (☎ 041/5298711) has detailed information about daily events.

Each year new costume events spring up during Carnevale, but the most popular balls and parties fill up fast, so if you want to take part you should book ahead. Balls cost roughly €350–€450 per person, dinner included, and though you can rent a standard costume for as little as €200–€400 (not including shoes or masks), you can spend over €1000 renting attire for the night. Candlelit **Ballo del Doge** (☎ 041/5233851 🖷 041/5287543 ⊕ www.ballodeldoge.com) is held at Palazzo Pisani-Moretta the last Saturday of Carnevale. Also at Pisani-Moretta is **Ballo Tiepolo** (☎ 041/717065 🖷 041/722285 ⊕ www.meetingeurope.com). Lively **Ballo dei Sospiri** (☎ 041/2411607 🖷 041/52335558 ⊕ www.venicemasquerade.com) is held in Palazzo Ca' Zenobio,

THE BIENNALE, AN ARTS FEAST

A Venetian cultural institution, the **Biennale** (as the name suggests) started as an art festival held every two years, but during the century-plus of its existence it's outgrown the name, becoming one of the world's major interdisciplinary art expositions. "Biennale" now refers to the group that coordinates festivals of art, film, music, dance, theater, and architecture. For information on all events, contact **La Biennale di Venezia** (✉ Ca' Giustinian, San Marco 1364/a ☎ 041/5218711 🖷 041/5227539 🌐 www.labiennale.org).

The **Biennale dell'Arte** (also known as the Esposizione Internazionale d'Arte) was originated in 1894 and, except for World War interruptions, has taken place every two years since. In 1910 Klimt and Renoir had their own exhibition rooms, while Picasso was removed from the Spanish salon over concern his paintings were too shocking. Picasso's work was finally shown in 1948, the same year Peggy Guggenheim brought her collection to Venice at the Biennale's invitation.

The Biennale dell'Arte currently takes place from mid-June to early November in odd-numbered years. The Giardini della Biennale, located in the Castello sestiere, was developed specifically for the event. In this parklike setting overlooking the lagoon, 30 countries have permanent pavilions to exhibit works by their native artists. In the neighboring Arsenale's Corderie, a long, beautiful building otherwise off-limits to visitors, works by artists from smaller nations, as well as some more avant-garde installations, are shown. Numerous palaces, warehouses, and churches all over town also hold exhibits, often allowing you to visit buildings not normally open to the public. Expect to see anything from huge realistic sculptures to a plain room painted white, then black, then white again every day of the five-month exhibition.

The **Biennale del Cinema** (also known as the Mostra Internazionale del Cinema, or Venice Film Festival) was first held in 1932 and soon turned into an annual event. Though not as famous as Cannes, it's nonetheless a world-class festival. Films are shown in several theaters at the **Palazzo del Cinema** (✉ Lungomare Guglielmo Marconi 90, Lido ☎ 041/2726511 🖪 Lido Casinò or S.M. Elizabetta), a low, boxy structure that from the outside could be mistaken for a train station. Closed most of the year, it comes to life in August with fresh paint, bright lights, and thousands of film fans and stars. Ten days of 9 AM to 2 AM screenings include films vying for awards as well as retrospectives and debuts of mainstream releases. Films are shown in their original language, with subtitles in Italian and English. Advance tickets are recommended for the most eagerly awaited films (the tourist office has details). The night after films play the Palazzo del Cinema, they're shown at Campo San Polo's open-air cinema and at the Giorgione Movie d'essai. San Polo screens the winner of the Leone d'Oro (Golden Lion) prize the night following the awards ceremony.

Since its launch in 1930, the **Biennale Musica** (also known as the Festival Internazionale di Musica Contemporanea) has attracted world-famous composers and performers. Igor Stravinsky premiered his Rake's Progress during the 1951 festival, and four years later it was George Gershwin's turn with Porgy and Bess. In 1984, San Lorenzo church was filled by a wooden structure that served as stage, seating area, and resonance chamber for Luigi Nono's opera Prometeo. The annual event stretches over several months, with performances in some of the city's smaller venues.

Scheduling is similar for the newest addition to the cultural family, **Biennale Danza,** as well as the **Biennale Teatro,** both of which stage some performances in the city's campi. The Theatro Verde, an outdoor amphitheater on the island of San Giorgio, was restored for Biennale use, and whether the performance is Spanish Flamenco or New Zealand's Maori dancers, you can't beat the Venetian lagoon as a backdrop. The least established of the Biennale events, the **Biennale of Architecture,** began in 1980 but has yet to develop a regular pattern of exhibits.

known for its elegant mirrored ballroom. **Count Emile Targhetta d'Aud-iffret** (✉ Cannaregio 6293, 30121 ☎ 041/5230242) opens his palazzo on the Fondamente Nuove for evenings of masquerade, dancing, and follies; write for information.

If you're not planning on joining in the revelry, you'd be wise to choose another time to visit Venice. Enormous crowds clog the streets (which become one-way, with police directing traffic), bridges are designated "no-stopping" zones to avoid gridlock, and prices absolutely skyrocket.

Concerts

The band Pink Floyd made rock history with a 1989 concert staged aboard a pontoon floating near Piazza San Marco. Fans made such a mess of the piazza and loud music stirred up such antipathy that the show was destined to become the city's first and last rock happening. Nearby Mestre, Padua, Verona, Trieste, and Treviso sometimes host artists on their European tours. Though the Biennale Musica and some clubs in Venice do spotlight contemporary music, the vast majority of the city's concerts are classical.

Local publications have up-to-date information, as do **Tourist Offices** (⇨ Smart Travel Tips, *Visitor Information*). **Vela** (✉ Calle dei Fuseri, San Marco 1810 ☎ 041/2424 ✉ Piazzale Roma), which handles vaporetto and bus ticket sales, and sells tickets for some musical events. It has sales kiosks at key vaporetto landings.

If you hear something you like and want to take a recording home with you, stop by **Vivaldi** (✉ Fontego dei Tedeschi 5537, opposite Rialto Post Office ☎☎ 041/5221343), a shop that specializes in Venetian classical music of all kinds and handles tickets for some concerts. Open Monday–Saturday 9:30–7:30 and Sunday 11–7, it's a good source of information about the musical events in town.

Classical

Many of Venice's myriad orchestras perform "greatest hits" programs marketed toward tourists, complete with musicians and ticket vendors in period costume. Groups may have a semi-permanent venue, such as a church or scuola, but these change frequently. In addition to the commercial groups, other professional orchestras perform less regularly, usually in museums or palazzi. Churches, scuole, palazzi, and museums sometimes sponsor concerts of their own, especially around the holidays, often featuring touring musicians. During summer months, costumed musicians sometimes play aboard a specially built boat with the audience riding along nearby in 10–12 gondole; suffice it to say, sound quality varies but acoustics are not this activity's draw.

L'Offerta Musicale, the city's main chamber orchestra, is one of the best classical groups giving concerts, often in Museo Ca' Rezzonico's lovely ballroom. The young, talented musicians perform works by a variety of composers rather than focusing on Vivaldi, as other local groups are apt to do. Call for information about performances. ☎ *041/5241143.*

Gruppo Accademia di San Rocco plays baroque music on original 17th-and 18th-century instruments throughout the summer at beautiful **Scuola Grande di San Rocco**, where concertgoers can enjoy more than 60 works by Tintoretto. ✉ *Campo San Rocco, San Polo 3054* ☎ *Venue: 041/5234864, booking: 041/962999* ⊕ *www.musicinvenice.com* ✉ *€20–€30* Ⅴ *San Tomà.*

Interpreti Veneziani string ensemble performs most evenings at **Chiesa di San Vidal.** Their repertoire frequently includes Vivaldi's *Four Seasons.*

☒ *Campo Santo Stefano, San Marco 2862/b* ☎ *041/2770561* ⊕ *www.interpretiveneziani.com* ▩ *€21* Ⓥ *Accademia.*

Musici Veneziani perform in 18th-century costume year-round at the **Scuola Grande di San Teodoro.** Vivaldi will be there, as always, and twice a week they're joined by a soprano and baritone for a bit of opera. ☒ *Campo San Salvador (near Rialto) San Marco 4811* ☎ *Booking: 041/5210294* ⊕ *www.musicaemusicasrl.com* ▩ *€21–€31* Ⓥ *Rialto.*

Museo Querini-Stampalia stays open late Friday and Saturday evenings to host *musica antica,* concerts featuring centuries-old music played on antique instruments. Your museum ticket includes the concert, and Florian Art e Caffè on the premises has food and drink available. ☒ *Campo Santa Maria Formosa, Castello 5252* ☎ *041/2711411* ▩ *€6.*

Cini Foundation, located on the island of San Giorgio, often has concerts, which are generally free. It's well worth attending, even if only to visit the lovely Benedictine monastery, which is normally closed to the public. ☒ *Isola di San Giorgio* ☎ *041/5289900* ⊕ *www.cini.it.*

Contemporary

Contemporary music options are at their richest during Biennale Musica (⇨ *see Biennale close-up box*), when concerts are held throughout Venice and advertised on billboards in all major campi. **Vortice—Associazione Culturale** hosts modern, ethnic and avant-garde concerts and dance at **Teatro Fondamente Nuove.** ☒ *Near Chiesa dei Gesuiti, Cannaregio 5013* ☎ *041/713913 office, 041/5224498 venue* ⊕ *www.provincia.venezia.it/vortice.*

Festivals

Festa della Madonna della Salute

This thanksgiving festival celebrates not a harvest, but survival. Every November 21, Venetian make pilgrimage to the church of Madonna della Salute, where they light candles to thank the Virgin Mary for liberating the city from the plague of 1630–31 and to pray for health in the year to come. It was while the plague was raging that the church was commissioned, but before the saint could intervene nearly one third of the city's 145,000 inhabitants were dead. To make the pilgrims' progress more expedient, a temporary bridge is erected across the Grand Canal between Campo Santa Maria del Giglio (near the Gritti Palace hotel) and the sestiere of Dorsoduro. The weather is usually cold and foggy, and the winter season is traditionally ushered in with a traditional stew called *castradina.* Outside the church is a carnival-like atmosphere, with *frittelle* (fritters), *palloncini* (balloons on strings), clowns, and votive candles.

Festa della Sensa

The oldest Venetian festival, the Festival of the Ascension, was initiated by Doge Pietro Orseolo II in the year 1000, after he led the Venetian fleet to victory over the Slavic pirates (who had invaded the Istrian-Dalamatian coast) on Ascension Day. Originally the Ascension was a very simple ceremony in which the doge led a procession of boats to the entrance of the port of San Nicolò di Lido to meet the religious leader of the period, the bishop of San Pietro di Castello, who blessed the waters as a sign of peace and gratitude.

In 1177, with the famous "Peace of Venice" between Emperor Frederick Barbarossa and Pope Alexander III, the festival was transformed into the so-called "wedding with the sea." The story goes that following the occupation of Rome by Barbarossa's troops, Alexander III escaped to Venice disguised as a pilgrim, and after having passed the first night in the open air on the Sottoportego della Madonna near the Church of Sant'Aponal (now marked by a wooden plaque), he found work in the kitchens of the Convento della Carità (today home of the Gallerie dell'Accademia). Some time later, Alexander III was recognized by a Roman high prelate who was visiting the monastery. When the doge Sebastiano Ziani heard of this, he immediately began peace talks with the emperor. But Barbarossa did not want to make peace, so the doge armed a strong fleet and with the blessing of Alexander III set off from Piazzetta di San Marco to attack the imperial ships in the Istrian waters. The Venetians won and captured Barbarossa's son, thereby forcing the emperor to negotiate. In gratitude the pope gave a gold ring to the doge, with which he could remarry Venice with the sea every year.

In Republican times, the Ascension began with a series of performances and celebrations that went on for 15 days and culminated with a large fair in Piazza San Marco. Today the Ascension is held on the Sunday following Ascension Day, the Thursday that falls 40 days after Easter, and begins at about 9 AM with a procession of ships led by the mayor, who tosses a ring into the water and pronounces the ritual phrase *"In segno di eterno dominio, noi, Doge di Venezia, ti sposiamo o mare!"* (As a symbol of our eternal dominion, we wed you, o sea!). Masses in the Chiesa di San Nicolò and boat races follow later in the afternoon. In the Sala del Maggior Consiglio in Palazzo Ducale, you can see several objects that are part of the ceremony, such as the thick candle, the umbrella, the gilded throne, and the eight white, red, blue, and yellow banners. The Museo Storico Navale has an 18-ft-long scale model of the gilded boat used by the doge.

Festa del Redentore

On the third Sunday of July, crowds of pilgrims cross the Canale della Giudecca by means of a pontoon bridge, which is traditionally built every year to commemorate the doge's annual visit to Palladio's Chiesa del Redentore to offer thanks to the Redeemer for the end of a 16th-century plague. Over the course of the Saturday before, neighbors mark off picnic turf with tables and chairs along the fondamente on Giudecca and Zattere, and even off in Sant'Elena park. As evening falls, thousands take to the streets and tables, and thousands more take to the water. Boats decorated with colored lanterns, well-provisioned with wine, watermelon, and snacks, jockey for position to watch the grand event. Around midnight, from a barge floating in the Bacino di San Marco, Venice kicks off a fireworks display right over the top of the boat fleet, moored so densely across the bacino that you could almost walk from San Marco and San Giorgio. Hotels overlooking the Bacino organize terrace dinners and parties (reserve well ahead), and many tourist boats host evening excursions. Anywhere along Piazza San Marco, Riva degli Schiavoni, or Giardini you'll find good viewing, or try Zattere, as close to Punta Dogana as you can get. Anywhere along the Giudecca is good, but the Zitelle end is the most popular. The show is not held in the rain, but no one can recall the last time it rained for Festa del Redentore. After the fireworks you can join the young folks staying out all night and greeting sunrise on the Lido beach, or rest up and make the procession to mass Sunday morning.

Festa di San Marco

The festival honoring the Evangelist who for 1,000 years protected his city is somewhat eclipsed by the fact that April 25 is also Italian Liberation Day, a national holiday. On St. Mark's Day men traditionally buy *boccoli* (red roses) for ladies in their lives (wives, mothers, sisters, cousins, friends)—the longer the stem the deeper the token of love. Legend tells of a soldier enamored of the doge's daughter who was mortally wounded in a far-off battle. As it spilled his blood bore red roses, which he entrusted his companion to bring to the girl. The story doesn't say if the flowers arrived on the saint's day, but by tradition Venetians celebrate the miracle on this date.

Opera and Ballet

Teatro La Fenice, located between Piazza San Marco and Campo San Stefano, is one of Italy's oldest opera houses and a shrine for opera lovers. It has witnessed many memorable operatic premieres, including, in 1853, the dismal first-night flop of Verdi's *La Traviata.* It has also witnessed its share of disasters. The most recent was a terrible fire, deliberately set in January 1996, followed by delays in reconstruction. However, in keeping with its name (which translates as The Phoenix, coined when it was built over the ashes of its predecessor in 1792), La Fenice will rise again, according to current estimates some time in late 2004.

Until Fenice reopens, symphony, opera, and ballet performances alternate between two venues. **Teatro Malibran** (⊠ Campo San Giovanni Crisostomo, Cannaregio 5873 Ⓥ Rialto), built by the powerful Grimani family in 1677, was one of Europe's most famous opera theaters. It was converted into a movie theater in 1927 and reopened in 2001 after lengthy restoration. Tentlike **Palafenice** (⊠ Tronchetto parking area, Ⓥ Tronchetto) will never rank among best opera houses, but after fire claimed La Fenice, music lovers were forced to make do with this semi-permanent structure. Visit (⊕ www.teatrolafenice.it) for a calender of performances and to buy tickets for either venue. You can also purchase tickets by faxing La Fenice (🖷 041/786580), calling the Vela Call Center (☎ 041/ 2424 ⊙ 8 AM–8 PM), going to the one of the Vela sales offices (⊠ Piazzale Roma, Ferrovia, or in Calle dei Fuseri), or going to the theater box office an hour before showtime.

Theater

Though most theatrical performances are in Italian or in the local Venetian dialect, they can still be entertaining, especially if the production is a classic play you're already familiar with. Venetian Carlo Goldoni (1707–93), a leading figure in Venice's Commedia dell'Arte, wrote many works based on simple stories that should be easy to follow even if you don't understand the language.

Venice's **Teatro Carlo Goldoni** produces many plays by Goldoni, as well as works by other playwrights. ⊠ *near Rialto San Marco 4650b* ☎ *041/ 2402011* ⊕ *www.teatrogoldonive.it.*

On the mainland, **Teatro Toniolo** hosts an assortment of concerts, opera, fringe theater pieces, and classic plays. ⊠ *Piazzetta Battisti 1, near central Piazza Ferretto, Mestre* ☎ *041/971666* ⊕ *www.boxoffice.it.*

NIGHTLIFE

Nightspots in and around Venice can be difficult to categorize. Pubs, of the English or Irish variety, with beer on tap and occasional live music, are easy to identify and are especially popular with local and traveling youth. When you're looking to dance, things get murkier: lounge-type piano bars generally have small dance floors, while dance clubs often serve snacks and even late-night meals. Bars and cafés are even harder to classify, as availability of snacks, meals, beverages, and music varies with the time of day and the season. Many also decorate their walls with works by local artists, whose paintings are for sale.

Bars

Al Chioschetto is among Venice's "nonbars," consisting only of a kiosk set up to serve some outdoor tables. Located on the Zattere, it's popular in nice weather for late-night *panini* (sandwiches) or a sunny breakfast. Live funk, reggae, jazz, or soul is on tap once a week, usually Friday or Saturday. ⊠ *near Ponte Lungo, Dorsoduro 1406/a* ☎ *338/1174077* Ⓥ *Zattere*.

Bácaro Jazz has hot jazz on the sound system and hot meals until 2 AM. It also has a very interactive owner and staff, so you're not likely to feel lonely even if you arrive alone. ⊠ *In front of Rialto Post Office* ☎ *041/5285249* Ⓥ *Rialto*.

Comfortably warm **Bagolo,** with its contemporary Murano glass sconces that are never too bright, welcomes clientele of all ages and all lifestyles. It's open daily except Monday from 7 AM until midnight or later. ⊠ *Campo San Giacomo dell'Orio, Santa Croce 1584* ☎ *041/717584* Ⓥ *San Stae*.

Caffè Blue is an unusual hybrid that reserves a bar area for top-shelf whiskey drinkers yet serves afternoon tea with samovar and pastry cart. Sandwiches are available from noon until 2 AM, and there's a no-smoking room until 8 PM. They feature live music on Friday and frequently have art openings. ⊠ *Calle dei Preti, near San Pantalon, Dorsoduro 3778* ☎ *041/710227* Ⓥ *San Tomà*.

Codroma is one of the few bacari that often stays open late, but its hours are utterly unpredictable. Sometimes there's live jazz, but the biggest attraction is the after-hours drinks, served Monday through Saturday. This Venetian institution was founded in the early 1900s by the bearded cook whose picture is near the window. ⊠ *Ponte del Soccorso, near Carmini Church, Dorsoduro 2540* ☎ *041/5246789* Ⓥ *San Basilio*.

★ **Il Caffè**, commonly called "Bar Rosso" for its bright-red exterior, hosts occasional summer jazz concerts and has far more tables outside than in. A favorite with students, it's famous for strong *spritz,* the preferred Venetian aperitif, of white wine, Campari or Aperol, soda water, and a twist of lemon. ⊠ *Campo Santa Margherita, Dorsoduro 2963* ☎ *041/5287998* Ⓥ *Ca' Rezzonico*.

Paradiso Perduto (Paradise Lost) has been catering to night owls since the '70s with drinks, wine, and reasonably priced fish dishes. It also serves up live music on weekends, mainly jazz and ethnic music. With closely placed tables, this huge room is full of conviviality; however, the only smoke-free zone is outdoors. ⊠ *Fondamenta della Misericordia, Cannaregio 2540* ☎ *041/720581* ◷ *Thurs.–Mon.* Ⓥ *San Marcuola*.

With a hundred tables set near a sunny canal, **Suzie,** at the west end of the Zattere, is a cheerful lunch stop and a popular nightspot on summer Fridays, when live music and university students fill the breezy campo. It has a decidedly friendly atmosphere and welcomes gay clientele. You'll find a good selection of panini and a limited pasta menu. ⊠ *Campo San Basilio, Dorsoduro 1527* ☎ *041/5227502* ◷ *Weekdays* Ⓥ *San Basilio*.

Nothing special by day, **Torino@notte** is a lively nightspot, often spilling out into the campo in summer. Cocktails, served until 2 AM, include the popular *cubino* (rum and Coke). Snacks are available until 7 PM. ⊠ *Campo San Luca, San Marco 459* ☎ *041/5223914* Ⓥ *Rialto*.

Zanzibar is a kiosk bar that's very popular on warm summer evenings, especially Fridays, when there's live music. The fare is limited to sandwiches and ice cream, but the location along the canal near Chiesa di Santa Maria Formosa makes it a pleasant place to sip a drink. ⊠ *Campo Santa Maria Formosa, Castello 5840* ☎ *347/1460107* Ⓥ *San Zaccaria.*

Casinos

The city-run gambling casino in splendid **Palazzo Vendramin-Calergi** is a classic scene of well-dressed high-rollers playing French roulette, Caribbean poker, chemin de fer, 30–40, and slots. You must be 18 to enter and men must wear jackets. ⊠ *Cannaregio 2040* ☎ *041/5297111* 🖼 *€10 entry includes €10 in chips* ⏱ *Slots 2:45 PM–3 AM; tables 3:30 PM–3 AM* Ⓥ *San Marcuola.*

Mestre's **Ca' Noghera** casino, near the airport, has slots, blackjack, craps, poker, and roulette. The minimum age is 18, and there's no dress code. ⊠ *Via Triestina 222, Tessera, Mestre* ☎ *041/5297111* 🖼 *€10 entry includes €10 in chips* ⏱ *Slots 11 AM–5 AM; tables 3:30 PM–5 AM.*

Dance Clubs

With only two discos in the historic center, Venice's club scene is rather skimpy. Dedicated dancers are often ready to face long and dangerous drives to reach the celebrated seaside clubs in Rimini and Riccione, south of Venice. On the mainland around Venice, clubs come and go frequently, and their opening hours are often seasonal and unpredictable. The discos listed here are well established, but it's still a good idea to call ahead. If you go to Mestre or Jesolo, you can plan your night so your return to Venice coincides with sunrise over the lagoon, but make sure you check public transportation details before you leave town.

Disco and live music are the lure at **Acropolis,** a trendy spot on the Lido with a large marble dance floor, a pedestal for *cubiste* (provocative dancing girls), and a view of the sea. In summer you can dance on the spacious terrace jutting out over the beach. The kitchen serves sandwiches, snacks, and pasta from 10 PM to 2 AM. ⊠ *Lungomare Marconi 22, Lido* ☎ *041/5260466* 🖼 *€15 includes 1 drink* ⏱ *Closed Sun.–Tues., Thurs., and Oct.–Feb.* Ⓥ *S.M. Elizabetta Lido.*

Metallic walls, red leather couches, and theme nights at **Casanova** attract a young and often wild clientele. By day they serve up meals and internet access; by night, it's disco and football matches on large-screen TV. ⊠ *Lista di Spagna, Cannaregio 158/a* ☎ *041/2750199* 🖼 *Fri. and Sat., €10 includes 1 drink; other nights free* Ⓥ *Ferrovia.*

An artistic blend of iron beams with silver candlesticks, old brick with white tablecloths, has transformed a vintage refrigerated warehouse into casually sophisticated **Frigo.** You'll be taken back to the old supper-club days, when diners got up and danced any time during their meal, as Frigo's DJ varies the music with the night's clientele. (The well-designed sound system means dancing and dinner conversation aren't mutually exclusive.) A menu ranging from pizza to pepper steak is available from 7:30 to 1:30 AM and though it's a five-minute taxi ride from Piazzale Roma (or buses 80 and N2 drop you within a 10-min. walk), your dining dollars go a lot farther in Mestre. ⊠ *Viale Ancona, 18 Mestre* ☎ *041/5319293.*

★ **Piccolo Mondo,** a tiny venue with few lights and some small tables arranged around the dance area, welcomes anyone looking for a late-night drink and a dance floor. The place is gay friendly, and the music (mostly commercial house) is not so loud as to make conversation impossible. ⊠ *Calle Contarini, near Gallerie dell'Accademia, Dorsoduro 1056/a* ☎ *041/5200371* 🖼 *Free* Ⓥ *Accademia.*

Cult favorites such as Jimi Hendrix and the Cure are daily fare at **Sound Garden Rock Café**, a club favored by the youth of Venice. On the weekend cutting-edge local bands often play, and they give away an electric guitar, so you can join in the music. Along with dancing, you can play pool and other games, surf the internet, and stroll the beach, just 20 yards away. From Piazzale Roma it's about an hour by **ATVO bus** (☏ 041/5205530), or from San Marco take the **motonave** (☏ 041/2714747 or 899/909090) to Punta Sabbione, where you pick up a bus; this trip that also takes about an hour, and boats stop running at midnight or 1 AM. ✉ *Piazza Mazzini, Jesolo Lido* ☏ *338/8752823* 💶 *€7 includes 1 drink* ⊙ *Closed Oct.–Dec. and Sun.–Thurs. Jan.–May.*

Late-Night

Campo Santa Margherita, where you'll find Il Caffè, Margaret Duchamp, and Pier Dickens, is one of the livelier gathering places in town after dark.

Midnight Snacks

Venice may be a sleepy city, but there are a number of places where you can answer the call of late-night hunger.

Karaoke nightly and four specialty brews on tap set **Brasserie Vecchia Bruxelles** apart from other late-night eateries. There's no cover charge for table seating or live music, and it serves pizza and light entrées until 11 PM and sandwiches until 2 AM. ✉ *near San Pantalon Santa Croce 81* ☏ *041/710636.*

★ **Gelateria il Doge** has over 30 flavors of gelato and several lighter varieties of milk-free sorbet. Try their decadently rich chocolate or the unique *strabon* (Venetian for extra good) made with vanilla, chocolate, and almond brittle. In summer you'll also find refreshing granita that isn't pumped out of a machine. It stays open until 2 AM. ✉ *Campo Santa Margherita, Dorsoduro 3058/a* ☏ *041/5234607* ⊙ *Closed Nov.–Feb.*

Tables along a canal and an oh-so-rare no-smoking room make **Gibo Bar** a dependable address all year round. Board games and an internet corner don't encourage fast turnover, but if tables are full you can sit Venetian style on the canal wall while dining on cicheti and sandwiches, served lunchtime to late in the night. ✉ *Ponte della Donna Onesta, San Polo 2925* ☏ *041/5229969* ⊙ *Closed Sun.* Ⓥ *San Tomà.*

Festooned with sombreros, **Iguana** is a bustling nightspot with live music once a week and a wide selection of Mexican beers and tequilas. It's open until 2 AM, and the more-Italian-than-Mexican kitchen stays open until midnight. ✉ *Fondamenta della Misericordia, Cannaregio 2515* ☏ *041/713561* ⊙ *Closed Mon.* Ⓥ *San Marcuola.*

The French-sounding name **Margaret Duchamp** befits this café-brasserie with an artfully minimalist decor. Warm sandwiches and light salads take the place of cicheti, but you won't pay more for the "designer's touch." It's open till 2 AM. ✉ *Campo Santa Margherita, Dorsoduro 3019* ☏ *041/5286255* Ⓥ *Ca' Rezzonico.*

Moscacieka is a wine bar with *bruschette* (toasted bread with toppings), grilled sandwiches, and salads. The name means "Blind Fly" (it also translates as "Blindman's Bluff"), and the ceiling features huge, blue Styrofoam flies. You'll find a matching blue Murano-glass bar and a dozen wooden tables. Though there's no live music, the location is handy, and it's open until 1 AM. ✉ *Calle dei Fabbri, San Marco 4717* ☏ *041/5208085* ⊙ *Closed Sun.* Ⓥ *Rialto.*

If you've never heard of a *spaghettata*, stick around **Pier Dickens Inn** until 1 AM to find out about the communal spaghetti bowl (where you don't get to choose the sauce). There's other food available until midnight, one night a week, usually Tuesday, there's live music. ⊠ *Campo Santa Margherita, Dorsoduro 3410* ☎ *041/2411979* Ⓥ *Ca' Rezzonico.*

The Hole-in-the-wall **Pizza al Volo** sells whole pies and slices to go until 1 or 1:30 AM in all the classic styles: *margarita* (tomato and mozzarella), *ai funghi* (with mushrooms), and *al prosciutto* (with ham). ⊠ *Campo Santa Margherita, Dorsoduro 2944/a* ☎ *041/5225430* Ⓥ *Ca' Rezzonico.*

Nightcaps

During Carnevale, many ordinary bars, which close around dinnertime the rest of the year, stay open around the clock.

If you can manage to turn your back on the San Marco's piazza and basilica, you'll enjoy the incredible view of San Giorgio and the Giudecca from the waterside tables of **Bar Al Todaro.** There's no inside seating, but it's a good place for sunny cocktails or midnight moonlit snacks. ⊠ *Piazzetta San Marco 3* ☎ *041/5285165* ⊘ *Closed winter* Ⓥ *Vallaresso.*

★ **Caffè Florian** opened up in 1720 as Venezia Trionfante (Triumphant Venice) but was soon renamed after its founder, Floriano Francesconi. The café started as a fashionable spot for a hot chocolate, but during the Austrian domination of Venice it became the favorite meeting place of Italian patriots and intellectuals who boycotted the rival Caffè Quadri across the piazza because of its Austrian military clientele. Stuccoes, mirrors, wooden carvings, and intimate booths date back to 1859, but the historical atmosphere comes at a price: though an espresso at the bar costs €2, sitting doubles that price, and live music will double it again. Afternoon tea can end up costing as much as a meal, but they do take credit cards, and it's certainly less painful than textbooks for absorbing world history. ⊠ *Piazza San Marco 56 Procuratie Nuove* ☎ *041/5205641* Ⓥ *Vallaresso.*

Caffè Quadri may be less glamorous and less intimate than the Florian across the piazza, but it too opened in the 18th century, making it equally historic (and pricey). This café has had its fair share of famous regulars, including Stendhal and Balzac. It's open late for starlit music on summer nights. ⊠ *Piazza San Marco 120 Procuratie Vecchie* ☎ *041/5289299* Ⓥ *Vallaresso.*

No Venice watering hole is more famous for a nightcap or an aperitif than **Harry's Bar,** once a favorite haunt of Ernest Hemingway. With a loan from an American named Harry Pickering in the 1930s, Giuseppe Cipriani turned an old rope factory into a cozy, wood-paneled bar, and today, his son Arrigo runs the place. If you'd like to follow in Hemingway's footsteps, ante up for a Bellini, the trademark blend of white peach juice and sparkling prosecco—it's a treat you shouldn't miss during summer peach season, even though you will pay for the privilege. ⊠ *Calle Vallaresso, San Marco 1323* ☎ *041/5285777* Ⓥ *Vallaresso.*

Piano Bars

Just outside Piazza San Marco (near Museo Correr), Hotel Luna Baglioni's **Caffè Baglioni** is perfect for an intimate chat in the cold winter months. There's live piano music from 6 until midnight Wednesday, Friday, and Saturday. ⊠ *Calle Larga de l'Ascension, San Marco 1243* ☎ *041/5289840* Ⓥ *Vallaresso.*

Historic Teatro Ridotto, an eighteenth-century casino, is the site of the piano bar of the **Hotel Monaco & Grand Canal.** The room exudes elegance, and from 7 PM to midnight, October through June, live music really brings its old-fashioned romance to life. ⊠ *Calle Vallaresso, San Marco 1325* ☎ *041/5200211* Ⓥ *Vallaresso.*

Attached to the fashionable restaurant of the same name, **Martini Scala Club** is the only place in town where you'll find full meals served until 2 AM. The dance floor is big enough and the lights are low enough in this elegant piano bar to dance away your Venice nights from 10 PM until 3:30 AM. ⊠ *Calle del Cafetier, San Marco 1007* ☎ *041/5224121* ☉ *Closed Tues. and July–Aug.* Ⓥ *Santa Maria del Giglio.*

Pubs

Thirsty sailors can find night moorage at **Capo Horn Pub,** a roomy watering hole on two floors, decked out like an old ship, with wooden benches, ropes, and brass lamps. Thirty different beers, twenty aged whiskies, and an assortment of wine should slake the thirst of even the briniest deckhand. It opens at 10 AM weekdays, 5 PM weekends, and the galley whips up tasty salads, sandwiches, and pasta until 2 AM every night. ⊠ *San Pantalon Dorsoduro 3740* ☎ *041/5242177* Ⓥ *San Tomà.*

Devil's Forest Pub, not far from Rialto Bridge, is one of the more popular Irish pubs in town, and one of the best decorated—right down to its proper red phone booth. There are plenty of board games and Irish beers on tap, and they serve up some tasty pasta at lunch. ⊠ *Calle dei Stagneri 5185, off Campo San Bartolomeo* ☎ *041/5200623* Ⓥ *Rialto.*

Fiddler's Elbow, a typical Irish pub (of the Italian variety), serves plenty of Guinness and gab from 5 PM to 1 AM. There are four Irish brews, plus cider, on tap, as well as sports on TV and occasional live music, either Irish or rock. ⊠ *Corte dei Pali, off Strada Nova, Cannaregio 3847* ☎ *041/5239930* Ⓥ *Ca' d'Oro.*

The popular Italo-Irish pub **Innishark,** located midway between San Marco and Rialto, is known for its variety of international brews. It's open until 1:30 AM. ⊠ *Calle Mondo Novo, near San Lio, Castello 5787* ☎ *051/5235300* ☉ *Closed Mon.* Ⓥ *Rialto.*

Olandese Volante (The Flying Dutchman) is decorated to look like an old ship, but the tables outside in the pretty campo are even more scenic. The central location makes this a convenient late-night stop for a simple bite and a beer. ⊠ *Campo San Lio, Castello 5658* ☎ *041/ 5289349* Ⓥ *Rialto.*

Senso Unico is a popular neighborhood hangout, decorated in wood and brick with a couple of tables that have a great view of the canal. There are four brews on tap and plenty of wine and sandwich choices from 10 AM to 1 AM. ⊠ *Past Campo San Vio, before the Guggenheim, Dorsoduro 684* ☎ *348/3720847* ☉ *Closed Mon.* Ⓥ *Accademia.*

SPORTS &
THE OUTDOORS

5

Updated by
Elaine Eliah

WITH ALL THE BRIDGES TO CROSS and streets to walk, getting from place to place in their carless world is the principal exercise for most Venetians—and it serves them well, to judge from the level of fitness you see, especially among the older residents. You'll find recreational facilities here, but as is the case with so many aspects of life in Venice, you have to put conventional expectations aside and accept the city on its own terms. A jog in La Serenissima, though not obstacle-free, will certainly be memorable.

While the soccer team struggles for respectability, the most distinctive spectator sports, fittingly enough, take place on the water. The city's annual rowing races are a melding of sports and centuries-old tradition that's uniquely Venetian.

Beaches

★ The **Lido's** 12 km (8 mi) of beaches have very fine sand (unlike many other Italian beaches), which makes for wonderful barefoot walks but which also turns the water murky—a shame, since this part of the Adriatic is much less polluted than other Italian waters. Unless there's a storm, Lido rarely sees breaking waves, and the water is so shallow you have to walk out at least 100 ft before you can swim. It makes these beaches ideal for toddlers and young children, who can safely play in the water and hunt for the few surviving crabs. The best times to visit the Lido beaches are in June and September, when you can enjoy long walks, play *racchettoni* (a paddle game), and swim without human obstacles. April–May and October are great for walks, but it's too cold to swim. July and August are, predictably, the busiest months of the year.

Most beaches are within 2 km (1 mi) of the vaporetto landing. A straight bus ride or 15-minute walk down Gran Viale takes you to the sea. There's a narrow stretch of free beach close to where Gran Viale meets the sea, but aside from that you have to travel north to San Nicolò or, for a bit more space, to the south end of the island at Alberoni to find *spiagge libere* (free beaches). These have no amenities, so you have to come prepared with food, water, and sunscreen. Technically, the law says "private beaches" can't throw you out as long as you're in the water or on the first couple yards of sand; you aren't likely to get hassled as long as you don't call attention to yourself. Although nonguests aren't permitted to use private beach facilities, including bathrooms, in practice many locals discreetly use them anyway.

Privately run beaches have such facilities as hot showers, shady porches, *capanne* (cabanas), mini-bungalows with eating areas, bars serving drinks and snacks, and even surfing—the Internet variety. Just left of where Gran Viale meets the sea are **Lungomare G. D'Azzunzio** (☎ 041/5260236, 041/5261249 in winter), which, along with the neighboring **San Nicolò**, is operated by Venezia Spiagge. They rent *camerini* (private dressing rooms where you can lock your valuables) for daily rates between €15.40 and €22.20 (prices highest in July). *Ombrelloni* (umbrellas) cost €9.70–€14.80 per day, and *sdraii* (chaise lounges) cost €5.10–€8.60. Often less crowded than larger beaches, **Sorriso** (✉ Lungomare Marconi 150 yards past Excelsior ☎ 041/5261066, 041/5260729 in winter) has good prices, with camerini as low as €3 and capanne for €7. It's a good base for exploring the rockier Murazzi coastline nearby, where water can be less murky. Just right of where Gran Viale meets the sea is **Bagni Des Bains** (☎ 041/2716836). On the left as you enter are a few of the old straw-roofed bungalows that survived the flood of 1966. Des Bains beach and hotel featured prominently in Luchino Visconti's haunting film *Death in Venice*. The Oriental-looking dome of the Westin Excelsior towers over the Lido's most famous beach, the **Bagni Excelsior** (✉ Lungomare Marconi ☎ 041/2716836). From the 1930s, when the Venice Film Festival began right here at the Excelsior, this beach has been a favorite of movie stars and their wealthy companions. At **Consorzio** (also known as Capli; ✉ Lungomare Marconi ☎ 041/5260356), you can rent a well-furnished hut for €30–€85 (maximum eight people). They also rent small private changing rooms where you can lock your clothes for €20 (for two to three people) and then lay out on the sand. At most private beaches you can rent a *pedalò* (paddleboat) or *moscone* (wooden pontoon) by the hour: these are the best ways to get a good tan under the breeze or to go for a swim away from the crowds.

Biking

Fodor's Choice
★
Bikes are popular on the long, flat island of **Lido,** and though there are no official bike lanes, cars are accustomed to sharing the road. Single or tandem bikes are available for rent, as well as quadricycles with canopy roofs that make it easy for families with small children to get around. Note that helmets are not mandatory in Venice, nor are they available for rent. As soon as you leave the Lido vaporetto stop, you'll find **Gardin** (✉ behind the Panorama Hotel ☎ 041/2760005), which has the island's best prices for bike rentals: €2.60 per hour or €7.75 per day. March through October it's open 9–1 and 2–7:30; November through February it's closed Sunday and hours other days are 9:30–1 and 4–7. **Bruno Lazzari** (✉ Gran Viale 21/b ☎ 041/5268019), two minutes from the vaporetto, is open March through October, 8–8, and November through February, Monday–Saturday 8:30–1 and 2:30–7). Prices are €3 an hour or €9 a day. **Giorgio Barbieri** (✉ Via Zara 5 ☎ 041/5261490) rents and repairs bikes. The location is at the intersection of Gran Viale and Via Zara, a five-minute walk from the vaporetto landing. Hours are March–October, 8:30–8; bikes rent for €3 an hour or €9 a day.

The Lido is too narrow to get lost—even without a map. Don't miss riding down Via Lepanto. It runs along a canal at the island's center and is lined with shade trees and lovely art deco villas. For a full, adventurous day you can take your bike on the ferry to Pellestrina, an equally long sandbar beach, minus the crowds, located to the south of the Lido, or even visit Chioggia, a canal-laced city beyond Pellestrina on the mainland.

Boating

For those sailing into Venice, slip space for boats up to 45 ft is available at **Diporto Velico** (✉ Sant'Elena ☎ 041/5231927). Although you can't reserve a slip, it doesn't hurt to call a few hours ahead. Boats pay by length, from €13 to €55, plus €3 per person per day. Directly opposite Piazza San Marco, **Compagnia della Vela** (✉ San Giorgio Maggiore ☎ 041/5210723 ⊕ www.compvela.com) is one of the world's most beautiful marinas. Docking fees range from €32 to €120 (maximum 48 ft), and you may book a day ahead.

If you've fallen in love with the lagoon, **Mare di Carta** (✉ Fondamenta dei Tolentini, Santa Croce 222, across from train station, ☎ 041/716304 ⊕ www.maredicarta.com) can help you get out and enjoy the water. In this full-service nautical store you'll find up-to-the-minute information about rentals and cruises, as well as books and charts to help you explore safely. Those planning to explore on their own need to be aware that some rules of the road are unique to Venice. Keep in mind that the lagoon has vast, unmarked shallow areas, and that weather changes can be unpredictable and abrupt—*trombe d'aria* (waterspouts) are not uncommon.

At €20 per hour or €130 per day including fuel, **Brussa** (✉ near Ponte delle Guglie, Cannaregio 331 ☎ 041/715787 ⊙ weekdays 7–5:30; weekends by arrangement) rents small skiffs with 15hp motors. **Noleggi Oscar** (✉ near Scuola di San Giorgio degli Schiavoni, Castello 3255 ☎ 041/739767, 0335/259435 mobile) rents skiffs with 25hp outboards at €150 for five hours. **Vela Club Venezia** (☎ 041/5352088 ⊕ www.velaclubvenezia.it) rents sailboats by day or week starting at €100 per day. Pietro Tosi's **Big Game Sport Fishing** (✉ Campo Stringari 13, Sant'Elena ☎ 041/5239042, 335/6276725 ⊕ www.biggamesportfishing.it) organizes expeditions that have landed record-size tuna and shark.

Boat Races

La Vogalonga

★ A cannon fires, oars are hoisted high in the air, and a cry of "Viva San Marco!" echoes across Bacino San Marco. Then the oars drop in the water and the **Vogalonga** (long row), a 30-km (19-mi) lagoon race from San Marco through Burano, Murano, and Cannaregio, gets underway. The event takes place on a Sunday in May and is open to any oar-powered boat. It began in 1975 as a way to spark more interest in *Voga alla Veneta*, Venetian-style stand-up rowing, and to protest *moto ondoso*, the destructive wave action created by motorboats, which damages building foundations far more than centuries of high water have. Participation has risen from 500 boats and 1,500 local rowers in its first year to nearly 2,000 boats and 5,000 rowers from around the world. The rediscovery of Venetian rowing triggered a boom in rowing clubs and has helped keep the crafts of the *squeri* (builders of traditional wooden boats) and the *forcole* (carvers of oars and oarlocks) alive. The Vogalonga begins at 9 AM and the finish line closes at 2 PM. For a view of the start, you can't beat the campanile of either San Marco or San Giorgio, but Piazzetta San Marco isn't a bad option as well. Around noon rowers start returning through narrow Canal de Cannaregio, and though it's quite a bottleneck, you get a close-up look at all the different boats. Entrants pay a registration fee of €10 and show up with their own boat. All rowers must be over 16. Information and registration is available from **Comitato Organizzatore Vogalonga** (✉ Rosa Salva, San Marco 951 ☎ 041/5210544 ☒ 041/5200771 ⊕ www.vogalonga.it).

Regata delle Befane

On January 6, Bucintoro Rowing Club celebrates the Epiphany with the first rowing race of the year. The Regata delle Befane features the club's senior members dressed in tattered clothes like a Befana, a mythical old woman with hooked nose, warts, and a scarf over her gray hair, who, in Santa-like fashion, brings candy to good kids and charcoal (black sugar lumps) to bad ones. The Bucintoro club members dispense hot cocoa, mulled wine, candy (to good and bad alike), and cookies called *galani*.

Regata Storica

Fodor'sChoice
★ The first Sunday in September all of Venice turns out for the **Regata Storica**, the Olympics of Venetian-style (stand-up) rowing. There are four races through the Grand Canal, culminating with the season championship of the *gondolini* (two-oared, gondola-like boats). The day kicks off with a lively procession of historic boats, full of crews and passengers in Renaissance costumes. This procession honors the return to the city of Venetian-born Caterina Cornaro (1454–1510), who "gave" the island of Cyprus to Venice after her husband, King James II of Cyprus, died.

The first race of the Regata Storica series is for teen pairs, the second for women pairs racing *mascarete* (shorter, wider boats). *Caorline* (heavy transport boats) are then raced by teams of six men, followed by the gondolini race. The top four crews in each event receive cash prizes and coveted flags: blue for fourth, green for third, white for second, and the prized *Bandiera Rossa,* or red flag, for first place. The races vary in length, but the longest, the two men's events, start at the entrance to the Grand Canal, round a mark at Piazzale Roma, and finish at Ca' Foscari. A window overlooking the Grand Canal provides the best view in town, but Riva del Vin or Riva del Carbon near the Rialto Bridge aren't bad, nor are Campiello San Vio, or Campo San Samuele.

Fitness Centers

There are a few modern fitness centers around town open to short-term visitors. Most exercise classes are conducted in Italian.

Fitness Point (⊠ near Campo Santa Maria Formosa, Calle del Pestrin, Castello 6141 ☎ 041/5209246), open weekdays 8 AM–10 PM and Saturday 8–3, has daily aerobic and step classes. One visit costs €15.50, and passes for one month are €40–€60.

Palestra Club Delfino (⊠ Zattere, Dorsoduro 788/a ☎ 041/5232763 ⊕ www.palestraclubdelfino.com) has English-speaking personal trainers by appointment, intensive wellness weeks, cardio machines, and classes. One visit costs €13, and you can buy a week's admission for €44. It's open September–June, weekdays 9 AM–10 PM and Saturday 9–noon; July–August, weekdays 9 AM–9:30 PM.

Wellness Center (⊠ Calle della Pietà, 3697 Castello, off Riva degli Schiavoni ☎ 041/5231944) has English-speaking trainers by appointment, a sauna, and a tanning center in a 2,000-square-ft space on two floors. One entry costs €15.50, and a three-day pass is €40. It's open September–June, weekdays 8 AM–9 PM, Saturday 9–1; July–August, Monday, Wednesday, and Friday 8 AM–9 PM, Tuesday and Thursday 3–9, Saturday 9–1.

Golf

The eighteen-hole course of the **Lido Golf Club** (⊠ Strada Vecchia 1, Alberoni, Lido ☎ 041/731015) isn't exceptional, but it fulfills the basic needs of golf addicts. Greens fees are €55–€65; you can rent clubs for €15 and pullcarts for €6. It's closed Monday.

Serious golfers will find it well worth the seven-mile taxi ride to **Ca' Della Nave** (⊠ Piazza della Vittoria 14, Mestre ☎ 041/5401555 🖷 041/5401926). Wednesday through Monday you can play this beautiful 18-hole, par-72 course for €50–€60 or the executive 9-hole course for €15. Rental clubs are available for €15 and carts for €25.

Horseback Riding

The iron rings on some buildings around town were once used to tie up horses. These days, you'll only find horses on the Lido. **Circolo Ippico Veneziano** (⊠ Ca' Bianca, Lido ☎ 041/5265162 🖷 041/5268091) rents horses for use in its riding arena or on nearby trails and beaches (though beach riding is prohibited in midsummer). It can also refer you other clubs around the Veneto region. It's closed Sunday afternoon and Monday.

Rowing

FodorsChoice
★

All kinds of rowing are popular here, but the lagoon's quintessential sport is **Voga alla Veneta,** the gondolier-style, stand-up rowing used in many types of traditional boats. You can arrange lessons from one of Venice's more than thirty *remiere* or *canottieri* (rowing clubs), as long as you don't insist that the instructor speak English. The easiest place for beginning rowers to get their sealegs is the calmest part of the lagoon; **Giudecca** (⊠Fondamente del Ponte Lungo, Giudecca 259 ☎041/5287409) offers five lessons for €40 or eight for €60. Venice's oldest rowing club, **Bucintoro** (⊠ Zattere, Dorsoduro 15 ☎041/5205630), has a package of eight lessons for €80, or you can become a nonresident member for €142 and receive lessons for free. **Querini** (⊠ Fondamente Nuove, Castello 6576 ☎041/5222039), in the north lagoon, gives eight lessons for €60.

Running

Jogging through Venice can certainly combine exercise with your sightseeing, but be ready to slalom around both people and dog droppings, and look out for slippery pavement and steps. Northern exposure makes **Fondamente Nuove**, near Campo Santi Giovanni e Paolo, one of the cooler places to jog in summer. It's enough off the beaten track that you can enjoy a long uninterrupted stretch. You can return to the center on Calle Racchetta and Strada Nova or take Via Barbaria delle Tole and Campo Santa Maria Formosa in the opposite direction. **Zattere** promenade is definitely scenic, but unless you're out very early in the day, there are likely to be lots of people to dodge. A pleasant, central route is along **Riva degli Schiavoni** starting from Hotel Danieli and heading east to Sant'Elena. You can return by way of San Pietro di Castello and Via Garibaldi. A good place for distance trainers is long, flat **Lido**, where drivers are surprisingly polite to bikers and pedestrians. Beaches have compact sand near the water, but from June through September you'll find them too crowded between 9 AM and 7 PM. From San Zaccaria, Line 6 gets you to Lido in 10 minutes and a 10-minute run down Gran Viale S.M. Elisabetta will have you on the beach.

The last Sunday in October is usually the date for the world-class **Venice Marathon** (⊠ In Italy: Venicemarathon, Via Felisati 34, Mestre 30172 ☎041/940644 ☏041/940349 ⊕ www.venicemarathon.it ⊠ In US: Marathon Tours & Travel, 261 Main St., Boston, MA 02129 ☎800/444–4097 ☏617/242–7686). The course, covering the standard 42 km (26 mi), begins in the mainland town of Strà near Padua, follows the Brenta River to Mestre, and crosses Ponte della Libertà into historic Venice. It continues along the Zattere, through Dorsoduro, then crosses a floating bridge, erected just for the event, to Piazza San Marco, and reaches the finish line at Sant'Elena. The field is limited to 6,500 runners. Fees are lower with early registration.

Su e Zo per i Ponti (☎ Up and Down the Bridges, contact the tourist office, 041/5298711 ⊕ www.suezoperiponti.org), held on a Sunday in March or April, is a family fun run, more popular with local children and joggers-for-a-day than with elite athletes. It begins around 9 AM in Piazza San Marco, where you can register right before the start. Various itineraries let you choose runs from 3 km (2 mi) to 14 km (9 mi) in length, and all participants receive a souvenir medal.

Swimming

The first public swimming pool in Venice opened only in 1986. It was not too long ago that most children learned to swim with their waist securely tied to a rope held by a teacher standing on top of a bridge. Until boat traffic got too heavy after World War II, daily swimming races from Piazzetta di San Marco to the Lido were part of Venetian summers.

Venice's two public pools are open certain hours for *nuoto libero* (open swim) but both are closed in July and August. Entry costs €4.50 per visit, and a €30 monthly pass allows swimming two mornings a week. Though neither facility has lockers, receptionists will usually keep valuables for you. With eight lanes and a glass wall overlooking the lagoon, 26-meter **Piscina Comunale** (✉ Island of Sacca Fisola, Giudecca ☎ 041/5285430 Ⓥ Sacca Fisola), is by far the better of Venice's two public pools. Four-lane, 25-meter **Sant'Alvise** (✉ Cannaregio 3161 ☎ 041/713567 Ⓥ Sant'Alvise) is located near the Sant'Alvise church in a building that was once the community laundry. **Club Ca' del Moro** (✉ Via F. Parri 6 Lido ☎ 041/770965) has an outdoor pool (no lanes) open May through September (€15.50 per day).

Tennis

The Lido is the place where tennis players can find court space. **Lido Tennis Club** (✉ Via Sandro Gallo 163 ☎ 041/5260954) has courts available for €14 to €28 per hour. **Club Ca' del Moro** (✉ Via F. Parri 6 ☎ 041/770965) has indoor tennis courts for €14 to €25 per hour and outdoor courts for €8 to €14 per hour. (Rates vary according to the number of players.)

Soccer

After more than 30 years in the minor leagues, Venice's soccer team, **Venezia,** was promoted to Serie A (First Division) in 1998, to the jubilation of its fans. Their joy was short-lived, for since then Venezia has been down- and upgraded repeatedly. The team's tired-looking stadium, located on Sant'Elena island at the east end of the Castello sestiere, does little to boost morale; built in 1913 and neglected for decades along with its once-hapless team, it now ranks as one of the worst facilities in Italy. Plans for a new stadium near Mestre on the mainland blossomed and subsequently wilted. The lengthy Italian soccer season runs from early fall to late spring, with matches usually played in the early afternoon on Sunday; if you want to sit among the local green-and-black-clad fans, reserve ahead through your hotel, or buy tickets through **Vela** (✉ Calle dei Fuseri, San Marco 1810 ☎ 041/2418029 ☻ Mon.–Sat. 7:30–7). For further information about professional soccer in Venice, contact **Venezia Calcio** (✉ Via Alfredo Ceccherini 19, Mestre 30175 ☎ 041/2380711 ⊕ www.veneziacalcio.it).

SHOPPING

FODOR'S CHOICE

Barbieri, *women's fashions, Castello*

Fruttaeverdure, *women's fashions, Cannaregio*

Gilberto Penzo, *woodwork, San Polo*

Scheggi di Arlecchino, *masks, Castello*

Venetia Studium, *fabrics, San Marco*

HIGHLY RECOMMENDED

Bevilacqua, *fabrics, San Marco*

Jesurum, *fabrics, San Marco*

Laboratorio Artigiano Maschere, *masks, Castello*

Laboratorio Orafo Guido Carbonich, *jewelry, Cannaregio*

Ma.Re, *glass, San Marco*

Macri, *leather goods, San Marco*

Trois, *fabrics, San Marco*

Updated by
Patricia Rucidlo

BRING AN EXTRA SUITCASE for all your newfound treasures, because Venice is a paradise for shoppers of all varieties. There's no better place for gifts and souvenirs, from kitschy to one-of-a-kind. The hunting ground is vast, and while warrens in the city center are devoted to high fashion, glass artwork, and antiques, quieter parts of town are home to a number of artisans' shops, where paper is glued, pressed, and shaped into masks, and gilded cherubs are born from the hands of wood-carvers.

Alluring shops abound. You'll find countless vendors of trademark Venetian wares such as glass and lace; the authenticity of some goods can be suspect, but they're often pleasing to the eye regardless of their heritage. For more sophisticated tastes (and deeper pockets), there are jewelers, antiques dealers, and high-fashion boutiques on a par with those in Italy's larger cities but often maintaining a uniquely Venetian flair.

It's always a good idea to mark the location of a shop that interests you on your map; otherwise you may not be able to find it again in the maze of tiny streets. Regular store hours are usually 9–12:30 and 3:30 or 4–7:30 PM; some stores are closed on Saturday afternoon or Monday morning. Food shops are open 8–1 and 5–7:30, and are closed all day Sunday and on Wednesday afternoon. However, many tourist-oriented shops are open all day, every day. Some shops close for both a summer and a winter vacation. If you plan on a major purchase, take advantage of tax-free shopping with the value-added tax (VAT, or IVA in Italian) refund, whereby non-EU residents are entitled to a tax refund (roughly 13% of the purchase price) on purchases greater than €155 (pretax) of clothing and luxury goods made in one store.

Department Stores

You wouldn't expect to find a big department store sandwiched between Venice's canals and narrow alleys, but two of Italy's three department-store chains have managed to settle into some of Venice's largest storefronts. Middle-market **Standa** (✉ Ponte San Felice, on the Strada Nova, Cannaregio 3659–60 ☎ 041/5238046 Ⓥ Ca' d'Oro ✉ Via Corfù 1/a, Lido ☎ 041/5265720 Ⓥ Venice Lido) has clothing, perfume, housewares, and a supermarket. Upscale **Coin** (✉ Salizzada San Crisostomo, near Campo San Bartolomio ☎ 041/5203581 Ⓥ Rialto) sells clothing, leather goods, and housewares. Coin has a second outlet called **Coin Beauty** (✉ San Marco 4546, Campo San Luca ☎ 041/5238444 Ⓥ Rialto or Sant'Angelo) where they sell only perfume and lingerie.

Markets

The itinerant flea markets operating on the mainland never include Venice in their tours, and the only markets left in town trade in food. The morning open-air **fruit and vegetable market** on the Santa Croce side of the Rialto Bridge in the Rialto district (open Monday–Saturday, roughly 8–1) has been in business since the 11th century. It offers animated local color and gorgeous produce that's tantalizing to browse through even if you have no plans to buy. The same holds true for the adjacent **Rialto Fish Market,** or *pescheria,* which offers an impressive lesson in ichthyology, with species you've certainly never seen before (open Monday–Saturday, roughly 8–1). Smaller, lively food markets are located on Via Garibaldi, near the Giardini della Biennale, and on Strada Nova, not far from the train station (both open Monday–Saturday, roughly 8–1).

Shopping Districts

Piazza San Marco

The rule here is simple: the closer you are to Piazza San Marco, the higher the prices. The serious jewelry and glasswork in the windows of the shops of the Procuratie Vecchie and Nuove make for a pleasant browse, and during the summer your stroll will be accompanied by the music from the bands that set up in front of Caffè Quadri and Florian. Under the arcades you'll also find an art gallery, a few old-fashioned shops selling kitschy souvenirs, and an assortment of lace, linen blouses, and silk ties and scarves. Masks haven't yet landed here.

Mercerie

The network of streets between the tower clock in Piazza San Marco and Campo San Salvador near Rialto is called the Mercerie. For centuries this was where Venetians came to shop—the word *merceria* comes from *merce* (goods). Only a few refined shops survive—the rest are spread out along other streets in the center of town—and a run of anonymous clothing shops and cheap souvenir boutiques has taken their place. On Campo San Zulian is Cartier, worth a look for its rather dour facade, and around the corner in Merceria San Zulian is a long-established jewelry shop (with no name) selling exquisite antique pieces.

Gucci is on Merceria dell'Orologio, but it has little of the flair and selection you'll find at its sister shops in Florence and Milan. Venice's top lace retailer, Jesurum, opened a second showroom on Merceria del Capitello, and from there it's a short walk (in the direction of Campo San Salvador) to Rosa Salva, one of the best pastry shops in town. Up ahead on the campo is the lingerie boutique La Perla, with lingerie so elegant you could wear it to a party, and Marforio, Venice's standby for high-quality leather.

Campo San Bartolomeo & Rialto

Other good shopping areas surround Campi San Salvador and San Bartolomeo. The department store Coin is just past the central post office and down Ponte dell'Olio. The Rialto district is the mecca for buyers of traditional, inexpensive souvenirs: *pantofole del gondoliere,* velvety slippers with rubber soles that resemble the traditional gondoliers' shoes; 18th-century-style wooden trays and coasters that will look better after a little wear; and glass "candies," which make a nice, inexpensive (if inedible) gift. Clothing and shoe shops are concentrated between the Rialto Bridge and San Polo, along Ruga Vecchia San Giovanni and Ruga Ravano, and around Campo Sant'Aponal.

West of Piazza San Marco

The San Marco sestiere has its fair share of boutiques, jewelry shops, antiques dealers, and the most important art galleries in the city, including Bugno.

Specialty Shops

Antiques & Art Dealers

You may not ship home a 19th-century bed from Venice, and even a relatively common item like an Art Deco chest of drawers is more easily found in Rome, Florence, or Naples. But if you have a taste for odd accessories from another age, Victorian silver plate, prints, or portable antiques with a *je ne sais quoi* to fill an empty corner, you might just find what you weren't even looking for.

Antichità Pietro Scarpa, next to the Gallerie dell'Accademia, sells Old Master paintings—originals, not copies—with accordingly rarified prices.

If your budget doesn't accommodate such an indulgence, you can always fantasize about having one in your next life. ✉ *Campo della Carità, Dorsoduro 1023/a* ☎ *041/5239700* Ⓥ *Accademia.*

Antiquus, a cozy shop from another era, sells a bit of everything, from Old Master paintings to jewelry. Among the hottest items are the lovely earrings and brooches in the shape of Moors' heads. ✉ *Calle delle Botteghe, San Marco 3131* ☎ *041/5206395* Ⓥ *San Samuele.*

Claudia Canestrelli is a tasteful shop with a limited choice of antiques, small paintings, and plenty of interesting-looking bric-a-brac, including silver ex-votos and period souvenirs such as brass ashtrays in the shape of lions' heads. ✉ *Campiello Barbaro, near the Peggy Guggenheim Collection, Dorsoduro 364/a* ☎ *041/5227072 or 340/5776089* Ⓥ *Accademia or Salute.*

Kleine Galerie is a good address for antique books and prints, majolica, and ceramics. ✉ *Calle delle Botteghe, San Marco 2972* ☎ *041/5222177* Ⓥ *San Samuele.*

Luisa Semenzato offers a good selection of furniture, a few paintings by minor masters, and European ceramics, as well as a miscellanea of more affordable objets d'art. ✉ *Merceria San Zulian, San Marco 732* ☎ *041/ 5231412* Ⓥ *San Marco.*

Art Galleries

Art galleries have become a burgeoning business in Venice. After centuries of commercial slumber, the city seems on its way to finally catching up with the world's contemporary art scene.

Bac Art Studio was founded in 1977 by Paolo Baruffaldi and Cadore, two etchers with a soft spot for angels, views of Venice and the lagoon, flowers, cats, and insects. The gallery also hosts exhibits of other local artists. Prices start around €10 for a 2-inch x 1-inch etching. ✉ *Fondamenta Venier, near the Gallerie dell'Accademia, Dorsoduro 862* ☎ *041/5228171* ⊕ *www.bacart.com* Ⓥ *Accademia.*

Bugno, a retailer of contemporary art, puts together windows representative of the whole gallery—most notably, Missagia's fruit and apples on textured backgrounds made of pasted newspaper and cardboard and Demarchi's sexy wooden sculptures. ✉ *Campo San Fantin, San Marco 1996/d* ☎ *041/5231305* Ⓥ *Sant'Angelo.*

Contini shows only 20th-century artists, including such household names as Picasso, Chagall, Magritte, and Giacometti. It's also Italy's only dealer for Botero, Navarro Vires, Zoran Music, and the marble and bronze sculptures by Mitorag. ✉ *Campo Santo Stefano, San Marco 2765* ☎ *041/5207525* Ⓥ *Accademia.*

Gallery Holly Snapp focuses on the works by the eclectic English-born artist Geoffrey Humphries, including paintings, drawings, and etchings ranging from landscapes to portraits; he also sells watercolors of Venetian views and vistas. ✉ *Calle delle Botteghe, San Marco 3133* ☎ *041/ 5210030* Ⓥ *San Samuele.*

At **Le Sculture di Livio de Marchi,** Signor De Marchi's swift hands turn wood into outstanding full-scale sculptures that perfectly reproduce everyday objects such as hats, laundry hung out to dry, telephones, jackets, books, fruit, lace—even underwear. Prices start at about €80 but can easily reach four figures. The shop is closed weekends. ✉ *Salizzada San Samuele, near Palazzo Grassi, San Marco 3157/a* ☎ *041/5285694* ⊕ *www.liviodemarchi.com* Ⓥ *San Samuele.*

San Marco Shopping

Melori & Rosenberg shows young Italian artists on their way up, including Luigi Rocca (hyper-realist scenes of modern life), Francesco Mancini (views of Venice and impressionistic nudes), Michele Giorgio Riva (still lifes), and expressionist Henry Vigino. ⊠ *Campo del Ghetto Nuovo, Cannaregio 2919* ☎ *041/2750039* ⊕ *www.melori-rosenberg. com* Ⓥ *San Marcuola.*

Negozio d'arte simply means "art shop." In it, Laura and Alberto Lo Verso sell original etchings in ink and watercolors, as well as prints of Venice and Palladian villas. ⊠ *Calle Seconda dei Saonieri, San Polo 2671* ☎ *041/275 9367* Ⓥ *Rialto.*

Ravagnan has been the exclusive dealer since 1967 of some of the most famous living artists on the Italian scene, including Venetian surrealist Ludovico de Luigi and metaphysical painter Andrea Vizzini. Glass sculptures by Primo Formenti and collages by Piero Princip are also available here. ⊠ *Procuratie Nuove, Piazza San Marco 50/a* ☎ *041/5203021* ⊕ *www.ravagnangallery.com* Ⓥ *San Marco.*

Ceramics

With all the glass around town, it's not surprising that Venice has never been known for its pottery. You can find replicas of 19th-century chocolate cups, usually cream-white and delicately gilded (not for daily use); pottery from Bassano, typically decorated with reliefs of fruit and vegetables; and some modern, handmade plates and mugs.

Angela Greco, a must for collectors and lovers of antique ceramics, has affordable items such as replicas of 19th-century Venetian chocolate cups. ⊠ *Campo Santa Maria del Giglio, San Marco 2433* ☎ *041/5234573* Ⓥ *Santa Maria del Giglio.*

Atelier stocks black-and-white ceramics with subjects inspired by famous erotic Italian cartoons. There are also more chaste pieces, some reminiscent of pop art. It's closed mornings and all day Wednesday. ⊠ *Calle del Pestrin, near Campo dell'Arsenale, Castello 3876* ☎ *041/5225895* or *348/7249249* Ⓥ *Arsenale.*

Margherita Rossetto creates faience-style majolica on a white background, with figures of animals, flowers, and fruit designed in oxidized copper. ⊠ *Sotoportego della Siora Bettina, off Campo San Cassiano, Santa Croce 2345* ☎ *041/723120* Ⓥ *S. Stae or Rialto.*

Rigattieri sells pottery from Bassano, ranging from white plates with a lace border to serving bowls in the shape of hens and geese to platters with asparagus in relief. They sell lanterns in blown glass that will give a Venetian touch to your garden or porch, as well as other objects in porcelain and silver. ⊠ *Calle dei Frati, between Campo Santo Stefano and Campo Sant'Angelo, San Marco 3532* ☎ *041/5231081* Ⓥ *Sant'Angelo.*

Clothing

Venetian streets are lined with so many designer boutiques and tiny, pricey stores that you may wonder where Venetians buy their everyday clothes. The truth is that fancy garments are not worn much here. Venice is a town without office buildings, banks, or government offices, and a casual dress code agrees with the mileage usually covered on foot everyday. You will undoubtedly see a few impeccably dressed *signore* (ladies) who manage the bridges in high heels without a misstep, but most Venetians prefer a more relaxed and creative style than that of the fashion-conscious Milanese and Romans. Bargain-hunters should know that the best clothing sales typically occur from January 7 until mid–February and from mid- to late July to early September.

Agnona has incredibly warm cashmere and wool knitwear and winter coats—all in soft natural colors (creamy white and various shades of beige). If you're undecided what to buy the guy or gal who has everything, consider one of the luscious scarves. ⊠ *Calle Vallaresso, San Marco 1316* ☎ *041/5205733* Ⓥ *San Marco.*

Al Pupo is one of the few surviving Venetian shops selling clothes for infants and children. They offer a good selection at good prices, and they even make Carnevale costumes for toddlers. ⊠ *Campo Santa Fosca, Cannaregio 2215* ☎ *041/721748* Ⓥ *San Marcuola.*

Armani, in a rather grand space, delivers its superlative signature style and service—women's silk shirts are especially striking for quality, design, and price. Those waiting for the dressing rooms can rest on comfortable couches. ⊠ *Calle Goldoni, San Marco 4412* ☎ *041/5234758* Ⓥ *San Marco.*

Camiceria San Marco is the town's top custom shirtmaker, with a fine assortment of blouses and shirts. Only the finest fabrics are used (they can also be bought by the meter). Elegant pajamas, gowns, and ladies' dresses complete the scene. ⊠ *Calle Vallaresso, San Marco 1340* ☎ *041/ 5221432* Ⓥ *San Marco.*

Elysée stocks mostly Armani and Armani-like clothing. ⊠ *Calle Goldoni, San Marco 4485* ☎ *041/5223020* Ⓥ *Rialto or San Marco* ⊠ *Frezzeria, San Marco 1693* ☎ *041/5236948* Ⓥ *San Marco.*

Emporio Armani flaunts the famous stylist's casual line, with his eagle symbol fastened onto just about everything. ⊠ *Calle dei Fabbri, San Marco 989* ☎ *041/5237808* Ⓥ *Rialto or San Marco.*

Fiorella Mancini Gallery is your best bet for original creations and the craziest look in town. ⊠ *Campo Santo Stefano, San Marco 2806* ☎ *041/ 5209228* Ⓥ *Accademia or San Samuele.*

La Coupole, with three shops a stone's throw from one another, offers an excellent selection of name-brand *alta moda* (high fashion). ⊠ *Calle Larga XXII Marzo, San Marco 2366* ☎ *041/5224243* Ⓥ *San Marco* ⊠ *Calle Larga XXII Marzo, San Marco 2031* ☎ *041/5232754* Ⓥ *San Marco* ⊠ *Calle Larga XXII Marzo, San Marco 2254* ☎ *041/5231273* Ⓥ *San Marco.*

La Tour carries labels such as Versace, Ferré, and the unparalleled Malo cashmere-wear. ⊠ *Calle Larga San Marco, San Marco 287* ☎ *041/ 5225147* Ⓥ *San Marco.*

Venice's **Prada** is one of the largest Prada stores in Italy. Suit up in clean-cut, modern-looking articles made out of high-tech materials, leather, or natural fibers. ⊠ *Campo San Moisè, San Marco 1479* ☎ *041/ 5283966* Ⓥ *San Marco.*

Florentine native **Roberto Cavalli** finally got around to opening a Venetian shop in 2002; rock stars and rock star wannabees need look no further. ⊠ *Calle Vallaresso, San Marco 1314* Ⓥ *San Marco.*

Trussardi sells the clothing, shoes, and bags of its namesake Italian designer. ⊠ *Spadaria, San Marco 695* ☎ *041/5285757.* Ⓥ *San Marco.*

MEN'S FASHIONS **Al Duca d'Aosta** stocks such classics as Burberry and Ralph Lauren. ⊠ *Merceria del Capitello, San Marco 4946* ☎ *041/5220733* Ⓥ *Rialto or San Marco.*

Ceriello is the only place in town selling Brioni suits. ⊠ *Campo SS. Filippo e Giacomo, San Marco 4275* ☎ *041/5222062* Ⓥ *San Zaccaria.*

Élite is the source for not-so-casual Italian outdoor wear as well as those quintessentially English Aquascutum coats that so many Italians favor. Silk ties and cashmere scarves complete the English country look. ⊠ *Calle Larga San Marco, San Marco 284* ☎ *041/5230145* Ⓥ *San Marco.*

La Bottega is the place to go if you like the comfort and style of leading Italian classic designers Cerruti and Ermenegildo Zegna. ⊠ *Merceria dell'Orologio, San Marco 223* ☎ *041/5225608* Ⓥ *Rialto or San Marco.*

Otello has a great selection of brightly colored waistcoats and bow ties—not for the conservative dresser. ⊠ *Calle dell'Acqua, San Marco 4989* ☎ *041/5223142* Ⓥ *Rialto.*

WOMEN'S FASHIONS

Al Duca d'Aosta, no longer the Venetian bulwark of classy Italian fashion, now offers a selection of international pret-a-porter on its two floors: Jil Sander, Rebecca Moses, Donna Karan, and Ralph Lauren. ⊠ *Merceria del Capitello, San Marco 4922* ☎ *041/5204079* Ⓥ *Rialto or San Marco.*

Arras sells exclusive scarves as well as a few blouses and jackets, all handwoven in wool or silk. It also occasionally organizes weaving workshops. ⊠ *Campiello Squellini, Dorsoduro 3234* ☎ *041/5226460* Ⓥ *Ca' Rezzonico.*

Fodor'sChoice
★

Barbieri has scarves and shawls for women in a myriad of colors as well as textures, and you can also pick up fine men's ties while you're here. They've been successfully plying their wares since 1945. ⊠ *Ponte dei Greci, Castello 3403* ☎ *041/522 8177* Ⓥ *San Zaccaria.*

Caberlotto has cornered the market on fabulous fur coats and hats. They sell interesting wool blazers for those cold walks about town, and pashmina shawls by Rosenda Arcioni Meer to wrap around your neck. They also have a complete line of luxurious cashmere clothing. ⊠ *Larga Mazzini, San Marco 5114* ☎ *041/5229242* Ⓥ *Rialto.*

Fodor'sChoice
★

Fruttaeverdure has a lively collection of scarves, purses, and hair accessories in brightly colored rainbow hues, for the young at heart and those who love bursts of color. ⊠ *Campo SS. Apostoli, Cannaregio 4451–2* ☎ *041/2411572* Ⓥ *Ca' d'Oro.*

Gucci sells shoes, bags, accessories, and some clothes as well in two side-by-side shops. ⊠ *Merceria dell'Orologio, San Marco 258* ☎ *041/5229119* Ⓥ *San Marco.*

Hermès offers the famous French foulards and accessories. ⊠ *Procuratie Vecchie, San Marco 127* ☎ *041/5210117* Ⓥ *San Marco.*

Hibiscus is a hip boutique selling loose-fitting women's clothing (which look better on you than they do drooping from hangers) and matching accessories. The style is very youthful, the prices very adult. ⊠ *Calle dell'Olio, near the Rialto Market, San Polo 1060* ☎ *041/5208989* Ⓥ *Rialto.*

La Fenice has an assortment of the wares of major Italian and international designers, including evening dresses and shoes to match. ⊠ *Calle Larga XXII Marzo, San Marco 2255* ☎ *041/5231273* Ⓥ *San Marco.*

La Perla specializes in extremely elegant lingerie that's comfortable, too. ⊠ *Campo San Salvador, San Marco 4828* ☎ *041/5226459* Ⓥ *Rialto.*

Le Ragazze di Cima carries the best Italian brands of lingerie, from glossy silk to cotton lace. ⊠ *Strada Nova, near Ponte San Felice, Cannaregio 3683* ☎ *041/5234988* Ⓥ *Ca' d'Oro.*

Malo is recognized as one of Italy's highest-quality producers of cashmere garments. Its styles are tasteful and refined, designed and made to be worn for many years. ☒ *Calle de le Ostreghe, San Marco 2359* ☏ *041/5232162* Ⓥ *San Marco or Santa Maria del Giglio.*

Missoni sells scarves and clothing made of wool, linen, or cotton, all rigorously knitted and dramatically colorful. ☒ *Calle Vallaresso, San Marco 1312* ☏ *041/5205733* Ⓥ *San Marco.*

The **Shirt Shop** specializes in good-quality cotton shirts and blouses and well-made stockings. ☒ *Campo Sant'Angelo, San Marco 3820* ☏ *no phone* Ⓥ *Sant'Angelo.*

Valentino only sells clothing signed by the famous eponymous Roman designer. ☒ *Salizzada San Moisè, San Marco 1473* ☏ *041/5205733* Ⓥ *San Marco.*

Valeria Bellinaso designs expensive, attractive straw hats, perfect for a romantic spring gondola ride. The store also features shawls full of character and foldable silk bags that are light as a feather yet large enough to pack for the weekend. ☒ *Campo Sant'Aponal, San Polo 1226* ☏ *041/ 5223351* Ⓥ *San Silvestro.*

Costumes & Accessories

Atelier Pietro Longhi rents and sells costumes inspired by 18th- and 19th-century models, with masks (for sale only) to match. Large sizes are available for both sexes. ☒ *Rio Terrà dei Frari, San Polo 2604/b* ☏ *041/ 714478* Ⓥ *San Tomà.*

Flavia is a good address for historical costumes, either made-to-order or for rent; you can also rent tuxedos all year round. When you walk into the shop, ask for either Adriano or Susan, both of whom speak flawless English, to take you to the atelier nearby. ☒ *near Campo San Lio, Castello 6010* ☏ *041/2413200* Ⓥ *Rialto.*

Laboratorio Arte & Costume is the place if you are making your own costume and need some professional sartorial assistance. Monica Daniele will fix your problem as quickly as her sewing machine will go. In the meantime you can take a look at the assorted hats, bags, and vintage clothing. ☒ *Calle del Scaleter, near Campo San Polo, San Polo 2235* ☏ *041/5246242* Ⓥ *San Tomà.*

At **Laboratorio Parrucche Carlotta** wig maker Carlotta Carisi believes that at Carnevale details count, and her sensational creations are the ideal way to top off an elegant costume. Note that the quality comes at a price (€230–€500), and credit cards are not accepted. ☒ *Campo Widman, Cannaregio 5415* ☏ *041/5207571.*

Nicolao Atelier is the largest costume-rental showroom in town, with nearly 7,000 choices ranging from the historical to the fantastic, including thematic costumes ideal for group masquerades. At the **tailor's workshop** (☒ Calle del Bagatin, near Campo SS. Apostoli, Cannaregio 5565 Ⓥ Ca' d'Oro) you can see the costumes being made (by appointment only). ☒ *Calle del Magazin, near Campo SS. Apostoli, Cannaregio 5590/a* ☏ *041/5209749* Ⓥ *Ca d'Oro.*

At **Venetia** the colorful, fanciful display window of 18th-century Venetian outfits often makes passersby stop to admire the mannequins. Lessglamorous medieval-style garments, masks, and accessories are kept behind the curtains inside. ☒ *Frezzeria, San Marco 1286* ☏ *041/5224426* Ⓥ *San Marco.*

English-Language Books

Venice, unlike Rome or Florence, does not have an English-language bookstore. However, some places carry small selections of books in English.

For newspapers and magazines in English, the best-stocked newsstand is on Bocca di Piazza near the Museum Correr.

Ca' Foscarina is the bookstore of nearby Università di Venezia Ca' Foscari, with the town's largest selection of books in English. Shelves teem with literature and history, but there's also a handful of travel books, as well as the latest best-sellers. ⊠ *Campiello Squellini, Dorsoduro 3259* ☎ *041/5229602* Ⓥ *Ca' Rezzonico.*

Fantoni specializes in coffee-table books on art, architecture, photography, and design, mostly in Italian, but the beautiful illustrations speak for themselves. You'll find books in English on Venice and Italian food. ⊠ *off Campo San Luca, San Marco 4119* ☎ *041/5220700* Ⓥ *Rialto or Sant'Angelo.*

Libreria San Pantalon sells children's books (some in English), minor arts and crafts, and books on music and opera (in Italian). ⊠ *Crosera, also known as Calle Lunga San Pantalon, Dorsoduro 3950* ☎ *041/5224436* Ⓥ *San Tomà.*

Studium is a good stop for books in English, especially guidebooks and books on Venetian culture and food. It's also particularly strong on English-language fiction with Italian, mostly Venetian, settings and themes; in addition, it has a small but worthy collection of recent hardcover fiction. ⊠ *Calle della Canonica, San Marco 337/C* ☎ *041/5222382* Ⓥ *San Marco.*

Gifts

At **Angelo Dalla Venezia,** Signor Angelo crafts objects in wood including "eggs" for mending socks and knitwear. He also has hard-to-find wooden bobbins for lace making. ⊠ *Calle del Scaleter, off Campo San Polo, San Polo 2204* ☎ *041/721659* Ⓥ *San Tomà.*

Antichità Santomanco della Toffola sells Russian and English silver work, paintings, period glass and jewelry, and bric-a-brac. ⊠ *Ramo Secondo Corte Contarina, San Marco 1567* ☎ *041/5236643* Ⓥ *San Marco.*

Fusetti Diego Baruch has all manner of handmade Jewish handicrafts, including copies of antique menorahs, in glass, bronze, gold, silver, and mosaic. It's closed Saturday. ⊠ *Ghetto Vecchio, Cannaregio 1218* ☎ *041/720092* ⊕ *www.shalomvenice.com* Ⓥ *Ferrovia Santa Lucia.*

The workshop of **Giro Vago** produces trendy, up-to-the-minute handmade copper jewelry and leather bags. It's almost always open, but sometimes the owner is out of town at markets and fairs, so it's a good idea to call ahead. ⊠ *Ponte dei Miracoli, near the Chiesa dei Miracoli, Cannaregio 6019* ☎ *041/5225217* Ⓥ *Ca' d'Oro.*

Giuliana Longo is a hat shop that's been around since 1901; it has a special corner dedicated to accessories for antique cars. You could also use the leather goggles and helmets for skiing. ⊠ *Calle del Lovo, San Marco 4813* ☎ *041/5226454* Ⓥ *San Marco.*

Il Baule Blu specializes in *orsi artistici,* teddy bears to collect and treat with great care. All are painstakingly handmade and have articulated paws and glass eyes; when squeezed on their tummy, they can either grumble or play a carillon tune. Some are stark naked; others are dressed in old baby garments trimmed with lace and ribbons. They come in many sizes and colors. ⊠ *Calle Prima, off Campo San Tomà, San Polo 2916/a* ☎ *041/719448* ⊕ *www.ilbauleblu.com* Ⓥ *San Tomà.*

La Stamperia del Ghetto sells black-and-white prints of the old Ghetto. It's closed Saturday. ⊠ *Calle del Ghetto Vecchio, Cannaregio 1185/a* ☎ *041/2750200* Ⓥ *San Marcuolo or Ponte delle Guglie.*

La Venexiana, an Aladdin's cave full of last-minute gift treasures, sells mostly Carnevale-oriented keepsakes. ⊠ *Frezzeria, San Marco 1135* ☎ *041/5286888* Ⓥ *San Marco.*

Perle Veneziane, two minutes from Piazza San Marco, fits the bill when you've got last-minute gifts to buy. There's an assortment of necklaces, faux-period Venetian glass jewelry and loose modern beads, but also *murrine,* pour tops for olive oil bottles, and an assortment of glass curios. ⊠ *Ponte della Canonica, San Marco 4308* ☎ *041/5289059* Ⓥ *San Marco.*

Signor Blum makes solid large-piece puzzles (painted or in natural wood colors) depicting animals, views of Venice, and trompe l'oeil scenes. Ideal toys for toddlers, the puzzles also look nice hanging on a wall. ⊠ *Fondamenta Gherardini, off Campo San Barnaba, Dorsoduro 2840* ☎ *041/5226367* ⊕ *www.signorblum.com* Ⓥ *Ca' Rezzonico.*

Strafanti & Cavalieri is operated by Luigina Checchini, a Venetian who returned home in 1999 after 10 years spent in Kenya. In her small shop she sells African pottery, hand-printed clothing, and necklaces made of painted beads and brass. The "Venetian corner" features soap made according to a medieval recipe and a selection of collectible handmade books about the region. Like jewelry made with *vetro murrina*? Luigina will tell you in fluent English how she is the only one in town to have the real McCoy. The shop is closed Monday. ⊠ *Campo del Ghetto Nuovo, Cannaregio 2920* ☎ *041/2440176* Ⓥ *Ferrovia Santa Lucia.*

Glass

Glass, most of it made in Murano, is Venice's number one product, and you'll be confronted by mind-boggling, often kitschy displays of traditional and contemporary glassware. Take your time and be selective. If you want to make an investment, the important producers to remember are Barovier, Pauly, Poli, Seguso, Toso, and Venini. Freelance designers create pieces for more than just a single glasshouse: look for signatures and certificates of authentication. Bear in mind that the value of any piece—signature and shape apart—is also based on the number of colors, the presence of gold, and, in the case of goblets, the thinness of the glass. Prices are about the same all over, but be warned that some shops sell glass made in Taiwan. All shops will arrange for shipping.

Al Campanil specializes in replicas of antique Murano pieces and jewelry made with tiny glass Venetian beads. ⊠ *Calle Lunga Santa Maria Formosa, Castello 5184* ☎ *041/5235734* Ⓥ *Rialto.*

Antichità displays attractive period objects made with the tiniest Murano glass beads "woven" on linen threads, as well as more modern creations, such as stunning flowers and necklaces in the shape of snakes. The antique and the modern are hard to tell apart, as they are crafted with the same antique beads. You can also purchase small quantities of antique beads for making your own jewelry. ⊠ *Calle della Toletta, Dorsoduro 1195* ☎ *041/5223159* Ⓥ *Accademia.*

Do Maghi means "two magicians," but in fact there's only one at work here, Hans Peter Neidhardt, who despite his name is a native Venetian and has been making glass since 1982. Though he's clearly cognizant of the Murano tradition, he injects humor and whimsy into his creations, from his goldfish in bowls to single long-stemmed red roses. ⊠ *Calle Dolfin, Cannaregio 5621* ☎ *041/5208535* ⊕ *www.evercom.it* Ⓥ *Ca' d'Oro.*

Domus has a selection of smaller objects and jewelry from the best glassworks. ⊠ *Fondamenta dei Vetrai 82, Murano* ☎ *041/739215* Ⓥ *Murano.*

Ferro & Cimegotto uses glass, enamel, and gold to make traditional Venetian plaques, coats-of-arms, and crucifixes, all for wall display. They take custom orders. ✉ *Ramo dei Saoneri, San Polo 2672/a* ☎ *041/5227794* Ⓥ *San Tomà.*

Galleria San Nicolò is owned by the American glass expert Louise Berndt. The gallery shows the best of contemporary glass, including superb work by Micheluzzi, Michael Groot, and Maria Brandolini. It's closed Sunday and Monday. ✉ *Calle della Fenice, San Marco 1920* ☎ *041/ 5221535* Ⓥ *San Marco.*

Genninger Studio is the retail outlet for Leslie Ann Genninger, an American from Ohio who was the first woman to enter the male-dominated world of Murano master bead makers. She established her own line of jewelry, called Murano Class Act, in 1994 using period glass beads, and when she could no longer find antique beads she started designing her own. Here you'll also find glasswork signed by Venetian Lucio Bubacco. ✉ *Calle del Frutariol, San Marco 1845* ☎ *041/5239494* Ⓥ *San Marco* ✉ *Calle del Traghetto, off Campo San Barnaba, Dorsoduro 2793/a* ☎ *041/5225565* Ⓥ *Accademia.*

Gianfranco Penzo decorates Jewish ritual vessels in glass and makes commemorative plates. He takes special orders. ✉ *Campo del Ghetto Nuovo, Cannaregio 2895* ☎ *no phone* Ⓥ *Ferrovia Santa Lucia.*

L'Isola has chic, contemporary glassware signed by Carlo Moretti. ✉ *Campo San Moisè, San Marco 1468* ☎ *041/5231973* Ⓥ *San Marco.*

★ **Ma.Re** sells Salviati glass, as well as blown and solid glass. It also sells one-of-a-kind objects by leading glass artists. ✉ *via XXII Marzo, San Marco 2088* ☎ *041/5231191* 🖷 *041/5285745* ⊕ *www.mareglass.com* Ⓥ *San Marco.*

Marina Barovier's Gallery has an excellent selection of collectible contemporary glass. It's open Monday through Friday, and on Saturday by appointment. ✉ *Calle delle Botteghe, off Campo Santo Stefano, San Marco 3216* ☎*041/5236748* 🖷*041/2447042* ⊕*www.barovier.it* Ⓥ*San Samuele.*

Paropàmiso sells stunning Venetian glass beads and jewelry from all over the world. ✉ *Frezzeria, San Marco 1701* ☎ *041/5227120* Ⓥ *San Marco.*

Pauly has a large showroom in Piazza San Marco, with a wide array of glassware and chandeliers. ✉ *Ala Napoleonica, San Marco 73–77* ☎ *041/5209899* Ⓥ *San Marco.*

Tre Erre is a reliable and respected firm for both traditional and contemporary glass designs. ✉ *Piazza San Marco 79/b* ☎ *041/5201715* Ⓥ *San Marco.*

Venini has been an institution since the 1930s, attracting some of the foremost names in glass design. ✉ *Piazzetta dei Leoncini, San Marco 314* ☎ *041/5224045* ⊕ *www.venini.it* Ⓥ *San Marco.*

Vetri d'Arte offers moderately priced glass jewelry. ✉ *Piazza San Marco 140* ☎ *041/5200205* Ⓥ *San Marco.*

Gold, Wood & Metalwork

Venice's passion for glittering golden objects, which began with the decoration in the Basilica di San Marco and later spread into the finest noble homes, kept specialized gold artisans (called *doradori*) in business for several centuries. They still produce lovely cabinets, shelves, wall lamps, lanterns, candleholders, banisters, headboards, frames, and the like by applying gold leaf to wrought iron and carved wood. Numerous skilled silversmiths still cater to the faithful; in their workshops you'll find silver devotional icons of the Madonna della Salute and of the Madonna Nicopeia, traditionally hung in Venetian bedrooms. Most foundries have long since closed their doors, but you can still find top-quality brass pieces at Valese Fonditore.

Cornici Trevisanello has wonderful handcrafted frames, made of gold-leafed wood and inset with antique glass beads, mosaic tesserae, and small ceramic tiles. Either Byzantine or rich Renaissance in appearance, the more elaborate pieces are at their best when used to frame an old mirror. ⊠ *Fondamenta Bragadin, off Campo San Vio* ☎ *041/5207779* Ⓥ *Accademia.*

Dorador trades in gilded carved wood, including flying cherubs playing trumpets. ⊠ *Campo San Barnaba, Dorsoduro 2808* ☎ *no phone* Ⓥ *San Tomà or Accademia.*

E. Pandian e Figli creates artisanal silver work, most notably icons of venerated Venetian Madonnas. ⊠ *Campo Santa Maria Mater Domini, Santa Croce 2171* ☎ *041/5241398* Ⓥ *S. Stae.*

Fodor'sChoice ★ **Gilberto Penzo** is the gondola expert in Venice. He creates scale models of gondolas and lagoon boats and real gondola *forcole* (oarlocks) in his *laboratorio* (workshop) nearby. (If the shop is closed, a sign posted on the door will explain how to find Signor Penzo.) When he's not busy sawing and sanding, Mr. Penzo writes historical and technical books about gondola building. Here you'll also find gondola model kits, a great gift for the boatbuilder in your life. ⊠ *Calle Seconda dei Saoneri, San Polo 2681* ☎ *041/719372* ⊕ *www.veniceboats.com* Ⓥ *San Tomà.*

Jonathan Ceolin, makes traditional wrought-iron chandeliers, wall lamps, and Venetian lanterns, either plain black or gilded (like in the old days), in his tiny workshop near Campo Santa Maria Formosa. ⊠ *Ponte Marcello off Campo Santa Marina, Castello 6106* ☎ *041/5200609* Ⓥ *Rialto.*

Luca Sumiti carries on the work of his father, Maurizio; this is a great place for traditional wrought-iron chandeliers and lamps. They come unadorned, gilded, or tastefully enameled in bright colors. Here you'll also find conspicuous, 5-ft-tall wooden sculptures of *mori veneziani* (Venetian Moors). ⊠ *Calle delle Bande, Castello 5274* ☎ *041/5205621* Ⓥ *Rialto or San Marco.*

At **Studio d'Arte Artù**, Tobia Morra practices wood and stone restoration. He also sells painted tables and chairs. ⊠ *Barbaria delle Tole, near Campo dei Santi Giovanni e Paolo, Castello 6656* ☎ *041/2777838* 🖷 *041/2777783* Ⓥ *Fondamenta Nove.*

Valese Fonditore, the Valese foundry, here since 1913, works in brass, bronze, copper, and pewter. The various metals are then cast into artistic handles, menorahs, Carnevale masks, and real gondola decorations (which make great paperweights, bookends, or shelf pieces). The coups de grâce are the brass chandeliers, exactly like those that hang in the Oval Office in the White House. The foundry is open every day, but things only get interesting when they pour, which is usually on Thursday and Friday. Call to arrange a visit. ⊠ *Calle Fiubera, San Marco 793* ☎ *041/ 5227282* Ⓥ *San Marco* ⊠ *foundry: Cannaregio 3535, near Madonna dell'Orto* ☎ *041/720234* Ⓥ *San Marcuola.*

Jewelry

Venetians have always liked gold, and the city is packed with first-class jewelry shops, as well as more modest shops found outside the San Marco area, most notably around the Rialto district. One of the most typical pieces of inexpensive jewelry that you can buy is a *murrina,* a thin, round slice of colored glass (imagine a bunch of colored spaghetti firmly held together and sliced) encircled with gold and sold as pendants or earrings. The Museo del Vetro at Murano nicely explains how they're made.

Bastianello has classic jewelry as well as pieces made with semiprecious stones. ⊠ *Via Due Aprile, off Campo San Bartolomio, San Marco 5041* ☎ *041/5226751* Ⓥ *Rialto.*

Bulgari is one of the best-known Italian jewelry designers. ⊠ *Calle Larga XXII Marzo, San Marco 2282* ☎ *041/2410553* ⊕ *www.bulgari. com* Ⓥ *San Marco.*

Cartier has watches and jewelry by the famous designer. ⊠ *Campo San Zulian, San Marco 606* ☎ *041/5222071* Ⓥ *San Marco.*

Elena carries pieces designed by world-famous firms such as Buccellati and Omega. ⊠ *Merceria dell'Orologio, San Marco 214-216* ☎ *041/ 5226540* Ⓥ *San Marco.*

Gualti makes creative jewelry in colored resin that looks as fragile as glass but is as strong and soft as rubber. Earrings take the shape of mysterious sea creatures—sea anemones or jellyfish—broaches look like fall leaves, and necklaces are reminiscent of Queen Elizabeth's ruffled collars. Silk shoes can be custom "garnished" with jewelry. ⊠ *Rio Terà Canal, near Campo Santa Margherita, Dorsoduro 3111* ☎ *041/5201731* ⊕ *www.gualti.it* Ⓥ *Ca' Rezzonico.*

★ At **Laboratorio Orafo Guido Carbonich,** Guido Carbonich's interest in Byzantine and Oriental art comes out in his unique jewels, made from silver, coral, and precious and semiprecious stones. Huge rings (meant for men more than for women), sensual serpentine bracelets, and earrings in the shape of Moors' heads are his strong points. For unique yet affordable bracelets and rings, this is *the* place. ⊠ *Ponte delle Guglie, Cannaregio 1297* ☎ *041/720461.*

Missiaglia is a landmark in Piazza San Marco, selling fabulous jewelry and a few silver accessories. ⊠ *Procuratie Vecchie, San Marco 125* ☎ *041/5224464* Ⓥ *San Marco.*

Nardi sells exquisite *moretti*—earrings and brooches in the shape of Moors' heads—studded with diamonds, rubies, or emeralds. ⊠ *under Procuratie Nuove, San Marco 69* ☎ *041/5225733* Ⓥ *San Marco.*

Pomellato is a leading Italian designer, with shops also in Rome and Milan. ⊠ *Calle Seconda dell'Ascensione, San Marco 1298* ☎ *041/5201048* Ⓥ *San Marco.*

Rizzo has no sign posted but is the place to come for antique brooches, earrings, pendants, and ceramic display pieces. With discretion and tact, prices can be bargained down a bit. ⊠ *Merceria San Zulian, San Marco 706* ☎ *041/5229380* Ⓥ *San Marco.*

Salvadori specializes in precious watches, but it also has sparkling diamonds and other precious stones set in their own designs. ⊠ *Merceria San Salvador, San Marco 5022* ☎ *041/5230609* Ⓥ *Rialto.*

Leather Goods

In Venice you'll find a good assortment of leather goods, especially shoes and ladies' bags. All shoe shops listed below are for both men and women. Unless stated otherwise, these shops tend to carry rather upmarket designer articles. For less fancy items, explore the areas of Rialto and Campo San Polo.

Bottega Veneta is a prestigious Italian chain selling bags typically made with intertwined strips of leather, plus smooth bags and elegant low-heeled shoes (for women only). ⊠ *Calle Vallaresso, San Marco 1337* ☎ *041/5228489* Ⓥ *San Marco.*

Emporium has traveling bags and suitcases by Alviero Martini, typically decorated with maps in light colors, and Trussardi accessories. ✉ *Spadaria, San Marco 670* ☎ *041/5235911* Ⓥ *San Marco.*

Fanny, run by a family of market stall sellers, combines good value, friendly service, and cheerful design. Leather and suede bags come in many different colors and sizes and can be embroidered; soft leather gloves are warm but not bulky. ✉ *Calle dei Saoneri, San Polo 2723* ☎ *041/5228266* Ⓥ *San Tomà.*

Fendi carries bags, shoes, and leather and fur winter clothing designed by the Fendi sisters. ✉ *Salizzada San Moisè, San Marco 1474* ☎ *041/2778528* Ⓥ *San Marco.*

Fratelli Rossetti has bags, boots, leather jackets, and shoes of the Rossetti brothers—for once, the selection here is better than in the Rome shop. ✉ *Campo San Salvador, San Marco 4800* ☎ *041/5230571* Ⓥ *San Marco.*

Glamour is a tiny neighborhood shop with a sign proudly stating CHAUSSURE DE TENDENCE (trendy shoes). Vic Matiè and Shilla are designers on the rise, who make cute, reasonably priced low-heeled sandals; you'll also find cork platform shoes and boots. ✉ *Ponte delle Guglie, Cannaregio 1298* ☎ *041/716246* Ⓥ *San Marcuola.*

Kalimala should not be missed if you are looking for soft leather bags, a perfect match for almost any outfit, or very pretty, inexpensive copper jewelry. ✉ *Salizzada San Lio, near Campo Santa Maria Formosa, Castello 5387* ☎ *041/5283596* ⊕ *www.kalimala.it* Ⓥ *Rialto.*

La Parigina is a Venetian institution, with five large windows spread in two neighboring shops. You'll find the house collection here, plus a dozen lesser-known designers such as Piero Guidi, Alexander Nicolette, and Testoni. ✉ *Merceria San Zulian, San Marco 727* ☎ *041/5226743* Ⓥ *San Marco* ✉ *Merceria San Zulian, San Marco 733* ☎ *041/523155* Ⓥ *San Marco.*

Louis Vuitton, the famous French maker of travel bags and boxes, has marvelous window displays. ✉ *Calle Larga dell'Ascensione, San Marco 1255* ☎ *041/5224500* Ⓥ *San Marco.*

★ The evening shoes at **Macri** are so glamorous and over-the-top that you might feel compelled to buy a pair and create an occasion to wear them to. René Caovilla's shoes are meant for showing off, not walking around town (especially in Venice). These high-heeled works of art are studded with sparkling bits of multicolored leather and crystal and decorated with feathers, flowers, and butterflies. Prices start at €350. ✉ *Calle dell'Ascensione, San Marco 1296* ☎ *041/5231221* Ⓥ *San Marco.*

Marforio beautifully balances quality with price, selling a wide range of bags, suitcases, belts, wallets, and somewhat-offbeat leather accessories such as cases for glasses and shoe-polish boxes. Also for sale here are items by Valentino and Armani. ✉ *Campo San Salvador, San Marco 5033* ☎ *041/5225734* Ⓥ *Rialto or San Marco.*

Mariani is one of Venice's best shoe shops, with very affordable prices. ✉ *Calle del Teatro, off Campo San Luca, San Marco 4775* ☎ *041/5222967* Ⓥ *Rialto or Sant'Angelo.*

Rolando Segalin founded the custom shoe workshop bearing his name in 1932. The team of artisans here can give life to your wildest shoe fantasy (see the gondola and cat-paw creations in the window) as well as make the most classic designs. ✉ *Calle dei Fuseri, San Marco 4365* ☎ *041/5222115* Ⓥ *San Marco.*

VENETIAN MASKS UNVEILED

VENETIAN MASK MAKING has experienced a rebirth. In the time of the Republic, the mask trade was vibrant—Venetians used masks all year round to go about town incognito—but it was suppressed by Napoléon, a by-product of his effort to end Carnevale. When Carnevale was revived in the late 1970s, mask making returned as well. Though many workshops use centuries-old techniques, none have been in business for more than 30 years.

A landmark date in the history of Venetian masks is 1436, when the mascareri (mask makers) founded their own guild. By then the techniques that are replicated today were well established: a mask is first modeled in clay, then a chalk cast is made from it and lined with layers of papier-mâché, glue, gauze, and wax. (You can buy a molded mask at this stage of production and paint it yourself.)

But masks were popular well before the mascareri's guild was established. Local laws regulating their use appeared as early as 1268, intended to prevent wearers from carrying weapons and masked men disguised as women from entering convents to seduce nuns. Masks were commonly used by Venetians going to the theater or attempting to avoid identification at brothels and gaming tables.

In the 18th century masks started being used by actors playing the traditional roles of the commedia dell'arte. Arlecchino, Pantalone, Pulcinella, and company would wear leather masks designed to amplify or change their voices. Inexpensive papier-mâché versions of these traditional masks can be found everywhere. Arlecchino has the round face and surprised expression, Pantalone is the one with the curved nose and long mustache, and Pulcinella has the protruding nose.

The least expensive mask is the white Bauta, smooth and plain with a short, pointed nose. Invented in the 18th century as a disguise, a properly made Bauta will alter the tone of the wearer's voice. It was particularly popular for women going to the theater; whether worn by a man or woman, it was accompanied by a black three-cornered hat and a black cloak. The pretty Gnaga, which resembles a cat's face, was used by gay men to "meow" proposals to good-looking boys. The basic Moretta is a black oval with eyeholes. The most interesting of the traditional masks may be the Medico della Peste (the Plague Doctor), with an enormous beaklike nose and a pair of glasses. During the plague of 1630 and 1631, doctors used masks as a form of protection; inside the nose they put herbs and fragrances thought to filter infected air, while the glasses protected the eyes.

Following the boom of mask shops, numerous costume rental stores opened in the 1990s. They have an assortment of masks and simplified versions of 18th-century costumes. If you plan to rent a costume during Carnevale, it's a good idea to make a reservation several months in advance.

Vogini is well stocked with designer bags by Moschino, Fendissime (Fendi's less expensive line), Bianchinardi, Roberta di Camerino, and Versace; it also has its own line of classic bags in crocodile, lizard, and ostrich. ✉ *Salizzada San Moisè, San Marco 1292* ☎ *041/5222573* Ⓥ *San Marco.*

Masks

Not everyone knows that the boom of mask shops started only in the early '80s, due to the resurrection of the Carnevale tradition, which the municipality dreamed up in 1979 as a way to draw tourists to Venice during what used to be the city's dead season. The mask business has grown so large that, while in the past it was enough to say visitors rarely left Venice without a piece of glass, now you must add "or a mask of some sort."

Scores of mask shops cluster around famous sights. You'll encounter countless sizes, colors, designs, and materials. Prices go up dramatically for leather and gilded masks, and you might come across expensive *pezzi da collezione* (collectors' items)—unique pieces whose casts are destroyed. In general, you'll get better deals direct from producers, so make a point to visit several of the largest workshops.

Ca' Macana, a large workshop offering lots of gilded creations, both traditional and new, is a must-see. ⊠ *Calle delle Botteghe, off Campo San Barnaba, Dorsoduro 3172* ☎ *041/2776142* ⊕ *www.camacana.com* Ⓥ *San Tomà.*

Il Canovaccio is a treasure trove of papier-mâché objects, panels, and masks designed for the theater stage. Mask-making classes are offered by appointment. ⊠ *Calle delle Bande, Castello 5369* ☎ *041/5210393* Ⓥ *Rialto or San Marco.*

★ **Laboratorio Artigiano Maschere** is home to Giorgio Clanetti, credited with starting the current revival in mask making; here you'll find the town's best masks of the Commedia dell'Arte, fashioned from papier-mâché and gold. ⊠ *Barbaria delle Tole, near Campo dei Santi Giovanni e Paolo, Castello 6657* ☎ *041/5223110* Ⓥ *Fondamenta Nove.*

Mondo Novo is a cut above most other mask stores and a real pleasure to browse through. ⊠ *Rio Terrà Canal, off Campo Santa Margherita, Dorsoduro 3063* ☎ *041/5287344* Ⓥ *Ca' Rezzonico.*

Fodor'sChoice
★ Family-owned and operated **Scheggi di Arlecchino** has windows full of the usual assortment of masks. What makes the shop distinctive are its masks inspired by the works of famous painters, including Picasso, Klimt, and de Chirico, to name but a few. ⊠ *Calle Longa Santa Maria Formosa, Castello 6185* ☎ *041/522 5789* Ⓥ *Rialto.*

Tragicomica has a good selection, and it's a useful resource for information about Carnevale parties. It also turns out a limited number of Carnevale costumes and hats made in hand-printed cotton fabric. ⊠ *Calle dei Nomboli, off Campo San Tomà, San Polo 2800* ☎ *041/721102* ⊕ *www. tragicomica.it* Ⓥ *San Tomà.*

Paper Goods

Twenty years ago there was only one *legatoria* (bookbindery) in town. Nowadays you find dozens of them, usually next door to a mask shop. Hand-printed paper and ornate leather-bound diaries marked with St. Mark's lion are hot souvenirs, and the young folks who run these shops come out with new ideas all the time, the latest invention being a glass pen to dip into colored ink (a matching ink bottle is, of course, available)—a necessary desk accessory to go along with your handmade writing paper, wax, and seals.

Antica Legatoria Piazzesi, the oldest bookbindery in Venice, used to make wonderful hand-printed paper using carved wood *stampi* (plates for a press), which the artisans carefully filled with colored inks. The stampi are on exhibit in the shop, and the last of this gorgeous paper is slowly being sold off. Due to the high production costs, this kind of paper is now only made to order. Although Piazzesi is a charming little place of great historical value, you'll probably find a more attractive selection in the new, more upmarket places. ⊠ *Campo della Feltrina, near Campo Santa Maria del Giglio, San Marco 2511* ☎ *041/5221202* Ⓥ *Santa Maria del Giglio.*

Cartavenezia stands out in the showy panorama of Venetian bookbindery shops. From handmade writing paper to cards and paper objects, everything is white here, so you'll be kindly asked to wear gloves while browsing. ⊠ *off Campo Santa Maria Mater Domini, Santa Croce 2125* ☎ *041/5241283* Ⓥ *S. Stae.*

Il Pavone, whose name aptly translates as "The Peacock," offers a great selection of *coda di pavone*, a kind of paper with colors and patterns resembling peacock feathers. Little prints with grapes, cherubs, and more peacocks make inexpensive gifts. The artisans here are particularly proud of their hand-painted paper. ⊠ *Fondamenta Venier, Dorsoduro 721* ☎ *041/5234517* Ⓥ *Zattere.*

La Ricerca is the biggest bookbindery in town. Here you'll find marbled paper, writing paper, bookmarks, leather-bound diaries, notepads, photo albums, colored prints of Venice to send as postcards, and even a medieval writing kit, complete with personalized wax seal. ⊠ *Ponte delle Ostreghe, near Campo Santa Maria del Giglio, San Marco 2431* ☎ *041/ 5212606* Ⓥ *Santa Maria del Giglio.*

Legatoria Polliero has the usual array of beautiful leather-bound blank books, desk accessories, and picture frames, at some of Venice's most reasonable prices. ⊠ *Campo dei Frari, San Polo 2995* ☎ *041/5285130* Ⓥ *San Tomà.*

Tabaccheria Grandesso stocks old-fashioned school writing tablets and notebooks, as well as period postcards. ⊠ *Campo Santa Margherita, Dorsoduro 2979* ☎ *041/5238626* Ⓥ *Ca' Rezzonico.*

Precious Fabrics, Lace & Linen

Not everyone knows that in Venice the tradition of weaving brocades, damasks, and velvets is still very much alive, with top manufacturers catering to royal courts, theaters, and the movie industry. With the tourist boom in the 1980s, the descendants of underpaid embroiderers opened up fine lace and handicraft boutiques. Prices range from €120 per meter for old-style fabrics woven on power looms to €1,500 per meter for handmade silk velvets of unparalleled softness and beauty. On the lower end of the price range are striking lampases, brocades, and damasks, which come in different floral and striped patterns as well as solid colors. Sometimes the fabrics are hand-dyed after they've been woven to obtain mellow watercolor effects. It's always worth inquiring about sales for discontinued designs—you might want to give a Venetian look to your favorite reading chair.

Although most of the lace sold in town is machine-made in China or Taiwan, you can still find something that more closely resembles the real thing in the best shops. Surprisingly, period lace (made between 1900 and 1940) is easier to find and less expensive than contemporary lace, even though the former is a finer product, made *ad ago* (with the needle), while the latter is made with thicker threads or *a fusello* (with the bobbin). A visit to the Museo del Merletto (Lace-Making Museum) in Burano will give you an idea of how lace once looked. Despite the reopening of the Scuola del Merletto (Lace-Making School), students and teachers no longer sell their creations in shops, but older lace makers might accept jobs on commission. The best way to contact them is to ask around in Burano (as they object to having their names put down in print), but consider that a 10-inch doily takes about 400 hours to make, and the price will show it. So go ahead and buy what you like, but do not believe any "handmade in Burano" signs.

Annelie has some lace baby clothing and a small selection of nightgowns and towels. ⊠ *Calle Lunga San Barnaba, Dorsoduro 2748* ☎ *041/ 5203277* Ⓥ *San Tomà or Accademia.*

★ **Bevilacqua** has kept the weaving tradition alive in Venice since 1875, using 18th-century hand looms for its most precious creations. Its repertoire of 3,500 different patterns and designs yields a ready-to-sell selection of hundreds of brocades, Gobelins, damasks, velvets, taffetas, and satins.

In the little shop near Piazza San Marco you'll also find tapestry, cushions, and braiding. Fabrics made by this prestigious firm have been used to decorate the Vatican, the Royal Palace of Stockholm, and the White House. ⊠ *Shop: Campo di Santa Maria del Giglio, San Marco 2520* ☎ *041/2410662* Ⓥ *Santa Maria del Giglio* ⊠ *Shop: Fondamenta della Cqnonica, San Marco 337/b* ☎ *041/5287581* Ⓥ *San Marco* ⊠ *Factory: Campiello della Comare, Santa Croce 1320* ☎ *041/721576* ⊙ *visits by appointment only* Ⓥ *Riva di Biasio.*

Capricci e Vanità, a small shop near the Church of San Pantalon, is where owner and lace-lover Signora Giovanna Gamba sells her wonderful authentic Burano lace. She specializes in tablecloths and lingerie made on the bobbin as well as more rare and precious pieces made with a needle in the extralight Burano stitch. ⊠ *Calle San Pantalon, Dorsoduro 3744* ☎ *041/5231504* Ⓥ *San Tomà.*

Frette sells high-quality sheets and bath towels—lace and embroidery are machine made, but the general effect is nonetheless luxurious and elegant. ⊠ *Calle Larga XXII Marzo, San Marco 2070/a* ☎ *041/5224914* Ⓥ *San Marco.*

G. Scarpa is an old-fashioned shop with no dressing room: you'll have to make do in a tiny corner behind a foldable screen. Its top-of-the-line silk lace shirts, from €40 to €50, are well worth the trouble, as are the lace cooking aprons. ⊠ *Campo San Zaccaria, Castello 4683* ☎ *041/5287883* Ⓥ *San Zaccaria.*

You need to ring the bell to be admitted inside **Gaggio,** one of Venice's most prestigious fabric shops. Bedcovers, cushions, tapestry, and the like are available, plus a line of delightful small bags made in silk velvet with dark wooden frames. The colors of the fabric are never garish—they tend toward mellow autumn tones. ⊠ *Calle delle Botteghe, near Campo Santo Stefano, San Marco 3451* ☎ *041/5228574* ⊠ *041/5228958* ⊕ *www. gaggio.it* Ⓥ *San Marco.*

Il Merletto, reached from Piazza San Marco by way of a private bridge, seems to make a point of putting on display just the low end of what's sold upstairs. To see the difference, ask for the authentic, handmade lace kept in the drawers behind the counter. This is the place to arrange lace-making demonstrations in Venice. ⊠ *Sotoportego del Cavalletto, under the Procuratie Vecchie, Piazza San Marco 95–96* ☎ *041/5208406* Ⓥ *San Marco.*

★ **Jesurum** is Venice's top name for lace and embroidered linen. Here you'll find an assortment of dreamy gowns and nightshirts, sheets, bedcovers, and towels ready to buy, or you can order yours custom-made. ⊠ *Procuratie Nuove, San Marco 60–61* ☎ *041/5229864* Ⓥ *San Marco* ⊠ *Merceria del Capitello, San Marco 4857* ☎ *041/5206177* Ⓥ *Rialto or San Marco* ⊕ *www.jesurum.it.*

La Bottega di Cenerentola, or "Cinderella's Workshop," creates unique handmade lamp shades out of silk, old lace, and real parchment, embroidered and decorated with gold braids and cotton or silk trim. The pieces on display are a perfect match for country- and antique-style furniture. The owner, Lidiana Vallongo, will be happy to discuss special orders. ⊠ *Calle dei Saoneri, San Polo 2718/a* ☎ *041/5232006* ⊕ *www. cenerentola.net* Ⓥ *San Tomà.*

La Fenice Atelier sells attractive lace nightdresses and handwoven bath towels at affordable prices. ⊠ *Calle dei Frati, down the bridge on Campo Sant'Angelo, San Marco 3537* ☎ *041/5230578* Ⓥ *Sant'Angelo.*

Lorenzo Rubelli offers the same sumptuous brocades, damasks, and cut velvets used by the world's most prestigious decorators. ⊠ *Campo San Gallo, San Marco 1089* ☎ *041/2584411* Ⓥ *San Marco.*

Norelene sells hand-printed scarves and clothing, either in solid colors or in geometric patterns inspired from the mosaic floors in the Basilica di San Marco. Tapestries and cushion covers are available and can also be made to order. Prices start at €100, but you can treasure a velvety souvenir for free: just step inside and ask for a business card. It's closed Sunday and Tuesday. ⊠ *Calle della Chiesa, near the Peggy Guggenheim Collection, Dorsoduro 727* ☎ *041/5237605* Ⓥ *Accademia.*

Pina Bonzio offers the usual array of inexpensive lace souvenirs, from handkerchiefs and baggy blouses to lovely bookmarks; the draw is that, despite the proximity to Piazza San Marco, the prices can't be beat. ⊠*Merceria dell'Orologio, San Marco 298* ☎ *041/5226791* Ⓥ *San Marco.*

★ **Trois** is one of those humble little shops often overlooked by passersby. But the Trois family has the exclusive rights to the "Tessuti Artistici Fortuny," the handwoven and hand-dyed fabrics "invented" by Mariano Fortuny, which are great for curtains, bedspreads, cushions, and more. The stunningly vibrant colors of these fabrics are all obtained from natural pigments. You can browse through a catalog of roughly 400 patterns. All fabrics are sold for the same price, currently €240 for 100 x 150 centimeters, a bargain if you consider that it takes each worker a full day to make 40 centimeters. ⊠ *Campo San Maurizio, San Marco 2666* ☎ *041/5222905* Ⓥ *San Marco.*

Fodor'sChoice **Venetia Studium** creates exclusive velvet fabrics in a splendid array of col-
★ ors and turns them into scarves, bags, stoles, and pillows of various sizes. They also make the famous pleated Fortuny dress and Fortuny lamps. ⊠ *Calle Larga XXII Marzo, San Marco 2403* ☎ *041/5229281* ⊠ *Merceria San Zulian, San Marco 723* ☎ *041/5229859* Ⓥ *San Marco* ⊠ *Merceria San Zulian, San Marco 2425* ☎ *041/5236953* 🖨 *041/5227353* Ⓥ *San Marco* ⊠ *Calle della Madonnetta, off Campo San Polo, San Polo 3006* ☎ *041/52713393* Ⓥ *San Tomà* ⊕ *www.venetiastudium.com.*

Venetian Floors

Another traditional Venetian craft is flooring made from cement and marble dust. One of the last surviving places where this centuries-old art is kept alive is worth seeking out for the dozens of different samples on display. You won't actually see workers laying out floors, but you can get a general idea of how the job gets done.

Benito Turco started making *terrazzi alla veneziana* (Venetian floors) when still in primary school, and he may very well be Venice's last artisan capable of laying down these gorgeous floors without the help of any modern machinery. One wall of his tiny showroom is covered with samples of many different colors, but the technique is basically the same: multicolored pebbles or marble particles are scattered (either at random or following a design for "carpetlike" effects) onto a bed of cement dyed with colored marble dust; the floor is pressed flat and left to dry, then polished to a high shine and waxed. The whole operation takes several months, but prices are not as high as you'd expect, due to the low cost of the materials involved. The logistics of getting a floor shipped are difficult, but not impossible. For most visitors, though, this is primarily a place to see a uniquely Venetian craft. ⊠ *Calle della Lacca, San Polo 2458* ☎ *041/5240999* Ⓥ *San Tomà.*

SOUTHERN VENETO

PADUA, VERONA, VICENZA, LAKE GARDA

7

FODOR'S CHOICE

Arena di Verona

Arquade, *restaurant near Verona*

Cappella degli Scrovegni, *Padua*

Gabbia d'Oro, *hotel, Verona*

San Zeno Maggiore, *Verona*

Villa La Rotonda, *Vicenza*

Villa Pisani, *hotel, near Este*

HIGHLY RECOMMENDED

SIGHTS   Basilica di Sant'Antonio, *Padua*

Musei Civici degli Eremitani, *Padua*

Palazzo Chiericati, *Vicenza*

Praglia

Sirmione

Teatro Olimpico, *Vicenza*

Villa Pisani, *Stra*

RESTAURANTS   Antico Brolo, *Padua*

Aubergine, *Abano Terme*

Il Desco, *Verona*

La Rucola, *Sirmione*

Taverna, *Rovigo*

Vecchia Lugana, *near Sirmione*

HOTELS   Aldo Moro, *Montagnana*

Armando, *Verona*

Majestic Toscanelli, *Padua*

Venetian Hostel, *Monselice*

Villa Cortine Palace, *Sirmione*

Villa del Quar, *near Verona*

Updated by
David Graham

THE ARC THAT STRETCHES WEST FROM VENICE to Verona and south as far as Rovigo falls under the historical and spiritual influence of its great seafaring namesake city. The region's architecture, paintings, and way of life all bask in the reflected splendor of La Serenissima, and much of the pleasure of exploring this area comes from discovering the individual variations on the Venetian theme, conferring special charm on the towns you'll visit.

Whether in the cities or the small towns, the winged lion of St. Mark, the emblem of Venice is very much in evidence, either emblazoned on palazzi or atop a lofty column. Long before its arrival, however, Ezzelino III da Romano (1194–1259), the larger-than-life scourge who was excommunicated by Pope Innocent IV and even had a crusade launched against him, laid claim to as much land as he could, seizing the cities of Verona, Padua, Este, Montagnana, and Monselice and their surrounding territory. After he was finally done away with in 1259, powerful families such as the Carrara in Padua and the della Scala (Scaligeri) from Verona vied with each other during the 14th century to annex these towns.

When not destroying each other, the noble families of the region bestowed on their progeny a rich legacy of architectural and artistic jewels, infusing the area with an opulence that is today the hallmark of Padua, Vicenza, and Verona. This trio of cities, though sharing the Venetian patrimony, has a diverse and multifaceted appeal, their individual characters well defined long before Venice arrived on the scene. Padua had established itself as a city-state during the 12th century. Its university, founded in 1222, counted Galileo among its teachers and drew the poets Dante and Petrarch into its orbit. In the 14th century, the cultural flowering found its most sublime expression in the frescoes of Giotto, a landmark in the history of art, and later in the painters and sculptors of the Renaissance, most notably Donatello and Mantegna.

Vicenza lays claim to a scion who was to have a predominant influence on the course of western architecture, Andrea di Pietro della Gondola—better known as Palladio, whose mark can be seen in practically every capitol in the United States. Not only did Palladio create new buildings, he grafted his classically inspired designs on the existing Gothic palazzi; his spirit prevails also in numerous villas in the surrounding countryside. In Verona, on the other hand, there's no escaping a much earlier epoch, for this was once a Roman city, its awe-inspiring arena the third largest in Italy. Here "circuses" still astound audiences, though the spectacles have moved on from the gladiatorial to the operatic, in the form of large-scale productions complete with animals. Among the performances, the Roman theater currently hosts an annual Shakespeare Festival, as who can forget that this is the home of that most fabled of love stories, *Romeo and Juliet*?

In the hinterland, redbrick castles and fortifications with fishtail or square crenellations bear testimony to the struggles of the medieval warring families. A better example would be hard to find than walled Montagnana—a town that changed hands 13 times in the course of its history—or Monselice, with its beautifully restored castle. Once Venice had established its presence in the region, a time of relative peace ensued, exquisitely marked by the blooming of Venetian palazzi and the works of masters. The three Ts—Titian, Tintoretto, and Tiepolo—have all contributed to the impressive heritage of the zone. These sophisticated traces of art contrast with the simpler delights of the Euganean Hills, south of Padua, where the unspoiled medieval village of Arqua Petrarca seems to exist in a separate dimension, unruffled by time's encroachments. A similar sense of peace reigns in and around Lake Garda, of which the German poet Goethe wrote, "I could have reached Verona by nightfall, but only a few steps away was this spectacular exhibition of nature, this stupendous panorama known as Lake Garda, and I simply could not tear myself away." Similar sentiments have been echoed by throngs of newcomers, who have added the joys of windsurfing and other lake sports to the delights of walking and taking in grand mountain scenery.

When Venetians took vacations, they made sure they did it in style, their retreats designed by the best architects and decorated by the best painters of the day. Needless to say, the architect Palladio was first choice for the job, and his work is nobly illustrated by the superlative Villa La Rotonda, near Vicenza, and at Villa Foscari, near Venice. For two centuries, villas in the style of the master sprouted up in prime locations, such as along the Brenta Canal. Many of these are now in private hands, but some open to the public. For requirements of the flesh, Abano Terme and Montegrotto Terme provide an excuse for pampering the body and rolling in mud, while the bustling fishing port of Chioggia is *the* place to savor fish.

Exploring Southern Veneto

Lake Garda and the trio of towns Padua, Verona, and Vicenza are easily and quickly reached from Venice by the A4 autostrada and the parallel S11 running west as far as Milan. Public transport is frequent and fast, with regular services from Verona, the jumping-off point for buses and trains to Peschiera and buses to Sirmione, both on the southern shore. The S249 hugs the lake's eastern shore and leads to Garda and Malcesine.

About the Restaurants & Hotels

In the main cities of the Veneto region, restaurants are generally moderately priced. In smaller towns and in the countryside you can find some real bargains.

The area around Venice has been playing host to visitors for centuries, and the result is a range of comfortable accommodations at every price. As with dining, common sense should tell you that the slightly out-of-the-way small hotel will cost you less than its counterpart in a bigger town, especially at trade-fair time. Expect to pay more as you approach Venice, since many of the mainland towns absorb the overflow when Venice becomes most crowded, such as Carnevale (Carnival, the 10 days preceding Lent) and throughout the summer. However, at no time do prices approach those in Venice proper. Padua, in fact, can be used in dire circumstances as a base for day trips to Venice. Be aware that prices in the Lake Garda area as much as double during high season.

Verona has a free hotel booking service through **Cooperativa Albergatori Veronesi** (⌧ Via Patuzzi 5, 37100 ☎ 045/8009844 🖷 045/8009372). Vicenza's **Consorzio di Promozione Turistica** (⌧ Via Fermi 34, 36100 ☎ 0444/964380) can provide information about hotel and restaurant discounts.

WHAT IT COSTS In euros				
	$$$$	**$$$**	**$$**	**$**	**¢**
RESTAURANTS	over €22	€17–€22	€12–€17	€7–€12	under €7
HOTELS	over €210	€160–€210	€110–€160	€60–€110	under €60

Restaurant prices are for a second course (secondo piatto). Hotel prices are for two people in a standard double room in high season, including tax and service.

7

Hard as it may seem to leave the unique beauty of Venice behind, the Venetian Arc is the perfect complement to a stay in La Serenissima. The towns are often beautiful, flawlessly mixing grand architecture and medieval ambience. One of these, Verona, has also produced one of the world's most tragic *storie d'amore* (love stories)—*Romeo and Juliet*—which it has never allowed visitors to forget.

You could visit most of the towns and cities in this chapter on day trips from Venice. A three-day itinerary would limit you to the principal cities. Five days would give you time to take in the cities and either the mountain scenery of Lake Garda or the group of smaller walled towns south of Padua, which you could combine with a visit to Chioggia, by the sea. A seven-day trip would allow a fuller exploration of the area embracing all of these possibilities.

Numbers in the text correspond to numbers in the margin and on the Southern Veneto; Padua; Vicenza; and Verona maps.

If you have 3 days

If you only have a short time, Padua, Vicenza, and Verona are the three cities that beckon, steeped as they are in art and architecture and all easily connected by the A4 autostrada. ⊞ **Padua** ❶–❻ ► holds the wondrous Giotto frescoes in the Cappella degli Scrovegni and the Venetian masters, Titian, Tiepolo, and Tintoretto in the nearby Musei Civici degli Eremitani. As you head west, ⊞ **Vicenza** ❻–❷⓼, the Palladian city, is home to the Teatro Olimpico, the oldest theater in Europe, with an alarmingly tilted backdrop. Try to find time for the Palladian villa par excellence, La Rotonda, close by. Continuing west along the A4, visit ⊞ **Verona** ❷❾–❹❺, whose awesome Arena offers a night at the opera, leaving time in the afternoon to browse among the fabulous shops along Via Mazzini. And you can't leave Verona without viewing that most famous of balconies, at the Casa di Giulietta.

If you have 5 days

Having visited the essential sights at ⊞ **Padua** ❶–❻ ►, ⊞ **Vicenza** ❻–❷⓼, and ⊞ **Verona** ❷❾–❹❺, it's only a short hop to Lake Garda, where the resort of ⊞ **Sirmione** ❺❶ has inspiring views across the azure water to the mountains from the Grotte di Catullo. Then head north up the lake's eastern shore to **Malcesine** ❹❾, where you can take a cable car up Monte Baldo for alpine views and fine walks. Spend your last night in ⊞ **Montagnana** ❻⓪ or ⊞ **Monselice** ❺❼, both walled towns with admirable castles; or, if you long for the beach, in the ⊞ **Chioggia-Sottomarina** ❹❼ area, where you can take a dip in the sea and then stuff yourself with seafood.

If you have 7 days

Spend the first four nights as outlined above. Next, head to ⊞ **Monselice** ❺❼, within striking distance of the equally atmospheric ⊞**Montagnana** ❻⓪ and ⊞**Este** ❺❾. From here, you can drive south to spend the night in the quiet inland town of ⊞ **Rovigo** ❹❽, with its 16th-century Palladian-style church, or spend some time exploring the Euganean Hills and the charming medieval village of **Arqua Petrarca** ❺❽ and pampering yourself at the baths at ⊞ **Abano Terme** ❺❺ or **Montegrotto Terme** ❺❺. Spend your last night in ⊞ **Chioggia-Sottomarina** ❹❼, with a celebratory evening meal at one of the fish restaurants of Chioggia.

Timing

To get the most out of your stay, consider coming in May, June, July, or September, when weather conditions are most comfortable and opera and theater are performed outdoors. Spring, the season of blossom, is always enchanting, and Lake Garda is especially enticing during the summer months, when there's always a cooling breeze blowing from the mountains and the water is comfortably warm. Summer also sees crowds, however, and neither will you be alone in such places as Verona and Sirmione during this period.

You'll have more elbowroom during winter, but the sights will have shorter opening hours, and hotels are often closed in November and February. This is also the season for fog, and you'll certainly find snow on the higher ground. Visitors in February or March, however, will encounter Carnevale shenanigans—Carnevale is not only the preserve of Venice—and you could find yourself sitting next to bearded nuns on the train, being served cappuccino by a long-tailed cat in the local bar, or smiling at a clown dining with a mouse at the next table.

PADUA

Bustling with bicycles and lined with frescoes, Padua has long been one of the major cultural centers in northern Italy. It's home to the peninsula's—and the world's—second-oldest university, founded in 1222, which attracted the likes of Dante (1265–1321), Petrarch (1304–74), and Galileo Galilei (1564–1642), thus earning the city the sobriquet *La Dotta* (The Learned). Padua's Basilica di Sant'Antonio, begun not long after the university in 1234, is dedicated to St. Anthony, the patron saint of lost and found objects, and attracts grateful pilgrims in droves, especially on his feast day, June 13. Three great artists—Giotto (1266–1337), Donatello (circa 1386–1466), and Mantegna (1431–1506)—left great works here, with Giotto's Scrovegni chapel one of the best-known, and most meticulously preserved, works of art in the country. Today, cycle-happy students still rule the roost, flavoring every aspect of local culture. Don't be surprised if you spot a *laurea* (graduation) ceremony marked by laurel leaves, mocking lullabies, and X-rated caricatures. If you plan to visit many of the local sites, consider a cumulative ticket, *Padova Arte*; at €14 it's a good deal, allowing entry to the Cappella degli Scrovegni, Musei Civici degli Eremitani, Palazzo della Ragione, Battistero, Scoletta del Santo, Musei Antoniani, and the Orto Botanico. It is available from the tourist office or any of the sites it covers.

Exploring Padua

The train station lies a few minutes' walk north of the main thoroughfare, Corso del Popolo, the bus station a few minutes east. The *corso* leads south through the walls into the heart of the city and the oval square, Prato della Valle, changing its name as it goes to Corso Garibaldi and, where it meets the university, to Via VIII Febbraio. The core of the city spreads north and west from here and includes the central squares of Piazza delle Frutte and Piazza delle Erbe. To the south, the Basilica di Sant'Antonio (Il Santo) and the Prato della Valle are within easy walking distance.

If you arrive by car, leave your vehicle in one of the parking lots on the outskirts or at your hotel, as much of the center is given over to pedestrians. Coming to Padua by autostrada, exit at Padova Est; there's a parking area in Via Tommaseo. Coming from Padova Ovest or Sud, park in Prato della Valle. Buses 3, 8, 10, and 12 go to the center. If you're staying in a central hotel, expect to pay to park.

a good walk

Start your tour at the **Cappella degli Scrovegni** ❶ ▶ for the Giotto frescoes. The **Musei Civici degli Eremitani** ❷ and the **Chiesa degli Eremitani** ❸ are close by. Following Corso Garibaldi will bring you to the university and its main building, the **Palazzo del Bo'** ❹. Stop at the Piazza della Frutta or Piazza delle Erbe for a quick bite from the market, or pop into one of the many bars and cafés around here before visiting the famed equestrian statue in the **Palazzo della Ragione** ❺, which straddles the two squares. Head west to the **Piazza dei Signori** ❻ to see the clock tower, and then on to the **Duomo** ❼ and the **Battistero del Duomo** ❽ to see Giusto de'Menabuoi's frescoes. Retrace your steps to the Via VIII Febbraio and stop for a coffee at **Caffè Pedrocchi** ❾; then head south along Via Roma and Via Umberto I to the spacious **Prato della Valle** ❿, site of the **Basilica di Santa Giustina** ⓫. From here, Via Belludi leads north to the monumental **Basilica di Sant'Antonio** ⓬, where you can mingle with the pilgrims and explore the **Musei Antoniani** ⓭. Next to the basilica are the **Oratorio di San Giorgio and Scuola del Santo** ⓮. Finally, take a well-deserved rest in the shady **Orto Botanico** ⓯.

TIMING You could easily spend a day following this walk, but if you don't want to stop at every sight, a half day will be enough.

What to See

⓫ **Basilica di Santa Giustina.** Two red marble griffins flank the steps of the unclad brick facade of this church, whose eight cupolas are reminiscent of Sant'Antonio's basilica. Inside are finely carved and inlaid 15th-century choir stalls and a colossal altarpiece, *The Martyrdom of St. Justina*, by Veronese (1528–88). Among the monuments are the sarcophagus that once contained the body of St. Luke, and in the Chapel of St. Luke, the resting place of Elena Piscopia, the first woman to receive a university degree. ⊠ *Prato della Valle* ☎ *049/8751628* ◷ *8:30–noon and 3–7.*

★ ⑫ **Basilica di Sant'Antonio.** Thousands of worshipers throng to Il Santo, a cluster of Byzantine domes and slender, minaretlike towers that gives it an Asian-inspired style reminiscent of San Marco, in Venice. The interior is sumptuous, too, with marble reliefs by Tullio Lombardo (1455–1532), the greatest in a talented family of marble carvers who decorated many churches in the area, among them Venice's Santa Maria dei Miracoli. The artistic highlights here, however, bear Donatello's name; the 15th-century Florentine master did the remarkable series of bronze reliefs illustrating the life of St. Anthony—whose feast day, June 13, draws pilgrims from all over Europe—as well as the bronze statues of the Madonna, the saints on the high altar, and the life-size bronze crucifix. The **Cappella del Santo** was built to house the green marble tomb of the saint and is now the object of votive offerings. Reconstructed in the 16th century, it shows Italian High Renaissance at its best. Note the nine panels of sculpted reliefs that commemorate the saint's miraculous healing powers. The **Cappella del Tesoro** (◷ daily 8–noon and 2:30–7) holds the not-so-pristine tongue of the saint in a 15th-century reliquary. In front of the church is Donatello's powerful statue of the *condottiere* (mercenary general) *Gattamelata,* which was cast in bronze—a monumental technical achievement—in 1453 and had an enormous influence on the development of Italian Renaissance sculpture. ⊠ *Piazza del Santo* ☎ *049/8242811* ⊕ *www.santantonio.org* ◷ *Weekdays 6:30 AM–7 PM, weekends 6:30 AM–7:45 PM.*

⑧ **Battistero del Duomo.** The baptistery next to the Duomo is more interesting than the cathedral itself. A prime example of Romanesque Lombardic art, the 1378 interior is covered with the finest example of frescoes by the Florentine painter Giusto de'Menabuoi (died 1397).

The vibrant cycle starts in the cupola with a depiction of Paradise and the *108 Saints,* a compendium of Paduan saints commissioned by the Carrara family to watch over their tomb. ⊠ *Piazza del Duomo* ☏ *049/ 656914* 🎫 *€2.50 or €1.50 with Padova Card* ☉ *Apr.–Oct., daily 10–7; Nov.–Mar., daily 10–6.*

❾ Caffè Pedrocchi. This neoclassical building was designed by Giuseppe Jappelli (1753–1852) in 1831 for Antonio Pedrocchi, called by Stendhal "the best caterer in Italy." Take the outside staircase up one flight to the *piano nobile* (first floor) for a delightful series of rooms decorated in a melee of antique styles—Etruscan, Roman, Egyptian, Renaissance—not to mention themed rooms such as the Rossini Room and the Herculaneum Room. ⊠ *Piazzetta Pedrocchi* ☏ *049/8205007* 🎫 *€3* ☉ *Daily 9:30–12:30 and 3:30–6.*

❶ Cappella degli Scrovegni (Scrovegni Chapel). Perhaps the most famous chapel in Italy after Michelangelo's magnum opus in the Vatican, this one was erected in the 13th century by a wealthy Paduan, Enrico Scrovegno, to atone for the usury of his deceased father, Reginaldo, as chronicled in Dante's *Inferno.* The fresco above the door, which depicts the dedication of the chapel, shows Enrico dressed in violet, the color of penitence. Scrovegno called on Giotto to decorate its interior, a task that occupied the great artist and his helpers from 1303 to 1305. They created a magnificent fresco cycle, arranged in typical medieval comic-strip fashion, illustrating the lives of Mary and Christ, allegorical forms of the seven deadly sins and the seven virtues, and the Last Judgment. The realism in these frescoes—which include the first blue skies in Western painting—was revolutionary. Today, in glorious restoration, Giotto's starry firmament glows in splashes of brilliant color. Entrance is only by reservation, which must be made at least two days ahead. Visits are scheduled every 20 minutes, and punctuality is essential. ⊠ *Piazza Eremitani 8* ☏ *49/2010020 for reservations* ⊕ *www. cappelladegliscrovegni.it* 🎫 *€11 or Padova Card* ☉ *Daily 9–7.*

Fodor'sChoice ★

❸ Chiesa degli Eremitani. The 13th-century church contains some fragments of frescoes—most, however, were destroyed by the Allied bombing of 1944—by Andrea Mantegna, the brilliant locally born artist. In the vestibule is a bronze copy of a *Pietà* by Antonio Canova (1757–1822). ⊠ *Piazza Eremitani 10* ☏ *049/8204550* 🎫 *Free* ☉ *Daily 8:30–5:30.*

❼ Duomo. Padua's cathedral was designed by a pupil of Michelangelo. The 17th- to 18th-century interior contains many paintings dating from the same era, as well as some 14th-century pieces in the sacristy such as *Virgin and Child* and *Life of St. Sebastian,* both by Nicolò Semitecolo (1353–70). ⊠ *Piazza del Duomo* ☏ *049/662814* ☉ *Mon.–Sat. 7:30–noon and 3:45–7:30, Sun. 7:45–1 and 3:45–8:30.*

off the beaten path

LA SPECOLA – See the astronomical instruments used by Galileo himself, and use the more up-to-date versions for observing the Italian sky at night. ⊠ *Vicolo dell'Osservatorio 5* ☏ *049/8293469* ⊕ *www.pd.astro.it/museo-laspecola* 🎫 *€7. Tickets must be purchased in advance from S. Michele Oratory (50 yards from La Specola) Tues.–Fri. 10 AM–1 PM, weekends 3–6 PM* ☉ *Guided visits Sat. and Sun. at 4 PM only.*

⓭ Musei Antoniani. To mark the 800th anniversary of the birth of St. Anthony in 1195, new galleries were opened in 1995 on the first floor of the church cloister building, with 300 exhibits relating to the image of the saint and of the basilica. ⊠ *Piazza del Santo* ☏ *049/8225656* 🎫 *€2.50* ☉ *9–1 and 2:30–6. Closed Mon.*

★ ❷ **Musei Civici degli Eremitani** (Civic Museum). The museum is housed in what used to be the monastery of the church and divided into three parts. The ground floor houses the **archaeological section** containing Etruscan, Roman, Egyptian, Greek, and early Christian objects. The **Pinacoteca** (art gallery) upstairs displays the work of Veneto masters from the 14th through 19th centuries and some Flemish and Dutch painters. Notable are the Giotto Crucifix, which was once in the Scrovegni chapel, the *Heavenly Host in Battle* by Guariento (1338–1368 or 1379), and the *Portrait of a Young Senator* by Bellini (1432–1516). The corridors are hung with 19th- and 20th-century prints and paintings, and the **Museo Bottacin** holds an important collection of more than 50,000 coins and medals. ⊠ *Piazza Eremitani 10* ☎ *049/8204551* ⊠ *Church free; museum €9 or Padova Card* ⊙ *Feb.–Oct. 9–7, Nov.–Jan. 9–6. Museum closed Mon.*

⓮ **Oratorio di San Giorgio and Scuola del Santo.** The San Giorgio Oratory and adjoining gallery are next to the Basilica di Sant'Antonio. The Romanesque oratory served as a prison in Napoleonic times. It displays frescoes dating from 1384 by two pupils of Giotto, Altichiero di Zevio and Jacopo Avanzo, that illustrate the lives of St. George, Catherine of Alexandria, and St. Lucy. The scuola, up a pretty stairway on the first floor, came into being after the canonization of St. Anthony in 1231; the present building was completed in 1504. The walls of the upper part are lined with frescoes, four of which are attributed to Titian. They depict the life and work of St. Anthony, including the saint reattaching the foot of a young man and bringing back to life a child who had fallen into a cauldron of boiling water. ⊠ *Piazza del Santo* ☎ *049/8755235* ⊠ *€2* ⊙ *Apr.–Sept., daily 9–12:30 and 2:30–7; Oct.–Mar., daily 9–12:30 and 2:30–5.*

⓯ **Orto Botanico.** The botanic garden was founded in 1545 by order of the Venetian Republic to supply the university with medicinal plants, and is one of the few Renaissance gardens to retain its original layout. The so-called Palm of St. Peter, planted in 1585, still stands, protected in its private little greenhouse. It was admired by Goethe (1749–1832) on his travels through Italy in 1786. Take time to wander through interesting hothouses, beds of plants that were first introduced to Italy in this garden, and the arboretum. ⊠ *Via Orto Botanico 15, a few steps south of the basilica* ☎ *049/8272119* ⊠ *€2.58* ⊙ *Apr.–Oct., daily 9–1 and 3–6; Nov.–Mar., weekdays 9–1.*

❹ **Palazzo del Bo'.** The 16th-century palace houses the **Università di Padova**, founded in 1222. The building, which now features an 18th-century facade, is named after the Osteria del Bo' (Bo' is Italian for "ox"), an inn that once stood on the site. The exquisite and perfectly proportioned anatomy theater was built in 1594. William Harvey (1578–1657), famous for his theory of the circulation of the blood, took a degree here in 1602, at the same time as Galileo was teaching. Galileo's *cattedra* (lectern) is still on display. In the courtyard there's a statue of Elena Lucrezia Cornaro Piscopia (1646–84), who, in 1678, was the first woman in the world to be confirmed with a university degree. If you're superstitious, don't jump over the chain in this courtyard, as, according to students, it will bring you bad luck. ⊠ *Via VIII Febbraio* ☎ *049/8273047* ⊠ *€3* ⊙ *Guided visits only. Apr.–Oct., Mon., Wed., and Fri. at 3, 4, and 5; Tues., Thurs., and Sat. at 9, 10, and 11. Nov.–Mar., Mon., Wed., and Fri. at 3 and 4; Tues., Thurs., and Sat. at 10 and 11.*

❺ **Palazzo della Ragione.** Also known as Il Salone, this impressive palace was built in the Middle Ages as the seat of Padua's parliament. Today its street-level arcades shelter shops and caffès. The **Salone** on the upper

ON THE MENU

SEAFOOD IS THE SPECIALTY along the coast, naturally—there's almost an embarrassment of choices. Both saltwater fish (sea bass, gilthead, sardines, eel) and freshwater (carp, trout, tench) are abundant, as are crustaceans. Inland, you'll encounter delicate and creamy risotto, radicchio di Treviso, and asparagus, all of which can accompany hearty grilled meat. (Don't be surprised to find horse meat on the menu and shops devoted to its sale.) Jewish influence has made its mark in such dishes as risi e bisi (rice and peas), sarde in saor (fried sardines marinated in vinegar, onions, pine nuts, and raisins), and bigoli in salsa (thick, rough spaghetti in anchovy sauce). Montagnana is famous for its deliciously sweet prosciutto and schizoto, an unleavened bread. Polenta, a creamy cornmeal concoction, is a staple throughout the area, served with thick, rich sauces or grilled as an accompaniment to meat.

The Veneto produces more D.O.C. (Denominazione di Origine Controllata) wines than any other region in Italy. The country's main trade wine fair, Vinitaly, takes place in Verona in April. The southern shores of Lake Garda and the gentle Euganean Hills provide optimum conditions for growing wine grapes. Amarone, by far the region's crowning achievement, is a robust and powerful red wine with an alcohol content as high as 16%. Valpolicella and Bardolino are other notable varietals. Ripasso is made from adding unpressed or partially dried grape skins to Amarone wines after spring fermentation and strikes a balance between the powerful Amarone and the more mild Valpolicella. The best of the whites are Soave; sweet, sparkling Prosecco; Pinot Bianco (Pinot Blanc); and Tocai (though the best of this variety comes from Friuli).

level is, at 85 ft high, one of the largest and most architecturally pleasing halls in Italy, covered by a wooden roof and frescoed with religious and astrological subjects. Inside pride of place is taken by an enormous wooden horse, a replica of the bronze steed in Donatello's equestrian statue of Gattamelata and originally built for a tournament held in the Piazza dei Signori in 1446. In the northeast corner is the Railing Stone where debtors had to sit three times repeating "Cedo bonis" (I give up all worldly goods) before leaving the city. At this writing the palazzo was being restored but entrance to the Salone was still possible and temporarily free of charge; call ahead to ask current status. ✉ *Piazza della Ragione, enter from Via VIII Febbraio* ☎ *call the main tourist office for info: 049/8767911.*

⑥ **Piazza dei Signori.** The large, sequestered square exhibits examples of 15th- and 16th-century buildings. On the west side the **Palazzo del Capitanio** sports an impressive **Torre dell'Orologio,** which has a fine astronomical clock dating from 1344.

⑩ **Prato della Valle.** Laid out in 1775, this immense space with a central oval park is surrounded by a canal along which stand 78 statues of local worthies. It hosts a general market on Saturday and an antiques market on the third Sunday of the month.

Where to Stay & Eat

★ **$$$$** ✕ **Antico Brolo.** Housed in a 16th-century building not far from central Piazza dei Signori, charming Antico Brolo is one of the best restaurants in town. Seasonal specialties are prepared with flair and might include starters like tiny flans with wild mushrooms and herbs or fresh pasta dressed with zucchini flowers. The wine list doesn't disappoint. ✉ *Corso*

Milano 22 ☎ *049/664555* ▤ *AE, DC, MC, V* ⊘ *Closed Mon. and 1 wk in mid-Aug. No lunch Tues.*

$$$ ✕ **La Vecchia Enoteca.** The ceiling is mirrored, the shelves are filled with books and wine, the silver service on which your meal arrives once belonged to a shipping line, and the flower displays are extravagant. In this luxurious ambience enjoy *branzino in crosta di patate* (sea bass with a potato crust) or beef with rosemary and balsamic vinegar, followed by a homemade dessert such as *crema catalana* (cream caramel). Reservations are advised. ⊠ *Via Santi Martino e Solferino 32* ☎ *049/8752856* ▤ *MC, V* ⊘ *Closed Sun., last week in July, first three weeks in August. No lunch Mon.*

$$ ✕ **Bastioni del Moro.** The genial owner devises his own recipes according to season, with vegetarians and calorie watchers in mind, although carnivores are well cared for, too. Gnocchi, eggplant, artichokes, and pumpkin all appear on the menu in different guises. For starters, you could try *tagliolini gratinati con prosciutto* (thin ribbons of egg noodles with prosciutto) or *gnocchi con capesante e porcini* (gnocchi with local fish and field mushrooms). The garden is put to good use in summer. Reservations are recommended. ⊠ *Via Pilade Bronzetti 18* ☎ *049/ 8710006* ▤ *AE, DC, MC, V* ⊘ *Closed Sun.*

$ ✕ **Ristorante Vecchia Padova.** The low-beamed and vaulted ceilings are hung with copper cauldrons, and a medley of antiques covers the walls. Locals flock here at lunchtime for the low-priced but good-quality self-service menu, offering three types of pasta, a range of grilled and roasted meats (and fish), and an extensive salad buffet. In the evening it becomes a fairly standard restaurant and pizzeria with waiter service. ⊠ *Via Zabarella 41* ☎ *049/8759680* ▤ *AE, DC, MC, V* ⊘ *Closed Mon.*

¢ ✕ **Brek.** Fast food Italian style: serve yourself from the hot and cold buffet islands and then dine comfortably at your table. This is one of a chain of individually decorated and efficiently operated self-service restaurants that have become the preferred lunchtime option for many city workers in northern Italy. Watch the pasta sauces of olives and tuna or ricotta and tomato being expertly created before your eyes over hot fire bricks; wait a few minutes while your steak grills, then choose from peppers, zucchini, and roast potatoes to accompany your meal. Brek is a satisfying choice for an easy and very cheap lunch or dinner. ⊠ *Piazza Cavour 54* ☎ *049/8753788* ▤ *AE, DC, MC, V.*

$$$ ▥ **Grand' Italia.** The art nouveau decorative detail on the outside of this superbly converted palace continues inside to the dramatic, sweeping stairway and curvy reception desk—both in sculpted marble. High ceilings, wooden floors, and elegant furnishings make the chic, modern rooms both spacious and inviting. Right across the road from the train station, this is an ideal base for visiting Venice. ⊠ *Corso del Popolo 81, 35131* ☎ *049/8761111* 🖶 *049/8750850* ⊕ *www.hotelgranditalia.it* ⬎ *61 rooms* ♿ *Bar, in-room data ports, in-room safes, minibars, cable TV, meeting rooms, parking (fee), some pets allowed* ¶◯¶ *CP.*

$$$ ▥ **Donatello.** Directly opposite the Basilica di Sant'Antonio, the Donatello has rooms with a view of the square and church, though the back rooms are quieter. The entrance hall is all mirrors, marble, and chandeliers, and gives direct access to the separately managed bar and restaurant out front and to the basement garage. ⊠ *Via del Santo 102, 35123* ☎ *049/ 8750634* 🖶 *049/8750829* ⊕ *www.hoteldonatello.net* ⬎ *45 rooms* ♿ *Bar, in-room safes, minibars, cable TV, parking (fee), some pets allowed* ▤ *AE, DC, MC, V* ⊘ *Closed Dec. 15–Jan. 15* ¶◯¶ *CP.*

★ $$–$$$ ▥ **Majestic Toscanelli.** The elegant entrance, with potted evergreens flanking the steps, sets the tone in this stylish, central hotel close to the Piazza della Frutta. Plants feature strongly in the breakfast room as well, and the charming bedrooms are furnished in different styles from 19th-century mahogany and brass to French Empire. ⊠ *Via dell'Arco 2, 35122* ☎ *049/663244* 🖷 *049/8760025* ⊕ *www.toscanelli.com* 🛏 *28 rooms, 6 suites ⚲ Bar, in-room data ports, some in-room safes, minibars, cable TV, meeting room, parking (fee), some pets allowed, no-smoking floor* ☰ *AE, DC, MC, V* ↿◖ *CP.*

$ 🏨 **Al Fagiano.** Close to the Basilica di Sant'Antonio and the river, this modest hostelry has basic facilities (some with shower only), an amiable staff, and a calm atmosphere. Some rooms have views of the church's spires and cupolas. ⊠ *Via Locatelli 45 35100* ☎ *049/8750073* 🖷 *049/8753396* ⊕ *www.alfagiano.it* 🛏 *30 rooms ⚲ Bar* ☰ *AE, DC, MC, V* ↿◖ *CP.*

¢–$ 🏨 **Casa del Pellegrino.** Facing the Basilica di Sant'Antonio, this rather austere hotel has something of a monastic air, with simple, fairly Spartan rooms arranged hospital-fashion off long, polished corridors. Rooms in the newer annex, 100 yards behind the main hotel, are more luxurious (and quieter), and offer more amenities, including air-conditioning. A cavernous restaurant downstairs serves cheap, simple fare. Breakfast is not included in the price. ⊠ *Via Cesarotti 21, 35123* ☎ *049/8239711* 🖷 *049/8239780* 🛏 *162 rooms, 115 with bath ⚲ Restaurant, bar, parking (fee); no a/c in some rooms* ☰ *AE, MC, V* ☉ *Closed last week Dec. to end Jan.* ↿◖ *EP.*

Nightlife & the Arts

The Arts

The **Auditorium Pollini** (⊠ Via Carlo Cassan 15 ☎ 049/8759880) puts on recitals and concerts. Ticket prices vary according to show. The **Teatro Verdi** (⊠ Via dei Livello 32 ☎ 049/8777011 ⊕ www.teatrostabileveneto.it) has a top-quality program of classical and modern theater year-round.

Nightlife

BARS **Limbo** (⊠ Via San Fermo 44 ☎ 049/656882) has a pool table and game room upstairs and live music downstairs. **Victoria** (⊠ Via Savonarola 149 ☎ 049/8721530) is a *birreria* (Italian-style pub) with live jazz concerts on Thursday.

CAFÉ **Caffè Margherita** (⊠ Piazza delle Frutte 44 ☎ 049/8760107) is the perfect place to watch the busy piazza and admire the nearby Palazzo della Ragione. It's closed on Sunday.

The ever-popular **Caffè Pedrocchi** (⊠ Piazzetta Pedrocchi ☎ 049/8781231), in a monumental 19th-century neoclassical coffeehouse, looks like a cross between a museum and a stage set, with rooms ranging in color from red to white to green. You can indulge in a full-scale lunch or just sip a cappuccino here. In days gone by it was a haunt for the city's intellectuals, who hung out all hours of the day and night. It's closed on Monday during the summer only.

NIGHTCLUB **Big Club** (⊠ Via Armistizio 68 ☎ 049/680934) has pizza and live music on Thursday and Sunday; on Friday and Saturday it becomes a disco. It's closed Monday and Tuesday.

Shopping

Markets

You could be forgiven for spending more time on the ground floor of Padua's **Palazzo della Ragione** (⊠ Piazza della Ragione) than in the gallery upstairs: it is the city's mouth-watering permanent food market, with shops offering choice salami and cured meats, fresh local cheeses, wine, coffee, and even tea. A fruit and vegetable market is held weekday mornings and all day Saturday in the **Piazza delle Erbe.** In the nearby **Piazza delle Frutte,** a general market is held Monday, Tuesday, and Wednesday mornings and all day Thursday through Saturday. Padua's Saturday market in **Prato della Valle** has a wide range of goods. An antiques market is held the third Sunday of every month with some 220 stalls—you're sure to find a bargain, but it's more likely to be '50s or '60s bric-a-brac than a genuine antique. **Padova Fiere** (Padua Trade Fair ⊠ Via Tommaseo 59 ☎ 049/840111) is the venue for conventions and exhibitions, including regular antiques and art fairs.

Specialty Stores

CLOTHING   There's no lack of fashion boutiques in Padua's center. You'll find many in the **Galleria Ezzelino** just off the Piazza delle Erbe. Close to the same piazza is **Paolo Prata** (⊠ Via Santi Martino e Solferino 42 ☎ 049/ 665508), specializing in women's clothes.

CRYSTAL   **Swarovski** (⊠ Via Cesare Battisti 15 ☎ 049/8753721), established more than 100 years ago, specializes in crystal miniatures with prices ranging from €35 to €125.

FOOD & WINE   **R. Vignato** (⊠ Via Roma 64 ☎ 049/8751320) is well known for its cheese, salami, olive oil, honey, and wine. It sells potato chips by the scoop, too.

JEWELRY   **Alberto Cesarotto** (⊠ Corso Milano 7 ☎ 049/8761550) specializes in designer jewelry and silverware with names such as Christian Dior and Gucci.

VICENZA

Vicenza bears the distinctive signature of the 16th-century architect Andrea Palladio (1508–80), whose name is the root of the style referred to as "Palladian." He gracefully incorporated elements of classical architecture—columns, porticoes, and domes—into a style that reflected the Renaissance celebration of order and harmony. His elegant villas and palaces were influential in propagating classical architecture in Europe, especially Britain, and later in America—most notably, at Thomas Jefferson's Monticello.

In the mid-16th century, Palladio was given the opportunity to rebuild much of Vicenza, which had suffered great damage during the bloody wars waged against Venice by the League of Cambrai, an alliance of the Papacy, France, the Holy Roman Empire, and several neighboring city-states. He imposed upon the city a number of his grand Roman-style buildings—rather an overstatement, considering the town's status. With the basilica, begun in 1549 in the very heart of Vicenza, he ensured his reputation and embarked on a series of lordly buildings, all of which proclaim the same rigorous classicism. Today Vicenza—one of Europe's biggest producers of gold jewelry and home to a diversity of light industry—is among the richest cities in Italy. This is readily apparent in the mod style of dress, the elegance of the shops, and the large number of late-model BMWs and Mercedes.

Exploring Vicenza

Vicenza can easily be covered in a day or less. The broad main street, Corso Palladio, cuts through the historical center, leading east from Piazza del Castello to Piazza Matteotti. Palladio's buildings line this street along with banks, offices, and elegant boutiques. The main square, Piazza dei Signori, lies to the south of the corso; from there it's an easy walk to the Teatro Olimpico. Make sure you save some time to visit the Villa La Rotonda, just south of the city.

a good walk

Two of Palladio's gems, the **Palazzo Chiericati** ⑯ ▶ and the **Teatro Olimpico** ⑰ across the road, make a good starting place for a tour of the city. From here it's a short walk along Corso Palladio to the church of **Santa Corona** ⑱, with works by Veronese and Bellini. Cross Contrà Santa Corona and go down Contrà Santo Stefano, site of the church of **Santo Stefano** ⑲ and its fine *Madonna and Child*. Head down Contrà Riale to **Contrà Porti** ⑳ to see the Palazzo Porto Festa, one of Palladio's works. Turning back toward the main corso takes you to the Palazzo Barbaran da Porto and Palazzo Thiene, which face one another across the Contrà Porti. If you cross the Corso Palladio and head for the Piazza dei Signori, you'll come to Palladio's earliest work, the **Basilica** ㉑, with the landmark **Torre di Piazza** ㉒ adjacent. Take a break for a drink at the Pasticceria Sorarù, some shopping, or for a bite to eat. The **Loggia del Capitaniato** ㉓, also in the square, is an unfinished work by Palladio. Passing through Piazza delle Erbe on the south side of the basilica, find the narrow Contrà Pigafetta for the **Casa Pigafetta** ㉔, from where it's not far to the **Duomo** ㉕. Retracing your steps, Contrà Fogazzaro is home to the Palazzo Valmarana Braga, with its armored statues in place of columns. For a further dose of Palladio, look for the majestic Palazzo Bonin Longare, at the end of the **Corso Palladio** ㉖.

Even if you think you've had your fill of Palladio, it's worth the half-hour walk or a quick bus ride south of the city center to see perhaps his greatest accomplishment, **Villa La Rotonda** ㉗, as well as the neighboring **Villa Valmarana ai Nani** ㉘.

What to See

㉑ **Basilica.** At the heart of Vicenza, Palladio's **Palazzo della Ragione** is commonly known as the basilica, though it was built to serve as a courthouse and public meeting hall. Palladio made his name by successfully modernizing the medieval building, grafting a graceful two-story exterior loggia onto the existing structure. Note that the massive main hall is open to the public only when there's an exhibition. ⊠ *Piazza dei Signori* ☎ *0444/323681.*

㉔ **Casa Pigafetta.** This ornate, red marble house was built shortly before the birth of the sailor after whom it is named. Antonio Pigafetta (1491–1534) was a crew member of Magellan's when the latter circumnavigated the globe in 1519. ⊠ *Contrà Pigafetta.*

㉑ **Contrà Porti.** A fine cluster of Palladio's buildings occupies this short street. The architect contributed a wing to **Palazzo Thiene**, at No. 47, which was started in 1484 and incorporates another Renaissance palace (1489) by Lorenzo da Bologna. At Contrà Porti 21, the **Palazzo Porto Festa** (1552) was begun but not finished by Palladio. With its mullioned windows, the strikingly Gothic **Palazzo Porto Breganze**, on the corner with Contrà Riale, is not Palladio's work, but his **Palazzo Barbaran da Porto** (1570), beyond, is the home of the International Center of Palladian Architectural Studies (CISA). On Via Fogazzaro, **Palazzo Valmarana Braga** (1566) is a perfect example of Palladio's ability to integrate his buildings with the surroundings. All these buildings can be admired from the outside.

㉖ **Corso Palladio.** The main street is lined with a succession of imposing palaces and churches that run the gamut from Venetian Gothic to Baroque. At the start of the Corso, near the Piazza del Castello, **Palazzo Bonin Longare** was probably built by Palladio's follower, Vincenzo Scamozzi (1552–1616), and has a good courtyard.

㉕ **Duomo.** Vicenza's Gothic cathedral is notable for a gleaming altarpiece by the 14th-century Venetian painter Lorenzo Veneziano (1356–72). The marble high altar could be an early work of Palladio as it comes from the workshop of Pedemuro, where he was employed as a novice. The cathedral itself was partly destroyed in World War II, but nearly all the damaged areas have been restored. The Romanesque bell tower stands apart from it. ⊠ *Piazza del Duomo* ☉ *Sun.–Fri. 10:30–noon and 3:30–7, Sat. 10:30–noon.*

㉓ Loggia del Capitaniato. Opposite the Basilica in Piazza dei Signori, this building was commissioned for the commander of the city and designed by Palladio, but never completed. The reliefs on the facade celebrate the defeat of the Turks at Lepanto in 1571. ⊠ *Piazza dei Signori.*

★ ▶ **⑯ Palazzo Chiericati.** This exquisite and unmistakably Palladian palace houses the **Museo Civico**, with a representative collection of Venetian paintings including Tiepolo (1696–1770) and Tintoretto (1519–94). Also noteworthy are the stucco relief *Madonna and Child* by Sansovino (1486–1570) and, in the Flemish room, another *Madonna and Child* attributed to Brueghel the Elder (circa 1520–69) and *Three Ages of Man* by Van Dyck (1599–1641). ⊠ *Piazza Matteotti* ☎ *0444/321348* 🖂 *€8 includes admission to Teatro Olimpico and Museo Naturalistico e Archeologico* ☉ *Sept.–June, Tues.–Sun. 9–5; July–Aug., Tues.–Sun. 9–7.*

⑱ Santa Corona. Begun in 1261 to house a thorn from Christ's crown, a gift from Louis IX of France, this church is said to possess the oldest Gothic interior in the Veneto. In addition to the Holy Thorn, which is kept in a gold reliquary and displayed only on Good Friday, it also holds an exceptionally fine *Baptism of Christ* (1500) by Giovanni Bellini (1430–1516) over the altar on the left, just in front of the transept, and an equally fine *Adoration of the Magi* by Paolo Veronese (1528–88). The high altar is a splendid example of 18th-century craftsmanship in inlaid marble and mother-of-pearl. The church was the original burial place of Palladio until his remains were transferred in the 19th century to the cemetery of Santa Lucia. The cloisters are now home to the **Museo Naturalistico-Archeologico**, containing remains of a Roman theater excavated in the 19th century and a natural history and geology section upstairs. ⊠ *Contrà Santa Corona* ☎ *0444/320440* 🏛 *Museum €7 includes Teatro Olimpico and Palazzo Chiericati* ۞ *Church Mon. 4–6, Tues.–Fri. 8:30–noon and 3–6, weekends 3–5. Museum Tues.–Sun. 9–5.*

⑲ Santo Stefano. This small church is worth tracking down for the fine painting contained within, the *Madonna and Child with Sts. George and Lucy* by Palma Vecchio (1480–1528), who was to influence Veronese's paintings. ⊠ *Contrà Santo Stefano* ۞ *Daily 8:30–noon and 2:30–6.*

★ ⑰ Teatro Olimpico. This is Palladio's last, and perhaps most exciting, work. It was completed in 1584 by Vincenzo Scamozzi (1552–1616), who was also responsible for the permanent set. Based closely on the model of the ancient Roman theater, it nonetheless represents an important development in theater and stage design and is noteworthy for its acoustics and the cunningly devised false perspective of a classical street in the permanent backdrop. The anterooms are all frescoed with important figures in Venetian history. ⊠ *Piazza Matteotti* ☎ *0444/222800* 🏛 *€8 includes admission to Palazzo Chiericati and Museo Naturalistico e Archeologico* ۞ *Sept.–June, Tues.–Sun. 9–5, July–Aug., Tues.–Sun. 9–7.*

㉒ Torre di Piazza. This slender tower at the corner of the basilica was built in the 12th century and is all that remains of the original structure to which Palladio made his additions. ⊠ *Piazza dei Signori.*

㉗ Villa La Rotonda. This is the most famous Palladian villa of all. In truth it can hardly be called a villa, since the architect was inspired by ancient Roman temples. Take the time to admire it from all sides, and you'll see that it was in turn inspiration not just for Monticello but for nearly every state capitol in the United States. The interior is typical of Palladio's grand style, with a distinctive use of negative space. It is a 20- to 30-minute walk from the center of Vicenza, along a pleasant route well away from the busy traffic. Go through the Palladio triumphal arch where Viale Margherita meets Viale Risorgimento and climb the steps. Turn left into Via Bastian, which becomes Via dei Nani and leads to the Villa ai Nani. A pedestrian path (Via Valmarana) then winds down to Villa La Rotonda. Or take Bus 8 from Viale Roma and ask the driver to let you off at La Rotonda. Note that the interior is open only on Wednesday, from April through October. ⊠ *Via della Rotonda 29* ☎ *0444/321793* 🏛 *€6; grounds only €3* ۞ *Grounds Apr.–Oct., Tues.–Sun. 10–noon and 3–6; villa Apr.–Oct., Wed. 10–noon and 3–6.*

Fodor'sChoice ★

㉘ Villa Valmarana ai Nani. A short walk from Villa La Rotonda, this 18th-century country house is decorated with a series of marvelous frescoes by Giambattista Tiepolo. These are fantastic visions of a mythological world, including one of his most stunning works, the *Sacrifice of Iphegenia.* The neighboring Foresteria, or guest house, holds more frescoes depicting vignettes of 18th-century Veneto life at its most charming, executed by Tiepolo's son, Giandomenico (1727–1804). In case you're wondering, *nani* means "dwarves": story has it that the villa was protected by the dwarf servants of a girl who used to live here. The dwarves were subsequently turned to stone, and you can see their statues all along the garden wall. ⊠ *Via dei Nani 2/8* ☎ *0444/54386, 0444/321803 for the Foresteria* 🏛 *€6* ۞ *Mar.–Oct., Wed., Thurs., and weekends 10–noon; Tues.–Sun. 2:30–5:30.*

Where to Stay & Eat

$$ ✕ **Antico Ristorante agli Schioppi.** Gli Schioppi is an attractive, family-run restaurant established in 1897. The low-key decor in the Veneto country style matches the simple yet imaginative cuisine. Begin with the Parma ham served with eggplant mousse and Parmesan. The *baccalà* (salt cod) is a must, as are the *petto d'anitra all'uva moscata e indivia* (duck breast with muscat grapes and endive) and *coniglio alle olive nere* (rabbit with black olives). Desserts include ever-so-light fruit mousse and a pear cake with red wine sauce. ✉ *Contra' del Castello 26* ☎ *0444/ 543701* 🖬 *AE, DC, MC, V* ⊗ *Closed Sun., last week of July–mid-Aug., Dec. 24, 25, and Jan. 1–6. No dinner Sat.*

$ ✕ **Il Cursore.** The front section of this cozy, 19th-century osteria is given over mainly to bar service, offering local wines and typical savory snacks like *cotechino* (boiled sausage) and *soppressa* (premium salami). There are some cramped tables against the wall, but the back rooms are better for a sit-down meal of local classics such as *bigoli* (thick, whole wheat spaghetti) with duck, spaghetti with salt cod and, in spring, *risi e bisi* (rice with peas). Desserts include the ubiquitous tiramisu and fruit tarts. ✉ *Stradella Pozzetto 10* ☎ *0444/323504* 🖬 *V.* ⊗ *Closed Tues. and last week July–Aug. 15.*

¢ ✕ **Brek.** See review under "Where to Stay & Eat in Padua," above. ✉ *Corso Palladio 10–12* ☎ *0444/327829* 🖬 *AE, DC, MC, V* ⊗ *Closed Mon.*

¢ ✕ **Righetti.** Simple, local cuisine is what keeps the locals coming back to this traditional self-service restaurant, especially for lunch: *orzo e fagioli* (bean and barley soup); pasta and risotto with asparagus, red radicchio, or *all'Amatriciana* (tomato and bacon); *stinco* (roast shin of pork); salt cod; and grilled vegetables or salads. Find a table and stake it out with paper placemats and cutlery, then line up at the food counters. Help yourself to bread, wine, and water on tap; after you've dined, tell the cashier what you've had so he can total up your (very reasonable) bill. ✉ *Piazza Duomo 3* ☎ *0444/543135* 🖬 *No credit cards* ⊗ *Closed weekends.*

$$$–$$$$ 🛏 **Campo Marzio.** This elegant hotel sits right in front of the city walls and is a five-minute walk from the railway station. The more expensive rooms are furnished in different styles; choose from Oriental, neoclassical, and floral themes. Many bathrooms have whirlpool baths. A special perk is the use of bicycles free of charge. ✉ *Viale Roma 21, 36100* ☎ *0444/545700* 🖨 *0444/320495* ⊕ *www.hotelcampomarzio.com* ➥ *35 rooms* ♿ *Restaurant, bar, bicycles, free parking, some pets allowed* 🖬 *AE, DC, MC, V* 🍽 *CP.*

$$ 🛏 **Giardini.** You're in good company here: the other sides of the central piazza on which the hotel stands are flanked by Palladio's Teatro Olimpico and Palazzo Chiericati, while the town center itself is just a few steps away. The hotel is tastefully furnished in modern Italian style. ✉ *Viale Giruioli 10, 36100* ☎ *0444/326458* 🖨 *0444/326458* ➥ *18 rooms* ♿ *Bar, in-room safes, minibars, cable TV, meeting room, some free parking* 🖬 *AE, DC, MC, V* ⊗ *Closed Dec. 23–Jan. 2* 🍽 *CP.*

$ 🛏 **Due Mori.** In the heart of Vicenza off Piazza dei Signori, this is allegedly the first hotel in town, dating from 1883, and is a favorite with regular visitors. It's light and airy, yet at the same time cozy. The rooms are individually furnished with antiques and wood detail in the bathrooms. Breakfast is not included in the price. ✉ *Contrà Do Rode 26, 36100* ☎ *0444/321886* 🖨 *0444/326127* ➥ *30 rooms, 3 without bath* ♿ *Some pets allowed; no air-conditioning, no room TVs* 🖬 *AE, MC, V* ⊗ *Closed last 2 wks in July* 🍽 *EP.*

Nightlife & the Arts

The Arts

MUSIC & THEATER The monthly *Informa Città,* available from the tourist office, will give you details of all events, including walking trips. Contact the tourist office for details of **Concerti in Ville,** a series of concerts held in nearby villas during June and July. Vicenza's **Teatro Olimpico** (☎ 0444/222800, box office: 0444/222801 ⊕ www.comune.vicenza.it) hosts a jazz festival in May, classical music concerts in June, and classical drama performances in September. Even if your Italian is dismal, it's particularly thrilling to see a performance in Palladio's magnificent theater.

Nightlife

BARS **Rebar** (✉ Via Zugliano 43 ☎ 0444/500151) has live rock, jazz, and funk on Friday nights.

Shopping

Markets

A daily fruit and vegetable market is held in **Piazza delle Erbe,** behind the basilica. A general market is held Thursday in **Piazza dei Signori.**

Shopping Districts

Shops center on the main Corso Palladio, Contrà Cavour, and Piazza dei Signori.

Specialty Shops

CERAMICS & GLASS A good place to pick up a gift is **L'Idea** (✉ Piazza dei Signori 56 ☎ 0444/ 542052), which sells contemporary ceramics and glass.

MEN'S CLOTHING For seriously elegant Italian men's fashion, step into **Pal Zileri** (✉ Corso Palladio 33 ☎ 0444/540768).

JEWELRY Vicenza is one of Italy's leading centers for the production and sale of jewelry. For gold, silver, jewelry, and watches at factory prices, visit **Cash & Gold** (✉ Viale della Scienza 14 ☎ 0444/965947), a complex of more than 100 traders. Buses 20 and 21 from the train station will get you there. **Fiera di Vicenza** (✉ Via dell'Oreficeria ☎ 0444/969111) holds a series of trade fairs selling mainly jewelry, pictures, ceramics, and coins. Most shows are open to the general public.

PASTICCERIE If you see a procession of people carrying beribboned packages across the Piazza dei Signori, you can bet they're coming from one of two great pastry shops. In addition to its wonderful old-fashioned look and great pastries, **Pasticceria Sorarù** (✉ Piazzetta Palladio 17 ☎ 0444/320915) is equally famous for its hot chocolate. **La Meneghina** (✉ Corso Cavour 18 ☎ 0444 323305), also with a delectable, quaint appeal, doubles as a wine bar.

VERONA

On the banks of the fast-flowing Adige River, enchanting Verona lays claim to classical and medieval monuments, a picturesque town center where bright geraniums bloom in window boxes, and a romantic reputation, thanks to its immortalization as the setting of Shakespeare's *Romeo and Juliet.* It is one of Italy's most alluring cities, despite extensive industrialization and urban development in its newer sections. There's an opulence in the air and in the shops that line the red Verona marble pavements with their enticing and elegant wares. Inevitably, with its lively Venetian feel, proximity to Lake Garda, and renowned summer opera season, it attracts hordes of tourists, especially vacationing Germans and Austrians, who drive over the Brenner Pass.

Verona grew to power and prosperity within the Roman Empire as a result of its key commercial and military position in northern Italy. After the fall of the Empire, the city continued to flourish under the guidance of Barbarian kings such as Theodoric, Alboin, Pepin, and Berenger I, reaching its cultural and artistic peak in the 13th and 14th centuries under the della Scala (Scaligeri) dynasty. You'll see the *scala*, or ladder, emblem all over town. In 1404, Verona traded its independence for security and placed itself under the control of Venice; the winged lion of St. Mark, symbol of Venetian rule, is another symbol often seen throughout the historical center. Verona remained under Venetian protection until 1797, when Napoléon invaded. In 1814 the entire Veneto region was won by the Austrians, and it was finally united with the rest of Italy in 1866.

Exploring Verona

With its small streets, secret courtyards, elegant boutiques, and comely air, Verona is an extremely walkable city. Please note that the Duomo and churches in Verona enforce a strict dress code: no tank tops, sleeveless shirts, shorts, or short skirts. You might want to consider buying the €5 combined ticket that allows admittance to most churches in town, including the Duomo, San Zeno, and Sant'Anastasia. Alternately, buy a Verona Card for one or three days (€8 or €12), which gains you admission to most of the city's major museums and churches as well as access to public transportation. Cars are not allowed in the historic center from 7:30 to 10 and 1:30 to 4:30. Numerous parking areas are found beyond the center, and one-hour disk parking (⇨ Parking *in* Smart Travel Tips) is permitted in the nearby streets.

a good walk

Start at the **Arena di Verona** ㉙ ▶ in Piazza Brà, the vast and airy square at the center of the city. Built by the Romans in the 1st century AD, the arena is one of the largest and best-preserved Roman amphitheaters anywhere. Take Via Mazzini, the main shopping street in town, to **Piazza delle Erbe** ㉚, a busy square surrounded by elegant old homes. The **Casa di Giulietta** ㉛, with the most famous balcony in Italy, is a block down Via del Cappello. Return and take a few moments to stroll around **Piazza dei Signori** ㉜, and admire the **Palazzo della Ragione** ㉝, **Loggia del Consiglio** ㉞, and **Palazzo degli Scaligeri** ㉟. Don't miss the **Arche Scaligere** ㊱, and, if you've time, take a trip to the top of the **Torre dei Lamberti** ㊲ for the view. From here it's a short walk to Ponte Nuovo and across the river toward the **Santa Maria in Organo** ㊳ and the **Giardino Giusti** ㊴. Then follow Via Santa Maria in Organo up to the Teatro Romano, site of the **Museo Archeologico** ㊵. The Romanesque **Duomo** ㊶ is just over Ponte Pietra. From there either walk down Via Duomo and Corso Sant'Anastasia to **Sant'Anastasia** ㊷ and then along Via Forti to the **Galleria d'Arte Moderna** ㊸. Or, turn toward the riverbank and stroll (or alternately take Bus 76) down to the 14th-century **Castelvecchio** ㊹, looking like a fairy-tale castle guarding the bridge over the Adige River. The stunning Romanesque **San Zeno Maggiore** ㊺ is another few minutes' walk downriver.

TIMING   It takes about an hour or two to walk the route, and four to six hours to see the sights.

What to See

㊱ **Arche Scaligere.** The impressive marbled Gothic monuments of the Scaligeri family tombs are set in the grounds of the church of Santa Maria Antica. Cangrande I ("Big Dog") looks down from atop his pinnacled

Verona

300 meters
300 yards

Via Santa Maria in Organo
Via Carducci
Via Trezza
Via XX Settembre
Piazza Fra Giovanni
Acqua Morta
Interrato dell'
Via
Lung. Re Teodorico
Lungo Sanmicheli
Lungo Bart. Rubele
Adige
Ponte Nuovo
Ponte Navi
TOMBA DI GIULIETTA
Piazza Independenza
Via Cappello
Ponte Pietra
Pza. Duomo
Via Duomo
Via Pigna
Corso S. Anastasia
Via Emilei
Via Stella
Via Leoncino
Corso Porta Borsari
Via Garibaldi
Ponte Garibaldi
Lungadige Panvinio
Via Mazzini
Via Catullo
Via Oberdan
Via Anfiteatro
Piazza Brà
Ponte della Vittoria
Lungadige G. Matteotti
V. Prato Santo
V. F. Anzani
Via del Mille
Via IV Novembre
Piazza Vittorio Veneto
Via C. Ederle
Via Menotti
Via Risorgimento
Viale della Repubblica
V. Arsenale
Corso Cavour
V. C. Cattaneo
V. Roma
Ponte Scaligero
STAZIONE F.S.
Ponte Risorgimento
Lungadige Cangrande
Adige
Rigaste S. Zeno
Via Cristoforo Colombo
v. Porta Catena
Via Tommaso Da Vico
Piazza Corrubio
Via Barbarani
Piazza S. Zeno
V.S. Pellico
Via Scarsellini
Piscina
Can. Camuzzoni

tomb—this statue is a copy of the original that stands in the Castelvecchio. Mastino II ("Mastiff") is buried to the left of the church close to Cansignorio ("Top Dog"). Look for the ladder motif on the wrought-iron grille surrounding the tombs. ⊠ *Via Arche Scaligere* ☼ *Visible at all times.*

Fodor'sChoice
★

Ⓒ **㉙ Arena di Verona.** Only the Colosseum and the arena in Capua can outdo this amphitheater in size. Just four arches remain of the arena's outer arcade, but the main structure is so complete that it takes little imagination to picture it as the site of the cruel deaths of countless gladiators, wild beasts, and Christians. Today it hosts, among other events, Verona's summer opera, famous for spectacular productions before audiences of up to 16,000. The best productions to see here are the big splashy ones that demand huge choruses, enormous sets, lots of color and movement, and, if possible, camels, horses, and/or elephants. The music can be excellent, and the acoustics are fine, too. If you book a place on the cheaper terraces, be sure to take or rent a cushion—four hours on 2,000-year-old marble can be an ordeal. ⊠ *Arena di Verona, Piazza Brà 5* ☎ *045/8003204* ⌨ *€3.10 or Verona Card; €1 1st Sun. of month* ☼ *Mon. 1:45–7:30, Tues.–Sun. 8:30–7:30, on performance days 8:30–3; last entry 45 mins before closing.*

㉛ Casa di Giulietta (Juliet's House). The balcony in the small courtyard will help to bring Shakespeare's play to life, even if it was built in the 20th century. Historians now believe that the couple had no real-life counterparts, but this hasn't discouraged anyone from imagining that they did. After all, historians are not as renowned for their storytelling as Shakespeare is. You can see the balcony without paying to enter. ⊠ *Via Cappello 23* ☎ *045/8034303* ⌨ *€3.10* ☼ *Mon. 1:30–7:30, Tues.–Sun. 8:30–7:30; last entry 45 mins before closing.*

Casa di Romeo. Folklore has it that Romeo's house was in Via Arche Scaligere, where at No. 4 a plaque marks the spot.

㊹ Castelvecchio (Old Castle). This crenellated, russet brick building with massive walls, towers, turrets, and a vast courtyard was built for Cangrande II della Scala in 1354. It presides over a street lined with attractive old buildings and palaces of the nobility. Inside, the **Museo di Castelvecchio** gives you a good look at the castle's vaulted halls and some treasures of 15th- to 18th-century Veronese painting and sculpture. Look out for the precious, 14th-century Via Trezza jewels, Cangrande's belt and sword in Room VIII, and the original painted walls of Room XI. In the courtyard Cangrande I stands imposingly on a pedestal. ⊠ *Corso Castelvecchio 2* ☎ *045/594734* ⌨ *€3.10 or Verona Card, free 1st Sun. of month* ☼ *Mon 1:45–7:30, Tues.–Sun. 8:30–7:30; last entry 45 mins before closing.*

off the beaten path

TOMBA DI GIULIETTA – Romantic souls may want to see the pretty spot claimed to be Juliet's tomb, near the river just a few minutes walk from the Arena. Authentic or not, it is still popular with lovesick Italian teenagers, who leave notes for the tragic lover. A small museum of frescoes is inside. ⊠ *Via del Pontiere 5* ☎ *045/8000361* ⌨ *€2.60 or Verona Card, free 1st Sun. of month* ☼ *Mon. 1:45–7:30, Tues.–Sun. 8:30–7:30; last entry 45 mins before closing.*

GIARDINI DI VILLA ARVEDI – Formal gardens surround a 17th-century villa 8 km (5 mi) northeast of town. ⊠ *Statale per Grezzana* ☎ *045/907045* ⌨ *€5.20* ☼ *By appointment only, minimum 8–10 people.*

41 **Duomo.** The ornate red-and-white striped Romanesque Duomo, dating back to the 12th century, has a grand organ and a wealth of decorative architectural detail, especially around each chapel. The first chapel on the left holds an *Assumption* (1535) by Titian. Fine reliefs on the 12th-century south porch depict *Jonah and the Whale,* and on the west porch are statues of *Roland* and *Oliver,* paladins of Charlemagne. ⊠ *Piazza Duomo* ☎ *045/592813* 🎫 *€2.00, €5.00 for combined churches ticket, or Verona Card* 🕙 *Nov.–Mar., Tues.–Sat. 10–1 and 1:30–4, Sun. 1–5; Apr.–Oct., Mon.–Sat. 10–5:30, Sun. 1:30–5:30.*

43 **Galleria d'Arte Moderna** (Gallery of Modern Art). The handsome Palazzo Forti was the 13th-century home of Ezzelino III and once provided lodgings for Napoléon. The gallery hosts contemporary painting exhibitions of well-known artists such as Marcel Duchamp (1887–1968) and Andy Warhol (1928–87). ⊠ *Via Forti 1 entrance vicolo Volto Due Mori 4* ☎ *045/8001903* ⊕ *www.palazzoforti.it* 🎫 *Fee varies according to exhibition* 🕙 *Hours vary according to exhibition.*

39 **Giardino Giusti.** Laid out on several levels around a 16th-century villa, the formal gardens are a symbol of things long gone. There's a fine view of the city from the terrace, from which the German poet and dramatist Johann von Goethe recorded his inspiration. Formal box hedges, cypresses, statues, fountains, and a maze provide a diversion from city sightseeing. ⊠ *Via Giardino Giusti 2* ☎ *045/8034029* 🎫 *€4.50* 🕙 *Apr.–Sept., daily 9–8; Oct.–Mar., daily 9–5.*

34 **Loggia del Consiglio.** This graceful structure was built in the 12th century to house city council meetings and still serves as the seat of the provincial government. Over the door is the inscription bearing testimony to Verona's loyalty to Venice and Venice's love for Verona, *Pro summa fide summa amor MDXCII* ("Greatest love for the greatest loyalty 1592"). ⊠ *Piazza dei Signori.*

40 **Museo Archeologico.** An old monastery above the **Teatro Romano** houses fine Greek, Roman, and Etruscan artifacts. The theater, built in the same era as the Arena di Verona and now restored, is still used for dramatic productions and a jazz festival. ⊠ *Regaste del Redentore 2* ☎ *045/8000360* 🎫 *€2.60 or Verona Card, free 1st Sun. of month* 🕙 *Mon. 1:30–7:30, Tues.–Sun. 8:30–7:30; last entry 45 mins before closing.*

35 **Palazzo degli Scaligeri.** This was the medieval stronghold from which the della Scalas ruled Verona with an iron fist. Admire it from the outside only; it's not open to the public. ⊠ *Piazza dei Signori.*

33 **Palazzo della Ragione.** The 12th-century palace has a somber courtyard, a Gothic staircase, and a medieval tower overlooking the piazza. ⊠ *Piazza dei Signori.*

32 **Piazza dei Signori.** Verona's great piazza has been at the center of things for more than 1,000 years, but the impressive facades and arched entrances surrounding it date from the early Renaissance.

30 **Piazza delle Erbe.** A Roman forum once bustled on this site and until recently it housed the daily fruit and vegetable market. The stalls have now gone, but the surrounding frescoed town houses still merit a visit.

45 **San Zeno Maggiore.** Possibly the finest Romanesque church in Italy is set between two medieval bell towers and has a 12th-century portal. The 13th-century rose window represents the Wheel of Fortune. Of special note are the 11th- and 12th-century bronze doors depicting biblical scenes and episodes from the life of San Zeno, Verona's patron saint, and Mantegna's triptych the *Madonna and Saints* over the main altar. San

Fodor'sChoice
★

Zeno is buried in the crypt, and a peaceful cloister lies off the left nave. ✉ *Piazza San Zeno* ☎ *045/8006120* 🎫 *€2, €5 for combined churches ticket, or Verona Card* 🕐 *Nov.–Feb., Tues.–Sat. 10–1 and 1:30–4, Sun. 1–5; Mar.–Oct., Mon.–Sat. 8:30–6, Sun. 1–5.*

38 Santa Maria in Organo. The choir and sacristy of this medieval church are decorated with inlaid-wood masterpieces by the 15th-century monk Fra Giovanni. A series of panels depicts varied scenes—local buildings, an idealized Renaissance town, wildlife, and fruit—that radiate a love of life and reveal the artist's eye for detail. ✉ *Via Interrato dell'Acqua Morta* ☎ *045/591440* 🕐 *Apr.–Oct., daily 8:30–noon and 3–6; Nov.–Mar., daily 8:30–noon.*

42 Sant'Anastasia. Verona's largest church, completed in 1481, is a fine example of Gothic brickwork. The Gothic interior contains numerous frescoes; the most outstanding are the richly decorative and glowing *St. George and the Princess* by Pisanello (1377–1455) above the Pellegrini Chapel and one by Altichiero (1320–95) in the sacristy. As you come in, look for the *gobbi* (hunchbacks), with holes in their pants, supporting the holy water stoup. ✉ *Piazza Sant'Anastasia* ☎ *045/8004325* 🎫 *€2, €5 for combined churches ticket, or Verona Card* 🕐 *Nov.–Feb., Tues.–Sat. 10–1 and 1:30–4, Sun. 1–5; Mar.–Oct., Mon.–Sat. 9–6, Sun. 1–6.*

37 Torre dei Lamberti. Standing 285 ft above Piazza dei Signori, this tower was begun in the 12th century and finished in the 15th. Taking the elevator costs only slightly more than walking up the 368 steps for the panoramic view. ✉ *Piazza dei Signori* ☎ *045/8032726* 🎫 *Elevator €2.10, stairs €1.50* 🕐 *Tues.–Sun. 8:30–6:45; Mon. 1:30–6:45.*

Where to Stay & Eat

$$$$ ✕ **Arquade.** Master chef Bruno Barbieri and his team present *nouveau* Italian cuisine that is a delight to both eye and palate in this highly acclaimed restaurant at the Villa del Quar hotel. The best tables are in the softly lit converted chapel, furnished with antiques. The creative menu may include such delicacies as baked scallops with sautéed Treviso radicchio, crunchy speck (smoked ham), and egg and vinegar custard, or suckling pig stuffed with lamb medallions served with new potatoes, confit of shallots, and fried quail eggs. The sommelier will then complement your choices with treasures from his wine cellar. ✉ *Via Quar 12 Pedemonte di San Pietro in Cariano, 5 km (3 mi) northwest of Verona* ☎ *045/6800681* 🖨 *045/6800604* ♟ *Reservations essential* 🖃 *AE, DC, MC, V* 🕐 *Closed Jan.1–Mar.14 and Mon. Mar–Apr.*

FodorsChoice ★

$$$$ ✕ **Dodici Apostoli.** Vaulted ceilings, frescoed walls, and a medieval ambience make this an exceptional place to enjoy classic regional dishes. Near Piazza delle Erbe, it stands on the foundations of a Roman temple. Specialties include gnocchi *di zucca e ricotta* (with squash and ricotta cheese) and *vitello alla Lessinia* (veal with mushrooms, cheese, and truffles). ✉ *Vicolo Corticella San Marco 3* ☎ *045/596999* 🖃 *AE, DC, MC, V* 🕐 *Closed Mon.; no dinner Sun. Closed Jan. 1–6 and mid-June–early July.*

★ **$$$$** ✕ **Il Desco.** Treat yourself to one of Italy's most renowned temples to its cuisine. The menu changes constantly, but entrées like *tagliolini al nero di seppia con piccoli legumi e seppioline* (pasta with new legumes and baby cuttlefish) and mains such as the *petto di faraone con purea di topinambur, salsa al ll'aceto balsamico e cioccolato* (breast of guinea fowl with Jerusalem artichoke purèe and a chocolate and balsamic vinegar sauce) proclaim the elegant style you can expect in this classic restaurant. The richness of the food is matched by the elegant decor, with fine tapestries, paintings, and an impressive 16th-century lacunar ceiling. ✉ *via Dietro San Sebastiano 7* ☎ *045/595358* ♟ *Reservations es-*

sential ⊟ DC, MC, V ⊘ *Closed Sun. Closed Dec. 25–Jan.10 and June 15–30. No lunch Mon. No dinner Mon. Jan.–June and Sept.–Nov.*

$$$ ✕ **La Greppia.** The classic decor with vaulted ceilings sets the tone in this bustling restaurant off Via Mazzini between the Arena and Piazza delle Erbe. The kitchen produces fine versions of local and regional dishes, especially *tortelli di zucca* (pasta filled with squash) and *bolliti* (assorted boiled meats served with a choice of sauces). Service is courteous and efficient. ⊠ *Vicolo Samaritana 3* ☎ *045/8004577* ⊟ *AE, DC, MC, V* ⊘ *Closed Mon., last 2 wks of Jan. and June.*

$$ ✕ **La Stueta.** This friendly trattoria is located between the Teatro Romano and the Giardino Giusti. Try the gnocchi *con la pastisada* (with a horse-meat sauce), *baccalà mantecato con polenta* (salt cod cooked in milk and served with polenta), or *maiale all'amarone* (pork shin in a red wine sauce with seasonal vegetables). Finish up with a homemade tart or mousse. ⊠ *Via del Redentore 4/b* ☎ *045/8032462* ⊟ *AE, DC, MC, V* ⊘ *Closed Mon. and 2 wks in July. No lunch Tues.*

¢ ✕ **Brek.** See review under "Where to Stay & Eat in Padua," above. ⊠ *Piazza Brà 20* ☎ *045/8004561* ⊟ *AE, DC, MC, V.*

$$$$ ⌂ **Gabbia d'Oro.** Set in a historic building off Piazza delle Erbe in the ancient heart of Verona, this hotel is a tasteful fantasia of romantic ornamentation, lavish trimmings, exquisite fabrics, and gorgeous period pieces. Rooms—each one different and more attractive than the last— have frescoes, beamed ceilings, pretty wallpaper, antique prints and furnishings, and canopy beds, some festooned with rosy-cheeked cherubs. You can relax outdoors in the medieval courtyard, in the leafy orangerie, or on the roof terrace. The breakfast spread (not included in the price during the summer opera season) is to die for. ⊠ *Corso Porta Borsari 4/a, 37121* ☎ *045/8003060* 🖷 *045/590293* ⊕ *www.hotelgabbiadoro. it* ⇆ *8 rooms, 19 suites* ⌂ *Restaurant, bar, in-room safes, minibars, cable TV, parking (fee), some pets allowed* ⊟ *AE, DC, MC, V* ⦿| *CP.*

FodorśChoice
★

★ **$$$$** ⌂ **Villa del Quar.** This tranquil 16th-century villa is surrounded by gardens and vineyards in the Valpolicella country, 10 minutes by taxi from the city. Architect Leopoldo Montresor and his wife, Evelina, who live here with their children, converted part of the villa into a stylish and sophisticated hotel. No expense has been spared: all rooms have marble bathrooms (some with whirlpool baths) and European antiques. ⊠ *Via del Quar 12, 37020 Loc. Pedemonte, S. Pietro Incariano, 5 km (3 mi) north of Verona* ☎ *045/6800681* 🖷 *045/6800604* ⊕ *www.relaischateaux. com/de/delquar* ⇆ *19 rooms, 2 suites* ⌂ *Restaurant, bar, pool, gym, massage, sauna, Internet, meeting room, some pets allowed* ⊟ *AE, DC, MC, V* ⊘ *Closed Jan.1–Mar.14* ⦿| *CP.*

$–$$ ⌂ **Torcolo.** The warm welcome extended by the owners, Signoras Diana and Silvia, the pleasant rooms decorated unfussily, and the central location on a peaceful street close to Piazza Brà and the Arena make the Torcolo a good value in its class. Breakfast, which costs an extra €7–€10, is served outside on the terrace in front of the hotel in summer. ⊠ *Vicolo Listone 3, 37121* ☎ *045/8007512 or 045/8003871* 🖷 *045/8004058* ⇆ *19 rooms* ⌂ *Some pets allowed* ⊟ *AE, MC, V* ⦿| *CP.*

★ **$** ⌂ **Armando.** Located in a largely residential area a few hundred yards southeast of the Arena, this bright, contemporary family hotel is a welcome respite from the busy city center just a few minutes' walk away. (Parking is easier here, too.) The rooms are decorated with light, modern furniture, and there are family rooms sleeping up to five. In the airy breakfast room downstairs, Signora Diana serves a hearty breakfast (not included in the price) of yogurt, fresh fruit, cheese, rolls and coffee, with melon and prosciutto in summer. ⊠ *Via Dietro Pallone 1, 37120* ☎ *045/ 8000206 or 045/ 8036015* 🖷 *045/8036015* ⇆ *19 rooms* ⊟ *MC, V* ⊘ *Closed Dec. 24–Dec. 31* ⦿| *CP.*

Nightlife & the Arts

The Arts

MUSIC &
CONCERTS

The beautiful **Teatro Filarmonico** (✉ Via dei Mutilati 4/k ☎ 045/8005151 ⊕ www.arena.it) puts on a varied program of traditional and experimental concerts, opera, and ballet attracting international artists. In addition, many churches put on concerts throughout the year.

In the first week of June, an **International Jazz Festival** (✉ Via Regaste del Redentore 2 ☎ 045/8077500 ⊕ www.estateteatraleveronese.it) is held at the Teatro Romano, with added venues in the Arena and Teatro Nuovo. The city is awash in cultural events in July and August—the Arena doesn't have a monopoly on all the entertainment. From Thursday through Saturday in both the afternoon and evening, free concerts called **I Concerti Scaligeri** (☎ 045/8077500 for information) take place in Piazza dei Signori. There's a wide range of national and international offerings, from Mozart to Gershwin, country to Indian ragas.

OPERA

FodorśChoice
★

Of all the venues for enjoying opera in the region, the best is probably the **Arena di Verona**. The season runs from July through August, and the audience is seated on stone terraces dating from the time when gladiators fought to the death, or in modern cushioned seats in the stalls. The opera stage is huge and best suited to grand operas such as *Aïda*, but the experience is memorable no matter what is being performed. Sometimes, while sipping a drink in a caffè at **Piazza Brà**, you can overhear the opera. Tickets can be ordered by phone, on-line, or from the Arena box office. *Fondazione Arena di Verona ✉ Piazza Brà 28, 37121 Verona ☎ 045/8051811 ✉ box office ✉ Via Dietro Anfiteatro 6B ☎ 045/8005151 ⊕ www.arena.it ⊙ Box office open weekdays 9–noon and 3:15–5:45, Sat. 9–noon. From June 21–Aug. 31, 10–9 on performance days and 10–5:45 on nonperformance days.*

THEATER

The Teatro Romano is the setting for annual summer events, including the **Shakespeare Festival** (✉ Via Regaste del Redentore 2 ☎045/8077201). From the end of August through September, strolling players perform Shakespeare's *Romeo and Juliet* (☎ 045/8000861 for tourist office) in the very place where the story is said to have unfolded.

Nightlife

DISCOS

Alter Ego (✉ Via Torricelle 9 ☎ 045/915130) packs a twentysomething crowd with a vague alternative edge. It's open weekends only from 9 PM to 4 AM. **Berfi's** (✉ Via Lussemburgo 1 ☎ 045/508024) is a popular and expensive spot. It's open from 8:30 in the evening to 4, Friday to Sunday only. **Penelope** (✉ Via Provolo 24 ☎☎ 045/597858) attracts a young crowd.

Enocibus (✉ Vicolo Pomodoro 3 ☎ 045/594010), one block off Piazza Brà, serves great wine and great food—and is no-smoking, a rarity in Italy.

Shopping

Markets

On the third Saturday of every month an antiques and arts-and-crafts market is held in **Piazza San Zeno**.

Specialty Stores

ANTIQUES, GIFTS
& HOUSEWARES

The area around the Gothic church of Sant'Anastasia is full of antiques shops, most of them catering to serious collectors. (After a strenuous day of antiques hunting, it's pleasant to picnic on the Piazza dei Signori.) Try **La Bottega del Tempo** (✉ Corso S. Anastasia 1 ☎ 045/8005999) for "portable" antiques: the shop specializes in watches and jewelry. Mod-

LOVE & DEATH IN VERONA

*"While Verona by that name is known,
There shall no figure at such rate be set
As that of true and faithful Juliet."*

(Romeo and Juliet, Act V, Scene 3)

SO PROMISED LORD MONTAGUE to Lord Capulet, as they ended the ancient family feud that doomed Romeo and Juliet to their tragic end. By the looks of things, he's kept his vow. Romeo and Juliet are said to have made their ill-fated match in the 13th century, and Shakespeare's play dates to the 16th, but no matter—English literature's best-known lovesick teenagers are even today the first couple of Verona, and they've turned this somewhat staid northern town into a mecca for romantic pilgrims with a literary bent.

Italy was a favorite dramatis loca for Shakespeare, and he set plays all along the peninsula, from Messina (Much Ado About Nothing) to Venice (The Merchant of Venice). No other city, however, wears its Shakespearean legacy as much on its sleeve as "fair Verona." In fact, the timeless story of doomed love was originally Verona's, not Shakespeare's—the tale of young lovers torn apart by feuding between the Montecchi (Montagues) and Cappellelli (Capulets) was first published in the 16th century by Veronese Luigi Da Porto, then popularized by retellings in French and English, one of which, Brooke's Romeus and Juliet: Being the Original of Shakespeare's Romeo and Juliet, by Arthur Brooke, is thought to have inspired Shakespeare's play.

Shakespeare's play, in turn, seems to have inspired Verona—or at least the tourists that flock there. Romeo and Juliet live on in the names of restaurants and hotels, and star-crossed-lover postcards and T-shirts are sold at every turn. The city hosts a Shakespeare festival every summer, with guess what play taking center stage? (Hint: it's not Two Gentlemen of Verona.) Some Veronese romantics have formed a Juliet Club, dedicated to answering letters for Juliet they say arrive from all over the world. Each year, they sponsor a love-letter writing contest on Juliet's birthday, September 16. The City of Romeo and Juliet basks in its reputation for romance, attracting flocks of lovebirds every year.

Starry-eyed visitors can stroll down not one but two Lovers' Lanes (Via Amanti and Vicolo Amanti), gaze up at the balcony of Juliet's house (Via Cappello 23), and dab moist eyes at Juliet's marble tomb next to the Museo degli Affreschi on Via del Pontiere. The more literal-minded will note that historians doubt Romeo and Juliet ever lived, much less loved, and that "Juliet's Balcony," built in the 20th century, is attached to a house that was not the Cappellellis' (although the Casa di Romeo, at Via Arche Scaligere, was indeed the Montecchi home). But what's in a name? What are authentic are the remains of the more than 700 defense towers and fortresses dating from the 13th century, testament to the real family feuding that took many more lives than Romeo's poison and Juliet's dagger.

ern, high-end jewelry can be found at **Canestrari** (✉ Via Mazzini 50 ☎ 045/594763), which is also a licensed repair shop. **Borsi** (✉ Corso Anastasia 2 ☎ 045/8005744) sells leather and footwear in one of Verona's historic shops.

CLOTHING & ACCESSORIES Via Mazzini is full of the well-known names—Maxmara, Versace, and Marina Rinaldi to name but a few. **Furla** (✉ Via Mazzini 60 ☎ 045/8004760) displays distinctive bags, watches, umbrellas, and key rings. **Pollini** (✉ Via Mazzini 64 ☎ 045/8032247) is nirvana for shoe collectors. **Prada** (✉ Corso Porta Borsari ☎ 045/8013861) features Miuccia's postmodern designs.

ENGLISH-LANGUAGE BOOKS The **Bookshop** (✉ Via Interrato dell'Acqua Morta 3/a ☎ 045/8007614) has a good range of English-language books and an English-speaking staff.

THE LAGOON & THE ADRIATIC

Crossing the lagoon from Venice over the Ponte della Libertà to the mainland, you'll be confronted with the sight of oil tankers and red-and-white striped cranes. Nevertheless, it can make a less-hectic and less-expensive base for exploring the Veneto and Venice itself, which is a mere 10 minutes away by bus or train, and some attractive hotels and restaurants are worth seeking out. What's more, you'll have no parking problems here. Crossing the flat expanse of the lagoon from Venice in the other (southerly) direction brings you to Chioggia, scene of a decisive naval battle between the rival sea powers Venice and Genoa in 1379. Now a bustling fishing port, it's based on a grid alleyway system and has excellent fish restaurants. The long strip of beach at nearby Sottomarina makes it a popular vacation spot for Italians. Rovigo, an inland town due south of Padua on A16, is a working city that's not geared up for tourists, but it does have a good art gallery and its own fine Rotonda. The area between Rovigo and the sea, the Po delta, with its slow-moving rivers, fields, and marshes, offers opportunities for quiet walks, bird-watching, and contemplation.

Mestre

46 *9 km (5½ mi) northwest of Venice.*

The Italian playwright Carlo Goldini (1707–93) likened Mestre to a "little Versailles"—but that was in the days when the Venetians were building numerous villas in the area for their country retreats and rural enjoyment. Since then, and particularly with the development of the port at Marghera in 1919, Mestre has become the focus for industrial development and the destination for an exodus of Venetians forced out by high rents and sinking houses. Although in many ways it is the town where the "real Venetians" now live, Mestre hardly fits the tourist idea of Italy. Most of it is more '70s-style suburb than culture-infused outskirt. However, the small historic center still reveals a few remnants of the medieval defense system: the tower in the main square, Piazza Ferretto; the 14th-century **Scuola dei Battuti**, now a retirement home; and the **Torre dell'Orologio** in Piazzetta Mattei. This brick tower with typical dovetail battlements dates from 1100, but the clock was added in the 16th century. Via Palazzo, the main street, makes for a pleasant stroll, lined as it is with arcaded buildings from the 16th to the 20th century. Note that the train station is marked "Venezia Mestre."

Where to Stay & Eat

$ ✕ **La Pergola.** The rustic atmosphere in this convivial *osteria* is a welcome break from Mestre's brash modernity. You can take a break from the usual seafood of the Venice area here, too: the menu is strictly meat. The seasonal selection may include starters like *orechiette con broccoli e pancetta crocante* (pasta with broccoli and crunchy bacon) and mains such as *sella di maialino da latte al forno* (roast saddle of suckling pig). ⊠ *Via Fiume 42* ☎ *041/974932* ⊟ *MC, V* ⊘ *Closed Sun. No lunch Sat.*

$–$$ ⊡ **Cris.** Completely restored and modernized in 2002, the Cris is still excellent value for a cheaper visit to Venice. This charming, green-shuttered building is on a quiet side-street just 200 yards from the train station and a ten-minute walk from Mestre city center. There is access for disabled guests, and the entire hotel is strictly no-smoking. ⊠ *Via Montenero 3, 30171* ☎ *041/926773* ⊟ *041/937106* ⊕ *www.hotelcris.it* ⊅ *18 rooms* ♿ *Bar, in-room data ports, free parking; no smoking* ⊟ *MC, V* ⦿ *CP.*

$ ▦ **Vivit.** Many of the rooms look directly out over one of the few historic parts of Mestre: its main piazza and medieval tower. This area and much of the rest of this busy city center are closed to traffic, so from here you can walk almost everywhere. The bar on the first floor has a cool terrace for relaxing away from the crowds and for enjoying an *al fresco* breakfast in summer. ⊠ *Piazza Ferretto 73, 30174* ☎ *041/951385* 🖨 *041/958891* ⊕ *www.hotelvivit.com* 🛏 *33 rooms, 2 suites* ♨ *Bar, in-room data ports, in-room safes, minibars, cable TV, free parking, no-smoking rooms* ☰ *AE, DC, MC, V* ⦿| *CP.*

Chioggia-Sottomarina

㊼ *44 km (27 mi) south of Mestre, 35 km (22 mi) south of Venice.*

Only a thin strip of the lagoon separates Chioggia from Sottomarina, but they're as different as chalk from cheese. If you skip the outskirts of Chioggia (after Venice it's the largest settlement on the lagoon), you'll find a gridded series of *calli* (alleyways) and a busy fishing port. Cross the Ponte Translagunare and you'll come to Sottomarina, with 9 km (5 ½ mi) of beach stretching to the river Brenta, and all the glitz of a popular resort. A regular public transport service (No. 11) involving two ferries and two buses leaves hourly from Chioggia for Venice's Lido, offering both an enjoyable lagoon trip and a cheap visit to Venice. In summer a direct service is operated privately. Contact the **Chioggia tourist office** (⊠ *Lungomare Adriatico 101, 30019 Chioggia* ☎ *041/401068*) for details. Practically all the hotels are situated in Sottomarina; you'll find the good restaurants in Chioggia.

Chioggia suffered terrible destruction from 1379 to 1380, when the Republics of Genoa and Venice clashed in the bid for supremacy of the Adriatic Sea, from which Venice emerged triumphant. The city then enjoyed a long period of calm under the sway of Venice until Napoléon arrived on the scene in 1797. Topped by the ubiquitous symbol of Venice, St. Mark's lion (irreverently known as "the cat"), the **Vigo Column** marks the eastern end of wide Corso del Popolo, which runs the length of the town and along which you'll find the main monuments. It's impossible to get lost in this grid plan. Parallel to the Corso, the Canale Vena is spanned by eight bridges, the most picturesque of which is the **Ponte Vigo** at the eastern end, Chioggia's version of the Rialto. Take an hour or so to stroll along the main drag, or poke around the fish market (held Tuesday through Saturday) and the narrow alleys with gently flapping washing strung across their balconies.

Walking down the corso from the Vigo column, you'll pass the 18th-century church of **Sant'Andrea.** After going by Sant'Andrea, you'll soon arrive at the **Palazzo del Granaio** (1322), formerly the town granary and one of the few buildings to have survived the sea battle. A niche on the facade has a *Madonna and Child* by the sculptor Jacopo Sansovino (1486–1570). The **Chiesa della Santa Trinità** contains paintings by the schools of Tintoretto and Veronese. ⊠ *Piazzetta XX Settembre* ⊙ *Open for Mass.*

The Romanesque bell tower predates the **Duomo** designed by Baldassare Longhena (1604–82). The interior holds some fine 18th-century paintings including work by Piazzetta (1683–1754) and Tiepolo (1696–1770). ⊠ *Piazza del Duomo 77* ☎ *041/400496* ⊙ *Daily 7–noon and 4–6.*

San Domenico has stood on a little island of the same name since 1745. The church's high altar is dominated by a 12-ft-high wooden crucifix said to have been carved by fishermen. Found within are the last work of Vittore Carpaccio (1455–1526), *San Paolo,* along with the *Appari-*

tion of Jesus to St. Thomas Aquinas by Tintoretto (1518–94). ✉ *Fondamenta San Domenico* ☎ *041/403526* ◷ *Call to check opening hrs.*

The **Museo Civico** is housed in the former monastery of San Francesco Fuori le Mura, and the collection illustrates the history of lagoon life, with a number of traditional boats on display. ✉ *Campo Marconi* ☎ *041/5500911* ✑ *€3.50* ◷ *Tues.–Wed. 9–1; Thurs.–Sun. 9–1 and 3–6.*

At the Sottomarina end of the bridge, the Venetian-Gothic church of **San Martino** was built by the townspeople after the battle of 1379. It holds two polyptychs by Veronese. ✉ *Piazza Ballarin* ☎ *041/40054* ◷ *Daily 7–noon and 4–7:30.*

It's not churches but hotels that are the dominant feature in this part of town. They stretch out along the **Lungomare Adriatico**, scene of a permanent *passeggiata* (stroll), even in winter. The beach is visible from the upstairs windows of hotels but not from the road, so encumbered is it with a barrier of buildings. You'll have to pay to get on the beach unless you walk to the far west end, though many hotels will have their own strip for guests. You'll find the usual crop of discos, swimming pools, bars, entertainment, opportunities for horseback riding, sailing, boat trips, and a teeming nightlife with karaoke on the beach and outdoor films. In summer, classical concerts are held in the town's churches and in the museum garden.

Where to Stay & Eat

$$ ✕ **Antico Toro.** In bygone days, a great spectacle at Carnevale time was to let 12 ferocious dogs chase a bull that was customarily housed in this restaurant before its release. Don't worry, though, if you see *al toro* on the menu; you won't be getting bull, just a special fish sauce. It comes with *gnocchetti* (little potato dumplings). The spaghetti with vongole or *granseola* (spider crabs) is worth fighting for. ✉ *Corso del Popolo 1306* ☎ *041/400560* ⚷ *Reservations essential* ▭ *AE, DC, MC, V* ◷ *Closed Wed. and Nov.*

$–$$ ✕ **Ai Vaporetti.** This restaurant overlooks the lagoon and Ponte Lagunale: a perfect spot for a summer evening. Downstairs, the whole of the ceiling is covered by a canvas fishing boat's sail, and above the intimate alcoves is a mezzanine level with a wrought-iron balcony. The menu is restricted to fish cooked over a wood fire. You could go for the eels, or maybe the clams in tomato sauce. There's a good local wine list. ✉ *Campo Traghetto 1256* ☎ *041/400841* ⚷ *Reservations essential* ▭ *AE, DC, MC, V* ◷ *Closed Tues. and 3 wks in Nov.*

$–$$ ✕ **Bella Venezia.** In summer you can eat in the courtyard amid the glory of the plants. The chef recommends *branzino al carpaccio* (marinated slices of raw sea bass) and *bianco nero alla scoglio* (a mix of cuttlefish-ink pasta with shrimp, clams, and squid), a specialty to this area. Try chilled port or grappa with it. ✉ *Calle Corona 51* ☎ *041/400500* ⚷ *Reservations essential* ▭ *AE, DC, MC, V* ◷ *Closed Thurs. and Jan. No dinner Wed. and Oct.–Feb.*

$–$$ ✕ **El Gato.** Signor Silvano cooks the vegetables grown in his own garden and Signora Alba is an old hand at the *dolci* (desserts). It's a winning combination. Try a creamy risotto with shrimp or fish, *cappellacci* ("little hat" pasta) with a fish sauce, and the linguine *con molluschi* (with smoky-tasting shellfish). The brick arches and wooden ceiling give a rustic air to the proceedings. ✉ *Campo Sant'Andrea 653* ☎ *041/401806* ⊕ *www.elgato.it* ⚷ *Reservations essential* ▭ *AE, DC, MC, V* ◷ *Closed Mon. and late Jan.–mid-Feb. No lunch Tues.*

$$–$$$ ⊞ **Grande Italia.** An important waterside landmark in Chioggia since 1914, the Grande marks the beginning of town from the lagoon side. Facing directly onto the *ponte Vigo*, its elegantly furnished rooms look

out over the sea on one side or down the pedestrian-only *Corso* on the other. Spacious, marble-lined bathrooms add a real sense of luxury to a hotel that is perfectly placed for visiting Venice: a one-hour ferry ride up the lagoon. The very renowned (and expensive) restaurant closes on Tuesday. ⊠ *Rione Sant'Andrea 597, 30015* ☎ *041/400515* 🖷 *041/400185* ⊕ *www.hotelgrandeitalia.com* ⮑ *49 rooms, 8 suites* ♿ *Restaurant, bar, health club, sauna, parking (fee)* 🖃 *AE, DC, MC, V* ⍟ *CP.*

$$ 🖹 **Bristol.** Of the many hotels along the Lungomare, this is one of the most tasteful and spacious, with service that does not take itself too seriously. All rooms have a terrace and sea view. There's an opulent restaurant, and piano accompaniment in the evenings. ⊠ *Lungomare Adriatico 46, 30019* ☎ *041/5540389* 🖷 *041/5541813* ⊕ *www.hotelbristol.net* ⮑ *70 rooms* ♿ *Restaurant, in-room safes, minibars, cable TV, pool, beach, piano bar, children's programs (all ages), meeting rooms, free parking, some pets allowed, no-smoking rooms* 🖃 *AE, DC, MC, V* ⍟ *CP.*

$ 🖹 **Airone.** Another high-rise, beach-front hotel, the Airone is set back a little from the road. The big lobby is all bright yellows and blues, and gives onto a relaxing restaurant and lively bar overlooking the pool. There's a private section of beach for guests, and some rooms have sea views. This is essentially a family hotel, offering an array of holiday programs and entertainment. ⊠ *Via Lungomare Adriatico 50, 30019* ☎ *041/492266* 🖷 *041/5541325* ⊕ *www.boscolo.com* ⮑ *97 rooms* ♿ *Restaurant, bar, in-room safes, minibars, pool, beach, children's programs (all ages), laundry service, meeting rooms, free parking, some pets allowed, no-smoking rooms* 🖃 *AE, DC, MC, V* ⍟ *CP.*

¢–$ 🖹 **Stella d'Italia.** Set back a little from the Lungomare and full of clutter and greenery, this is one of the smaller hotels to stay open all year, so it's always busy and most likely full of children. It's a 'no-frills' hotel, but all rooms have air-conditioning and the price goes down the longer you stay. ⊠ *Viale Veneto 37, 30019* ☎ *041/400600* 🖷 *041/400322* ⊕ *www.hotelstelladitalia.net* ⮑ *40 rooms* ♿ *Restaurant, bar, free parking* 🖃 *AE, DC, MC, V* ⍟ *CP.*

Nightlife & the Arts

FESTIVALS The Palio **La Maciliana** takes place in the third week of June with medieval fun and games. The **Sagra del Pesce** (Fish Festival; ⊠ tourist office: Lungomare Adriatico 101, 30019 Chioggia ☎ 041/40106) celebrates the lagoon's bounty the third week in July, with fish-tasting, music, poetry, and theater.

Sports & the Outdoors

BOATING **Rendez-vous Fantasia** (⊠ Via San Marco 1720 ☎☎ 041/5540016) rents houseboats by the week. For sailing boats with or without a skipper, contact **Morgan Yachting** (⊠ Viale Trieste 31/a ☎ 0335 5606251 cell), which also runs short cruises in July and August.

Rovigo

➍ *70 km (44 mi) southwest of Venice, 53 km (33 mi) southwest of Chioggia-Sottomarina.*

Between Chioggia and Rovigo the land is flat, given over to market gardening and agriculture. Rovigo itself is a fairly quiet, personable town that is noticeably less prosperous than its northern neighbors, reflected in generally lower prices, especially for accommodation. Join the farmers doing their town business in the wood-panelled **Caffè Borsa** (⊠ Piazza Garibaldi 2 ☎ 0425/21999) for an espresso and snack. It's closed Thursday. If you're in the center of the city, the first thing to catch your eye will most likely be the **Torre Dona**, one of the tallest towers in Italy, and the **Torre Mozza,** the one remaining tower of the castle built in 920 by the Bishop of Adria. Both appear to be rather alarmingly out of kilter. Like other towns and cities in the area, Rovigo submitted to the yoke of Venice, which controlled the town from 1482 until the end of the Republic.

The main **Piazza Vittorio Emanuele II** holds some fine palaces, including the **Palazzo Roncale** designed in 1555 by Sanmichele (1484–1559). Also in the main square is the **Accademia dei Concordi,** which was founded in 1580 and now houses the Pinacoteca (Art Gallery), with a fine, intimate collection of Veneto masters. Stop and admire Bellini's *Madonna*, the portraits of Alessandro Longhi (1733–1813), and the paintings of the late-17th-century artist Elizabeth Marchioni, a native of Rovigo. A small Roman, Greek, and Egyptian collection includes a touching mummy with child and in a room downstairs some Flemish tapestries by pupils of Rubens (1577–1640). ⊠ *Piazza Vittorio Emanuele II 14* ☎*0425/21654* ⊠*€3* ☉ *Sept.–June, weekdays 9:30–noon and 3:30–6:30, weekends 10–noon; July–Aug., Mon.–Sat. 9:30–1.*

An impressive dual row of pine trees leads up to the church of Santa Maria del Soccorso di Rovigo, better known as **La Rotonda.** Contrasting against the trees stands the white, Palladian-influenced octagonal structure, surrounded by a portico of Tuscan columns. It was designed by Francesco Zamberlan (1529–1606) in 1594, and the brick campanile was added in 1673 by Baldassare Longhena. The interior, both walls and dome, is entirely and sumptuously covered by 17th-century Veneto paintings. ⊠ *Piazza XX Settembre 37* ☎ *0425/24914* ⊠ *Free* ☉ *Easter–Oct., daily 8–noon and 4–8; Nov.–Easter, daily 8–noon and 3:30–7:30.*

Where to Stay & Eat

$$ ✕ **Tavernetta Dante.** The comprehensive menu of Veneto specialties, including plenty of seafood, is complemented by an excellent choice of wines in this convivial, long-established restaurant. The main room is decorated in warm tones of pink plaster and brick; the other (no-smoking), in cool shades of green, gives onto a plant-filled terrace for outdoor summer dining. The menu changes frequently according to season, with dishes like radicchio and sausage risotto, *tagliata con rucola e grano* (beef steak with arugula and parmesan), or a tempting mixed grilled seafood. ⊠ *Corso del Popolo 212* ☎ *0425/26386* ⊟ *MC, V* ☉ *Closed Sun. and Aug. 10–31.*

★ **¢** ✕ **Taverna.** This no-nonsense restaurant with its cheerful plaid tablecloths is a real find and very popular. At lunchtime, the city's workers stream in and out for a quality, low-priced, three-course meal. The excellent salads are complete meals in themselves: a big bowl of *radicchio, rucola, pere, grana a scaglie e mandorla* (radicchio, arugula, pear, flakes of Grana Padano, and almonds) or *verdure crude, uove, tonno, mozzarella, mais e olive* (tuna, egg, and mozzarella salad) will sustain you for the rest of the day. ⊠ *Piazza Merlin 20* ☎ *0425/21653* ⊟ *AE, DC, MC, V* ☉ *Closed Fri. and last 2 wks in Aug. No lunch Sat.*

$ ▦ **Corona Ferrea.** Right in the center of the city but well away from any busy roads, this hotel offers polite, friendly service. The decor bears the same hallmark of discretion—modern and elegant, the colors understated and quiet. Relax over breakfast in the bright dining room upstairs, flooded with morning sunshine. ⊠ *Via Umberto I 21, 45100* ☎ *0425/ 422433* ⊟ *0425/422292* ⌦ *30 rooms* ♻ *Bar, minibars, cable TV, parking (fee), some pets allowed* ⊟ *AE, DC, MC, V* ❙❘❙ *CP.*

$ ▦ **Villa Regina Margherita.** The most attractive of Rovigo's hotels, this early 20th-century villa glows a welcoming pink and reflects an art nouveau style. Large comfortable armchairs, velvet upholstery, and potted palms give an air of luxury, and the restaurant is very highly regarded. Book ahead, as rooms fill quickly. ⊠ *Viale Regina Margherita 6, 45100* ☎ *0425/361540* 🖶 *0425/31301* 🛏 *20 rooms, 2 suites* ♿ *Restaurant, bar, free parking, some pets allowed* ⊟ *AE, DC, MC, V* †○† *CP.*

Nightlife & the Arts

The **Teatro Sociale** (⊠ Piazza Garibaldi 14 ☎ 0425/25614) puts on musicals and symphony concerts as well as plays.

Antico Canevone (⊠ Vicolo Canevone 4, off Via X Luglio ☎ 0425/27787) offers light snacks and music presented by the resident deejay till the early hours, Tues.–Sun.

LAKE GARDA

Lake Garda is the most popular of the Italian lakes as well as the largest, spanning the borders of three regions—the Veneto, Trentino, and Lombardy. The size of the lake actually has an impact upon the climate, making the summers cooler and the winters warmer. Vacationers on packages love it, especially the German and the French, who invade the large number of hotels. If you plan to spend any time during the summer in the busiest resorts, such as Sirmione, book well ahead. Of course, if you're a windsurfer or a sailor, then this is your heaven, with breezes tailor-made for you. The funicular ride up the slopes of Monte Baldo is spectacular. You can even arrange for a mountain bike to meet you at the top or take a paragliding trip. Glorious walking can be enjoyed in the mountains that enclose the narrow northern part of the lake, tapering off to the south to give way to flatter country. On the gentle slopes are lush olive and lemon groves, oleanders and palm trees, and the vines that provide the grapes for the local wines such as Valpolicella and Bardolino. Enchanting castles and little medieval towns complete the picture.

Malcesine

49 *179 km (111 mi) northwest of Venice, 67 km (42 mi) northwest of Verona.*

One of the loveliest areas along the upper eastern shore of Lake Garda, Malcesine is principally known as a summer resort with sailing and windsurfing schools. The 13 campsites and tourist villages do tend to make the town a little crowded in summer. There are, however, some nice walks from the town toward the mountains behind. The town hall was the seat of the Captains of the Lake during the 16th and 17th centuries. Dominating the town is the 13th- to 14th-century **Castello Scaligero**, built by the della Scalas. Inside are several small museums, one of which is devoted to Goethe, who in 1786 spent a short spell in prison here—while sketching the lake he was thought to be an Austrian spy and promptly arrested. Another contains paintings of the ships being hauled to Torbole. There's a fine view from the tower. ⊠ *Via Castello* ☎ *045/7400837* 🎫 *€4* ⊙ *Apr.–Oct., daily 9–6:30; Nov.–Mar., weekends only, 10:30–5.*

> **off the beaten path**
>
> **MONTE BALDO –** If you are fond of cable cars take the 15-minute *funivia* ride to the top of Monte Baldo (5,791 ft) for a great view of the whole lake in summer, or possibly a short ski run in winter (expect a wait). The area is also a great place for mountain biking, and you can even arrange for bikes to meet you at the top. Because of the variety of vegetation found here, from olive and lemon groves to beech woods, not to mention the profuse Alpine flowers, the mountain was once known as the *hortus europae* (garden of Europe).

Sports & the Outdoors

MOUNTAIN BIKING **Furioli** (✉ Piazza Matteotti 11 ☎ 045/7400089) rents bikes by the day. Contact **Funivia Malcesine-Montebaldo** (☎ 045/7400206) for mountain-bike rentals and paragliding.

WINDSURFING Malcesine **Wind Square** (✉ Località Sottodossi ☎ 045/7400413) offers windsurfing courses and rents equipment. **Marco Segnana** (✉ Foci del Sarca, Torbole ☎ 0464/505963) just north of Malcesine, can arrange windsurfing weekends, including lessons and equipment rental, and also arranges mountain-bike rentals and hotel accommodation.

Peschiera

⑤⓪ *46 km (29 mi) southwest of Malcesine, 140 km (90 mi) west of Venice.*

At the southern end of the Lake Garda, Peschiera is a pleasant place to wander around for a half day or so. It's less touristy than other lake towns and makes an alternative to staying in Sirmione if that resort is full or if you fancy a lower-key scene. Sports enthusiasts will find all the usual water sports on hand. The town is surrounded by hefty bastion walls that were begun by the Venetians in 1553 and subsequently strengthened by Napoléon and later the Austrians. Crossing the bridge from the harbor brings you through the defenses to the historic center and the *lungolago* (lake promenade) lined with villas now defended by dogs. The Roman writer Pliny (AD 23–79) noted that Peschiera was the place for eels, and indeed the eel is featured on the town's coat of arms. So don't be surprised if you see them on the menu.

off the beaten path

PARCO GIARDINO SIGURTÀ – Over a period of 40 years, Count Doctor Carlo Sigurtà transformed the hillside into a sumptuous garden, introducing walkways through lawn carpets, woods, canals with water lilies, surrealist sculptures in boxwood, rosebushes, grottoes, and cypresses. It makes a magical place to spend an afternoon. ✉ *Valeggio sul Mincio, 8 km (5 mi) south of Peschiera* ☎ *045/6371033* ☑ *€8* ☉ *Mar.–Nov., daily 9–6.*

Where to Stay & Eat

$–$$ ✕ **Bellavista.** Right on the lake with an outdoor terrace and view, this is a pleasantly old-fashioned restaurant and pizzeria with brisk service. Inside, the gold tablecloths and gilt mirrors give it a glitzy air. The menu includes grilled lavaret from the lake, seafood, and meat dishes such as fillet of beef with green peppercorns. ✉ *Lungolago Mazzini 1* ☎ *045/7553252* ☰ *AE, DC, MC, V* ☉ *Closed Thurs. and mid-Nov.–mid-Dec.*

$–$$ ✕ **Il Cantinone.** This quiet courtyard in the historic center is an ideal place to sample tagliolini *al ragù di trota* (with trout) or gnocchi *alla polpa di granchio* (with crab meat). Follow it with fish from the lake, such as lavaret, or eel. If it's not warm enough to eat out, the inside is cozy with lots of reproduction paintings on the walls. ✉ *Via Galileo Galilei 14* ☎ *045/7551162* ⌲ *Reservations essential* ☰ *AE, DC, MC, V* ☉ *Closed Tues. Oct.–Mar.*

$ ⊞ **Bell'Arrivo.** This pink-washed, family-run hotel on the banks of the Mincio River makes for an attractive place to stay in the center of town. The front rooms have big windows offering a spectacular, close-up lake view. There's a tempting, rather grand marbled *pasticceria* (pastry shop) underneath. ✉ *Piazza Benacense 29, 37019* ☎ *045/6401322* 🖷 *045/6401311* ⊕ *www.hotelbellarrivo.it* ⇄ *27 rooms* ⌂ *Boating, bicycles, bar* ☰ *AE, DC, MC, V* ☉ *Closed Jan. 11–Feb. 7* ⦿ *FAP, MAP.*

$ ⊞ **San Marco.** Many of the rooms in this smart lakeside hotel have views and all guests have access to a large sun terrace. The restaurant also has a covered terrace for outdoor dining in summer. The spacious comfort of the public areas is repeated in the rooms, with stylish bathrooms featuring pink marble. ⊠ *Lungolago Mazzini 37019* ☎ *045/7550077* ↘ *36 rooms, 4 suites* ⚭ *Restaurant, bar, minibars, cable TV, free parking* ▭ *AE, DC, MC, V* ⦿⦾ *CP.*

Sports & the Outdoors

BOAT TRIP **Gestione Governativa** (⊠ Piazza Matteotti 2, Desenzano ☎ 030/9149511 or 167/551801) runs a daily ferry to Riva del Garda from April through September, costing €18. It leaves Peschiera at 9:45 AM and returns at 7:55 PM.

Sirmione

★ ⑤ *14 km (9 mi) northwest of Peschiera, 150 km (94 mi) west of Venice.*

The ruins at this enchanting town on an isthmus at the southwestern shore of Lake Garda, complete with narrow, cobbled streets that wind their way through medieval arches, are a reminder that Garda has been a holiday resort for the well-to-do since the height of the Roman era. Most of the historic town, which stretches the length of the spit, is inaccessible to cars, so you must park at the bottom of the historic center and walk the rest of the way. The locals will almost certainly tell you that the so-called **Grotte di Catullo** (Grottoes of Catullus) were once the site of the villa of Catullus, one of the greatest pleasure-seeking poets of all time. Present archaeological wisdom, however, does not concur, and there is some consensus that this was the site of two villas of slightly different periods, dating from about the 1st century AD. But never mind—the view through the cypresses and olive trees is lovely, and even if Catullus didn't have a villa here, he is closely associated with the area and undoubtedly did once plop down somewhere nearby. The ruins are at the top of the isthmus and are badly signposted: walk through the historic center and past the various villas to the top of the spit; the grottoes are on the right. The whole peninsula is best avoided on Sundays, when the huge car parks and tiny historic center are packed solid with throngs of Italian visitors. ⊠ *Grotte di Catullo, Sirmione* ☎ *030/916157* ⚏ *€4* ⊘ *Mar.–Sept., Tues.–Sun. 8:30–7; Oct.–Feb., Tues.–Sun. 8:30–5:30.*

The **Castello Scaligero** was built, along with almost all the other castles on the lake, by the della Scala family. As hereditary rulers of Verona for more than a century before control of the city was seized by the Visconti in 1402, they counted Garda among their possessions. The inside of the castle offers a nice view of the lake from the tower. Entry to the old part of town is gained through the castle's gates, over what was originally a drawbridge. ⊠ *Piazza Castello, Sirmione* ☎ *030/916468* ⚏ *€4* ⊘ *Call the local tourist office for opening hours* ☎ *030/916114.*

> **off the beaten path**

GARDALAND AMUSEMENT PARK – This park has more than 40 different rides and water slides and is one of Italy's biggest amusement parks. It is 16 km (10 mi) east of Sirmione. There is a free transfer service from Peschiera train station, less than 5 km (3 mi) up the road. ⊠ *Castelnuovo del Garda* ☎ *045/6449777* ⚏ *€22* ⊘ *Apr.1–June 20 and Sept. 9–30, daily 10–6; June 21–Sept. 8, daily 9–midnight; Oct. weekends only 10–6. Closed Nov.–Mar.*

Where to Stay & Eat

★ **$$$$** ✕ **Vecchia Lugana.** At the base of the peninsula and outside the town, this restaurant is considered one of Italy's best. Adventurous diners will reap the most rewards, by sampling such wonders as wood mushroom soup with river prawns or venison fillet with artichoke puree. The menu changes seasonally. There's also an elegant garden. ⊠ *Piazzale Vecchia Lugana 1, Lugana di Sirmione* ☎ *030/919012* ⊟ *AE, DC, MC, V* ⊘ *Closed Mon., Tues. and Jan.–mid-Feb. and Mon.–Thurs. in Nov.*

★ **$$$–$$$$** ✕ **La Rucola.** This secluded restaurant prides itself on attention to detail in its courteous service, elegant surroundings, and, of course, the food. The young chef, Gionatha Bignotti, offers mouth-watering set meals based on fish or meat, or tempting *nouveau* creations from the menu. This changes regularly, but dishes like *portafoglio di spigola, carciofi e fegato d'anatra con pureè di patate e aceto balsamico* (sea-bass with artichokes, and duck liver with Italian-style mashed potatoes and balsamic vinegar) are typical of the rich selection. The spiced and iced zabaglione is also worth dipping into. ⊠ *Vicolo Strentelle 7* ☎ *030/916326* 🪑 *Reservations essential* ⊟ *AE, DC, MC, V* ⊘ *Closed Thurs. and Jan. No lunch Fri.*

$–$$$ ✕ **Ristorante Al Pescatore.** The specialty of this simple, rustic, and very popular restaurant is lake fish. Try grilled trout with a bottle of local white wine and finish your meal with a walk in the nearby public park. ⊠ *Via Piana 20* ☎ *030/916216* ⊟ *DC, MC, V* ⊘ *Closed Jan.–Feb. and Wed. Oct.–May.*

★ **$$$$** 🏨 **Villa Cortine Palace.** A formidably decorative early 19th-century villa in a secluded park, Villa Cortine is in danger of being just plain ostentatious, but only just. It is saved by the sheer luxury of its setting and the extraordinary professionalism of its staff, which, although a little too formal and cold, will leave you wanting for virtually nothing—except your wallet. It dominates a low hill, and the grounds—a colorful mixture of lawns, trees, statues, and fountains—go down to the lake. Rooms in the original villa have old-world charm, while those in the newer wing have better lake views. ⊠ *Via Grotte 12, 25019* ☎ *030/9905890* 🖷 *030/916390* ⊕ *www.hotelvillacortine.com* 📞 *48 rooms, 6 suites* 🍴 *Restaurant, bar, in-room safes, minibars, cable TV, tennis court, pool, beach, some pets allowed* ⊟ *AE, DC, MC, V* ⊘ *Closed Oct. 20–Mar. 31* ⦿ *MAP.*

$$$–$$$$ 🏨 **Hotel Sirmione.** Just inside the city walls, near the Castello, this hotel and spa sits amid lakeside gardens and terraces. Some rooms display superb execution, with comfortable Scandinavian slat beds, matching floral draperies and wall coverings, and built-in white furniture. Many guests have been returning for years, largely due to the homespun feel and the attentiveness of the staff. ⊠ *Piazza Castello 19, 25019* ☎ *030/916331* 🖷 *030/916558* 📞 *76 rooms* 🍴 *Restaurant, bar, in-room safes, minibars, cable TV, pool, sauna, spa, meeting room, free parking, some pets allowed* ⊟ *AE, DC, MC, V* ⊘ *Closed Nov.–Mar. (incl.)* ⦿ *FAP, MAP.*

Bosco Chiesanuova

㉜ *68 km (42 mi) northeast of Sirmione, 125 km (78 mi) northwest of Venice.*

Bosco Chiesanuova is the stopping-off point for exploration of **Parco Regionale della Lessinia** (Lessinia Regional Park). Best reached from Verona (31 km [19 mi] south), the park lies between the Adige Valley to the west and the Piccoli Dolomiti to the north. Featuring a gentle but rugged landscape, it is ideal for exploring either on foot, by mountain bike, or on horseback and, in winter, on cross-country skis. Among the cherry trees, beech groves, and meadows edged with dry-stone walls are houses made from the local *pietra di Prun*, a type of stone that, in the not-so-distant past, was used in the construction of underground ice houses where ice was stored to be sold for summer use. This is a karst limestone area, so the pastures are riven with deep gorges and sprinkled with small lakes and waterfalls. At **Ponte di Veja,** the natural attraction is the stone bridge that has been created purely by water erosion. The area is renowned for its fish fossils. The small **Museo Civico** has a nice display of artifacts and photographs of the traditions, art, and costumes of the area. ⊠ *Bosco Chiesanuova* ☎ *045/7050022* 🎟 *€1.50* ⊗ *Sept.–June, weekends 4:30–6:30; July–Aug., Tues., Fri., Sat., and Sun. 4:30–6.*

Where to Stay

¢ 🏨 **Lessinia.** This modern, functional hotel is vaguely Tyrolean in style. The plain, cheerful rooms are furnished with pine and some have mountain views. There's a big restaurant downstairs (closed Wednesday), offering local specialties featuring Monte Veronese cheese, and a big billiard room in the basement. ⊠ *Piazzetta Alpini 2, 37021* ☎ *045/ 6780151* 🖨 *045/6780098* ⇨ *20 rooms* ⚒ *Restaurant, bar, recreation room, meeting rooms, free parking* 🖭 *MC, V* 🍴 *FAP, MAP.*

Sports & the Outdoors

MOUNTAIN BIKING From June 6 until September 13 you can take your mountain bike on the special bus that leaves Verona for Bosco Chiesanuova at 9 AM, returning at 7:30 PM (€9.30 round-trip). You can get tickets from the **Verona bus station** (☎ 045/8057911) and information on biking trails from the tourist office in Verona (☎ 045/8068680).

SKIING For latest skiing information, contact **Lessinia Turistsport** (⊠ Piazza della Chiesa 3 ☎ 045/7050088 ⊕ www.leturispo.it)

WALKING & HIKING Bosco's **tourist office** (⊠ Piazza della Chiesa 34, 37021 Bosco Chiesanuova ☎🖨 045/7050088) has information on walks.

THE BRENTA

Once upon a time, the Brenta River was a constant source of trouble to the settlers of the area, as it was prone to flooding and caused the lagoon to silt up. Steps had been taken to regulate matters since the 11th century, but it was not until Venice took control of the area in 1405 that matters were really taken in hand. Diversions were created, banks strengthened, and the deposit of silt controlled. By the 16th century the land was safe enough for extensive farming and for wealthy Venetians to enjoy *villeggiatura,* a vacation from harried city life, by building princely residences on their country estates. The best architects, sculptors, and artists were summoned, and elegant symmetry and Baroque sumptuousness remain the characteristic style. Some of the 100 or so villas built served as farmhouses, while others were just used for pleasure. A handful of these are now open to the public, often for only a couple of days a week, so check before arranging your itinerary. Two of the best villas, each reflecting the different basic designs of Palladio, are the Villa Pisani and the Villa Foscari.

Malcontenta/Villa Foscari

❸ *8 km (5 mi) west of Venice.*

Malcontenta is the first village along the Brenta River from Venice. Legend has it that the name "Malcontenta" (unhappy) was derived from the wife of one of the Foscari brothers, the lady having been banished here for "inappropriate behavior," but the real explanation is likely to be more prosaic, as the name was already in use before the arrival of the Foscari. Built in 1560 by—who else—Palladio, **Villa Foscari** is not one of his long, low designs but one of his large cubes with portico and dome, its lawn running down to the river. Giovanni Batista Zelotti (1526–78) lent his hand in decorating the walls inside, covering them with allegorical and mythological figures in mock architectural effects. ✉ *Malcontenta* ☎ *041/ 5470012* 🎟 *€7* ◷ *Apr.–Oct., Tues. and Sat. 9–noon.*

Stra/Villa Pisani

★ ☾ 🔢 *37 km (23 mi) west of Malcontenta, 34 km (21 mi) west of Venice.*

Extensive grounds with rare trees, ornamental fountains, and garden follies surround this extraordinary 18th-century palace in Stra. It was one of the last of many stately residences constructed along the Brenta River from the 16th to 18th centuries by wealthy Venetians for their vacation and escape from the mid-summer humidity. The *trompe l'oeil* frescoes by Giambattista Tiepolo (1696–1770) on the ceiling of the ballroom alone are worth the visit. If you have youngsters in tow surfeited with old masters, explore the gorgeous **park** and the **maze** (open April through September only). ✉ *Stra* ☎ *049/502074* 🎟 *Villa, maze, and grounds €5; maze and grounds only, €2.50* ◷ *Apr.–Sept., Tues.–Sun. 9–7; Oct.–Mar., Tues.–Sun. 9–4; last entry 1 hr before closing.*

Euganean Hills: Abano Terme/Montegrotto Terme

🔢 *12 km (7 mi) south of Padua, 49 km (30 mi) west of Venice.*

Rising abruptly out of the plain, the volcanic Euganean Hills are a pleasure to explore in any season, the gentle slopes strewn with chestnut trees, olive groves, and vineyards that encroach upon the road. The hills themselves enfold unspoiled villages, and at their feet you'll find abbeys and villas. Take time to wander along the paths marked for walkers, look for wild mushrooms, and enjoy the microclimates that produce Mediterranean and Alpine flowers, myrtle, and even prickly pears. In spring the blossom of almond and cherry trees turns the hills a frothy pink and white. For information about the regional park here contact the **Parco Regionale dei Colli Euganei** (✉ Via Rana Cà Mori 8, Este ☎ 0427/612010).

Fango (mud) is the one thing that draws people in droves to these two conjoined resorts, considered among the foremost in Europe. There is no escaping the steam that rises from streets and gardens at every turn and is channelled into the collection of hotels and thermal clinics that make up Abano Terme and Montegrotto Terme. Water emanates from the Dolomites after a journey deep underground and resurfaces at a temperature of 87°F, full of salt, bromine, and iodine. Each hotel will have its series of slimy mud basins and clients in dressing gowns submitting to mud massage, inhalations, or irrigations. If it's not mud you're after, or indulgence in one of the nine five-star hotels, you'll get more out of your trip by staying in one of the small towns in the area.

Abano Terme shows its Roman origin in its name, Abano deriving from the Roman god of healing, Aponeus. Although some buildings were a result of the design by Giuseppe Jappelli in the early 19th century, most hotels and parks have appeared in the 20th century.

The small **Museo D'Arte** contains 16th- and 17th-century Venetian and Flemish masters. ✉ *Via Pietro d'Abano 20* ☎ *049/8617901* 🎟 *Free* ◷ *Apr.–Oct., Tues.–Sun. 10–noon and 4–7; Nov.–Mar., Tues.–Sun, 10–noon and 3–6.*

The name **Montegrotto Terme** derives from "Mons Aegrotorum" (Mount of the Sick). It became a Roman colony in 184 BC, was the birthplace of the historian Livy (59 BC–AD 17), and was much praised for the properties of its algae by a succession of Roman worthies—Pliny, Suetonius, and Plutarch to name but three. The **archaeological zone** consists of the remains of Roman Baths (Terme Romane), and a theater dating from the era of Augustus (63 BC–AD 14) can be seen from the outside at all times. If you spot a statue of a medieval dame rotating, it'll be the one commemorating the story of Berta che Filava (Bertha Spinning), to whom the wife of Henry IV of Germany gave as much land as could be surrounded by the thread on her spinning wheel. Visits had been suspended at press time, but inquiries can be made through the library in Via Scavi (☎ 049/892883)

Where to Stay & Eat

$$–$$$ ✕ **Victoria.** Step out of brash, modern Abano into the tasteful elegance of this fine restaurant. The seafood dishes are of a quality that requires no dressing up, such as whole bream or sea bass simply grilled or steamed, and barbecued scampi: each served with seasonal vegetables to complement its flavors. An extensive wine list, tempting sweets, and efficient service allow the Victoria to win customers from the town's several five-star hotels. ⊠ *Via Monteortone 30* ☎ *049/667684* ⚱ *Reservations essential* ▤ *AE, D, MC, V* ⊘ *Closed Mon.*

★ **$$** ✕ **Aubergine.** An unusual combination of classical, semi-formal restaurant, pizzeria, and mini-golf course—all run by one family. The restaurant menu changes regularly to focus on seasonal specialties, creatively interpreted by the lady of the house who presides over the kitchen. Before dipping into the tempting selection of chocolate desserts, try the polenta with truffles (fall), chicken breasts with ham and sage (summer), or spinach and cheese gnocchi (winter). A range of pizzas includes one, of course, with eggplant. ⊠ *Via Ghislandhi 5* ☎ *049/8669910* ▤ *AE, DC, MC, V* ⊘ *Closed Wed. and first 2 wks of Aug.*

$ ✕ **Al Bosco.** A 3-km (2-mi) drive out of Montegrotto in the Torreglia direction (signposted left) brings you to this hilltop setting near the woods. The restaurant's rustic decor features large copper pans and cowbells. Cooking is done *alla brace* (barbecued) in summer and the accent is on meats such as *scottadito di agnello* (barbecued lamb chops) and *fiorentina* (char-grilled T-bone steak, priced according to weight). ⊠ *Via Cogolo 8, Parco dei Colli Euganei* ☎☎ *049/794317* ▤ *AE, MC, V* ⊘ *Closed Wed. and Jan. 10–31.*

$$$ ▥ **Bristol Buja Spa.** One of Abano's modern, first-class hotels, the Bristol Buja offers all the usual mud treatments, diet regimes, and exercise classes in outdoor pools. The indoor pool is covered by a colorful stained-glass roof. The bright, well-furnished, luxurious rooms all look out over the tree-studded front lawns. Most guests come for several days to subject themselves to all the treatments on half- or full-board arrangements, but single-night guests are also welcome. ⊠ *Via Monteortone 2, 35031 Abano Terme* ☎ *049/8669390* ⊟ *049/667910* ⊲ *116 rooms* ⚘ *Restaurant, bar, in-room safes, minibars, driving range, golf privileges, tennis courts, 3 pools, fitness classes, gym, health club, sauna, spa, bicycles available, bocce, meeting rooms, free parking, pets allowed, nosmoking rooms* ▤ *AE, DC, MC, V* ⊘ *Closed Nov. 21–Dec. 19* ⦿ *CP.*

Praglia

★ ㊏ *8 km (5 mi) west of Abano Terme, 12 km (7 mi) southwest of Padua.*

You can tour the evocative 15th-century halls and cloisters of this Benedictine monastery set at the foot of the Euganean Hills. The monastery was founded in the 11th century, but the present buildings date from the 15th and 16th centuries and consist of four cloisters, two refectories—one with a fine *Crucifixion* by Montagna—and the church with its Romanesque campanile containing paintings by Veneto masters. Known for book restoration, the monastery has a library of more than 100,000 books on its 16th-century shelves. The monks sell the wine and

honey produced here. ☎ 049/9900010 ⚏ *Free; donations appreciated*
⊙ *Tours Apr.–Oct., Tues.–Sun. 3:30, 4:10, 4:50, and 5:30; Nov.–Mar.,*
Tues.–Sun. 2:30, 3:10, 3:50, and 4:30.

Monselice

⑤⑦ *7 km (4½ mi) south of Montegrotto Terme, 61 km (38 mi) southwest*
of Venice.

Rising out of the Paduan plain, Monselice's defensive walls skirt the base
of the volcanic hill around which the town is ranged, making its lofty
position unique in this part of the country. The foremost building of the
town is the **Castello di Monselice,** or Ca' Marcello—a must to visit. Passing through the hands of Ezzelino III da Romano, who extended the original 12th-century building, and then to the Carrara and Marcello
families, this castle has been lovingly and meticulously restored by
Count Vittorio Cini, into whose care it came after World War I. As you
enter the Salone d'Onore, you will immediately notice the wonderful
chimney with its tiered arches on columns of majolica set against the
red-and-white checkerboard walls. It's everything a medieval castle
should be, both inside and out. ⊠ *Via del Santuario 24* ☎ *0429/72931*
⚏ *€5.50* ⊙ *Guided tours only. Apr.–Nov., Tues.–Sun. 9–noon and 3–6*
pm; Dec.–Mar. by appointment only.

The Via Santuario leads to the **Via Sette Chiese,** a private road that climbs
up the hill to the **Villa Duodo,** summer residence of the Duodo family
built in 1593 by Scamozzi. At the lower end of the street stands the Romanesque Gothic **Duomo Vecchio** (☎ 0429/72130) and six little pilgrimage churches, where those in need of forgiveness could stop and
pray on their way to the seventh, San Giorgio. **San Giorgio** houses relics
of some of the first Christian martyrs. These were transferred from the
catacombs of Rome at the behest of the Duodo family and are displayed
in glass cases. Among the relics are those of St. Valentine, and surely
it's no surprise to hear that there's an annual pilgrimage here on February 14. San Giorgio is open on Sunday; contact the tourist office (⊠ Piazza Mazzini 15, ☎☎ 0429/783026) for opening hours at other times.

Where to Stay & Eat

$$–$$$ ✕ **La Torre.** You can't dine in the castle, but the next best thing is a meal
in the medieval walls. The accent here is on seasonal ingredients, especially vegetables. If you're here in April you can sample the local white
asparagus, but just as delightful are the *fior di zucca* (zucchini blossoms),
which in summer, along with wild porcini, are picked as fillings for the
homemade ravioli. You'll find truffles as well, but you'll be digging deep
in your pocket for the tubers. ⊠ *Piazza Mazzini 14* ☎ *0429/73752*
⚐ *Reservations essential* ▭ *AE, DC, MC, V* ⊙ *Closed Mon. and Aug.*
No dinner Sun.

¢–$ ✕ **Savellon Molini.** A 2-km (1-mi) drive from Monselice toward Padua
will bring you to this converted barn, with its wooden beams and
benches, set among log stacks and vineyards. The first courses are all
of homemade pasta, while seconds are based on *carni alla brace* (grilled
meats)—there's a huge barbecue grill in summer—and local vegetables.
⊠ *Via Savellon Molini 52* ☎ *0429/73135* ▭ *AE, DC, MC, V*
⊙ *Closed Mon.*

$$ ▢ **Hotel Ceffri.** Hidden away on its own leafy grounds, the Ceffri is only
a few minutes from the Monselice *autostrada* exit, on the outskirts of
town. The rooms are spacious and quiet, each with its own balcony.
There's a pleasant garden next to the pool, a perfect place for sipping
a long drink or a *thè freddo* (iced tea) in summer. The adjacent restau-
rant associated with the hotel, the Villa Corner, provides local and in-

ternational dishes. To be recommended is the dessert *strudel con crema e pinoli* (strudel with cream and pine nuts). ✉ *Via Orti 7/b, 35043* ☎ *0429/783111* 🖶 *0429/783100* ⊕ *www.ceffri.it* ⇆ *42 rooms, 2 suites ⚒ Restaurant, minibars, pool, piano bar, meeting rooms, free parking, no-smoking rooms* ▭ *AE, DC, MC, V* ⭗ *FAP, MAP.*

★ ¢ 🖾 **Venetian Hostel.** The massive wooden beams spanning the terracotta-tiled foyer of this beautifully restored 16th-century mansion are just a taste of the Renaissance elegance and fine furnishings throughout. Several larger rooms—some for families, others dormatory-style—explain the 'hostel' designation, but all rooms have bathrooms and air-conditioning. ✉ *Via Santo Stefano 33, 35043* ☎🖶 *0429/783125* ⇆ *13 rooms, 6 dorms ⚒ Internet, meeting rooms, free parking* ▭ *No credit cards* ⊘ *Reception closed 12:30 PM–5PM* ⭗ *CP.*

Nightlife & the Arts

FESTIVALS Monselice relives the Middle Ages with a festival on the first three Sundays of September. It culminates in the medieval festival **Giostra della Rocca** on the third Sunday, when muscle men perform feats of strength with millstones, archers strive for glory, and riders on horseback gallop around the town in the *quintana*. To add to it all, there's a market with vendors in medieval costume. For more information contact the tourist office (✉ Piazza Mazzini 15, 35043 Monselice ☎🖶 0429/783026)

MUSIC A classical music performance is given on Sunday mornings at the castle during April and sometimes in May and September. For information call 0429/72931 or the Monselice tourist office.

Shopping

MARKETS A general market is held year-round on Monday and Friday in **Piazza Mazzini**; a flea market is held there from May through September on the last Saturday of the month.

Arqua Petrarca

❺❽ *22 km (14 mi) south of Padua, 9 km (5½ mi) northeast of Este.*

It would be a shame to miss this little jewel of a village tucked away in the Euganean Hills. The narrow cobbled streets wind their way between carefully restored medieval houses and pretty gardens surrounded by the mellow green of the hills and vineyards. It's a good spot for lunch. The poet Francesco Petrarca, more often referred to by his Anglicized name: Petrarch (1304–74) spent the last four years of his life in this little haven: his house, **Casa Petrarca,** is visitable and his life traceable through the medieval frescoes on its walls (they were retouched in the 17th century). You can see his chair and desk here and later visit his sarcophagus by the church in the center of the village. ✉ *Via Valesella 4* ☎ *0429/718294* 🖾 *€5.10* ⊘ *Mar.–Oct., Tues.–Sun. 9–12:30 and 3–7; Nov.–Feb., Tues.–Sun. 9–noon and 2:30–5:30.*

Where to Eat

$$–$$$ ✕ **La Montanella.** The oil used here is cold pressed from the century-old olive trees in the garden, which you can admire from the restaurant's veranda. The strictly local cuisine highlights homemade pasta, poultry, and game—including venison and boar. Only fresh, seasonal vegetables are used and in summer these will include delicacies like wild herbs and nettles. Try the orange blossom or quail risotto, or the *papero alla frutta* (duck with pear, grapes, or cherries), made to an original 17th-century recipe, complemented with a full-bodied Merlot or Carbenet from the Euganean hills. ✉ *Via Costa 33* ☎ *0429/718200* ⊕ *www.montanella. it* ▭ *AE, DC, MC, V* ⊘ *Closed Wed., Jan. 1–Feb. 13, and Aug. 7–21. No dinner Tues.*

The **Festa delle Giuggiole** (Jujube Festival) on the first and second weekends of October involves local food and wine tastings, buskers, and flag-waving performances. Call the **Comune di Arqua Petrarca** (☎ 0429/ 777100) for information.

Este

⑤⑨ *9 km (5½ mi) southwest of Monselice, 80 km (50 mi) southwest of Venice.*

Este was an important center of the Veneto before becoming Roman Ateste, retaining its prominent role under the rule of the Este family, later to become dukes of Ferrara. Power was then transferred to Venice. Dominating the town is the **Castello dei Carraresi**, now in ruins, although the gardens are open to the public. Abutting the walls, housed in a 16th-century palace, is the **Museo Nazionale Atestino**, where you can see the Veneto's best collection of pre-Roman and Roman artifacts, including some fine bronzes such as the 7th-century *Situla Benvenuti* and the *Dea di Caldevigo* dating from the 5th century. ⊠ *Via Guido Negri 2* ☎ *0429/2085* ☜ *€2* ☉ *Open daily 9–8.*

The Baroque **Duomo** is dedicated to Santa Thecla, who is represented in a large painting by Tiepolo. ⊠ *Piazza Santa Thecla 6* ☎ *0429/2009* ☉ *Apr.–Sept. 9:30–noon and 4–6; Oct.–Mar. 9:30–noon and 3–6.*

$–$$ ✕ **Sapio.** Tucked up a little alley in the center of town, this is the place for wine lovers, for it's a well-stocked *enoteca* (wine shop/bar) as well as a restaurant. There's no set menu—the chef is inventive and likes to use local ingredients such as lamb, goose, and seasonal vegetables. Homemade desserts such as *torta della nonna* ("grandma's tart," made with pine nuts), *torta al cioccolato* (chocolate cake), and seasonal fruit tarts are a specialty. The decor is plain with terra-cotta accents, and there's a quiet garden for alfresco eating in warm weather. ⊠ *Via Madonetta 2/c* ☎ *0429/602565* ☜ *Reservations essential* ☰ *AE, DC, MC, V* ☉ *Closed Mon.*

$$ ▥ **Villa Pisani.** The spacious, high-ceilinged rooms in this enormous
FodorśChoice 16th-century villa are completely furnished with period furniture—
   ★   some even have fully frescoed walls. All rooms look out over stunning formal gardens and beyond to a 15-acre park with rare trees, a chapel, a theater, and a concealed swimming pool. You'll also have access to three big *sale* (lounges), where you can chat with the few other lucky guests and Signora Scalabrin, who shares her patrician living areas, music, and books. With breakfast served on silver platters, this is a bed and breakfast that outstrips almost all the competition. ⊠ *Via Roma 19, 35040 Vescovana, 11 km (7 mi) south of Este* ▦▦ *0425/920016* ⊕ *www. villapisani.com* ➥ *8 rooms, 1 suite* ⌂ *Bar, pool, meeting room, some pets allowed; no a/c* ☰ *AE, DC, MC, V* ᴼᴵ *CP.*

$ ▥ **Beatrice d'Este.** The statues set among the trees leading up to the entrance to this hotel against the backdrop of the castle walls make you think it's going to be rather grand. It is, but it's also family run and very good value, with quiet sunny rooms. The hotel is named after one of the most renowned women of her day (1475–97), an intelligent and cultured beauty married at the age of 16 to the seventh Duke of Milan (who commissioned Leonardi da Vinci to paint *The Last Supper*). ⊠ *Viale delle Rimembranze 1, 35042,* ☎ *0429/600533* ▤ *0429/601957* ➥ *30 rooms* ⌂ *Restaurant, bar, cable TV, free parking, some pets allowed* ☰*AE, DC, MC, V* ᴼᴵ *CP.*

$ ▥ **Castello.** Some of the rooms in this centrally located hotel look out over the medieval castle walls; all are smartly furnished with style and taste. The small lobby downstairs leads straight into a busy café full of gossiping locals and serving coffee, drinks, and snacks all day. Breakfast is not included in the price. ⊠ *Via San Girolamo 7/a, 35042* ☎ *0429/602223* 🖷 *0429/602418* ⇆ *12 rooms* ⚿ *In-room data ports, minibars, parking (fee), some pets allowed* �′ *AE, DC, MC, V* ⑩ *EP.*

Nightlife & the Arts

FESTIVALS The **Settembre Euganeo** in September heralds theater performances, an antiques market, an exhibition of local handicrafts, and a pumpkin feast. Contact the tourist office (⊠ Via Guido Negri 9, 35042 Este ☎ 0429/ 600462) for information.

Montagnana

60 *42 km (26 mi) west of Este, 85 km (53 mi) southwest of Venice.*

You could almost be forgiven for thinking that you have been transported back to the 1300s as you approach the medieval walls and tall, crenellated towers that surround Montagnana, glowing pink against the green of the moat. Might you even hear the noise of the hooves of horses galloping past? If you're here in September, then your ears may not be deceiving you, as this is when the 10 bareback jockeys compete for the *pallium* (a red cloth), from which the name *palio* is derived. In this the whole town celebrates the end of the rule of the tyrant Ezzelino III, who in 1242 practically destroyed the town by fire. It was thanks to the Carrara family that the defensive walls, with their 24 towers and four gates, were subsequently put in place; these now rank among the best preserved in Europe, and even boast two castles directly abutting their ramparts. One of these, the **Rocca degli Alberi**, was built in 1362 to defend the western approaches but now, functioning as a youth hostel, is only subject to invasions by backpackers.

Montagnana's eastern gate (Porta Padova) is defended by the town's oldest fortification, the **Castello di San Zeno**, a survivor from Ezzelino's time. It presently houses the **Museo Civico**, consisting of memorabilia of two famous tenors born in the town in 1885, Giovannni Martinelli and Aureliano Pertile. For a panoramic view over the red roofs and a different perspective on the walls, take a trip up the tower. ⊠ *Piazza Trieste 15* ☎ *0429/804128* 🎟 *Castle and museum €2.07, tower €1.03* ⏱ *Museum, guided tours only: Wed.–Fri. at 11 and Sat. at 10:30, 11:30, 3, 4, and 5; Sun. at 11, noon, 3, 4, and 5. Castle and tower: Apr.–Oct., 9:30–12:30 and 4–7; Nov.–Mar. 9:30–12:30 and 3–6, closed Mon. and Tues. morning.*

The brick **Duomo** reflects both Gothic and Renaissance styles. In its spacious nave, your eye might be caught by the altarpieces by Veronese and Buonconsiglio (died circa 1536) but will probably dwell longer on the lively painting of the decisive *Battle of Lepanto* (1571) by Vassilacchi (known as Aliense), fought against the Turkish invaders. ⊠ *Piazza Vittorio Emanuele* ☎ *0429/83736* 🎟 *Free* ⏱ *Apr.–Oct., daily 8–noon and 3–6; Nov.–Mar., daily 8–noon and 1–5.*

need a break? Whatever the time of year, it's worth a stop for a delicious ice cream at the **Bottega del Gelato** (☎ 0429/800855), across the square from the cathedral. Also, don't leave town without strolling through the cobbled streets and buying some prosciutto *di Montagnana*, as sweet and tasty as any you'll find in Italy.

The Duomo is the dominant feature of the main square, **Piazza Vittorio Emanuele.** Of the Quattrocento buildings gracing the rest of the square, perhaps the finest is the Venetian Gothic **Palazzo Lombardesco,** with its balconies and five-paned windows. Notice the ornamental chimneys sprouting like flowers from the roofs.

Where to Stay & Eat

$$$ ✕ **Marco Polo.** This is a serious fish restaurant full of locals concentrating on their food. It's a bit outside the town center, but worth the walk (about ten minutes) if you're hankering for simply prepared, fresh seafood. Most dishes are steamed or boiled, then dressed with simple sauces to highlight their natural flavor. Make your way past the stacked-up piles of plates in this no-frills place and try out the risotto with prawns, scampi, or *polipo* (octopus). ⊠ *Via San Zeno 37* ☎ *0429/81509* ♨ *Reservations essential* ▭ *AE, MC, V* ☾ *Closed Mon.*

★ $ ✕▢ **Aldo Moro.** Pink marble, parquet floors, and polished furniture imbue this little hotel with ineffable charm. Formerly an inn, the building is steeped in style and warmth, enhanced by beamed ceilings and creaking floors. Bathrooms are pink marble, too. If you dine in the restaurant ($$; closed Monday), make sure you taste the prosciutto di Montagnana, then perhaps some *oca* (goose) or, as an extravagant novelty, tagliolini *al cacao con funghi porcini e tartufo* (with cocoa, mushrooms, and truffles). For secondi, try *filetto di cervo in salsa "mercante di vino"* (fillet of venison in a wine sauce). ⊠ *Via Guglielmo Marconi 27, 35044* ☎ *0429/81351* ♨ *0429/81842* ♫ *29 rooms, 5 suites* ♨ *Restaurant, bar, meeting rooms, free parking; no a/c in some rooms* ☾ *Closed Aug. 1–15* ❡❨ *CP.*

¢ ✕▢ **Concordia.** Whether you come to eat or stay here, you'll be sure of a warm welcome in this family-run establishment. You're not in the historic center, but you're surrounded by a modest, homey atmosphere with folksy furnishings to match. There are only a small number of rooms, so book ahead. A full meal ($) of traditional home cooking chosen from the simple menu will cost you around €16 and might include bigoli (thick, whole-wheat spaghetti) *con ragù,* local prosciutto, or *pollo alla griglia* (grilled chicken). An inexpensive house wine from the Colli Euganei will set it all off nicely. ⊠ *Via San Zeno 148, 35044* ☎☎ *0429/81673* ♫ *8 rooms* ♨ *Restaurant, bar, free parking* ☾ *Restaurant closed Sun.* ▭ *AE, MC, V* ❡❨ *CP.*

Nightlife & the Arts

The **Palio** takes place on the first Sunday in September. Ten districts compete in a horse race around the outside of the ancient walls. You can get information from the **Comitato Palio dei 10 Communi** (☎ 0429/80448) or the **tourist office** (⊠ Piazza Trieste 3, 35044 Montagnana ☎☎ 0429/81320).

SOUTHERN VENETO A TO Z

To research prices, get advice from other travelers, and book travel arrangements, visit www.fodors.com.

AIRPORTS & TRANSFERS

The main airport serving the Venetian Arc is Aeroporto Marco Polo, 10 km (6 mi) north of Venice, which handles international and domestic flights. A few European airlines schedule flights to Verona's Aeroporto Catullo di Villafranca, also served by charter flights.

🔲 Airport Information **Aeroporto Catullo di Villafranca** ⊠ 10 km [6 mi] southwest of Verona ☎ 045/8095666 ⊕ www.aeroportoverona.it. **Aeroporto Marco Polo** ☎ 041/2609260 or 041/2609240 ⊕ www.veniceairport.it.

TRANSFERS From Padua, Landomas Service provides a minibus to Venice's Marco Polo airport. A regular bus service connects Villafranca with Verona's Porta Nuova railway station.

🚕 Taxis & Shuttles **Landomas Service** ☎ 049/8808505.

BOAT & FERRY TRAVEL

ACTV operates a once-daily direct boat service in the summer connecting Venice (San Zaccaria) with Chioggia and Sottomarina, along with its regular No.11 service between Chioggia and Venice's Lido via Pellestrina (an island en route).

🚤 Boat & Ferry Information **ACTV** ☎ 041/5287886.

BUS TRAVEL TO & FROM VENICE & THE VENETO

Frequent buses from Venice to the region's major cities are operated by ATVO and ACTV, both operating from the bus station at Piazzale Roma in Venice. There are interurban and interregional connections throughout the Veneto. Local tourist offices may be able to provide details of timetables and routes; otherwise contact the local bus station, or in some cases the individual bus companies operating from the station. Lake Garda is more easily explored by bus; frequent services run between the towns.

FARES & 🚌 Bus Information **ACTV** ✉ Piazzale Roma, Venice ☎ 041/2424. **ATVO**
SCHEDULES ✉ Piazzale Roma, Venice ☎ 041/5205530.

BUS TRAVEL WITHIN THE VENETO

Contact ACTV for buses from Venice to Brenta Riviera, Padua, and Chioggia; ATVO covers the Conegliano–Vittorio Veneto–Cortina routes. Contact APT for Lake Garda, Montagnana, and Bosco Chiesanuova. In Verona, AMT gets you around; in Padua it's the APS, while FTV serves the Vicenza region. AIM takes you around the city; minibuses run every few minutes from the parking lots to the town center Monday through Saturday. Take Line A from Via Bassano, Line B from Via Farini and Via Cairoli, and Line C from Viale Cricoli.

🚌 Bus Information **ACTV** ✉ Piazzale Roma, Venice ☎ 041/5287886. **AIM** ✉ Via Fusinieri 83/h, Vicenza ☎ 0444/394909. **AMT** ✉ Via Torbido 1, Verona ☎ 045/887120. **APS** ✉ Via Rismondi 28 Padua ☎ 049/8241111. **APTV** ✉ Autostazione di Verona Porta Nuova, Piazzale XXV Aprile, Verona ☎ 045/8057911 ⊕ www.aptv.it. **ATVO** ✉ Piazzale Roma, Venice ☎ 041/5205530. **FTV** ✉ Viale Milano 138, Vicenza ☎ 0444/223115.

CAR RENTAL

🚗 Local Agencies **Avis** ✉ Piazza Stazione 1 Padua ☎ 049/664198 ✉ Via Marzan 4, Peschiera ☎ 045/6401164 ✉ Corso del Popolo 329, Rovigo ☎ 0425/23028 ✉ Stazione FS, Verona ☎ 045/8006636 ✉ Viale Milano 88, Vicenza ☎ 0444/321622. **Hertz** ✉ Piazza Stazione 1-VI, Padua ☎ 049/8752202 ✉ Stazione FS, Verona ☎ 045/8000832 ✉ Stazione FS Vicenza, Vicenza ☎ 0444/231728.

CAR TRAVEL

The main access roads to the region are both linked to the A1 (Autostrada del Sole), which connects Bologna, Florence, and Rome. They are the A13, which culminates in Padua, and the A22, which passes through Verona in a north–south direction. The road linking the region from east to west is the A4, the primary route from Milan as far as Trieste.

The main highway in the region is the A4, which connects Verona, Padua, and Venice with Trieste. The A13 connects Padua with Monselice and Rovigo. The A4 and SS11 pass the southern edge of Lake Garda, and the A22, which connects Verona with Trento, runs along the lake's eastern shore.

EMERGENCIES

For first aid, ask for *pronto soccorso,* and be prepared to give your address. All pharmacies post signs on the door with addresses of *farmacie di turno,* pharmacies that take turns staying open after normal business hours: at night, on Saturday afternoon, and on Sunday.

🔲 Emergency Services **Police, Ambulance, Fire** ☎ 113.

🔲 Hospitals **Ospedale Civile** ⊠ Via Rodolfi 37, Vicenza ☎ 0444/993111. **Ospedale Civile e Policlinico dell'Università** ⊠ Via Giustiniani 2, Padua ☎ 049/8211111. **Ospedale Civile Maggiore** ⊠ Piazza Stefani, Verona ☎ 045/8071111.

LODGING

APARTMENT & VILLA RENTALS

The Landmark Trust offers vacation rentals self-catering accommodation in the Villa Saraceno, a carefully restored Palladio villa in Finale di Agugliaro, south of Vicenza. It can sleep up to 16 people for minimum stays of one week from June 1 to mid–Oct, and short stays of 3 nights (min.) in winter. Bookings must be made well in advance.

Local agencies that rent out villas around Malcesine include La Costa Blu and Little Villa.

🔲 Local Agents **La Costa Blu** ⊠ Via Gardesana 62, 37018 Malcesine ☎ 045/7400699. **Little Villa** ⊠ Via Gardesana 32, 37018 Malcesine ☎ 045/7401547

🔲 Rental Listings **The Landmark Trust** ⊠ Shottesbrooke, Maidenhead, Berkshire SL6 3SW, England ☎ 01628/825925 🖷 01628/825417 ⊕ www.landmarktrust.co.uk.

TOURS

You'll find that many of the best tours begin and end in Venice because so much of the region is accessible from there. Local tourist offices will be able to provide you with a list of authorized guides, for whom there is an official tariff rate.

BOAT TOURS

Between March and November, the Burchiello excursion boat makes an all-day villa tour along the Brenta Canal, departing from Padua on Wednesday, Friday, and Sunday, and from Venice on Tuesday, Thursday, and Saturday. You can admire more than 50 villas en route and stop and visit three: the Villas Pisani, Valmarana, and Foscari. There's a lunchtime break at the Burchiello restaurant at Oriago. Contact American Express for details, or book online at ⊕ www.ilburchiello.it.

🔲 Fees & Schedules **American Express** ⊠ Salizzada San Moisè, 1471 San Marco, Venice ☎ 041/5200844 🖷 041/5229937.

SPECIAL-INTEREST TOURS

You can have a free tour of "Chioggia by Night" on Monday and Thursday, June through September. Get details from the tourist office. During July and August you can take guided tours by night for "music and culture under the stars" in the towns of the Euganean Hills (Monselice, Montagnana, Este, Arqua Petrarca). Call Centro Guide Padova for information.

🔲 Fees & Schedules **Centro Guide Padova** ☎ 049/8209711. **Chioggia Tourist Office** ☎ 041/401068. **Sottomarina Tourist Office** ☎ 041/5540466

PRIVATE GUIDES

For an individual guide in Padua, call the Sindacato Guide Turistiche. Ippogrifo in Verona can provide escorted trips on foot, by car, or bus.

🔲 **Ippogrifo** ⊠ Via Roncisvalle 76 ☎ 045/8278959. **Sindacato Guide Turistiche** ☎ 049/8209711.

WALKING TOURS

The Comune di Padova organizes nocturnal tours of Padua.

🔲 Fees & Schedules **Comune di Padova** ☎ 049/8204562.

TRAIN TRAVEL

Trains on the most important routes from the south stop almost every hour in Verona, Padua, and Venice. From northern Italy and the rest of Europe, trains usually enter via Milan to the west or through Porta Nuova station in Verona. Call Trenitalia for fare and schedule information.

From Venice, the main line running across the north of Italy connects Padua (20 mins), Vicenza (1 hr), and Verona (1½ hrs) with most routes continuing west to Milan (3 hrs). From Padua, there are regular connections for Monselice, Este, Montegrotto Terme, and Rovigo, which in turn connect with Chioggia. The nearest train stations for Lake Garda are Peschiera, in the south, and Rovereto (in Trentino), from which there are frequent bus connections for Riva del Garda. Again, call Trenitalia for train information.

🚆 Train Information **Trenitalia** ☎ 892021 (no area code).

TRAVEL AGENCIES

🚆 Local Agents **A. Palladio Viaggi** ✉ Contrà Cavour 16, Vicenza ☎ 0444/546738. **Caldieri** ✉ Via Negrelli 1, Monselice ☎ 0429/783396. **Felicity** ✉ Riviera Magellano 4, Mestre ☎ 041/980899. **Freeworld Travel** ✉ Via Carrarese 29, Montagnana ☎ 0429/804278. **Garbellini Viaggi** ✉ Via Portello 13, Rovigo ☎ 0425/361319. **Giramondo Viaggi** ✉ Via Roma 12, Verona ☎ 045/595555. **Piacere Viaggi** ✉ Viale Veneto 8/a, Chioggia ☎ 041/5500470. **Welcome Travel Group** ✉ Via Risorgimento 20, Padua ☎ 049/666133.

VISITOR INFORMATION

Italian tourist office staff all speak good English, but hours vary so wildly that it's impossible to list or describe with any accuracy.

🚆 Tourist Information **Abano Terme** ✉ Via Pietro d'Abano 18, 35031 ☎ 049/8669055 **Arqua Petrarca** ✉ Via Castello 6, 35032 ☎ 0429/777240 **Bosco Chiesanuova** ✉ Piazza Chiesa 34, 37021 ☎ 045/7050088 **Chioggia** ✉ Lungomare Adriatico 101, 30019 ☎ 041/401068 **Este** ✉ Via Guido Negri 9/a, 35042 ☎ 0429/60042 **Malcesine** ✉ Via Capitanato del Porto 6, 37018 ☎ 045/7400044 **Mestre** ✉ Rotonda Marghera, 30174 ☎ 041/937764 **Monselice** ✉ Piazza Mazzini 15, 35043 ☎ 0429/783026 **Montagnana** ✉ Piazza Trieste 3, 35044 ☎ 0429/81320 **Montegrotto Terme** ✉ Viale Stazione 60, 35036 ☎ 049/793384 **Padua** ✉ Stazione Ferroviaria, 35100 ☎ 049/8752077; ✉ Piazza del Santo, 37019 Padua ☎ 049/8753087 **Peschiera** ✉ Piazza Municipio, 37019 ☎ 045/7551673 **Rovigo** ✉ Via Dunant 10, 45100 ☎ 0425/361481 **Verona** ✉ Stazione Ferroviaria, Porta Nuova, 37100 ☎ 045/8000861; ✉ Piazza Brà, 37121 ☎ 045/8068680 ⊕ www.tourism.verona.it **Vicenza** ✉ Piazza Matteotti 12, 36100 ☎ 0444/320854.

NORTHERN VENETO
TREVISO, THE DOLOMITES

8

FODOR'S CHOICE

Cortina d'Ampezzo

Da Bastian, *restaurant, Maser*

Due Mori, *hotel, Marostica*

Osteria Terraglio, *restaurant, Bassano del Grappa*

Toni del Spin, *restaurant, Treviso*

HIGHLY RECOMMENDED

SIGHTS Asolo

Cittadella

San Nicolò, *Treviso*

Villa Barbaro, *Maser*

RESTAURANTS Al Castello Superiore, *Marostica*

Alla Cima, *Valdobbiadene*

Alle Mura, *Castelfranco Veneto*

Città di Venezia, *Conegliano*

La Chiusa, *near Pieve di Cadore*

Locanda al Postiglione, *Vittorio Veneto*

Osteria degli Artisti, *Cittadella*

HOTELS Al Moretto, *Castelfranco Veneto*

Al Sole, *Asolo*

Bonotto Belvedere, *Bassano del Grappa*

Hotel Calvi, *Vittorio Veneto*

Miramonti Majestic, *Cortina d'Ampezzo*

Villa Cipriani, *Asolo*

Updated by
David Graham

THE REGION AROUND TREVISO called Marca Trevigiana was known by its early admirers as *gioiosa et amorosa* ("joyful and lovely"), which remains a good encapsulation of its attractions today. Towns here have spawned some of Italy's supreme painters and sculptors, whose magnificent works of art and architecture are very much in evidence. The region to the north provides a natural complement to these works of men in the form of the mighty Dolomites.

The arcaded town of Treviso, dubbed "the painted city" for its prolific frescoes, yields abundant artwork by Giotto's heir, Tomaso da Modena. The walled town of Castelfranco boasts a much-admired altarpiece by the Renaissance painter Giorgione. Great art and architecture can be discovered in the same building at the Villa Barbaro at Maser, the only point where the two geniuses of the 16th century, Palladio and Veronese, coincided. Conegliano—wine capital of the Veneto—is the birthplace of the 15th-century painter Cima. The unassuming village of Possagno displays one of the largest collections of Canova's sculptures and plaster casts anywhere. Last but not least, the mountain village of Pieve di Cadore has produced yet another master, Titian, whose modest house still remains.

The Dolomites are masterpieces in their own right, particularly when the last rays of the setting sun shed their pink spell on the sheer and jagged heights. Here, follow your whim, either to hobnob in Cortina d'Ampezzo's bars and restaurants during the ski season or to experience the thrill of the mountains while walking, fishing, or horseback riding—best done on the gentler slopes of the southerly Pieve di Cadore districts. Higher up are some of the most dramatic driving routes in Italy. You'll find some excellent restaurants in these parts, many tucked away in the woods, as well as a wide range of upmarket or cozy hotels.

The shadow of Venice, of course, is ever present, its influence stretching to Belluno, strategically placed as its northernmost ally. La Serenissima was responsible for rebuilding the town of Feltre after it was sacked by Emperor Maximilian in 1509, thus making Feltre one of the best places to absorb the feel of small-scale 16th-century Italy. The lion of St. Mark sits proudly atop a column in the piazza at Bassano del Grappa, a town made even more picturesque by the wooden bridge designed by Palladio. Marostica, famous for its human chess match held each September, was ruled by Venice for nearly 400 years and vaunts two castles with walls that tier down the hillside. Imposing defense works also gird the small centers of Castelfranco and Cittadella.

With its red walls rising above and sheltering the town within, Cittadella is perhaps the supreme example of a small fortified Italian town. It was one of the strongholds of Ezzelino III da Romano (1194–1259), a name that comes up in any account of this area. A much-hated man who terrorized the region during the 13th century, he was known as the "Son of Satan"—so monstrous and tyrannical were his deeds that he was condemned to boil in a river of blood in Dante's *Inferno*. When Ezzelino died, the remainder of his family was massacred by the citizens of Asolo to prevent his like from ever being seen again.

Exploring Northern Veneto

A half hour's drive due north of Mestre on the A27 brings you to Treviso, the chief town of the region. Set among gentle hills, the area's numerous walled and medieval towns lie to the north and west of this town, though the region becomes more mountainous at Bassano del Grappa in the west and at Vittorio Veneto, farther north of Treviso. From Belluno, dramatically placed on the Piave River on the edge of the Dolomites, the S51 continues north to Pieve di Cadore and Cortina d'Ampezzo in the heart of Dolomites. If you're without a car, this range is most easily explored by bus, and it's easy to connect with any of the other smaller towns in this region by public transportation.

About the Restaurants & Hotels

Hotels in the small towns of the region offer excellent value. Treviso caters largely to the business sector, with hotels sited away from the historic center. If you're planning a stay in Cortina in the peak skiing season, be sure to book well ahead. The quieter resorts will have more low-key hotels, but still check on availability. Bear in mind that many hotels in the mountains and some restaurants close between Easter and June.

WHAT IT COSTS In euros					
	$$$$	**$$$**	**$$**	**$**	**¢**
RESTAURANTS	over €22	€17–€22	€12–€17	€7–€12	under €7
HOTELS	over €210	€160–€210	€110–€160	€60–€110	under €60

Restaurant prices are for a second course (secondo piatto). Hotel prices are for two people in a standard double room in high season, including tax and service.

Timing

Touring the Treviso region or the Dolomites in late spring or early summer is a visual feast, when the vines are in full leaf and the meadows lush with flowers (the cherry blossom is a sight to behold in April and May). Many of the smaller towns hold festivals in the fall, when there is much feasting and gaiety. In winter the crucial question is: snow or no snow? Snowfalls can make driving treacherous, though main roads are kept clear and tourist offices always have up-to-the-minute reports on conditions. Skiing varies wildly year by year but is almost always best in late February and March, after a full season of snow. Whatever time you plan your trip, you'll always be here at the right time for the mountains, which are stunning in all seasons.

TREVISO & ENVIRONS

The prosperous city of Treviso provides easy access to a handful of towns in the region, including the beautiful walled towns of Castelfranco, home to one of Giorgione's most famous paintings, and Cittadella, resonant with reminders of its long history. Bassano del Grappa, with its lovely Palladian bridge and ceramics, is only a hop away, as are Marostica, renowned for its checkerboard square, and Asolo, antique retreat of the Venetian aristocracy. North of Treviso, the Renaissance can be savored in the streets of Vittorio Veneto and the thriving wine center of Conegliano. If you're interested in white wine, the abundant wine trails in the area invite exploration, while if sculpture's your bag, you can refresh your spirit by gazing on Canova's masterpieces in his museum at Possagno. And if you really can't leave the region without shopping, you'll find all the well-known names in Treviso, as well as a plethora of crafts and ceramics shops here and in the smaller towns, not to mention the gourmet delicatessens bulging with local specialties.

Treviso

▶ ❶ *30 km (19 mi) north of Venice.*

"Little Venice" is probably a somewhat inflated claim for Treviso, though the town does have canals and a Venetian air; "the painted city"

Numbers in the text correspond to numbers in the margin and on the Northern Veneto map.

If you have 3 days

Even with only three days at your disposal, you can experience both the mountains and towns of this area. Starting off in "the painted city" of **Treviso** ①►, browse around the town's artworks and diverse shops in the morning before heading west to make a brief circuit of the medieval walls of **Cittadella** ⑤. After a bite of lunch, head off to the lovely Palladian bridge in ▨**Bassano del Grappa** ⑥, the place to indulge in a grappa (and a possible hotel stop); alternatively, spend the night in ▨**Asolo** ②, a town famed for its "hundred vistas." From either of these places, head north toward the Dolomites, perhaps stopping in **Belluno** ⑪ for lunch. The grandeur of the mountains becomes a constant presence as you progress up the Piave River valley to ▨**Cortina d'Ampezzo** ⑭ or to the quieter ▨**Pieve di Cadore** ⑬ for your second night, dining well in one of the local restaurants. Your third day could be spent walking and admiring the stunning mountain views before returning south, on the way passing through **Vittorio Veneto** ⑩ and ▨**Conegliano** ⑨, both with fine artistic and architectural treasures on view, before returning to Treviso.

8

If you have 5 days

Five days would allow you to tour the area at a more leisurely pace. Following the same basic route from **Treviso** ①► as before, you could take in ▨**Castelfranco Veneto** ④ for the Giorgione connection en route to ▨**Cittadella** ⑤, spending the night in ▨**Bassano del Grappa** ⑥. From here, it's a short hop west to **Marostica** ⑦ to see the famous checkered square. Doubling back through Bassano, head northeast to Possagno to admire Canova's graceful sculptures; then spend your second night at ▨**Asolo** ②, where you'll have time for the famous vistas and the Palladian villa at **Maser** ③. Taking the road north, you should stop next in the walled Venetian town of **Feltre** ⑫, and then visit **Belluno** ⑪, beautifully sited against the backdrop of the mountains, before spending your third night in either ▨**Cortina d'Ampezzo** ⑭ or **Pieve di Cadore** ⑬. If you're a fan of mountain scenery, spend a second night here; otherwise drive south to **Vittorio Veneto** ⑩, still within the shadow of the mountains, and then continue on for your fourth night at ▨**Conegliano** ⑨. Here you can pick up the wine route almost all the way back to Treviso.

---

is a less extravagant title, and an apt one: you'll come across frescoes practically everywhere you look. This is a busy commercial center, with fashionable shops and boutiques at every turn. Treviso was already well established long before it came within the sphere of Venetian influence in the late 14th century, minting its own coins as early as the 8th century and becoming a center for literary and artistic excellence by the 13th. Much of the city was embellished by Tomaso da Modena (1325–79), the foremost northern Italian painter following the death of Giotto, responsible for decorating many of the Gothic churches with his frescoes.

Most of the frescoes on the outside of Treviso's buildings were put there by happy accident—the lack of suitable stone with which to finish the facades in the 13th century. Together with the arcaded streets and mossy banked canals, where weeping willows trail their fronds in the water, these help to create an appealing town center, unmarred by the postwar

Northern
Veneto

constructions erected after a bombing raid on Good Friday 1944, when about half the city was destroyed. Other buildings, some dating from the 15th century, have been expertly restored.

The early 15th-century walls are best preserved around the Porta dei Santa Quaranta, the main gate west of the center. Borgo Cavour leads past the Museo Civico to Via Calmaggiore and the main **Piazza dei Signori,** in the heart of the medieval city. Some impressive public buildings line the piazza. Behind one of them, the early 13th-century **Palazzo dei Trecento** (restored after the bombing raid of 1944), follow a small alley for about 200 yards to the *pescheria* (fish market) on an island in one of the canals flowing through town. The nearby church of **Santa Lucia** holds frescoes by Tomaso da Modena.

> **need a break?**
>
> Nearby, **Nascimben** (✉ Via Calmaggiore 32 ☎ 0422/540871), closed Monday, is the best *pasticceria* (pastry shop) in town, a good place for the requisite sampling of the local tiramisù before more exploring.

Treviso's seven-domed **Duomo** was founded in the 12th century. Within, the Malchiostro Chapel contains fine paintings and frescoes: an *Annunciation* by Titian (circa 1488–1576) and frescoes by Pordenone (1484–1539), including the *Adoration of the Magi.* The crypt is worth a visit for its array of 12th-century columns. ✉ Piazza del Duomo ☎ 0422/545720 ☉ Daily 7:30–noon and 3–7.

Housed in the Canoniche Vecchie near the Duomo, the **Museo Diocesano d'Arte Sacra** contains archaeological material, a frescoed lunette by Tomaso da Modena, church silver, and vestments. ✉ Canoniche Vecchie, Via Canoniche 9 ☎ 0422/410700 ☞ Free ☉ Mon.–Thurs. 9–noon, Sat. 9–noon and 3–6.

★ The most important church in Treviso is **San Nicolò**, an imposing Gothic building with an ornate vaulted ceiling. San Nicolò has more frescoes of the saints by Tomaso da Modena on the columns. Particularly charming is the depiction of *St. Agnes* on the north side, but the artist's best work here is the remarkable series of 40 portraits of Dominican friars in the seminary next door. These are astoundingly realistic considering that some were painted as early as 1352 and include one of the earliest-known portraits of a subject wearing glasses. ⊠ *Capitolo dei Domenicani, Seminario Vescovile, Via San Nicolò* ☎ *0422/3247* ⊙ *Mon.–Sat. 8:15–noon and 3–5, Sun. 3–5.*

The **Museo Civico** holds an archaeological section on the ground floor, including a collection of bronze sword blades dating from the 7th and 6th centuries BC and Roman remains. Upstairs is the picture gallery, the **Galleria Communale d'Arte Moderna.** Room 11 holds the best: portraits by Titian and Lorenzo Lotto (circa 1480–1556) and a *Crucifixion* by Jacopo Bassano (circa 1510–92). In contrast to these are the 19th- and 20th-century sculptures, bronzes, ceramics, and charcoal drawings by the Trevisan artist Arturo Martini (1889–1947) and the painter Gino Rossi (1884–1947). ⊠ *Borgo Cavour 24* ☎ *0422/591337* ⊠ *€3* ⊙ *Tues.–Sat. 9–12:30 and 2:30–5, Sun. 9–noon.*

The **Chiesa di Santa Caterina,** on the east side of the city, holds more frescoes by da Modena, including his *Ursula Cycle.* Other frescoes attributed to his school are found in the **Cappella degli Innocenti** (⊠ tourist office: Piazzetta del Monte di Pietà, 31100 ☎ 0422/547632). This deconsecrated church is in the process of being restored and is currently closed. Contact the Museo Civico or the tourist office for information. ⊠ *Piazzetta Mario Botter.*

Where to Stay & Eat

$–$$ ╳ **Toni del Spin.** Wood-paneled and styled with '30s decor, this place oozes
Fodor'sChoice delightful, old-fashioned character. Locals love the friendly and bustling
★ feel as well as the wholesome food. The menu changes twice a week and is chalked on a hanging wooden board: try the filling *zuppa d'orzo e fagioli* (barley and bean soup) or the pasta e fagioli, delivered with panache and care. You shouldn't leave without quaffing a glass or two of Prosecco. ⊠ *Via Inferiore 7* ☎ *0422/543829* ⊰ *Reservations essential* ⊟ *AE, MC, V* ⊙ *Closed Sun. and Aug. No lunch Mon.*

¢–$ ╳ **Osteria Muscoli's.** The bar is always busy with locals popping in for an *ombra* (glass of wine), but there are rustic wooden tables out back where you can sit and enjoy the offerings of this traditional osteria. The young, efficient staff will prepare a generous platter of savory delights, possibly with chunks of ham off the bone, a wedge of potato-and-porcini pie, pepper cheese, stuffed pickled tomatoes, and *crostini* (grilled bread) with *sfilacci* (shredded, cured horse meat). The menu, posted on a blackboard, changes daily. ⊠ *Via Pescheria 23* ☎ *0422/583390* ⊟ *No credit cards* ⊙ *Closed Sun. and 3 wks in Sept.*

¢ ╳ **Brek.** See review under "Where to Stay & Eat" in Padua, Chapter 7. ⊠ *Corso del Popolo 25* ☎ *0422/590012* ⊟ *AE, DC, MC, V.*

$–$$ ╳⌂ **La Colonna.** Everything in this small hotel, set in a vine-covered 15th-century courtyard, is crisp and white. Flower-frescoed ceilings and old-fashioned washstands in the bathrooms add to the charm. It's essential to book one of the six rooms well ahead. You can feel the history seeping through the walls in the associated restaurant of the same name ($$–$$$), where you can dine among the pillars, beamed ceiling, and low arches of the main room or on the mezzanine floor. The chef favors fish, and beef with rosemary is a perfumey delight. The wine bar next door is also worth a visit. ⊠ *Via Campana 27, 31100* ☎ *0422/ 544804* ⊟ *0422/419177* ⇥ *6 rooms* ⌂ *Restaurant, bar, some pets al-*

ON THE MENU

THE CUISINE OF THE TREVISO AREA combines robust country cooking and more refined dishes. Great use is made of what grows in the wild, especially in the hills. Chestnuts, berries, mushrooms, herbs, and verdure (greens) all have their place on the menu. You can't make a journey through this zone without encountering radicchio and white asparagus, the two vegetable specialties. Game figures on the menu in the mountain zones, and in winter steaming bowls of pasta e fagioli (pasta and bean soup), creamy risotto, and polenta are staples. Treviso is reputedly the birthplace of tiramisù (literally "pick me up"), that delight composed of espresso, mascarpone cheese, sugar, ladyfingers, liqueur, and cocoa powder.

The cattle that graze on the mountain pastures and the fertile lowlands produce excellent cheese that comes with a D.O.C.

(Denominazione di Origine Controllata) mark, a guarantee of quality. Look for Montasio and Asiago, both in mild, medium, and strong varieties. Grana Padano and Provolone Val Padana are piquant and flavorful. In summer try Morlacco, a soft, salty cheese that comes from the mountains, and Casatella, a creamy cheese made by local farmers.

Regional wine production is dominated by Prosecco, the white wine of choice here (and also in Venice). Prosecco tranquillo (still) goes well with starters, spumante (sparkling) is recommended as an aperitif, and frizzante (lightly sparkling, the most popular type) is suitable for any occasion. Prosecco is often sold with a distinctive string tied round the cork, recalling the traditional means of keeping the cork in during the second fermentation. The most highly rated is Superiore di Cartizze.

---

lowed ⊟ AE, DC, MC, V ⊘ Restaurant closed Mon. and 2 wks in mid-Aug. No dinner Sun. ⧀ CP.

$$–$$$ ▣ **Cà del Galletto.** This modern, functional hotel on the outskirts of town offers plenty of personal and public space while being just five minutes by car or city bus from the center. Facilities include a pool (summer only), gym, sauna, and elegant restaurant. Free use of bikes means you can park the car here and visit the historic center at a leisurely pace. ⊠ Via Santa Bona Vecchia 30, ☎ 0422/432550 🖷 0422/432510 ⊕ www.hotelcadelgalletto.it ⟿ 37 rooms ⌂ Restaurant, in-room data ports, tennis court, pool, gym, sauna, bicycles, bar ⊟ AE, DC, MC, V ⧀ CP.

¢ ▣ **Il Cascinale.** A five-minute urban bus ride will get you here from the center of town, but this agriturismo, or farmstay, is in the open country. Don't expect time-worn rustic charm though: this is a modern block of bright, spacious rooms above the owners' equally modern residence. Rooms are smartly furnished to hotel standards, and a hearty, country breakfast (not included in the room rate) is on offer downstairs. The restaurant is open for other meals on weekends only. A big front lawn provides plenty of play space for children. ⊠ Via Torre d'Orlando 6/B, 31100 🖷🖷 0422/402203 ⊕ www.agriturismoilcascinale.it ⟿ 8 rooms ⌂ Restaurant, minibars, playground, meeting room, free parking; no a/c ⊟ No credit cards ⧀ CP.

Nightlife & the Arts

ART EXHIBITIONS The **Casa dei Carraresi** (⊠ Via Palestro 33-35 ☎ call center 0438/21306 ⊕ www.lineadombra.it) hosts big, international impressionist art exhibitions annually. Contact the call center for information on current exhibits.

CONCERTS **Estate Trevigiano** (☎ 0422/547632 tourist office), a series of open-air events consisting of music, concerts, theater, and dance, takes place in the summer.

BARS The piano bar **Nilo Blu** (✉ Via della Repubblica 7/c ☎ 0422/420469), 3 km (2 mi) north of the center on the road to Vittorio Veneto and Conegliano, features live jazz and rock bands most evenings but is primarily a place to lounge and talk. **Soda Pop** (✉ Via Fonderia 46 ☎ 0422/424487) has live music and a young crowd.

Shopping

The wrought iron and copper for which Treviso is known might be a little difficult to transport home, but there are plenty of small shops to explore in addition to the usual well-known names. A general market is held Tuesday and Saturday mornings just behind the **Piazza dei Signori.**

CERAMICS For ceramics, visit **Ceramiche Artistiche di Visentin** (✉ Piazza Garibaldi 16 ☎ 0422/590990) where you can watch the owner hand-painting beautiful pieces with reproduction antique or made-to-order patterns.

GIFTS At **Mangiafuoco-Vecchi Giochi** (✉ Via Riccati 12 ☎ 0422/541738) you can find handcrafted puppets, models of characters from fairy tales, and handmade paper items. **De Pol** (✉ Via Calmaggiore 33 ☎ 0422/412343) sells fine leather bags, belts, and shoes.

Asolo

★ ❷ *35 km (22 mi) northwest of Treviso, 65 km (41 mi) northwest of Venice.*

The romantic, charming hillside hamlet of Asolo was the consolation prize of an exiled queen. At the end of the 15th century, Venetian-born Caterina Cornaro was sent here by Venice's doges to keep her from interfering with their administration of her former kingdom of Cyprus, which she had inherited upon the death of her husband, James II Lusignan of Cyprus. To soothe the pain of exile, she established a lively and brilliant court in Asolo. In this court Cardinal Pietro Bembo (1470–1547), one of the foremost literary figures of the time, wrote the love letters *Gli Asolani,* coining the word *asolare,* meaning to while away the time in idle pleasures. Over the centuries, Venetian aristocrats continued to build gracious villas on the hillside, and in the 19th century Asolo once again became the idyllic haunt of musicians, poets, and painters. The man of letters and ideologue Gabriele d'Annunzio (1863–1938) was smitten with the beauty of the place, as was the English poet Robert Browning (1812–89). From the outside, you can see villas once inhabited by Browning and also the actress Eleonora Duse (1850–1924), called "*La Divina del teatro italiano.*" She was famous as much for her stormy love life as for her roles in Ibsen and Shakespeare. Her tomb can be found in the cemetery of the church of Sant'Anna, along with that of the English explorer and writer Freya Stark (1893–1993), who lived here for most of her life.

Asolo has not always been a scene of tranquillity. In the early 13th century it fell, like many other towns of the area, under the sway of the tyrant Ezzelino III da Romano. Upon his death in 1259 the people of Asolo made sure that his ilk was never seen again by massacring all remaining members of his family. The peaceful Old World ambience vaporizes on holiday weekends when the crowds pour in. Book your accommodation well ahead if you can.

Asolo's town center, **Piazza Maggiore,** is the site of Renaissance palaces and antique cafés. The Piazza Maggiore is also home to the frescoed 15th-century **Loggia del Capitano,** which contains the **Museo Civico,** displaying memorabilia of Asolo's dead coterie—manuscripts, Eleonora Duse's correspondence, Browning's spinet, and portraits of Caterina Cornaro. ✉ *Piazza Maggiore* ☎ *0423/952313* 💶 *€4, or €5 for a combined ticket giving access to the Gypsotech in Possagno and a discount on entry to the Villa Barbaro* ☉ *Wed.–Sun. 10–12:30 and 3–7.*

need a break?

While away some idle moments at the famous **Caffè Centrale** (☒ Via Roma 72 ☎ 0423/952141 ⊕ www.caffecentrale.com ☉ Closed Tues.), which has overlooked the fountain in Piazza Maggiore and the Duomo since about 1700.

The **Duomo** was rebuilt in 1747 on the site of Roman baths. Caterina Cornaro donated the baptismal font, and Jacopo Bassano (circa 1510–92) and Lorenzo Lotto (1480–1556) both painted *Assumption* altarpieces. ☒ *Piazzetta S. Pio X 192* ☎ *0423/952376* ☉ *Daily 7–noon and 3–6.*

Walking along Via Browning takes you past smart shops, Browning's house at No. 153, and the enoteca **Alle Ore** (☒ Via Browning 183 ☎ 0423/952070), where you can sample the local wine and grappa. It's closed Monday. Uphill from the piazza, you'll go past Caterina's ruined **Castello** (☒ Piazzetta E. Duse ☎ 0423/952361), whose theater was transported to Florida in 1930. The castle is closed for renovation. Then as you go farther past some Gothic-style houses, you'll find the medieval fortress **La Rocca** From this summit is a view of Asolo's "hundred horizons." The site closes when the weather turns bad. ☒ *Monte Ricco* ☎ *0423/529046 (tourist office)* ⊠ *€1.50* ☉ *Daily 10–12.30 and 3–7.*

off the beaten path

POSSAGNO – Just 8 km (5 mi) northwest of Asolo, this small town nestling at the foot of Monte Grappa merits a visit for its **Gipsoteca Museo Canoviano,** birthplace of the sculptor and architect Antonio Canova (1757–1822). Set in a typical Venetian garden, with vistas over the mellow countryside, the *gipsoteca* (collection of plaster casts) was built in 1836 and contains about 300 plaster, wax, and terra-cotta models that illustrate Canova's way of working. Little nails (*rèpere*) were first studded all over the plaster cast; then by means of a pantograph (measuring device) the proportions were transferred to the final marble version. This is documented in his studio, part of his native house, alongside his charming and elegant paintings, mainly of disporting Greek nymphs. In the airy halls, marvel at the force of *Hercules and the Lion* and the beauty of *The Three Graces*. ☒ *Piazza Canova* ☎ *0423/544323* ⊠ *€4, or €5 for a combined ticket giving access to the Asolo museum and a discount on entry to the Villa Barbaro* ☉ *Tues.–Sun. 9–noon and 3–6.*

On the other side of the road an imposing drive leads to the **Tempio,** a church—reminiscent of the Pantheon—designed by Canova as the resting place for his mortal remains. ☒ *Stradone del Tempio* ☉ *Tues.–Sun. 9–noon and 3–6.*

Where to Stay & Eat

$$–$$$ ✕ **Hosteria Ca'Derton.** Opposite the entrance to the castle, Ca'Derton is pleasantly old-fashioned, with early photos of Asolo and bouquets of dried flowers. Proprietor Nino and his wife, Antonietta, serve both local and international dishes, and take pride in their homemade pasta, bread, and desserts. From November through April, try the *sopa coada,* a local soup made with pigeon meat and bread that takes two days to prepare; the recipe is several centuries old. ☒ *Piazza Gabriele D'Annunzio 11* ☎ *0423/529648* ⊟ *AE, DC, MC, V* ☉ *Closed Mon., last wk in July and 1st wk in Aug. No dinner Sun.*

$ ✕ **Al Bacaro.** Simple but authentic traditional specialties like stewed game, tripe, snails, and cooked cheese dishes are served in this rustic little osteria, or you can choose from the tempting selection of big open sandwiches generously topped with fresh salami, speck, or other cold cuts. Founded in 1892, it is also renowned for its local and Apulian wines. ☒ *Via Browning 165* ☎ *0423/55150* ⊟ *AE, DC, MC, V* ☉ *Closed Wed.*

★ $$$$ 🏨 **Villa Cipriani.** A romantic garden surrounded by gracious country homes on a hillside below Asolo is the setting for this historic villa, now part of the Starwood chain. Tastefully furnished with 19th-century antiques, it offers an old-fangled atmosphere, every creature comfort, and discreet service. Past guests have included Prince Philip, Aristotle Onassis, and Queen Juliana. The superb restaurant has a terrace overlooking the garden, a perfect place to sip an aperitif. ⊠ *Via Canova 298, 31011* ☎ *0423/523411* 🖷 *0423/952095* ⊕ *www.starwood.com/italy* 🛏 *31 rooms* ⚷ *Restaurant, bar, in-room data ports, in-room safes, minibars, cable TV, Internet, meeting room, some pets allowed (fee), no-smoking floor* ▤ *AE, DC, MC, V* ⎩ *CP.*

★ $$$–$$$$ 🏨 **Al Sole.** The smell of the polished wood floor greets you as you enter this 1920s pink-washed hotel overlooking the main square. All the rooms are large and furnished in antique style; the more expensive ones overlook the town, but the back rooms have leafy, rural views that are equally pleasant. The decoratively tiled bathrooms come equipped with hydro-massage showers. ⊠ *Via Collegio 3, 31011* ☎ *0423/528111* 🖷 *0423/528399* ⊕ *www.albergoalsole.com* 🛏 *22 rooms, 1 suite* ⚷ *Bar, in-room data ports, in-room safes, minibars, cable TV, golf privileges, gym, free parking, some pets allowed* ▤ *AE, MC, V* ⎩ *CP.*

$$ 🏨 **Duse.** Rooms in this centrally located hotel are prettily decorated, but some are fairly small. Those higher up have beamed ceilings and views across to the Duomo. Best of all is the attic suite up a winding staircase, with different levels. ⊠ *Via Browning 190, 31011* ☎ *0423/55241* 🖷 *0423/950404* ⊕ *www.hotelduse.com* 🛏 *13 rooms, 1 suite* ⚷ *Bar, minibars, cable TV, meeting room* ▤ *AE, MC, V* ⎩ *CP.*

Nightlife & the Arts

FESTIVALS During the third weekend of September a **Palio** is held, commemorating the history of Asolo from Roman times until the arrival of Caterina Cornaro. It takes the form of a Roman chariot race through the streets and is attended by much feasting.

Shopping

An **antiques market** sets up in Piazza Maggiore on the second Sunday of the month (except July and August).

FOOD For a shop that is pure theater, make sure you visit the century-old **Ennio** (⊠ Via Browning 151 ☎ 0423/529109). Once you've ogled longingly in front of the many windows, where food is displayed in all its glory—the biggest bowls of preserves and olives you've ever seen, graceful bottles of grappa, jars of truffle, enticing pastries, formidable cheeses—a visit inside is obligatory, as all these delights will be lovingly extolled by the expansive owner.

GIFTS You can see the ceramic artist at work at **La Guizza Ceramiche** (⊠ Via Browning 166 ☎ 0423/55430). **Rosso** (⊠ Via Regina Cornaro 221 ☎ 0423/55544) sells tasteful jewelry.

Maser

❸ *7 km (4½ mi) northeast of Asolo, 33 km (20½ mi) northwest of Treviso.*

★ **Villa Barbaro** is one of Palladio's most gracious Renaissance creations. The fully furnished villa, just outside the town of Maser, is still inhabited by its owners, who make you wear heavy felt slippers over your shoes to protect the highly polished floors. The elaborate stuccos and opulent frescoes by Paolo Veronese bring the 16th century to life. After La Rotonda in Vicenza, this is Palladio's greatest villa and is definitely worth going out of your way for (before making the trip, note the restricted hours). On the grounds, the **Tempietto** (little church) is one of

Palladio's last projects, the only church designed by him lying outside Venice. The Tempietto is currently closed for restoration, but a **cantina** on the grounds offers wine tastings. ⊠ *Via Cornuda 2* ☎ *0423/923004* 🖅 *€5* ⏰ *Mar.–Oct., Tues. and weekends 3–6; Nov.–Feb., weekends 2:30–5. Closed Dec. 24–Jan. 6.*

Where to Eat

$–$$ ✕ **Agnoletti.** In the town of Giavera del Montello, about 25 km (16 mi) east of Maser, Agnoletti is an 18th-century inn of a bygone era with a lovely summer garden. The kitchen can produce an all-mushroom menu; but if you order something else, at least try the mushroom *zuppa* (soup) or *tortina di funghi* (mushroom tart). ⊠ *Via della Vittoria 190, Giavera del Montello* ☎ *0422/776009* 🖃 *AE, DC, MC, V* ⏰ *Closed Tues., 1 wk in Jan., and 2 wks in July.*

$ ✕ **Da Bastian.** A good place to stop for lunch in Maser before visiting
FodorśChoice the Villa Barbaro (a five-minute walk away), this excellent restaurant
★ has a pleasant garden for outdoor dining. Everything on the menu is seasonal; autumn and winter offerings include grilled mushrooms, homemade pumpkin tortelli, and, for second courses, baccalà, snails, and *trippa alla Veneta* (tripe cooked in a tomato and white wine sauce). The dessert trolley is laden with mouthwatering homemade cakes and fruit tarts. ⊠ *Via Cornuda (follow sign), Loc. Muliparte, Maser* ☎ *0423/565400* 🖃 *No credit cards* ⏰ *Closed Thurs. and Aug. No dinner Wed.*

Castelfranco Veneto

❹ *27 km (17 mi) west of Treviso, 45 km (28 mi) northwest of Venice.*

The stocky, battlemented walls with green banks and trees running down to the moat are not quite in the league of Cittadella's, but they nevertheless lend character to this small town. Erected in the 12th century by the Trevisans as protection against Padua, they encircle the old center, or Castello. The most famous name associated with this town is that of Giorgione (1478–1510), the least known of all the figures of the High Renaissance. Dying young, possibly of the plague, graced with physical beauty and musical talents, he possessed all the attributes of poetic remembrance. The **Casa Giorgione** contains a small museum about the artist and, on the first floor, a chiaroscuro frieze attributed to him. ⊠ *Piazzetta San Liberale* ⏰ *Closed for restoration at press time. Contact the library for information* ☎ *0423/735690.*

The neoclassical **Duomo**, modeled on Palladio's Chiesa del Redentore in Venice, holds frescoes by Paolo Veronese (1528–88) and Zelotti (1526–78). Castelfranco's greatest treasure, however, is Giorgione's altarpiece *Madonna and Child with SS. Francis and Liberale*, known as *La Pala*. The poetic and enigmatic mood his paintings evoke is ably demonstrated here. Commissioned in 1504 to commemorate the death of a young man of 18, Matteo Costanza, it shows three figures gazing dolefully out of the picture. Mary is set apart, at one with the landscape and isolated from the two saints in the foreground. ⊠ *Via Francesco Maria Preti* ☎ *0423/495202* ⏰ *Daily 9–noon and 3–6.*

The restored **Teatro Accademico** was built to a design of F. M. Preti, also responsible for the cathedral. It's an elegant example of 18th-century work, in which concerts and performances can still be enjoyed in season. ⊠ *Via Garibaldi* ☎ *0423/735571* 🖅 *Free* ⏰ *By appointment.*

Outside the city walls are some fine palaces, notably the stuccoed 18th-century **Palazzo Soranzo Novello** (⊠ Corso XXIX Aprile), now a bank.

The broad road Borgo Treviso leads to the **Parco Revedin Bolasco**, a tranquil garden with lakes, canals, little bridges, and hillocks. It complements the villa built in the 19th century by Giovan Battista Meduna. Here you'll find a Moorish greenhouse on an island and a circle of statues surrounding an amphitheater that was originally used as an exercise ground for horses. ☎ *337 805304* ✆ *Free* ⊙ *Mar.·21–May 31 and Sept. 21–Nov. 2, Tues. and Thurs. 10–12:30 and 3–5:30, Sun. 10–1 and 2:30–5:30; June 1–Sept. 20, Tues. and Thurs 10–12:30 and 3–5:30, Sun. 10–1 and 3–7:30.*

Where to Stay & Eat

★ **$$$–$$$$** ✕ **Alle Mura.** Castelfranco is not the sort of town where you would expect to find this tropical-style restaurant, where the exotic festoons of fruit and flowers, chirping birds, and leopard-skin chairs are a veritable assault on the eye. If that is not enough, the pictures on the wall might suggest you've been transported to the South Seas, as do the Pacific island recipes, which include fish and shellfish specialties. ⊠ *Via Francesco Maria Preti 69* ☎ *0423/498098* ⚐ *Reservations essential* ▤ *AE, DC, MC, V* ⊙ *Closed Thurs., Jan. 10–31, and Aug.*

$$ ✕ **Ai Do Mori.** Typical dishes from the Veneto are served in this small restaurant up a little street just within the walls. If you've never got around to tasting *trippa* (tripe), now is your chance, but if you're not tempted by the trippa *alla parmigiana* (with Parmesan), maybe you'll feel safer with the *polenta e oca* (goose with polenta and herbs). ⊠ *Vicolo Montebelluna 24* ☎ *0423/495725* ▤ *AE, DC, MC, V* ⊙ *Closed Thurs.*

★ **$$** ▥ **Al Moretto.** In the hands of the same family for generations, this refined but understated hotel offers welcoming service. The public rooms are intimate and at the same time light, soothing, and summery, with wicker furniture and chintz armchairs. In summer, breakfast is served in the leafy garden. ⊠ *Via San Pio X 10, 31033* ☎ *0423/721313* 🖷 *0423/721066* ◀ *36 rooms* ⚑ *Bar, in-room data ports, in-room safes, minibars, cable TV, free parking, some pets allowed, no-smoking floor* ▤ *AE, DC, MC, V* ▯⊙▮ *CP.*

$ ▥ **Alla Torre.** The clock tower of Castelfranco's medieval castle overlooks this hotel, and the original brick wall is even incorporated into some of the suites. Rooms are modern and spacious, and the plaid carpets add a touch of hominess. A terrace gives onto the square. ⊠ *Piazzetta Trento Trieste 7, 31033* ☎ *0423/498707* 🖷 *0423/498737* ◀ *46 rooms, 9 suites* ⚑ *Bar, in-room safes, minibars, cable TV, free parking, some pets allowed* ▤ *AE, DC, MC, V* ▯⊙▮ *CP.*

Cittadella

★ ❺ *13 km (8 mi) southeast of Marostica, 61 km (38 mi) northwest of Venice.*

Of all the walled cities in the Brenta Valley, Cittadella conveys most fully the sense of enclosure and protection. The lofty and battlemented walls rise up on either side as you enter through the brick arches of the Porta Padua, painted with the red *carra* (wagon) emblem of the Carrara family. Imagine, as you pass the **Torre di Malta,** the plight of the prisoners abandoned here to die of starvation by the tyrant Ezzelino III da Romano. The town was built on a Roman site by the Paduans as a counter to Castelfranco, a Trevisan stronghold, and then passed to a succession of powerful families including, of course, Ezzelino's. The lines of the streets follow the original Roman plan, with gates at the four cardinal points.

Via Garibaldi leads to the main plaza, **Piazza Pierobon** and the early 19th-century square **Duomo** with its massive columns and, inside, paintings by Jacopo Bassano, including *La Cena in Emmaus* in the sacristy. ⊠ *Via Marconi 5* ☎ *049/5970237* ⊙ *Daily 7:30–12:30 and 3–7.*

For the best view over the red-tiled roofs, pale ocher houses, and soaring walls, climb the bell tower of the Duomo, the **Torre Campanaria,** which doubles as a museum. As you go up, you'll see the walls festooned with vestments, candelabra, and other ecclesiastical exhibits. ⊠ *Duomo, Via Marconi 5* ☎ *049/5970237* ⊘ *Open by appointment only, phone for information.*

On Via Indipendenza, the neoclassical **Teatro** has a facade by Japelli (1783–1852). The **Palazzo Pretorio** on Via Marconi, with a fine 16th-century marble portal and frescoes, was headquarters of whoever was in control of the city. You can visit upon request; contact the **tourist office** (⊠ Via Marconi 3, ☎☎ 049/5970627).

A pleasant end to your visit can be a walk around the exterior of the walls through the **Giardini Pubblici,** open daily 8:30–5:30.

Where to Stay & Eat

★ $ ✕ **Osteria degli Artisti.** Colorful tablecloths, ceramic dishes, and numerous paintings decorating the bright, airy dining rooms contribute to the homey atmosphere. Before tucking into *petto di pavoncella con erbette di campo* (breast of peafowl with wild vegetables), try the *tortelli di fagiano ai Carletti e crudo di Parma* (homemade tortelli pasta filled with pheasant and Parma ham) or macaroni with wild hops and salt cod. ⊠ *Via Mura Rotta 11* ☎ *049/9402317* ⊟ *AE, MC, V* ⊘ *Closed Tues. No dinner Mon.*

$$ 🏨 **La Cittadella.** The accent is emphatically floral in this beautifully decorated hotel, from the dried flower arrangements to the frescoes and wallpaper. The rooms are bright and spacious, and some have small terraces with potted plants and chairs. It's in a quiet location just outside the walls and represents very good value for the money. ⊠ *Via Monte Pertica 3, 35013* ☎ *049/9402434* 🖷 *049/5975544* ⤶ *26 rooms, 9 suites, 14 apartments with kitchen* ⚭ *Restaurant, bar, in-room safes, minibars, cable TV, indoor pool, gym, sauna, baby-sitting, meeting room, free parking* ⊟ *AE, DC, MC, V* ⦿ *CP.*

$$ 🏨 **La Filanda.** A 19th-century spinning factory has been restored and adapted to house one of Cittadella's most stylish hotels. You can still see the tall brick chimney and old machinery, but the interior is now bright, spacious, and furnished to a high standard. The restaurant (closed August) serves local and national dishes, in summer under a garden gazebo. ⊠ *Via Palladio 34, 35013* ☎ *049/940000* 🖷 *049/9402111* ⤶ *70 rooms, 1 suite* ⚭ *Restaurant, bar, in-room safes, minibars, cable TV, gym, hot tub, sauna, free parking* ⊟ *AE, DC, MC, V* ⦿ *CP.*

Bassano del Grappa

❻ *13 km (8 mi) north of Cittadella, 76 km (47 mi) northwest of Venice.*

Beautifully positioned directly above the swift-flowing waters of the Brenta River at the foot of the Monte Grappa massif (5,880 ft), Bassano has old streets lined with low-slung buildings flanked by wooden balconies and pretty flowerpots. Bright ceramic wares produced here and in nearby Nove are displayed in shops along byways that curve uphill toward a centuries-old square, and, even higher, to a belvedere with a good view of Monte Grappa and part of the Val Sugana.

Bassano's most famous landmark is the **Ponte degli Alpini** (also called Ponte Vecchio), which has spanned the Brenta since the 13th century. Rebuilt countless times (floods are frequent), the present-day bridge is a postwar reconstruction using Andrea Palladio's 16th-century design. The great architect astutely chose to use wood as his medium, knowing that it could be replaced quickly and cheaply. For the best view, cross to the far side; then take Via Marcello and follow the *Veduta Panoramica* (panoramic view) sign. The bridge itself is named after the Alpini regiment who fought in the World War I campaigns on Monte Grappa and above Asiago and who were responsible for the present-day reconstruction. The small **Museo degli Alpini** documents this in the Taverna al Ponte. ⊠ *Via Angarono 2* ☎ *0424/503662* ☜ *Free* ⊙ *Tues.–Sun. 8:30–8.*

Almost as famous as the bridge is the liquor shop **Nardini** (⊠ Ponte Vecchio 2 ☎ 0424/527741), right by the bridge, where grappa has been distilled for more than two centuries. Stop in for a sniff or a snifter. It's closed Monday October–May.

The center of town focuses on two adjacent squares, the Piazza Libertà and the Piazza Garibaldi. Most of the buildings date from the 16th century, a period of stability under Venetian rule. Looking down on the bustle of Piazza Garibaldi is the **Torre Civica**, once part of the earlier 13th-century defense system. Also dominating the piazza is the campanile of the Gothic church of **San Francesco**, which houses an interesting 13th-century wooden crucifix, on the arms of which are carved the sun and moon. The cloister of this church is home to the **Museo Civico**, whose downstairs section is devoted to archaeological finds, notably the Chini collection of 1st-century BC vases from Apulia, a good collection of 18th-century engravings, and theatrical memorabilia and costumes of the baritone Tito Gobbi (1913–84), who was a native of the town. Upstairs, the museum features paintings from three generations of the da Ponte family, predominantly Jacopo Bassano (1510–92). Note the dirty feet and wrinkled skin of the peasants in *The Adoration of the Shepherds,* a prosaic touch that heralded a new realism in Venetian painting. One room is devoted to the works of Canova; the library owns 2,000 of his drawings and 7,000 letters. ⊠ *Piazza Garibaldi* ☎ *0424/522235, 0424/ 523464 campanile* ☜ *€4.50; campanile €2* ⊙ *Tues.–Sat. 9–6:30, Sun. 3:30–6:30; campanile daily 9:30–12:30 and 3–7.*

need a break? A table set outside the **Bar Daniele** (⊠ Piazza Garibaldi 39 ☎ 0424/ 529322) is a great place from which to watch life unfold on the piazza. It's closed Tuesday afternoon and Wednesday.

The civic museum's ceramics collection is found in the 18th-century **Palazzo Sturm**, on the river's east bank. Walk through the attractive courtyard, past frescoes by Giorgio Anselmi (1723–97), to view the town's famed majolica pieces including 17th-century Manardi ware and later ware from Nove and Faenza. ⊠ *Via Ferracina 16* ☎ *0424/524933* ☜ *€4.50* ⊙ *Apr.–Oct., Tues.–Sun. 9–12:30 and 3:30–6:30; Nov.–Mar., Fri. 9–12:30, weekends 3:30–6:30.*

Where to Stay & Eat

$$ ✕ **Al Sole.** The walls of this highly renowned restaurant are decorated with hefty ceramic whistles in the shape of men astride animals. These oddities were typical of the area in bygone days when they were used to warn of the approach of enemies. In the two large dining areas, you can taste such dishes as *anitra al melograna* (duck with pomegranate, Torcolato wine, and rosemary), seasonal game, and white asparagus in season. ⊠ *Via Jacopo Vittorelli 41/43* ☎ *0424/523206* ▭ *AE, DC, MC, V* ⊙ *Closed Mon. and July 15–Aug. 15.*

$$ ✕ **Ristorante Birreria Ottone.** Excellent cuisine and an old central-European beer-hall atmosphere keep the locals coming back to this Old World restaurant. It is run by the friendly Wipflinger family, headed by

Otto, whose Austrian forebear founded it as a beer hall a century ago. Equally good for a simple lunch or more elaborate dinner, Ottone offers specialties that include a delicious goulash cooked with cumin. ⊠ *Via Matteotti 48/50* ☎ *0424/522206* ⊟ *AE, D, MC, V* ☺ *Closed Tues. and first 3 wks in Aug. No dinner Mon.*

$–$$ ✕ **Osteria Terraglio.** The creative, modern menu here focuses on absolute freshness, in the wonderful array of savory snacks, the big, crisp *insalatone* (main-course salads with tuna or various cheeses), and even the fillet steak, sliced to order. Special tasting sessions of local delicacies like asparagus, cold-pressed olive oil, and fine wines are a regular feature, while there is live jazz on Tuesday evenings. ⊠ *Piazza Terraglio 28* ☎ *0424/521064* ⊟ *AE, DC, MC, V* ☺ *Closed Mon.*

FodorsChoice
★

★ $$ ⌂ **Bonotto Belvedere.** This historic hotel has richly decorated public rooms with period furnishings and Oriental rugs; the lounge has an open fireplace and a piano. Guest rooms are decorated in traditional Venetian or contemporary style. There are two rooms with facilities for people with disabilities. The elegant, separately managed Belvedere restaurant offers classic Italian cuisine, focusing equally on seafood and meat dishes. ⊠ *Piazzale Giardino 14, 36061* ☎ *0424/529845* 🖷 *0424/529849* ⊕ *www.bonotto.it* ⇆ *83 rooms, 4 suites* ⌂ *Restaurant, bar, Internet, meeting rooms, some pets allowed (fee)* ⊟ *AE, DC, MC, V* ⊠❙ *CP.*

$ ✕⌂ **Al Bassanello.** Established for more than 50 years, this neat, white, family-run hotel is about a ten-minute walk from the center in a quiet residential area. The restaurant is locally renowned for its fresh seasonal food, especially Bassano's famous asparagus, grown on the owners' nearby farm. ⊠ *Via Trozzetti 2, 36061* ☎ *0424/35347* 🖷 *0424/35347* ⇆ *24 rooms* ⌂ *Restaurant, bar, minibars, cable TV, free parking* ⊟ *AE, DC, MC, V* ⊠❙ *CP.*

$ ⌂ **Al Castello.** In a restored town house at the foot of the medieval Torre Civica, the Cattapan family's Castello is a reasonably priced, attractive choice. The simply furnished rooms all differ in shape and size. The best ones at the front have a small balcony offering a wonderful view of the charming inner-city square below. ⊠ *Piazza Terraglio 20, 36061* ☎🖷 *0424/228665* ⇆ *11 rooms* ⌂ *Café* ⊟ *AE, MC, V* ⊠❙ *CP.*

Nightlife & the Arts

ROMAN FEASTS   Throughout the year, the dining group **Ristoratori Bassanesi** arranges special dinners featuring either a traditional ingredient such as white asparagus or the whole works in a gala dinner. Contact the **tourist office** (☎ 0424/524351) or **Promo Bassanopiù** (☎ 0424/228651) for dates and participating restaurants.

FESTIVALS   During July and August, Bassano stages the **Opera Estate Festival** (☎ 0424/524214 for information and reservations), a season of classical and jazz music, dance, opera, cinema, and theater. You can also contact the tourist office for information.

Shopping

There's a general market on Thursday and Saturday in **Piazza Garibaldi** and the surrounding streets.

CERAMICS   Bassano del Grappa and nearby Nove are the best bets in the region for ceramic items. A large number of shops in town feature wrought-iron and copper utensils, many made on the premises. **Luigi Parise** (⊠ Salita Ferracina 4 ☎ 0424/228359) sells hand-painted ceramics.

LAMPS   **Lumi Vecchio Ponte** (⊠ Via Angarano 19 ☎🖷 0424/503651) is a real treasure trove of copper, wrought iron, and stained-glass antique and art lamps, along with brass compasses and baroque mirrors.

Marostica

❼ *18 km (11 mi) west of Asolo, 82 km (51 mi) northwest of Venice.*

Ruled by Venice between 1404 and 1797, Marostica exudes a powerful sense of history, immediately apparent at the first glimpse of its formidable fortifications. From the **Castello Superiore**, perched on a hill overlooking the surrounding countryside, the ramparts tier down to enclose the main square and a second castle. The enclosed castle, the **Castello Inferiore**, affords marvelous views in all directions. The castle was built by the Scaligeri family in the 13th century, ousting the despotic Ezzelino III da Romano, who had taken over from Ezzelino the Stutterer and Ezzelino the Monk. If you take a guided tour of the castle, you'll see the oldest and largest ivy in Europe, which is more than 420 years old, as well as a reconstructed catapult, the frescoed Sala del Consiglio, where the town council still meets, and the costumes used for the historic chess game on which the fame of the town rests. ⊠ *Piazza Castello* ☎ *0424/72127* 🎟 *€1* 🕑 *Mon.–Sat. 9–noon and 3–6, Sun. 3–6.*

The harmonious Piazza Castello is marked out in red and white stone checkerboard fashion and on the second weekend in September in even-numbered years is the venue for a human chess game, the ***partita a scacchi.*** In 1454, rival suitors for the hand of a fair maiden decided to fight it out, not by means of the sword but with chess pieces. Nowadays a set game is enacted to the accompaniment of solemn proclamations, fanfares, processions, and flag waving, with a total of 500 participants dressed in medieval garb and 20 horses in attendance, the whole thing culminating in a dramatized wedding ceremony. If you want to see it, have your tickets bought by June.

After you've admired the square, drop into the nearby **Osteria alla Madonetta** (⊠ Viale Vajenti 21) to see a model of Marostica, handmade in wood by the proprietor. It looks like a bed but is in fact a seating arrangement in which to play chess, using the miniature piazza as the board. Take a seat at the long, polished wood tables by the fireplace for a glass of Moscato wine, while absorbing the quaint charm of the clutter here. There's a ceramics shop next door at No. 23, **Alla Vecia Bottega** (☎ 0424/73674), where you can see the ceramicist in action and buy some of his wares. The 15th-century church **Sant'Antonio** contains a fine 16th-century altarpiece by the painter Jacopo Bassano. ⊠ *Via Sant'Antonio* ☎ *0424/72007* 🕑 *Daily 8–11.*

Marostica's soil and climate conspire to produce Italy's most luscious cherries. During May and June, the square is covered with stalls selling Morello, Sandre, Roane, and Marostegane varieties.

Where to Stay & Eat

★ **$$** ✕ **Al Castello Superiore.** This place is right in the hillside castle: wind up the corkscrew road and through the gate to be greeted by stupendous views of the town and the hills behind. The castle's heyday is evoked by suits of armour and various iron implements; there's a terrace for summer eating and a welcoming fireplace for winter. Try the *tagliatelle ai torresani* (pasta with a sauce of pigeon spiced with sage and onions) or the veal with asparagus. If you haven't tasted tiramisù, now's your chance. ⊠ *Via Consignorio della Scala* ☎ *0424/73315* 🖃 *AE, DC, MC, V* 🕑 *Closed Wed., last wk in Jan., 1st wk in Feb., and 1 wk in mid-Aug. No lunch Thurs.*

$$ 🛏 **Due Mori.** Modern, design-conscious rooms with wooden floors and beige marble bathrooms offer classy Italian elegance in the heart of FodorsChoice ★ this medieval town center. Some rooms have magical views of the olive-studded terraces behind the town, the upper castle, and ancient city wall. With its chic, minimalist restaurant downstairs, Due Mori is an excellent base for visiting the surrounding hills and towns of the northern Veneto. ⊠ *Corso Mazzini 73, 36063* ☎ *0424/471777* 🖷 *0424/476920* 🌐 *www.duemori.it* 🗗 *10 rooms* ⚬ *Minibars, cable TV, restaurant, free parking* 🖃 *AE, DC, MC, V* ⊘ *Closed 1st wk Jan., 1 wk mid-Aug.* ⦿| *CP.*

$ 🖻 **La Rosina.** All the rooms in this quiet country hotel, a couple of miles into the hills north of Marostica, have terraces and fabulous views back toward the castle. The hotel features wooden furniture and polished parquet floors, while the restaurant (closed Mon. and Tues.) prides itself on the freshness of seasonal ingredients. ⊠ *Contrà Marchetti 4, 36063 Valle San Floriano* ☎ *0424/470360* 🖷 *0424/470290* 🗗 *12 rooms* ⚬ *Restaurant, minibars, cable TV, bar* 🖃 *AE, DC, MC, V* ⦿| *CP.*

Nightlife & the Arts

FESTIVALS Marostica's **partita a scacchi** (human-scale chess game) takes place on the second weekend in September in even-numbered years (tickets go on sale in April). For information, contact **Associazone Pro Marostica** (☎ 0424/72127 🖷 0424/72800). The **Sagra delle Ciliege** (Cherry Festival) is held on the last Sunday in May in the castle yard. Growers from the surrounding regions attend, and plenty of eating and drinking accompanies the revelry.

Shopping

Soffieria Parise (⊠ Corso della Ceramica 18 ☎ 0424/470262), out of the center toward Nove, specializes in handblown glass.

Conegliano

❽ *28 km (17 mi) north of Treviso, 60 km (37 mi) northwest of Venice.*

Situated in the heart of wine-producing country, Conegliano is an attractive town with Venetian-style villas, frescoed houses, arcades, and cobbled streets. The walls that once girded the city did not succeed in repelling the series of assaults between the 12th and 14th centuries, when after being subjected to Padua, Treviso, Feltre, Belluno, the Carraresi, and Scaligeri families, the city finally declared its allegiance to Venice. It turned out to be a good move: Conegliano enjoyed nearly 300 years of peace and stability after the pact.

Shops, bars, and restaurants now line Conegliano's main street, the Via XX Settembre, housed in former palaces that bear witness to the Venetian influence. As well as being known as a thriving center of wine, Prosecco in particular, Conegliano is also the birthplace of the painter Giambattista Cima (1460–1518), a follower of Giorgione who enjoyed great popularity in Venice.

The **Casa del Pittore Giambattista Cima,** the modest house where Cima died in 1517, contains reproductions of his paintings and some archaeological pieces discovered when the house was restored. ⊠ *Via Cima 24* ☎ *0438/21660* 🖾 *€1* ⊘ *Open on request only. Call 0438/21660 or 0438/411026 for an appointment.*

The 14th-century **Duomo** has an arcaded facade frescoed in the 16th century by Ludovico Pozzoserrato (1550–1603/05). Inside, Cima's 1493 masterpiece, *La Madonna in Trono e Santi,* graces the altar, as well as paintings by Palma the Younger (1548–1628) and frescoes by Pordenone (1484–1539). ⊠ *Via XX Settembre* ☎ *0438/22606* ⊘ *Daily 9–noon and 3–6.*

TRAVELING THE WINE ROADS

The Veneto is one of Italy's distinguished wine-making regions, producing more wines that earn the DOC seal of excellence than anywhere else in the country. First-rate varieties from the Veneto include Soave, Tocai, Prosecco, Riesling, and Pinot among the whites, and Bardolino, Valpolicella, Merlot, Cabernet, and Pinot Nero among the reds.

One of the most hospitable areas in the region for wine enthusiasts is the stretch of country north of Treviso, where you can follow designated wine roads—tours that blend a beautiful rural setting with the culture and delights of the grape. Authorized wine shops where you can stop and sample are marked with a sign showing a triangular arrangement of red and yellow grapes. There are three routes to choose from, and they're manageable enough that you can do them all.

Montello & Asolo Hills

This route provides a good balance of vineyards and non-wine-related sights. It winds its way from Nervesa della Battaglia, a couple of miles south of Conegliano, through two prime destinations in the area, the lovely village of Asolo and the Villa Barbaro at Maser. Asolo produces good Prosecco, whereas Montello favors Merlot and Cabernet. Both areas also yield Pinot and Chardonnay.

Piave River

The circular route starts and ends in Conegliano. It follows the river Piave and runs through orchards, woods, and hills. Of the red and white wines here, the Raboso del Piave ages well and is the perfect complement for local dishes such as beans and pasta or goose stuffed with chestnut. The other reds are Cabernet, Merlot, and Cabernet Sauvignon. As an accompaniment to fish, choose a Verduzzo del Piave or, for an aperitif, the lovely warm-yellow Pinot Grigio del Piave. The gems of the area are the D.O.C. Torchiato di Fregona and Refrontolo Passito, both made according to traditional methods.

Prosecco

This route runs for 47 km (29 mi) between Valdobbiadene and Conegliano, winding through knobby hills covered in grapevines. These hang in festoons on row after row of pergolas to create a thick, luxuriant mantle of green. Turn off the main route to explore the narrower country lanes, most of which eventually join up. They meander through tiny hamlets and past numerous family wineries where you can taste and purchase the wines. Spring is an excellent time to visit, with no fewer than fifteen local wine festivals held between March and early June.

The Duomo gives onto **Sala dei Battuti**, which was previously the meeting place for the Confraternità dei Flagellanti—a brotherhood of 13th-century self-flagellating mystics). It is covered with frescoes by Girolamo da Treviso (circa 1455–97) and Jacopo da Montagnana (15th century) among others. ⊠ *Via XX Settembre* ☎ *0438/22606* ◷ *Sun. 10–12:30 and 3:30–7, or weekday mornings by appointment (find a parishioner).*

It's a steep walk up the cobbled Calle Madonna della Neve to the Castello, where you'll find the **Museo Civico** in the tower. It's full of local artifacts and memorabilia, some frescoes by Pordenone, and a good bronze by Giambologna (1529–1608). Make your way to the roof and you'll be rewarded with a fine view over the city to the gentle hills and their vines. ⊠ *Piazzale San Leonardo* ☎ *0438/22871* 🎟 *€2* ◷ *Apr.–Sept. 10–12:30 and 3–6:30; Oct.–Mar. 10–12:30 and 3:30–7. Closed Mon. and Nov.*

Where to Stay & Eat

$ ✕ **Al Salisà.** Taking its name from the Venetian dialect word for a cobbled street, this restaurant is cool and fresh, with white walls and wrought iron and a big, sunny terrace. Fish ranks high on the menu, though the friendly, English-speaking owner, Giorgio, will certainly urge you to try the *lumache alla corsa* (literally, "racing snails") made to his secret recipe. Reservations are advised in summer. ⊠ *Via XX Settembre 2* ☎ *0438/24288* ▤ *AE, DC, MC, V* ⊘ *Closed Wed.*

★ $$ ✕ **Città di Venezia.** It's no surprise to see the lions and striped poles in this restaurant, for it was here that the doges came on vacation. It is the oldest eating place in the town, with a 14th-century room featuring heavy ceiling beams and an ancient, time-polished marble floor. Seafood predominates, with delicacies like crab served in the shell, scallops, *risotto al nero di seppie* (risotto with cuttlefish ink) and fillet of gilthead with capers and gherkins. The local version of *saor* sauce (onions marinated in vinegar and fried with sultanas and pine nuts) is also renowned. Reservations are advised. ⊠ *Via XX Settembre 77/79* ☎ *0438/23186* ▤ *AE, DC, MC, V* ⊘ *Closed Mon. and Aug. 10–31. No dinner Sun.*

$ ✕ **Al Bacareto.** Little wooden compartments divide up this snug osteria where the jovial owner, Mario, will recite the menu (in English). Specialties include *porchetta* (suckling pig) with roast potatoes, and cuttlefish with tomato and polenta. There's also a good range of pasta dishes, open sandwiches, and pizza slices for a quick lunch, all washed down with the excellent, local Zahre beer. ⊠ *Via Cavour 6* ☎ *0438/411666* ▤ *No credit cards* ⊘ *Closed Mon.*

$–$$ ▦ **Canon d'Oro.** The town's oldest inn, the Canon d'Oro is in an arcaded and frescoed 16th-century building in a central location within walking distance of the train station. The antique furniture, lovely bed linen, and terraced garden all add to its charm. ⊠ *Via XX Settembre 129, 31015* ☎ *0438/34246* 🖨 *0438/34246* ⊕ *www.hotelcanondoro.it* ⇗ *51 rooms* ⚬ *Restaurant, bar, in-room data ports, in-room safes, minibars, cable TV, free parking, some pets allowed* ▤ *AE, DC, MC, V* ⦿ *CP.*

$ ▦ **Sporting Hotel Ragno d'Oro.** Just out of the center amid the greenery of the Parco Rocca, this modern hotel offers generous facilities for relaxing or exercising. There's an 8-km (5-mi) running course nearby if all that good Italian food and wine has gone to your waistline. Guest rooms are plain and wood-paneled. ⊠ *Via Diaz 37, 31015* ☎ *0438/412300* 🖨 *0438/412310* ⊕ *www.hotelragnodoro.it* ⇗ *17 rooms* ⚬ *Bar, minibars, 2 tennis courts, pool, sauna, free parking, some pets allowed* ▤ *AE, DC, MC, V* ⦿ *CP.*

The Arts

Musical and literary events take place each weekend in September, leading up to the **Dama Castellana** on the first weekend in October—a human chess match in celebration of victory over Treviso in 1241. Processions, flag-waving, and fireworks accompany the proceedings.

Shopping

For gifts, **Follies** (⊠ Via Beato Ongaro 5 ☎ 0438/21201) has a wide selection of antiques and craftwork. **Ornamenta** (⊠ Via Beato Ongaro 7 ☎ 0438/35527) carries local crafts and antiques.

Valdobbiadene

◉ *36 km (22 mi) north of Treviso, 66 km (41 mi) northwest of Venice.*

If you're following the Prosecco Wine Road (⇨ Pleasures & Pastimes, *above*), Valdobbiadene will be your end destination. As you wind your way through the hills, the vines practically creep up onto the road.

The pasticceria **Emilio Carnia** (✉ Viale Vittoria 1 ☎ 0423/972209), established as a family-run business since 1935, doubles as a wine shop. Signor Carnia, the versatile pastry maker, not only makes excellent biscuits and pastries but chooses the grapes for the prestigious Cartizze Prosecco wine. The terrace will tempt you to indulge in a breakfast croissant, a Mozart *plait* (a kind of biscuit), or an evening aperitif before continuing on your way. It's closed Wednesday.

Where to Stay & Eat

★ **$–$$** ✕ **Alla Cima.** A big, circular, open fire where one of the chefs performs the art of char-grilling your preferred cut of meat has center stage here, about a five-minute drive outside town. Starters reflect local produce, like gnocchi with fresh walnut sauce, while the mains delight serious meat-eaters with thick beef steaks, pork, and veal. The wine list has a concise selection of white wines and a large range of reds from virtually every region in Italy, while the house wine is Prosecco from the owners' vineyards. Excellent food and service make this an excellent place to stop for a meal; if you want a table on the roofed wooden terrace—with its sweeping vineyard views and refreshing breeze in summer—by all means book ahead. ✉ *Via Cima 13 S. Pietro di Barbozza, Valdobbiadene* ☎ *0423/972711* 🖨 *0423/971040* ⚘ *Reservations essential (evenings, rooftop terrace)* ▭ *AE, DC, MC, V* ☉ *Closed Tues. and Jan. No dinner Mon.*

$ ▦ **Diana.** The warm hues of the exposed stone walls and tiled floors of this modern hotel are set off by discreet lighting and colorful rugs. There's plenty of comfortable space for relaxation in the large, sprawling public lounges, while some rooms have views of the surrounding hills. The large, airy restaurant has an impressive trussed wooden roof under which to dine. Service is courteous. ✉ *Via Roma 49, 31049* ☎ *0423/976222* 🖨 *0423/972237* ⤺ *57 rooms* ⚭ *Restaurant, bar, in-room data ports, in-room safes, minibars, cable TV, meeting rooms, free parking* ▭ *AE, DC, MC, V* ⦿ *CP.*

Vittorio Veneto

❿ *14 km (7 mi) north of Conegliano, 70 km (43 mi) northwest of Venice.*

Vittorio Veneto owes its name to the unification of Italy in 1866 and its first king, Vittorio Emanuele II. The two towns of Ceneda and Serravalle were joined to form Vittorio Veneto, with a new town hall and train station built between them. The town extends along the main road, with Ceneda, the commercial center, in the south. To the north, Serravalle is the historic quarter enclosed within a gorge that sports a more Alpine feel. After Serravalle's annexation to Venice in 1337 it became an important economic center and money market, with one of the largest Jewish communities in the north of Italy.

Although Serravalle is by far the more attractive of the two parts, Ceneda does have two sights, the first of which is the church of **Santa Maria del Meschio,** which holds a heavenly *Annunciation* by Andre Previtali (circa 1470–1528). ✉ *Piazza Meschio* ☎ *0438/53581* ☉ *Daily 8–noon and 3–7.*

The second reason to visit Ceneda is the **Museo della Battaglia,** dedicated to the Battle of Vittorio, which in 1918 marked the final engagement of the Italian army in World War I. It is housed in the graceful **Loggia del Cenedese,** which is attributed to Jacopo Sansovino (1486–1570). ✉ *Piazza Giovanni Paolo I* ☎ *0438/57695* 🎟 *€3 includes Museo del Cenedese and San Lorenzo dei Battuti* ☉ *May–Sept., 9:30–12:30 and 3:30–7; Oct.–Apr., 9:30–12:30 and 2–5. Closed Mon.*

Franco Zeffirelli was so taken by Serravalle that he used it as a location for his 1970s film *Romeo and Juliet,* and indeed its charm rests on the fact that nothing much has changed since the 16th century. Via Martiri della Libertà leads up to the main square, lined with 15th- and 16th-century buildings and ending at the Loggia Serravalle, a fine building emblazoned with shields. The Loggia Serravalle is now the home of the **Museo del Cenedese,** a collection of local archaeological bits and pieces, minor paintings, and frescoes. ⊠ *Piazza Flaminio* ☎ *0438/57103* 🖾 *€3 includes Museo della Battaglia and San Lorenzo dei Battuti* ⊙ *May–Sept., 9:30–12:30 and 3:30–7; Oct.–Apr., 9:30–12:30 and 2–5. Closed Mon.*

The church of **San Lorenzo dei Battuti** houses an excellent fresco cycle painted in the mid-15th century. The damage suffered when Napoléon's men used the church as a kitchen has since been rectified. ⊠ *Piazza Vecellio* ☎ *0438/57103* 🖾 *€3 includes Museo della Battaglia and Museo del Cenedese* ⊙ *May–Sept., 9:30–12:30 and 3:30–7; Oct.–Apr., 9:30–12:30 and 2–5. Closed Mon.*

Crossing the river Meschio from Piazza Flaminio, you come to the **Duomo,** notable for its Titian altarpiece *The Virgin with S. Peter and S. Andrew.* ⊠ *Piazza Giovanni Paolo I* ☎ *0438/53401* ⊙ *May–Sept., daily 6:30–noon and 2:30–7:30; Oct.–Apr., daily 6:30–noon and 2:30–6:30.*

Where to Stay & Eat

★ $ ✕ **Locanda al Postiglione.** A post office in the time of Emperor Franz Josef, this restaurant preserves its 18th-century atmosphere with beamed ceilings and wood paneling. The menu changes daily. Regional dishes prevail, but the choice extends wider to encompass international dishes, too. Specialties include roast shank of pork, duck, and grilled porcini mushrooms; fish is served on Thursday and Friday. Make sure you save room for the enticing berry tarts and other homemade sweets on the dessert trolley. ⊠ *Via Cavour 39* ☎ *0438/556924* ▭ *AE, DC, MC, V* ⊙ *Closed Tues. and July 20–Aug. 10.*

$ ✕ **Taverna da Peo.** Typical Veneto cooking is served at plain wooden tables in this bustling osteria-cum-trattoria, which stays open until 1 AM (till 2 on Fridays and Saturdays). The local fare is all homemade and includes standards like *pasta e fagioli* (pasta and beans), several varieties of seasonal vegetable risotti, and mains such as *bigoli con ragù di anatra* (thick spaghetti with duck ragout) and *salsiccetta con polenta* (sausage and polenta). Service is friendly. ⊠ *Via Martiri della Libertà 25* ☎ *0438/554930* ▭ *DC, MC, V* ⊙ *Closed Tues., 2nd wk in Jan., and 3 wks in July. No dinner Mon.*

¢–$ ✕ **Club degli Spaghetti.** Enjoy a light, modern Italian lunch in sunny surroundings here off the square in Ceneda. Seasonal pasta dishes top the list, served with fresh asparagus and cream in season, or perhaps with artichokes, porcini, champignons, and parsley. There are then 15 varieties of *insalatone* (big, single-dish salads) with crab, Greek feta cheese, mozzarella, and melon, or your own combination, and a rich variety of well-filled sandwiches. In addition to these generous starters, save room for main courses such as steaks, wurstel, and cooked cheese with grilled vegetables, along with desserts such as tiramisù or fresh strawberries with wine. ⊠ *Piazza Giovanni Paolo I #10* ☎ *0438/57474* ▭ *AE, DC, MC, V* ⊙ *Closed Mon. and 1st 2 wks in July.*

★ $ ▦ **Hotel Calvi.** Tasteful architectural and interior design have given this 19th-century inn an air of elegant comfort. The spacious lounge and breakfast room has a high, wood-beamed ceiling, big open fire, and large windows looking across the Meschio river (here just a stream), which separates the restful garden from the hills behind. Since it's handily located on the main road, about 50 yards from the north end of Serravalle, you can leave the car here and visit the town on foot, soaking up its romantic lanes and medieval architecture. ✉ *Via Calvi 19, 31029* ☎ *0438/941682* 🖷 *0438/947331* ⊕ *www.hotelcalvi.it* ⇴ *11 rooms* 🛆 *Bar, minibars, cable TV, free parking, no-smoking rooms* ⊟ *AE, DC, MC, V* ⊘ *Closed Dec. 10–Jan. 7* ⏐⊙⏐ *CP.*

$ 🖭 **La Casa del Podestà.** An upstairs wing of this fine old patrician mansion (the podestà was the mayor) has been converted into a quality bed and breakfast. All rooms have their own bathrooms and feature exposed wooden roof beams and garden views. Start your day in the big breakfast room, then comfortably visit the whole town on foot. A spacious apartment is also available for longer stays (min. 1 week) at the same price. ✉ *Piazza G. Paolo 65, 31029* ☎ *0438/53448* ⊕ *www.vittorioveneto.net/podesta/podesta.htm* ⇴ *4 rooms, 1 apartment* ⊟ *No credit cards* ⏐⊙⏐ *CP.*

Shopping

Distilleria de Negri (✉ Via Martiri della Libertà 43 🖭 no phone), closed Wednesday, has a large stock of grappa. **Tochetti** (✉ Via Martiri dei Libertà ☎ 0438/450025) is good for a range of fresh mountain cheeses.

THE DOLOMITES

Turn northward to enter one of Italy's grandest mountain landscapes, an exhilarating land of lush, flower-laden meadows cut through by lakes and river valleys. The towns of Belluno and Feltre lie on the mighty Piave River, the first of these a relatively neglected holiday destination dramatically sited against the jagged mountain backdrop. Feltre, a walled city perched high on a ridge with stunning views, reveals some unexpected examples of Renaissance architecture. For a more glamorous aspect of the Alps, repair to the ritzy Cortina d'Ampezzo ski resort. The scenery around Cortina is as good as anything you'll find in these mountains and can be just as scintillating in summer as in the winter months, and certainly more accessible for rambling through. The rich and creamy food here, including fondues, polentas, and barley soups, reflects the Alpine climate and Austrian and Swiss influence; there are a number of dishes unique to the zone. If your doctor permits it, try the *schiz*: fresh cheese that is sliced and fried in butter, sometimes with cream added.

Belluno

⓫ *78 km (49 mi) north of Treviso, 108 km (67 mi) north of Venice.*

The Dolomites set the mood in Belluno, spread over a plateau above the junction of the Piave and Ardo rivers. It's the northernmost town of the Veneto and, given its strategic position, prospered as an ally of Venice. Now a provincial capital and busy commercial center, the city attracts a few tourists, though most prefer to stay higher in the mountains; Belluno's hotels are fairly quiet. You could spend a rewarding half day wandering around the old town, and there are some good spots for lunch. It's best to park on the lower side near the river and take the escalator up, enjoying the panorama as you go.

Take a stroll around the impressively broad main square, **Piazza dei Martiri**, complete with a grove of evergreens and bordered on one side by a unified row of arcaded palaces. To the south lies the Piazza del Duomo, where the pale-ocher **Duomo**, built in the 16th century to a design of Tullio Lombardo (1455–1532), had to be rebuilt after two earthquakes, once in 1873 and again in 1936. Inside there are 16th-century paintings by Jacopo Bassano. Next to it, topped by a green onion-shape cupola, stands the tall campanile, Belluno's most prominent monument, built in the 18th century by the Sicilian architect and stage designer Filippo Juvara (1678–1736). ⊠ *Piazza del Duomo* ☎ *0437/941908* ☉ *Daily 7–noon and 3–7.*

The **Palazzo dei Rettori,** an ornate 15th-century building with baroque touches, seat of the Venetian governors and now an administrative building, fills one side of the square. The best view of the river and surrounding countryside is from **Porta Ruga** at the end of the main street, Via Mezzaterra.

The **Museo Civico,** housed in a 17th-century palazzo, has a good collection of work by the locally born painters Sebastiano Ricci (1659–1734) and Marco Ricci (1679–1729), and the sculptor Andrea Brustolon (1662–1732). ⊠ *Piazza del Duomo 16* ☎ *0437/944836* ⊡ *€2.30* ☉ *Mid-Apr.–Sept., Tues.–Sat. 10–noon and 4–7, Sun. 10:30–12:30. Closed Mon. and Aug. 15; Oct.–mid-Apr., Mon., Wed., Thurs., Sat. 10–noon, Tues. and Fri. 3–6. Closed Sun. and Nov. 11.*

Where to Stay & Eat

$$ ✕ **Al Borgo.** Cross the river to find this lovely rustic restaurant, an 18th-century villa in a park, colored in shades of terra-cotta, green, and cream. The chef uses wild herbs and greenery from the mountains: whatever's in season. Spring might produce risotto *selvatico e lupolo* (with hops and herbs), while in summer you can find gnocchi with *zucca* (pumpkin) and lamb with rosemary. On rare occasions you might be offered *pinza da noze,* a traditional wedding cake made with ricotta cheese. ⊠ *Via Anconetta 8* ☎ *0437/926755* ⚓ *Reservations essential* ⊟ *AE, DC, MC, V* ☉ *Closed Tues. and last 2 wks in Jan. No dinner Mon.*

$–$$ ✕ **Terracotta.** This small restaurant serves meat, game, and seafood, with a focus on traditional Bellunese dishes such as *formai schiz e rösti di patate* (cheese and roasted potatoes). The tiny, candle-lit terrace offers intimate dining on summer evenings, with glimpses of the surrounding mountains. ⊠ *Via Garibaldi 61* ☎ *0437/942644* ⊟ *AE, MC, V* ☉ *Closed Wed. No dinner Tues.*

$ ▦ **Cappello e Cadore.** Specially crafted wooden furniture typical of the area adds personality to the spacious, warmly decorated rooms here. There's private car parking out front, but you won't be needing your car: the hotel is in a quiet lane just a few steps behind the Piazza dei Martiri from where all the sights can be visited on foot. ⊠ *Via Ricci 8, 32100* ☎ *0437/940246* ⊞ *0437/292319* ⊕ *www.albergocappello.com* ⇱ *32 rooms* ⚬ *Bar, in-room data ports, minibars, cable TV, meeting rooms, free parking, some pets allowed, no-smoking rooms* ⊟ *AE, DC, MC, V* ⊙⫶ *CP.*

Feltre

⑫ *31 km (19 mi) east of Belluno, 88 km (55 mi) northwest of Venice.*

Approaching along one of the river valleys below the town, you'll soon see the mellow tones of Feltre's historic center rearing above you on its narrow fortified ridge. To reach the old quarter, either wend your way up the main cobbled street from the modern zone, or opt for the steeper but more rewarding toil up one of the various flights of stone steps that thread up through the old town. Either way, you'll be stepping back into the 16th century, when Venice had Feltre almost completely rebuilt after it was sacked in 1509 by the League of Cambrai, as punishment for the town's allegiance to La Serenissima.

Via Mezzaterra, marked by gates at either end, is lined with harmonious houses, many of which are adorned with frescoes by Lorenzo Luzzo (died 1526), the town's best-known painter, who bore the unfortunate nickname of "Il Morto da Feltre" (the Dead Man of Feltre) due to his pallid complexion. Midway along, the road pans out into the **Piazza Maggiore**, the main square that holds the medieval **Castello** and the **Palazzo della Ragione**, with its Palladian portico. Here you can see the frescoed Sala Consiglio and the little wooden theater, La Scena, rebuilt in 1802 by Gian Antonio Selva, the designer of La Fenice in Venice. Call the Museo Civico for visiting hours.

Via Mezzaterra continues into Via Luzzo to the **Museo Civico**, containing a collection of paintings by Luzzo including his *Madonna with S. Vitus and S. Modestus,* as well as a portrait by Gentile Bellini (1429–1546) and a triptych by Cima da Conegliano (1460–1518). Luzzo's masterpiece, a *Transfiguration,* is housed in the sacristy of the **Chiesa di Ognissanti**. ⊠ *Via Lorenzo Luzzo 23* ☎ *0439/885242* ⊠ *€4* ☉ *Tues.–Fri. 10:30–12:30 and 4–7, weekends 9:30–12:30 and 4–7. Closed Mon.*

In the street parallel to Via Mezzaterra, the **Galleria d'Arte Moderna Carlo Rizzarda** has wrought-iron work on display, mostly by Carlo Rizzarda (1883–1931), whose decorative pieces reveal art nouveau and art deco influences. In 1929 Rizzarda presented the town with his collection and his house. ⊠ *Via Paradiso 8* ☎ *0439/885234* ⊠ *€4* ☉ *Apr.–Sept., weekdays 10:30–12:30 and 4–7, weekends 9:30–12:30 and 4–7; Oct.–Mar. weekdays 10:30–12:30 and 3–6, weekends 9:30–12:30 and 3–6.*

At the bottom of the 16th-century stairway that leads from Piazza Maggiore you'll reach the Porta Pusterla and the **Duomo** with its baptistery. Look for the 6th-century carved Byzantine cross inside the much-altered 15th-century cathedral. ⊠ *Piazza del Duomo* ☎ *0439/2312* ☉ *Daily 8–noon and 3–7.*

Where to Stay & Eat

$$–$$$ ✕ **Hostaria Novecento.** One of the few dining places in the old city, it has recently moved up the hill to the 'dress circle' on the main square. Dine on seafood or meat dishes here, including *spiedini di scampi e seppie* (scampi and cuttlefish kebabs), *petto d'oca con crostini caldi* (breast of goose with hot croutons), or a simple steak fillet with porcini mushrooms. Or you may choose just to settle in on the terrace with an ice cream or coffee and enjoy the rich surroundings of medieval architecture. ⊠ *Via Mezzaterra 24* ☎ *0439/80193* ▭ *MC, V* ☉ *Closed Mon.*

¢–$ ✕ **Osteria Mezzaterra.** Get a sandwich or roll made to order or sit down with a simple dish of cold cuts, pickles, cheeses and bread in one of the growing number of places in Italy boasting "slow food." The rustic, wooden decor and fine selection of wines by the glass suggest an ideal rest stop after trudging up the hill to the main square. ⊠ *Via Mezzaterra 5* ☎ *0439/89020* ▭ *No credit cards.*

$ ▨ **Doriguzzi.** The mountains are clearly visible from the windows of this modern hotel, which is handily located a few minutes walk from the town center. Ask for one of the two huge attic rooms with skylights that open, making you feel you could almost touch the inspiring Alpine scenery. ⊠ *Viale Piave 2, 32032* ☎ *0439/2003* 🖷 *0439/83660* ⤶ *23 rooms* ⟁ *Bar, in-room data ports, minibars, cable TV, meeting rooms, some pets allowed* ▭ *AE, DC, MC, V* ⑂ *CP.*

$ ▨ **Nuovo.** This is a small, modern hotel near the river in the town center. An open fireplace crackles in winter; in summer relax in the garden or on the terrace. The rooms are light and airy and full of plants; most have mountain views. The management is cheerful and hospitable.

⊠ Via Fornere Pazze 15, 32032 ☎ *0439/2110* 🖷 *0439/89241* 🖘 *23 rooms* ⚲ *Bar, in-room data ports, minibars, cable TV, meeting rooms, some pets allowed* 🖃 *AE, DC, MC, V* ⑩ *CP.*

Pieve di Cadore

🔞 *43 km (27 mi) north of Belluno, 130 km (81 mi) northwest of Venice.*

The Cadore region of the Dolomites extends as far as the Austrian frontier. Pope John Paul II has vacationed in the area for years, as do many other overheated city folk, though it does not have the feel of a tourist zone. The region's most important artistic center, Pieve di Cadore, is small, scenic, set on a hill, and quickly explored. A bronze statue of Pieve's most illustrious son, the painter Titian (circa 1480–1576) guards the **Casa di Tiziano**, where he was born. It's furnished as in Titian's time but contains none of his possessions or works. ⊠ *Via Arsenale* ☎ *0435/32262* 🖘*€1.50* ◷ *June–mid-Sept., Tues.–Sun. 9:30–12:30 and 4–7; other times by appointment.*

The **Museo dell'Occhiale** claims to be the only one of its kind in the world. It exhibits more than 2,000 glasses (spectacles) from medieval times to the present day, including the earliest French, English, and Chinese models, and the first pair of sunglasses, used by the 18th-century Venetian dramatist Carlo Goldoni. ⊠ *Via degli Alpini 39* ☎ *0435/500213* 🖘 *€3* ◷ *June–Sept. 10, 8:30–12:30 and 4:30–7:30; Sept. 11–May, 8:30–12:30. Closed Sun.*

The pretty church **Parrochiale di Santa Maria Nascente** was completed in the early 19th century and the mosaicked facade dates from 1876. Inside, the Titian altarpiece in the Cappella di San Tiziano is said to bear likenesses of the painter's family, his daughter Lavinia representing the Virgin Mary and his son Pomponio, Bishop Tiziano. ⊠ *Piazza Tiziano 41* ☎ *0435/32261* ◷ *Daily 8–noon and 3–6.*

If you're here before Christmas, drop a note at the **Casa di Babbo Natale** (House of Father Christmas), on the nearby hill of Montericco, and maybe Father Christmas will bring you what you've asked for.

Where to Stay & Eat

★ **$$–$$$** ✕ **La Chiusa.** It may be the secluded position in a hillside copse that entices you here, or the smell of the wood smoke in winter. Within, the ceiling beams are tree trunks and the wood paneling is imported from Turkey and Pakistan. But the star attraction is the fare itself. The genial owner, Benito Perismascietti, encourages you to linger over your victuals (the menu has a poem to this effect). Try the pasta stuffed with potatoes, walnuts, and sage, or the carrot dumplings with a cream and arugula sauce. This gourmet heaven is 20 km (12 mi) southeast of Cortina and 10 km (6 mi) west from Pieve di Cadore on the SS51. ⊠ *Località La Chiusa, Ruvignan, Vodo di Cadore* ☎ *0435/489288* 🖷 *0435/488048* ⚲ *Reservations essential* 🖃 *AE, DC, MC, V* ◷ *Closed Mon., Tues., and last 2 wks in Oct.*

$$ 🏠 **Villa Marinotti.** This lovely wooden chalet set on a gentle slope was once a private home, now converted into suites, and there are a pair of bungalows on the grounds. All the accommodations are beautifully furnished with a luxuriously light and spacious feel. In winter there's a *fogher* (open fireplace). It makes an ideal center for walking, horseback riding, and fishing. The gracious and hospitable owner speaks excellent English. ⊠ *Via Manzago 21, Tai di Cadore, 32040* ☎ *0435/32231* 🖷 *0435/33335* 🖘 *5 suites, 2 bungalows* ⚲ *Restaurant, tennis court* 🖃 *AE, DC, MC, V* ⑩ *CP.*

Sports & the Outdoors

BIKING From June through September, mountain bikes can be rented from **Dynamic Line** (⊠ Via XX Settembre 63, Valle di Cadore ☎ 0435/519260).

FISHING Permits can be bought from **Cadore Sport Camping** (⊠ Via Cortina 63/65, Pieve di Cadore ☎ 0435/30251).

HORSEBACK Contact **Agriturismo di Masi Alessandro** (⊠ Via Campo Sportivo, Vallsella
RIDING di Domegge ☎ 0435/7284).

WALKING For walking trips, contact **Gruppo CAI di Pieve di Cadore** (⊠ Località Valcalda ☎ 0435/31515).

Cortina d'Ampezzo

⑭ *30 km (19 mi) northwest of Pieve de Cadore, 155 km (97 mi) north-
Fodor'sChoice west of Venice.*
★

"The Pearl of the Dolomites" is set in a lush meadow 4,000 ft above sea level. Dense forests adjoin the town, and mountains encircle the whole valley. The town sprawls on the slopes along a fast-moving stream; a public park extends along one bank. Luxury hotels and the villas of the rich are conspicuously scattered over the slopes above the town—identifiable by their attempts to hide behind stands of fir and spruce.

The bustling center of Cortina d'Ampezzo has little nostalgia for days gone by, despite its Alpine appearance. The tone is set by elegant shops and stylish cafés, as opulent as their well-dressed patrons, whose corduroy pants may well have been tailored by Armani. Don't look for authentic Tyrolean gemütlichkeit here: Cortina is the place for a whiff of the heady aromas of wealth and sophistication, and retains a more Italian feel than some of its German-speaking Alto Adige neighbors.

Where to Stay & Eat

$$$$ ✕**Leone e Anna.** Decorated in Sardinian style in dusky pink, with leather sofas, this warm and welcoming restaurant specializes in Sard cuisine. To be recommended are spaghetti *alla bottarga* (with tuna eggs seasoned with oil and lemon), *porceddu alla sarda* (roast piglet with raw seasoned vegetables), and the homemade Sard desserts. ⊠ *Via Alverà 112* ☎ *0436/2768* ⌖ *Reservations essential* ⊟ *AE, DC, MC, V* ⊘ *Closed Tues., May–June, and Nov.*

$-$$ ✕**Birreria Vienna.** A hearty meal at a fair price is a welcome find in Cortina and, despite the name, this is more restaurant (no-smoking) than pub. Alpine specialties like green gnocchi with gorgonzola and smoked saddle of pork line up alongside excellent *insalatone,* or single-dish salads with tuna, cheese, olives, and plenty of other goodies, and tempting pizzas with seasonal toppings. ⊠ *Via Roma 66/68* ☎ *0436/866944* ⊟ *AE, DC, MC, V* ⊘ *Closed Wed. and May and Nov.*

$$$$ ▦**De la Poste.** Skiers who want to see and be seen return year after year to this lively hotel, one of Cortina's social centers. The hotel has been run by the same family management since 1826, and the furnishings feature antiques in characteristic Dolomite style. Almost all rooms have wooden balconies. ⊠ *Piazza Roma 62, 32043* ☎ *0436/4271* ⊟ *0436/868435* ⊕ *www.hotels.cortina.it/delaposte* ↘ *83 rooms* ⌂ *Restaurant, in-room data ports, in-room safes, minibars, cable TV, bar* ⊟ *AE, DC, MC, V* ⊘ *Closed Apr.–mid-June and Oct.–mid-Dec.* ⦿ *MAP, FAP.*

★ $$$$ ▦**Miramonti Majestic.** This luxurious, historic hotel has a magnificent location about 1 km (½ mi) south of Cortina and undoubtedly the best Alpine panorama in the area. A touch of Old World formality accompanies the imperial Austrian design. There's always a roaring fire in the cozy bar, and the hotel's recreation rooms are framed by plate-glass windows overlooking mountain vistas. The history of Cortina is intricately tied to the Miramonti, and you'll feel a part of it all here. ⊠ *Località Peziè 103, 32043* ☎ *0436/4201* 🖷 *0436/867019* ⊕ *www.geturhotels. com* 🛏 *105 rooms* ⚹ *Restaurant, bar, in-room data ports, in-room safes, minibars, cable TV, golf course, tennis courts, indoor pool, gym, sauna, bicycles, billiards, bocce, Ping-Pong, ski storage, piano bar, recreation room, theater, playground, meeting rooms, some pets allowed* ▤ *AE, DC, MC, V* ⊗ *Closed Apr.–June and Sept.–Dec. 21* ⦿| *CP.*

$$ 🖾 **Meublè Oasi.** The tasteful, modern furnishings, homey atmosphere and quiet, handy location mean you'll have to book early here. It's right next to the bus station and just a few minutes walk from both the town center and the main ski lift. Some front rooms have big balconies and dramatic views of the Tofane peaks across town. ⊠ *Via Cantore 2, 32043* ☎ *0436/862019* 🖷 *0436/879476* ⊕ *www.hoteloasi.it* 🛏 *10* ⚹ *Ski storage, free parking* ▤ *MC, V* ⊗ *Closed Oct.* ⦿| *CP.*

Nightlife & the Arts

At **Europa hotel** (⊠ Corso Italia 207 ☎ 0436/3221) you can expect to mingle with the couture set at the VIP disco; nonguests are welcome, but don't expect to spend less than €20–€30 on drinks.

Sports & the Outdoors

The **tourist office** (⊠ Piazzetta San Francesco 8, ☎ 0436/3231 🖷 0436/ 3235) will supply a good trail map and information about hiking paths.

Cortina d'Ampezzo has downhill slopes to challenge all levels of skiers. The most impressive views (and steepest slopes) in town are on **Monte Cristallo,** based at **Misurina.** The **Faloria** gondola runs from the center of town. From its top, you can get up to most of the other central mountains. Farther out of town, don't miss the **Cinque Torri** and **Passo Falzarego** runs either. All runs are covered by the **Dolomiti Superski pass** (☎ 0471/ 795397 ⊕ www.dolomitisuperski.com), good for the entire region.

NORTHERN VENETO A TO Z

To research prices, get advice from other travelers, and book travel arrangements, visit www.fodors.com.

AIRPORTS & TRANSFERS

Treviso's Aeroporto San Giuseppe is served by charter and commercial flights. There is a coach service between the airport and Piazzale Roma in Venice, also stopping in Mestre, for all flights; otherwise there is local bus service via ATVO to Treviso every 30 minutes during the day, or a taxi will come from Treviso, only 6 km (4 mi) away, to pick you up.

🛧 Airport Information **Aeroporto San Giuseppe** ⊠ 5 km [3 mi] southeast of Treviso, 32 km [19 mi] north of Venice ☎ 0422/315131.

🛧 Taxis & Shuttles **Taxi** ☎ 0422/431515.

BUS TRAVEL TO & FROM TREVISO

Taking one of the frequent ACTV buses from Venice will get you to Treviso in a half hour. An equally frequent service runs from Padua with La Marca bus line.

FARES & 🚌 Bus Information **ACTV** ⊠ Piazzale Roma, Venice ☎ 041/2424. **La Marca**
SCHEDULES ⊠ Lungosile Mattei 29, Treviso ☎ 0422/577311.

BUS TRAVEL WITHIN TREVISO & THE DOLOMITES

More so than elsewhere in Italy, bus travel is a reasonable choice in the Dolomites. La Marca has connections throughout the province, including the Conegliano bus station. From Bassano del Grappa, FTV runs hourly buses to Marostica and Vicenza. ACTM serves Asolo, Maser, and

Possagno. The Dolomites are served by Dolomiti Bus. Buses run frequently between Conegliano and Valdobbiadene along the Prosecco Wine Road.

FARES & SCHEDULES Bus Information **ACTM** ✉ Via Vittorio Veneto 13, Castelfranco Veneto ☎ 0423/493464 **Conegliano Bus Station** ✉ Piazza Fili Zoppas ☎ 0438/21011. **Dolomiti Bus** ✉ Piazzale Stazione, Belluno ☎ 0437/941237. **FTV** ✉ Viale Europa 25, Romano d'Ezzelino ☎ 0424/30850. **La Marca** ✉ Lungosile Mattei 29, Treviso ☎ 0422/577311.

CAR RENTAL

 Local Agencies **Ad Hoc** ✉ Via Maggio 24, Cortina ☎ 0436/868061 **Alfieri** ✉ Viale Italia 170 Conegliano ☎ 0438/32399 **Autonoleggio Kappa** ✉ Via Col di Salle 5/A Belluno ☎ 0437/915140 **Avis** ✉ c/o Garage Cima, Conegliano ☎ 0438/34687 ✉ Piazzale Duca d'Aosta 1 Treviso ☎ 0422/542287. **Garage Dolomiti** ✉ Corso Italia 186 Cortina ☎ 0436/861345 **Hertz** ✉ Treviso airport ☎ 0422/264216 ✉ Via Trevigiana 1, Feltre ☎ 0439/80373. **Maggiore Budget** ✉ Via Medaglia d'Oro 46 Belluno ☎ 0437/932044.

CAR TRAVEL

The SS11 connects Venice with Mestre, from where the SS13 leads due north to Treviso. The autostrada A4 runs north of Mestre and continues north of Belluno. From Padua, the SS47 goes north to Bassano del Grappa.

Westward from Treviso, it's a straight run on the SS53 to Castelfranco and Cittadella. The SS47 connects Cittadella with Bassano del Grappa. Joining the autostrada A27 at Treviso Nord takes you as far as Belluno. A continuation of the A27, the SS51 heads up to Pieve di Cadore following the River Piave, and then northwest to Cortina d'Ampezzo. The SS13 and SS51 connect Treviso with Conegliano and Vittorio Veneto.

ROAD CONDITIONS Beware: wind and snow conditions in the region can be treacherous at times in the winter.

EMERGENCIES

For first aid, ask for *pronto soccorso,* and be prepared to give your address. All pharmacies post signs on the door with addresses of *farmacie di turno,* pharmacies that take turns staying open after normal business hours: at night, on Saturday afternoon, and on Sunday.

 Emergency Services **Ambulance, Police, and Fire** ☎ 113. **First aid** ☎ 118.

 Hospitals **Bassano del Grappa** Ospedale Civile ✉ Via dei Lotti 40 ☎ 0424/888111. **Belluno** Ospedale Civile ✉ Viale Europa ☎ 0437/216111. **Treviso** Ospedale Generale ✉ Viale Vittorio Veneto 18 ☎ 0422/4281. **Vittorio Veneto** Ospedale Civile ✉ Via Forlanini 71 ☎ 0438/5671.

TOURS

Contact the tourist office at Castelfranco (⇨ Visitor Information, *below*) for tours of the town. Free guided tours of Feltre are offered on weekends in summer from 10 to 1 and 4 to 7 and at other times by appointment. Call the number listed below Tuesday through Friday between 9:30 and 10:30 AM for information. Vichival Tour will arrange a gastronomic or cultural tour of the Treviso area.

 Fees & Schedules **Feltre Tours** ☎ 0439/83879. **Vichival Tour** ✉ Via Mazzini 4, 31049 Valdobbiadene ☎ 0423/976322.

TRAIN TRAVEL

The Treviso train station lies on the FS line from Venice to Udine. Trains run several times an hour, and the journey takes a half hour. The FS line connects Treviso with Castelfranco, Cittadella, and Conegliano. On the Padua–Belluno line you pass through Castelfranco and Feltre. Bassano del Grappa has frequent trains to Cittadella, Venice, and Padua. Belluno connects with Conegliano and Padua. The nearest station to Cortina d'Ampezzo is at Calalzo, 32 km (19 mi) southeast, where there are frequent connecting buses.

FARES & SCHEDULES 🚆 Train Information **FS** 🕿 892021. **Treviso Train Station** ✉ Piazzale Duca d'Aosta.

TRAVEL AGENCIES

🚩 Local Agents **Agenzia Esprit Tour** ✉ Viale d'Alviano 52, 31100 Treviso 🕿 0422/410999. **ASVI** ✉ Piazza Martiri 27/e, 32100 Belluno 🕿 0437/941746. **Tai di Pieve di Cadore** ✉ Piazza Venezia 20, 32044 Pieve di Cadore 🕿 0435/31644. **Giorgione** ✉ Piazza Giorgione 46, 31033 Castelfranco 🕿 0423/493601. **Grizzly Viaggi** ✉ Piazzetta Trento e Trieste 16, 32032 Feltre 🕿 0439/2222 ✉ Galleria Caffi, Belluno 🕿 0437/942726 🌐 www.grizzlyviaggi.it. **Viaggi Montegrappa** ✉ Via Giuseppe Barbieri 40, 36061 Bassano del Grappa 🕿 0424/523007.

VISITOR INFORMATION

🚩 Tourist Information **Asolo** ✉ Piazza Garibaldi 73, 31011 🕿 0423/529046 🖨 0423/524137 **Bassano del Grappa** ✉ Largo Corona d'Italia, 36061 🕿 0424/524351 🖨 0424/525301 **Belluno** ✉ Piazza dei Martiri 7, 32100 🕿🖨 0437/940083 **Castelfranco** ✉ Via Francesco Maria Preti 66, 31033 🕿 0423/495000 🖨 0423/720760 **Cittadella** ✉ Via Marconi 3, 35013 🕿🖨 049/5970627 **Conegliano** ✉ Via XX Settembre 61, 31015 🕿 0438/21230 🖨 0438/428777 **Cortina d'Ampezzo** ✉ Piazzetta San Francesco 8, 32043 🕿 0436/3231 🖨 0436/3235 **Feltre** ✉ Piazzetta Trento e Trieste 9, 32032 🕿 0439/2540 🖨 0439/2839 **Marostica** ✉ Piazza Castello, 36063 🕿 0424/72127 🖨 0424/72800 **Pieve di Cadore** ✉ Piazza Venezia 1, 32044 🕿 0435/31644 🖨 0435/31645 **Treviso** ✉ Piazzetta del Monte di Pietà, 31100 🕿 0422/547632 🖨 0422/419092 **Vittorio Veneto** ✉ Piazza del Popolo 18, 31029 🕿 0438/57243 🖨 0438/53629.

FRIULI-VENEZIA GIULIA

9

FODOR'S CHOICE

Antipastoteca di Mare, *restaurant, Trieste*

Castello di Miramare

Duchi d'Aosta, *hotel, Trieste*

HIGHLY RECOMMENDED

SIGHTS Tempietto Longobardo, *Cividale del Friuli*

Vitello d'Oro, *Udine*

RESTAURANTS Montecarlo, *Trieste*

Trattoria Dominissini, *Cividale del Friuli*

HOTELS Al Pomo d'Oro, *Cividale del Friuli*

Alla Posta, *Trieste*

Hotel Clocchiatti, *Udine*

La Dama Bianca, *Duino*

Riviera and Maximilian's, *Trieste*

Updated by
David Graham

TUCKED AWAY in Italy's northeastern corner, Friuli-Venezia Giulia is off most tourist tracks and gains as a result. It's a packed wedge of extremes, from the green, mountainous region of Carnia to the ragged coast of the Golfo di Trieste, a hodgepodge of cultures and climates, marched through, fought over, hymned by patriots and poets, and scene of war atrocities. The capital is the old Hungarian port of Trieste, a longtime symbol of Italian nationalist aspirations that, together with the medieval city of Udine, makes a perfect excursion base.

In the 19th century, the great Italian novelist Ippolito Nievo described this region as "a small abridged version of the universe." Bounded by the Adriatic to the south, the Slovenian and Austrian borders to the north and east, and a ring of mountains to the north, this part of Italy is also as diverse in its culture, architecture, and cuisine as it is in its landscape.

The region has in turn suffered invasions from Romans, Lombards, Cossacks, and Nazis. The rule of Venice was felt at Udine, and the Habsburgs dominated Trieste. During the 19th century, Trieste was the focus for Irredentism, a movement that sought liberation from Austrian rule and ended with the arrival of Italian troops in 1918. Some of the fiercest fighting of World War I took place on the Carso hinterland behind Trieste—now remembered in war memorials and cemeteries containing thousands of fallen soldiers—at Oslavia, Udine, and, with as many as 100,000 interred, Redipuglia. During World War II, Italian fascism found a stronghold in Trieste, the city holding one of Italy's two concentration camps, still visitable. In 1991 border posts witnessed confrontations between Yugoslav and Slovene troops in the battle for Slovenian independence. Trieste's culture and architecture remain distinctly Eastern compared with the rest of the country.

The landscape of Fruili-Venezia Giulia shows an extraordinary diversity, from the mountainous north, essentially Alpine in character, and the limestone karst of the plateau around the Slovenian border, to the flat lagoons and dramatic coastline of the Adriatic. The varied topography is reflected in the patchwork past of this border zone. Whereas the palazzi of Udine reveal Venetian influence, Grado and Aquileia are strongly redolent of their Roman and early Christian past. Trieste, the capital of the region, only became Italian soil after World War II. Its peculiar frontier ambience proved a breeding ground for literary talent in the early years of the 20th century, providing refuge for James Joyce, Richard Burton, Rainer Maria Rilke, and the native Ettore Schmitz. Joyce (1882–1941) lived in Trieste with his wife for spells before and after World War I and wrote *Portrait of the Artist as a Young Man* and part of *Ulysses* here. Sir Richard Burton (1821–90), explorer and writer, was British consul from 1872 until his death and completed his translation of *A Thousand and One Nights* in Trieste. Rilke (1875–1926) composed the *Duino Elegies* near here, and Schmitz, better known as Italo Svevo, wrote his masterpiece, *Confessions of Zeno*.

Exploring Friuli-Venezia Giulia

The region is easily accessed from Venice by the A4 autostrada, which terminates at Trieste. Palmanova (90 km [56 mi] from Venice) marks a crossing point for the region. From here the A23 heads north to Udine and border country with Slovenia to the east, or farther north to connect with the S52, which bisects the mountainous Western Carnia region, following the line of the River Tagliamento, the longest river of the region. Heading farther west will entail taking a tortuous mountain pass—not so easy in winter. South from Palmanova, the historic towns

9

Numbers in the text correspond to numbers in the margin and on the Friuli-Venezia Giulia and Trieste maps.

**If you have
3 days**

Spend your first day and night in ⊡ **Trieste** ①–⑪ ⌐, where your first port of call should be the panoramic **Castello di San Giusto** ⑦ and the nearby cathedral. Break from your perambulations in a buffet-restaurant for lunch; then head outside the city to take in the dramatically positioned **Castello di Miramare** ⑫ in all its opulence, perhaps leaving time for a walk along the coastline at **Duino** ⑬. The next day, make the short journey west to ⊡ **Aquileia** ⑭ to explore the unmissable early Christian treasures and mosaics in the basilica, as well as the remains and museum exhibits from the Roman era. For your last day, head north via the city of **Udine** ⑰, home to some stunning work by Tiepolo, en route to the mountains of Carnia, the place to sample game or wild produce and do some hill walking, spending a quiet night at the village of ⊡ **Forni di Sopra** ⑲. Alternatively, spend a day at the picturesque town of ⊡ **Cividale del Friuli** ⑱, with its early Christian and Roman treasures and delightful setting by the river. Carry on from here to venture farther into the Dolomites, or retrace your steps to Trieste.

**If you have
6 days**

Spend your first two days as above in ⊡ **Trieste** ①–⑪ ⌐ and ⊡ **Aquileia** ⑭, making excursions to the **Castello di Miramare** ⑫, the coast around **Duino** ⑬, and the island town of **Grado** ⑮. On your third day, head north to **Gorizia** ⑯, right on the Slovenian border, then northwest to stay the night at ⊡ **Udine** ⑰. Spend the next day here exploring the town's Venetian art and architectural heritage; then head east to ⊡ **Cividale del Friuli** ⑱ for your fourth night in this charming town in sight of the mountains. For your last day, head north again into the Carnia region for idyllic alpine scenery, perfect for sampling the bracing mountain air, ideally on a hike. Just set off in your car and pick your spot. A good base here would be the village of ⊡ **Forni di Sopra** ⑲, where there's a choice of hotels for your fifth night, and plenty of opportunity to sample rural specialties in the local restaurants. From Forni, you can retrace your steps south to Udine, alternatively continue west, either to further penetrate the Alps or to catch the SS51 south toward Belluno, the Lakes, Treviso, and Venice.

of Aquileia and Grado can easily be reached by the straight Roman road. All towns are well served by public transportation.

About the Restaurants & Hotels

In 1784 a decree was passed allowing peasants around Trieste to sell their own produce for eight days a year. This led to the setting up of *osmizze,* eateries where local food and wine were offered, a tradition that still continues today. Osmizze provide probably the best, and certainly the cheapest, way to experience authentic home cooking in the region—fresh cheeses, bread, prosciutto, soups, and wine in a rustic setting. Look for the *frasco,* a bunch of leaves on a post.

As this area is not very well known to tourists, apart from Austrians, it shouldn't be too hard to find accommodations. In the rural districts you'll certainly find good value for your money. The smaller country hotels often have a restaurant with an open *fogher* (hearth), which gives an intimate and cozy air and is more than welcome in chilly winter months. Your options on the seaside vary from the plethora of hotels in Grado to tranquil spots in Duino. Trieste is busy and caters mainly to the business crowd. You'll find excellent hotels along the water here.

WHAT IT COSTS In euros				
$$$$	**$$$**	**$$**	**$**	**¢**
RESTAURANTS over €22	€17–€22	€12–€17	€7–€12	under €7
HOTELS over €210	€160–€210	€110–€160	€60–€110	under €60

Restaurant prices are for a second course (secondo piatto). Hotel prices are for two people in a standard double room in high season, including tax and service.

Timing

The beauty of being in the shadow of tourist-hungry Venice is that there is never an overwhelming presence of other visitors. Any season is a pleasure here, though winter snows may make the roads difficult in Carnia, which sees a fair number of ski enthusiasts between December and March. Spring and autumn will bring walkers to this mountain zone, but never enough to spoil your enjoyment. Friuli would also be a cool haven from the heat of summer, when the coastal regions can be sultry. Tourist offices can update you about the weather and offer advice on walking conditions.

TRIESTE

Surrounded by rugged countryside and beautiful coastline, Trieste is a lovely architectural melange built on a hillside above what was once the

ON THE MENU

TRIESTE IS KNOWN for its self-service buffets, from which the aromas of cren (horseradish), paprika, capuzi garbi (sweetkraut), and jota (sauerkraut and bean soup) waft invitingly through the streets—don't be surprised to hear these Slavic syllables spoken or to find a strange dialect on menus. These dishes are what give a distinctive flavor to the cuisine of this corner of the Italian peninsula. Seafood abounds here, in some restaurants to the exclusion of everything else. Look for soups made from a diverse range of seafood—mackerel, sardines, clams, squid, and octopus to name but a few. When sated on seafood, try acclaimed San Daniele ham, either cooked or cured. In the Carnia district you're sure to come across cjalsòns—ravioli stuffed with ricotta and spinach. Here and in other rural areas, make a point of savoring the verdure (greens picked from the mountains) and the wild fruits and berries. Sweet specialties include gnocchi stuffed with prunes and coated in cinnamon and sugar.

Friuli produces some of the best wines in northeast Italy. The local wine par excellence is Tocai Friulano, a dry, lively white made from Tocai grapes that has attained international stature. The red of choice is Terrano, a deep, dry, ruby wine produced from Refosco vines. Esteemed reds also come from Isonzo, Carso, and Grave del Friuli. The D.O.C. (Denominazione di Origine Controllata e Garantita) wines, which meet production and quality standards, include Malvasia Carso and Carso Terrano. The Collio designation indicates wines from vineyards in the eastern part of Friuli, near the Slovenian border. The Collio Pinot Bianco from here, a fragrant white, is cool and refreshing. The highly regarded sauternes-like Picolit is made in very limited quantities.

chief port of the Austro-Hungarian Habsburg Empire. The spacious streets hold a lively mix of monumental, neoclassical, and art nouveau styles, granting an air of stateliness to the city. On the downside, Trieste is also brash and clogged with traffic and can be a little overwhelming until you settle in.

Trieste was the Roman city of Tergeste. Having chafed under a brief Venetian dominion, in 1382 the city placed itself under the protection of Leopold III of Habsburg, whose overlordship gradually developed into Austrian possession. In 1719 the city was proclaimed an imperial free port, its economy taking an upturn at the instigation of Maria Teresa, Empress of Austria (1717–80), under whom a program of building started around the Grand Canal. From this anchorage for sailing ships, a regular pattern of spacious streets developed to the west of Piazza Unità d'Italia, called the Borgo Teresiano, an area still lined with grand neoclassical buildings and embellished with statues and bas-reliefs. Much of the city's pre-19th-century identity, in fact, has been submerged under this Austrian layer. The feeling of a Mittel-European city is compounded by the many cafés that grew up at the end of the 19th century. Like Vienna's coffeehouses, these are the social and cultural centers of the city, and much-beloved refuges from the city's prevailing northeast wind, the bora.

On becoming Italian in 1918, the port lost much of its business and Trieste suffered a period of decline. The quays are now used as parking lots, and the container port has moved to the south side of Trieste. In recent years, however, the city has undergone a degree of rejuvenation and has become something of a center for science and the computer industry. Having absorbed new waves of Slavic and Eastern European immigrants, Trieste still has an international air, a tattered romance, and the offbeat ambience of a remote frontier town.

Exploring Trieste

If you're bringing a car into Trieste, find a space to park along the quay, as negotiating the city's system of one-way streets can be a nightmare. From the Stazione Centrale the Corso Cavour leads westward to the Riva, the broad quay that changes its name five times—Rivas Tre Novembre, del Mandracchio, Nazario Sauro, Tommaso Gulli, Grumula—as it skirts the seafront. The Borgo Teresiano sector of the city extends behind the Corso and the Riva's first section (Riva Tre Novembre); adjoining this area, the main Piazza Unità d'Italia opens out onto the sea. Behind the piazza, you can wind your way up through the historical center, pausing along the way at places of interest before reaching the Castello and a rewarding view of the city. On the seafront beyond the piazza, the long white building on the pier, formerly the Stazione Marittima, is now a conference center. From Piazza Oberdan a *tranvia* (cable car) runs every 20 minutes to Opicina and the Carso plateau.

a good walk

Start at **Piazza Unità d'Italia** ❶ ☛ and walk south along Riva Mandracchio and Riva Nazario Sauro past the fish market. Turn left into Piazza Venezia for the **Museo Revoltella e Galleria d'Arte Moderna** ❷. From the square, take Via Torino and turn left into Via di Cavana to return to Piazza Unità d'Italia. Head south to the Scala Medaglie, steps that lead to the churches of **San Silvestro** ❸, dating from the 11th century, and the Baroque **Santa Maria Maggiore** ❹. From here it's only a few paces to Piazza Barbacan. At the far end of the piazza, stop at the Roman **Arco di Riccardo** ❺ before winding your way uphill along Via della Cattedrale to the **Cattedrale di San Giusto** ❻ for its exquisite mosaics and to the **Castello di San Giusto** ❼ for the view and the museum within. The **Museo Civico di Storia ed Arte** ❽ lies across Via della Cattedrale from here. If you're set to visit the **Museo Morpurgo** ❾, follow Via Spellico (the continuation of Galleria Sandrinelli), turning left onto Corso Italia and right onto Via Imbriani. Alternatively, head down Via Rota from the cathedral to the **Teatro Romano** ❿ and the **Piazza della Borsa** ⓫, where you can stop for an espresso, or else wait until you return to Piazza Unità d'Italia, just on the other side of Teatro Verdi.

TIMING   The route would take a couple of hours to walk, a half day to tour the sites on the hill, and longer still if you're going to stop in the museums.

What to See

❺ **Arco di Riccardo.** The Roman arch was built in AD 33 in honor of the Emperor Augustus (63 BC–AD 14) and served as a city gate. Its name recalls the belief that Richard I of England, "the Lionheart," (1157–99) was imprisoned here after a spell in the Holy Land. ⊠ *Piazza Barbacan.*

❼ **Castello di San Giusto.** The Venetians, who always had an eye for the best vantage point in the cities they controlled, built the castle in the 15th century during one of their brief sojourns in Trieste. The Habsburgs enlarged it to its present size in the 18th century. Inside, some of the best exhibits in the **Museo Civico del Castello di San Giusto** are the weaponry and armor, but you can also admire an array of Flemish tapestries, a painted ceiling by Andrea Celesti (1637–1712), and period furnishings. From the ramparts, you can have a view of the area as far as the Dolomites. ⊠ *Piazza Cattedrale* ☎ *040/309362* ⊑ *Castle €1.03, museum and castle €1.55* ◷ *Museum Tues.–Sun. 9–1; castle Apr.–Sept., daily 9–7; Oct.–Mar., daily 9–5.*

❻ **Cattedrale di San Giusto.** Fragments of Roman tombs and temples can be seen among the jumble of styles on the exterior of this 14th-century cathedral; you can see these most clearly on the pillars of the main door-way. The structure incorporates two much older churches, one dating from the 5th century. The facade has a fine and lovely Gothic rose win-dow. The highlights of the interior are the 13th-century mosaics and fres-coes, green and golden and beautifully decorated. Look up and you'll see the wooden ceiling studded with stars. ⊠ *Piazza Cattedrale* ☎ *040/309666* ☾ *Apr.–Sept., daily 8–7:30; Oct.–Mar., daily 8–6:30.*

❽ Museo Civico di Storia ed Arte. Statues from the Roman theater and ar-tifacts from Egypt as well as Greece and Rome are on show at the eclec-tic Civic Museum of History and Art, including sculptures, glass, and manuscripts. From here you can gain access to the **Orto Lapidario** (Lap-idary Garden), where you'll find classical statuary and pottery and a small Corinthian temple that houses the remains of the archaeologist and proponent of neoclassicism, J. J. Winckelmann (1717–68). He was murdered here in Trieste by a thief who coveted his collection of gold coins. ⊠ *Via Cattedrale 15* ☎ *040/310500* ▦ *€3* ☾ *Tues. and Thurs.–Sun. 9–1, Wed. 9–7.*

❾ Museo Morpurgo. The building and its contents were left to the city in 1943 by Mario Morpurgo, a wealthy banker. It's still very much as it was in the last decades of the 19th century, and you can wander through the rooms with their glass, ceramics and porcelain, 19th-century paint-ings, and Japanese prints. ⊠ *Via Imbriani 5* ☎ *040/636969* ▦ *€2* ☾ *Tues. and Thurs.–Sun. 9–1, Wed. 9–7.*

need a break? For the best ice cream in town, head for **Zampolli** (⊠ Via Ghega Carlo 10 ☎ 040/364868).

② **Museo Revoltella e Galleria d'Arte Moderna.** In 1872 the Venetian Baron Revoltella left the city his palace, library, and art collection. Original furniture, inlaid floors, and enameled stoves set the tone in the older part of the museum. A modern annex designed by Carlo Scarpa (1906–78), holds one of the most important collections of 19th- and 20th-century art in Italy, including work by the metaphysical painter Giorgio De Chirico (1878–1978). In July and August the museum is open until midnight with a bar on the terrace featuring splendid views. ☒ *Via Diaz 27* ☎ *040/311360* ☒ *€5* ☉ *Sept.–June, 10–1 and 3–7; July–Aug., 10–1 and 3–midnight. Closed Mon.*

⑪ **Piazza della Borsa.** This square contains Trieste's original stock exchange, the **Borsa Vecchia,** a neoclassical building with a four-columned portico, now serving as the Chamber of Commerce. The statues on the top represent Asia, Europe, Africa, and the Americas, along with Mercury and Vulcan. Presiding over the square from a column is a **Statue of Leopold I** (died 994), Emperor of Austria. In the same square, you can sample art nouveau style à la Trieste in the lightly decorated facade of the **Casa Bartoli,** designed in 1905 by Max Fabiani.

① **Piazza Unità d'Italia.** This spacious square inevitably recalls Piazza San Marco in Venice. Both are focal points of architectural interest abutting the water. Inhabitants of Trieste, however, argue that their piazza is superior to that of San Marco, as it opens out directly onto the seafront. Imposing late 18th- and 19th-century buildings flank the square, most prominently the **Palazzo Comunale** (Town Hall) taking up the entire southern end of the piazza, designed in grand imperial style in 1877. The sidewalk cafés here have always been popular meeting places for literary and political figures and still make grand watering holes.

off the beaten path

RISIERA DI SAN SABBA – Originally used for the preparation of rice, this building was turned into a prison and subsequently became, in 1943, one of the only two concentration camps used by the Germans in Italy. A railway line ran to the crematorium, where it is estimated that 5,000 inmates were burned before liberation by the Yugoslavs on May 1, 1945. Now a museum, it serves as a reminder of the Fascist past. Bus 10 will get you here, or drive southeast out of town on Via Gabriele D'Annunzio. ☒ *Ratto della Pileria 43* ☎ *040/826202* ☒ *Free* ☉ *Tues.–Sun. 9–1.*

③ **San Silvestro.** Now used by Evangelicals, this solid little church is the oldest place of worship in Trieste. It's of plain-fronted Romanesque construction, dating from the 11th century, and said to have been erected on the site where two local martyrs, Sts. Tecla and Eufemia, once lived. ☒ *Piazza di San Silvestro* ☎ *040/632770* ☉ *Mon.–Sat. 9:30–12:30 and Sun. for Mass.*

④ **Santa Maria Maggiore.** In contrast to San Silvestro next door, this church, begun in 1627, has a square Baroque facade with slender columns giving height and lightness. The interior has an altarpiece by Francesco Maffei (circa 1625–60). ☒ *Via del Collegio 6* ☎ *040/632920* ☉ *Mon.–Sat. 8:30–noon and 4:30–7; Sun. 8:30–noon only.*

⑩ **Teatro Romano.** Quintus Petronius Modestus, procurator of the Emperor Trajan, endowed Tergeste, as Trieste was known in Roman times, with this amphitheater in the late 1st century AD. The 6,000 spectators it once held have been replaced with grass and flowers. The statues that once adorned the proscenium arch are now in the Museo Civico di Storia ed Arte. The theater only resurfaced in 1938 after demolition work in the area. ☒ *Via del Teatro Romano.*

off the beaten path	**GROTTA GIGANTE –** This is the largest cave in the world open to tourists. It is more than 300 ft high, 900 ft long, and 200 ft wide, with spectacular stalactites and stalagmites. Reserve 45 minutes for the tour. It is not far from Trieste, about 10 km (6 mi) north of the city (take Bus 42 from Piazza Oberdan). ☎ *040/327312* ✉ *€7.50* ☼ *Apr.–June and Sept., Tues.–Sun. 10–6; July–Aug., daily 10–6; Mar. and Oct., Tues.–Sun. 10–4; Nov.–Feb., Tues.–Sun. 10–noon and 2–4. Apr.–Sept. tours leave every 30 mins; other months, every hr.*

Where to Stay & Eat

$$$ ✕ **Hostaria alle Bandierette.** Try to keep from bumping into the tank of crayfish; then squeeze past the beds of flatfish and shellfish on crushed ice—yes, you're in seafood territory. In fact, this restaurant serves nothing else but. It's small, hectic, and full of serious eaters admiring the cooks in full view. Fish risottos, squid spaghetti, and lobsters with capers will all hit the spot. Dine on the outdoor patio in summer. ⊠ *Riva Nazario Sauro 2* ☎ *040/300686* ⌕ *Reservations essential* ▭ *AE, DC, MC, V* ☼ *Closed Mon. and Jan. 1–15.*

$$–$$$ ✕ **Città di Cherso.** Light, white, and restful in atmosphere, this restaurant right in the heart of downtown specializes in fish. Try the gnocchi *çon seppie* (with cuttlefish, brandy, tomatoes, and cream) or the *rana pescatrice al trancio* (angler-fish steaks). Desserts are a must: there are wonderful concoctions of chocolate and cream. ⊠ *Via Cadorna 6* ☎ *040/366044* ⌕ *Reservations essential* ▭ *AE, DC, MC, V* ☼ *Closed Tues. and Aug.*

★ **$–$$** ✕ **Montecarlo.** Four warmly furnished rooms give this fine restaurant a cozy atmosphere, but with first-class food and service. Help yourself (and be generous!) from the excellent antipasto buffet to sample from more than a dozen exquisite seafood delicacies—baby octopus in oil and garlic, marinated herring and anchovy, shrimp, and *baccalà mantecato* (whisked salt cod)—along with sautéed zucchini and Russian salad. Mains include both seafood and meat dishes and there is an extensive wine list—though the house wine is also good. ⊠ *Via San Marco 10* ☎ *040/662545* ⌕ *Reservations essential on weekends* ▭ *MC, V* ☼ *Closed Mon.*

$–$$ ✕ **Suban.** Though in the hills on the edge of town, this historic trattoria is worth the taxi ride. The rustic decor is rich in dark wood, stone, and wrought iron, and you'll find typical regional fare with imaginative variations. Among the specialties are *jota carsolina* (typical local minestrone made of cabbage, potatoes, and beans) and duck breast in Tokay sauce. Finish with the Hungarian-influenced *rigo jançi* (a mousse-like chocolate pudding). ⊠ *Via Emilio Comici 2/d,* ☎*040/54368* ▭ *AE, DC, MC, V* ☼ *Closed Tues., 3 wks in Aug., and 1 wk in early Jan. No lunch Mon.*

$ ✕ **Antipastoteca di Mare.** Hidden away halfway up the hill to the Castello

Fodor'sChoice di San Giusto, Roberto Surian's simple little restaurant is well worth ★ seeking out during the day and booking for the evening. You'll find here some of the tastiest of hot and cold seafood combinations, from calamari and barley salad to scallops, mussels, and sardines with basil. The extraordinary fish soup of sardines, mackerel, and tuna, sprinkled with lightly fried, diced garlic bread and polenta, won Roberto first prize in Trieste's prestigious Sarde Day competition. Fish is everything here, accompanied only by a simple salad, potatoes, polenta, and house wine. ⊠ *Via della Fornace 1* ☎ *040/309606* ▭ *No credit cards* ☼ *Closed Mon. No dinner Sun.*

¢ ✕ **Brek.** See review under "Where to Stay & Eat in Padua," Chapter 7. ⊠ *Via S. Francesco 10* ☎ *040/371331* ▭ *AE, DC, MC, V* ☼ *Jan.–Feb., no dinner Fri.*

TRIESTE'S CAFFÈ CULTURE

TRIESTE IS JUSTLY FAMOUS for its coffee, and so it is perhaps no coincidence that its former mayor is Riccardo Illy, patriarch of the eponymous über-roaster, Illycaffè, which can be credited with supplying caffeine fixes to most Italians and much of the free world. The elegant civility of Trieste plays out beautifully in a café culture that rivals Vienna. In Trieste, as in all of Italy, ask for a caffè and you'll get a thimbleful of high-octane, but no less delicious, espresso. Know that in Trieste your cappuccino will come in said espresso cup, with only half as much frothy milk and a dollop of whipped cream. Many cafés are part of a torrefazione (roasting shop), so you can sample the beans before you buy. You can taste the local brews at both the Cremecaffè and Caffè La Colombiana.

Few cafés in Trieste, Italy, and the world, can rival **Antico Caffè San Marco** (⊠ Via Cesare Battisti 18 ☎ 040/363538) for its glimmering art deco style and Old World patina. It was completely destroyed in World War I, and when it was rebuilt in the 1920s, it became the meeting place for local intellectuals. On Friday and Saturday it hosts live music; it's closed Monday. **Caffè Tommaseo** (⊠ Riva Tre Novembre 5 ☎ 040/362666) has been the haunt of politicians and businessmen since 1830. Sober and elegant, it has mirrors that were imported from Belgium more than 100 years ago. It's also closed Monday.

Caffè Pasticceria Pirona (⊠ Largo Barriera Vecchia 12 ☎ 040/636046) was patronized by the likes of James Joyce. Imagine him garnering inspiration for his Ulysses as he sipped his macchiato (literally "stained," espresso with a touch of steamed milk). Founded in 1900 by Alberto Pirona and still in the family, the place has maintained an old-fashioned look with its cherry-wood fittings but has no place to sit down: it's a spot for coffee and its famously scrumptious cakes on the go. It's closed on Monday. **Cremecaffè** (⊠ Piazza Goldoni 10 ☎ 040/636555), closed Sunday, may not be the place to sit down and read the paper, lest you get jostled by the caffeine-craving crowd, but it's nonetheless one of the most-frequented cafés in town, with 20 different blends to choose from.

One of the city's finest roasting shops, **Caffè La Colombiana** (⊠ Via Carducci 12 ☎ 040/370855), closed Sunday, has stood here since the 1940s—still without tables or eats, but the coffee hasn't changed since those days. There is no better location in town than **Caffè Piazza Grande** (⊠ Piazza Unità d'Italia 5 ☎ 040/369878), with a great view of this grand square. It's closed Sunday. **Il Gran Bar Malabar** (⊠ Piazza San Giovanni 6 ☎ 040/636226) is yet another wonderful stop for a coffee or an aperitif, with an excellent wine list as well and tastings every Friday.

$$$$ 🏨 **Duchi d'Aosta.** On the spacious Piazza Unità d'Italia, this hotel, beautifully furnished in Venetian-Renaissance style, has come a long way since its original incarnation as a 19th-century dockers' café. Each of the rooms is decorated in elegant "one-off" style, with dark-wood antiques, rich carpets, and plush fabrics. On the ground floor is Harry's Grill, one of the city's most select restaurants. ⊠ Piazza Unità d'Italia 2/1, 34121 ☎ 040/7600011 🖷 040/366092 ⊕ www.grandhotelduchidaosta.com 🛏 53 rooms, 2 suites ⟜ Restaurant, bar, minibars, cable TV, hot tubs, Turkish bath, meeting rooms, parking (fee), some pets allowed ⊟ AE, DC, MC, V ⧖ CP.

FodorsChoice ★

★ **$$–$$$** 🏨 **Riviera and Maximilian's.** Seven kilometers (4 miles) north of Trieste, this lovely hotel commands stunning views across the Golfo di Trieste to Castello di Miramare. There's no sand on this stretch of coast, but an elevator leads to the hotel's own private bathing quay below. Rooms are well furnished in modern style and all have sea-view balconies. The breakfast restaurant and main Le Terrazze restaurant both have similarly stunning sea views. ✉ *Strada Costiera 22, 34010* ☎ *040/224551* 🖷 *040/224300* 📞 *57 rooms, 1 suite* ♿ *Restaurant, bar, no a/c in some rooms, minibars, cable TV, beach, Internet, meeting rooms, free parking, some pets allowed* ▤ *AE, DC, MC, V* ⋈ *MAP, FAP.*

★ **$$** 🏨 **Alla Posta.** The reading lounge—with its high-backed armchairs, parquet floor, and potted plants, plus a roaring fire in winter—will entice you into this elegant, central hotel. Upstairs, stylishly decorated guest rooms are outfitted with high-tech controls for amenities such as heating, air-conditioning, and wake-up calls. The spacious bathrooms are done in Italian marble. ✉ *Piazza Oberdan 1* ☎ *040/365208* 🖷 *040/ 633720* 📞 *47 rooms* ♿ *In-room data ports, in-room safes, minibars, cable TV with movies* ▤ *AE, DC, MC, V* ⋈ *CP.*

$$ 🏨 **Best Western San Giusto.** Oriental rugs on the marble floor, potted palms, and chandeliers complement the elegant art deco style of this hotel. Only a 10-minute walk from the center of town, on the hill behind the castle, it's away from the concentration of hotels and restaurants downtown in a less touristy area with a mix of small shops, apartment buildings, offices, and some very good restaurants. ✉ *Via dell'Istria 7, 34137* ☎ *040/764824* 🖷 *040/763826* 🌐 *www.hotelsangiusto.it* 📞 *62 rooms* ♿ *Bar, cable TV, parking (fee), some pets allowed, no-smoking rooms* ▤ *AE, DC, MC, V* ⋈ *CP.*

$ 🏨 **Alabarda.** The bright, spacious rooms in this restored, family-operated hotel are the best value in central Trieste, only 10 minutes' walk from the train station. You can check your e-mail at the computer in the lobby and catch an English news broadcast on the satellite TV in your room. The friendly staff will offer assistance with local services, maps, and city bus tickets. Some front rooms can be noisy. ✉ *Via Valdirivo 22,* ☎ *040/630269* 🖷 *040/639284* 🌐 *www.hotelalabarda.it* 📞 *18 rooms, 9 rooms without bathroom* ♿ *Internet; no a/c* ▤ *AE, DC, MC, V* ⋈ *CP.*

Nightlife & the Arts

The Arts

CONCERTS, OPERA & BALLET The concert, opera, and ballet season in Trieste runs from October through May, with events taking place in the **Teatro Verdi** (✉ Piazza Giuseppe Verdi ☎ 040/6722298 🌐 www.teatroverdi-trieste.com). Various music and dance events are held at the **Sala Tripcovich** (✉ Piazza Libertà); for information and tickets contact Teatro Verdi. The **Festival Internazionale dell'Operetta** is held in July and August. Prices start at €7.75; for information and tickets contact Teatro Verdi.

FESTIVALS Details of events and festivals are published in the daily paper, *Il Piccolo*.

Films from central and eastern Europe are shown during the **Alpe-Adria Film Festival**, held in December and January. Contact the **Teatro Miela** (✉ Piazza Duca degli Abruzzi 3 ☎ 040/365119).

The **Barcolana Autumn Cup Regatta** gets under way on the second Sunday in October, attracting more than 1,000 sailing boats.

Four kilometers (2½ miles) south of Trieste, Muggia is famous for its **Carnevale,** a moveable feast in February that goes back as far as 1420, but it also has a crowd-pulling "summer edition" in July and August with music, dancing, and theater. Call the **Commune di Muggia** (☎ 040/ 3360340) for further information.

Nightlife

DISCOS   **Machiavelli** (⊠ Viale Miramare 285 ☎ 040/44104) attracts a lively crowd. **Tor Cucherna** (⊠ Via Chiauchiara 7 ☎ 040/368874), another hopping discotheque, has an American bar (one with a full range of well drinks).

Shopping

You'll find several big department stores like "Coin" and "Rinascente," and most of Italy's big fashion names along Trieste's busy shopping street, **Corso Italia.** Trieste has some 60 antiques dealers, jewelers, and secondhand shops. For small items of glass and porcelain, the nameless antiques shop at Piazza Vecchia 2/c is excellent. You'll find similar shops along the Via del Ponte.

Markets

Markets are held Tuesday through Saturday. You'll find general markets in Piazza della Libertà and Via Carducci and fish, fruit, and flowers in Piazza di Ponterosso and at Riva Nazario Sauro 1. Antiques markets crowd the streets of the city's old center on the third Sunday of each month. At the beginning of November, Trieste plays host to the region's biggest antiques fair—a good opportunity to find those art nouveau pieces. Contact **Promotrieste** (Centro Congressi ⊠ Stazione Marittima ☎ 040/304888) for information.

Specialty Shops

CHINA–CRYSTAL   An elegant range of Venetian glass and fine china from names like Venini and Versace can be found at Orietta Spangher's **Bottega** (⊠ Piazza Unità d'Italia 5 ☎ 040/366200).

CLOTHING   **Alexandra** (⊠ Via XXX Ottobre 14 ☎ 040/634401) has fine Italian selections of clothing. **Annamaria Costantini** (⊠ Via Mazzini 22/B ☎ 040/369643) sells slightly off-beat evening wear. **Confezione Wallner** (⊠ Via Roma 13 ☎ 040/631570) clothes men, women, and children.

JEWELRY   For nice stocks of silverware and watches, visit **Cavallar** (⊠ Via S. Lazzaro 15 ☎ 040/630335). The proprietor of **G. Bin** (⊠ Via Giulia 10/c ☎ 040/569450) is a registered gemologist specializing in unset stones.

FROM THE COAST TO SLOVENIA

From Trieste, the road eastward follows the coast under the shadow of the huge geological formation called the Carso, a barren expanse of limestone that forms a giant ledge, most of which is across the border in Slovenia. Italian territory extends only a couple of miles inland on this narrow strip, and Italy's small Slovene minority ekes out an agricultural existence in the region, which has changed hands countless times since the final days of Imperial Rome. Forty or so kilometers (25 miles) west of Trieste, Aquileia was the principal Roman center in the region. In 313, Theodore became its first Christian patriarch (bishop), founding a basilica whose richly allegorical early Christian mosaics are among the finest to be seen in Italy today.

The Roman population of Aquileia found safe refuge from the ravaging Huns and Lombards in the island town of Grado, whose small historic center lies adjacent to some of the region's best beaches. There is more than a passing resemblance to Venice in the layout of this port and resort, and no lack of hotels just a short walk from the sands, not to mention fish restaurants galore. Between Trieste and Grado, Miramare and Duino offer more coastal pleasures but without the bustling beach culture of other resorts along this stretch. The shore here is picturesquely cliffy, the tramping ground and inspiration for both Dante and Rilke.

To the north, Gorizia lies right on the Slovenian border, literally bisected by it. The hilltop castle here holds a World War I museum, recalling the conflict that devastated this region. The Slavic element is strong here; make sure you sample the local goulash.

Castello di Miramare

12 *8 km (5 mi) northwest of Trieste, 138 km (86 mi) east of Venice.*

Fodor'sChoice
★

This waterfront castle in Miramare is a 19th-century extravaganza in white stone, built for the Archduke Maximilian of Habsburg (1832–67, brother of Emperor Franz Josef). Maximilian spent a brief, happy time here until Napoléon III of France took Trieste from the Habsburgs and sent the poor archduke packing. He was given the title of emperor of Mexico in 1864 as a compensation but met his death before a Mexican firing squad in 1867. The interiors preserve much of the original fittings and ornaments: Bohemian glass chandeliers, inlaid furniture, and ornately molded ceilings, including the elaborate Gothic ceiling in the vast throne room. Lush grounds surround the castle, affording stupendous views over the Adriatic. In summer, son-et-lumière shows are staged here, including a version in English. ⊠ *Miramare* ☎ *040/224143* ⊕ *www. castello-miramare.it* ⊠ *Castle €4, plus €3 for optional guided visit (reservation required for guided visit); grounds free* ☉ *Castle and grounds daily 9–6.30; last entry 30 mins before closing.*

Duino

13 *20 km (12 mi) northwest of Trieste, 12 km (8 mi) northwest of Castello di Miramare.*

The small fishing village of Duino is a picture of tranquillity, largely unspoiled, consisting of a few houses, hotels, and a police station. The contrast with the neighboring bay of Sistiana, which is chock-full of yachts and pleasure boats, couldn't be greater. You can walk the 2-km (1-mi) path from Sistiana, passing through woodland along the panoramic rocky coast, where you might even glimpse a peregrine falcon. Duino has two castles—one, the **Castello Vecchio**, is in ruins; the other **Castello** once hosted the German poet Rilke and is still inhabited by descendants of the original owners, the Della Torre e Tasso family (part of it now belongs to an international school). Rilke used the path for his musings and composed the *Duino Elegies,* among his last and most famous works, while staying here. This castle is not open to the public, but you can reach the Castello Vecchio easily enough, crowning an impressive headland jutting out to sea. The site is famed for the Dama Bianca (White Lady), a white rock named after a legendary episode in which the Lord Duino hurled a woman for whom he had no further use out of the castle. Before hitting the water, she turned to stone, the white rock. The locality is also said to have been a favorite haunt of Dante (1265–1321); the cliff on which he meditated bears his name.

Where to Stay & Eat

★ **$** ✕⊡ **La Dama Bianca.** Right on the shore, with glorious sunset views, the balconied rooms just a few yards from the water's edge are blue, cool, light, and airy. With lush foliage and twinkling of the lights on the tables at night and on the boats out to sea, the hotel's restaurant ($$–$$$) is romantic indeed. From the catch of her fisherman husband, the affable Branca Miladinovic concocts crab served in its shell, and crescent-shape ravioli with shrimp, basil, and poppy seeds. The desserts, Signora Branca's own recipes, are to die for, and there's an excellent local wine list. ⊠ *Duino Porto 61/c, 34013* ☎ *040/208137* ⊟ *040/208258* ⊕*www.*

alladamabianca.com ⤷ *7 rooms* ⚲ *Restaurant, bar, some pets allowed; no a/c in some rooms.* ▤ *AE, DC, MC, V* ⦿ *EP Mar.–Oct.* ⊗ *Hotel closed Dec. 15–Jan. 31; restaurant closed Thurs.* ⦿ *CP.*

$$ ▣ **Duino Park Hotel.** This is a nice, quiet lodging a little way up the hill from the sea and run by genial management. Rooms are individually furnished, some with balconies overlooking the bay. The wicker furniture in the public area, set off by big terra-cotta floor tiles, adds to the charm. Breakfast is taken on the terrace in warm weather. ✉ *Via Duino 60/c, 34013* ☎ *040/208184* 🖷 *040/208526* ⤷ *18 rooms* ⚲ *Bar, minibars, pool, sauna, free parking* ▤ *AE, DC, MC, V* ⊗ *Dec.15–Feb. 15* ⦿ *CP.*

Aquileia

⑭ *77 km (48 mi) west of Trieste, 18 km (11 mi) west of Monfalcone.*

Nowadays it's difficult to believe that this sleepy little town was, in the time of Emperor Augustus, Italy's fourth most important city (after Rome, Milan, and Capua). The patriarchate (bishopric) of Aquileia was founded here around 314, the basilica commissioned shortly afterward, and, after several centuries of decline and frequent pillaging, the town regained its prominence from the 11th to the end of the 14th century. Prominent past visitors include Herod the Great, who was received by Augustus in 10 BC; Sts. Jerome and Ambrose, who attended a council of bishops in AD 381; and Attila the Hun, who sacked the town in 452. Aquileia's magnificent Roman and Byzantine remains are strongly evocative of this patchwork past, beautifully preserved right in the middle of the serene village and refreshingly free of the mass tourism that you might expect to find given its cultural riches.

Aquileia's **Basilica** was founded by Theodore, its first patriarch, and later extended. It owes its present form to the patriarch Poppo (or Popone) who rebuilt it between 1021 and 1031, though it has accumulated different elements including the Romanesque portico and the Gothic bell tower. But the highlight of this monument is the staggering 4th-century mosaic covering the entire floor, one of the finest relics of the early Christian period in Italy and the biggest of its kind. From the vibrancy of the colors, the floor appears as if it has just been laid, and with good reason, as it was only uncovered at the beginning of the 20th century. It survived a major earthquake in 1328—just: it now ripples in corrugated waves as a consequence. Christian images combine with the pagan in this marine extravaganza of dolphins, squid, and lobsters, among which Jonah is swallowed and spewed out of an extraordinary sea monster, and cherubs fish from a boat.

Before the Edict of Constantine (the proclamation in 313 that established religious toleration for Christianity under the Romans), Christians adopted images of pagan symbolism to express their faith, some of which can be seen here. The winged figure of Victory with her laurel wreath and palm frond equates with triumph over death; the tortoise with its carapace symbolizes darkness, and the cockerel, which crows at dawn, is light. Fish, of course, represent Christ, from Ichthos—Greek for fish and an acronym for Jesus Christ, Son of God, Savior—and birds such as peacocks represent immortality. Down a flight of steps, the **Cripta degli Affreschi** contains soft-hued frescoes, among them St. Peter sending St. Mark to Aquileia and the beheading of Saints Hermagoras and Fortunatus, to whom the basilica is dedicated. The **Cripta degli Scavi** contains another huge area of mosaic paving surrounding the base to the campanile and allows you to see how the successive layers of building took place from the 4th century on. ✉ *Piazza Capitolo* ☎ *0431/*

91067 ✉ *Basilica free; both crypts €2.60; campanile €1.10* ⊙ *Apr.–Oct., Mon.–Sat. 8:30–6, Sun. 8:30–6:30; Nov.–Mar. 8:30–12:30 and 2:30–5:30. Visits suspended during Sunday mass (10:30–11:15).*

Beyond the basilica and across the road from it, the **archaeological site** among the cypresses reveals Roman remains of the forum, houses, cemetery, and port. The little stream was once a navigable and important waterway extending to Grado. The area is well signposted. ⊕ *www. museoarcheo-aquileia.it* ✉ *Free* ⊙ *Daily 8:15–one hr before sunset.*

Of the town's two museums, the **Museo Archeologico** is the most rewarding, containing a wealth of material from the Roman era. Notable are the portrait busts from Republican times, semiprecious gems, amber- and gold-work—including preserved flies—a fine glass collection in iridescent hues, and miniature priapic bronzes. ⊠ *Via Roma 1* ☎ *0431/ 91096* ⊕ *www.museoarcheo-aquileia.it* ✉ *€4* ⊙ *Tues.–Sun. 8:30–7:30, Mon. 8:30–2.*

The **Museo Paleocristiano** houses more mosaics and traces the development of art from Roman to Christian times. ⊠ *Località Monastero* ☎ *0431/91131* ⊕ *www.museoarcheo-aquileia.it* ✉ *Free* ⊙ *Daily 8:30–1:45.*

Where to Stay & Eat

¢–$ ✕ **La Colombara.** The large, open fireplace in this friendly, family-run restaurant about 2 km (1 mi) northeast of Aquileia is used for cooking, and the fare is mainly fish and game. Try the stuffed calamari with artichokes or ravioli with mixed fish, or, in spring, any of several dishes based on asparagus. Everything is homemade—pasta, bread, and cakes. In August and September the restaurant organizes Roman evenings (come in a toga) when the tables are cleared for the triclinia (reclining couches). ⊠ *Via San Zilli 42* ☎ *0431/91513* ⊕ *www.lacolombara.it* ▭ *AE, DC, MC, V* ⊙ *Closed Mon.*

$ ✕▥ **Patriarchi.** You can open your shutters onto a view of the basilica from this hotel. It's well run and very friendly, and offers good service. Colorful rugs enliven modern rooms with plenty of space. Book ahead for stays in July and August, when an umbrella on Grado's beach is included in the price. The simple restaurant ($; closed Wed.) serves its own salami or baby octopus in *salsa piccante* (spicy sauce) as antipasti on unusual glass plates. Follow it with gnocchi with salmon and cognac or *scarpena alla siciliana* (scorpion fish with black olives, tomato, and oregano). Everything is deliciously light. ⊠ *Via Giulia Augusta 12, 33051* ☎ *0431/919595* 🖷 *0431/919596* ⊕ *www.hotelpatriarchi.it* ⬙ *22 rooms* ⚷ *Restaurant, bar, some in-room safes, minibars, cable TV, some pets allowed* ▭ *AE, DC, MC, V* ⊙ *Closed Nov. 10–20.* ▯◎▯ *CP.*

Grado

⓯ *11 km (7 mi) south of Aquileia, 52 km (32 mi) west of Trieste.*

Grado is an island town set among lagoons and approached by causeway from Aquileia or Monfalcone. The town has a compact and attractive historic center, but most people flock here for its 20 km (12 mi) of sandy beaches, as clean and safe as you'll find anywhere in Italy. All the usual sunning and swimming facilities are on hand, as well as thermal baths, but it's worth leaving the serried ranks of umbrellas to take a stroll round the harbor and the alleys and piazzas of the old town. This small quarter has an engaging, slightly decaying air to it and holds the best restaurants. With Grado still an active fishing port, seafood is abundant.

The old town's Venetian architecture sets the tone, a legacy of the period when Grado came under the Republic's sway in the 15th century. Its history, however, extends back further, for this was an outpost of Roman Aquileia, the place to which the inhabitants of that inland town fled in the 5th century to escape the invasions of Huns. In the 6th century, Grado became the principal patriarchal seat and grew in importance. Three engaging buildings remain from that time, in each of which you can see mosaic pavements from the 6th century.

The 6th-century **Basilica di Sant'Eufemia** has some 20 different columns with Byzantine capitals, a patterned geometrical mosaic floor, and an embossed, silver Venetian altar frontal dating from the 14th century. Remarkable, too, is the lovely 13th-century hexagonal *ambo* (pulpit) decorated with bold symbols of the Evangelists and covered by an Oriental cupola. ⊠ *Campo Patriarca Elia* ☎ *0439/80146* ☉ *Apr.–Oct. 7:30 AM–9 PM; Nov.–Mar. 7:30 AM–6:30PM.*

Next to the Basilica in Campo dei Patriarchi, the 6th-century **Battistero** (Baptistery) also has a mosaic pavement. In the same square, the church of **Santa Maria delle Grazie** displays more Byzantine columns and mosaics.

Where to Stay & Eat

$$–$$$ ✕ **De Toni.** Right in the old town, this pretty restaurant exposes its floor so that you can see the foundations of the old Roman structure beneath it. Dining outside in summer is almost de rigueur. The chef has his own special recipe for fish soup the *zuppa di vongole* (clam soup) is good, too, as is *triglia* (red mullet) in bread crumbs with vinaigrette. Reservations are advised in summer. ⊠ *Piazza Duca d'Aosta 37* ☎ *0431/80104* ⊟ *AE, DC, MC, V* ☉ *Closed Jan. and Wed. Sept.–June.*

$–$$ ✕ **Al Balaor.** As you might expect in this fishing port, seafood is the specialty. Pull up a button-backed chair in this elegant and plush restaurant with blue-green furnishings, and tuck into the fresh fish antipasti, scallops St. Jacques with polenta, *frogolezzi* (small gnocchi) with shrimp, or swordfish. As the restaurant has its own pasticceria, the cakes are superb. Reservations are advised in summer. ⊠ *Calle Zanini 3* ☎ *0431/80150* ⊟ *AE, DC, MC, V* ☉ *Closed Thurs. and 10 days in Nov.*

$$$ ▦ **Hannover.** The best thing about this small four-star hotel is its position overlooking the tiny fishing port. Rooms are spacious and modern in a standard way, offset by the pink and green marble of the public rooms. The beach is also nearby, and access to this and the changing rooms is included in the price. ⊠ *Piazza XXVI Maggio, 34073* ☎ *0431/82264* 🖷 *0431/82141* ⤶ *23 rooms, 3 suites* ⚬ *Restaurant, bar, in-room safes, minibars, health club, hot tub, sauna, parking (fee), some pets allowed* ⊟ *AE, DC, MC, V* ☉ *Closed 2 wks in Jan.* ⑴ *CP.*

$$–$$$ ▦ **Savoy.** Light and spacious, this is the only Grado hotel to offer both indoor and outdoor swimming pools. Guest rooms are elegantly minimalist. The stately striped sofas in the lobby combine with the modernistic pink and white columns to lend an almost 18th-century flavor. ⊠ *Via Carducci 33, 34073* ☎ *0431/897111* 🖷 *0431/83305* ⊕ *www.hotelsavoygrado.it* ⤶ *83 rooms* ⚬ *Restaurant, in-room safes, minibars, cable TV, golf privileges, saltwater pool, indoor-outdoor pool, gym, health club, hot tub, sauna, steam room, bicycles, bar* ⊟ *AE, DC, MC, V* ☉ *Closed Nov.–Mar.* ⑴ *CP.*

$$ ▦ **Antares.** A pleasant, small, plant-filled hotel, it's just a step back from the waterfront in a quiet location. All rooms have a balcony and there's a terrace for sunbathing. Breakfast is served on the quiet, sunny terrace in summer and includes a range of freshly sliced cold cuts and cheeses. ⊠ *Via delle Scuole 4, 34073* ☎ *0431/84961* 🖷 *0431/82385* ⊕ *www.antareshotel.info* ⤶ *19 rooms* ⚬ *Bar, in-room safes, minibars, cable TV,*

parking (fee), some pets allowed ⊟ *No credit cards* ⊙ *Closed Nov. 20–Feb. 10.* ⦙◉⦙ *CP.*

Sports & the Outdoors

BEACH Before or after sightseeing in the old town, take a dip in the sea: the beach umbrellas are backed by cabins on lidos where you pay a small daily fee, and there's a free beach at the west end. The water is shallow and clean, making it ideal for kids.

BOAT TRIPS The **Motonave Cristina** (☎ 0431/81412) sails twice a day from Grado to Portobuso, with a stop for lunch on the isle of Anfora.

Gorizia

🖲 *51 km (39 mi) northwest of Trieste, 43 km (27 mi) north of Grado.*

Like Trieste, Gorizia bears the hallmark of the Habsburgs, having remained under the control of the Austrian dynasty until 1916. After World War II, the Treaty of Paris split the town, Italy keeping the western half and Yugoslavia the eastern, which is now Nova Gorica. A quiet place, Gorizia is still imbued with a mixture of Italian and Slavic cultures, and a stroll around town reveals grand streets, arcades, parks, and gardens.

A pleasant garden surrounds the Borgo Castello, a hilltop fortified by the Venetians. Climb up the steps on the steep west side, or take the Viale D'Annunzio on the gentler south side to reach the red-roofed and battlemented **Castello.** The walls were reinforced in 1508 by the Venetians, who left their ubiquitous mark in the form of a winged lion in bas-relief over the castle entrance. In the inner court it's possible to see the original 11th- and 12th-century foundations of the keep. ⊠ *Borgo Castello 36* ☎ *0481/535146* ⊡ *€2.60* ⊙ *Nov.–Mar. 9:30–6, Apr.–Oct. 9:30–1 and 3–7:30. Closed Mon.*

Within the castle complex is the church of **Santo Spirito,** built in 1398. It's notable for the hanging porch and large 16th-century wooden crucifix on the facade—actually a copy, the original squirreled away for safekeeping. ⊠ *Borgo Castello* ☎ *0481/530193* ⊙ *Church rarely open; check at the Musei Provinciali for entry.*

Also in the Borgo Castello, the **Musei Provinciali di Borgo Castello** houses the Museo della Grande Guerra (Museum of the Great War) and the Museo della Moda e delle Arti Applicati (Fashion and Applied Arts Museum), along with some smaller exhibitions. ⊠ *Borgo Castello* ☎ *0481/ 533926, 530382* 🖷 *0481/534878* ⊡ *€6* ⊙ *Tues.–Sun. 9:30–1 and 2–7:30.* The **Palazzo Attems** is a fine neoclassical building, designed in 1745 by Nicolò Pacassi (1711–90), which stages major temporary exhibitions. ⊠ *Piazza de Amicis* ☎ *0481/531798 for information.*

Where to Stay & Eat

$–$$ ✕ **Ai Tre Soldi Goriziani.** This long dining room with plain white walls and a refined atmosphere is popular with locals on their night out. Try dishes with an East European flair such as the *gnocchi di pane al sugo di goulasch* (bread gnocchi with goulash) or the Wiener schnitzel. ⊠ *Corso Italia 38* ☎ *0481/531956* ⚭ *Reservations essential* ⊟ *AE, DC, MC, V* ⊙ *Closed Mon. and Aug. No dinner Sun.*

$ ✕ **Ristorante 1803.** Whitewashed plaster, terra-cotta floors, and soft lighting set a rustic tone in this seafood restaurant. Antipasti may include such delicacies as thinly sliced smoked swordfish with arugula, or grilled cuttlefish. The Sardinian owners are very friendly and will offer additional delights from their own traditions, such as the famous *carta di musica*, a superbly crunchy, salted, paper-thin bread. ⊠ *Piazza Cavour 6* ☎ *0481/30333* ⊟ *MC, V* ⊙ *Closed Sun.*

$ ╳ **Rosenbar.** There's a predominantly dark-red tone at this restaurant with wood paneling and a copper bar. One part is more formal, the other around the bar less so. It's a popular spot, usually fairly lively, and with hospitable service. The small menu is handwritten and changes regularly. Try the pumpkin soup and the strudel of potato and radicchio, both delicious. Homemade puddings are a delight. ⊠ *Via Duca d'Aosta 96* ☎ *0481/522700* ⊟ *AE, DC, MC, V* ⊘ *Closed Sun.–Mon. and 2 wks in Feb.*

$ 🏨 **Euro Diplomat.** Fancy trimmings at this modern hotel right in the center of town are confined to the impressive glass chandelier in the lobby. The place is a bit tattered around the edges, but it's conveniently priced, offers standard comfort, and has surprisingly little competition in this delightful, little-visited city. ⊠ *Corso Italia 63, 34170* ☎ *0481/82166* 🖶 *0481/31658* ➥ *70 rooms* ⚴ *Restaurant (closed weekends), bar, minibars, meeting rooms, free parking, some pets allowed.* ⊟ *AE, DC, MC, V* ⦿ *CP.*

UDINE & POINTS NORTH

Infused with the spirit of Venice, the inland town of Udine holds a cluster of absorbing attractions and is also the starting point for some fine sights in the vicinity, including a couple of the region's best museums. Although there are good lodgings to be found at Udine, you might prefer the quieter milieu of Cividale del Friuli, almost within spitting distance of the Julian Alps and washed through by the lovely Natisone River. Some excellent museum collections are here, particularly the Museo Cristiano annexed to the Duomo.

You don't have to venture far from Cividale to feel the Alpine earth under your feet. Carry on northward, past Tolmezzo, to enter the charmed environment of Carnia, a mountain region lacking the epic grandeur of the Dolomites but containing enough natural beauty to impress even the most jaded urban sensibility. Aside from a few larger hotels catering to skiers and hikers, the lodgings here are generally small and inexpensive. Hospitality is the watchword, and the meals are designed to cure the deep hunger induced by the clean air and healthy exertions.

Udine

🔞 *64 km (40 mi) north of Trieste, 100 km (62 mi) east of Venice.*

The second-largest city in the Friuli-Venezia Giulia region, Udine has a very different atmosphere than Trieste. Almost sleepy in its provincialism, Udine commands a view of the surrounding plain and the Alpine foothills. According to legend, it stands on a mound erected by Attila the Hun so he could watch the burning of the important Roman center of Aquileia, to the south. Udine flourished in the Middle Ages, thanks to its good location for trade and the rights it gained from the local patriarch to hold regular markets. There is a distinct Venetian feel to the city, noticeable in the architecture of Piazza della Libertà, which lies under the stern gaze of the lion of St. Mark. Like Venice, the city has a rich artistic patrimony, including a good selection of works by Tiepolo.

Udine's **Duomo,** consecrated in 1335—completed in the 15th century but much altered in the baroque period—is an essential stop for its altarpieces and frescoes by the great Venetian artist, Giambattista Tiepolo (1696–1770). ⊠ *Piazza Duomo* ☎ *0432/506832* ⊘ *Daily 9–noon and 4–6.*

Opposite the cathedral, the **Oratorio della Purità** is well worth a visit for more Tiepolo frescoes and, by his son, Giandomenico, grisaille (gray-toned) biblical friezes. Ask the sacristan at the cathedral to let you in; late afternoon is probably the best time. ⊠ *Piazza Duomo* ☎ *0432/505032.*

The Palazzo Arcivescovile houses the **Galleria del Tiepolo**, which contains superlative examples of Tiepolo's frescoes from the Old Testament, depicting the stories of Abraham, Isaac, and Jacob and the *Judgment of Solomon* in beautiful pastel colors. In the same building, the **Museo Diocesano** features a collection of sculptures from Friuli churches from the 13th through the 18th centuries. ⊠ *Piazza Patriarcato 1* ☎ *0432/25003* 🖃 *€4 includes Museo Diocesano* ⊙ *Wed.–Sun. 10–noon and 3:30–6:30.*

Udine's large main square, **Piazza Libertà,** features the Palazzo del Comune, a typical 15th-century Venetian palace, built in imitation of the Palazzo Ducale in Venice. Opposite is the Renaissance Porticato di San Giovanni and the Torre dell'Orologio, a clock tower complete with naked *mori* (the Moors who strike the hours) on the top—another reference to Venice and the Torre d'Orologio in Piazza San Marco.

Pass through the **Arco Bollani,** a triumphal arch by Palladio, and climb the steps to the castle hill. From Udine's **Castello,** rebuilt after earthquakes in 1511 and 1976, the stunning panoramic views extend as far as Monte Nero (7,360 ft), in neighboring Slovenia. The castle now holds the city's two main museums: the Civici Musei and the Galleria di Storia ed Arte Antica. In summer, concerts are held in the gardens. ⊠ *Castello di Udine* ☎ *0432/502872* 🖃 *€2.60, free Sun. morning* ⊙ *Tues.–Sat. 9:30–12:30 and 3–6, Sun. 9:30–12:30.* The **Civici Musei** is the best place to trace the history of the area and the importance of Udine and nearby Cividale del Friuli in the formative period following the collapse of the Roman Empire. A large collection of Lombard artifacts includes weapons, jewelry, and domestic wares from this warrior race, which swept into what is now Italy in the 6th century.

The **Galleria di Storia ed Arte Antica** is a wide-ranging collection of local and Italian art including canvases by the prolific Neapolitan Luca Giordano (1632–1705), the Venetians Vittore Carpaccio (circa 1460–1525) and Tiepolo, and a painting of St. Francis receiving the stigmata, attributed to Michelangelo Merisi Caravaggio (circa 1571–1610).

Also within the castle area is the 13th-century church of **Santa Maria di Castello,** which contains frescoes contemporary with the building. It can be opened on request; inquire at the Galleria d'Arte Antica.

West of Piazza Libertà, **Piazza Matteotti,** surrounded on three sides by arcades and on the fourth by the church of San Giacomo, is the central piazza of Udine. The balcony of San Giacomo has an outside altar, which was built so that Mass could be said while business went on uninterrupted in the market below.

Where to Stay & Eat

★ $$$ ✕ **Vitello d'Oro.** Udine's very elegant, landmark restaurant is the one reserved by most local people for special occasions. The big terrace in front is popular for *al fresco* dining in summer. The menu features both meat and fish in classic regional dishes as well as more innovative creations. You might start with an antipasto of *scaloppa di fegato d'oca con mele al marsala* (escalope of goose liver with apples in Marsala wine), followed by roast saddle of wild boar in its cooking juices, served with crushed potatoes. You'll also want to leave room for the rich range of sweets. ⊠ *Via Valvason 4* ☎ *0432/508982* 🖎 *Reservations essential* 🖃 *AE, DC, MC, V* ⊙ *Closed Sun. July–Sept. and Wed. Oct.–June.*

$$ ✕ **Al Marinaio.** An entirely seafood menu is offered in this historic osteria, which, though spruced up, has retained its original character. The mixed seafood antipasto is enormous: a large serving dish is laden with baby octopus, cuttlefish, prawns, shrimp, and other delicacies. Spaghetti *con le vongole* (with clams) is a standard entree, while winter main courses

may include such unusual delights as *orata con funghi porcini* (gilthead bream with porcini mushrooms). ⊠ *Via Cisis 2* ☎ *0432/295949* ⊟ *MC, V* ⊗ *Closed Tues.*

$ ✕ **Al Vecchio Stallo.** Hidden away in a narrow alley, this popular osteria offers a great selection of wine by the glass and a few well-prepared traditional soups and meat dishes, including *zuppa d'orzo* (barley soup) and *cinghiale in umido* (stewed wild boar). Seasonal vegetables, *frittate* (thick omelets), and fish on Friday round out the menu. ⊠ *Via Viola 7* ☎ *0432/21296* ⊟ *No credit cards* ⊗ *Closed Sun.*

¢ ✕ **Ai Provinciali.** Line up with the locals at this popular self-service osteria in the city center. Local cuisine is evident in pasta choices such as gnocchi with cream and speck, and *orecchiette* (small, ear-shaped pasta) with sausage. Main courses include roast chicken leg, boiled meats, and seasonal vegetables. ⊠ *Via Prefettura 3* ☎ *0432/297816* ⊟ *No credit cards* ⊗ *Closed Sun.*

$$$ ⊞ **Astoria Hotel Italia.** The facade of this elegant, arcaded building in the heart of the old city overlooks a big plaza, providing interesting city views from many of the rooms. The spacious public areas and lounges offer contemporary elegance, while the guest rooms are individually furnished in traditional style. ⊠ *Piazza XX Settembre 24, 33100* ☎ *0432/505091* 🖷 *0432/509070* ⤳ *73 rooms, 2 suites* ⌂ *Restaurant, bar, minibars, in-room data ports, meeting rooms, some pets allowed* ⊟ *AE, DC, MC, V* ○| *CP.*

★ $$ ⊞ **Hotel Clocchiatti.** The large, comfortable rooms in this converted late-19th-century city mansion are individually furnished with antiques and fine fabrics. They all differ in size and shape, and many offer something unique: one has a comfortable lounge area with armchairs and sofa, while another has its own large balcony. A terrace provides a peaceful place to relax overlooking the garden with its centuries-old trees. ⊠ *Via Cividale 29, 33100* ☎🖷 *0432/505047* ⊕ *www.hotelclocchiatti.it* ⤳ *13 rooms* ⌂ *Bar, in-room safes, minibars, cable TV, bicycles, laundry service, free parking, some pets allowed* ⊟ *AE, DC, MC, V* ○| *CP.*

$ ⊞ **Quo Vadis.** A 10-minute walk from the train station, this modest, plant-filled hotel has an older part and modern annex with its own small terrace. Rooms are small but comfortable. Choose one facing away from the main road to cut down on traffic noise. Facilities are basic and there's no restaurant, but Udine has a good choice of eating places. ⊠ *Piazzale Cella 28, 33100* ☎ *0432/21091* 🖷 *0432/21092* ⤳ *14 rooms* ⌂ *Bar, free parking* ⊟ *AE, DC* ○| *CP.*

Cividale del Friuli

⑱ *17 km (11 mi) east of Udine, 52 km (29 mi) north of Trieste.*

For space, serenity, and beautiful scenery, venture east of Udine to the foothills of the Julian Alps and the town of Cividale del Friuli, one of the most pleasant and picturesque towns of the region. The Natisone River tumbles down from the Alps to cut a limestone swath through the town, where it is crossed by the Ponte del Diavolo (Devil's Bridge). Legend has it that the devil himself threw into the river the large stone on which the central pier of the bridge rests. The town dates from the time of Julius Caesar, who was commander of Roman legions in the area and who had it named the Forum Julii—from which the Friuli region is named. In AD 568 it became the first Lombard duchy formed in Italy after the demise of the Lombards, it was dominated by Franks, when the name was changed to Civitas Austriae—hence the name Cividale. Until 1238 it was the seat of the patriarchs of Aquileia, becoming a university town in 1353, though it declined from 1420 onward when it fell to Venice with the rest of Friuli and lost much of its influence to Udine. As a result, it has maintained a small, manageable size and is brimming with the impressive relics of various periods, all easily seen in less than a day. The **Duomo**, with its Gothic-Renaissance facade, contains a magnificent 12th-century silver altarpiece, a gift of the patriarch Pellegrino II (in office 1195–1204). It depicts a multitude of saints who surround the archangels Michael and Gabriel, who in turn flank the Virgin Mary. ⊠ *Piazza del Duomo* ☎ *0432/731144* ⊙ *Apr.–Oct., Mon.–Sat. 9:30–noon and 3–7, Sun. 3–7; Nov.–Mar., Mon.–Sat. 9:30–noon and 3–6, Sun. 3–6.*

Two masterpieces of Lombard sculpture are preserved in the **Museo Cristiano,** right next door to the Duomo and accessible from there. First of these is the octagonal baptistery, which incorporates 5th-century columns and capitals. This was named after Callisto, the first patriarch of Aquileia to live in Cividale (between 730 and 756). It was he who commissioned this baptistery, which is beautifully decorated with bas-reliefs, to stand originally beside the cathedral. The second piece is the altar that was carved for Ratchis, the Duke of Cividale and King of the Lombards from 744 to 749. The sides of the altar hold more bas-reliefs, depicting *Christ in Triumph,* the *Visitation,* and the *Adoration of the Magi.* Look, too, for the sculpted rhinoceros elsewhere in the museum. ⊠ *Piazza del Duomo* ☎ *0432/731144* ✉ *Free* ⊙ *Apr.–Oct., Mon.–Sat. 9:30–noon and 3–7, Sun. 3–7; Nov.–Mar., Mon.–Sat. 9:30–noon and 3–6, Sun. 3–6.*

Also in Piazza del Duomo is the **Museo Archeologico,** installed in a building dating from the late 16th century and ascribed to Palladio. It houses an important and well-displayed collection of artifacts, including Roman mosaics and bronzes, Romanesque reliefs, and the Psalter of St. Elizabeth of Hungary. Cividale was a flourishing artistic center during Lombardic times, particularly in the goldsmith's field, to which the many finely crafted and delicate pieces here attest. ⊠ *Piazza del Duomo* ☎ *0432/700700* ✉ *€2* ⊙ *Mon. 9–2; Tues.–Sun. and holidays 8:30–7:30.*

Heading toward the river, you'll soon come to the **Ipogeo Celtico,** reached by a flight of steep steps at the bottom of which are underground chambers thought to be either a Celtic place of burial or a Roman prison. On the walls are crudely carved heads possibly dating from the 3rd century BC. ⊠ *Via Monastero Maggiore 6* ☎ *0432/701211* ✉ *Free* ⊙ *Daily 8 AM–10 PM (get key from adjacent Bar Ipogeo).*

★ Farther down Via Aquileia lies the river and the **Ponte del Diavolo,** the double-arched bridge crossing the Natisone. On the other side, you can browse among the stalls selling basketwork. The pretty, cobbled Via Monastero Maggiore leads along the river to one of the most evocative early medieval buildings in Italy. The **Tempietto Longobardo,** a little gem of Lombard church-building, stands in a perfect and peaceful location above the meandering river. Though damaged by earthquakes, there remains a remarkable 8th-century stucco procession of female figures on either side of an arch, and lovely friezes with a vine motif. The carved and canopied wooden stalls date from the 14th century, as do the frescoes. The epiphany scene is unique in that instead of the usual three kings it depicts two kings and a queen, the last in the procession, possibly in recognition of Giseltrude, a Lombard queen at the time of the chapel's construction. ⊠ *Via Monastero Maggiore* ☎ *0432/700867* ✉ *€2* ⊙ *Apr.–Sept., Mon.–Sat. 9:30–12:30 and 3–6:30, Sun. 9:30–1 and 3–7:30; Oct.–Mar., Mon.–Sat. 9:30–12:30 and 3–5, Sun. 9:30–12:30 and 2:30–6.*

need a break? The **Caffè Longobardo** (⊠ Via Carlo Alberto 6 ⊙ closed Mon.) is a pleasant place to sit and sample a grappa or a slice of traditional *gubana,* a light, spongy cake filled with pine nuts and raisins, as you watch the passersby on the piazza.

Where to Stay & Eat

$–$$ ✕ **Al Monastero.** You can dine under the wooden roof or in an arcade whose walls were frescoed in the 1930s by an itinerant painter. There's an open fireplace, and if you happen to be here in January you might catch a medieval-style banquet. If not, don't fret: today's dishes, such as *calciones del Monastero* (gnocchi filled with spinach, pine nuts, ricotta, and raisins with a Montasio cheese sauce sprinkled with smoked ricotta) or a grilled venison steak will still go down very nicely. The restaurant serves wine from its own vineyards. ✉ *Via Ristori 11* ☎ *0432/700808* ⊕ *www.almonastero.com* ⌖ *Reservations essential* ⊟ *AE, DC, MC, V* ⊘ *Closed Mon. No dinner Sun.*

★ **¢–$** ✕ **Trattoria Dominissini.** The rustic wood furnishings and simple decor here are perfectly in keeping with Cividale's Old-World charm. The menu features typical dishes of game and cheese. If you've got a soft spot for melted cheese, try the wonderful *frico di patate*, a mixture of potato and local Montasio cheese cooked in the pan like an omelette; game dishes may include *cinghiale in umido con polenta* (stewed wild boar with polenta). There's a healthy selection of vegetables along with mixed salads, tempting desserts, and excellent Friuli wines. ✉ *Via Jacopo Stellini 18* ☎ *0432/733763* ⊟ *AE, DC, MC, V* ⊘ *Closed Mon. No dinner Sun.*

$–$$ ✕▥ **Locanda Al Castello.** Set on a peaceful hillside a few minutes drive out of town, this creeper-covered, crenellated hotel was once a monastery. Rooms are spacious and furnished in different styles, some antique, some modern, and with nice, big bathrooms. The redbrick restaurant ($–$$; closed Wed.), popular for Sunday lunch, has a Friulian open fireplace and serves national as well as local dishes, both fish and meat. Specialties include *polentina ripiena* (small rounds of polenta filled with porcini mushrooms in garlic, oil, and parsley, cooked au gratin in the oven), and *maltagliata alla lungobarda* (thinly sliced beef marinated in herbs and spices and char-grilled). ✉ *Via del Castello 12, 33043* ☎ *0432/733242* ☐ *0432/700901* ⊕ *www.alcastello.net* ⇆ *17 rooms* ⌖ *Restaurant, bar, fans, in-room data ports, in-room safes, minibars, cable TV, tennis court, meeting rooms, free parking, some pets allowed; no a/c* ⊟ *AE, DC, MC, V* ⊘ *Closed Jan. 15–31* ⊗ *CP.*

★ **$** ▥ **Al Pomo d'Oro.** Pink seems to be a predominant color for little hotels in Italy and this one is no exception, presenting a charming facade with its shutters and geraniums. It was an inn in the 12th century but has since undergone considerable renovation; rooms are furnished in a plain, modern style, some with wonderful views of the surrounding mountains. The location is excellent, a few steps away from the cathedral, and the elegant restaurant may well keep you in for the evening. ✉ *Piazza San Giovanni 20, 33043* ☎ *0432/731489* ☐ *0432/701257* ⊕ *www. alpomodoro.com* ⇆ *17 rooms* ⌖ *Restaurant, bar, in-room safes, minibars, cable TV, some pets allowed; no a/c* ⊟ *AE, DC, MC, V* ⊗ *CP.*

Shopping

A **general market** is held every Saturday morning in Piazza Garibaldi; by the bridge you'll find good stalls selling wicker baskets of every description.

Forni di Sopra

⑲ *100 km (62 mi) northwest of Cividale, 153 km (95 mi) northwest of Trieste.*

Forni di Sopra sits on the edge of the Parco Regionale delle Dolomiti Friulane and at the foot of the Passo di Mauria, the mountain pass connecting Carnia with the eastern Dolomites. In summer, the area is a walker's nirvana, although you'll find plenty of space to yourself, as the area is not on any major tourist routes. The lush meadows are filled with flowers, and there are trails for mountain biking and horseback riding. The **tourist office** (☎ 0433/886767) can furnish you with information on these activities as well as hikes. Excellent food can be found in small trattorias, many with an open fireplace, that make good use of wild plants and herbs in their cooking. Winter, of course, brings streams of skiers to the district, and there are places to rent equipment if you want to join them.

Where to Stay & Eat

$ ✕ **Osteria di Nonta.** Relax at this lovely, hospitable old restaurant in the village of Nonta di Socchieve, 26 km (16 mi) east of Forni di Sopra and 15 km (9 mi) west of Tolmezzo. It has long, polished wooden tables; an open fireplace with a cauldron; a frilly curtain; a wind-up telephone (that almost works); and lace lamp shades. The obliging lady of the house devises a different menu each day of extremely traditional food; taste the local specialty, *cjalsòns* (ravioli) if you haven't already, with various seasonings, such as ricotta, sultanas, and nutmeg. ⊠ *Nonta di Socchieve* ☎ *0433/80596* ⌂ *Reservations essential* ▭ *No credit cards* ♥ *Closed Mon.*

$ 🏨 **Davost.** This hearty, no-nonsense hotel is next to good sporting facilities, including an ice rink and tennis courts. The terrace has fine views of the mountains. In the basement there's a large pizzeria with a wood-burning oven and a reasonably priced tourist menu. Try the local specialty *frico* (cheese) with gnocchi, onion, speck, and mushrooms. ⊠ *Via Tagliamento 12, 33024* ☎ *0433/88103* 🖷 *0433/88550* ⇥ *34 rooms, 2 suites* ⌂ *Restaurant, bar* ▭ *MC, V* ♥ *Closed Mar.–May and Oct.–Dec. 15 Restaurant closed Mon.* ⦿⃝ *CP.*

$ 🏨 **I Larici.** This is a long, low hotel with clean, elegant lines and good facilities. It's a favorite hostelry for skiers (the bus to the ski lift is included in the price) and hikers, offering a range of evening entertainment and generous meals in its restaurant for those choosing the full-board option. ⊠ *Via Chianeit 5, 33024* ☎ *0433/886701* 🖷 *0433/886710* ⇥ *68 rooms, 3 suites* ⌂ *Restaurant, bar, minibars, cable TV, gym, sauna, dance club* ▭ *MC, V* ♥ *Closed Sept. 13–Dec. 20 and mid-Mar.–mid-June* ⦿⃝ *FAP.*

¢ 🏨 **Nuoitas.** In a quiet location 4 km (2½ mi) north of Forni di Sopra, circled by evergreens, this is a traditional chalet hotel with wooden furniture in an Alpine style. The bathrooms are attractive, and rooms have good views from their wooden balconies. It represents very good value for the money. The restaurant serves typical local fare and is closed Tuesday. ⊠ *Località Nuoitas Nord-Ovest, 33024* ☎ *0433/88387* 🖷 *0433/886956* ⇥ *18 rooms* ⌂ *Restaurant, bar* ▭ *AE, DC, MC, V* ⦿⃝ *CP.*

FRIULI-VENEZIA GIULIA A TO Z

To *research prices, get advice from other travelers, and book travel arrangements, visit www.fodors.com.*

AIRPORTS & TRANSFERS

There are domestic flights to Aeroporto Ronchi dei Legionari, 35 km (22 mi) northwest of Trieste, linked by regular SAF bus service to Via Flavio Gioia, near Trieste's train station. There is also a SAF connection to Udine and Gorizia from the airport.

🔲 Airport Information **Aeroporto Ronchi dei Legionari** ⊠ Redipuglia ☎ 0481/773224 ⊕ www.aeroporto.fvg.it. **SAF** ☎ 800/915303 (toll-free).

BOAT & FERRY TRAVEL

Boats from Greece, Albania, Slovenia, and Croatia dock in Trieste. Contact Adriatica di Navigazione through the agent Agemar.

🚢 Boat & Ferry Information **Adriatica di Navigazione** ✉ Piazza Duca degli Abruzzi 1/a ☎ 040/363737 📠 040/638172.

BUS TRAVEL

Interurban and interregional bus connections serve the Veneto and Friuli-Venezia Giulia. Regular buses run from Piazzale Roma in Venice to Trieste, and there are frequent connections from Padua and Treviso. Local tourist offices may be able to provide details of timetables and routes; otherwise contact the local bus station.

The bus station in Trieste is at Piazza della Libertà; ACT operates services in and around Trieste. SAF operates services within the province and to Slovenia and Croatia. Gradese buses travel between Trieste, Aquileia, Cividale, and Udine.

🚌 Bus Information **ACT** ☎ 800/016675 toll-free. **Gradese** ☎ 0432/503004. **SAF** ☎ 800/915303 toll-free. **Trieste Bus Station** ✉ Piazza della Libertà 11 ☎ 040/42520.

CAR RENTAL

🚗 Local Agencies **Avis** ✉ Molo Bersaglieri 3, Stazione Marittima, Trieste ☎ 040/300820 ✉ Aeroporto Ronchi dei Legionari, Trieste ☎ 0481/777085 ✉ Viale Leopardi 5/a, Udine ☎ 0432/501149. **Hertz** ✉ Molo Bersaglieri 3, Stazione Marittima, Trieste ☎ 040/3220098 ✉ Aeroporto Ronchi dei Legionari, Trieste ☎ 0481/777025 ✉ Via Crispi 17, Udine ☎ 0432/511211.

CAR TRAVEL

The good A4 autostrada runs eastward past or through Verona, Vicenza, and Venice to Trieste, off of which the A23 highway branches north to Udine; both are toll routes. The A27 links the A4 with Treviso and continues northward until it ends north of Belluno, from where you can pick up the SS51, then turn eastward on the SS52 to reach Carnia.

From Trieste the SS14 runs northwest along the coast to Monfalcone (and on to Venice), and the A4 takes the more inland route. The A23 runs from Palmanova to Udine and on to the Austrian border. The SS52 runs east from this through Tolmezzo to Carnia and Forni di Sopra. Aquileia is easily reached via the SS14, from where the straight SS352 traverses the causeway to Grado. Gorizia is accessed from Monfalcone, and Cividale from Udine along the SS54.

EMERGENCIES

All pharmacies post signs on the door with addresses of *farmacie di turno* (pharmacies taking shifts), which stay open at night, on Saturday afternoon, and on Sunday.

🚑 Emergency Services **Police** ☎ 112 or 113. **Ambulance** ☎ 118.

🏥 Hospitals **Ospedale Civile** ✉ Via Chiusaforte 41, Udine ☎ 0432/480062. **Ospedale Maggiore** ✉ Via Stuparich 1, Trieste ☎ 040/3991111.

TOURS

Guided tours to all the principle sights can be arranged through the tourist office or the Trieste association of authorized tour guides.

🎫 Fees & Schedules **A.G.A.T.A. tour guides** ☎ 333/5034942.

TRAIN TRAVEL

There are 14 daily trains between Venice and Trieste and hourly service between Treviso and Udine. Trieste also connects easily with Budapest, Ljubljana, and Vienna. All towns within this region are connected by train with the exception of Grado and Aquileia and Forni di Sopra, which are reachable by bus. Contact Trenitalia for train information.

FARES &
SCHEDULES 🚆 Train Information **Trenitalia** ☎ 892021. **Stazione Gorizia** ✉ Piazzale Martiri Libertà d'Italia. **Stazione Trieste Centrale** ✉ Piazza della Libertà 8. **Stazione Udine** ✉ Piazzale d'Annunzio.

TRAVEL AGENCIES
🚆 Local Agents **Gotour** ✉ Via Nazario Sauro 12, Gorizia ☎ 0481/531213. **No Stop Viaggi** ✉ Viale San Marco 38/a, Monfalcone ☎ 0481/791096. **Paterniti Viaggi/American Express** ✉ Corso Cavour 7, Trieste ☎ 040/366161. **Ribi** ✉ Viale Europa Unita 5, Grado ☎ 0431/80166. **Viaggi Uno** ✉ Viale Europa Unita 36, Udine ☎ 0432/25123.

VISITOR INFORMATION
🚆 Tourist Information **Aquileia** ✉ Piazza Capitolo, 33043 ☎ 0431/919491 **Cividale del Friuli** ✉ Corso Paolino d'Aquileia 10, 33051 ☎ 0432/731461 🖷 0432/731398 **Forni di Sopra** ✉ Via Cadore 1, 33024 ☎ 0433/886767 🖷 0433/886686 **Gorizia** ✉ Via Roma, 34170 ☎ 0481/386225 🖷 0481/386277 **Grado** ✉ Viale Dante 72, 34073 ☎ 0431/8991 🖷 0431/899278 **Trieste** ✉ Via San Nicolò 20, 34121 ☎ 040/67961 🖷 040/6796299 **Udine** ✉ Piazza I Maggio 7, 33100 ☎ 0432/295972 🖷 0432/504743.

UNDERSTANDING VENICE & THE VENETIAN ARC

VENETIAN ART: RENAISSANCE & ROCOCO

The Renaissance, that most vaunted period for the arts, did not evolve simply from a set of newfound artistic skills; the movement represented a revolution in attitudes whereby each individual was thought to play a specific role in the divine scheme of things. By fulfilling this role, it was believed the individual gained a new dignity. It was no coincidence that this revolution took place in Florence, which in the 15th century was an influential, wealthy, highly evolved city-state. Artists there had the leisure, prestige, and self-confidence to develop their talent and produce works that would reflect this new dignity and strength as well as their own prowess.

The new skills and realistic effects of Florentine painting rapidly found a sympathetic response among Venetian painters. Gentile Bellini and Antonio Carpaccio, just two of the many whose work fills the Accademia, took to covering their canvases with crowd scenes, buildings, canals, processions, dogs, ships, parrots, and chimneys. These were generally narrative paintings, telling the story of a saint's life or simply depicting everyday scenes.

It was the emphasis on color, though, that made Venetian art Venetian, and it was the late-15th-century masters of color, preeminently Giovanni Bellini and Giorgione, who began to use it no longer as decoration but as a means to create a particular atmosphere. How different the effect of Giorgione's *Tempest* (in the Accademia) would be with a sunny blue sky instead of the ominous grays and dark greens that fill the background! For the first time, the atmosphere, not the figures, became the central focus of painting.

Among the next generation of Venetian art, Titian's painting was a more virtuoso version of Bellini's and Giorgione's poetic style, but Titian later shifted the emphasis back to figures, rather than atmosphere, as the central focus of his paintings. Titian's younger contemporaries in Venice—Veronese, Tintoretto, and Bassano—wanted to make names for themselves. They started working on huge canvases—which gave them more freedom of movement—playing all sorts of visual games:

juggling with viewpoints and perspective and using dazzlingly bright colors. This visual trickery suggests a natural parallel with the self-conscious artifice of Florentine painting of the same period, but the exuberance of these Venetian painters, and the increasingly emotional quality of their work, remained significantly more vital than the arid and ever more sterile works of central Italy toward the end of the 16th century.

In the 18th century, Venice came back into its own. Venetian artists adopted the soft, overripe version of baroque—known as rococo—that had originated in France. Free from the spiritual ideals that motivated the baroque style, rococo celebrated sensuousness (and sensuality) for its own sake. Although Venice was nearing the last stages of its political decline, there was still immense wealth in the city, mostly in the hands of families who wished to make the world know about it—and what better way than through vast, dazzling rococo canvases, reassuringly stylized and removed from reality? The revival began with Sebastiano Ricci and was expertly elaborated on by Tiepolo. But it could never have taken place had there not been a return to the city's great artistic traditions. Late-16th-century color technique and expertise were drawn on and fused with what had been learned from the baroque to create the breathtaking, magical, decadent world of the Venetian rococo.

This was the final flowering of Venetian painting. The death of Francesco Guardi in 1793, compounded by the fall of the Republic of Venice in 1797, marked the effective end of the city's artistic life. Neoclassicism found no champion here, except for the sculptor Canova, who, in any case, did his finest work after he left Venice.

ARTISTICALLY SPEAKING: A GLOSSARY

The eloquence of the world's greatest masterpieces can be deafening, and Italy's treasures—their message made manifest in marble, pigment, and precious metals—instill a spirit of awe. You can enhance your enjoyment of this bounty by learning some of the terms of art-speak. Here is a limited glossary.

Acanthus: Sculptural ornamentation from antiquity; it's based on the foliage of the acanthus plant.

Apse: A semicircular terminus found behind the altar in a church.

Atrium: The courtyard in front of the entrance to an ancient Roman villa or an early church.

Badia: Abbey.

Baldacchino: A canopy—often made of stone—above a church altar, supported by columns.

Baptistery: A separate structure or area in a church where rites of baptism are held.

Baroque: A 17th-century European art movement in which dramatic, elaborate ornamentation was used to stir viewers' emotions. The most famous Italian baroque artists were Carracci and Bernini.

Basilica: A rectangular Roman public building divided into aisles by rows of columns. Many early churches were built on the basilican plan, but the term is also applied to some churches without specific reference to architecture.

Belvedere: Usually a lookout point for vistas; the word means "beautiful view."

Campanile: A bell tower of a church.

Capital: The crowning section of a column, usually decorated with Doric, Ionic, or Corinthian ornament.

Chiaroscuro: Literally "light/dark;" used to describe the distribution of light and shade in a painting, either with a marked contrast or a muted tonal gradation.

Cinquecento: Literally, "five hundred," used in Italian to refer to the 16th century.

Contrapposto: A dramatic pose of a sculpted figure in which the upper portion of the body is placed in opposition to the lower portion.

Cortile: Courtyard.

Cupola: Dome.

Duomo: Cathedral.

Fresco: A wall-painting technique, used in Roman times and again in the early Renaissance, in which pigment was applied to wet plaster.

Gothic: Medieval architectural and ornamental style featuring pointed arches, high interior vaulting, and flying buttresses to emphasize height and, symbolically, an ascension to heaven.

Grotesques: Decorations of fanciful human and animal forms, embellished with flowers; first used in Nero's Golden House and rediscovered during the Renaissance.

Loggia: Roofed balcony or gallery.

Maestà: The Virgin and Child enthroned in majesty often surrounded by angels, saints, or prophets.

Mannerism: Style of the mid-16th century, in which artists—such as Pontormo and Rosso Fiorentino—sought to replace the warm, humanizing ideals of Leonardo and Raphael with super-elegant, emotionally cold forms. Portraits in the Mannerist style feature lively colors and often strangely contorted bodies.

Nave: The central aisle of a church.

Palazzo: A palace, or more generally, any large building.

Perspective: The illusion of three-dimensional space that was obtained in the early 15th century with the discovery that all parallel lines running in one direction meet at a single point on the horizon known as the vanishing point.

Piano nobile: The main floor of a palace (the first floor above ground level).

Pietà: Literally "piety"; refers to an image of the Virgin Mary holding the crucified body of Christ on her lap.

Polyptych: A painting—often an altarpiece—on multiple wooden panels that are joined.

Predella: A series of small paintings found below the main section of an altarpiece.

Putti: Cherubs, cupids, or other images of infant boys in painting.

Quattrocento: Literally "four hundred"; refers to the 15th century.

Renaissance: Major school of Italian art, literature, and philosophy (14th century–16th century) that fused innovations in realism with the rediscovery of the great heritage of classical antiquity. After Giotto introduced a new naturalism into painting in the early 14th century, Florentine artists of the early and mid-15th century, such as Masaccio and Fra Filippo Lippi, paved the way for the later 15th-century realism of Botticelli and Ghirlandaio. The movement particularly flourished in Florence and Venice, but most other Italian cities were participants as well. Some scholars believe that the movement culminated in Rome with the High Renaissance (circa 1490–1520) and the masterpieces of Leonardo, Raphael, and Michelangelo.

Rococo: Light, dainty 18th-century art and architectural style created in reaction to heavy baroque. Tiepolo is the leading painter of the rococo style.

Romanesque: Architectural style of the 11th and 12th centuries that reworked ancient Roman forms, particularly barrel and groin vaults. Stark, severe, and magisterial, Romanesque basilicas are among Italy's most awe-inspiring churches.

Sacra conversazione: A "holy conversation" wherein saints act as intercessor to the Madonna and Child.

Tondo: Circular painting or sculpture.

Triptych: A three-panel painting executed on wood.

Trompe l'oeil: An artistic technique employed to "fool the eye" into believing that the object or scene depicted is actually real.

Veduta: A painting of a city or landscape as viewed from afar, popular in the 18th century.

BOOKS & MOVIES

Books

Italian history, art, and culture have been examined in countless English-language books. Their profusion is a testament both to the wonders of Italy and to the challenge of defining what exactly "Italian" is. *The Italians,* by Luigi Barzini, dates from 1964 but remains a valuable effort toward this end; its lively analysis of the national character is both enlightening and frustrating in ways that make reading it a genuinely Italian experience.

Before, during, and after a visit to Venice and the Venetian Arc, it's a pleasure to compare notes with your fellow travelers. Classics in the travel-essay genre, often mixing firsthand experience and selected history, include James and Jan Morris's *World of Venice,* Mary McCarthy's *Venice Observed,* and James Lees-Milne's *Venetian Mornings.*

Some English-speaking visitors have chosen to settle in Italy long-term, and the resulting expatriate memoirs make up their own literary subgenre. Notable among the contributions from the Venetian Arc is Tim Parks's *Italian Neighbors,* which tells with candor and good humor of his life in Verona. To get a native's perspective on contemporary Venice, read *Venice Revealed* by the charmingly cranky Paolo Barbaro.

For a general historical and art history framework, Harry Hearder's *Italy, A Short History* cuts right to the chase, with 2,000 years covered in less than 300 pages. Michael Levey's clear and concise treatments of the Renaissance, *Early Renaissance* and *High Renaissance,* are good introductions to the most vaunted of artistic periods. Two wonderfully written and beautifully illustrated volumes on the subject are John T. Paoletti and Gary M. Radke's *Art in Renaissance Italy* and Evelyn Welch's eloquent *Art and Society in Italy 1350–1500. The Civilization of the Renaissance in Italy,* by 19th-century Swiss historian Jacob Burckhardt, is the classic study of the culture and politics of the time. John Ruskin's *The Stones of Venice,* which examines Venetian architecture with unparalleled grace, is another 19th-century masterwork.

John Julius Norwich's exhaustive *A History of Venice* stands at the forefront of English-language accounts of the city's past. In *Venice: Lion City,* Garry Wills illuminates the Venetian Republic at the height of its powers in the 15th and 16th centuries. To some observers, the most beautiful book about the most beautiful city in the world is Richard de Combray's *Venice, Frail Barrier.*

Lovers of detective stories will likely enjoy the antics of Aurelio Zen, Michael Dibdin's bumbling detective. It's best to read them in order, as he builds on characters and situations; each novel is set in an Italian city. The series commences in Perugia with *Ratking* and finds its way to Venice in *Dead Lagoon.* If you like your fiction with a more literary bent, try *Zeno's Conscience* by Trieste native Italo Svevo; the bittersweet tale of a thoroughly common man was hailed by no less than James Joyce as a breakthough in modern psychological literature.

If you truly want to understand the Italian psyche, learn about the national passion for *calcio* (soccer). Tim Parks made a soccer odyssey with the Verona club and recorded his experiences in *A Season with Verona.*

Movies

Venice is the setting for numerous English-language movies. Few are cinematic gems, but the beautiful location can do a lot to compensate for other shortcomings. *Dangerous Beauty* (1998) may unintentionally venture into high camp, but it will give you an idea of what the life of a talented Venetian courtesan was like in the 16th century. *The Talented Mr. Ripley* (1999), set in sumptuous Italy of the 1950s, ends with a visit to Venice. *The Italian Job* (2003) is a heist film that starts with a hair-raising boat chase through the canals of Venice and a confrontation in the Dolomites. In the thriller *Don't Look

Now (1973), the dead daughter of Donald Sutherland and Julie Christie haunts Venice's streets. Some viewers cringe at and others delight in *Everyone Says I Love You*, Woody Allen's venture into the musical genre. Lucino Visconti's adaptation of the Thomas Mann novella *Death in Venice* (1971) also evokes strong feelings pro and con; don't watch it expecting an action movie. Among recent efforts from Italian cinema, *Pane e tulipani (Bread and Tulips,* 2001) is a charming romance.

CHRONOLOGY

753 BC	Traditional date for the founding of Rome.
133	Rome rules entire Mediterranean Basin except Egypt.
165 AD	A smallpox epidemic ravages the Empire.
238	The first wave of Germanic invasions penetrates Italy.
293	Diocletian reorganizes the Empire into West and East.
330	Constantine founds a new Imperial capital (Constantinople) in the East.
410	Rome is sacked by Visigoths.
476	The last Roman emperor, Romulus Augustus, is deposed. The Empire of Rome falls.
552	Eastern emperor Justinian (527–565) recovers control of Italy.
570	Lombards gain control of much of Italy, including Rome.
774	Frankish ruler Charlemagne (742–814) invades Italy under papal authority and is crowned Holy Roman Emperor by Pope Leo III (800).
ca. 800–900	The breakup of Charlemagne's (Carolingian) realm leads to the rise of Italian city-states.
811	Venice is founded by mainlanders escaping Barbarian invasions.
1054	The Schism develops between Greek (Orthodox) and Latin churches.
1077	Pope Gregory VII leads the Holy See into conflict with the Germanic Holy Roman Empire.
1152–90	Frederick I (Barbarossa) is crowned Holy Roman Emperor (1155); punitive expeditions by his forces (Ghibellines) are countered by the Guelphs, supporters of the powerful Papal States in central Italy. Guelph–Ghibelline conflict becomes a feature of medieval life.
1204	Crusaders, led by Venetian doge Dandolo, capture Constantinople.
1257	The first of four wars is declared between Genoa and Venice; at stake is the maritime control of the eastern Mediterranean.
1264	Charles I of Anjou invades Italy, intervening in the continuing Guelph–Ghibelline conflict.
1275	Marco Polo (1254–1324) reaches the Orient.
1355	Venetian doge Marino Falier is executed for treason.
1380	Venice finally disposes of the Genovese threat in the Battle of Chioggia.
1402	The last German intervention into Italy is repulsed by the Lombards.
1546	Andrea Palladio (1508–80), architectural genius, wins his first commission in Vicenza.
1571	The combined navies of Venice, Spain, and the Papacy defeat the Turks in the Battle of Lepanto.
ca. 1700	Opera develops as an art form in Italy.
1720–90	The Great Age of the Grand Tour: northern Europeans visit Italy and start the vogue for classical studies. Among the famous visitors are

Edward Gibbon (1758), Jacques-Louis David (1775), and Johann Wolfgang von Goethe (1786).

1796 Napoléon begins his Italian campaigns, annexing Rome and imprisoning Pope Pius VI four years later.

1815 Austria controls much of Italy after Napoléon's downfall.

1848 Revolutionary troops under Risorgimento (Unification) leaders Giuseppe Mazzini (1805–72) and Giuseppe Garibaldi (1807–82) establish a republic in Rome.

1849 French troops crush rebellion and restore Pope Pius IX.

1860 Garibaldi and his "Thousand" defeat the Bourbon rulers in Sicily and Naples.

1870 Rome is finally captured by Risorgimento troops and is declared capital of Italy by King Vittorio Emanuele II.

1900 King Umberto I is assassinated by an anarchist; he is succeeded by King Vittorio Emanuele III.

1915 Italy enters World War I on the side of the Allies.

1922 Fascist "black shirts" under Benito Mussolini (1883–1945) march on Rome; Mussolini becomes prime minister and later "Il Duce" (literally "leader") of Italy.

1940–44 In World War II, Italy fights on the side of the Axis powers until its capitulation (1943), when Mussolini flees Rome. Italian partisans and Allied troops from the landings at Anzio (January 1944) win victory at Cassino (March 1944) and force the eventual withdrawal of German troops from Italy.

1957 The Treaty of Rome is signed, and Italy becomes a founding member of the European Economic Community.

1968–79 The growth of left-wing activities leads to the formation of the Red Brigades and provokes right-wing reactions. Bombings and kidnappings culminate in the abduction and murder of Prime Minister Aldo Moro (1916–78).

1992 The Christian Democrat Party, in power throughout the postwar period, loses its hold on a relative majority in Parliament.

1993 Italians vote for sweeping reforms after the Tangentopoli (Bribe City) scandal exposes widespread political corruption, including politicians' collusion with organized crime.

1994 A center-right coalition wins in spring elections, and media magnate Silvio Berlusconi becomes premier—only to be deposed within a year. Italian politics seem to be evolving into the equivalent of a two-party system.

1995 Newly appointed Lamberto Dini takes hold of the government's rudder and, as president of the Council of Ministers, institutes major reforms and replaces old-line politicians.

1996 A league of center-left parties wins national elections and puts together a government coalition that sees the Democratic Party of the Left (PDS), the former Communist party, into power for the first time ever in Italy.

1997 Political stability and an austerity program put Italy on track toward the European Monetary Union and adoption of the single euro currency.

1998 Romano Prodi's center-left government, widely praised for its economic policies and lack of scandals, is brought down by a no-confidence vote in October, after the Reformed-Communist Party (PCI) withdraws its support for Prodi. The center-left regroups and forms a new government under Massimo D'Alema, leader of the former Communist Party, who in large part continues Prodi's policies.

2001 Media mogul Silvio Berlusconi is elected prime minister for the second time.

2002 The lira is supplanted by the euro as the currency of the land.

ITALIAN VOCABULARY

English	Italian	Pronunciation
Basics		
Yes/no	Sí/No	see/no
Please	Per favore	pear fa-**vo**-ray
Yes, please	Sí grazie	see **grah**-tsee-ay
Thank you	Grazie	**grah**-tsee-ay
You're welcome	Prego	**pray**-go
Excuse me, sorry	Scusi	**skoo**-zee
Sorry!	Mi dispiace!	mee dis-spee-**ah**-chay
Good morning/ afternoon	Buongiorno	bwohn-**jor**-no
Good evening	Buona sera	**bwoh**-na **say**-ra
Good bye	Arrivederci	a-ree-vah-**dare**-chee
Mr. (Sir)	Signore	see-**nyo**-ray
Mrs. (Ma'am)	Signora	see-**nyo**-ra
Miss	Signorina	see-nyo-**ree**-na
Pleased to meet you	Piacere	pee-ah-**chair**-ray
How are you?	Come sta?	**ko**-may **stah**
Very well, thanks	Bene, grazie	**ben**-ay **grah**-tsee-ay
And you?	E lei?	ay **lay**-ee
Hello (phone)	Pronto?	**proan**-to
Numbers		
one	uno	**oo**-no
two	due	**doo**-ay
three	tre	tray
four	quattro	**kwah**-tro
five	cinque	**cheen**-kway
six	sei	say
seven	sette	**set**-ay
eight	otto	**oh**-to
nine	nove	**no**-vay
ten	dieci	dee-**eh**-chee
eleven	undici	**oon**-dee-chee
twelve	dodici	**doe**-dee-chee
thirteen	tredici	**tray**-dee-chee
fourteen	quattordici	kwa-**tore**-dee-chee
fifteen	quindici	**kwin**-dee-chee
sixteen	sedici	**say**-dee-chee

seventeen	diciassette	dee-cha-**set**-ay
eighteen	diciotto	dee-**cho**-to
nineteen	diciannove	dee-cha-**no**-vay
twenty	venti	**vain**-tee
twenty-one	ventuno	vain-**too**-no
twenty-two	ventidue	vain-tee-**doo**-ay
thirty	trenta	**train**-ta
forty	quaranta	kwa-**rahn**-ta
fifty	cinquanta	cheen-**kwahn**-ta
sixty	sessanta	seh-**sahn**-ta
seventy	settanta	seh-**tahn**-ta
eighty	ottanta	o-**tahn**-ta
ninety	novanta	no-**vahn**-ta
one hundred	cento	**chen**-to
one thousand	mille	**mee**-lay
ten thousand	diecimila	dee-eh-chee-**mee**-la

Useful Phrases

Do you speak English?	Parla inglese?	**par**-la een-**glay**-zay
I don't speak Italian	Non parlo italiano	non **par**-lo ee-tal-**yah**-no
I don't understand	Non capisco	non ka-**peess**-ko
Can you please repeat?	Può ripetere?	pwo ree-**pet**-ay-ray
Slowly!	Lentamente!	**len**-ta-men-tay
I don't know	Non lo so	non lo **so**
I'm American/ British	Sono americano(a) Sono inglese	**so**-no a-may-ree-**kah**-no(a) **so**-no een-**glay**-zay
What's your name?	Come si chiama?	**ko**-may see kee-**ah**-ma
My name is . . .	Mi chiamo . . .	mee kee-**ah**-mo
What time is it?	Che ore sono?	kay **o**-ray **so**-no
How?	Come?	**ko**-may
When?	Quando?	**kwan**-doe
Yesterday/today/ tomorrow	Ieri/oggi/domani	**yer**-ee/**o**-jee/ do-**mah**-nee
This morning/ ternoon	Stamattina/Oggi pomeriggio	sta-ma-**tee**-na/**o**-jee af-po-mer-**ee**-jo
Tonight	Stasera	sta-**ser**-a
What?	Che cosa?	kay **ko**-za
What is it?	Che cos'è?	kay ko-**zay**
Why?	Perché?	pear-**kay**
Who?	Chi?	kee
Where is . . . the bus stop?	Dov'è . . . la fermata dell'autobus?	doe-**veh** la fer-**mah**-ta del ow-toe-**booss**

the train station?	la stazione?	la sta-tsee-**oh**-nay
the subway station?	la metropolitana?	la may-tro-po-lee-**tah**-na
the terminal?	il terminale?	eel ter-mee-**nah**-lay
the post office?	l'ufficio postale?	loo-**fee**-cho po-**stah**-lay
the bank?	la banca?	la **bahn**-ka
the . . . hotel?	l'hotel . . .?	lo-**tel**
the store?	il negozio?	eel nay-**go**-tsee-o
the cashier?	la cassa?	la **kah**-sa
the . . . museum?	il museo . . .?	eel moo-**zay**-o
the hospital?	l'ospedale?	lo-spay-**dah**-lay
the first aid station?	il pronto soccorso?	eel **pron**-to so-**kor**-so
the elevator?	l'ascensore?	la-shen-**so**-ray
a telephone?	un telefono?	oon tay-**lay**-fo-no
Where are the restrooms?	Dov'è il bagno?	do-**vay** eel **bahn**-yo
Here/there	Qui/là	kwee/la
Left/right	A sinistra/a destra	a see-**neess**-tra/a **des**-tra
Straight ahead	Avanti dritto	a-**vahn**-tee **dree**-to
Is it near/far?	È vicino/lontano?	ay vee-**chee**-no/lon-**tah**-no
I'd like . . .	Vorrei . . .	vo-**ray**
a room	una camera	**oo**-na **kah**-may-ra
the key	la chiave	la kee-**ah**-vay
a newspaper	un giornale	oon jor-**nah**-lay
a stamp	un francobollo	oon frahn-ko-**bo**-lo
I'd like to buy . . .	Vorrei comprare . . .	vo-**ray** kom-**prah**-ray
a cigar	un sigaro	oon see-**gah**-ro
cigarettes	delle sigarette	**day**-lay see-ga-**ret**-ay
some matches	dei fiammiferi	**day**-ee **fee**-ah-**mee**-fer-ee
some soap	una saponetta	**oo**-na sa-po-**net**-a
a city plan	una pianta della città	**oo**-na **pyahn**-ta **day**-la chee-**tah**
a road map of . . .	una carta stradale di . . .	**oo**-na **cart**-a stra-**dah**-lay dee
a country map	una carta geografica	**oo**-na **cart**-a jay-o-**grah**-fee-ka
a magazine	una rivista	**oo**-na ree-**veess**-ta
envelopes	delle buste	**day**-lay **booss**-tay
writing paper	della carta da lettere	**day**-la **cart**-a da **let**-air-ay
a postcard	una cartolina	**oo**-na car-toe-**lee**-na
a guidebook	una guida turistica	**oo**-na **gwee**-da too-**reess**-tee-ka
How much is it?	Quanto costa?	**kwahn**-toe **coast**-a
It's expensive/cheap	È caro/economico	ay **car**-o/ay-ko-no-mee-ko
A little/a lot	Poco/tanto	**po**-ko/**tahn**-to
More/less	Più/meno	pee-**oo**/**may**-no

Enough/too (much)	Abbastanza/troppo	a-bas-**tahn**-sa/**tro**-po
I am sick	Sto male	sto **mah**-lay
Call a doctor	Chiama un dottore	kee-**ah**-mah oon doe-**toe**-ray
Help!	Aiuto!	a-**yoo**-toe
Stop!	Alt!	ahlt
Fire!	Al fuoco!	ahl **fwo**-ko
Caution/Look out!	Attenzione!	a-ten-**syon**-ay

Dining Out

A bottle of . . .	Una bottiglia di . . .	**oo**-na bo-**tee**-lee-ah dee
A cup of . . .	Una tazza di . . .	**oo**-na **tah**-tsa dee
A glass of . . .	Un bicchiere di . . .	oon bee-key-**air**-ay dee
Bill/check	Il conto	eel **cone**-toe
Bread	Il pane	eel **pah**-nay
Breakfast	La prima colazione	la **pree**-ma ko-la-**tsee**-oh-nay
Cocktail/aperitif	L'aperitivo	la-pay-ree-**tee**-vo
Dinner	La cena	la **chen**-a
Fixed-price menu	Menù a prezzo fisso	may-**noo** a **pret**-so **fee**-so
Fork	La forchetta	la for-**ket**-a
I am diabetic	Ho il diabete	o eel dee-a-**bay**-tay
I am vegetarian	Sono vegetariano/a	**so**-no vay-jay-ta-ree-**ah**-no/a
I'd like . . .	Vorrei . . .	vo-**ray**
I'd like to order	Vorrei ordinare	vo-**ay** or-dee-**nah**-ray
Is service included?	Il servizio è incluso?	eel ser-**vee**-tzee-o ay een-**kloo**-zo
It's good/bad	È buono/cattivo	ay **bwo**-no/ka-**tee**-vo
It's hot/cold	È caldo/freddo	ay **kahl**-doe/**fred**-o
Knife	Il coltello	eel kol-**tel**-o
Lunch	Il pranzo	eel **prahnt**-so
Menu	Il menù	eel may-**noo**
Napkin	Il tovagliolo	eel toe-va-lee-**oh**-lo
Please give me . . .	Mi dia . . .	mee **dee**-a
Salt	Il sale	eel **sah**-lay
Spoon	Il cucchiaio	eel koo-kee-**ah**-yo
Sugar	Lo zucchero	lo **tsoo**-ker-o
Waiter/Waitress	Cameriere/cameriera	ka-mare-**yer**-ay/ka-mare-**yer**-a
Wine list	La lista dei vini	la **lee**-sta **day**-ee **vee**-nee

MENU GUIDE

English	Italian
Set menu	Menù a prezzo fisso
Dish of the day	Piatto del giorno
Specialty of the house	Specialità della casa
Local specialties	Specialità locali
Extra charge	Extra . . .
In season	Di stagione
Cover charge/Service charge	Coperto/Servizio

Breakfast

Butter	Burro
Croissant	Cornetto
Eggs	Uova
Honey	Miele
Jam/Marmalade	Marmellata
Roll	Panino
Toast	Pane tostato

Starters

Assorted cold cuts	Affettati misti
Assorted seafood	Antipasto di pesce
Assorted appetizers	Antipasto misto
Toasted rounds of bread, fried or toasted in oil	Crostini/Crostoni
Diced-potato and vegetable salad with mayonnaise	Insalata russa
Eggplant parmigiana	Melanzane alla parmigiana
Fried mozzarella sandwich	Mozzarella in carrozza
Ham and melon	Prosciutto e melone
Cooked sausages and cured meats	Salumi cotti
Filled pastry shells	Vol-au-vents

Soups

"Angel hair," thin noodle soup	Capelli d'angelo
Cream of . . .	Crema di . . .
Pasta-and-bean soup	Pasta e fagioli
Egg-drop and parmesan cheese soup	Stracciatella

Pasta, Rice, and Pizza

Filled pasta	Agnolotti/ravioli/tortellini
Potato dumplings	Gnocchi
Semolina dumplings	Gnocchi alla romana
Pasta	Pasta
with four cheeses	*al quattro formaggi*
with basil/cheese/pine nuts/ garlic sauce	*al pesto*

with tomato-based meat sauce	*al ragù*
with tomato sauce	*al sugo* or *al pomodoro*
with butter	*in bianco* or *al burro*
with egg, parmesan cheese, and pepper	*alla carbonara*
green (spinach-based) pasta	*verde*
Rice	Riso
Rice dish	Risotto
with mushrooms	*ai funghi*
with saffron	*alla milanese*
Noodles	Tagliatelle
Pizza	Pizza
Pizza with seafood, cheese, artichokes, and ham in four different sections	Pizza quattro stagioni
Pizza with tomato and mozzarella	Pizza margherita
Pizza with oil, garlic, and oregano	Pizza marinara

Fish and Seafood

Anchovies	Acciughe
Bass	Persico
Carp	Carpa
Clams	Vongole
Cod	Merluzzo
Crab	Granchio
Eel	Anguilla
Lobster	Aragosta
Mackerel	Sgombro
Mullet	Triglia
Mussels	Cozze
Octopus	Polpo
Oysters	Ostriche
Pike	Luccio
Prawns	Gamberoni
Salmon	Salmone
Shrimp	Scampi
Shrimps	Gamberetti
Sole	Sogliola
Squid	Calamari
Swordfish	Pescespada
Trout	Trota
Tuna	Tonno

Methods of Preparation

Baked	Al forno
Cold, with vinegar sauce	In carpione
Fish stew	Zuppa di pesce
Fried	Fritto
Grilled (usually charcoal)	Alla griglia
Seafood salad	In insalata
Smoked	Affumicato
Stuffed	Ripieno

Meat

Boar	Cinghiale
Brain	Cervella
Braised meat with wine	Brasato
Chop	Costoletta
Duck	Anatra
Lamb	Agnello
Baby lamb	Abbacchio
Liver	Fegato
Pheasant	Fagiano
Pork roast	Arista
Rabbit	Coniglio
Steak	Bistecca
Sliced raw steak with sauce	Carpaccio
Mixed boiled meat	Bollito misto

Methods of Preparation

Battered with eggs and crumbs and fried	. . . alla milanese
Grilled	. . . ai ferri
Grilled (usually charcoal)	. . . alla griglia
Raw, with lemon/egg sauce	. . . alla tartara
Roasted	. . . arrosto
Very rare	. . . al sangue
Well done	. . . ben cotta
With ham and cheese	. . . alla valdostana
With parmesan cheese and tomatoes	. . . alla parmigiana

Vegetables

Artichokes	Carciofi
Asparagus	Asparagi
Beans	Fagioli
Brussels sprouts	Cavolini di Bruxelles
Cabbage	Cavolo
Carrots	Carote
Cauliflower	Cavolfiore
Cucumber	Cetriolo
Eggplants	Melanzane
Green beans	Fagiolini
Leeks	Porri
Lentils	Lenticchie
Lettuce	Lattuga
Mushrooms	Funghi
Onions	Cipolle
Peas	Piselli
Peppers	Peperoni
Potatoes	Patate
Roasted potatoes	*Patate arroste*
Boiled potatoes	*Patate bollite*
Fried potatoes	*Patate fritte*
Small, roasted potatoes	*Patatine novelle*
Mashed potatoes	*Purè di patate*

Radishes	Rapanelli
Salad	Insalata
vegetable	*mista*
green	*verde*
Spinach	Spinaci
Tomatoes	Pomodori
Zucchini	Zucchini

Sauces, Herbs, and Spices

Basil	Basilico
Bay leaf	Lauro
Chervil	Cerfoglio
Dill	Aneto
Garlic	Aglio
Hot dip with anchovies (for vegetables)	Bagna cauda
Marjoram	Maggiorana
Mayonnaise	Maionese
Mustard	Mostarda *or* senape
Oil	Olio
Parsley-based sauce	Salsa verde
Pepper	Pepe
Rosemary	Rosmarino
Tartar sauce	Salsa tartara
Vinegar	Aceto
White sauce	Besciamella

Cheeses

Fresh:	Caprino fresco
	Mascarpone
	Mozzarella
	Ricotta
Mild:	Caciotta
	Caprino
	Fontina
	Grana
	Provola
	Provolone dolce
	Robiola
	Scamorza
Sharp:	Asiago
	Gorgonzola
	Groviera
	Pecorino
	Provolone piccante
	Taleggio
	Toma

Fruits and Nuts

Almonds	Mandorle
Apple	Mela
Apricot	Albicocca
Blackberries	More
Black currant	Ribes nero

Blueberries	Mirtilli
Cherries	Ciliege
Chestnuts	Castagne
Coconut	Noce di cocco
Dates	Datteri
Figs	Fichi
Green grapes	Uva bianca
Black grapes	Uva nera
Grapefruit	Pompelmo
Hazelnuts	Nocciole
Lemon	Limone
Melon	Melone
Nectarine	Nocepesca
Orange	Arancia
Pear	Pera
Peach	Pesca
Pineapple	Ananas
Plum	Prugna/Susina
Prune	Prugna secca
Raisins	Uva passa
Raspberries	Lamponi
Red currant	Ribes
Strawberries	Fragole
Tangerine	Mandarino
Walnuts	Noci
Watermelon	Anguria/Cocomero
Dried fruit	Frutta secca
Fresh fruit	Frutta fresca
Fruit salad	Macedonia di frutta

Desserts

Custard filed pastry, with candied fruit	Cannoli
Ricotta filled pastry shells with sugar glaze	Cannoli alla siciliana
Ice cream with candied fruit	Cassata
Ricotta filed cake with sugar glaze	Cassata siciliana
Chocolate	Cioccolato
Cup of ice cream	Coppa gelato
Caramel custard	Crème caramel
Pie	Crostata
Fruit pie	Crostata di frutta
Ice cream	Gelato
Flaked pastry	Millefoglie
Chestnuts and whipped-cream cake	Montebianco
Whipped cream	Panna montata
Pastries	Paste
Sherbet	Sorbetto
Chocolate-coated ice cream	Tartufo
Fruit tart	Torta di frutta
Apple tart	Torta di mele
Ice-cream cake	Torta gelata

Vanilla	Vaniglia
Egg-based cream with sugar and Marsala wine	Zabaione
Ice-cream filled cake	Zuccotto

Alcoholic Drinks

On the rocks	Con ghiaccio
Straight	Liscio
With soda	Con seltz
Beer	Birra
light/dark	*chiara/scura*
Bitter cordial	Amaro
Brandy	Cognac
Cordial	Liquore
Aniseed cordial	Sambuca
Martini	Cocktail Martini
Port	Porto
Vermouth	Vermut/Martini
Wine	Vino
blush	*rosé*
dry	*secco*
full-bodied	*corposo*
light	*leggero*
red	*rosso*
sparkling	*spumante*
sweet	*dolce*
very dry	*brut*
white	*bianco*
Light wine	Vinello
Bottle	Bottiglia
Carafe	Caraffa
Flask	Fiasco

Nonalcoholic Drinks

Mineral water	Acqua minerale
carbonated	*gassata*
still	*non gassata*
Tap water	Acqua naturale
Tonic water	Acqua tonica
Coffee with steamed milk	Cappuccino
Espresso	Caffè espresso
with milk	*macchiato*
decaffeinated	*decaffeinato*
lighter espresso	*lungo*
with cordial	*corretto*
Fruit juice	Succo di frutta
Lemonade	Limonata
Milk	Latte
Orangeade	Aranciata
Tea	Tè
with milk/lemon	*col latte/col limone*
iced	*freddo*

INDEX